MW01087712

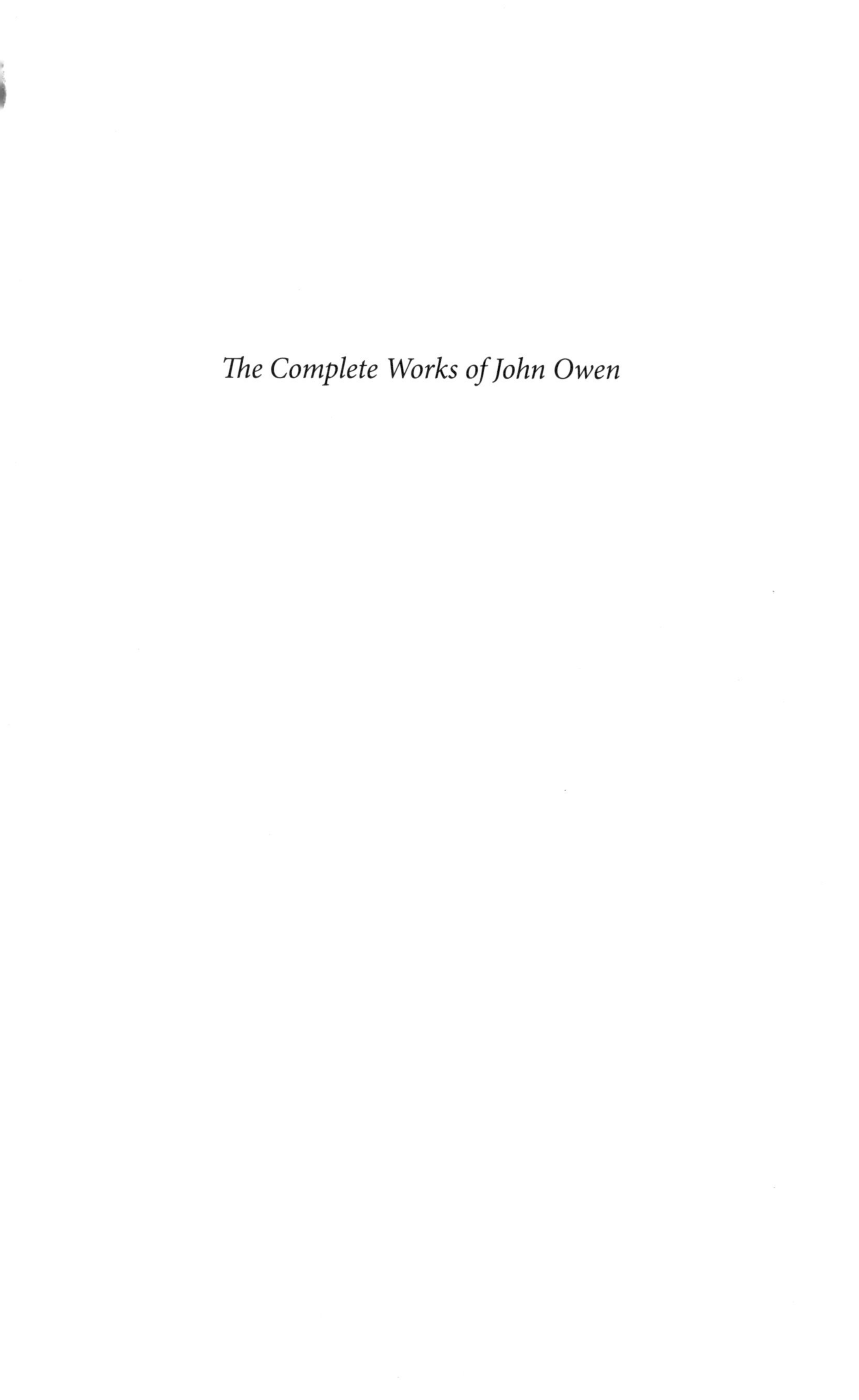

The Complete Works of John Owen

The Complete Works of John Owen

The Trinity

Vol. 1 *Communion with God*

Vol. 2 *The Trinity Defended: Part 1*

Vol. 3 *The Trinity Defended: Part 2*

Vol. 4 *The Person of Christ*

Vol. 5 *The Holy Spirit—His Person and Work: Part 1*

Vol. 6 *The Holy Spirit—His Person and Work: Part 2*

Vol. 7 *The Holy Spirit—The Helper*

Vol. 8 *The Holy Spirit—The Comforter*

The Gospel

Vol. 9 *The Death of Christ*

Vol. 10 *Sovereign Grace and Justice*

Vol. 11 *Justification by Faith Alone*

Vol. 12 *The Saints' Perseverance: Part 1*

Vol. 13 *The Saints' Perseverance: Part 2*

Vol. 14 *Apostasy from the Gospel*

The Christian Life

Vol. 15 *Sin and Temptation*

Vol. 16 *An Exposition of Psalm 130*

Vol. 17 *Heavenly-Mindedness*

Vol. 18 *Sermons and Tracts from the Civil Wars (1646–1649)*

Vol. 19 *Sermons from the Commonwealth and Protectorate (1650–1659)*

Vol. 20 *Sermons from the Early Restoration Years (1669–1675)*

Vol. 21 *Sermons from the Later Restoration Years (1676–1682)*

Vol. 22 *Miscellaneous Sermons and Lectures*

The Church

Vol. 23 *The Nature of the Church: Part 1*

Vol. 24 *The Nature of the Church: Part 2*

Vol. 25 *The Church Defended: Part 1*

Vol. 26 *The Church Defended: Part 2*

Vol. 27 *The Church's Worship*

Vol. 28 *The Church, the Scriptures, and the Sacraments*

Hebrews

Vol. 29 *An Exposition of Hebrews: Part 1, Introduction to Hebrews*

Vol. 30 *An Exposition of Hebrews: Part 2, Christ's Priesthood and the Sabbath*

Vol. 31 *An Exposition of Hebrews: Part 3, Jesus the Messiah*

Vol. 32 *An Exposition of Hebrews: Part 4, Hebrews 1–2*

Vol. 33 *An Exposition of Hebrews: Part 5, Hebrews 3–4*

Vol. 34 *An Exposition of Hebrews: Part 6, Hebrews 5–6*

Vol. 35 *An Exposition of Hebrews: Part 7, Hebrews 7–8*

Vol. 36 *An Exposition of Hebrews: Part 8, Hebrews 9–10*

Vol. 37 *An Exposition of Hebrews: Part 9, Hebrews 11–13*

Latin Works

Vol. 38 *The Study of True Theology*

Shorter Works

Vol. 39 *The Shorter Works of John Owen*

Indexes

Vol. 40 *Indexes*

The Complete Works of John Owen

THE CHRISTIAN LIFE

VOLUME 19

Sermons from the Commonwealth and Protectorate (1650–1659)

John Owen

INTRODUCED AND EDITED BY

Martyn C. Cowan

GENERAL EDITORS

Lee Gatiss and Shawn D. Wright

WHEATON, ILLINOIS

Sermons from the Commonwealth and Protectorate (1650–1659)

Published by Crossway
1300 Crescent Street
Wheaton, Illinois 60187

Cover design: Jordan Singer

Cover image: Marble Paper Artist: Vanessa Reynoso, Marbled Paper Studio

First printing 2025

Printed in China

Hardcover ISBN: 978-1-4335-6048-4
ePub ISBN: 978-1-4335-8612-5
PDF ISBN: 978-1-4335-8610-1

Library of Congress Cataloging-in-Publication Data

Names: Owen, John, 1616–1683, author. | Cowan, Martyn C., editor.
Title: Sermons from the Commonwealth and Protectorate (1650–1659) / John Owen ; introduced and edited by Martyn C. Cowan ; general editors Lee Gatiss and Shawn D. Wright.
Description: Wheaton, Illinois : Crossway, [2025] | Series: The complete works of John Owen ; volume 19 | Includes bibliographical references and index.
Identifiers: LCCN 2024028364 (print) | LCCN 2024028365 (ebook) | ISBN 9781433560484 (hardcover) | ISBN 9781433586101 (pdf) | ISBN 9781433586125 (epub)
Subjects: LCSH: Sermons, English—17th century.
Classification: LCC BX5201 .O496 2025 (print) | LCC BX5201 (ebook) | DDC 252/.059—dc23/eng/20240923
LC record available at https://lccn.loc.gov/2024028364
LC ebook record available at https://lccn.loc.gov/2024028365

Crossway is a publishing ministry of Good News Publishers.

RRD 34 33 32 31 30 29 28 27 26 25
15 14 13 12 11 10 9 8 7 6 5 4 3 2 1

Volume 19
Contents

Works Preface

JOHN OWEN (1616–1683) is one of the most significant, influential, and prolific theologians that England has ever produced. His work is of such a high caliber that it is no surprise to find it still in demand more than four centuries after his birth. As a son of the Church of England, a Puritan preacher, a statesman, a Reformed theologian and Bible commentator, and later a prominent Nonconformist and advocate of toleration, he is widely read and appreciated by Christians of different types all over the globe, not only for the profundity of his thinking but also for the depth of his spiritual insight.

Owen was born in the year that William Shakespeare died, and in terms of his public influence, he was a rising star in the 1640s and at the height of his power in the 1650s. As chaplain to Oliver Cromwell, dean of Christ Church, and vice-chancellor of Oxford University, he wielded a substantial degree of power and influence within the short-lived English republic. Yet he eventually found himself on the losing side of the epic struggles of the seventeenth century and was ousted from his position of national preeminence. The Act of Uniformity in 1662 effectively barred him from any role in the established church, yet it was in the wilderness of those turbulent post-Restoration years that he wrote many of his most momentous contributions to the world of theological literature, despite being burdened by opposition, persecution, family tragedies, and illness.

There was an abortive endeavor to publish a uniform edition of Owen's works in the early eighteenth century, but this progressed no further than a single folio volume in 1721. A century later (1826), Thomas Russell met with much more success when he produced a collection in twenty-one volumes. The appetite for Owen only grew; more than three hundred people had subscribed to the 1721 and 1826 editions of his works, but almost three thousand subscribed to the twenty-four-volume set produced by William H. Goold from 1850 onward. That collection, with Goold's learned introductions and notes, became the standard edition. It was given a new lease on life when the Banner of Truth Trust reprinted it several times beginning in 1965, though without some of Owen's Latin works, which had appeared in Goold's edition, or his massive Hebrews commentary, which Banner did eventually reprint in 1991. Goold corrected various errors in the original seventeenth- and eighteenth-century publications, some of which Owen himself had complained of, as well as certain grammatical errors. He thoroughly revised the punctuation, numeration of points, and Scripture references in Owen and presented him in a way acceptable to nineteenth-century readers without taking liberties with the text.

Since the mid-nineteenth century, and especially since the reprinting of Goold's edition in the mid-twentieth century, there has been a great flowering of interest in seventeenth-century Puritanism and Reformed theology. The recent profusion of scholarship in this area has resulted in a huge increase of attention given to Owen and his contribution to these movements. The time has therefore come to attempt another presentation of Owen's body of work for a new century. This new edition is more than a reprint of earlier collections of Owen's writings. As useful as those have been to us and many others, they fail to meet the needs of modern readers who are often familiar with neither the theological context nor the syntax and rhetorical style of seventeenth-century English divinity.

For that reason, we have returned again to the original editions of Owen's texts to ensure the accuracy of their presentation here but have conformed the spelling to modern American standards, modernized older verb endings, updated some punctuation for clarity, reduced the use of italics where they do not clarify meaning, updated some hyphenation forms, modernized capitalization both for select terms in the text and for titles of Owen's works, refreshed the typesetting, set lengthy quotations in block format, and both checked and added Scripture references in a consistent format where necessary. Owen's quotations of others, however, including the various editions of the Bible he used or translated, are kept as they appear in his original. His marginal notes and footnotes have been clearly marked in footnotes as his (with "—Owen" appearing at the end of his content) to distinguish them from editorial comments. Foreign languages such as Greek, Hebrew, and Latin (which Owen knew and used extensively) have been translated into modern English, with the original languages retained in footnotes for scholarly reference (also followed by "—Owen"). If Goold omitted parts of the original text in his edition, we have restored them to their rightful place. Additionally, we have attempted to regularize the numbering system Owen employed, which was often imprecise and inconsistent; our order is 1, (1), [1], {1}, and 1st. We have also included various features to aid readers' comprehension of Owen's writings, including extensive introductions and outlines by established scholars in the field today, new paragraph breaks marked by a pilcrow (¶), chapter titles and appropriate headings (either entirely new or adapted from Goold), and explanatory footnotes that define archaic or obscure words and point out scriptural and other allusions in the text. When a contents page was not included in the original publication, we have provided one. On the rare occasions when we have added words to the text for readability, we have clearly marked them using square brackets. Having a team of experts involved, along with the benefit of modern online database technology, has also enabled us to make the prodigious effort to identify sources and citations in Owen that Russell and Goold deliberately avoided or were unable to locate for their editions.

Owen did not use only one English translation of the Bible. At various times, he employed the Great Bible, the Geneva Bible, or the Authorized Version (KJV), as well as his own paraphrases or translations from the original languages. We have not sought to harmonize his biblical quotations to any single version. Similarly, we have left his Hebrew and Greek quotations exactly as he recorded them, including the unpointed Hebrew text. When it appears that he has misspelled the Hebrew or Greek, we have acknowledged that in a footnote with reference to either *Biblia Hebraica Stuttgartensia* or *Novum Testamentum Graece*, though Greek accents and breathing marks have been silently corrected.

This new edition presents fresh translations of Owen's works that were originally published in Latin, such as his *Θεολογούμενα Παντοδαπά* (1661) and *A Dissertation on Divine Justice* (which Goold published in an amended eighteenth-century translation). It also includes certain shorter works that have never before been collected in one place, such as Owen's prefaces to other people's works and many of his letters, with an extensive index to the whole set.

Our hope and prayer in presenting this new edition of John Owen's complete works is that it will equip and enable new generations of readers to appreciate the spiritual insights he accumulated over the course of his remarkable life. Those with a merely historical interest will find here a testimony to the exceptional labors of one extraordinary figure from a tumultuous age, in a modern and usable critical edition. Those who seek to learn from Owen about the God he worshiped and served will, we trust, find even greater riches in his doctrine of salvation, his passion for evangelism and missions, his Christ-centered vision of all reality, his realistic pursuit of holiness, his belief that theology matters, his concern for right worship and religious freedom, and his careful exegetical engagement with the text of God's word. We echo the words of the apostle Paul that Owen inscribed on the title page of his book *Χριστολογία* (1679), "I count all things but loss for the excellency of the knowledge of Christ Jesus my Lord, for whom I have suffered the loss of all things, and do count them but dung that I may win Christ" (Phil. 3:8).

Lee Gatiss
CAMBRIDGE, ENGLAND

Shawn D. Wright
LOUISVILLE, KENTUCKY, UNITED STATES

Editor's Introduction

THIS VOLUME CONTAINS some of the most important sermons delivered by Owen in the 1650s. Many of these sermons were delivered on the national stage and address the turbulent events associated with a search for a lasting settlement for the English Revolution. Some of his other important sermons from Westminster have not come down to us. For example, there is no known record of the following: Owen's weekly preaching to the executive of the new regime, the Council of State, in 1649–1651; his sermons to the Rump Parliament in June 1649, the Nominated Assembly in August 1653, and the Recalled Rump in May 1659; and finally, there is no known record of his preaching to the Council of State at Whitehall each Sunday in the highly fraught months of October and November 1659 (something Crawford Gribben described as the Council "keeping its friends close, and its enemies even closer").[1]

The sermons in volume 19 are not to be regarded as representative of all Owen's preaching during that decade. For example, we have no extant record of the sermons he preached while in Ireland. Writing from Dublin Castle in December 1649, Owen described how he was constantly preaching to "a numerous multitude, *of as thirsting a people after the Gospel as ever yet I conversed withal*."[2] Indeed, there is some evidence that a number of people were converted through his ministry in and around Dublin.[3]

There are, however, numerous examples of the fruit of Owen's pulpit ministry in Cromwellian Oxford that are found in other volumes in this edition

1 Crawford Gribben, *John Owen and English Puritanism: Experiences of Defeat* (New York: Oxford University Press, 2016), 115, 202; Peter Toon, *God's Statesman: The Life and Work of John Owen* (Exeter, UK: Paternoster, 1971), 88, 113.

2 John Owen, *Of the Death of Christ, The Price He Paid* (1650), 97. See also *Complete Works of John Owen*, vol. 9.

3 Crawford Gribben, *God's Irishmen: Theological Debates in Cromwellian Ireland* (Oxford: Oxford University Press, 2007), 26, 135, 225n37.

of Owen's works. These help provide a fuller record of the themes that Owen addressed in preaching. In Oxford, Owen was preaching at Christ Church and delivering fortnightly Sunday afternoon sermons at the University Church of St Mary's. Around the middle of the decade, a new wooden pulpit was installed in St Mary's on the old stone pedestal.[4] Some of this expository material was adapted into treatises for the press. For example, the material in important treatises such as *Communion with God* (1657) and *Mortification of Sin in Believers* (1656) found its first expression in Owen's preaching in the 1650s. The former was a series of sermons from 1651 that took a number of years, and some persuasion from others, to finally make its way into print.[5] In the latter Owen notes in passing that his preaching on the doctrine of mortification had enjoyed "some comfortable success" and that it was adapted for publication "with such additions and alterations as I should judge necessary."[6] Nonetheless, in works like these Gribben has detected "the strategies of the pulpit" in Owen's "pithy soundbites."[7] Unlike much of what is contained in this volume, the application in the preaching from which these treatises evolved was often aimed at the individual believer rather than being directed to the duties and responsibilities of those in government. Nonetheless, the content of Owen's political preaching ought not to be too sharply distinguished from his other preaching. For example, Owen's work *Of Temptation* (1658) was based on sermons from Cromwellian Oxford delivered at the time when Owen was losing influence both at Oxford and Westminster. Owen emphasized that his message was particularly "suited to the times that pass over us,"[8] in which "providential dispensations, in reference to the public concernments of these nations" had seen all things "shaken."[9] It is striking to note that Owen himself stated that he was not dealing with temptation in a general sense: he was providing a probing analysis of the "hour of temptation" that comes to "try them that dwell upon the earth" (Rev. 3:10). He spoke of a time of "backsliding" in which "thousands" had apostatized "within a few years."[10] Now increasingly

4 T. G. Jackson, *The Church of St. Mary the Virgin, Oxford* (Oxford: Clarendon, 1897), 180–81.

5 John Owen, *Communion with God, the Father, Sonne, and Holy Ghost* (Oxford, 1657), sig. A2r; *Complete Works of John Owen*, vol. 1. See what are the notes from these (or at least very similar) sermons: Bodleian Library, University of Oxford, MS Don F. 40, fols. 113–17 (Notebook of Thomas Aldersey).

6 John Owen, *Of the Mortification of Sinne in Believers* [. . .] (Oxford, 1656), sig. A3r; *Complete Works of John Owen*, 15:76.

7 Gribben, *John Owen and English Puritanism*, 165.

8 John Owen, *Of Temptation* [. . .] (Oxford, 1658), sig. A2r–v; *Complete Works of John Owen*, 15:203.

9 Owen, *Of Temptation*, sig. A2r–v; *Complete Works of John Owen*, 15:204.

10 Owen, *Of Temptation*, 66–67; *Complete Works of John Owen*, 15:233.

alienated, he highlighted how "the prevailing party of these nations, many of those in rule, power [and] favour" had formerly been regarded as lowly "Puritans," but their attitudes had changed once they had been "translated by a high hand to the mountains they now possess." Owen lamented, "How soon they have forgot the customs, manners, ways, of their own old people, and are cast into the mould of them that went before them."[11] He specifically referred to those "in high places" who were particularly tempted to pursue "Crownes, Glories, *Thrones*, pleasures, [and] profits of the world."[12] Owen's litany of sins resonated with the temptations that he believed accompanied the monarchical drift of the Protectorate.[13] Thus, even something like *Of Temptation* displays many of the hallmarks of the sermons contained in this volume. The potentially subversive tenor of some of his pulpit ministry helps explain why he was replaced at St Mary's. Owen's rather provocative response was to set up a rival lecture at St Peter's in the East.[14] In the summer of 1659, John Locke mocked the dispirited preaching about the state of the nation that he, as a student, presumably heard from Owen's other pulpit in Christ Church.[15] It is highly plausible that the undated sermon *Providential Changes, an Argument for Universal Holiness* was preached in Cromwellian Oxford, most likely in the first half of 1657, and this is included in this volume to help readers follow the development of Owen's preaching across the decade. Some of the sermons from volume 22 may tentatively be assigned a date in the 1650s, but the lack of certainty means that they are included among the other undated sermons.[16]

Owen's sermons from this decade are best described as a form of "prophetic preaching."[17] Taking the voices and assuming tropes of the biblical prophets, Owen offered an explanation of the events of the English Revolution and

11 Owen, *Of Temptation*, 66–67; *Complete Works of John Owen*, 15:243.

12 Owen, *Of Temptation*, 160; *Complete Works of John Owen*, 15:286.

13 Owen, *Of Temptation*, 175–76; *Complete Works of John Owen*, 15:292–93.

14 Tim Cooper, *John Owen, Richard Baxter, and the Formation of Nonconformity* (Farnham, UK: Ashgate, 2011), 122–23; Gribben, *John Owen and English Puritanism*, 176.

15 John Locke, *The Correspondence of John Locke*, ed. Esmond S. de Beer, 8 vols. (Oxford: Clarendon Press, 1976–1989), 1:83. Locke wrote of those whose message was "of noe thing but fire sword and ruine."

16 *Complete Works of John Owen*, vol. 22.

17 The shorthand of "prophetic preaching" has been usefully employed by the following scholars: Patrick Collinson, "Biblical Rhetoric: The English Nation and National Sentiment in the Prophetic Mode," in *Religion and Culture in Renaissance England*, ed. Claire McEachern and Debora Shuger (Cambridge: Cambridge University Press, 1997), 27; Alexandra Walsham, *Providence in Early Modern England* (Oxford: Oxford University Press, 1999), 284; Mary Morrissey, "Elect Nations and Prophetic Preaching: Types and Examples in the Paul's Cross Jeremiad," in *The English Sermon Revised: Religion, Literature and History 1600–1750*, ed. Lori Anne Ferrell and Peter McCullough (Manchester: Manchester University Press, 2000), 43–58.

urged his hearers and readers to make a proper response. Patrick Collinson helpfully summarizes the message of this genre as "always the same: most favoured, more obligated, most negligent."[18] This pattern is certainly evident in Owen's preaching as he drew attention to the undeserved blessings of apocalyptic significance that the nation had experienced, set forth the obligation incumbent upon it to respond appropriately to this unique providential moment, and as he lamented the nation's failures to do so, with warnings of the consequent threat of divine judgment.

THE STEADFASTNESS OF THE PROMISES, AND THE SINFULNESS OF STAGGERING

Context of Owen's Parliamentary Fast Sermon

Recently returned from the Irish expedition, where he had served as a military chaplain, Owen preached to the Parliament on the occasion of a national fast. On January 29, 1650, the Rump had ordered a committee to draw up a declaration for this solemn day of fasting and public humiliation. The act appointing that a fast be held on Thursday, February 28, was read on February 2 and approved after two readings on February 4.[19] As regular monthly humiliations had now been abolished, public fasts were now called only for specific purposes. Those reasons were set out in the published act.[20] It began by making reference to the Lord, "who Ruleth over the Nations, who disposeth and ordereth all things, according to the Good pleasure of his own Will." It explained how God's intention was to "warn and awaken the inhabitants of the Earth" to live faithfully and fruitfully before him. It rehearsed how, in recent days, God had intervened decisively to deliver England from "Tyranny, Popery and Superstition." The receipt of such goodness and mercy should evoke duty and obedience. The nervous new regime had introduced a test of loyalty that took the form of the Engagement Oath, and in January 1650 an act for nationwide subscription to this engagement was passed. This required all men to declare their allegiance to the Commonwealth "as now established

18 Collinson, "Biblical Rhetoric," 28.

19 *Journals of the House of Commons*, 13 vols. (London: HMSO, 1802–1803), 6:352, 356–57; Bulstrode Whitelocke, *Memorials of the English Affairs* [. . .], 4 vols. (Oxford: Oxford University Press, 1853), 2:517; Natalie Mears et al., eds., *National Prayers: Special Worship Since the Reformation*, vol. 1, *Special Prayers, Fasts and Thanksgivings in the British Isles, 1533–1688* (Woodbridge, UK: Boydell, 2013), 515–16.

20 *An Act Appointing Thursday the Last Day of February, 1649. For a Solemn Day of Humiliation, Fasting and Prayer: And Declaring the Grounds Therof* (London, [February 4,] 1650).

without a single person, kingship or the house of peers."[21] This was the cause of significant debate at the time when this sermon was delivered and prepared for publication.[22] In an attempt to broaden the support base for the new regime, particularly among Presbyterians, the engagement cautiously avoided religious language; indeed, people were told to regard it "not as a thing of Religion, but a civill action," and some who promoted it encouraged subscribers to swear "equivocally."[23] As a result, some Presbyterians made much less than half-hearted promises of loyalty to the new republic.[24] In this sermon, Owen appears to commend the Engagement Oath of fealty to the new regime.

The act establishing the fast lamented how "we finde . . . crying sins, hideous Blasphemies, and unheard of Abominations (and that by some under pretence of Liberty, and greater measure of Light)."[25] This was, most likely, a reference to the uproar caused by groups such as the so-called Ranters. Of particular relevance for this sermon was this act's call for prayer and supplication concerning the propagation of the gospel, and this was a major theme that Owen chose to address in this sermon by offering "more specific guidance than heretofore" about how this might be done, all informed by his own recent experience across the Irish Sea.[26]

The other preacher that day was the Welsh radical Vavasor Powell (1617–1670), whose sermon, like Owen's, was also published. Powell was listed as one of the approvers of a parliamentary act that had established the Commission for Better Propagation of the Gospel in Wales and that had been passed the week beforehand, on February 22.[27] This was part of a wider scheme designed to advance the gospel in Wales and the north of England.[28] Powell appears to have been sponsored by Thomas Harrison, who had a key role in this propagation scheme.[29] Powell's sermon was distinctly millenarian,

21 *Severall Proceedings in Parliament 14* (December 28, 1649–January 4, 1650), 180.

22 Blair Worden, *The Rump Parliament, 1648–1653* (Cambridge: Cambridge University Press, 1977), 226–32.

23 *Severall Proceedings in Parliament*, 180.

24 Edward Vallance, *Revolutionary England and the National Covenant: State Oaths, Protestantism and the Political Nation, 1553–1682* (Woodbridge, UK: Boydell, 2005), 168–73.

25 *An Act Appointing Thursday the Last Day of February, 1649, For a Solemn Day of Humiliation, Fasting, and Prayer* (London, 1650).

26 *History of Parliament*, s.v. "Owen, Dr John (?1614–83)."

27 *Journals of the House of Commons*, 6:350, 365–70.

28 *Journals of the House of Commons*, 6:335–37, 352, 365, 370, 396, 416, 420–21; David Underdown, *Pride's Purge: Politics in the Puritan Revolution* (Oxford: Clarendon, 1971), 273; Worden, *Rump Parliament*, 120–21, 234–36, 271–73.

29 Worden, *Rump Parliament*, 234; David Farr, *Major-General Thomas Harrison: Millenarianism, Fifth Monarchism and the English Revolution 1616–1660* (Farnham, UK: Ashgate, 2014), 131.

announcing that 1650 was "to be the Saints yeare of Jubilee." He rejoiced in God's providence both in England and Ireland and pleaded with members of Parliament to examine themselves to ensure that they were favoring the cause of the saints and being gentle to those with "tender consciences, who peradventure cannot subscribe and submit to your power and authoritie."[30]

If the choice of Powell as a preacher was linked to the Welsh scheme for the propagation of the gospel, then this was something of a two-pronged movement, with Owen's sermon concentrating on the need for similar action in Ireland. Toby Barnard comments that the Rump Parliament had to be "goaded into action" by Cromwell through the action of some of his military chaplains from the Irish expedition and claims that this sermon by Owen "breathed new life" into the ordinance first read at the end of November 1649.[31]

Somewhat unusually, the parliamentary order was not included in the printed version of the sermon. On Friday, March 1, the Commons instructed Sir. William Masham to communicate thanks to Owen for the sermon he delivered at the previous day's fast and requested that the sermon be published.[32] Masham, a well-established member of the Essex gentry, had been the most prominent prisoner during the siege of Colchester and one of those to whom Owen dedicated *Ebenezer* (1648).[33] He was readmitted to the House in February 1649 and elected to the new Council of State.[34]

The sermon was printed by Peter Cole (ca. 1613–1665) to be sold at his shop at the sign of the printing press in Cornhill, near the Royal Exchange, where he had been operating since 1643.[35] Cole was a prominent London bookseller and printer, best remembered for printing works on medicine, particularly those of Nicholas Culpeper. In the year that he printed this sermon, Cole also produced Owen's *Of the Death of Christ, the Price He Paid* (1650) and works by a variety of ministers such as Jeremiah Burroughes, William Bridge, and John Cardell. The book collector George Thomason acquired his copy on April 30.

30 Vavasor Powell, *Christ Exalted Above All Creatures by God His Father* [. . .] *the Last Day of the Last Month Called February 1649* (London, 1651), 74–77, 87.

31 Toby C. Barnard, *Cromwellian Ireland: English Government and Reform in Ireland, 1649–1660* (Oxford: Clarendon, 2000), 96–97.

32 *Journals of the House of Commons*, 6:374.

33 See *Complete Works of John Owen*, vol. 18.

34 See *History of Parliament: The House of Commons, 1640–1660*, ed. Stephen K. Roberts, 9 vols. (Woodbridge, UK: Boydell and Brewer, 2023), *1660*, s.v. "Masham, Sir William, 1st bt. (1591–1656)."

35 See Elizabeth Lane Furdell, "'Reported to be Distracted': The Suicide of Puritan Entrepreneur Peter Cole," *The Historian* 66, no. 4 (2004): 772; Henry R. Plomer, *A Dictionary of the Booksellers and Printers Who Were at Work in England, Scotland and Ireland from 1641–1667* (London: Bibliographical Society, 1907), s.v.

Summary and Analysis of the Sermon

Owen took as his text Paul's description of Abraham's faith: "He staggered not at the promise of God through unbelief" (Rom. 4:20).[36] He called the saints to follow Abraham, setting out with trustworthy promises, even if they were unsure of exactly where their journey might lead. While Owen's exposition of the text addressed the application to individual believers, given his context, his concerns lay with members of Parliament. Parliament had, like Abraham, triumphed over a king and enjoyed "outward success and glory" and yet was in many ways perplexed and in danger of stumbling in unbelief because of a refusal to believe the promises, not least about the "propagation and establishment" of the kingdom of Christ, because of "all the difficulties that lie in the way for the accomplishment of it." Owen explained how this led to hesitation and indecision. The need was for "consolation and establishment" so that as rulers they would embrace the promise that "peace and prosperity" would be "the inheritance of the nation" in due "subordination to the kingdom of Christ" (Isa. 60:11; Jer. 30:20–21). Owen set about doing this by demonstrating the reliability of the promises of God because of "the ability of the promiser" and "the means whereby he works." Consequently, the cause of staggering was unbelief. Opposition may, "for a season," impede the fulfillment of the promise, but "the appointed hour" would come, and, like water welling up behind a dam, the promise would break through in great power.

Owen turned to illustrate this by means of "the affair of Ireland," where, despite the "mountains of opposition" seeming so great, he was confident of "deliverance for Ireland." He believed that the "mountains" there included the following: the English Civil Wars that had delayed the Long Parliament's plans to take action in Ireland; the Levellers ("that mighty mountain" that some "misnamed a Level") who had tried to influence a significant part of the army soldiers not to participate in the expedition; and the "many congregations in this nation" failing to engage in "prayers, tears, and supplications for carrying on of the work of God in Ireland." Owen claimed that even with respect to the "choicest and most rational advices of the army," had they not been "overswayed" by providence, the cause would not have been as far advanced as it was. According to Patrick Little, the commanders of the expeditionary force initially planned that the main assault would land in Munster, but events took a different course, and the entire force eventually disembarked at Ringsend in Dublin.[37]

36 Two years later, in Henry Ireton's funeral sermon, Owen portrayed Ireton as an exemplary godly magistrate precisely because he "staggered not" but was "steadfast in faith." See *The Laboring Saint's Dismission to Rest* (1652), which is included in this volume.

37 Patrick Little, "Cromwell and Ireland before 1649," in *Oliver Cromwell: New Perspectives*, ed. Patrick Little (Basingstoke, UK: Palgrave Macmillan, 2009), 134.

This change of plan, which Owen attributed to the hand of God, had significant bearings on the outcome of the invasion because of three events. First, the Marquess of Ormond took the fateful decision to divide his army, sending his most able commander, Murrough O'Brien (d. 1674), the Earl of Inchiquin, south in the belief that Cromwell would land in Munster.[38] Second, Colonel Michael Jones (d. 1649) won a remarkable victory at Rathmines, outside Dublin, over Lieutenant General Purcell's royalists, killing up to four thousand, capturing two thousand five hundred, and seizing Ormond's artillery, ciphers, and supplies. This was "a stupendous reversal of royalist fortunes, with incalculable psychological and strategic consequences."[39] From a parliamentarian perspective, this was hugely significant: according to Whitelocke, "There never was any day in Ireland like this."[40] The invasion force heard of this "astonishinge mercie" just before embarkation and believed it provided clear evidence of God's favor.[41] Third, although Henry Ireton set sail with a smaller force to the original target of Kinsale, unable to land, he diverted to Dublin. Thus, with no field army to face them, Cromwell's full army assembled with its large train of siege artillery at Dublin. Once Drogheda had been taken, and the area north of Dublin secured, the main army marched south and met Lord Broghill (d. 1679), who had by this stage managed the successful mutiny of the garrisons in Munster against Lord Inchiquin.[42] It is likely that these are the unplanned events in which Owen saw the hand of providence advancing the cause of the Cromwellian conquest of Ireland. Powell concurred in his sermon, telling members of Parliament that one of the "signes of the Lords presence, with you" was the "concurrence of Gods Providence in effecting those great things which you have undertaken, both in this land and in *Ireland*."[43] The members of Parliament whom Owen addressed, as well as the wider public hungry for news, would have been well aware of the ongoing successes that Cromwell was enjoying early on in the

38 Micheál Ó Siochrú, *God's Executioner: Oliver Cromwell and the Conquest of Ireland* (London: Faber and Faber, 2008), 72.

39 Ian Gentles, *The English Revolution and the Wars in the Three Kingdoms, 1638–1652* (Harlow, UK: Pearson Longman, 2007), 391; Pádraig Lenihan, *Consolidating Conquest: Ireland, 1603–1727* (Harlow, UK: Pearson Longman, 2008), "Map Five," 127–28; William Strong's Thanksgiving sermon for this victory, titled "Babylons Ruine, the Saints Triumph," in his *XXXI Select Sermons, Preached on Special Occasions* [. . .] (London, 1656), 55.

40 Whitelocke, *Memorials of the English Affairs*, 3:85.

41 Oliver Cromwell, *The Letters, Writings, and Speeches of Oliver Cromwell*, ed. John Morrill et al., 3 vols. (Oxford: Oxford University Press, 2022), 2:72.

42 Little, "Cromwell and Ireland," 135; J. S. Morrill, "The Drogheda Massacre in Cromwellian Context," in *Age of Atrocity: Violence and Political Conflict in Early Modern Ireland*, ed. David Edwards, Pádraig Lenihan, and Clodagh Tait (Dublin: Four Courts Press, 2007), 251–59.

43 Powell, *Christ Exalted Above All Creatures*, 87 (italics original).

campaigning season of the year since news had been read to members of Parliament on February 25 and then subsequently published.[44]

The final "mountain" was the "combined opposition" that arose. He depicted the royalist coalition as a strong "Fivefold Cord" of ill-matched associates in an unholy alliance: (1) the Scottish Covenanters in Ulster under Sir George Monro;[45] (2) the Ormond Party united in its desire to maintain prelacy and the Book of Common Prayer; (3) the Roman Catholics of the Kilkenny Confederation; (4) the self-interested in the southern ports of Munster who had temporarily abandoned the parliamentary cause in April 1648 and who would need to be bribed to return; and (5) the native Irish rebels. These five groups now had joined forces after having spent the last seven years fighting one another in various combinations. For Owen, their union was reminiscent of the pact between the northern kingdom of Israel and Syria. This Syro-Ephraimite bloc had aimed to force Judah into alignment with them (Isa. 7–9), just as the enemies of the Commonwealth had been intent on doing. Owen cast their role in the drama as that of a monstrous "hydra" of "covenant," "prelacy, popery," "treachery," and "blood."[46] In these examples, Owen's portrayal of the enemy served to emphasize their strength that, in turn, highlighted the providential nature of their defeat.

Owen's first point of application was "unto temporals." He called members of Parliament to live by faith when "called out to public actings." Throughout the sermon, Owen was concerned with reliance on "carnal wisdom" and "carnal policy." He linked this to those who "plot, and contrive, and design." This is possibly an allusion to the continuing links that the Presbyterians maintained with Charles II. By this stage Charles had given up on securing help from Ireland and was turning to the Scots. In March 1650, negotiations began between Charles and the Covenanters in Breda in the Netherlands. Some London Presbyterians wished for "the presbyterian party in England" to be represented at Breda.[47] Another area

44 Cromwell, *Letters, Writings, and Speeches of Oliver Cromwell*, 2:207.

45 Owen does not dwell on the Scottish Kirk's rejection of the Second Ormond Peace in July 1649 and the rejection of it by the Ulster Presbytery. See David Stevenson, *Scottish Covenanters and Irish Confederates: Scottish-Irish Relations in the Mid-Seventeenth Century* (Belfast: Ulster Historical Foundation, 1981), 273–74. See also *A Seasonable and Necessary Warning and Declaration concerning Present and Imminent Dangers* [. . .] (Edinburgh, 1649), 12; and *A Declaration and Warning unto all the Members of This Kirk and Kingdom* [. . .] (Edinburgh, 1650), 5.

46 For a description of Ormond's uneasy coalition, see Jane H. Ohlmeyer, *Ireland from Independence to Occupation, 1641–1660* (Cambridge: Cambridge University Press, 1995), 60–61.

47 Elliot Vernon, "The Quarrel of the Covenant: The London Presbyterians and the Regicide," in *The Regicides and the Execution of Charles I*, ed. Jason Peacey (Basingstoke, UK: Palgrave, 2001),

in which Owen detected the operation of such "carnal wisdom" was in the parliamentary "management of religion." Here Owen criticized those for whom religious policy was simply a means to an end—for example, those who adopted policies specifically designed to gain the "assistance and compliance" of others. This could well be a reference to those in Parliament who were wishing to make concessions to the Presbyterian interest.[48] Owen appeared to commend the Engagement Oath but was preaching for much more than a merely de facto acceptance of the legitimacy of the new regime; he exhorted his hearers to "Engage your hearts" and to believe that God was fulfilling his promises.

Owen's second use was to ensure appropriate engagement in "the propagating of the kingdom of Christ." Thus, with respect to the reconquest of Ireland, members of Parliament ought not only consider "the sovereignty and interest of England" but should do their "utmost for the preaching of the gospel in Ireland." He exhorted them not to conceive of the Cromwellian conquest of Ireland simply in terms of the destruction of the influence of the antichrist in that place but instead to see it as an opportunity for Christ "to take possession of his long since promised inheritance" in that place. He believed Parliament's enemies in Ireland were "vassals of the man of sin" and "followers after the beast," and justice required that they be given "a cup of blood" to drink. Referring to the Irish Rebellion of 1641, he likened Irish rebels to the Amalekites, the first of the nations that attacked God's people who were seeking to enter their promised rest (Ex. 17). In doing so, they disobeyed the command "touch not mine anointed" and invited God's pronouncement that all Amalekites would "perish forever" (Num. 24:20).[49] Nonetheless, after the violence in which he claimed to see Christ "as a lion staining all his garments with the blood of his Enemies," he pressed Parliament to send preachers to the island in order to "hold [Christ] out as a lamb sprinkled with his own blood to his friends." He presented an impassioned firsthand account of what he had witnessed, speaking of the "tears and cries of the inhabitants of Dublin after the manifestations of Christ."[50] Elsewhere, he revealed how in Dublin he had been constantly preaching to "a numerous multitude, *of as thirsting*

202–24; Elliot Vernon, *London Presbyterians and the British Revolutions, 1638–64* (Manchester: Manchester University Press, 2021), 228.

48 Anthony Milton, *England's Second Reformation: The Battle for the Church of England, 1625–1662* (Cambridge: Cambridge University Press, 2021), 307–8.

49 Ethan H. Shagan, "Constructing Discord: Ideology, Propaganda, and English Response to the Irish Rebellion of 1641," *Journal of British Studies* 36, no. 1 (1997): 4–34.

50 For details of Owen's preaching in Dublin, see Gribben, *God's Irishmen*, 7, 11; Barnard, *Cromwellian Ireland*, 145.

a People after the Gospel, as ever yet I conversed withal."[51] This concern was accentuated by his fears about preachers who had already traveled to Ireland "without call, without employments," who were, he believed, "seducers and blasphemers" (he had previously called the magistrate to bring under his cognizance those who wander about with "no calling . . . under a pretense of teaching the truth, without mission, without call, without warrant").[52] Owen was suggesting that preachers who had been ejected in England could easily move to Ireland, bringing their heretical ideas with them.[53] If they do not to their utmost sow the "Seed of the word," then surely numerous "seducers and blasphemers" will sow their tares in "those fallowed fields."

Owen pressed for talk to turn into action: "This thing is often spoken of, seldom driven to any close!" He called his hearers and readers to pray that God would send "laborers" to Ireland (Matt. 9:38). Owen's sermon proposed that Parliament should send "one gospel preacher, for every walled town in the English possession in Ireland." Practically, he suggested that a committee be appointed to "hear what sober proposals" might come regarding how best to further this aim.

The day after Owen delivered the sermon, Whitelocke reported on amendments to the bill for "Advancement of the Gospel, and Learning, in Ireland," and the relevant committee was authorized to receive proposals for how to advance and maintain a preaching ministry in Ireland.[54] That Owen thought himself among those bringing sober proposals is clear from the sermon's dedicatory epistle, which describes the printed tract as "a serious proposal for the advancement and propagation of the Gospel in another nation." The ordinance for the propagation of the gospel in Ireland was passed on March 8, the day Owen penned his preface.[55] The rather sketchy ordinance was, according to Underdown, "uncontroversial" and lacked direct provisions beyond increasing the endowment of Trinity College Dublin, vesting the property of the late archbishop of Dublin and the dean and chapter of the cathedral in fifteen commissioners (of whom Owen was one).[56] It was supplemented by a decision

51 John Owen, *Of the Death of Christ, The Price He Paid* (1650), 97 (italics original). See *Complete Works of John Owen*, vol. 9.

52 See Owen, *Of Toleration* (1649), in *Complete Works of John Owen*, 18:396.

53 Barnard, *Cromwellian Ireland*, 99.

54 *Journals of the House of Commons*, 6:374.

55 "March 1650: An Act for the Better Advancement of the Gospel and Learning in Ireland," in *Acts and Ordinances of the Interregnum, 1642–1660*, eds. C. H. Firth and R. S. Rait, 3 vols. (London: HMSO, 1911), 2:355–57.

56 *Journals of the House of Commons*, 6:248; Barnard, *Cromwellian Ireland*, 95–98; Raymond Gillespie, "The Crisis of Reform, 1625–60," in *Christ Church Cathedral Dublin: A History*,

to "send over Six able Ministers" to Dublin, the place whose plight Owen had highlighted.[57] Barnard concludes that "compared with Ireland's needs, and with treatment of Wales and the north, the Rump's legislation was meagre, and had been achieved only at Cromwell's and his entourage's prompting."[58]

Owen appeared to be particularly concerned about the so-called Ranter threat: those preachers of a "high and heavenly notion which have an open and experimented tendency to earthly, fleshly, dunghill practices."[59] He told Parliament that if it failed to act, Ireland in particular was in danger of becoming a "frippery of monstrous, enormous, contradictious opinions."[60] Owen warned that some have fallen into "downright atheism." Care needs to be taken with the language because, according to Michael Buckley, early modern accusations of atheism "possessed all the accuracy of the newly developed musket."[61] It is unclear whether Owen was addressing practical or speculative atheism.[62] Several pieces of Parliamentary legislation that year would go some way to addressing his concerns. In June there was an act "for the better preventing and suppressing of the detestable sins of prophane swearing and cursing," which was intended to suppress the Ranters.[63] This was closely followed in August with the "Act against several Atheistical, Blasphemous and Execrable Opinions, derogatory to the honor of God, and destructive to humane Society." There was an anti-Ranter element to this legislation against blasphemy.[64] It was against "divers men and women . . . most monstrous in

ed. Kenneth Milne (Dublin: Four Courts Press, 2000), 209–10; Gribben, *God's Irishmen*, 40; Underdown, *Pride's Purge*, 273–74.

57 *Journals of the House of Commons*, 6:379.

58 Barnard, *Cromwellian Ireland*, 98.

59 The "Ranter" phenomenon of 1650–1651 is controversial, with some historians suggesting it was a myth projected by the pulpit and press. E.g., J. C. Davis, *Fear, Myth and History: The Ranters and the Historians* (Cambridge: Cambridge University Press, 1986), 11, 83. An alternative view is argued by Nigel Smith, ed., *A Collection of Ranter Writings from the Seventeenth Century* (London: Junction Books, 1983), 7–39.

60 For a discussion of some of the extremists in Dublin, such as the radical prophet Elizabeth Avery, see Gribben, *God's Irishmen*, 160–73.

61 Michael J. Buckley, *At the Origins of Modern Atheism* (New Haven, CT: Yale University Press, 1987), 10.

62 For the "frequent division of atheism into its practical and speculative components," see Kenneth Sheppard, *Anti-Atheism in Early Modern England, 1580–1720: The Atheist Answered and His Error Confuted* (Leiden: Brill, 2015), 19–21.

63 "June 1650: An Act for the Better Preventing of Prophane Swearing and Cursing," in *Acts and Ordinances of the Interregnum*, 2:393–96; *Journals of the House of Commons*, 6:427; Whitelocke, *Memorials of the English Affairs*, 3:206.

64 J. F. McGregor, "Debate: Fear, Myth and Furore: Reappraising the 'Ranters,'" *Past and Present* 140, no. 1 (1993): 157–58.

their opinions, and loose in all wicked and abominable practices . . . not only to the notorious corrupting and disordering, but even to the dissolution of all humane society; who rejecting the use of any gospel ordinances, do deny the necessity of civil and moral righteousness among men."[65]

Owen was also horrified by "poor parentless children, that lie begging, starving, rotting in the streets, and find no relief." In particular, he called on Parliament to provide for the families of soldiers who had "lost their dearest relations in your service" but who were now "seeking for bread, and finding none." Powell concurred with the sentiments about the poor in his sermon, urging members of Parliament to remember prisoners and poor "Beggers."[66] By the summer of 1649, the Rump had resolved to reform the excise but would only complete those plans in September 1650.[67]

His final three uses were "purely spiritual" and involved calling his hearers to learn how "to believe for your own souls" so that they would, in turn, be able "to believe for a nation." Owen believed that there had been too many excuses for inactivity that were nothing but the consequences of the sin of unbelief, a sin that grieved, provoked, and dishonored God. It was unbelief and "carnal reasonings" that threatened the fulfillment of the promise: "Oh stop not success from Ireland, by unbelief."

Owen's influence as a spokesman for the regime continued to increase in the wake of this sermon. On the day he penned the dedication to the version intended for publication, the Council of State appointed him to deliver sermons to it for the next year "every Lord's day in the afternoon," and to facilitate this it provided him with "fit lodgings" in Whitehall.[68]

THE BRANCH OF THE LORD, THE BEAUTY OF SION

Context of Owen's Preaching in Scotland as an Army Chaplain

After the defeat of the Scottish Engagers' army at Preston in August 1648, the government of Scotland that had sanctioned the Engagement with the king was overthrown with the establishment of the more militant Kirk Party

65 "August 1650: An Act Against Several Atheistical, Blasphemous and Execrable Opinions, Derogatory to the Honor of God, and Destructive to Humane Society," in *Acts and Ordinances of the Interregnum*, 2:409–12.

66 Powell, *Christ Exalted*, 94.

67 Worden, *Rump Parliament*, 167–68, 216; *Acts and Ordinances of the Interregnum*, 2:168–91, 422–23.

68 *Calendar of State Papers, Domestic: Interregnum*, ed. Mary Anne Everett Green, 13 vols. (London, 1875–1886), 9:30. Toon suggests that these lodgings might have been those formerly used by the late Archbishop Laud. See Toon, *God's Statesman*, 42.

regime. Following the execution of Charles I, the Covenanters proclaimed his son to be Charles II on February 5, 1649, but they did not permit him to return to Scotland to exercise his authority until he subscribed to the Covenant and promised to implement Presbyterianism across his three kingdoms. By mid-1650, the king knew that any real hope of support from Ireland had disappeared, and he grudgingly consented to Scottish demands, signing the Covenant and sailing into the Moray Firth in June.[69] It now seemed as if another Scottish invasion was likely in order to recapture England for Charles, and so the Council of State, having recalled Cromwell from Ireland, decided to conduct a preemptive invasion of Scotland with Cromwell as commander in chief. The invasion was unpopular with many; indeed, General Fairfax resigned rather than lead the army into Scotland.[70] Owen was to serve on the Scottish expedition, and on June 26 the Council of State dealt with "his employment with the Lord General in the expedition to the North."[71] In mid-July, Cromwell's forces had reached Newcastle, where *A Declaration of the Army of England upon Their March into Scotland* (1650) was composed and printed; it is possible that Owen had a hand in it since it set out to justify the invasion in largely religious terms. Rather than being directed to the Committee of Estates or the institutional Kirk, it was addressed to "all that are Saints and Partakers of the Faith of Gods Elect in Scotland."[72] It sought to distinguish the godly elect from those who refused to recognize the "finger of God" in recent acts of providence.[73] The English Parliament's recourse to providence angered the Kirk, which complained that the English used providence as a pretext to justify its invasion.[74]

At the border in Berwick on July 21, just before the English army crossed into Scotland, Owen delivered a sermon that would, with another sermon delivered in several months, evolve into what was published as *The Branch of the Lord, the Beauty of Sion: or, The Glory of the Church, in Its Relation unto*

69 Anna Keay, *The Magnificent Monarch: Charles II and the Ceremonies of Power* (London: Bloomsbury, 2008), 46–47.

70 David Stevenson, *Revolution and Counter-Revolution, 1644–1651* (Edinburgh: John Donald, 2003), 170–71; Martyn Bennett, *The Civil Wars in Britain and Ireland, 1638–1651* (Oxford: Blackwell, 1997), 339.

71 *Calendar of State Papers, Domestic*, 9:217.

72 Cromwell, *Letters, Writings, and Speeches of Oliver Cromwell*, 2:278–79; Spurlock, *Cromwell and Scotland*, 20–30.

73 Cromwell, *Letters, Writings, and Speeches of Oliver Cromwell*, 2:283, 287.

74 *A Short Reply unto a Declaration Intituled the Declaration of the Army of England, upon Their March into Scotland. By the Generall Assembly of the Kirk of Scotland* [. . .] (Edinburgh, 1650), 7.

Christ (1650).[75] The text for the sermon was Isaiah 56:7, but the title of the published work drew on language used earlier in the prophecy: "In that day shall the branch of the Lord be beautiful and glorious, and the fruit of the earth *shall be* excellent and comely for them that are escaped of Israel" (Isa. 4:2 KJV). Owen would explain his understanding of the purpose of these verses from Isaiah 4 in his treatise *The Doctrine of the Saints' Perseverance* (1654). He summarized how they laid out God's gracious promises to Israel in the context of her present painful experience of exile. In particular, there were promises of justification (4:2), sanctification (4:3–4), and perseverance (4:5–6). All these were given on account of Christ, who is both "the branch of the Lord" and "the fruit of the earth."[76]

The text of scripture emblazoned on the title page of the printed sermon was Psalm 48:12–14. (In his 1649 sermon *Human Power Defeated*, Owen had expressed confidence that those who embarked for Ireland would be made "sensible" of the truth of these verses—in particular, that it was far more dangerous to fight against Christ than to fight against the antichrist.)[77] The leading Scottish Covenanter, Archibald Johnston of Wariston (1611–1663), heard a report about the sermon and noted in his diary that Owen had warned that "God would bring doun Cromwell and his airmy, who was so proud as to say that at the sight of his face wee would all flye."[78] According to Whitelocke, when orders were given for the army to march, "they went on shouting as they entered Scotland."[79]

Cromwell's invasion force of some sixteen thousand troops found the land stripped bare of crops, with even the animals driven north, and the weather was cold and wet.[80] Despite Cromwell's best efforts to bring the Scots to battle, the Covenanter army remained entrenched behind the fortified line of earthworks and gun emplacements that they had built from Edinburgh to Leith.[81] Owen wrote to the Lord Commissioner John Lisle (ca. 1609–1664),

75 Gribben, *John Owen and English Puritanism*, 119.

76 See Edwin E. M. Tay, *The Priesthood of Christ: Atonement in the Theology of John Owen (1616–1683)* (Milton Keynes, UK: Paternoster, 2014), 171–72.

77 See *Complete Works of John Owen*, vol. 18.

78 Archibald Johnston of Wariston, *Diary of Sir Archibald Johnston of Wariston* [. . .], ed. D. H. Fleming et al., 3 vols (Edinburgh: Scottish History Society, 1911–1940), 2:16. For a discussion of this diary entry, see Crawford Gribben, "Owen and Politics," in *The T&T Clark Handbook of John Owen*, ed. Crawford Gribben and John W. Tweeddale (London: T&T Clark, 2022), 92.

79 Whitelocke, *Memorials of the English Affair*, 3:223–24.

80 Frances Dow, *Cromwellian Scotland, 1651–1660* (Edinburgh: John Donald, 1979), 8.

81 Kenneth Charles Corsar, "David Leslie's Defence of Edinburgh," *Journal of the Society for Army Historical Research* 25, no. 103 (Autumn, 1947): 96–105.

a member of the Council of State, about a skirmish that took place at the end of July. This short letter reveals something of Owen's understanding of how the Scottish army viewed their own cause and the invasion of the army of "sectaries."[82] Cromwell took the time to engage in a further theological offensive against the Scottish Presbyterian clergy. Writing to the Commissioners of the Kirk, he asserted the providential mandate that Owen had done so much to construct: "The Lord hath not hid his face from us since our approach so near unto you."[83] He accused them of pride and "Spirituall Drunkennesse" and urged them to read Isaiah 28:5–15 with its stinging denunciation of "dissolute priests."[84] (Owen would quote from this chapter in this sermon.) Cromwell told them that the Scots had made a covenant with "wicked and carnall men," one that amounted to "a *Covenant . . . with Death and Hell*."[85] Owen may well have had a hand in *The Declaration of the English Army Now in Scotland*, written from Musselburgh on August 1, and a number of ideas from that tract are found in this sermon.[86]

Following the Cromwellian invasion, a number of significant leaders within the Covenanter movement denounced the king for his manifest insincerity in subscribing to the covenant and called for the Scottish army to be purged of all known royalists and former Engagers according to the 1646 and 1649 Acts of Classis.[87] In August, the Kirk Party insisted that Charles issue a declaration making clear his commitment to the covenanting cause by repudiating popery and prelacy and his alliance with the Irish Roman Catholics. He was also forced to express shame concerning the faults of his father and the idolatry of his mother. By the end of the month, a significant (and damaging) purge of the army had been carried out, perhaps reducing it in size by as much as one third.[88]

Five weeks after the invasion commenced, the English army withdrew to Dunbar. Cromwell's forces were reduced to some eleven thousand men because of sickness and desertion, and they were significantly outnumbered and effectively stranded on the coast, with the Scots occupying a more stra-

82 *A True Relation of the Proceedings of the English Army Now in Scotland: From the Two and Twentieth Day of July, to the First of August. Contained in, and Extracted Out of the Several Letters Sent from the Army and Read in Parliament, the Sixth of August, 1650* [. . .] (London, 1650), 14.

83 Cromwell, *Letters, Writings, and Speeches of Oliver Cromwell*, 2:309.

84 Cromwell, *Letters, Writings, and Speeches of Oliver Cromwell*, 2:309–10.

85 Cromwell, *Letters, Writings, and Speeches of Oliver Cromwell*, 2:309–10 (italics original).

86 See the discussion in R. Scott Spurlock, *Cromwell and Scotland: Conquest and Religion, 1650–1660* (John Donald: Edinburgh, 2007), 21.

87 Dow, *Cromwellian Scotland*, 2–12.

88 Stevenson, *Revolution and Counter-Revolution*, 145, 169–70, 176–7.

tegic defensive position. Nonetheless, among the English army there was a significant culture of prayer and preaching and confidence in the intercessions of the godly in England.[89] Cromwell launched his attack before first light on September 3 by calling out "let God arise and his enemies be scattered" (Ps. 68:1). (Owen had quoted from this Psalm in two of his published sermons: *Ebenezer* [1648] and *The Shaking and Translating of Heaven and Earth* [1649].) In what was a stunning victory, the English apparently lost only twenty soldiers, compared to the loss of some three thousand Scots (according to Cromwell "the enemy made by the Lord of Hosts as stubble" to his cavalry) and the capture of around ten thousand prisoners.[90] It was taken to be "an especially significant declaration of God's favour."[91] According to Cromwell, it was "one of the most signal mercies God hath done for England and His people"[92] and an act of divine punishment on the Scots for "not beholding the glory of Gods wonderfull dispensations in this Series of his Providences in *England*, *Ireland* and *Scotland*."[93]

It appears that Owen's responsibilities as a preacher to the Council of State had necessitated a return to Westminster, so he was not present to witness this victory, against all the odds, at Dunbar. On September 10, the House of Commons ordered that he and Joseph Caryl would preach a thanksgiving sermon for the victory on October 8 at St Margaret's, Westminster.[94] However, two days later, on September 12, the Council of State determined that Owen and Caryl were needed in Scotland, and the following day the Commons ordered both preachers to go "forthwith" to Scotland "according to the Desire of the Lord General."[95] Accordingly, on September 20, £50 was to be paid to Owen, Caryl, and two other ministers who were to serve in Scotland.[96] Their presence was necessary because in the aftermath of Dunbar Cromwell "renewed his

89 Ian Gentles, *The New Model Army: Agent of Revolution* (New Haven, CT: Yale University Press, 2022), 209, 212.

90 Stevenson, *Revolution and Counter-Revolution*, 178.

91 Blair Worden, "Providence and Politics in Cromwellian England," *Past and Present* 109 (1985), 81–82.

92 Cromwell, *Letters, Writings, and Speeches of Oliver Cromwell*, 2:328.

93 Cromwell, *Letters, Writings, and Speeches of Oliver Cromwell*, 2:362 (italics original).

94 *Journals of the House of Commons*, 6:464. The two preachers would actually be William Strong (d. 1654) and Thomas Brooks (1608–1680). Many in both Scotland and England refused to honor such national days of thanksgiving to celebrate the English Parliament's victories. See, e.g., William Prynne's scathing comments about the October 1651 thanksgiving in his *Sad and Serious Politicall Considerations Touching the Invasive War against Our Presbyterian Protestant Brethren in Scotland, Their Late Great Overthrow* [. . .] (London, 1650), 6, 8, 9, 21.

95 *Calendar of State Papers, Domestic*, 11:336; *Journals of the House of Commons*, 6:468.

96 *Calendar of State Papers, Domestic*, 11:348.

theological offensive," and the "religious warfare" began in earnest; he clearly wished to have Owen and other ministers alongside him.[97] Owen "embraced his call" and traveled north with "thoughts of peace," intending "to pour out a savour of the gospel upon the sons of peace in this place." Back in Scotland, he was involved in "a vigorous culture of preaching" in which it also appears that officers including Cromwell and his second in command, the brilliant cavalry officer Major General John Lambert (ca. 1619–1684), participated.[98] However, as R. Glynne Lloyd notes, Owen's preaching did not seem to be as well received in Scotland as it was in Dublin.[99] While few specifics are known, part of that preaching in Edinburgh involved a celebration of the submission of the city to the Cromwellians.

When the Cromwellians had entered the capitol in September, they quickly seized control of Edinburgh's presses.[100] Cromwell prayed that the Lord would give the Scots "a cleare sight of the great worke, he is now in these last dayes carrying on."[101] In order to facilitate this, he had his press in Leith printed this sermon by Owen and another by fellow English Congregationalist minister Nicholas Lockyer (1611–1685). This sermon was published in November under the name of the printer Evan Tyler.[102] The London book collector George Thomason acquired his copy on November 26. Owen's sermons were, as Gribben describes, combined into "one seamless discourse" that was both a "celebration of Independent ecclesiology" and a "searing critique of the Presbyterian position."[103] Tellingly, the title page of the sermon contained the text of Psalm 48:12–14, a text whose interpretation for matters of

97 Gentles, *New Model Army*, 214.

98 Henry Reece, *The Army in Cromwellian England, 1649–1660* (Oxford: Oxford University Press, 2013), 119.

99 R. Glynne Lloyd, *John Owen: Commonwealth Puritan* (Pontypridd: Modern Welsh Publications, 1972), 72.

100 J. D. Ogilvie, "Papers from an Army Press, 1650," *Edinburgh Bibliographical Society Transactions* 2 (1938–45): 420.

101 *Letters from the Head-Quarters of our Army in Scotland: Being a Diary of All Proceedings in the Army to Octob. 30. 1650* [. . .] (London, [5 Novembers] 1650), sig. A3r.

102 The print house of the Englishman Evan Tyler (fl. 1639–82) had published for the king and the Covenanter regime. In 1647 it was purchased by the London Stationers' Company, and by 1650 John Twyn was operating it printing pro-English propaganda under the imprint of the former owner. See David Stevenson, "A Revolutionary Regime and the Press: The Scottish Covenanters and Their Printers, 1638–51," in Stevenson, *Union, Revolution and Religion in Seventeenth-Century Scotland* (Aldershot, UK: Ashgate, 1997), 315–30; R. Scott Spurlock, "Cromwell's Edinburgh Press and the Development of Print Culture in Scotland," *Scottish Historical Review* 90, no. 2 (2011): 179–203.

103 Gribben, *John Owen and English Puritanism*, 121; Crawford Gribben, "Polemic and Apocalyptic in the Cromwellian Invasion of Scotland," *Literature and History* 23, no. 1 (2014): 12.

ecclesiology was contested—for example, it had appeared on the title page of Samuel Rutherford's *A Peaceable and Temperate Plea for Pauls Presbyterie in Scotland* (1642).[104] The goal of these sermons was the same: to help define the purpose behind the Commonwealth invasion and persuade the Scots to accept it.[105] *The Branch of the Lord* would help answer Cromwell's desire that the Lord would give the Scots a clear vision of the work that he was doing through the revolutionary English regime.

Alongside it, Cromwell's Scottish press would publish Nicholas Lockyer's sermon titled *A Litle Stone, Out of the Mountain. Church-Order Briefly Opened* (1652). It revealed his eager expectation of the church being "raised from its corruptions, intrusions and ruine made by unsound men."[106] Lockyer's polemical description of the Scottish church shows remarkable similarities to what Owen had preached during the Scottish campaign.[107] Both contrasted gathered churches comprised of "living stones" with the churches of the Kirk, which they believed to be comprised of "dead, rotten stones." Lockyer declared the Kirk to be beyond hope of regeneration and rejected the idea that a national church could be purged. Instead, he called for the gathering of "Gospell Churches out of a Legall Nationall Church."[108] As Scott Spurlock recognizes, Owen's sermon was subtler than Lockyer's "openly anti-Kirk" sermon, but both would have been provocative, especially given that, since 1647, the Kirk had enforced strict censorship on the writings of the English Congregationalists.[109]

The Kirk Party's ascendancy was coming to an end, and as the sermon was published the party split between its more extreme and moderate members. For the more radical Covenanters, their defeat at Dunbar was a sign not of divine favor toward the English but of divine judgment on the ungodly Scots because the purging had not gone far enough.[110] The emerging ideological differences within the Kirk Party came to the fore in the Western Association's Remonstrance of October 1650. This announced that support for Charles II should not be forthcoming until he demonstrated sincere repentance and genuine commitment to the Covenant. *The Branch of the Lord* was published

104 Owen would use this text once again on the cover of *God's Work in Founding Zion* (1656).

105 Spurlock, *Cromwell and Scotland*, 45.

106 Nicholas Lockyer, *A Litle Stone, Out of the Mountain. Church-Order Briefly Opened* (Leith, 1652), 13–14.

107 Lockyer, *Litle Stone*, 16, 33.

108 Lockyer, *Litle Stone*, 47.

109 Spurlock, *Cromwell and Scotland*, 46; *Acts of the General Assembly of the Church of Scotland, 1638–1842* (Edinburgh, 1843), 75–76.

110 Spurlock, *Cromwell and Scotland*, 14–15.

in the context of the November debates on the Western Remonstrance, which brought about open division of the Kirk Party. On November 28, the moderate Commission of the Kirk condemned this Remonstrance. Soon after Owen's sermon was published, on December 1, the English defeated the forces of the Western Association at Hamilton. Later in the month, public resolutions led to the repeal of the Acts of Classes, thus allowing royalists and Engagers back into the Covenanter armies and public office. This was condemned by the minority Remonstrants, later termed Protesters.

Owen's published sermons found a warm reception from at least some in Scotland. In early January 1651, the officer and regicide Robert Lilburne wrote to Cromwell asking "that some able minister were here to speake in publique, and that I had some of Mr Owen's sermons, and other books to disperse." Many of the Scots had apparently told Lilburne that "they would gladly see and reade them," particularly because "they have been keptt from them, and have not beene truely informed concerning our proceedings."[111] Cromwell would, presumably, have been delighted to receive Lilburne's request since it was in line with his existing policy of disseminating preaching, which supported the regime.

One of Owen's perhaps most paradigmatic conversions occurred during this time—namely, that of the Scottish politician Alexander Jaffray (1614–1673).[112] In his diary, Jaffray, a member of the Scottish Committee of Estates, described being seriously wounded in the fighting at Dunbar and his subsequent imprisonment by the English, during which months he "had good opportunity of frequent conference" with both Cromwell and Owen. Through these encounters, he came to understand the "dreadful appearance of God against us at Dunbar," in which the Covenanters were "visibly forsaken." Previously, Jaffray had been "zealous for presbytery," but he came to abandon it, instead adopting Congregationalism. Significantly, Jaffray even appealed to a text frequently employed by Owen: Revelation 11:1–2.[113] Owen persuaded Alexander Jaffray that "the sinful mistake of the good men of this [Scottish] nation" concerned "the knowledge and mind of God as to the exercise of the magistrate's power in matters of religion—what the due

111 *The Original Letters and Papers of State, Addressed to Oliver Cromwell: Concerning the Affairs of Great Britain* [. . .], ed. J. Nickolls (London, 1743), 48–49; Anne Laurence, *Parliamentary Army Chaplains, 1642–1651* (Woodbridge, UK: Boydell, 1990), 71–72.

112 Austin Woolrych, *Britain in Revolution: 1625–1660* (Oxford: Oxford University Press, 2002), 492; G. D. Henderson, *Religious Life in Seventeenth-Century Scotland* (Cambridge: Cambridge University Press, 1937), 107–16; Spurlock, *Cromwell and Scotland*, 107–8.

113 Alexander Jaffray, *Diary of Alexander Jaffray*, ed. J. M. G. Barclay (Aberdeen, 1856), 45–48, 60.

bounds and limits of it are."[114] He accepted Owen's interpretation of providence, particularly in regard to its civil and ecclesiastical implications. This accords with the *Declaration of the Army upon the March into Scotland* (July 15, 1650), which stated that ministers should preach rather than "medling with, or engaging the Authorities of the World." Too many clergy had "seduced" the people by mingling "the Presbyterian with the Kingly Interest."[115] In other words, they had failed to recognize the due bounds of church and state. Similarly, Jaffray's testimony resonates with Cromwell's comments to Speaker William Lenthall after the battle of Dunbar, in which he described how God had dealt a blow to the "Ministers of Scotland" for "medling with worldly Pollicies & mixtures of earthly power, to sett up, that which they call the Kingdome of Christ."[116]

Summary and Analysis of the Sermon

Owen took the text as a description of "Christ's church of saints," gathered out of the nations, with its appointed ordinances and worship. This was, in the first instance, the church universal but, in a secondary sense, "every particular church of his saints," which Owen styled as "every holy assembly of mount Zion." This house is built on the foundation of Jesus Christ and is made up of living stones—that is, elect believers. The principal builder of God's house is the Holy Spirit, who makes instrumental use of "the prophets and apostles," first in their labors and then in the apostolic doctrine.

The resultant house is living, strong, and glorious: living because "Christ the foundation is a living stone, and they that are built upon him, are living stones"; strong because of the rock on which it is built; and glorious because Christ is present in each assembly and the glory of the ordinances of the gospel surpass all the glory of the worship of the tabernacle and temple. No opposition to this house has arisen or will arise that will not be broken in pieces. Owen listed persecutors of the church such as Pharaoh, Nebuchadnezzar, the pagan Roman emperors, the persecuting Laudian bishops, and others who had recently had their garments "rolled in blood." Owen was seeking to justify the invasion on account of freeing the saints in Scotland from those who were seeking to impose religious tyranny. At Musselburgh on August 1, the officers spoke of "the Antichristian Tyranny that was exercised by the late king and His Prelates" over "the True Spiritual Church of Jesus Christ;

114 Jaffray, *Diary of Alexander Jaffray*, 37.

115 Cromwell, *Letters, Writings, and Speeches of Oliver Cromwell*, 2:284–85.

116 See Cromwell's letter from September 4, 1650, in Cromwell, *Letters, Writings, and Speeches of Oliver Cromwell*, 2:329.

namely, Those that were born again, and united to him by his Spirit." They knew that "a time of Deliverance was to be expected to the Church of Christ, and destruction and ruine to *Babylon*."[117] They were "called forth by the Lord" to be "instrumental" in the "destruction of Antichrist" and the "Deliverance and Reformation of Christ's Church and people."[118] Owen depicted the true church of the saints as "a house, a palace hung round about with ensigns, spoils, and banners taken from the enemies." This is especially poignant given that in the rout, all the Scottish artillery and baggage were captured along with over two hundred regimental colors emblazoned with such slogans as "Covenant: for Religion, King and Kingdomes" and "Covenant: for Religion, Croune and Countrie." Parliament ordered them to be hung in Westminster Hall alongside those taken at Marston Moor, Naseby, and Preston.[119] Ian Gentles has analyzed banners from the civil wars to demonstrate how they were often "wrought from expensive materials," regularly with religious or political slogans, and thus had "high symbolic importance."[120] This action was well-known and controversial. For example, *Mercurius Politicus* reported on the images and mottos on some of the flags.[121] William Prynne was greatly exercised that Cromwell sent "all the Scots Colours to Westminster" in order to "hang up the Ensignes taken from them in Westminster Hall, as publicke trophies and testimonies to succeeding ages."[122]

Owen's main intention was to speak of how this house stands in a twofold relation to Jesus Christ. In the first instance, he developed four relevant motifs from the architecture and furnishings of this house. He began by considering what it means for Christ to be the foundation, distinguishing the different senses in which he is foundational for the church. From all eternity, God purposed that Christ would be the church's foundation. Christ is also first in that in the protevangelium he was announced as the one through whom grace would be given to the elect. Christ is first in that he is "laid in the heart of every individual stone, before they are laid up in this building." Finally, he is to be first and preeminent in every particular congregation. Owen developed this architectural metaphor by considering how foundations "must be hidden, and out of sight unto all those that outwardly look upon the house."

117 *The Declaration of the English Army Now in Scotland* (London, 1650), sig. B1r (italics original).

118 *Declaration of the English Army Now in Scotland*, sig. B1v–B2r.

119 C. H. Firth, "The Battle of Dunbar," *Transactions of the Royal Historical Society* 14 (1900): 19–52.

120 Ian Gentles, "The Iconography of Revolution: England 1642–9," in *Soldiers, Writers, and Statesmen of the English Revolution*, ed. Ian Gentles, John Morrill, and Blair Worden (Cambridge: Cambridge University Press, 1998), 95, 97.

121 *Mercurius Politicus* 14 (September 5–12, 1650), 224.

122 Prynne, *Sad and Serious Politicall Considerations*, 6, 9.

He extended the illustration by describing the ornamental features of a great house—for example, impressive carvings on the exterior of the building. Here he refers to a type of decorative plaster work particularly associated with Essex known as pargework. A foolish person may believe that these outward structures are load bearing when in reality "they bear not the house," but "there is a foundation in the bottom, which bears up the whole." Owen confessed that he himself had at times mistakenly thought that the church would not survive without the assistance of the civil magistrate or the army. The reality was the other way round. The "very best" in civil government and the army realized that they were supported and held up by the church. Those who were worldly had no apprehension of the hidden foundation and made the mistake of thinking that they could easily demolish the church, not realizing that in doing so they would "dash themselves all to pieces." His final use of the motif of the foundation is to say that without the foundation of faith "a man [may] be hewed and squared by the word and ordinances into outward conformity," but the stone has no support and "will quickly fall to the ground," leaving only a heap of rubbish.

In terms of the furnishings of this house, Christ is the ark, altar, and candlestick. He is the ark and "the mercy seat covering it" in the sense that he hides the law with its condemning power and contains in himself the new covenant. Furthermore, he is the altar of this house—that is, the altar of sacrifice and atonement as well as the golden altar of incense. Finally, he is the "one eminent candlestick" of the church, giving out the light that is necessary for the church's worship in revealing all that is necessary of the doctrine, worship, and discipline of the house. Others had attempted to "set up light in this house" by appeal to tradition, prudence, and ceremonies. The Commissioners of the Kirk had alluded to Jeremiah 9:14 and Isaiah 50:11 in regard to those who would tolerate error. They sought to portray the English army as comprised of those who "love to walk in the Immaginations of their own hearts, and in the light of their own fire, and in the sparkes that they have kindled, corrupting the truth of God, approving errors in themselves, and tolerating them in others."[123] Owen suggested that it was the Scottish Presbyterians who "compass themselves with sparks, and walk in the light of the fire which themselves have kindled, in the face of the Sun of Righteousness?" He exhorted his hearers and readers to "take heed of such *ignes fatui*, foolish misguiding fires." Such so-called lights were "not from Christ"

123 *A Seasonable and Necessary Warning concerning Present Dangers and Duties from the Commissioners of the Generall Assembly unto All the Members of This Kirk* (Edinburgh, 1650), 7.

and were nothing more than a will-o'-the-wisp. Furthermore, Christ is the candlestick in that by the "mighty efficacy of his Spirit" he opens the eyes of the blind by "creating a new power of life, and light upon the soul."

Having addressed how Christ stands in relation to the church in terms of its "fabric and building," he turned to consider Christ's fivefold relation to his house as owner, builder, watchman, inhibiter, and avenger. First, Christ is the owner of the church. He not only has the title to this inheritance as the rightful heir but also has paid the price of purchase with his own blood; furthermore, he has conquered the devil, the "unjust usurper" who "had taken possession of this house, and kept it in bondage." Owen raised three observations from Christ's ownership of his house. First, Christ will "defend his own possession" from all who upon "various pretenses" oppose, encroach, spoil, or meddle with it. To do so was to fight against God. The language of meddling is significant within the context of the Scottish invasion. Cromwell and his council of officers had written about how the Scottish ministers should preach rather than "medling with, or engaging the Authorities of the World," seducing the people by mingling "the Presbyterian with the Kingly interest."[124] After his victory, Cromwell wrote to Speaker William Lenthall, describing how God had dealt a blow to the "Ministers of Scotland" for "medling with worldly Pollices & mixtures of earthly power to sett up, that which they call the Kingdome of Christ."[125] Owen warns those whose actions appear to suggest that they are the owners: "Do not think it will excuse you to say, you wast mistaken." Here Owen is adopting the rhetoric that Cromwell had addressed "to the General Assembly of the Kirk of Scotland" in his letter from August 3: "I beseech you in the bowels of Christ, think it possible you may be mistaken."[126]

The second observation arising from the Christ's ownership was that he alone had the right to "order" the affairs of the house, and therefore no one should seek to tamper with it by ordering and regulating it for their own ends or according to their own wisdom. His final observation was pointedly anti-Presbyterian. Congregations in which "the far greatest part are dead stones" ought not to be called churches. Owen's treatments of "titles" is striking when located in its context. David Dickson (ca. 1583–1662), a member of the Commission of the Kirk and a Resolutioner wrote, "Whosoever are born within

124 Cromwell, *Letters, Writings, and Speeches of Oliver Cromwell*, 2:284–85

125 Cromwell, *Letters, Writings, and Speeches of Oliver Cromwell*, 2:329.

126 This is striking in the context of Cromwell's appeal to the Scots on August 3, 1650: See Cromwell, *Letters, Writings, and Speeches of Oliver Cromwell*, 2:309. This letter from the English Army's camp at Musselburgh was in response to the Kirk's Declaration on July 30.

the compasse of a Nationall covenant with God, are children of *the Kingdome*, that is, have an external title to be heirs of *the Kingdome*."[127] As John Coffey has argued, Samuel Rutherford was also committed to the idea that the visible church must be a comprehensive national church.[128] Owen claimed that such a view was a great provocation to Christ to give the title of church to what was "a sty of swine, a den of unclean beasts, a ruinous heap."[129] In the early 1650s, the Covenanter minister Hugh Binning (1627–1653) acknowledged that "the great blot on our visible church" was that "the most part are not God's children but are called so."[130]

Christ was also the Master-builder of his house, both the one mystical house and the congregations that comprised it, which he styles as "assemblies and dwelling places of mount Zion." Only Christ can build the church because he alone can give "life unto dead stones," meaning that the "workman" of free will "never placed stone in the house of Christ." Furthermore, he alone gives directions for the "institution" and "perfection" of this building. It was a great mistake to try to "hew and square" the stones by "vows, promises, resolutions, and engagements" or to attempt to "beautify" dead stones "with duties and services" because only Christ can produce living stones. This was not an unfamiliar line of argument against the Covenanters, who demanded from both elect and reprobate alike a commitment to live in the fullness of covenanted expectations. Rutherford, for example, knew that Presbyterians were accused of endeavoring to lay dead stones in a living temple but rejected the idea that the church should be composed only of visible saints.[131] The Covenanters believed in a covenanted nation and a church comprising both elect and reprobate alike. The visible church was not composed entirely of the elect but rather was an *ecclesia mixta*, comprised of both elect and reprobate.[132] Rutherford captured the differences between the view laid out in this sermon by Owen and that held by the Covenanters in his treatment of the constitution of the visible church in his *Due Right of Presbyteries* (1644):

127 David Dickson, *A Brief Exposition of the Evangel of Jesus Christ according to Matthew* (London, 1651), 86. For Dickson's role, see David Stevenson, *The Scottish Revolution, 1637–44: The Triumph of the Covenanters* (Newton Abbot, UK: David and Charles, 1973), 24.

128 John Coffey, *Politics, Religion and British Revolutions: The Mind of Samuel Rutherford* (Cambridge: Cambridge University Press, 1997), 206.

129 Lockyer described such churches as nothing but "a carcasse." See Locker, *Litle Stone*, 131.

130 Hugh Binning, *The Works of Hugh Binning*, 3 vols., ed. James Cochrane (Edinburgh: William Whyte, 1839–40), 2:409.

131 Samuel Rutherford, *Due Right of Presbyteries* [. . .] (London, 1644), 266.

132 Coffey, *Politics, Religion and the British Revolutions*, 166–67, 206.

> A visible profession of the Truth and Doctrine of godlinesse, is that which essentially constituteth a visible *church*, and every member of the visible *church*; onely our Brethren and we differ much about the nature of this profession which is required in members added to the *Church*. Our Brethren will have none members of the visible *Church*, but such as are satisfactory to the consciences of all the visible *church*, and give evidences so cleare, as the judgement of discerning men can attaine unto, that they are truly regenerated. We againe do teach, that the scandalously wicked are to be cast out of the *Church* by excommunication, and these of approved piety are undoubtedly members of the visible *Church*, so these of the middle sort are to be acknowledged members of the *Church*, though the *Church* have not a positive certainty of the judgement of charity, that they are regenerated, so they be knowen. 1 To be Baptized. 2. That they be free of grosse scandals. 3. And professe that they be willing hearers of the Doctrine of the Gospell. Such a profession, as giveth evidences to the positive certainty of the judgement of charity, of sound conversion, is not required to make and constitute a true visible *Church*.[133]

A distinction was made between external and internal covenanting: there was an external covenant to which all members of the visible church belonged that was distinguished from the internal covenant of which the elect, the members of the invisible church, were members. As Spurlock explains, "Rutherford understood the external covenant to stretch the canvas of a visible church over the whole population of Scotland."[134] In the aftermath of Dunbar, Protesters like Rutherford did lean in Owen's direction as they sought a purged church. However, those on the majority Resolutioner side, such as Robert Baillie, maintained their commitment to a mixed church that pragmatically embraced lapsed "malignants" in the interests of maintaining a unified national Kirk.[135] Owen's sermon would have been highly provocative because he implied that another of the ways in which the Kirk had become infected with popery was by admitting the unregenerate. He had effectively unchurched much of Scotland because his issue with the mixed constitution

133 Rutherford, *Due Right of Presbyteries*, 251 (italics original).

134 R. Scott Spurlock, "Polity, Discipline and Theology: The Importance of the Covenant in Scottish Presbyterianism, 1560–c.1700," in *Church Polity and Politics in the British Atlantic World, c. 1635–66*, ed. Elliot Vernon and Hunter Powell (Manchester: Manchester University Press, 2020), 84.

135 Alexander D. Campbell, *The Life and Works of Robert Baillie (1602–1662): Politics, Religion and Record-Keeping in the British Civil Wars* (Woodbridge, UK: Boydell, 2017), 110.

of the Kirk could however be addressed satisfactorily only by the gathering of congregations of visible saints. That is exactly what Jaffray and several other Protesters were openly advocating in May 1652.[136]

Owen then addressed what it meant for Christ to be the "great watchman or keeper of this house." Christ appointed other watchmen—principally pastors—to be watchmen, but too often "they have been, and oftentimes are" guilty of self-interest, meddling, or abuse. Consequently, it was a mercy that Christ watched over the state and condition of his people "to eye them in their distresses, and to give them timely and suitable deliverance." If there was a delay to his intervention, it was because he was allowing the godly to "strive and wrestle with great oppositions" in order "to draw out and exercise" faith. The "enemies of the church" should know that "the eye of Christ" is on them in "all their counsels and undertakings." Owen described this in a way that resonated with recent events. The enemy may be "digging deep," but their undertakings would come to nothing because Christ was "continually present" in all their planning. Owen pointed to an episode from the life of Elisha where the perplexed king of Syria could not comprehend how his Israelite enemies had prior knowledge of all his military maneuvers, knowledge that extended to "the words that thou speakest in thy bedchamber" (2 Kings 6:8–12 KJV). As Owen applied this, he attributed the intelligence that enabled Cromwell to identify the weakness in Leslie's army to the hand of providence.

Owen outlined a threefold sense in which Christ is the inhabiter or indweller of the church: it is his "habitation" and "his court." First, he dwells in his house and in every stone of it by his Spirit. He clarified that "Christ does not assume the saints into a personal subsistence with himself, but dwells in their persons by his Spirit." Perhaps Owen was aware of how the Congregationalist point about the visible church consisting only of those who were "partakers of the divine nature" might be misunderstood (2 Pet. 1:4). Rutherford, for example, had engaged with the Congregationalists' use of this terminology. While Christ indwelled all his saints, he did not do so equally when it came to his "workings," "operations," and "manifestations." Second, Christ dwells in his house by the "graces" of which his people are made partakers. These graces, such as "light, and life, and love," are the "the ornaments of the living stones." Third, Christ dwells in his church by his "ordinances." From this Owen entered into a discussion about the "intimacy" that Christ has with his saints, drawing upon the Song of Songs in order to describe "the choicest communion." This was a common theme among

136 Coffey, *Politics, Religion and the British Revolutions*, 221.

Congregationalists, and Owen's treatment of these texts is similar to that adopted by William Strong in *The Saints Communion with God* (1655), and it anticipates his own sermons from the following year that would in time be published as *Communion with God* (1657). Once again, contextualization brings Owen's point into clarity because Rutherford had claimed something very different: "The faithfull may become and stand members, and have a spirituall communion with a people . . . that are Idolaters, thieves, murtherers, worshippers of Baal, so being they worship the true God publickly as he commandeth, and be in externall covenant with him."[137]

Owen then warned about grieving the indwelling Spirit of Christ by "unbelief, unruly passions, worldly desires, [and] foolish imaginations." In response, Christ would "hide his face," and all sense of his presence would be lost. Although Owen was clear that the application was not limited to the Scots, the implication was that this is exactly what the Covenanters had done as he paraphrased Isaiah's warning of how God would act to make "your heart ache, your joints tremble, and break all your bones in pieces" (see Isa. 38:13). Owen's point would have been heard by many engaged in significant heart-searching after the events at Dunbar which, as Spurlock notes, resulted in "a number of queries about the very nature of a covenanted nation."[138] Owen pressed the point by insisting that the indwelling Christ could be grieved by calling the appearances of the grace of Christ in others "hypocrisy, humor, folly, pride, [and] singularity." The implication was that this is what the Scots had done by describing the English army as nothing more than an army of sectaries.[139]

The final consideration of Christ's relationship to his house was as its "great avenger," the one who would "destroy all the enemies of his holy dwelling." Here Owen returned to texts and motifs from his sermons from the previous two years to argue that "every instrument of persecution in the world" would be called to account, "sooner or later, temporally or eternally." For example, the old pagan Roman Empire had been judged, and anti-Christian Rome would also be destroyed, tellingly, "with all its adherents." In the Declaration of Musselburgh, the junior officers in the army announced that they were fighting for "the destruction of Antichrist, [and] the advancement of the Kingdom of

137 Samuel Rutherford, *A Peaceable and Temperate Plea for Pauls Presbyterie in Scotland* (London, 1642), 136.

138 R. Scott Spurlock, "Boundaries of Scottish Reformed Orthodoxy, 1560–1700," in *The History of Scottish Theology*, vol. 1, *Celtic Origins to Reformed Orthodoxy*, ed. David Fergusson and Mark W. Elliott (Oxford: Oxford University Press, 2019), 367.

139 Spurlock, *Cromwell and Scotland*, 24.

Jesus Christ."[140] Owen's point here was that the Scots had effectively "roused" the lion and so had been destroyed by the avenger.

Owen closed the sermon with three brief but significant applications. The first concerned the "eminent privilege of them which are indeed stones of this house." It was a great honor to serve Christ and be "safeguarded as his." Second, it was "vanity" to trust in "outward church privileges" because Christ actually "abhors those assemblies" comprised of "dead rubbish." By implication, this was a call to abandon such assemblies and to be gathered into churches made up of living stones. Finally, Owen explained that persecution appeared "in various forms," some "old ones new painted," and others "new pretenses." Regardless of the form it took, persecutors would be destroyed.

THE ADVANTAGE OF THE KINGDOM OF CHRIST IN THE SHAKING OF THE KINGDOMS OF THE WORLD

Context of Owen's Sermon Celebrating the Victory at the Battle of Worcester

The Scots crowned Charles at Scone in January 1651 in the hope that he would be a covenanted monarch reigning over three kingdoms.[141] Charles's intention was that with the support of the Scots he would invade England in the hope that this might exploit disillusionment with the republican regime and northern royalists would rally to his standard. At the beginning of August, around thirteen thousand Scottish royalist troops crossed the border into England. There was, however, no general uprising, and Charles's army began to dwindle because of desertion and dysentery. With Parliament's army in pursuit, the depleted royalists arrived at the loyal but weakly fortified city of Worcester, tired and exhausted after the long march from Stirling. By now, the Parliamentary army had caught up with them, and the king found himself outnumbered and effectively trapped in the city. On September 3, this covenanted king and his Scottish army suffered an overwhelming defeat. Cromwell attacked the city from the east and south, and after the walls were breached, bitter street fighting ensued. The aftermath was, as Gentles explains, "a scene of desolation," with the streets "choked" with corpses and "the stench of death everywhere."[142] It was said that perhaps nearly three thousand royalists were killed, compared to only two hundred parliamentarians, and more than six

140 *Declaration of the English Army Now in Scotland*, sig. B2r.

141 Kirsteen M. MacKenzie, *The Solemn League and Covenant of the Kingdoms and the Cromwellian Union, 1643–1663* (Abingdon, UK: Routledge, 2018), 76–77.

142 Gentles, *English Revolution*, 430.

thousand were taken prisoner. Charles fled and eventually escaped to France. It was not lost on anyone that this was the first anniversary of the victory at Dunbar. The day after his sweeping victory, Cromwell wrote to William Lenthall, expressing his desire that this "Crowning mercy," as he put it, would "provoake those that are conserned in it to thankfull nes, & the Parliamt. to doe the will of him, who hath done his will for it, & for the Nation." He warned that "the fatnes of these continued mercies may not occasion pride, & wantonnes, as formerly the like hath don [illegible], to a chosen Nation." He demanded that "justice rightuousnes, mercie & trueth, may flow from you, as a thankfull returne to our gratious God."[143]

On Saturday, September 6, having heard about "the great Success God was pleased to give the Army, in a total Rout of the Enemy," the Rump Parliament resolved to hold a day of solemn thanksgiving across England, Wales, Scotland, and Ireland, and that "Mr. *Thomas Goodwyn* and Mr. *Owen*, be desired to preach before the Parliament that Day." Earlier in the summer, Joseph Caryl (1602–1673) had replaced Owen as preacher to the Council of State, but the invitation is evidence that Owen "still moved on the national stage." Sir Henry Mildmay was, once again, tasked with giving him notice.[144] The thanksgiving was originally scheduled to take place on Thursday, October 2, but on September 26 it was pushed back to October 24 (the reasons for this were not stated).[145] After the service, Parliament had been due to dine at the Banqueting House on Whitehall, but for some unknown reason that feast was canceled. Details were duly published as *An Act for Setting Apart Friday the Four and Twentieth Day of October, One Thousand Six Hundred Fifty One, for a Day of Publique Thanksgiving: Together with a Narrative Declaring the Grounds and Reasons Thereof* (1651). Such a celebration was an occasion of great rejoicing for some.[146] However, such days of public thanksgiving were not universally well received. For example, the minister of Doulting in Somerset did not attend any service of thanksgiving and chose to pass the

143 Cromwell, *Letters, Writings, and Speeches of Oliver Cromwell*, 2:491.

144 *Journals of the House of Commons*, 7:12–13; *History of Parliament*, s.v. "Owen, Dr John (?1614–83)." Mears et al., *National Prayers*, 1:573. Mildmay, a member of the Essex County Committee, had also been tasked with issuing the invitation to Owen to preach the fast sermon on January 31, 1649.

145 *Journals of the House of Commons*, 7:20, 22.

146 For example, John Goodwin published *Two Hymns, or Spirituall Songs* [. . .] (London, 1651), and William Barton produced *Hallelujah, Or Certain Hymns, Composed out of Scripture, to Celebrate Some Special and Publick Occasions* [. . .] *Upon Occasion of those Two Glorious and Most Remarkable Appearances of God for them, at Dunbar and Worcester: Both upon That Memorable Day Septem. 3 1650. 1651* (London, 1651).

day in an alehouse.[147] In Dorchester in Dorset, a collection was held as part of the celebration, but only a paltry sum was given, even less than the small sum collected to mark the victory at Dunbar the previous year. This was indicative of "the townsmen's ambivalence towards the Commonwealth."[148] Unsurprisingly, in Scotland, the ministers of the Kirk refused to participate in the thanksgiving, judging it instead a day "to fast and murne" because of their "miserie and destruction."[149]

The sermon was printed by Leonard Lichfield (1604–1657), a "jobbing printer" who styled himself "printer to the university."[150] It was sold by the Oxford bookseller Thomas Robinson at his shop by the junction of St Mary's Church and High Street.[151] A London edition was printed probably in the same year as the Oxford edition.[152] It was dedicated to the members of Parliament of the House of Commons, "the supreme authority of the nation." Owen sought to impress upon them that they were living in unprecedented days and were themselves instrumental in the fulfillment of God's providential purposes. In particular, as was befitting the occasion, he drew their attention to the "wasting and desolation" of "the late grand attempt of those in Scotland" to oppose the cause of Jesus Christ. For Owen, despite its appeal to "zeal" and "reformation," the covenanted interest was no more than a hypocritical pretense, and its supporters were motivated by "revenge" and a desire to persecute and enslave. This was a provocation to God who executed "dreadful vengeance" against them at Worcester. Owen informed members of Parliament that his sermon dealt with the obligations placed upon them to make an appropriate response to such a gracious deliverance. In other words, this was a sermon calling for Parliament to demonstrate reforming zeal. This accords with Cromwell's words to the Rump via Speaker Lenthall on the day

147 Imogen Peck, *Recollection in the Republics: Memories of the British Civil Wars in England, 1649–1659* (Oxford: Oxford University Press, 2021), 125.

148 David Underdown, *Fire from Heaven: Life in an English Town in the Seventeenth Century* (New Haven, CT: Yale University Press, 1992), 213–14, cf. 228–29.

149 John Nicoll, *A Diary of Public Transactions and Other Occurrences Chiefly in Scotland, from January 1650 to June 1667*, ed. David Laing (Edinburgh: Bannatyne Society, 1836), 61.

150 See Jason Peacey, "'Printers to the University' 1584–1658," in *The History of Oxford University Press*, vol. 1, *Beginnings to 1780*, ed. Ian Gadd (Oxford: Oxford University Press, 2013), 56, 69, 71.

151 J. G. Philip and Paul Morgan "Libraries, Books, and Printing," in *The History of the University of Oxford*, vol. 4, *Seventeenth-Century Oxford*, ed. Nicholas Tyacke (Oxford: Clarendon, 1997), 666.

152 Falconer Madan, *Oxford Books: A Bibliography of Printed Works Relating to the University and City of Oxford or Printed or Published There*, vol. 3, *Oxford Literature, 1651–1680* (Oxford: Clarendon, 1931), 9–10.

after Worcester, when he urged its members to respond with thankfulness and "to doe the will of him, who hath done his will for it."[153]

Now that Scottish and royalist resistance was collapsing, the regime was secure, and there were further moves to broaden the support base for the Commonwealth by securing an amnesty for former royalists through the Act of Oblivion. Not only had the Scottish army been defeated, but in the summer, the Presbyterian minister Christopher Love (1618–1651) had been executed for his alleged role in a royalist conspiracy. This had broken the back of pro-Covenant English Presbyterian resistance to the regime, and in the middle of October, Love's fellow conspirators received a reprieve.[154] However, this "reversion to peace" also brought "its anxieties."[155] In the turbulent political waters of the autumn, fissures in the regime were coming to light. The Rump Parliament was becoming more aware of the complexities of significant change and reform in matters of religion, law, and the electoral franchise. As the army officers (and their chaplains) returned from nearly two years of fighting, they discovered that a good deal of what they had been fighting for was now viewed as unrealistic.

Owen preached as part of a campaign to push a threefold reformist agenda. First, the army sought the dissolution of the Rump Parliament and fresh elections, even though the result could prove to be problematic; as Owen came to preach, the Rump had been discussing the bill for such a new representative. Second, there was a renewed demand to reform the English legal system. The Rump had debated legal reform on a number of occasions, but as Cromwell complained in June 1650, "the sons of Zeruiah are yet too strong for us: and we cannot mention the reformation of the law."[156] In the sermon, Owen lent his voice for a reform of the law. Third, there was the outstanding issue of the church settlement. Owen shared the Cromwellian desire for a settlement that would include all truly godly. After the victory at Dunbar, the army had prodded the Rump into agreeing to a measure of religious toleration with the repeal of the Elizabethan laws compelling attendance at parish church services on the Sabbath. That, however, had been the Rump's last effort at

153 Cromwell, *Letters, Wirings, and Speeches of Oliver Cromwell*, 2:491.

154 Worden, *Rump Parliament*, 247–48.

155 Blair Worden, "Oliver Cromwell and the Sin of Achan," in *God's Instruments: Political Conduct in the England of Oliver Cromwell* (Oxford: Oxford University Press, 2012), 19.

156 Edmund Ludlow, *The Memoirs of Edmund Ludlow: Lieutenant-general of the Horse in the Army of the Commonwealth of England, 1625–1672*, ed. C. H. Firth, 2 vols. (Oxford, 1894), 1:246. Cromwell was quoting 2 Sam. 3:39. John Morrill and Philip Baker, "Oliver Cromwell, the Regicide and the Sons of Zeruiah," in *The Regicide and the Execution of Charles I*, ed. Jason Peacey (Basingstoke, UK: Palgrave, 2001), 14–35.

religious reform, and at this point the broad national church settlement was still not in place.[157]

Summary and Analysis of the Sermon

Owen was aware that many were slow to recognize God's hand of providence. This had been the case with the wicked in the Old Testament, people like the Egyptians and Philistines, and often the reason for this was judicial blindness and hardening. In order to interpret the significance of the "providential alteration" that was being celebrated on the day of thanksgiving, Owen selected a text from a chapter in Ezekiel that described, in the form of a parable, how "God would destroy the outward visible monarchy of the Jews" because of idolatry and persecution (see Ezek. 17:24). Owen sought to trace obvious parallels to contemporary events, not least because the passage described how God "subdues the nation" and "takes away two kings, one after another." The Scots had been defeated, and two Stuart kings had been removed in quick succession, one by death and the other by exile. Owen took the opportunity to clarify that "kingly government" did not have any "eminency" in it: God had also employed rule by elders and judges at various times in biblical history. Although the monarchy did have an important typological role for the people of God, in time, the people began to idolize the type, embracing "the shadow instead of the substance," which led to "the neglect of the spiritual kingdom of Christ represented thereby." Owen noted how God's purposes in providential alterations of civil rule often involved the "plucking down of kings," with all the accompanying "tumults and embroilments of the nations"—namely, "the setting up" of the kingdom of Christ, "planting it in the church," advancing it, so that it would flourish. In "this nation" of England, such work involved the punishment of tyrants (the late king, Charles I) and the disappointment of "revengeful persecutors" (the Kirk Party in Scotland) and the establishment of godly "governors" (the new republican regime).

Using the arboreal metaphor of his text, Owen expounded several aspects of this great work of advancing the kingdom of Christ with respect to its author, responses to it, and the assurance of its accomplishment. First, considered negatively, this work of the Lord involves the rejection of all means of worldly glory, whether the monarchy in the days of Ezekiel or, in Owen's day, the rejection of the "mighty monarchy" of the house of Stuart, the "triumphing prelacy" of the Laudian bishops and all attempts at enforced "conformity." Considered positively, and contrary to the expectations of many, it involved

157 Underdown, *Pride's Purge*, 271–77.

the exaltation of "things, persons, [and] assemblies" that were instrumental in the advancement of the kingdom of Christ despite many viewing these instruments as "weak and contemptible." Second, in terms of responses to these providential observations, Owen observed that people were often reluctant or unwilling to see the hand of God at work when what was being done went against their expectations of what they judged reasonable. Nonetheless, he insisted that God would continue his work until all people acknowledged his mighty works of providence. The saints could be assured that despite opposition, God would continue to advance the kingdom of Christ. From his exposition of the verse, Owen raised two significant observations that he would spend the rest of the sermon proving and applying.

The first major observation was as follows: "In the carrying on the interest of Christ and the gospel, God will work wonderful providential alterations." Owen explained that there were three principal seasons of divine "appearances" to advance the kingdom of Christ and the gospel. The first was during the time of the promulgation of the gospel by Christ and his apostles. This included the "wars and rumors of wars" that Christ prophesied (Matt. 24:6) concerning the destruction of Jerusalem and for which Josephus recorded the unparalleled "destruction and desolation" that took place. The second such season involved the spread of the gospel across the Roman Empire and the dissolution of that pagan empire. Owen understood this to be a fulfillment of the opening of the six seals described in Revelation 6. The importance of this chapter for Owen's understanding of history is seen in his referencing it in five previously published sermons.[158] The third and final season of "wonderful providential alterations" was ongoing in the work of Christ "to recover his people from anti-Christian idolatry and oppression" in fulfillment of Revelation 17–19. Owen explained that when the Reformation began in the sixteenth century, it was attended by "wars, tumults, and destructions" and that work of deliverance and transformation was not yet complete. As he had argued in previous sermons, the interest of the antichrist was not restricted to its manifestation in Roman Catholicism. When Owen said that he would not speak about "any engagements of war with foreign nations," he simply did not need to do so because, as Gribben notes, "Owen had already made his position clear . . . he was calling for a global revolution."[159] As for what nation Owen might have in mind, Venning points out that France was, at this time, the "likeliest choice of target," especially since many in the army viewed

158 See *Complete Works of John Owen*, 18.

159 Gribben, *John Owen and English Puritanism*, 133.

the French as sharing some responsibly for the invasion from Scotland.[160] Colonel Edward Sexby and other English envoys were in Huguenot regions of southwest France, seeking to gain support from the radical party known as the *Ormée*. In the month Owen preached this sermon, the Council of State was considering sending an expeditionary force to La Rochelle in response to a request that had come via Conan, the agent of the Comte du Daugnon, the pro-Condé governor of La Rochelle.[161] Nonetheless, Owen argued that there was "work enough" to be done domestically, and Owen's thanksgiving sermon was a call to complete that work.

Owen offered two reasons why providential desolations like what had been witnessed at Worcester were necessary. The first was that in order for Christ to come into his possession, he had to act against the leaders of the Western nations who grasped onto his inheritance by seeking to oppress his people. He offered the example of how the Stuart kings James I and Charles I were committed to "holding fast prelacy"—that is, the system of episcopal church government that Owen provocatively styled as "a mere antichristian encroachment upon the inheritance of Christ."[162] This had to be shaken to pieces in the First Civil War. More recently, the Kirk Party in Scotland, "those who would have been our oppressors" by the imposition of Presbyterian uniformity, had been destroyed, and "the cockatrice" (a mythical dragon hatched by a serpent) had been crushed while it was still in its shell (Isa. 14:29). The second reason why such providential shakings were required was because God was delivering his people and taking revenge on those who oppressed them. Owen recognized that even in England there were those who wished to impose the yoke of false worship on others and persecute those who would not conform. In the run-up to the battle of Worcester, there were some supporters of this agenda and others who were simply complacent and unmoved at the plight of the godly. Owen was unequivocal: vengeance would be taken on all of them, and that could not happen "without great alterations." The trials that this inevitably would refine the godly and expose hypocrites.

Owen applied this first observation by way of two main uses. The first was for his hearers and readers to understand that the English revolution—which had caused such "amazement" as the world was turned upside down and set

160 Timothy Venning, *Cromwellian Foreign Policy* (Basingstoke, UK: Palgrave Macmillan, 1995), 40–41.

161 Philip A. Knachel, *England and the Fronde: The Impact of the English Civil War and Revolution on France* (Ithaca, NY: Cornell University Press, 1967), 162–64.

162 Samuel Parker quoted this as a provocative example of Owen's hostility to prelacy. See his *A Defence and Continuation of the Ecclesiastical Politie* [. . .] (London, 1671), 60.

ablaze—came about because God was advancing the interest of Christ and removing all obstacles that stood in the way. The house of Stuart was brought down, and Charles I was "brought to punishment for blood." The Scots had been exposed as hypocrites for forming an alliance with the English Parliament against the king and then entering into an alliance with English royalists against the English Parliament. In England, those who had once favored the cause of Parliament but who had turned away revealed their true identity in their "cursing, repining, [and] slighting the marvelous appearance of God" in support of the new republic. No obstacle could stand in the way of God's work of delivering Zion.

Owen's second use was to provide the rationale for why the saints ought to rejoice even in an "outwardly dreadful and horrible" dispensation such as the slaughter at Worcester. When the enemies of Christ were being destroyed, the saints were to sing the song of Moses and the Lamb (Rev. 15:3) because they had witnessed a deliverance that was both temporal and spiritual. Consequently, he contended that there was every reason to rejoice in the outcome at Worcester because the nation had been delivered from an Egyptian-like "tyrant full of revenge" (Charles II returned from exile) and a Babylonian "discipline full of persecution" (enforced Presbyterian uniformity). As Spurlock explains, Owen's assessment was that Scotland bore the responsibility for the conflict between the two nations "because it had attempted to impose its tyrannical anti-Christian form of church government upon England."[163] Therefore it was incumbent upon the nation "to rejoice" in the destruction of a Babylonian-like regime. For Owen, there was no place for neutrality, given that the hand of God was so obviously at work in these alterations.

The second major observation that Owen drew from his text was that "the actings of God's providence in carrying on the interest of Christ, are and shall be exceedingly unsuited to the reasonings and expectations of the most of men." Here Owen offered a number of examples as to why "the thoughts of God are 'not as our thoughts,' neither doth he look on 'outward appearances.'" He explained that this was the case with Jesus Christ, who was rejected by many because he did not conform to their expectations. Similarly, the apostles were "ignorant, weak, unlearned fishermen, despised upon all accounts," and yet they were the "instruments" that God made use of in the proclamation of the gospel to the pagan world. When it came to the destruction of Babylon, the Scots made the mistake of thinking that reformation would be accomplished "with might, power and strength" and so put their confidence in the king.

163 Spurlock, *Cromwell and Scotland*, 85.

They thought that if Charles II's "malignant" advisors were removed from the royal court, the king with "sound good men" next to him would further the covenanted interest and establish a system of enforced Presbyterian uniformity (what Owen termed the "iron yoke"). Contrary to their expectations of being lifted up and exalted to influence, they found themselves "shaken and broken with unparalleled destruction." The so-called army of sectaries that the Scots so despised was actually the great instrument employed by the Lord to achieve his purposes.

Owen explained that there were at least several reasons why the thoughts and expectations of many in his day were at odds with God's ways. The first was that corrupt hearts long for "carnal power and glory." For Owen, the Scots wanted to see Charles returned to his English throne so that they would "be great under him"; they were set on "re-enthroning . . . tyranny" under the guise of their covenant. Another reason was that by such works of providence, God gave people "a clear" and uneclipsed view of his power. Such manners of working also had a role in judicial hardening. Owen believed that the late king's heart had been hardened and that through his "stubbornness" many mighty providential alterations had been carried out. The application was straightforward; it was "vanity" (and "a great provocation") for proud hearts to reject the work of God simply because it did not conform to expectations: "our ways please not God, when his ways please not us."

Time did not permit Owen to deal with two other observations raised from the text, and so he closed with one final general point of application. This "use" was drawn from the prophet Amos's counsel for how to live during such a "great dispensation of providence": "prepare to meet thy God" (Amos 4:12 KJV). This was the duty incumbent upon the nation and its Parliament and army. Given the tensions that were developing between these two groups, this use was proposed as the way in which their unity could be restored. Owen was endeavoring to mediate between the Parliament and the army by calling for them to look back over the Second Civil War, the campaign in Ireland, and the defeat of the Scots through this shared providentialist and apocalyptic framework. This meant submission and acceptance of the mind and will of God in three areas: his works of providence, worship, and holiness.

With regard to God's works of providence, Owen laid out six things that were "clearly promised" for the period of latter-day glory. Here he returned to a number of texts that he had made reference to in earlier sermons, particularly ones from Isaiah and Revelation. Those in authority (and others among the godly) were to believe these promises because prayerful faith would hasten their fulfillment more than great armies. Owen then raised two areas in which action was required from Parliament as a response to the "constant appearing of God" in vindication of its cause against all opposition: "the advancement of the gospel" and "the administration of justice." Here he was referring to two issues in which Parliament and the army were increasingly at odds. Owen impressed on his hearers and readers that God's work in his days involved "staining the glory of all flesh" (Isa. 23:9) and "shaking and translating" the heavens and earth (Heb. 12:26–27). In the wake of this triumph on the battlefield, Owen was expecting the dawn of a new era, and that involved action in the areas of religion and law. The radical-moderate split over these two issues caused significant tension in Parliament at the time. With the former, Owen would the following year lead a broad coalition of ministers that made proposals for the better regulation and propagation of religion in the Commonwealth church. With the latter, the Rump had debated legal reform on a number of occasions and had made some progress—for example, in November 1650, an act was passed declaring that legal proceedings would take place in English rather than in Latin or French and that the paperwork would be written in ordinary script rather than in the antiquated "court hand." As others added their voice to the calls for further reform to the law, particularly the army's Council of Officers, two months later, in December 1651 Matthew Hale's Commission was established and charged with overhauling the English legal system.[164]

Owen tactfully raised the issue of the self-interest of those in government. This matter had generated a degree of tension in Rump-army relations, as it was thought that the Rump had been hesitant to embark on legal reform because its membership was dominated by lawyers intent on maintaining their position within the status quo. Owen called his hearers to loosen their grip on those things that were being shaken away and to instead find their riches in Christ.

A response was also required in the area of worship. Owen was concerned about a tendency to neglect God's ordinances or to utilize those institutions without an appropriate response of the heart. This was not confined to public worship and included "private worship, both personal and family," as well as Sabbath keeping. He made reference to the recent new laws that the Rump Parliament had passed concerning Sabbath observance and encouraged his hearers to set an example in this area.

The final area of response that Owen dealt with was in holy living. Here Owen appealed to a text that he would expound in depth in the posthumously

164 Worden, *Rump Parliament*, 271; Underdown, *Pride's Purge*, 277–79; *Acts and Ordinances of the Interregnum*, 2:455–56.

published sermon *Providential Changes, an Argument for Universal Holiness* (2 Pet. 3:11), which is included in this volume. Owen sought to harness the recent victory at Worcester, utilizing it as a further call to holiness of life, a responsibility that he believed was particularly important for those in government (2 Sam. 23:3).

The sermon was "an immediate success," being published in London and Oxford in 1651 and then in Leith in 1652.[165] Spurlock suggests that Robert Lilburne's earlier appeal for copies of Owen's sermon may have been the motivation for this sermon being printed by the "Evan Tyler" print house in Leith.[166] Four days after it was preached, Parliament ordered Owen and Thomas Goodwin to preach at the University of Oxford, and for the next five years they alternately delivered sermons from the pulpit of the University Church of St Mary's.[167]

THE LABORING SAINT'S DISMISSION TO REST

Context of Ireton's Funeral

Henry Ireton (1611–1651) was educated at Trinity College, Oxford, and underwent legal training at Middle Temple, London. During the First Civil War, he had fought at Marston Moor, Naseby, and the siege of Bristol. He entered the House of Commons as the member of Parliament for Appleby in 1645, and in 1646 he married Oliver Cromwell's oldest daughter, Bridget.[168] Ireton became the army's chief political strategist. He was involved in drawing up the Heads of the Proposals, the army's basis for attempted negotiations with the king in 1647, and he participated in the Putney Debates with the Levellers later in that year. During the Second Civil War, Ireton served in Kent and Essex. It is quite possible that Owen would have become acquainted with Ireton during the siege of Colchester. In the immediate aftermath of the siege of Colchester, it was Ireton who had led Lucas and Lisle out from the Council of War to be put to death as traitors.[169] In late 1648, he participated in the Whitehall debates and had an important role in orchestrating both

165 Crawford Gribben, "Becoming John Owen: The Making of an Evangelical Reputation," *Westminster Theological Journal* 79, no. 2 (2017): 313.

166 Spurlock, *Cromwell and Scotland*, 46.

167 *Journals of the House of Commons*, 7:31.

168 See David Farr's discussion of Ireton as Cromwell's "son" in David Farr, *Oliver Cromwell's Kin, 1643–1726: The Private and Public Worlds of the English Revolution and Restoration* (London: Routledge, 2024), 18–32.

169 Barbara Donagan, *War in England, 1642–1649* (Oxford: Oxford University Press, 2010), 364.

Pride's Purge and the regicide.[170] Ireton was convinced that the army was God's instrument and that the king must be brought to justice.[171] He was appointed Cromwell's second-in-command for the Irish expedition of 1649 and succeeded his father-in-law as Lord Deputy in Ireland. He died of a fever shortly after concluding the siege of Limerick on November 26, 1651.

Owen was chosen to preach at his high-profile funeral in London. As Gentles has shown, through the 1640s London provided the stage for a number of significant funerals, "each of which exploited the familiar idioms of civic pageantry for the purpose of forwarding a political agenda."[172] Ireton's funeral would be no different. Evelyn provided a full account of what he described as "the Magnificent Funeral of that arch-Rebell Ireton."[173] Evelyn was not the only one to mock the funeral. Anthony Wood recorded that a hatchment was hung at Somerset House while Ireton's body was lying in state, "with this Motto under his Arms depicted thereon, *Dulce est pro patria mori*, which was englished by an honest Cavalier thus, *It is good for his country that he is dead*."[174] There was all the pomp and grandeur of a state funeral with trumpeters and four heralds wearing new tabards bearing the arms of the Commonwealth.[175] Owen delivered the sermon at Westminster Abbey because, as Gribben notes, "preaching was central to [the] construction of godly memory."[176] And, as Jeanne Shami comments, funeral sermons in London were "reaching their apogee in the 1640s and 1650s."[177] Anthony Wood, a hostile detractor, claimed that Owen preached "not without some blasphemy."[178] Afterward, Ireton was buried in Henry VII's chapel at the abbey. Merritt notes how the funeral was "notorious for its lavish expense," with the Venetian ambassador describing

170 David Farr, *Henry Ireton and the English Revolution* (Woodbridge, UK: Boydell, 2006), 159–203.

171 A. S. P. Woodhouse, ed., *Puritanism and Liberty: Being the Army Debates (1647–49) From the Clarke Manuscripts with Supplementary Documents* (London: J. M. Dent, 1974), 87–88.

172 Ian Gentles, "Political Funerals during the English Revolution" in *London and the Civil War*, ed. Stephen Porter (Basingstoke, UK: Macmillan, 1996), 207.

173 John Evelyn, *The Diary of John Evelyn*, ed. E. S. de Beer, 6 vols. (Oxford: Clarendon, 1955), 3:57–58.

174 Anthony à Wood, *Athenae Oxonienses* [. . .], vol. 2 (London, 1692), 82. The phrase is drawn from the *Odes* 3.2.13 of the Roman lyric poet Horace and is properly translated: "It is sweet to die for one's country." For text and translation, see Horace, *Odes and Epodes*, ed. and trans. Niall Rudd, Loeb Classical Library 33 (Cambridge, MA: Harvard University Press, 2004), 144–45.

175 H. Stanford London, "The Heralds' Tabards under the Commonwealth," *Notes and Queries* 198 (1953): 276–77.

176 Gribben, *John Owen and English Puritanism*, 135.

177 Jeanne Shami, "Women and Sermons," in *The Oxford Handbook of the Early Modern Sermon*, ed. Peter McCullough, Hugh Adlington, and Emma Rhatigan (Oxford: Oxford University Press, 2011), 156.

178 Wood, *Athenae Oxonienses*, 2:82.

it as "sumptuous."[179] The government commissioned a substantial tomb to be completed by a prominent London mason.[180] After the Restoration, in January 1661, Ireton's remains were disinterred along with those of Cromwell and John Bradshaw.[181] Evelyn described how their "Carkasses" were "draged out of their superbe Tombs (in Westminster among the Kings)."[182]

Such a lavish funeral was likely at odds with Ireton's own austerity and views on how the dead should be commemorated. Ireton refused a number of opportunities to enrich himself during his career, and, as Farr comments, "it seems unlikely that Ireton received the funeral that he would have wanted."[183] There are perhaps hints of Owen seeking to disassociate himself with aspects of the funeral when he explained that he was charged to "preach the word, not to carry on a part of a funeral ceremony." Nonetheless, the funeral provided an important occasion for the new regime to demonstrate its legitimacy.

Owen dedicated the sermon to his friend, Colonel Henry Cromwell (1628–1674), who had served under Ireton, his brother-in-law, in Ireland and who had been alongside him when he died.[184] In the prefatory address to Cromwell's son, Owen described Ireton as an exceptional example of "righteousness, faith, holiness, zeal, courage, self-denial, love to his country, wisdom and industry."

The work was licensed by those appointed by Parliament, and the title entered on the register of the Stationers' Company on April 15, 1652.[185] It was printed by Robert and William Leybourn (or Leyborne), who were, most likely, brothers operating a printshop on Monkswell Street, Cripplegate.[186] It was published by Philemon Stephens, who had already been responsible for a number

179 J. F. Merritt, *Westminster, 1640–60: A Royal City in a Time of Revolution* (Manchester: Manchester University Press, 2013), 101; "Venice: March 1652," in *Calendar of State Papers Relating to English Affairs in the Archives of Venice*, vol. 28, *1647–1652*, ed. Allen B. Hinds (London: HMSO, 1927), 215–19.

180 Peter Sherlock, "The Revolution of Memory: The Monuments of Westminster Abbey," in *Revolutionary England, c.1630–c.1660: Essays for Clive Holmes*, ed. George Southcombe and Grant Tapsell (Abingdon, UK: Routledge, 2017), 211.

181 For a fuller account of Ireton's burial, funeral, and disinterment, see Farr, *Henry Ireton and the English Revolution*, 1–14.

182 Evelyn, *Diary of John Evelyn*, 3:269.

183 Farr, *Henry Ireton and the English Revolution*, 11.

184 Peacey cites this as an example of how printed sermons "tended to be dedicated to friends of both the author and the deceased." Jason Peacey, *Politicians and Pamphleteers: Propaganda during the English Civil Wars and Interregnum* (Aldershot, UK: Ashgate, 2004), 73.

185 See *Transcript of the Registers of the Worshipful Company of Stationers: From 1640–1708 A.D.*, ed. G. E. B. Eyre, 3 vols. (London, 1913–1914), 1:394.

186 William Leybourn (1626–ca. 1716) went on to become an important mathematician and land surveyor.

of Owen's earlier works. Owen's return to working with him may suggest that "Owen was now someone who could make money for his publishers."[187]

Summary and Analysis of the Sermon

Owen's text comprised the words of discharge spoken to Daniel upon which he formally took his leave to go to his rest: "But go thou thy way till the end be, for thou shalt rest, and stand in thy lot at the end of the days" (Dan. 12:13). He judged these words to be able to stand alone and so proceeded without his usual examination of the context. He divided the text into four parts and from it raised six observations, two of which he handled at length and two only briefly.

For Owen this was a fitting "parallel" between Daniel and Ireton because both were dismissed from their faithful service having demonstrated the same qualities of wisdom, love for God's people, and uprightness in the discharge of their offices and employments. Both showed "civil wisdom" in "the management of the affairs of men" and were men of "the most eminent abilities" and "most useful employments" who died doing their work.

Daniel was also one who received clear visions about the "providential alterations" that would take place from his own day to the end of the world, all of which were centered on the exaltation of the kingdom of Christ. Ireton was a model of one who listened to God's providential voice and who understood the times in which he was living, asking, "What saith the Lord?" and "What Israel ought to do." In Ireton's own *Declaration*, this outlook is obvious as he writes, for example, about how "the Lord our God" had stretched "his heavy hand over this Nation" in those "capital Judgements of Sword and Pestilence."[188] Ireton explained how he believed divine judgments were sent for "reproving, or restraining, for awakening, or quickening, for humbling, teaching or instructing, for purging or purifying, for trying or perfecting."[189] The godly were to seek God through "frequent exercise of Prayer with Fasting (such is without Superstition) and (suitable to the Faith, Simplicity, Truth and Purity

187 Gribben, *John Owen and English Puritanism*, 109. At this time "virtually every frontage in the Cross Yard either was, or had been, a bookshop." The different bookshops were known by their devices, in this case a gilded lion. Stephens remained at these premises "until at least 1665." See Peter W. M. Blayney, *The Bookshops of Paul's Cross Churchyard* (London: Bibliographical Society, 1990), 5, 40. In Thomason's copy of the sermon, the date was altered to 1651 in order to reflect the idea that the new year began on Lady Day, March 25.

188 Henry Ireton, *A Declaration of the Deputy-General of Ireland, concerning the Present Hand of God in the Visitation of the Plague; and for the Exercise of Fasting and Prayer in Relation Thereunto* (Cork, 1650), 3.

189 Ireton, *Declaration of the Deputy-General of Ireland*, 6.

of the Gospel)."[190] Recalling the title and theme of his parliamentary sermon from February 1650, Owen portrayed Ireton as an exemplary godly magistrate precisely because he "staggered not" and instead was "steadfast in faith." Owen presented Ireton as one fully aware that he was living during the period of the "vengeance of the Lord and his temple" before Christ would "reign in Righteousness and Peace." Owen spoke of how even in the "most dismal and black engagements," Ireton remained confident that, in "the appointed season," there would be "the coming in of the promised glory." Unlike those "swallowed up" in "applying secondary causes," Owen was able to hold up as an example Ireton's pattern of "receiving from God, and holding out to others, clear and express visions concerning God's wonderful providential alterations in kingdoms, and nations, which were to be accomplished, from the days wherein he lived."

Owen drew out further similarities between Daniel and Ireton in the area of love for their people. He mentioned Ireton's "great neglect of self," something for which others also remembered Ireton. John Cook (bapt. 1608–d. 1660), prosecutor at the trial of the king and Ireton's Chief Justice of Munster, shared this perspective: "If he erred in any thing (as error and Humanity are inseparable) it was in too much neglecting himselfe."[191] Similarly, John Hewson (d. 1660), the regicide governor of Dublin, also praised Ireton for his selflessness, writing the following on December 2, 1651: "Wee that knew him, can and must say truly, wee know no man like minded; most seeking their own things, few so singly minde the things of Jesus Christ, of publique concernment, of the interest of the precious sons of Zion."[192] Edmund Ludlow (ca. 1616–1692), who had served with Ireton in Ireland, also remembered his austerity and self-denial: he "was so diligent in the publick service, and so careless of food he used, what hour he went to rest, or what horse he mounted."[193] Ludlow recalled Ireton turning down Parliament's gift of land worth £2,000 a year, and, as such, he believed that Ireton would have despised the "pompous and expensive vanities" associated with his funeral.[194]

It appears that Owen sought to justify some of the changes in policy that Ireton engaged in during the late 1640s. For example, the Leveller leader John Lilburne (1615?–1657) described Ireton as "the cunningest of Machiavilians"

190 Ireton, *Declaration of the Deputy-General of Ireland*, 7–8. Ireton ordered twice as many acts of special worship in his two years as Lord Deputy than had taken place in the previous twenty-five years. See Mears et al., *National Prayers*, 1:526.

191 John Cook, *Monarchy No Creature of Gods Making* [. . .] (London, 1652), sig. G1r.

192 *Severall Proceedings* 115 (December 4–11, 1651), 1780.

193 Ludlow, *Memoirs of Edmund Ludlow*, 1:278–79.

194 Ludlow, *The Memoirs of Edmund Ludlow*, 1:286, 295.

and accused the regicide of playing "fast and loose with the King" by initially being willing to bargain with him in the *The Heads of the Proposals* (1647).[195] Similarly, Lilburne and the other Levellers were incensed that Ireton had appeared to court them in late 1648 before turning his back on their *Agreement of the People*.[196] He reasoned that "what is most wisely proposed in one season, may be most foolishly pursued in another." As Owen discussed Ireton's political involvement, he revealed something of his own political theory.[197] Political society is necessary because of human sinfulness and serves to mitigate the effects of the fall. For Owen, certain principles of natural law precede the formation of human government and serve as the foundation on which political society is built. These principles are "universally unchangeable and indispensable," and these "general rules of unchangeable righteousness, and equity" apply to "all times, places, ways and forms of government." The example that Owen offers is that of self-preservation. This had been an important principle for Ireton, for whom peace was "the central political value, which governments existed to maintain."[198] In the Whitehall debates, Ireton had argued that

> the necessary thing, that which *necessarily* leads all men into civil agreements or contracts, or to make commonwealths, is the necessity of it for preserving peace. Because otherwise, if there were no such thing, but every man [were] left to his own will, men's contrary wills, lusts and passions would lead every one to the destruction of another, and [every one] to seek all the ways of fencing himself against the jealousies of another.[199]

In Ireton's Army's Remonstrance, appeal was made to the principle that peace and safety is the highest law (*salus populi suprema lex*). However, when it came to particular forms of government, Owen, like Ireton, granted considerable freedom to human beings to shape their own political

195 John Lilburne, *Legall Fundamentall Liberties of the People of England* [. . .] (London, 1649), 35. *The Heads of the Proposals* (the most generous peace terms offered to the king) has, traditionally, been credited to Ireton. However, the parliamentary Independents and the Council of Officers also had input. Woolrych, *Britain in Revolution*, 374.

196 John Lilburne, *The Second Part of Englands New-Chaines Discovered* [. . .] (London, 1649), 17.

197 It is impossible to agree with Peter Toon's assertion that this sermon contained "no religiopolitical ideas." See Toon, *God's Statesman*, 83.

198 Glenn Burgess, "Religion and Civil Society: The Place of the English Revolution in the Development of Political Thought," in *The Experience of Revolution in Stuart Britain and Ireland: Essays for John Morrill*, ed. Michael J. Braddick and David L. Smith (Cambridge: Cambridge University Press, 2011), 277.

199 Woodhouse, *Puritanism and Liberty*, 130 (italics original).

communities.[200] For Ireton, "'Just principles of law, nature and nations' provided the ultimate sanction for any system of government."[201] At the Putney debates in 1647, Cromwell said that he was not "wedded and glewed to formes of Government." Forms of government were secondary matters, but "Drosse & Dunge in Comparison of Christ."[202] In 1648, the army leaders spoke of significant flexibility over forms of government, being prepared to believe that "any of them," "monarchical, aristocratical, or democratical," might be appropriate "as providence should direct us."[203] This is another example of what Owen refers to in saying that what is wisely proposed in one season would be foolish in another. Serving as an apologist for the revolution in which Ireton had engaged, Owen explained that under certain circumstances alterations to the form of government were permitted, and indeed required. This could be when an institution degenerated or even when it had outlived its usefulness. In such circumstances, change was required for the sake of "mutual preservation," a universal principle of natural law. The implication of what Owen was claiming is that the political institutions such as the monarchy and the House of Lords were, under certain circumstances, "alterable and dispensable." Owen alluded to Ireton's role in the regicide when he described him as "an eminent instrument in the hand of God in as tremendous providential alterations, as such a spot of the world has at any time received since Daniel." Owen allowed "prudence" to determine the manner in which individuals would be designated for office or their tenure in such positions. This had relevance for two matters that the army and others were pressing the Rump to consider—namely, the electoral franchise and the Rump's own dissolution.

The parallels between Daniel and Ireton continued in that both were "saints of the most eminent abilities, in the most useful employments," and they were dismissed from service before they could see "the issue and accomplishment of those glorious things wherein themselves have been most eminently engaged." They were dismissed for a variety of reasons, not least so that they were seen to be merely instruments in the hands of the one who was doing the work. The first application Owen made from this was to remind those of "eminent abilities" who were engaged in "eminent employments" that they had only an allotted season in which to do that work. It was therefore

200 Glenn Burgess, *British Political Thought, 1500–1660: The Politics of the Post-Reformation* (London: Palgrave Macmillan, 2009), 256.

201 Sarah Mortimer, "Henry Ireton and the Limits of Radicalism, 1647–9," in *Revolutionary England*, 57; and Woodhouse, *Puritanism and Liberty*, 404.

202 Cromwell, *Letters, Writings, and Speeches of Oliver Cromwell*, 1:451, 465.

203 Ludlow, *Memoirs of Edmund Ludlow*, 1:184–85.

incumbent upon them "to improve the time." It was possible to do "a world of work for God" in a short period of time, just as Ireton did in his forty years. Ireton had worked long hours in Ireland, something that Cromwell alluded to in one of the letters to his daughter, Ireton's wife, Bridget.[204] This meant that his hearers needed to "be diligent to pass through your work, and let it not too long hang upon your hands."

Owen pressed this home with a litany of areas in which parliamentary reform and action was necessary: the relief of oppressed persons (probably the poor and those imprisoned);[205] responding to requests from widows and orphans (perhaps a call for pensions for army widows and orphans); chastising offenders against God and man; encouraging the better administration of justice across the nation; and the propagation of the gospel. In all these areas of reform, there had been little action.

The Commons revived its committee for poor law reform in April 1652, which did succeed in passing a bill for the relief of poor prisoners. As for law reform, despite the lengthy debates that had taken place, it "now vanished from parliamentary view."[206] Ireton would have been disappointed because in Ireland he had supported Cook's legal reforms.[207] The propagation of the gospel, the last of the areas that Owen mentions, is of particular note. The energy of the relevant committee had "waned markedly," and the propagation bill had by this stage effectively "gone completely to sleep."[208] Owen was imploring his hearers to do something about it. The opportunity to do so arrived days later when, on Tuesday, February 10, Owen and some fellow Congregationalists appeared at the bar of the House of Commons to submit a petition calling for Parliament to take action over the recent republication of the Latin anti-Trinitarian tract known as the Racovian Catechism.[209] Hunter Powell suggests that the Council of State had Owen and his colleagues present its warrant for the seizure of all copies of the catechism.[210] Mortimer proposes that Owen may have hoped to take advantage of Ireton's legacy in order to call Parliament to greater religious

204 Cromwell, *Letters, Writings, and Speeches of Oliver Cromwell*, 1:354.

205 See "April 1652: A Further Additional Act for Relief of Poor Prisoners," in *Acts and Ordinances of the Interregnum*, 2:582.

206 Worden, *Rump Parliament*, 298.

207 Barnard, *Cromwellian Ireland*, 256.

208 Worden, *Rump Parliament*, 298; Underdown, *Pride's Purge*, 274.

209 *Journals of the House of Commons*, 7:85–86. The anonymous work in question was titled *Catechesis ecclesiarum quae in Regno Poloniae* [. . .] (London, 1651).

210 Hunter Powell, "'Promote, Protect, Prosecute': The Congregationalist Divines and the Establishment of Church and Magistrate in Cromwellian England," in *Church Polity and Politics in the British Atlantic World*, 226.

reform since it was well known that Ireton had been a supporter of the civil magistrate's authority in "spiritual" matters—namely, to ensure that there was tolerance for the orthodox godly and the exercise of restrictive power in order to restrain heresy.[211] This may have been what Owen had in mind when in this sermon he spoke about the need to chastise those who offended against God. In response, the Rump created two committees: one to consider the Racovian Catechism and the other to confer with Owen and the other petitioners and to receive proposals "for the better Propagation of the Gospel."[212] A week later, Owen and his colleagues submitted a blueprint for a church settlement to the committee in the form of a list of fifteen proposals, which they duly published as *The Humble Proposals of Mr Owen, Mr Tho Goodwin, Mr Nye, Mr Sympson and Other Ministers* (1652). The title page reveals its consistency with what Owen believed to be the two broad duties of the magistrate—namely, supplying "all Parishes in England with able, godly and Orthodox Ministers" and also dealing with "dangerous Errours and Blasphemies."[213] It included provision for the vetting, supervising, and maintenance of ministers.[214] All people were required to attend public worship, apart from those who out of a "scruple of conscience" would meet in alternative venues notified to the magistrate. Any ministers who opposed "those Principles of Christian Religion, without the acknowledgment whereof the Scriptures doe clearly and plainly affirme, that salvation is not to be obtained" would "not be suffered to preach or promulgate any thing in opposition unto such Principles."[215]

These *Humble Proposals* resulted in a barrage of criticism from the sects and other champions of a fuller toleration such as Roger Williams (just recently returned from New England), Sir Henry Vane, John Milton, and Marchamont Nedham.[216] They were, however, an attempt for a broad settlement within the Commonwealth's national church. As Coffey points out, even the Arminian John Goodwin was persuaded to subscribe to them, despite having criticized

211 Sarah Mortimer, *Reason and Religion in the English Revolution: The Challenge of Socinianism* (Cambridge: Cambridge University Press, 2010), 198; Woodhouse, *Puritanism and Liberty*, 126, 131, 143–44.

212 *Journals of the House of Commons*, 7:85–86.

213 *The Humble Proposals of Mr Owen, Mr Tho Goodwin, Mr Nye, Mr Sympson and Other Ministers* [. . .] (London, 1652), title page.

214 Jeffrey R. Collins, "The Church Settlement of Oliver Cromwell," *History* 87, no. 285 (2002): 24–25.

215 *The Humble Proposals of Mr Owen, Mr Tho Goodwin, Mr Nye, Mr Sympson and Other Ministers* [. . .], 4–6; Worden, *Rump Parliament*, 296.

216 Carolyn Polizzotto, "The Campaign against The Humble Proposals of 1652," *Journal of Ecclesiastical History* 38, no. 4 (1987): 570–71; Blair Worden, *Literature and Politics in Cromwellian England: John Milton, Andrew Marvell, Marchamont Nedham* (Oxford: Oxford University Press, 2007), 266–68.

the magistrate's power in matters of religion throughout the 1640s.[217] The committee called to consider Owen's proposals initially met regularly over the next few months, but then it stalled because of the Rump's internal divisions. There was another gesture toward toleration in June, with recusants no longer being forced to attend Protestant worship against their consciences.[218]

Owen offered two reasons why those employed in great works are so often called away before their work is done. The first was because of "secret provocations." There is every indication that Ireton would have agreed with Owen at this point because John Cook wrote about him in very similar terms: "upon the least losse we received by the Irish, or any disappointment; Oh, sayes he, is not our God angry with us? let us be fervent in prayer to know his minde in every checke or chastisement."[219] The second was because God had "better things in store for his saints." Consequently, if those who were engaged in the work of God were unlikely to see the end of their work, they should "seek for a reward of your service in the service itself."

Owen turned to offer comfort with his third observation about the dismissed saint being in a condition of rest: freed not only from the power of indwelling sin and its guilt but also from the trouble of this life. He presented Ireton as one whose pilgrimage was "consumed in travail"; but now there was "no more fighting, no more blood, no more sorrow." The one whom he described as "our deceased friend" no longer battled with "tyrants" and "rebels" but was at rest. Owen dismissed all ideas of purgatory and limbo. As Richard Muller states, these postmortem receptacles of souls were regarded by the Reformed orthodox "as inventions or fabrications of Rome."[220] Owen also dismissed the different conceptions of Christian mortalism, both *psychopannychism* (that the soul in some sense sleeps at death) and *thnetopsychism* (that the soul dies with the body).[221]

Owen closed with a rehearsal of Ireton's capacities: his exceptional "heroical virtues," particularly his "courage" and tenacity; his "ability, faithfulness, and industry" in his work in the civil state as a wise counselor and commitment to his work; and the fruit of the Spirit seen in Ireton's "faith, love,

217 John Coffey, *John Goodwin and the Puritan Revolution: Religion and Intellectual Change in Seventeenth-Century England* (Woodbridge, UK: Boydell, 2006), 233–35.

218 *Journals of the House of Commons*, 7:138.

219 Cook, *Monarchy No Creature of Gods Making*, sig. L2r.

220 Richard A. Muller, *Dictionary of Latin and Greek Theological Terms: Drawn Principally from Protestant Scholastic Theology*, 2nd ed. (Grand Rapids, MI: Baker, 2017), s.v. "*limbus*."

221 Norman T. Burns, *Christian Mortalism from Tyndale to Milton* (Cambridge, MA: Harvard University Press, 1972), 97–191; Richard Sugg, *The Smoke of the Soul: Medicine, Physiology and Religion in Early Modern England* (Basingstoke, UK: Palgrave Macmillan, 2013), 207–22.

and self-denial."[222] This set Ireton apart from those involved in government whose rule caused others to suffer by their "weakness, treachery [and] sloth" and "unsettled, pragmatical shuffling." Owen hoped that he could make his point "without offense," but the point would not have been missed by those present: in light of eternity, the nation had to engage in serious reform, and they could do that by seeking to emulate the example of Ireton.

CONCERNING THE KINGDOM OF CHRIST, AND THE POWER OF THE CIVIL MAGISTRATE ABOUT THE THINGS OF THE WORSHIP OF GOD

Context of This Fast Sermon during the First Anglo-Dutch War

On August 10, 1652, Parliament proposed that a fast would be held on September 8. When the act was read again on August 19, the matter was referred to the Committee for Propagating the Gospel, presumably to seek its guidance in crafting the rationale for the keeping of the fast. On Wednesday, September 1, the Rump Parliament passed the act for the fast but moved the day to Wednesday, October 13.[223] The preachers were to be Owen; Thomas Goodwin (1600–1680), president of Magdalen College, Oxford; and Christopher Feake (ca. 1611–ca. 1682), the Fifth Monarchist leader and lecturer at St Anne's Blackfriars.[224] Once again, Owen's invitation came via Sir Henry Mildmay, with Goodwin being nominated by Colonel William Purefoy (ca. 1580–1659), a regicide and member of the Council of State,[225] and Feake by the Army Office and regicide Thomas Harrison (1616–1660).[226] The act appointing the fast sought to discover "how the saving truth of the Gospel may be best advanced and propagated, and whatsoever is contrary to sound Doctrine & the power of Godliness suppressed." The act also spoke of the war between the Commonwealth and the United Provinces that had started in July, stating

222 This appraisal of Ireton's virtues corresponds to Ludlow's recollections of Ireton: he "erected for himself a more glorious monument in the hearts of good men, by his affection to his country, his abilities of mind, his impartial justice, his diligence in the public service, and his other virtues; which were a far greater honour to his memory than a dormitory among the ashes of kings." See Ludlow, *Memoirs of Edmund Ludlow*, 1:33.

223 Mears, *National Prayers*, 1:584.

224 The name of this religiopolitical movement came from the references in the book of Daniel to a fifth monarchy that would follow the great kingdoms of Babylon, Medo-Persia, Greece, and Rome. These millenarians believed that Christ was about to abolish the rule of papal Rome (the current manifestation of the fourth monarchy) and establish the rule of Christ on earth (the fifth monarchy).

225 *History of Parliament*, s.v. "Purefoy, William I (c. 1584–1659)."

226 *Journals of the House of Commons*, 7:162, 173.

that the fast would provide an opportunity to pray for God's "Presence with, and Blessing upon the Forces and Navy of this Commonwealth."[227]

The ongoing debate about the civil magistrate's role in the propagation of the gospel is one of the most important contexts in which to locate this sermon. Owen's *Humble Proposals* had been published in March, and these constituted what Hunter Powell refers to as the magisterial Congregationalists' "manifesto" for the church of the English republic.[228] These proposals envisaged a state-supervised national church with an educated ministry and a panel of triers to vet and discipline the clergy.[229] In order to define the boundaries of acceptable doctrine, a list of foundational doctrines was under consideration according to which no one would be permitted "to preach or promulgate any thing in opposition unto such principles."[230] These fundamentals were not published until December 1652, but they were known about by the end of March. These principles were generous in scope and had the potential to unify the Reformed orthodox middle ground of Congregationalists and Presbyterians.[231] The Congregationalists hoped that this would be a means to prevent heresy while maintaining toleration for the various Dissenters who were deemed to be within the bounds of orthodoxy. The issue was pressing because an English translation of the Socinian Racovian Catechism appeared in July, almost certainly a work of John Biddle (1615/16–1662), who had recently been released from prison.[232] The *Humble Proposals* had alarmed Separatists and, almost immediately, a significant campaign had been launched against them by Roger Williams, John Milton, Henry Vane, and Marchamont Nedham.[233] In the sermon, Owen provided "a telling summary of the tumultuous last year of the Rump Parliament."[234] For example, Owen could well have had Williams in view as one who advocated unlimited toleration, no involvement of the civil magistrate in matters of religion, and the disestablishment of the ministry.[235] Similarly, he may be alluding to the

227 *An Act for Setting Apart Wednesday the Thirteenth day of October, 1652, For a Day of Publique Fasting and Humiliation* [. . .] (London, 1652).

228 Powell, "'Promote, Protect, Prosecute,'" 226.

229 Jeffrey R. Collins, *The Allegiance of Thomas Hobbes* (Oxford: Oxford University Press, 2005), 167.

230 *Humble Proposals*, 6.

231 Woolrych, *Britain in Revolution*, 517.

232 Gribben, *John Owen and English Puritanism*, 137–38.

233 Polizzotto, "The Campaign against *The Humble Proposals* of 1652," 569–81; Blair Worden, "John Milton and Oliver Cromwell," in *Soldiers, Writers, and Statesmen*, 244–52.

234 Powell, "'Promote, Protect, Prosecute,'" 226.

235 Roger Williams, *The Fourth Paper; The Bloody Tenent Yet More Bloody* [. . .] (London, 1652). Thomason acquired his copy on April 28.

ideas put forward by Sir Henry Vane the Younger (1613–1662), author of the anonymously published *Zeal Examined*, which appeared in June. In early July, Milton praised Vane for his near unmatched understanding of "spirituall powre and civill."[236] Shortly beforehand, in his sonnet "To the Lord Generall Cromwell," Milton had warned of "new foes," "hireling wolves whose Gospell is their maw," who threatened "to bind our soules with secular chaines."[237]

As this debate about the magistrate's role in the propagation of the gospel continued, tensions were mounting between Parliament and the army, and, according to Gentles, by the autumn (the time Owen came to preach) the mood of the officers had "turned ugly."[238] There was a growing sense that the Rump was incapable of accomplishing the reforms that it believed were necessary.[239] The Dutch war was unpopular with the officers, not least because of the expenditure that it required and because it pushed domestic reform further down the political agenda. The army had issued a strong petition to Parliament on August 12, 1652, demanding wide-ranging reforms. (One of the officers who submitted the petition was Colonel John Okey [ca. 1606–1662], who also had subscribed to Owen's *Humble Proposals*.) It spoke of how the officers, having sought the Lord, desired that twelve articles be considered.[240] The first of these was, "That speedy and effectual means be used for promoting the gospel, profane and scandalous ministers be outed, good preachers encouraged, maintenance for them provided, and tithes taken away." This petition also included calls for legal reform, changes in public accounting, arrangement for soldiers' pay, and measures for dealing with poverty. The final article reminded the Rump that a bill settling the nature of a future Parliament was long overdue and that measures should be taken to ensure that those elected would be suitably qualified—that is, "well-affected," "pious, and faithful to the interests of the Commonwealth." The importance of this petition from August is seen in how the following year Cromwell and the officers justified the dissolution of the Rump on the basis that there had been so little progress on the matters laid out in it.[241]

236 John Milton, "To Sir Henry Vane the younger," lines 10–11, in *The Poetical Works of John Milton*, vol. 2, *Paradise Regain'd, Samson Agonistes, Poems upon Several Occasions, Both English and Latin*, ed. Helen Darbishire (Oxford: Clarendon, 1973), 154.

237 Milton, "To the Lord General Cromwell," lines 11–14 in *Poetical Works*, 154. See Worden, *Literature and Politics in Cromwellian England*, 241–54.

238 Gentles, *New Model Army*, 242.

239 Ludlow, *Memoirs of Edmund Ludlow*, 1:345–46.

240 *To the Supreme Authoritie the Parliament of the Commonwealth of England. The Humble Petition of the Officers of the Army* (London, 1652); *Journals of the House of Commons*, 7:164–65.

241 Austin Woolrych, *Commonwealth to Protectorate* (Oxford: Clarendon, 1982), 40.

After the sermons were preached at the fast, Owen and Goodwin were informally thanked by the house, but Feake was not, having caused controversy by being "very home in his applications."[242] At least two sources recounted how the fiery Fifth Monarchist spoke "plain English" to the Parliament. The resulting controversy was not unlike what happened when John Simpson preached on March 13, 1651.[243] Outside Parliament, although the fast was to be held across England and Wales, it was noted that while some kept it "very strictly," many of the Presbyterians "would not open their church doors."[244] Owen alluded to this in the sermon when he pointed out that public fasts were "neglected, despised, [and] spoken against." Owen's sermon was printed by Leonard Lichfield for Thomas Robinson.[245] In the previous month Owen had been nominated by Cromwell to be the vice-chancellor of the University of Oxford and had been duly elected by convocation. Nonetheless, on the title page the author is simply styled "John Owen" without any of his titles. The book collector George Thomason had acquired his copy by the end of October.

Summary and Analysis of the Sermon

As he had done at Ireton's funeral, Owen looked to the prophet Daniel to provide an example of a godly magistrate. The sermon reveals how Owen himself was in "a reflective mood"; like the prophet Daniel he too was "grieved" and "perplexed."[246] He presented Daniel as one who was seeking the truth—in particular, the interpretation of the things that he witnessed in order to understand the mind and will of God.

Daniel found himself in this state because of the very things that Owen had been describing in his various parliamentary sermons—namely, "the great works of the providence of God, in the shaking and overturning of kingdoms and nations, in a subserviency to his kingdom." The things that Daniel had witnessed were communicated to him in visions of violent "winds and seas." The language is particularly evocative in the midst of the First Anglo-Dutch War (1652–1654), which had started just some three months beforehand, and at that time it must have seemed as if the nations were indeed being "tossed with the winds of commotions, seditions, oppressions, [and] passions," resulting in "horrible tumults, shakings, confusions, and violence."

242 *A Perfect Account* (October 13–29, 1652), 745.

243 Worden, *Rump Parliament*, 315.

244 See "Newsletter from Henry Walker, Westminster, 16 October 1652," in *The Clarke Papers*, vol. 5, ed. F. Henderson (London: Camden Society, 2005), 67.

245 Madan, *Oxford Books*, 3:19.

246 Gribben, "Owen and Politics," 93.

Owen regarded all this as the work of God in "the setting up, and pulling down the powers of this world." As to the nature of the kingdom that Christ was establishing, Owen recognized the ongoing disputes about its "rise, and manner of government." Here he alluded to the Fifth Monarchists and their expectations of an earthly kingdom and claimed that they had made the mistake of adopting the erroneous views held by the pope and the Jews. He sought to correct this by insisting that the kingdom of Christ was "First and principally . . . internal and spiritual." The fast had been called in order to receive "strength and direction" for "carrying on" and propagating this kingdom. Owen recognized that such a task was difficult and that it was easier to complain about the Rump's inactivity in this matter than to guide and direct its members about how to do the work. Nonetheless, he proceeded to offer them five "brief observations" of what was "clear and certain from Scripture" about the nature of Christ's kingdom. Aware that there were "endless and irreconcilable" differences about the kingdom that it was believed Christ would set up, it appears that he himself believed that Christ's future reign would be "only differenced by more glorious degrees and manifestations of his power." "While never directly naming the Fifth Monarchists," Owen sought to correct their invective with five observations that offered a rebuttal of their radical millenarianism.[247] This had direct bearing on the matter of the magistrate's role in the propagation of the gospel and the search for a national church settlement because the Fifth Monarchists were calling for the overthrow of secular government in order to make way for the rule of the saints. First, Owen insisted that the saints in every age should pursue godliness and regard any "outward glory" that would appear in the world as "a shadow" of this; he described as "sin and folly" the attempts of some radical millenarians to try "to set up the kingdom of Christ in the world" while "pull[ing] it down in their own hearts."[248] Nonetheless, and second, it was indeed the case that an apocalyptic shaking of the nations would take place, and this would result in a transformation of their governments and constitutions. Owen reminded his audience that this was something he had "fully demonstrated elsewhere" and pointed to his sermon from April

247 Stella P. Revard, "Milton and Millenarianism: From the Nativity Ode to *Paradise Regained*," in *Milton and the Ends of Time*, ed. Juliet Cummins (Cambridge: Cambridge University Press, 2003), 52.

248 In September 1654, at the opening of the first Protectorate Parliament, Cromwell responded to the Fifth Monarchists by speaking of "a notion I hope we all honour, wait, and hope for; that Jesus Christ will have a time to set up his Reigne in our hearts." Cromwell, *Letters, Writings, and Speeches of Oliver Cromwell*, 3:74.

1649, *The Shaking and Translating of Heaven and Earth*. Third, Owen once again returned to Isaiah 60, a chapter that he had referenced in numerous previous sermons, to make the point that the civil powers of those nations would come to serve the interests of Christ as "his kingdoms" (Rev. 11:15). Fourth, Christ would advance his glorious kingdom through the conversion of the Jews and the destruction of the antichrist. Thus, any attempt to set up a kingdom for Christ in the world before these promises were fulfilled was, in effect, an attempt to "set up his kingdom here on a molehill." Finally, unlike the kingdoms of this world, the kingdom of Christ was not established by "outward force" through the actions of "the sword of man setting up a few to rule over others." Rather, it was a work of the Holy Spirit through the word of God.

Having "opened" the words of his text, Owen made three observations, the first of which was: "In the consideration of God's marvelous actings in the world, in order to the carrying on of the gospel and the interest of the Lord Jesus Christ, the hearts of his saints are oftentimes filled with perplexity and trouble." God's great works associated with the coming of Christ, either his coming in the flesh or his coming to advance his kingdom, were astonishing and beyond expectation. Even the saints had not been expecting such "shakings" as led to the regicide, the establishment of the English Republic, and, more recently, the banishment of Charles II. Owen engaged in what Gribben describes as "homiletical flattery" in order to portray the Rump as being united in a commitment to the further propagation of the gospel while, at the same time, acknowledging there was much that was unsettling.[249] He made what Hunter Powell describes as "dire warnings against sectary views of the magistrate's power."[250] His concerns reflect the debates of the past year, particularly about the *Humble Proposals* that had been before Parliament.[251] He laid out some of the views that he was most concerned about:

> Say some, "There is no gospel at all" say others, "If there be, you have nothing to do with it": some say, "Lo, here is Christ"; others "Lo, there": some make religion a color for one thing; some for another: say some, "The magistrate must not support the gospel"; say others, "The gospel must subvert the magistrate": say some, "Your rule is only for men, as men, you have nothing to do with the interest of Christ and the church": say others, "You have nothing to do to rule men but upon the account of being saints."

249 Gribben, "Owen and Politics," 93.

250 Powell, "'Promote, Protect, Prosecute,'" 226.

251 Worden, *Rump Parliament*, 234–35, 294.

For maximum impact, Owen reminded his hearers and readers of the anticlericalism of those who referred, shockingly, to the clergy as "chemarims" and "locusts"—something Feake's associate, John Simpson, had done.[252]

Parliament's problems were not only confined to the increasingly radical views of the sects, as Owen specifically drew attention to the opposition that the new regime had faced from the Scottish Covenanters and was now facing given that the Netherlands had joined "the great antichristian interest." This was all the more shocking given that in the previous year serious consideration had been given to a federal union of the two republics.[253]

Owen then turned to direct his hearers to the "ways and means of quietness"—namely, as suggested in the second observation, a discovery of God's will in "faith and prayer," both "public and private." Owen was convinced that public fasts were either neglected, criticized, or observed with cold formality. This was a far cry from the observance he remembered from the 1640s and evidence that the nation had "certainly backslidden." Nonetheless, he told his hearers that if his directions were followed, they would enjoy communion with God, the peace that flowed from it, and divine guidance.

Owen spoke of the "extremes" and "extravagances" of the various parties involved in the quest for a church settlement and, by contrast, sought to portray himself (and by implication the *Humble Proposals*) as being marked by moderation. On the one hand, he cautioned members of Parliament about neglecting their responsibilities: if "you shall say, you have nothing to do with religion as rulers of the nation, God will quickly manifest that he has nothing to do with you as rulers of the nation." On the other hand, he warned about those who seek to "set up forms of government, to compel men to come under the line of them," who wish the civil magistrate to "thrust in your sword to cut the lesser differences of brethren," or those engaged in "the great design" of the antichrist—namely, "grasping temporal power, upon a spiritual account." Owen portrayed his political theology as one characterized by moderation, summarizing his view in stating that the civil magistrate's responsibility was that the gospel be "protected, preserved, [and] propagated" in the nation.

This led Owen on to one of the express purposes of the public fast: seeking God's direction for the propagation of the gospel and preventing that which is contrary to sound doctrine and godliness. He began by offering a brief

252 *Original Letters and Papers of State, Addressed to Oliver Cromwell*, 82–83. The term *Chemarim* occurs in the Authorized Version (KJV) translation of Zeph. 1:4.

253 Steven C. A. Pincus, *Protestantism and Patriotism: Ideologies and the Making of English Foreign Policy, 1650–1668* (Cambridge: Cambridge University Press, 1996), 15–39.

summary of "what God has promised concerning magistrates, kings, rulers, judges, and nations, and their subserviency to the church." As he had done in previous sermons, Owen appealed to passages from Isaiah and Revelation in support of his contention that magistrates had a duty to support the interest of the church, acting for its "good, welfare, and prosperity." Owen insisted that these promises belonged to the gospel age and therefore "belong directly to us, and our rulers." This was important because proponents of far-reaching toleration were arguing against magisterial restraint or coercion in matters of religion, dismissing the Old Testament's teaching on the magistrate's responsibilities in religious matters as applicable only to national Israel.[254] They did this very well aware that those in favor of religious coercion rested their case on the Old Testament laws against blasphemers and idolaters. Owen was providing different grounds for the magistrate's power in matters of religion in these prophecies of a time when godly rulers would be raised up in the nations of the world. If the members of the Rump were to be such rulers, then they must

> *put forth their power, and act in that capacity, wherein he has placed them in the world, for the good, furtherance, and prosperity of the truth and church of Christ*: they shall protect them with their power, feed them with their substance, adorn them with their favor, and the privileges wherewith they are entrusted: they shall break their forcibly oppressing adversaries.

Owen then offered five further principles relevant to the propagation of the gospel. First, the magistrate's duty of protection extended to ensuring that the gospel was preached and propagated in the nation. Second, a nation that embraced the gospel would enjoy prosperity and be instrumental in the destruction of oppressive tyrants. Third, should a nation reject the gospel and refuse to serve Christ and his church, then Christ would, "sooner or later," come against that nation in judgment. Fourth, the magistrate was not only responsible for seeking the good, peace, and prosperity of the people but also charged to "prevent, obviate, remove, [and] take away" those things that cause "confusion, destruction, [and] desolation." The latter included not only threats to national security and various crimes but also those things that were "morally" opposed to the good and welfare of the nation, particularly those things that would bring God's judgment on a nation. He offered obvious examples, such as murder and adultery, but suggested that there were other

254 See, e.g., [Henry Vane], *Zeal Examined, or, A Discourse for Liberty of Conscience* [...] (London, 1652). George Thomason acquired his copy on June 15. For the attribution to Sir Henry Vane the younger, see Polizzotto, "The Campaign against *The Humble Proposals* of 1652," 579.

provocations that required a similar response. This may be an oblique reference to the magistrate's responsibilities to act against certain forms of heresy and blasphemy. Finally, he also argued that the judicial laws given to Israel were no longer in force, though the moral elements of those laws remained binding once they had been "unclothed of their Judaical form."

Owen closed by laying down three rules by way of direction, pointing his readers to *Of Toleration* (1649) for a fuller treatment of the matter.[255] First, his readers needed to be fully persuaded of what the truth of the gospel was and what constituted error. Second, he insisted that "error and falsehood" had no right to any protection from the civil magistrate. Finally, he noted that "the plea of conscience," far from serving as a justification, could, on occasion, be an aggravating factor.

GOD'S WORK IN FOUNDING ZION, AND HIS PEOPLE'S DUTY THEREUPON

Context of This Sermon to the Second Protectorate Parliament

In the summer of 1656, Oliver Cromwell, as Lord Protector, reluctantly issued writs for an extraordinary Parliament with elections set to take place in August. (Owen's brother Henry was one of those elected to an Irish constituency.)[256] The regime had little choice because of the "looming financial disaster" caused, not least, by the outbreak of war with Spain and the cost of maintaining armies in Ireland and Scotland.[257] Cromwell had thought that the conflict would have been funded by the seizure of Spanish silver, but this was not to be, given the blundering failure of the so-called Western Design in 1655.[258] The army Grandees and the Council of State failed to manage these elections quite as they had confidently intended. The elections had been fraught, and, from the regime's point of view, the results were even worse than those of the elections to the First Protectorate Parliament. Consequently, the decision was taken to exclude those members of Parliament who were hostile to the new constitution, the Instrument of Government, and critical of the political role of the army: nearly one hundred members out of four

255 See *Complete Works of John Owen*, vol. 18.

256 *History of Parliament*, s.v. "Owen, Henry (d. 1660?)." For evidence of his later career, see Gribben, *John Owen and English Politics*, 160–61, 257–61.

257 Peter Gaunt, "'The Single Person's Confidants and Dependents'? Oliver Cromwell and his Protectoral Councillors," in *Cromwell and the Interregnum: The Essential Readings*, ed. David L. Smith (Oxford: Blackwell, 2003), 115; Venning, *Cromwellian Foreign Policy*, 109.

258 An expeditionary force that had been sent to seize Hispaniola in the West Indies.

hundred sixty were purged, and around sixty others withdrew in protest.[259] This was done on the basis that under the terms of this constitution they were not "persons of known integrity, fearing God, and of good conversation." Those excluded included crypto royalists, rigid Presbyterians, and committed republicans. Of those who remained, there was "a sizeable bloc of MPs favourable to Presbyterianism who sought an anti-militarist return to the ancient constitution."[260] As Patrick Little describes it, "very strong Presbyterian undercurrents" had remained through the early 1650s, and these "broke the surface" in this Parliament.[261] Many in Parliament were critical of the regime's tolerant approach to religion, particularly where Quakers were concerned.

Owen addressed this second Protectorate Parliament on two occasions. The first was as the preacher at the grand and militaristic opening of the Parliament on September 17. On that day, the Lord Protector, accompanied in his coach by Lord Lambert, journeyed to the abbey with the members of the Council of State, and some three hundred soldiers. They arrived for ten o'clock in the morning to be greeted by the newly elected members of Parliament who had already gathered. The abbey where Owen would deliver this sermon was now "more than ever before the church of the state," serving as "the religious heart of the regime."[262] Although Austin Woolrych described Owen as preaching an "adulatory sermon," it was, as we shall see, actually somewhat more ambiguous.[263]

Those in the abbey to hear Owen preach would have been unaware that outside, Miles Sindercombe (d. 1657) was engaged in a conspiracy to assassinate Cromwell as he left the building and proceeded to Parliament. A house had been rented near the abbey, and scaffolding had been erected to provide an elevated position for the gunmen. The plot was aborted at the last moment because the would-be assassins lost their nerve in the presence of the gathering crowds of onlookers.[264] After the service, Cromwell met

259 Patrick Little and David L. Smith, *Parliaments and Politics during the Cromwellian Protectorate* (Cambridge: Cambridge University Press, 2007), 87–91; Blair Worden, "Oliver Cromwell and the Council," in *The Cromwellian Protectorate*, ed. Patrick Little (Woodbridge, UK: Boydell, 2007), 100–03.

260 Vernon, *London Presbyterians and the British Revolutions*, 255.

261 Patrick Little, *Lord Broghill and the Cromwellian Union with Ireland and Scotland* (Woodbridge, UK: Boydell, 2004), 233.

262 Merritt, *Westminster 1640–60*, 106–7.

263 Woolrych, *Britain in Revolution*, 646.

264 John Thurloe, *Collection of the State Papers of John Thurloe* [. . .], ed. Thomas Birch, 7 vols. (London, 1742), 5:774–77 (The examinations of John Cecil and John Toop, 9 Jan. 1656); *A Declaration of His Highness the Lord Protector and the Parliament for a Day of Publique Thanksgiving On Friday the Twentieth of February, 1656* (London, 1657), 3–5; *A True Narrative of the late Trayterous Plot Against the Person of His Highness, The Lord Protector* [. . .] (London, 1657), 5–6.

with the three hundred or so members of Parliament in the Painted Chamber of the medieval Palace of Westminster and gave a lengthy and at times rambling speech outlining the reasons for calling the present Parliament.[265] The heat was stifling, and Cromwell spoke for up to three hours. Security was a dominant theme in the light of the threat posed by royalists, Roman Catholics, and those radicals of the levelling sort. He praised the rule of the major generals and defended his war with Spain. In this address, the Lord Protector signaled his approval of what Owen had said, stating that he desired liberty for Presbyterians, Independents, and Baptists, stating that this was "the peculiar Interest all this while Contested for."[266] The members then moved to the House of Commons, and, after the election of the speaker of the House, it was agreed that the lieutenant of the Tower of London, Major Generals Sir John Barkstead (d. 1662),[267] and John Maidstone,[268] the steward of Cromwell's household, "should return the Thanks of the House to Doctor Owen for the pains by him taken in the Sermon preached before them" and that he be asked to prepare the sermon for publication.[269] News of Owen's preaching spread, as is evidenced by Ralph Josselin hearing about Owen's sermon two days after it was preached.[270] It was printed by Leonard Lichfield (d. 1657), so-called printer to the University of Oxford, for the Oxford bookseller Thomas Robinson. George Thomason had acquired his copy by October 25.

265 Cromwell, *Letters, Writings, and Speeches of Oliver Cromwell*, 3:288–317.

266 Cromwell, *Letters, Writings, and Speeches of Oliver Cromwell*, 3:306.

267 One of Cromwell's "most reliable colleagues," Barkstead was major general for Middlesex, London and Westminster and sat as the member of Parliament for Middlesex in the second Protectorate Parliament. He had commanded a regiment at the siege of Colchester and was a regicide. He described himself as "a follower of the congregational way" and was hostile to the Fifth Monarchism. He served as lieutenant of the Tower of London and was knighted by Cromwell at the beginning of 1656. Sir John went on to become a member of Cromwell's Other House in 1657. See Christopher Durston, *Cromwell's Major-Generals: Godly Government during the English Revolution* (Manchester: Manchester University Press, 2001), 29, 51, 141–42, 156–57; and *History of Parliament*, s.v. "Barkstead, John (c. 1612–62)."

268 From a minor gentry family in Essex, Maidstone had served in the Essex county militia. He became Cromwell's steward and cofferer and in the Second Protectorate Parliament he sat as member of Parliament for Colchester. See Andrew Barclay, "The Lord Protector and his Court," in *Oliver Cromwell: New Perspectives*, ed. Patrick Little (London: Palgrave Macmillan, 2009), 206–7; *History of Parliament*, s.v. "Maidstone, John (1606–67)"; and Owen's letter to Maidstone from January 1658 in which he and other Visitors of the University of Oxford wrote to Maidstone describing his "known respect to things of honesty and good repute."

269 *Mercurius Politicus* 327 (September 11–16, 1656), 7254; Thomas Burton, *Diary of Thomas Burton, Esq.* [. . .], ed. J. T. Rutt, 4 vols. (London, 1828), 1:cxlvi; and *Journals of the House of Commons*, 7:423.

270 Ralph Josselin, *The Diary of Ralph Josselin, 1616–1683*, ed. Alan Macfarlane, Records of Social and Economic History (Oxford: Oxford University Press, 1976), 381.

On the title page, Owen included the text of Psalm 48:12–14. The published sermon was dedicated to the Lord Protector and Parliament, but Gribben describes Owen's preface as offering only "rather faint praise" to Cromwell.[271]

Summary and Analysis of the Sermon

Owen expounded the text "What shall one then answer the messengers of the nation? That the Lord hath founded Zion, and the poor of his people shall trust in it" (Isa. 14:32). Owen had quoted this text in a previous sermon as a summary of "the great alterations that have been in these nations."[272] As Owen set this verse in its context, its relevance would have emerged to all contemporary hearers and readers. It came from a season when Judah was "low," "broken," and "divided" because of foreign enemies and domestic problems. The parallels would have been all too clear because at this time progress in the Anglo-Spanish war was slow, a far cry from the previous wars against the Scottish and the Dutch, and such was the nature of internal political tensions that the military and political leaders of the regime had felt forced to exclude over one hundred elected members of Parliament. Owen selected a text that drew particular attention to one of the most obvious errors of Hezekiah's reign.[273] Owen commented that "all would have been well" for Hezekiah "and his posterity" had he followed the clear instructions prepared for him by the prophet when the Babylonian envoys came. However, Hezekiah failed to act as required, and instead the man who had once stood firm against the threat of the Assyrian army now melted in the face of Babylonian flattery (Isa. 39:2). He made it very explicit that "His mistake herein, was the fatal ruin of Judah's prosperity," and this warning from the opening of the sermon frames all that follows.

It was Owen's contention that the "peculiar" work of God in the past few years had not been principally that of the setting up and pulling down of "new fabrics of government or ruling." He argued that God did not delight in one form of government more than another. This defense of the Protectorate was a tacit rebuke to civilian republicans like Sir Arthur Hesilrige, John Bradshaw, Thomas Scot, and John Weaver, who refused to accept the Protectorate and who were prominent among those members excluded from Parliament.[274] Rather, when it was asked, "What [God] has done in England," through the mid-seventeenth-century crisis, Owen's unequivocal answer was that God

271 Gribben, "Owen and Politics," 96.

272 *The Advantage of the Kingdom* (1651).

273 Woolrych, *Britain in Revolution*, 646.

274 Carol S. Egloff, "The Search for a Cromwellian Settlement: Exclusions from the Second Protectorate Parliament," parts 1–2, *Parliamentary History* 17, no. 3 (1998): 178–97, 301–21.

had acted to "found Zion" and "establish the interest of his chosen." By this Owen meant that God had destroyed those who sought "to overthrow Zion" and had given the peace, liberty, and freedom to gather gospel churches of "secret covenanted ones." Cromwell would echo this sentiment later in the day with his comment that securing toleration for the godly was "the peculiar interest all this while contended for."[275]

Owen summarized four "observations" "drawn from the words" of his text and then dealt with each in turn. He commented that he hoped to strike the balance of addressing his hearers with both due reverence and appropriate authority. He also voiced his conviction that not all in the abbey that day were regenerate. The first observation was about how the nations were "diligently inquiring concerning God's dispensations among his people." In the case of England, Owen thought that surrounding nations were making such inquiries because they envied the nation's unique and exalted position and feared how the nation would grow and develop. The second observation concerned the answer that should be given to the nations when they were inquiring about what God had done. Owen recognized that not all could see what God had done because their vision was clouded and distorted by being taken up and preoccupied with their own agendas and rivalries. This diverted their attention from the great "providential alterations of the late times that have passed over us." Owen was thinking of how the Laudian tyranny had been overthrown and those who had been imprisoned had been released and those exiled to the Netherlands or New England had been able to return home. He was horrified that some were contemplating a return to tyranny and superstition. His third observation was that "the great design of God in his mighty works and dispensations, is the establishment of his people and their proper interest." Those whom God "by his providence raises up to rule and government" had an instrumental role in ensuring that the people of God had this freedom to worship. Owen warned that God would "pull down" rulers who did not discharge this responsibility. His final observation was that it was "the common interest" of God's people that was to be preserved. Owen reiterated what he had "sundry years since, sundry times complained of to a parliament of this commonwealth"—namely, that too many were taken up with their own "peculiar interest" and therefore despised the "common interest." He confessed that his optimism that things would change was withering by the day. Owen regarded these four observations as "foundations . . . laid in the words of the text" that led him to application.

275 Cromwell, *Letters, Writings, and Speeches of Oliver Cromwell*, 3:306.

Owen's first "use" was a call on those in political power to consider how they would give an account of "what God has done in these nations." He hoped that their response would indicate enthusiastic support of "the old and common cause." This phrase was shorthand for the struggle of the civil war and was provocative because it was often used to rally opposition to the Protectorate. He warned against allowing personal "disquietness" to inadvertently "cast contempt on the work of God." Owen recognized that the counsel that he was about to offer would be regarded by many of his hearers as unlikely to yield results and potentially was even irrational. This was because Owen suggested that the godly themselves be consulted about what the common interest of Zion was, and he was aware that, to many, the various parties seemed hopelessly divided. He responded to this by employing a Ciceronian argument to prove what was the best option for a church settlement that would include all the godly of the nation. In a fragment of Cicero preserved in Augustine and mediated by Francis Bacon, Owen recounted how when asked which was the best school of philosophy, the ancient sects, such as the Stoics and the Epicureans, all put themselves first and assigned Plato to the second place. From this Cicero reasoned that because all parties were united in their views of what constituted the second-best option, it was in fact the best and preferred option. Owen applied this to the situation of the day: Presbyterians sought uniformity of doctrine, worship, and discipline; radical anticlericalists such as the Quakers sought an abolition of tithes and believed an ordained and educated ministry to be anti-Christian; and Fifth Monarchists were still calling for the rule of the saints. Owen reasoned that all the godly would put his own position, at the very least, in second place[276]—namely, that despite their differences, the godly would be able to live in peace with the civil magistrate, ensuring that the godly would be "preserved, protected, and secured."[277]

Owen offered five reasons in support of this. First, it comprehended all the godly, recognizing that not all churches were identical according to the degree of spiritual light they had received. Second, none who lived by faith

276 Others would employ this motif. For example, at the opening of the second session of the second Protectorate Parliament in January 1658, the Lord Commissioner, Nathaniel Fiennes, advocated unity through a shared acceptance of the next best thing. See *Commons Journals* 7:582–87.

277 Owen made a similar point in *The Kingdom of Christ* (1652), which is included in this volume, when he told members of Parliament of their responsibilities to ensure that the gospel may "be protected, preserved, propagated to and among the people which God has set you over." Similar language would be employed in chapter 24 of the Savoy Declaration of 1658. It stated that the magistrate was bound "to incourage, promote and protect the professors and profession of the Gospel." See *The Savoy Declaration of Faith and Order 1658*, ed. A. G. Matthews (Letchworth, UK: Independent Press, 1959), 37.

and prayer in the late dispensations were excluded. Third, such an option prevented coercion, oppression, and persecution. Fourth, all the godly were united by the opposition of those who sought to destroy them. Finally, reiterating a point from earlier in the sermon, he insisted that God's great work had been focused on the church rather than on the establishment of "this or that form of the civil administration of human affairs." Owen remained ambivalent to particular forms of government, stating that the only thing promised about government was that it would be "laid in an orderly subserviency, to the common interest of the saints." Owen had made a very similar point in *The Kingdom of Christ, and the Power of the Civil Magistrate* (1652) in saying that "the civil powers of the world, after fearful shakings and desolations, shall be disposed of into a useful subserviency to the interest, power, and kingdom of Jesus Christ."

The second major application was to call his hearers to go to this work. To aid the government in this task he offered two directions. The first was to refuse to engage with any counsel that was inconsistent with this common interest because to do so would be to contend against the work of God. He was aware that there was much discussion about clamping down on toleration and "establishing a discipline in the church" and rejected any suggestion that he was arguing "for errors and unsettlement." Rather, he was calling for "mutual forbearance" until God intervened to unite his people. Owen exhorted his hearers to be "instrumental" in this process. True reformation would come about through a personal reformation and a reformation of "families" and "parishes." It would be accomplished by prayer, preaching, and the other means of grace. In all of this it was imperative that people did not forget that this work of God had been what the Wars of the Three Kingdoms had been about "from the beginning to the end."

Owen's second direction regarding how the government could go about this task in all its consultations, actions, and proposals was to make the work of establishing Zion its "polestar." That would lead to two priorities: pursuing peace domestically and building a pan-Protestant alliance internationally.[278] The latter would involve a plan to "gather into one common interest, the Protestant nations abroad in the world, that we may stand or fall together." In his speech later that day, Cromwell spoke of the recently elected Pope Alexander VII and his plan to "unite all the Popish Interest in all the Christian world against this nation about any, and against all the Protestant Interest

278 Adam Quibell, "The Grounds, Method, Scope, and Impact of Independentism's Efforts for Union, 1654–1659," (PhD diss., Queen's University Belfast, 2024), 57–62.

in the world."[279] At this time, there were efforts to broker peace among the Protestant nations in the Baltic who were engaged in the Second Northern War (1655–1660) in order to forge a defensive alliance between Sweden and England as part of a plan for a Protestant League. Correspondingly, the Papacy and the Roman Catholic Habsburg Empire were increasingly aligned and strengthened because of conflict between various Protestant nations.[280]

Owen's third major "use" was to carry on the work of reformation, encouraging and resourcing it as required. This would involve taking action against those who "under pretense of religion . . . disturb the civil peace." By doing so, they would be "preservers of the good old cause of England." This would require sincere seeking after God's will and "love and forbearance" as they sought to "regard, cleave to, promote, [and] protect" the common interest of Zion.

GOD'S PRESENCE WITH A PEOPLE, THE SPRING OF THEIR PROSPERITY

Context of Owen's Fast Sermon

On September 18, 1656, the day after the second Protectorate Parliament assembled, it resolved that "a day of public fasting and humiliation" be held throughout England, Scotland, and Ireland. The Parliamentary preachers were to be Owen, his Oxford colleague Thomas Goodwin, and the prominent London preacher George Griffith. Owen was invited by Major General Thomas Kelsey (d. ca. 1676), Goodwin by Sir William Strickland (ca. 1596–1673), and Griffith by Major General Whalley (ca. 1607–ca. 1675). A committee was established to prepare the declaration for the fast. This received its second reading in Parliament on September 22 and was presented to Cromwell for approval. The date of the fast was changed to October 30, and the declaration was duly published on September 23.[281] It expressed concern about "the abominable Blasphemies vented and spread of late through the apostasie of, and the abuse of liberty by, many professing Religion" and sought for believers to be united by "Agreements in fundamentals." The declaration called for prayer that God would defeat the designs of those who opposed the interest of Christ and his people and that, furthermore, God would grant his presence

279 Cromwell, *Letters, Writings, and Speeches of Oliver Cromwell*, 3:299.

280 Woolrych, *Britain in Revolution*, 632–37; Barry Coward, *The Cromwellian Protectorate* (Manchester: Manchester University Press, 2002), 129–30; Michael Roberts, "Cromwell and the Baltic," *The English Historical Review*, 76 (July 1961): 406–8.

281 *Journals of the House of Commons*, 7:423–24, 426–27, 447; Burton, *Diary of Thomas Burton*, 1:clxxix; Mears et al., *National Prayers*, 1:610.

to those in government so that they would be united in the work to which they were called.[282]

In the intervening period prior to the fast, news of Captain Richard Stayner's capture of two vessels from the Spanish plate fleet off Cadiz had reached London giving "a needed boost to government morale."[283] This news came at the beginning of October and served for many as a long-awaited providential sign, especially in the context of the ongoing war against Spain. An official account of the victory was published on October 4, and the sermons from the public thanksgiving on October 8 were published as Joseph Caryl's *A Sermon Pressing to, and Directing in, That Great Duty of Praising God* (1657) and John Rowe's *Mans Duty in Magnifying Gods Work* (1656).[284] Rowe was confident that such a providential mercy had "silenced the secret thoughts and reasonings of some, touching the engagement in this war; and who are too apt to say, that God never owned you since you undertook this business."[285]

Reports of the fast sermons from the service held on Thursday, October 30, at St Margaret's were published in *Mercurius Politicus*. The weekly newsbook summarized Owen's message to the purged Parliament as follows: "the great concernment of any people, is to know where lies the Spring of all their Success, and to what it is proportioned." It continued by describing how after opening the text the following doctrine was "raised" from it: "That Gods special presence with any people in providential dispensations for their good, depends upon their obediential abiding with him in National Administrations for his glory."[286] The news report also recorded summaries of Goodwin's sermon on Romans 15:8–9 and that by Griffith on 2 Chronicles 20:12. Outside of Westminster, Owen's old acquaintance Ralph Josselin kept the fast by preaching on Isaiah 5:25 but confessed that he found his own heart "very dead and unaffected."[287] The preachers were thanked on Friday, October 31, and invited to publish their sermons. Owen's work was printed by "R.N."

282 *A Declaration of His Highnes the Lord Protector and the Parliament of the Commonwealth of England, Scotland, and Ireland, for a Day of Solemn Fasting and Humiliation in the Three Nations* (London, 1656), 2–4.

283 Worden, "Cromwell and the Sin of Achan," 22. For details of the naval engagement in September, see: Bernard S. Capp, *Cromwell's Navy: The Fleet and the English Revolution, 1648–1660* (Oxford: Clarendon, 1989), 98–99.

284 *A True Narrative of the Late Success Which It Hath Pleased God to Give to Some Part of the Fleet of This Common-Wealth against the King of Spain's West India Fleet in Its Return to Cadiz* [. . .] (London, 1656).

285 John Rowe, *Mans Duty in Magnifying Gods Work* [. . .] (London, 1656), 20.

286 *Mercurius Politicus* 334 (October 29–November 6, 1656), 7354–355.

287 Josselin, *Diary of Ralph Josselin*, 384.

This is almost certainly a reference to Roger Norton (d. 1664), a printer in Blackfriars.[288] It was published by Philemon Stephens and was entered on the Stationers' Register only days after it was preached on November 6, 1656.[289] On the title page, Owen styled himself with the DD that he had been awarded by diploma on December 23, 1653. This was qualified by a description of himself as "a servant of Jesus Christ, in the work of the gospel."

Summary and Analysis of the Sermon

Owen took as his text the record of the "thanksgiving sermon" delivered by the prophet Azariah to King Asa (2 Chron. 15:2). Despite the seeming incongruity of doing so on "a day of humiliation," Owen thought the "instruction" suitable for the occasion because it summarized the "rules, and exhortations" that were necessary, given "the event, and issue of our affairs." The text recorded an event in the aftermath of Judah's great victory against "the huge host of the Ethiopians" who had come against Jerusalem (2 Chron. 14). Owen drew an explicit parallel between his preaching of the sermon and the prophet going out to meet those returning to Jerusalem in triumph carrying "abundant spoils." The point would not have been lost on his hearers—that as the sermon was being delivered "the Spanish prizes," the spoils taken from the captured "Silver Gallion," were in the process of being transferred to the Tower of London.[290] As the title of the published version of the sermon suggests, Owen was interested in "the spring" of such mercies, something even "the best of men" were quick to forget, and the "duty" that this placed on the recipients to "use and improve their peace." The importance of "duty" had been prominent in the thanksgiving sermons celebrating the capture of the treasure fleet that were delivered earlier in the month by Joseph Caryl (1602–1673) and John Rowe (1626–1677), as is evident in their respective titles: *A Sermon Pressing to, and Directing in, That Great Duty of Praising God* (1657) and *Mans Duty in Magnifying Gods Work* (1656). As Owen delivered his fast sermon, he was aware of the divisions and conflicting agendas that existed among the rulers of the nation about how to respond "in making peace or war" in dealings "with neighboring princes, and nations." As Owen set about "the opening of the

288 Norton had printed John Trapp's commentary on the minor prophets for Philemon Stephens in 1654. Plomer, *Dictionary of the Booksellers and Printers*, s.v. "Roger Norton."

289 *Transcript of the Registers of the Worshipful Company of Stationers*, 2:94. At the end of the sermon, Stephens included a list of nineteen others titles by Owen which he was marketing. See Owen, *God's Presence with a People, the Spring of Their Prosperity* [. . .] (1656), 39.

290 *Mercurius Politicus* 333 (October 23–29, 1656), 7335; *Mercurius Politicus* 334 (October 29–November 6, 1656), 7365.

words," he explained that he would take his hearers to matters of "unspeakably greater importance" by dealing with two main questions.

First, Owen set about clarifying and explaining what exactly it meant for God to be with a people "in respect of providential dispensations." Not simply in that "general" sense of God's "ordering, disposing, guiding, [and] ruling" all the events of nations and their governments but in that "special" sense of being with a people in guidance, blessing, and preservation. This gave rise to his first "observation," the doctrinal proposition that the nation must recognize that the source of all its prosperity was the special presence of God and that it was therefore necessary "to attend to that which will give continuance thereunto."

Second, he posed the question about what it meant for a people to abide with God. Given the context, his particular concern here was abiding with God "in national administrations"—that is, how to order the affairs of the nation so that God would thereby be glorified. This led to the main doctrinal observation of the sermon, which stated that God's special presence with a people "depends on their obediential presence with him, in national administrations to his glory." A significant assumption underlying this position was that God's presence in respect of providential dispensations was "purely conditional," in the sense it was distinct from that of the gospel, resting on an entirely different "foundation" and operating according to a different principle. Nonetheless, God's presence with a people was always merciful rather than "merited," with the strength to fulfill the condition being itself given by God. For Owen, the evidence supporting this conditionality lay both in the history of God's dealings with his people of old and in the events of history. A king like Asa of Judah enjoyed seasons of blessing when he acted in obedience but also experienced divine curses for disobedience. For example, when Asa relied on King Ben-Hadad of Damascus for assistance against Baasha rather than trusting in the Lord, there was plague and war (2 Chron. 16:7–14). The same conditionality could be seen in the history of the Roman Empire. It flourished under those emperors "who ruled with God," and now, as Owen understood it, in its present form as the Holy Roman Empire, it endured "the fury and cruelty of Turk and Pope." This was because its present rulers were characterized by "unrighteousness, idolatry, luxury, and persecution." Owen was referring to how the Holy Roman Empire had been devastated by the Thirty Years' War (1618–1648), a struggle over religion and the power of the emperor, particularly in Habsburg lands. One example of the rulers that Owen had in mind would be Ferdinand II, Holy Roman emperor from 1619. He was a champion of the Counter-Reformation, and his determination to reestablish Roman Catholicism across all his lands had been a significant cause of that war.[291] At the same time, on the borders of the empire, the Ottomans were, once again, beginning to pursue their expansionist ambitions. As Owen saw it, the empire was experiencing all these things because its rulers did not abide with God. He issued two brief cautions by way of qualification. First, that outward "flourishing" and "prosperity" was not always proof of God's special presence. This was important because a number of Roman Catholic nations continued to prosper, as did the Ottoman empire, which was at the beginning of the period of the Köprülü revival (1656–1702). Second, periods of affliction and distress, like what the Protectorate had endured in recent years, did not necessarily mean that God had withdrawn his special presence.

Owen's first point of application was to give further instruction about how, through abiding with God, the nation could enjoy God's special presence. He explained how, at the time of the Exodus and wilderness wanderings, the pillar of cloud and fire that were symbolized God's presence with his people. This "eminent pledge of the presence of God" guided the people on their journey toward "their resting place" and offered them "protection and defense" along the way. In a similar manner, the "assembly of Parliament" was also being led and directed by God toward a resting place. Owen also believed that God's special presence had preserved the nation from enemies internal and external and, furthermore, "our own follies." Here he referred to the first Protectorate Parliament that met from September 1654 to January 1655. Despite the best intentions of some, it succeeded in passing no legislation during its entire sitting. Owen explained that it was as if the cloud had settled on them, and so "they could not see how to take one step forward."[292] As he saw it, England was still journeying through the wilderness, and God had been present at the last Parliament "to cause us to rest and cease."[293] Thomas Goodwin had also employed this motif as he preached at the opening of the first Protectorate Parliament on September 4, 1654. In Cromwell's speech as the nation's new head of state, he made reference to this otherwise unpublished sermon by Goodwin: "the only parallel of God's dealing with us that I know in the

291 For the question of the influence of the pope on the Holy Roman emperors at this time, see Rubén González Cuerva and Luis Tercero Casado, "The Imperial Court during the Thirty Years War: A Battleground for Factions?" in *Factional Struggles: Divided Elites in European Cities and Courts (1400–1750)*, ed. Mathieu Caesar (Leiden: Brill, 2017), 155–75.

292 See David L. Smith, "Oliver Cromwell, the First Protectorate Parliament and Religious Reform," in *Cromwell and the Interregnum: The Essential Readings*, ed. David L. Smith (Oxford: Blackwell, 2003), 167–82.

293 Owen had, controversially, been chosen as a member of that Parliament representing the University of Oxford. See Gribben, "Owen and Politics," 94; *History of Parliament*, s.v. "Owen, Dr John (?1614–83)."

world, which was largely and wisely held forth to you this day, [is] *Israels* bringing out of *Egypt* through a Wildernesse, by many Signes, and Wonders, towards a Place of Rest; I say towards it." According to the Lord Protector, Goodwin had spoken "largely and wisely" as he described how, even up to that point, the slow and painful journey through the wilderness had been delayed due to "unbelief, murmurring, repining, and other temptations and sinnes, wherewith God was provoked."[294] There had, of course, been times when God's presence had been "eclipsed," as for example in the failure of the campaign against the Spanish empire known as the Western Design. In April 1655, English forces were repulsed from Hispaniola having suffered heavy losses. News of the regime's first major defeat reached England in July. It was understood as a sign of divine displeasure and caused significant soul searching with days of fasting being held on November 21, 1655, and March 14, 1656.[295] Owen assured members of Parliament that not every defeat or disappointment was a sign of God's departure because often such providences were designed as trials whose purpose could be to bring about renewed enjoyment of God's presence. The cloud by which God ordinarily led his people was not the only "pledge of his presence with them." Owen explained that in "extraordinary seasons," there were "extraordinary manifestations" of God's glory, "eminent and glorious appearances," such as what occurred at Mount Sinai and the dedication of the tabernacle. Owen was confident that England had enjoyed such special providences. An example of what he had in mind could well have been the capture of the part of the Spanish treasure fleet.

In order to continue to enjoy God's special presence, the "rulers" of the nation had to abide with God. Owen distanced himself from the claims of the Fifth Monarchists, who advocated the rule of the saints over the masses, claiming that their methods "have not become sober men, much less saints of Christ."[296] Owen spoke favorably of how the present constitution, the

294 Cromwell, *Letters, Writings, and Speeches of Oliver Cromwell*, 3:71, 81 (italics original). See also John Coffey, *Exodus and Liberation: Deliverance Politics from John Calvin to Martin Luther King Jr.* (Oxford: Oxford University Press, 2014), 25.

295 Worden, "Oliver Cromwell and the Sin of Achan," 22–23.

296 In February 1655, there were intelligence reports that Thomas Harrison, Christopher Feake and John Rogers were plotting against the government. See William Clarke, *Clarke Papers* [. . .], vols. 1–4, ed. C. H. Firth (London: Camden Society, 1891–1901), 2:244. In November 1655, John Thurloe, secretary of state, wrote to Henry Cromwell saying that "It is certayne, that the 5th monarchy men, (some of them I meane) have designes of puttinge us into blood." See Thurloe, *Collection of the State Papers of John Thurloe*, 4:190–91. Despite its leaders enduring periods of imprisonment, Fifth Monarchist agitation continued throughout 1656. See Bernard Capp, *The Fifth Monarchy Men: A Study in Seventeenth-Century English Millenarianism* (London: Faber 2008), 114–15.

Instrument of Government (1653–1657), had been "framed" and "balanced": the Lord Protector governing with an elected unicameral Parliament and a Council of State, elected by the Parliament. As S. R. Gardiner memorably put it, that constitution steered "a middle course between the despotism of a 'single person' and the despotism of a 'single House.' "[297] Woolrych describes how the "ghost" of Owen's old friend Henry Ireton "hovers over the constitution of the Protectorate."[298] Even with such a constitution, Owen confessed that his "heart trembles" at the thought that those who governed the commonwealth had their "rise" from a people who were so "dark and profane . . . full of enmity against the remnant." He insisted that it was the duty of those in government "to consider all ways and means whereby the power of these nations may be in succeeding seasons, devolved on men of the like spirit."[299] By "all ways and means," Owen tacitly included the Council's exclusion of a hundred elected members under article 17 of the Instrument of Government. Major General Kelsey, who had sponsored Owen's invitation to preach, was a strong supporter of this policy of exclusion, stating, "The interest of God's people is to be preferred before a thousand Parliaments" in order to prevent a return to slavery under "Egyptian taskmasters."[300] By contrast, civilian republicans like Sir Arthur Hesilrige (1601–1661) and Thomas Scott (d. 1660), both of whom had been excluded, saw this as an act of "absolute arbitrary sovereignty" and further evidence of the army's continued influence on the direction of government.[301] However, for Owen, such actions were necessary because if those in power were not "men interested personally in Christ," then "England's glory and happiness" would come to an end. This was not a new theme in Owen's preaching. He told members of Parliament that this point was something that he had "delivered long ago, and many times in this place."

Owen continued with application as he turned to deal with how to ensure that as the rulers of the nation they did not act in such as manner as to be "the cause of God's departure from us." First, it was necessary for the rulers of the nation to seek counsel and direction from God in all things, seeking his glory, sensing their own unworthiness, and walking in integrity and uprightness.

297 S. R. Gardiner, *Constitutional Documents of the Puritan Revolution*, 3rd ed. (Oxford: Clarendon, 1951), lvi.

298 Woolrych, *Commonwealth to Protectorate*, 377.

299 Egloff, "Search for a Cromwellian Settlement," 178–97, 301–21; Little and Smith, *Parliaments*, 80.

300 *Journals of the House of Commons*, 7:424, 447; Thurloe, *Collection of the State Papers of John Thurloe*, 5:384; Major General Kelsey sent in a number of objections to those elected in his county of Kent. See *Calendar of State Papers, Domestic*, 10:87.

301 C. H. Firth, *The Last Years of the Protectorate, 1656–1658*, 2 vols. (1909; repr., New York: Russell and Russell, 1964), 1:21–23.

This involved public and private prayer and diligent use of days of fasting, such as the occasion on which Owen was preaching. Second, Owen urged his hearers to trust God for protection rather than relying on their own counsel and strength. God was glorified when his people trusted him in perplexing storms, submitting to God's providence rather than attempting to prescribe to God what must take place. Third, the rulers of the nation were to prioritize the interests of Christ and his people. He chose not to deal with this in detail because this had been a prominent theme in his sermon from the previous month at the opening of the Parliament, *God's Work in Founding Zion* (1656), which is included in this volume.

The concluding uses were threefold. First, as the prophet had said, the presence of God was to be the main concern of the Parliament rather than matters of military strength, political alliances, and foreign policy. Owen believed that through the events of the mid-century crisis, experience had taught that God's presence was the people's "life," "preservation," "protection," "prosperity," "safety," "success," and "peace." This was in line with Protectorate policy. Earlier that year, Cromwell had issued a fast-day declaration seeking to ascertain how the nation might recover God's "blessed presence."[302]

Second, with a pledge of God's presence, the Parliament could be confident in the face of all opposition. Owen rehearsed some of the difficulties that were raised by opponents of the government. There were those like Fifth Monarchists prophesying the "ruin and destruction" of the Parliament. Others raised the specter of the threat of Roman Catholic powers uniting against England. There were also concerns about how the war against Spain would be financed. Owen's response was simply, "If God be with us, who can be against us?"

The third "use" was to prioritize anything that would serve to confirm God's special presence. Here Owen underlined to them how on any occasion he had "opportunity to speak to you or any concerned in the government of this nation, in public or private," and he spoke about the need to protect and encourage "the remnant, the hidden people." This rehearsal of previous messages was useful because many members of Parliament were newcomers. Owen explained that this was because the civil power's treatment of the remnant would determine if God's presence would remain with the nation.

He closed the sermon by dealing with two areas of policy and reform that, if successfully implemented, could ensure God's presence would remain with his people. The first was the Cromwellian church settlement. Recognizing

302 *A Declaration of His Highness Inviting the People of England and Wales to a Day of Solemn Fasting and Humiliation on March 28, 1656* (London, 1656), unpaginated.

that many were unhappy with the current model, he nonetheless expressed his confidence that it would eventually be seen to have been good for all the godly in the nation.[303] He did take the time to remind members of Parliament about the situation in Wales, where, he claimed, nearly all were "running into extremes" to the detriment of the propagation of the gospel.[304] He thus presented his position as a moderate middle way between, on the one hand, the "misguided zeal" of those like the Fifth Monarchists and, on the other, those committed to "formality," who would be satisfied only by a return to "beggarly readers in every parish." By claiming the middle ground, he sought to make his proposed settlement more reasonable and thereby made other proposals appear extreme and lacking the potential to be truly comprehensive. Owen's confidence in the Cromwellian church settlement would be tested in the coming months during the debate about what to do with the notorious Quaker James Nayler (1618–1660). This would only increase the tensions between those who supported some measure of liberty of conscience and those who sought to suppress the sects.

Owen urged members of Parliament to set the wheels in motion for the "righteous administrations of justice." Mentioning how "many particulars lie before you; more will present themselves," he opined that "troublesome times have always produced good laws" and urged them to provide for "good execution" of justice.[305] The "particulars" before Parliament included those

303 Two Protectoral ordinances in March and September of 1654 established a national body of "Triers" to vet new clergy and county commissions known as "Ejectors" to expel "scandalous, ignorant, and insufficient ministers." Cromwell spoke of how Thomas Goodwin's sermon had described how this system "endeavoured to put a stop to that heady way . . . of every man making himself a Minister, and a Preacher." See Cromwell, *Letters, Writings, and Speeches of Oliver Cromwell*, 3:78. See also Ann Hughes, "'*The Public Profession of these Nations*': The National Church in Interregnum England," in *Religion in Revolutionary England*, ed. Christopher Durston and Judith Maltby (Manchester: Manchester University Press, 2006), 97–104; Christopher Durston, "Policing the Cromwellian Church: The Activities of the County Ejection Committees, 1654–1659," in *Cromwellian Protectorate*, 189–206.

304 See Lloyd Bowen, "'This Murmuring and Unthankful Peevish Land': Wales and the Protectorate," in *The Cromwellian Protectorate*, 147. Around this time James Berry (d. 1691), the Cromwellian major general governing Wales, wrote of how this reformation "hath many enemies, and indeed here wants matter." See Thurloe, *Collection of the State Papers of John Thurloe*, 5:334. Alexander Griffith (1600–1676), who had been ejected from his living, wrote a number of tracts against the Welsh commission for the propagation of the gospel. See Lloyd Bowen, "Preaching and Politics in the Welsh Marches, 1643–63: The Case of Alexander Griffith," *Historical Research* 94 (2001): 28–50.

305 Earlier in the month, Caryl had argued before Parliament that an appropriate response to the capture of the Spanish treasure fleet would be the promotion of justice in the nation. See Joseph Caryl, *A Sermon Pressing to, and Directing in, that Great Duty of Praising God* [. . .] (London, 1657), 37.

suggested by William Sheppard in *Englands Balme*. Owen's point was timely: two weeks after the second Protectorate Parliament convened, William Sheppard signed the preface to *Englands Balme*, at Whitehall. It was entered in the Stationers' Register on October 11, and by October 23 Thomason had acquired his copy.[306] The Protectorate administration indicated that it was prepared to back Sheppard's plan by creating him a sergeant-at-law just weeks later. Sheppard had spent the past two years working on this blueprint for the reform of English law aimed at establishing a new simplified and decentralized legal system. He proposed transferring much more responsibility to godly justices of the peace (assisted by a second rank of "all sober and civil men") while ensuring that "godless and wicked men" were "incapable of any office in the commonwealth."[307] Owen gave his endorsement to these serious and detailed plans for legal reform, hoping that the English Parliament might, at long last, make significant progress in this area. The sermon appears to have borne fruit. When the Lord Protector addressed the house on November 27, he praised members of Parliament for having achieved, in some measure, the very thing that Owen had been calling for: "though you have satte but A Little time . . . you have made manny good Lawes the Effects whereof the people of the Common-wealth will with Comfort find hereafter."[308]

PROVIDENTIAL CHANGES, AN ARGUMENT FOR UNIVERSAL HOLINESS

Dating and Context

This sermon was published posthumously in 1721, and, though undated, it is possible to suggest a plausible date for delivery early in 1657.[309] This was a particularly apt time for Owen to be reflecting on the changes brought by providence because by this stage "Owen was losing ground on all fronts."[310] Perhaps the most important initial clue to dating lies in Owen's lament of how "we scarce seem to be the same generation of men that we were fifteen

306 William Sheppard, *Englands Balme: or, Proposals by Way of Grievance and Remedy* [. . .] (London, 1656); *Transcript of the Registers of the Worshipful Company of Stationers*, 2:90; Nancy L. Matthews, *William Sheppard, Cromwell's Law Reformer* (Cambridge: Cambridge University Press, 2004), 58, 144–86.

307 Sheppard, *Englands Balme*, 41–42.

308 Cromwell, *Letters, Writings, and Speeches, of Oliver Cromwell*, 3:319.

309 In *A Complete Collection of the Sermons of the Reverend and Learned John Owen* [. . .], ed. John Asty (London, 1721), it is numbered as sermons 8–11, running pages 49–78, and is given the title *Providential Changes, an Argument for Universal Holiness.*

310 Gribben, *John Owen and English Puritanism*, 169.

or sixteen years ago." There are good reasons to believe that this is a reference back to the golden era of 1641–1642 and therefore to believe that this sermon was preached in 1657. Gribben notes that in the spring of that year, Owen's "changing fortunes reflected broader changes in the political landscape," and in this sermon Owen makes three references to "constitutions" of government, particularly highlighting debates between rival parties over "newly framed constitutions."[311] Owen described providential "alterations" that had shown that "forms of government of old established," but also "newly framed constitutions" were "obnoxious" (that is subject) to "dissolution." The "old established" form was almost certainly that of king, Lords and Commons. The "newly framed" constitution would appear to be the Instrument of Government by which, in December 1653, Oliver Cromwell became Lord Protector. Moves were underway to change this constitution by the autumn of 1656 in order to secure the regime by removing the influence of the army and placing it on a more parliamentary foundation. This sermon was not necessarily preached after the Instrument was replaced by another constitution called The Humble Petition and Advice in May 1657; rather, it could belong to earlier in the year when many had decided that the Instrument was unsatisfactory and stood in need of replacement.[312]

On two occasions, Owen spoke of "a plot," adapting the trope to rhapsodize about a plot for godly reformation that "the men of the world would have more just cause to fear, than ever they had of any," one that would "blow up their contrivance, disappoint their counsel, ruin their interest, shake heaven and earth." This evocative language is suggestive of the circumstances surrounding the arrest of the disgruntled former soldier and conspirator Miles Sindercombe, convicted of treason for plotting to bomb the protector's apartments at Whitehall and sentenced on February 9, 1657.[313] It is plausible to see Owen alluding to Sindercombe's plot because of its high profile at the time; secretary Thurloe's propaganda machine made great use of the foiled plot and the subsequent trial in order to give additional impetus to moves that were afoot for a new, more traditional constitutional settlement. The fact that Cromwell narrowly escaped death raised issues not only of security but also of political succession. In late February, a new draft constitution was introduced for debate; it would soon be renamed as the Humble Petition and

311 Gribben, *John Owen and English Puritanism*, 169.

312 For details of the debates of January–March 1657, see Little, *Lord Broghill*, 145–60; and Christopher Durston, "The Fall of Cromwell's Major-Generals," *English Historical Review* 113 (1998): 34–37.

313 *Mercurius Politicus* (February 5–12, 1657), 7588–592; *Publicke Intelligencer* (February 2–9, 1657), 1180.

Advice. Its supporters argued that it was essential for the long-term safety and stability of the three nations.[314] In the sermon, there are repeated references to how the three nations (England, Scotland, and Ireland) might be spared from God's punishment, and these are suggestive in the context of ongoing debates about how best to ensure the security of the nation.

The circumstantial evidence for a date in the first part of 1657 is strengthened with the realization that one of the reasons why Owen was willing to see the Instrument replaced was because of the unprecedented debate surrounding the trial of the Quaker preacher and writer James Nayler in December 1656. Upon his release from Exeter jail, Nayler achieved infamy by riding into Bristol with his followers in an attempt to recreate the events of Palm Sunday.[315] The parliamentary committee's report stated that "James Nayler did assume the gesture, words, honour, worship, and miracles of our blessed Saviour. Secondly, the names and incommunicable attributes and titles of our blessed Saviour." Therefore, he was deemed a "grand imposter and seducer of the people."[316] The intense debates over Nayler led to calls for his death, and the motion to do so was defeated by the narrow margin of ninety-six to eighty-two. Instead, he was whipped through the streets, had his tongue bored through, and was branded on his forehead as a blasphemer. All of this may lie behind Owen's reference to those who were prepared to contemplate "persecution, banishment, [and] blood" in order to enforce religious uniformity. The whole incident had demonstrated the inadequacies of the existing constitutional settlement because, under article 37 of the Instrument, Nayler was protected so long as he professed "faith in God by Jesus Christ."[317] Indeed, the Instrument had allowed Quakerism to flourish, and in this sermon Owen discusses how groups, like the Quakers, were seeking to emulate the outward practice of the Old Testament. The new constitution of the Humble Petition and Advice would avoid such debilitating ambiguity and define anti-Trinitarian heresy more clearly while, at the same time, offering a degree of liberty to the orthodox godly. It stated that "the true Protestant Christian religion . . . and no other" should be "held forth and asserted for the public profession of these nations" and it explicitly called for a "Confession of Faith."[318]

314 Patrick Little, "John Thurloe and the Offer of the Crown to Oliver Cromwell," in *Oliver Cromwell: New Perspectives*, 235.

315 John Coffey, *Persecution and Toleration in Protestant England, 1558–1689* (Harlow, UK: Pearson, 2000), 153–54.

316 Burton, *Diary of Thomas Burton*, 1:72–73.

317 Little and Smith, *Parliaments and Politics*, 214–15.

318 Gardiner, *Constitutional Documents of the Puritan Revolution*, 416, 442, 454.

A further clue as to the dating of the sermon in early 1657 lies in what appears to be a reference to, as yet, unsatisfactory meetings of ministers called to discuss their controversies. In February, Owen and other ministers were involved in high-level meetings in London designed to settle the split in the Scottish Kirk between the rival Protester (or Remonstrant) party and the majority Resolutioner party.[319] In these discussions, Owen and the leading army officers clearly favored the Protestors (men like Patrick Gillespie, Sir Archibald Johnston, Lord Wariston, and James Guthrie), while the Resolutioners had the support of Lord Broghill and the Cromwellian government.[320]

Together, the evidence about a change in constitution, the plot, the Naylor case, and the ongoing meetings of ministers provide strong circumstantial evidence that this sermon should be located in early 1657. This is particularly fascinating given the scant but intriguing details surrounding the Parliamentary fast held on February 27 of that year. Owen had been invited to assist along with Philip Nye, Thomas Manton, Joseph Caryl, and Patrick Gillespie.[321] According to Archibald Johnston of Wariston, recently arrived in London as a representative of the Scottish Protesters, the atmosphere in the House was heated and Owen was only invited to preach "after two houres debayte."[322] However, when reporting on the fast, the weekly newsbook *Mercurius Politicus* mentioned only the involvement of Caryl, Nye and Manton. Furthermore, according to Gilbert Mabbott, "Yesterday Mr. Galeaspey and Mr. Nye preached in the Parliament House before the Members. The first was bitter, the 2d more moderate against King-shippe."[323] Afterward, Parliament voted to thank Caryl, Gillespie, Manton, and Nye. No explanation is given for why Owen did not participate.[324] Dating this sermon offers a possible insight into the sorts of themes that Owen might have chosen to elaborate on had he delivered a sermon at the parliamentary fast. The potential for the sermon to reveal Owen's thought about the significance of political events at this time is heightened because careful examination reveals the material itself was designed to be delivered on a national stage to a body of auditors whom Owen believed were "contemptible to the nation" because of their divisions. Part of Owen's application in the sermon was specifically addressed to the civil magistrate, and, more generally, he was calling his

319 Johnston of Wariston, *Diary of Sir Archibald Johnston*, 3:62; *Register of the Consultations of the Ministers of Edinburgh and Some Other Brethren of the Ministry*, ed. William Stephen, 2 vols. (Edinburgh: Scottish History Society, 1921–1930), 1:349–50.

320 Vernon, *London Presbyterians and the British Revolutions*, 255–56.

321 *Journals of the House of Commons*, 7:497.

322 Wariston, *Diary of Wariston*, 3:67.

323 Clarke, *Clarke Papers*, 3:92.

324 *Journals of the House of Commons*, 7:497.

hearers to unite in a "project to save three nations" by accomplishing further reformation in "councils, counties, [and] cities."

Summary and Analysis of the Sermon

Owen opens this sermon with a reminder that 2 Peter was addressed to "strangers," those believing Jews who faced "extreme oppositions" from "their own countrymen, with and among whom they lived." In particular, they were mocked by "prophane persons and hardened sinners" because the "coming of the Lord" that they insisted on had not yet taken place. In response, Peter sets out to show the folly of such presumptuous scoffing while providing further instruction about the nature of the coming of Christ and the practical implications of this.

Owen began by setting his text in its context in order to show its "design" or purpose. This involved a discussion of Peter's appeal to the scoffing that Noah endured prior to the flood. By "word and deed," Noah warned of the approaching judgment of God through his preaching by constructing the ark. Those who witnessed this did not make "a due improvement" of it and continued to "live securely in sin," "willingly ignorant of the flood." An important point of Owen's interpretation turns on what is meant by the destruction of "the heavens and earth" by either water or fire (2 Pet. 3:5–7). He argued that this referred not to the destruction of "the fabric" of heaven and earth but to "persons." This was a prophetic "idiom" to describe the destruction of "the civil and religious state" (Isa. 34:4; Matt. 24; Rev. 6:14). Thus, for Owen, 2 Peter 3:7 did not refer in the first instance to the final day of judgment but was interpreted in a preterist manner as referring to the destruction of "the Judaical church and state." He understood the hope of a "new heavens and a new earth" to be a reference to the creation of "gospel ordinances" (cf. Heb. 12:26–28).

Owen turned to "open the words" of his text and to "fix upon the truth contained in them." He began with "the foundation" of the exhortation—namely, the certainty of Christ's coming in judgment against "the Judaical polity and church." For Owen, the political implications of this for his own day were abundantly clear, but it was not his "business" to deal with that beyond asserting that "there is no outward constitution nor frame of things in governments or nations, but it is subject to a dissolution, and may receive it, and that in a way of judgment." It was folly to think that a constitution that was "a mere human creation," "a mere product of the sayings and the wisdom of men," would endure once it had outlived its "usefulness to the great ends that Christ has to accomplish in the world." This was a theme in Owen's preaching from the late 1650s and one that would prompt the publication of his parliamentary sermon from February 1659. This contradicted the views of some of those advocates of a return to monarchy, or "kinglings" as they were called—men like George Downing, who in January 1657 had urged Cromwell to take the crown because "Government is the foundation of security . . . Men go away, but constitutions never fall."[325]

Having identified this "foundation," Owen argued that there was a necessary "inference," given "such providential alterations." That is to say, a particular kind of response was required from the saints, one that was "boundless and endless," concerned with all life (including a response acting in the capacity "as a magistrate"), and also "the worship of God according to the appointment and institution of Christ." He summarized this as a proposition: "Great providential alterations or destructions made upon the account of Christ and his church, call for eminency of universal holiness and godliness in all believers." Owen argued that all recognized that they were living in a "dispensation" in which there had been "many providential alterations" but expressed his astonishment that so few made a proper "improvement" of what they witnessed. There were "two great providential alterations and dissolutions" that concerned Christ and his church. The first concerned the events that Peter prophesied about in this text—namely, the destruction of Jerusalem in AD 70. The second was "the destruction of Antichrist and his Babylonish kingdom." For Owen, this was "the ocean of providence" into which "all the rivulets of lesser alterations do run."

He offered several "grounds" in support of this proposition. This first was that in all these providential alterations, there was a "peculiar coming of Christ," "the holy King of saints," and his "special presence" required special holiness from the saints. The second was that every such coming was "a lesser day of judgment," something to be understood "as pledges of the final judgment at the last day." Here he chose to deal with the "secret judiciary acts" that Christ usually undertook in these in the alterations and desolations that his comings bring about. These providences have "a voice" that pleads with people about their sins. They are trials that expose the false profession of many "hypocrites." Owen expostulated "Oh, that England might not yet be farther filled with instances and examples of this." They also serve in the "blinding and hardening" of the wicked who, despite the initial appearance of wisdom and prudence, are shown to lack understanding as to the nature of Christ's work of removing "old superstitions" and "forms of government." This was a damning assessment of those who were advocating that the Cromwellian

325 Burton, *Diary of Thomas Burton*, 1:364–66.

regime needed to return to traditional forms of government and enforce religious uniformity in worship. In such a dispensation, Christ also pleaded with the saints. Times of "peace and outward prosperity" brought with them "manifold temptations," and the "afflictions, trials, and troubles" that accompanied Christ's coming in judgment had the power to challenge the consciences of the godly about "secret lusts" and about ways in which they were out of step with Christ, particularly in endeavoring to hold on to "the shaken" and "passing things." In such seasons, the Spirit was poured out in a special manner and there was much spiritual light from "the dispensation of the word." Consequently, now was a time for "self-searching."

As Owen proceeded to "the use," he laid down two relevant "considerations" as initial premises for his application. The first was that not only the English but those in Europe and beyond knew that "we have had great providential alterations and dissolutions in these nations." Both "civil and ecclesiastical" government had been shaken in an "unparalleled" manner, removing "persons, things, [and] forms of government of old established." The shaking continued with Owen making clear that "newly framed constitutions" (such as the Instrument of Government) were also subject "to change or ruin." The second premise was that all these "revolutions," "desolations of nations, ruin of families, [and] alterations of government" had been brought about by a work of God. He then turned to "one principal inquiry" that would be the foundation of his application. He offered four reasons why "these providential alterations and dissolutions" related in a special way to "Christ and his interest in the world." The first reason was based on spiritual experience: the saints enjoyed genuine, "self-evidencing" communion with Christ "in and about the works of his providence among us." He was confident that this was not "the fancy or imagination of a deluded heart" because all the godly had shared in this experience during "the greatest straits and difficulties" (a reference to the 1640s). It was only since the nation had been delivered from its "bloody troubles" that this shared experience among the godly had been lost. Second, much had been accomplished for Christ, in particular the destruction of "false worship as established by a law" and "the casting down of combinations for persecution." This was a reference to the Laudian era and moves to establish "an outside, formal worship, in opposition unto the spiritual worship of the gospel," which led to the imprisonment and banishment of the godly. Now such "false worship" and "the most eminent persecutors of the saints" had been removed. Third, "glorious gospel light" had broken out, illuminating the nature of true worship. And, fourth, the events of recent history corresponded to "the predictions" of what would be accomplished in the last days regarding the latter-day glory of the kingdom of Christ. Together, these constituted four reasons why Owen could confidently claim that "for many years" Christ had been present in a special manner. This had been a significant theme in his parliamentary sermon from October 1656.

Owen's first "use" was an examination of whether or not "all or any of us have answered the mind of Christ in these dispensations." His assessment of "the generality of the people of the nation" was not positive. He feared for the future of England as he identified a litany of sins that demonstrated "contempt of the gospel": for example, adherence to "old superstitious ways of worship." Worship according to the Book of Common Prayer had, according to John Morrill, "earthed itself into the Englishman's consciousness and had sunk deep roots in popular culture," and many were willing to support clergy who used the traditional forms.[326] A protectoral proclamation from November 1655 had ordered that from January 1, 1656, no clergyman should use the Book of Common Prayer privately, but the government did often turn a blind eye to prayer book services.[327] As Coffey points out, the diary of John Evelyn illustrates that he had "no difficulty in finding Prayer Book services" to attend in the late 1650s.[328] Owen was concerned about those who remained committed to the old forms and rhythms of worship and piety. This was a matter in which Owen himself "continued to be the subject of polemical dispute."[329] Thomas Long (1621–1707) published his response to Owen's position in *An Exercitation concerning the Frequent Use of Our Lord's Prayer, in the Publicke Worship of God, and a View of What Hath Been Said by Dr Owen concerning the Subject* (1658).[330] However, Owen's main inquiry was to demonstrate how the saints themselves had failed to respond appropriately in several different ways. He first of all examined "their great differences among themselves about lesser things." Such a divisive attitude was something that Christ abhorred. It was evidenced in being taken up, speaking and writing books about lesser things, in the "judging and censuring" of fellow believers as "sectaries, heretics, [and] schismatics," and even in some being willing to entertain thoughts of "persecution, banishment, [and] blood" in order to enforce uniformity. This is striking in the context of the case of James Nayler, who had been tried and convicted by the second Protectorate Parliament under the Blasphemy Acts

326 John Morrill, *The Nature of the English Revolution* (Harlow, UK: Longman, 1993), 174.

327 Coward, *Cromwellian Protectorate*, 60.

328 Coffey, *Persecution and Toleration in Protestant England*, 159.

329 Gribben, *John Owen and English Puritanism*, 182.

330 This was entered on the Stationers' Register on July 13, 1658. See *Transcript of the Registers of the Worshipful Company of Stationers*, 2:187.

of 1650. As a first offender, he was sentenced to prison for six months. However, many members of Parliament demanded a harsher sentence; a vote to have Nayler executed was only narrowly defeated, and his punishment was instead to be flogged, branded, and have his tongue bored through with a hot iron.[331] Owen was clearly concerned at attempts to limit religious liberty for the godly in the face of the increasing alarm at the spread of Quakerism, and his response was to call the godly to unite around fundamental doctrines. If the godly were divided from one another in lesser things, they were also, secondly, indistinct from the world in "great things." Here he wished that the task in hand was more difficult. Owen gave particular attention to worldliness "in public actings" and "public aims." In evocative language, given the kingship controversy, Owen believed that too many sought to "enthrone" some god of their own "fleshly imagination" and were taken up with their own "wealth" and "power." The third area in which he believed there had not been an appropriate response lay in the area of "the advancement of the gospel." Owen contended that what had been an unprecedented moment of opportunity was being squandered. Once again, a particular problem lay in the "multitude" of divisions that existed among the godly. Owen then pointed to "the scandalous apostasies of many professors" and "the general backsliding" away from a godly agenda that had united the saints "fifteen or sixteen years ago." His examination revealed multiple provocations that required the saints to apply themselves to his second point of application.

Owen's second "use" was an exhortation to special holiness and godliness. This was not a consideration of the "general reasons" for holiness but "a peculiar pressing unto holiness" on the basis that this was a season in which "Christ is come among us, to the dissolution of the great things of the nations." He called for the godly to come together and unite around prioritizing holy living. Owen offered several words of caution at this point. First, there was the prevalent danger of self-righteousness, something that had caused "many in our days" to abandon the gospel of justification by faith alone.[332] Self-righteousness produced "a bondage frame of spirit" and also led to a focus on outward forms. One of the groups that Owen may have had in mind when he spoke of the those who in their "word and prophecy" followed the

331 For an account of the relevance of this debate about Nayler and the Quakers, see John Marshall, *John Locke, Toleration and Early Enlightenment Culture* (Cambridge: Cambridge University Press, 2006), 293–96.

332 For the debates about justification in the 1650s, particularly between Owen and Richard Baxter, see Cooper, *Fear and Polemic in Seventeenth-Century England*; and Cooper, *John Owen, Richard Baxter*, 55–100.

"outward appearance" of the Old Testament administration were the Quakers. Ecstatic prophecy was a distinctive practice of the Quakers at this time, and Owen himself had to contend with early Quakers who sought to emulate the prophetic acts of the Old Testament by walking seminaked through Oxford.[333] Perhaps the most high-profile example of such prophetic acts was Nayler's entrance into Bristol in imitation of Christ's entry into Jerusalem. Owen's second caution concerned the "wretched superstition" of "monastic uselessness" that he could detect in those who out of weariness deserted the work of God "and withdrew themselves into retirement." He insisted that those who did not do the work of God actually opposed it. His final caution concerned the "the great scandal that has befallen the days wherein we live"—namely, to make religion "a cloak for carnal and secular ends."

With these words of caution in place, Owen turned to address the motivations for such holy living. Since holiness was hindered by placing too much value on earthly things ("the power . . . riches, [and] pleasures of the world"), the realization that such things were perishing would promote holiness. The motivations that he chose to concentrate on were threefold. First, the duty of pursuing holiness would enable the believer to "maintain peace and quiet" in their souls, even in the midst of "outward pressures and calamities" such as those that came through "sword, fire, plots, [and] conspiracies." Such peace did not, ultimately, come by means of "parliaments" or "armies" but instead was "kept up by the holiness" that God required. Second, taking this duty seriously could be an effective means to save "the nation wherein we live" by turning away the indignation of the Lord. Owen remained convinced that Christ had "a controversy with these nations" and that the provocations were such that ruin was deserved. The controversy began prior to the "troubles" of the civil wars with the Laudian persecution of the saints. Now, however, Owen contended that "the root" of Christ's controversy with the three nations was because of "the sins of the saints themselves." The pursuit of holiness was "the only means" that would serve "to deliver England out of the hand of the Lord." This would require real reformation, "the great thing" that had been talked about for "many years," and putting away the "contemptible" divisions that existed among the godly. Finally, holiness would bring glory to Christ by bearing witness to the world a belief that Christ had "come forth among us" to advance his kingdom and interest. Owen recognized that nearly "every party" spoke of the kingdom of Christ and that many did so in what

333 See Hilary Hinds, *George Fox and Early Quaker Culture* (Manchester: Manchester University Press, 2011), 93–94; Toon, *God's Statesman*, 76; Kenneth L. Carroll, "Early Quakers and Going Naked as a Sign," *Quaker History* 67, no. 2 (1978): 69–79.

he regarded as a "carnal" manner, not least the Fifth Monarchists who had at this time renewed their agitation. By contrast, he insisted that while the kingdom we look for "be in this world," it was not to be "of this world." That meant that "a real difference" ought to be discernible in the lives of Christ's people. His word of exhortation concluded with his insistence that in "the dispensations among us" special holiness was the only way to appropriately honor and glorify Christ.

THE GLORY AND INTEREST OF NATIONS PROFESSING THE GOSPEL

Context of Owen's Sermon to Richard's Parliament

Oliver Cromwell had died on September 3, 1658, the anniversary of his triumphs at Dunbar and Worcester. His eldest surviving son, Richard Cromwell (1626–1712), was to be his successor as Lord Protector. The months that followed were, as Owen acknowledged in this sermon, a time of relative peace and stability, but this was to be simply the calm before the storm.[334] With Oliver's death, the end of the Protectorate was all but inevitable. Richard would soon lose control of the factions that his father had just managed to maintain in a delicate political balance.[335] The new protector did not have his father's influence within the army; nor did he share his sympathy toward the sects. Instead, Richard appears to have favored the Presbyterians in both religion and politics.[336]

Richard and his Council of State rather reluctantly called a parliament in an attempt to deal with a deepening financial crisis: the treasury was in massive debt, army pay was in serious arrears, and a parliament was needed in order to agree to new taxes. This was to be the Protectorate's third Parliament, and it was summoned on the basis of the electoral system that had been in place prior to the Instrument of Government and would include both Scottish and Irish members. Over half of the members elected to this very large and unmanageable Parliament were new to the house.[337] When it convened on January 27, 1659, the Protectoral Council made no attempt to exclude those

334 Godfrey Davies, *The Restoration of Charles II, 1658–1660* (San Marino, CA: Huntington Library, 1955), 36–40.

335 See for example Oliver's response to the challenge to his authority in February 1658 in Gentles, *New Model Army*, 284.

336 Ronald Hutton, *The Restoration: A Political and Religious History of England and Wales 1658–1667* (Oxford: Oxford University Press, 1986), 34.

337 Davies, *Restoration of Charles II*, 46–8; G. B. Nourse, "Richard Cromwell's House of Commons," *Bulletin of the John Rylands University Library* 60, no. 1 (1977): 98.

members who were hostile to the government.[338] This meant that the new Parliament was, in many ways, an unknown quantity. As Secretary Thurloe noted, there was "soe great a mixture in the house of commons, that no man knowes which way the major part will enclyne."[339] The majority of members were provincial gentry and they demonstrated conservative instincts in matters of religion, often being moderate Presbyterian supporters of the Humble Petition and Advice. Hard-line republican commonwealth's-men did exercise considerable influence in the House, but they remained a vocal minority. As Woolrych explains, they were "more anti-Cromwellian than a unified party," being held together through a shared opposition to the Protectorate state.[340] Their number included men like Sir Henry Vane (1613–1662) and Sir Arthur Hesilrige (1601–1661), who repeatedly voiced their anger and opposition as they disrupted debates. There were also older members who returned to the House after having been excluded a decade beforehand by Pride's Purge. They favored a more traditional settlement along the lines of the Treaty of Newport. Controlling these members of Parliament proved very challenging because men like Lord Broghill, who had been skilled in managing the politics of the Commons, had now been elevated to the Other House.[341] In all, this was a factious and deeply divided Parliament.

Thomas Goodwin preached at the opening of the Parliament, calling for unity and tolerance. The next day, Friday, January 28, the Commons agreed to hold a private fast the following week. The purpose of this "solemn Day of Humiliation" was for "Seeking of God, for his special Assistance and Blessing upon the Endeavours of this House."[342]

Dr. Edward Reynolds (1599–1676) and Thomas Manton (bapt. 1620–1677) were chosen unanimously as the first two minsters to take part in the proceedings. Reynolds was now the leader of moderate Presbyterianism and had preached only days beforehand at the opening session of the Parliament.[343]

338 Godfrey Davies, "The Election of Richard Cromwell's Parliament, 1658–9," *English Historical Review* 63 (1948), 488–501; Jason Peacey, "The Protector Humbled: Richard Cromwell and the Constitution," in *Cromwellian Protectorate*, 37; Little and Smith, *Parliaments and Politics*, 77–78.

339 Thurloe, *Collection of the State Papers of John Thurloe* 7:594.

340 Austin Woolrych, "Introduction," in *The Complete Prose Works of John Milton*, ed. Don. M. Wolfe, 8 vols. (New Haven, CT: Yale University Press, 1953–1982), 7:16.

341 Jonathan Fitzgibbons, *Cromwell's House of Lords: Politics, Parliaments and Constitutional Revolution, 1642–1660* (Woodbridge, UK: Boydell, 2018), 195–216.

342 *Journals of the House of Commons*, 7:594.

343 For Reynolds' activities at this time, see Christy Wang, "Edward Reynolds and the Making of a Presbyterian Bishop," in *Reformed Conformity in England, 1559–1714*, ed. Jake Griesel and Esther Counsell (Manchester: Manchester University Press, 2024), 199–221, esp. 212–13.

His invitation was to come from Francis Gerard (1617–1680), member of Parliament for Middlesex. Manton, rector of St Paul's, Covent Garden, was to be invited by Richard Knightley, member of Parliament for Northamptonshire and a known supporter of Presbyterianism. Knightley's London residence was in Manton's parish.[344] There was then some debate about the other ministers and the order in which they would be invited to participate. A broad range of figures favored the Presbyterian divine Edmund Calamy (1600–1666), including John Weaver (a leader of the republican commonwealth's-men), Dr. Thomas Clarges (General George Monck's agent in the Parliament), Edmund Hoskins (a traditionalist), and Sir Arthur Heselrige (another leader of the commonwealth's-men and a Presbyterian). Weaver was responsible for inviting Calamy to participate. Tellingly, Owen was supported by two senior figures in the army, his old supporter Major General Thomas Kelsey and also John Lambert. Kelsey was the member of Parliament for Dover and "a prominent opponent of the protectorate." He would soon emerge as "a prominent member of the Wallingford House party." Lambert had resigned on principle in July 1657 and had recently reemerged as the member of Parliament for Pontefract and "a leading figure in the anti-Cromwellian coalition."[345] Owen's invitation was to come from Kelsey. The venue was also the subject of debate. Some wished the fast to be held in public at St Margaret's Church, while others favored the sermons being heard in the privacy of the House. In the end, it was resolved to observe the fast in private despite the "inconveniences" such as "want of air" in a smaller and very crowded venue. It was argued that this would allow the ministers to speak "freely" in order to deal with the Parliament's "faults and duties." Furthermore, it was said that when the fasts were held at St Margaret's, "ill affected persons came frequently to such exercises not out of any zeal or devotion but to feel the pulse of the state, and to steer their counsels and affairs accordingly."[346]

It is possible to reconstruct something of what took place in the House on February 4 from contemporary reports. According to the parliamentary diary of Thomas Burton, it was an all-day event with "the exercises held from nine till six."[347] The Particular Baptist Colonel Sir Jerome Sankey (ca. 1621–ca. 1687) summarized Owen's message as comprising an urgent call to return to godly

344 See *History of Parliament*, s.v. "Knightley, Richard (c. 1610–61)."

345 Kelsey had issued the invitation and then thanked Owen for his sermon to the second Protectorate Parliament in October 1656, *God's Presence with a People* (1656). See *History of Parliament*, s.v. "Kelsey, Thomas (c. 1616–?1687)" and "Lambert, John (1619–84)."

346 Burton, *Diary of Thomas Burton*, 3:11–15.

347 Burton, *Diary of Thomas Burton*, 3:67.

reformation, as he wrote to inform Henry Cromwell of events: "Dr Owen preached first and very seriously asserted and pressed the whole cause and interest."[348] In terms of understanding Sankey's point, here it is worth noting that at that time his attachment to Major General Fleetwood (ca. 1618–1692) was "as strong as ever," and he hoped that "through God's mercy the foundations of a settlement will indeed be laid."[349] Sankey continued by outlining how Edward Reynolds followed and in his exposition of Philippians 2:1–2 "pressed hard to unity."[350] Sankey's summary is confirmed in the title of the version of the sermon that Reynolds prepared for the press, which he described as a plea for "Unity of Judgement and Love amongst Brethren."[351] These sermons were followed by Calamy preaching on how "The Lord Reigneth" from Psalm 93:4. Sankey judged the sermons by Reynolds and Calamy as "very moderate." Finally, Manton delivered a sermon on Deuteronomy 33:4–5, which was described as "the most earnest of them as to church worke."[352]

Parliament agreed to thank all four ministers for their "great Pains" in "carrying on the Work of Fasting and Humiliation this Day in the House, by Prayer and Preaching." Those who had invited them were charged with extending thanks and the invitation to print the sermons.[353]

Summary and Analysis of the Sermon

Owen selected a text whose purpose was to offer "relief against outward perplexing extremities" based on the presence of Christ with his remnant. It was, as Woolrych describes it, a "remarkable sermon" because Owen told the Parliament that the only reason why God had any regard for the English nation was for the sake of the saints but warned that God's glorious presence seemed to be departing.[354] Thus, as Cooper points out, "despite its title . . . there was very little glory about it."[355] William Goold detected "a spirit of anxiety

348 Henry Cromwell, *The Correspondence of Henry Cromwell, 1655–1659: From the British Library Lansdown Manuscripts*, ed. Peter Gaunt (Cambridge: Cambridge University Press for the Royal Historical Society, 2007), 449.

349 See *History of Parliament*, s.v. "Sankey, Jerome (c. 1621–86)"; Cromwell, *The Correspondence of Henry Cromwell, 1655–1659*, 459.

350 Cromwell, *Correspondence of Henry Cromwell*, 449–50.

351 Edward Reynolds, *The Substance of Two Sermons One Touching Composing of Controversies, Another Touching Unity of Judgement and Love Amongst Brethren* [. . .] (London, 1659), title page.

352 *Mercurius Politicus* 553 (Feb. 3–10, 1659), 215; Burton, *Diary of Thomas Burton* 3:67; Cromwell, *Correspondence of Henry Cromwell*, 449–50.

353 *Journals of the House of Commons*, 7:599.

354 A. H. Woolrych, "The Good Old Cause and the Fall of the Protectorate," *Historical Journal* 13, no. 2 (1957): 146–47.

355 Cooper, *John Owen, Richard Baxter*, 235.

as to the future developments of providence."[356] Owen told the members of Parliament who gathered in the House to hear him preach that they were "the remnant" that had survived the "great trials and desolations" of recent years. Now, at the beginning of this Parliament, great promises were being made to them, particularly concerning their "preservation and safety," both "spiritual and temporal." He summarized how the verse spoke of how "God by his creating power, in despite of all opposition will bring forth preservation for his people, guiding them in paths wherein they shall find peace and safety." The promise was, however, expressed in conditional form with the requirement being holiness. Then, having explained the biblical typology necessary for the correct interpretation of the verse, he argued that the "substance" of the mercy that was promised could be comprehended in two propositions: first, "the presence of Christ with any people, is the glory of any people" and; second, that "the presence of God in special providence over a people, attends the presence of Christ in grace with a people."

Owen explained that the true glory of a people did not lie in the "number" or "strength" of its armies; nor was it to be found the "wisdom," "counsel," and "politic contrivances" to order the affairs of the nation. Owen thought that he could give ample examples to prove this from "the days and seasons that have passed over [us]." Instead, he insisted that the glory of a people lay in the presence of Christ among them—not by way of a "bare profession" of the gospel, but as the saints, be they "few or many," united to Christ by the Spirit. Such people were precious in the eyes of Christ, even if the world treated them with contempt. Owen knew that the saints were often despised by the world, especially through the "many temptations" that they faced, sometimes those associated with "public employment." Yet it was the saints who were precious in God's sight rather than "the glittering shows" of the world's wealth and riches or "the state and magnificence of their governments" or "the beauty of their laws and order." These saints were the secret to both the "preservation" and "prosperity" of England. This had been the case throughout "all our late revolutions." The nation had not been preserved principally through the "prudence of councils" (they had been "divided, entangled, [and] ensnared") or even through the strength of its armies. Rather the presence of Christ among "his secret ones" had been "the preservation of England, in the midst of all the changes and revolutions." Owen contended that the oppressive regime of the 1630s was broken because of the prayers of those

356 See the editorial introduction by William Goold in John Owen, *The Works of John Owen*, ed. William H. Goold, 24 vols. (Edinburgh: Johnstone and Hunter, 1850–1855), 8:454.

dismissed as "the fanatic crew." He pointedly mentioned the "backsliding of some" from the cause, particularly by those who under various "pretenses" sought to undermine the freedom of the saints (this undoubtedly included those calling for Presbyterian uniformity). Such "slighting" of the saints led to the Second English Civil War and further conflict in Ireland and Scotland. In an autobiographical note, Owen reminded members of Parliament how through his preaching he had "opportunity to make observations of the passages of providence in those days, in all the three nations, in the times of our greatest hazards." What he had observed was God, in his mercy, prospering the work of those who prioritized "the preservation of the interest of Christ in and with his people."

Owen's application was to call members of Parliament "to promote the interest of Christ in these nations." This call applied to them as both individuals and civil magistrates. First, it was a call to those in that private fast to prioritize their own godliness in order to avoid the nation being brought through another providential shaking and alteration of government. Although he did not require each individual in government to be a converted believer, Owen had "no great expectation" of what magistrates who were not believers might accomplish.[357]

He then offered a very bleak assessment of national affairs. Despite the "outward peace" that the nation enjoyed, there was evidence that all was not well because he identified symptoms of "a profane, wicked, [and] carnal spirit." Promoting the interest of Christ in England, Scotland, and Ireland also involved the Parliament taking action to oppose "that overflowing flood of profaneness, and opposition to the power of godliness, that is spreading itself over this nation." In what must be seen as an indictment of the current Protectorate, he described how "the temptations of these days" had led to a return to "old forms and ways." As Woolrych captures it, Owen "had long been a watch-dog against the forces of reaction."[358] This "apostasy" also manifested itself in "rage and contempt of all the work of reformation that has been attempted among us." He feared that "our ruin should come with more speed, than did our deliverance" and that the nation would "quickly return to its former station and condition, and that with the price of your dearest blood." He employed an apt metaphor from Hosea to describe the state of the nation: "Gray hairs are here and there," and he knows it not (Hos. 7:9). In other words, England was like a man unaware that he had suddenly grown

357 Gribben, "Owen and Politics," 99.

358 Woolrych, "The Good Old Cause and the Fall of the Protectorate," 146.

old, weak, and near death.[359] Similarly, drawing on the Oracle of Doom from Amos 4:1–13, he suggested that the glory was departing. Gribben describes Owen as being alert to "a serious political danger" as he prayed that "we lose not our ground faster than we won it."[360] Owen then adapted the language of the Good Old Cause to call his hearers back to "our good old principles on which we first engaged." The Good Old Cause was a somewhat imprecise leitmotif that ran through the protests of the spring of 1659: "seldom explicitly defined, but always appealing emotionally to memories of a time when the Lord had lent His presence to all who fought His battles, and before their hopes of a new Jerusalem had dimmed amid the inevitable compromises with political realities during the last half-dozen years."[361] It was a rallying cry for a loose alliance of those who were critical of the Protectorate but who were not necessarily in agreement on how the cause might best be restored. For Owen, it could only be through those in Parliament committing themselves to "value, encourage, and close with" the saints. Here Owen was endeavoring to unite those who differed in both "civil affairs" and "church matters" behind this common cause. This was no easy task in early 1659, when many were asserting particular forms of both church polity and political constitutions. As Toon writes, "His view that the unity of the true saints and their encouragement was of far greater importance than the promotion of any theory of the government of Church or State was, needless to say, not a popular one. At this time it seemed that each religious and political group was intent on promoting its own ends without regard to the good of the nation and its people."[362]

Owen anticipated the objection that would be made that this task was almost impossible because the saints were hopelessly divided, mentioning "Prelatists," "Presbyterians," "Independents," "Anabaptists," and "Fifth Monarchy Men." His response was a well-worn one: the only party he was pleading for was "the party of Christ" and that although there was "a great noise" about the differences between the various "denominations," these differences were often "very little things in themselves." He retained a millenarian confidence that Christ would, eventually, remove these differences and the church would flourish and be at peace. Consequently, such an objection was actually nothing more than a Satanic "cheat" to keep members of Parliament from following through with this duty.

359 Jeremiah Burroughes, *Fourth, Fifth, Sixth, and Seventh Chapters of the Prophesy of Hosea* [. . .] (London, 1650), 679.

360 Gribben, "Owen and Politics," 100.

361 Woolrych, "Introduction," 22.

362 Toon, *God's Statesman*, 108–9.

Ominously, in the weeks that followed, Owen saw little evidence of the repentance and reformation he desired as the Commons became bogged down in constitutional wrangling. His fears were, it seemed, well founded: Richard was unable to manage the Parliament or to keep the support of the army.[363] At that time, Owen "gathered a church in the Independent way" among the grandees meeting at Wallingford House, the London home of Charles Fleetwood, one that was "not very well liked at Whitehall."[364] In those tense days, as Owen prepared his sermon for publication, he appears to have relied on the notes of auditors "that I might not preach one sermon and print another."

The work was entered on the Stationers' Register two months after it was preached on April 14, and it was published under the title *The Glory and Interest of Nations Professing the Gospel* (1659).[365] Gribben suggested this delay in publication may have been "politic," given "the ambiguous political context."[366] The timing was surely significant. The day beforehand, the officers of the army met at Wallingford House and spent "the whole day" of April 13 "in prayer and preaching."[367] On April 14, some five hundred officers attended a General Council of the Army.[368] Details in the dedicatory preface suggest that one of the reasons why Owen eventually decided to accept the opportunity to publish the sermon was to correct "some mistakes" about what he had said that had been "exposed in print unto public view." Owen may have been alluding to comments made about the Parliament's fast by the political theorist James Harrington (1611–1677), who in his pamphlet *The Art of Law-Giving* (1659) recounted a report he received about Owen's sermon: "But they say, Mr Dean Owen, to the Parliament at their fast, was positive that no government upon mere humane principles can be good or lasting." By contrast, Harrington claimed that Manton sought to prove "that the government instituted by Moses consisted of kings, lords and commons."[369] Harrington's work was prepared for the press on February 20 and was part of a pamphlet war over constitutional forms that raged that spring.[370] By April, the tensions

363 Godfrey Davies, "The Army and the Downfall of Richard Cromwell," *The Huntingdon Library Bulletin* 7 (1935): 131–67.

364 Cromwell, *Correspondence of Henry Cromwell*, 475; and Woolrych, "Introduction," 61.

365 *Transcript of the Registers of the Company of Stationers of London*, 2:221.

366 Gribben, *John Owen and English Puritanism*, 199.

367 Clarke, *Clarke Papers*, 3:189.

368 Gentles, *New Model Army*, 288; Reece, *Army in Cromwellian England*, 196.

369 James Harrington, *The Political Works of James Harrington*, part 1, ed J. G. A. Pocock (Cambridge: Cambridge University Press, 1977), 652–53.

370 Rachel Hammersley, *James Harrington: An Intellectual Biography* (Oxford: Oxford University Press, 2019), 233.

between Richard and his Parliament, on the one hand, and the army, on the other, had only increased. In this highly charged context, Owen sought to set the record straight about what he said in the sermon.[371] He claimed that there was nothing "from the beginning to the ending of the short discourse that does really interfere with any form of civil government in the world, administered according to righteousness and equity." This would suggest that in mid-April, Owen was still willing to support some sort of Protectorate government, provided that it re-embraced what he judged to be godly priorities. His concern was not with the form of government (a dominant theme in these debates of those months) but with the Protectorate appearing to drift in a direction that might reverse the godly gains of the revolution. The differences among members over "civil affairs" were minor compared to "the continuance of the presence of God among us." Owen encouraged members to reject party divisions and unite in order to promote the interest of Christ. As he saw it, a government based on "mere human" principles would not last, but should that government be based on godly principles, then there was a way forward. Here Owen differed from republicans who rejected the Protectorate on ideological grounds and the junior officers (among whom republican sentiment was spreading) who had already reached the point of regarding the Protectorate as being past fixing. Owen maintained that his principal design in the sermon, and one that he had "openly managed and pursued with all plainness of speech," was that "the true real interest of these nations" was one focused on "the interest of Christ." Nonetheless, there is little optimism in the sermon, and, indeed, "an element of disillusion may be read into his ambiguous dedication to Members."[372]

In order that a godly oligarchy might put the revolution back on sure footing, on April 22, Owen and the senior officers met at Fleetwood's Wallingford House in Whitehall and decided to force Richard to dissolve Parliament.[373] However, the Army Grandees quickly lost control of the situation and, with few options before them, decided to support the growing movement favoring the recall of the Rump Parliament.[374] The rationale was laid out in *A Declaration of the Officers of the Army* presented on May 6. It arose from reflection upon how their commitment to carrying on the "great work" of "the Good Old Cause" had declined and how they had "been led to look back

371 Woolrych, *Britain in Revolution*, 714–20.

372 *History of Parliament*, s.v. "Owen, Dr John (?1614–83)."

373 Gribben, "Owen and Politics," 100.

374 For the events associated with the recall of the Rump, see Henry Reece, *The Fall: Last Days of the English Republic* (New Haven, CT: Yale University Press, 2024), 78–122.

and examine the cause of the Lords withdrawing his wonted presence from us."[375] Such analysis is entirely consistent with the vision Owen had laid out in the February sermon. Furthermore, Owen's ambivalence toward political forms, articulated in this sermon, meant that he was willing to play an active role in facilitating this move and to preach to the reinstated Rump the day after it convened, on Sunday, May 8.[376] That morning was spent "in Praying and Hearing the Word, Dr. *Owen* praying and preaching before them." Owen was thanked and invited to publish the sermon "with all convenient Speed" by Colonel John Jones and Major Salwey.[377] It was reported that "Doctor Owen entertained them with a comfortable Sermon."[378] According to a Quaker source, Owen "calledst them dry Bones breathed into," thus invoking a prophetic trope to speak of Parliament being divinely resurrected (Ezek. 37).[379] It seems likely that Owen would have shared the hope of the Army Grandees that the Council of State and Upper House would be replaced by a godly Senate, which would see through a program of reformation.[380] This was not to be, and in the coming months Owen would find himself at the very center of national political turmoil and collapse.[381]

375 *A Declaration of the Officers of the Army, Inviting the Members of the Long Parliament, Who Continued sitting till the 20th of April, 1653 to Return to the Exercise and Discharge of Their Trust. Friday 6 May, 1659.* [. . .] (London, 1659), 2–3.

376 *Mercurius Politicus* 566 (May 5–May 12, 1659), 424; Gribben, "Owen and Politics," 101; Toon, *God's Statesman*, 113.

377 *Journals of the House of Commons*, 7:646. Jones, who had previously been a member of the Other House, became "an active member" of the restored Rump, playing "a prominent part in settling in the new government" and becoming a member of the new Council of State. The active republican Richard Salwey would also serve on the Council of State. He had been part of the group of Commonwealthsmen who met with the Army Grandees to agree to the recall of the Rump in late April and early May. See *History of Parliament*, s.v. "Jones, John I (c. 1597–1660)" and "Salwey, Richard (1615–85)."

378 *The Weekly Intelligencer of the Common-wealth* [. . .] (May 3–10, 1659), 8.

379 *A Serious Letter to Dr. John Owen, Sent by a Small Friend of His, Relating to the Intendments of Wallingford-House; Also a Short Friendly Reply to a Late Pamphlet of His concerning Tithes* ([Oxford], [1660]), single sheet.

380 Ludlow, *Memoirs of Edmund Ludlow*, 2:74.

381 For a treatment of the events which ensued, see Ruth E. Mayers, *1659: The Crisis of the Commonwealth* (Woodbridge, UK: Boydell, 2004). For Owen's specific involvement, see Reece, *The Fall*, 176, 183, 195–96, 222, 312; Gribben, *John Owen and English Puritanism*, 204–8.

Outlines

THE STEADFASTNESS OF THE PROMISES, AND THE SINFULNESS OF STAGGERING

- I. Introduction and contextualization
- II. A threefold description of Abraham's faith
  - A. Abraham's faith rested on the all-sufficiency of God
  - B. Abraham believed the promise of God
  - C. A fourfold description of the manner in which Abraham believed
    1. Abraham had hope
    2. Abraham's faith was strong
    3. Abraham was fully resolved
    4. Abraham did not stagger
- III. Main doctrinal observation: all staggering at the promises of God is from unbelief
  - A. The promise that Abraham would have seed of his own
    1. Abraham's situation when this promise was made
    2. The three elements of this promise of seed
    3. General and specific application
  - B. Staggering comes from unbelief
    1. Proof of this principle
    2. A twofold demonstration of the principle
       - a. Five theological reasons for confidence in the promises
         - i. God has done all that is necessary by way of confirmation
         - ii. God has the power and means to accomplish his promises

iii. God is sincere in what he promises
iv. God never forgets his promises
v. Divine immutability ensures that the promises will not change
b. Various providential reasons for confidence in the promises
3. Five applications of this principle
a. Those in power must learn to live by faith in all matters of policy and politics
b. God is faithful, so those in power must be faithful in propagation of the gospel, especially in Ireland
c. Those in power must believe the promises of the gospel
d. Warnings about the consequences of staggering in unbelief
e. Those in power must repent of all staggering in unbelief

THE BRANCH OF THE LORD, THE BEAUTY OF SION

I. Introduction and contextualization
II. Observation: Christ's church of saints is God's house
A. A threefold demonstration that the church is God's house
B. Three characteristics of God's house
1. The church is a living house
2. The church is a strong house
3. The church is a glorious house
C. The church's relation to Jesus Christ
1. Christ is the foundation, ark, altar, and candlestick of this house
a. Christ is the hidden foundation, supporting the whole weight of the building
b. Christ is the ark and mercy seat of this house
c. Christ is the altar of this house through his atonement and intercession
d. Christ is the candlestick, bringing light that shines out to the world

2. Christ is the owner, builder, watchman, inhabitant, and avenger of his house
    a. Christ is the owner with a threefold title to this house by inheritance, purchase, and conquest
    b. Three observations arising
        i. Christ will defend his house
        ii. Christ has the right to order his house
        iii. Christ is jealous for his house
    c. Christ builds his house with living stones
    d. Two observations arising from this
        i. The Master-builder puts life into dead stones
        ii. Vows, promises, resolutions, and engagements are insufficient
    e. Christ watches over his house in order to supply the needs of his people and to protect and avenge them
    f. Three observations arising
        i. Christ tries his church
        ii. Christ protects his church
        iii. Christ preserves his church
    g. Christ inhabits his house by the Holy Spirit
    h. Two observations arising
        i. Clarifying the nature of union with Christ
        ii. The Spirit is free to work as he pleases
    i. Christ graciously makes the believer's heart his dwelling place
    j. Christ inhabits the church as his royal court
    k. Three observations arising
        i. The intimacy of communion with Christ
        ii. The danger of grieving his Spirit
        iii. The value of the graces of Christ
    l. Christ brings vengeance on all who persecute the saints of his house
3. Three general points of application
    a. The privilege of being a living stone in this house
    b. Not all assemblies have such status and privilege
    c. History teaches persecutors of the true church will be destroyed

THE ADVANTAGE OF THE KINGDOM OF CHRIST IN THE SHAKING OF THE KINGDOMS OF THE WORLD

- I. God's works of providence
- II. The context of the text from Ezekiel
  - A. Two observations arising from a brief exposition of Ezekiel 17:22–23
    1. God's special work of advancing the kingdom of Christ
    2. All the nations will be brought into Christ's possession
- III. Exposition of the text
  - A. The work that God is doing
  - B. Introduction to the two main observations
    1. The reason for God's great works of providence
    2. The assurance that God's great work will be accomplished
- IV. First observation: In carrying on the interest of Christ and the gospel, God will work wonderful providential alterations
  - A. The three seasons in which these providential alterations take place
    1. The time of Christ and the apostles
    2. The growth of the church and the fall of the Roman Empire
    3. The Reformation and post-Reformation era
  - B. Two reasons for this observation
    1. Christ must take his inheritance out of the hands of his enemies
    2. The nature of this work involves vengeance, deliverance, and trial
  - C. Two applications arising
    1. In the British Civil Wars, God has been bringing down oppressors and raising up the saints
    2. Reasons to rejoice in these providential alterations
- V. Second observation: These providential alterations do not conform to the thoughts and expectations of many
  - A. Examples of this principle
    1. Examples from biblical history
    2. An example from recent history
  - B. Three reasons for this observation

1. The corrupt heart given over to judgment
2. The glory of God
3. Judicial hardening

C. One application arising: It is a foolish provocation to reject the work of God

VI. General conclusion: Prepare to meet God
A. A summary of what it means to prepare to meet the Lord
B. Meet God in his works of providence
1. Cast down all opposition to Christ's kingdom in anticipation of the latter-day glory
a. Believe and pray, and those in power must be active in reformation
b. Consider the lessons of providence
2. Reject all worldly glory
3. Treasure the things of the kingdom
C. Meet God in worship
D. Meet God through holy living

THE LABORING SAINT'S DISMISSION TO REST

I. Introduction and opening of the text
A. The servant is dismissed from his service
1. The godly character and work of this servant
a. A loving, wise, and upright servant
b. A servant who rightly understood God's providential alterations
2. A servant who died in service
3. Observation: There is an appointed time for all servants to be dismissed
a. Daniel and Ireton were servants of similar character
i. Men of wisdom
ii. Lovers of God's people
iii. Righteous in public service
b. Daniel and Ireton both understood providential alterations
B. The servant is dismissed before the completion of his work
1. The meaning of "the end"
2. Observation: Servants often do not see their work completed

C. The servant is released to rest
 1. Observation: Dismissed servants are at rest
D. The servant is dismissed to rest until the end of days
 1. Observation: The intermediate state precedes the eternal state
 2. Observations concerning the appointed lot

II. Treatment of the first observation: There is an appointed time for all servants to be dismissed
 A. Three reasons for this doctrine
 B. Two applications
  1. Servants should improve the time that has been allotted to them
   a. Take Ireton as an example
   b. A call to diligence
  2. Servants come and go, but the work is God's

III. Treatment of the second observation: servants often do not see their work completed
 A. Two reasons for this doctrine
 B. Two applications
  1. Servants should seek their reward in the service itself
  2. Servants should be confident in their eternal hope

IV. Treatment of the third observation: Saints are dismissed to their rest
 A. This rest is freedom from sin, oppression, and grief
 B. This glorious and satisfying rest is in God

V. Treatment of the fourth observation: The intermediate state precedes the eternal state

VI. Concluding application from Ireton's example

CONCERNING THE KINGDOM OF CHRIST, AND THE POWER OF THE CIVIL MAGISTRATE ABOUT THE THINGS OF THE WORSHIP OF GOD

I. Introduction and opening of the text
 A. The perplexing nature of the shaking of the nations
 B. A Survey of the establishment of the kingdom of Christ
  1. A survey of the progress within Daniel's vision
  2. The climax of the vision and a threefold analysis of Christ's kingdom

3. Five observations about the nature of Christ's kingdom

C. Seeking the mind of God

D. The peace that comes from a revelation of the mind of God

E. Summary of the three doctrines raised from the text

II. Treatment of the main doctrine: The advancement of the kingdom of Christ often leaves the saints troubled and perplexed

A. Four reasons why the saints find themselves in such a condition
   1. The astonishing nature of what God is doing
   2. The mysterious manner in which God works
   3. The unsettling influence of the ungodly
   4. The unsettling effects of sin

B. Application: Instruction in how to find peace
   1. Be guided by the second observation: draw near to God in prayer
      a. Three reasons to seek God in public and private prayer
   2. The magistrate should advance the cause of the gospel
      a. Protect, promote, and propagate the gospel
      b. Allow the church to be the church

C. Specific guidance to Parliament in the propagation of the gospel and in dealing with religious heterodoxy
   1. Understand the promises about God raising up godly rulers
      a. These promises are for today
      b. Magistrates are entrusted with particular responsibilities in matters of religion
      c. Magistrates have a duty to use their power for the good of the church
   2. Understand five relevant principles
      a. The gospel should be preached to every nation
      b. Blessing and prosperity come to a nation that embraces the gospel
      c. A nation that rejects the gospel will be rejected by God

- d. Magistrates have specific responsibilities in these matters
- e. Rightly understood, the Old Testament teaches these principles

3. Three rules for Parliament in the propagation of the gospel and in dealing with religious heterodoxy
   - a. Be committed to the truth of the gospel
   - b. There are no grounds for formally supporting error
   - c. The plea of conscience is insufficient grounds for rejecting this

D. Conclusion

GOD'S WORK IN FOUNDING ZION, AND HIS PEOPLE'S DUTY THEREUPON

- I. Introduction and context
- II. Opening of the text and raising of four doctrines
  - A. Exposition of the inquiry: What shall one answer the messengers of the nations?
    1. Two doctrines raised from the exposition of the inquiry
  - B. First part of the exposition of the answer to the question: The Lord has founded Zion
    1. Doctrine raised from this first part of the answer
  - C. Second part of the exposition of the answer to the question: The poor of his people shall trust in it
    1. Doctrine raised from this second part of the answer
- III. Treatment of the first doctrine
  - A. Statement of the doctrine
  - B. Two reasons why the nations make such inquiries
    1. The nations are prompted by envy
    2. The nations are driven by fear
  - C. Application of the first doctrine
- IV. Treatment of the second doctrine
  - A. Statement of the doctrine
  - B. Two reasons why God's glorious works of providence may not be seen
    1. People may be blinded by selfishness
    2. People may be distracted by strife

V. Treatment of the third doctrine
   A. Statement of the doctrine
   B. Three premises for this doctrine
      1. The people of God are to glorify him in their generation
      2. This generation should glorify God in the midst of divisions
      3. The people of God must submit to providence
   C. Reasons for this doctrine
   D. Application of the third doctrine, particularly to those in power

VI. Treatment of the fourth doctrine
   A. Statement of the doctrine
   B. Two reasons why those in power have been slow to be persuaded
      1. Unwillingness to pursue the common interest of God's people
      2. The presumption that seeks to determine how God should work
   C. First application: Those in power should be able to give an account of God's work in the English Revolution
      1. Objections answered
      2. Summary of what God has done for all the saints
      3. Specific application to those in power, supported by five reasons
      4. Summary of the answer that should be given
   D. Second application: Directions to those in power about how to respond to what God is doing
      1. First direction: Reject any proposals for a church settlement that is incompatible with the common interest of the saints
         a. Three words of caution
      2. Second direction: Be guided by the work of God in both domestic and foreign policy
   E. Third application: Those in power must encourage, preserve, promote, and defend the work of the gospel

VII. Concluding general directions

GOD'S PRESENCE WITH A PEOPLE, THE SPRING OF THEIR PROSPERITY

- I. Introduction and context
  - A. Doctrinal proposition raised from the preface
- II. Opening of the text in order to raise the main doctrinal observation
  - A. Distinguishing the four ways in which God may be said to be with a people
    1. By divine omnipresence
    2. By the incarnation
    3. By means of the covenant of grace
    4. By means of providence
  - B. Distinguishing the two ways in which a people may abide with God
    1. Personally
    2. Nationally
  - C. Main doctrine raised from the text
- III. Treatment of the main doctrine
  - A. Three initial premises
    1. The conditional nature of God's presence in respect of providential dispensations
    2. God's presence in providential dispensations is on the basis of mercy rather than merit
    3. God gives the ability to perform the conditions
  - B. Proofs confirming this doctrine
  - C. Two qualifications
    1. Outward prosperity is not necessarily evidence of God's special presence
    2. Trials do not necessarily mean that God has withdrawn his special presence
  - D. Application of the doctrine: Instruction
    1. Understand the nature of God's special presence with a nation
       - a. God will be present to guide and protect, even through political uncertainty
       - b. Special manifestations of God's presence with a nation, as seen in his works of providence, strengthen the saints

2. Understand how a nation can obtain and enjoy God's special presence
    a. An essential prerequisite is a nation having godly rulers
    b. Those in power must seek God's direction, trust him for protection, and submit to providence
    c. Objections answered
3. Those in power must prioritize the interest of Christ and his church

IV. Three concluding applications
- A. Prioritize abiding with God at a national level in order to maintain God's special presence
- B. Be reassured by providential signs of God's special presence with the nation
- C. Maintain God's special presence through the Cromwellian church settlement and legal reform

PROVIDENTIAL CHANGES, AN ARGUMENT FOR UNIVERSAL HOLINESS

I. Introduction and context
- A. Peter's audience
    1. Scattered strangers
    2. Scoffed at by their countrymen
- B. Peter's threefold purpose
- C. Excursus: Consideration of the prophetic idiom of "heaven and earth"

II. Opening the text in order to raise a doctrine
- A. The foundation: Providential alterations will come, despite what scoffers say
- B. The inference: This necessitates a heightened response of holiness
- C. The exhortation: This is a call to comprehensive holiness
- D. The call to universal holiness

III. Treatment of the doctrine raised from the text
- A. Statement of the doctrine
- B. Defining the two great periods of providential alterations
    1. The destruction of the Jewish church and state in AD 70
    2. The destruction of the antichrist's church and state

- C. First ground of this doctrine: In providential alterations there is a special coming of Christ
  1. Objection answered
  2. The one who comes is holy
  3. The one who comes has kingly power and authority
  4. The one who comes has a loving heart of compassion
  5. Summary of the first ground of this doctrinal observation
- D. Second ground of this doctrine: In providential alterations Christ comes as judge
  1. Christ pleads with nations about their sin
  2. Christ exposes false professions of faith
  3. Christ engages in judicial hardening of the wicked
  4. Christ pleads with his people about their sins and temptations through a range of different ways and means
- E. Conclusion of the treatment of the first doctrinal observation

IV. The providential alterations of the mid-century crisis is such a coming of Christ
- A. Two initial premises about what has occurred
  1. England has been shaken
  2. This is a mighty work of God
- B. Statement of the main question to determine
- C. Four reasons for confidence
  1. The saints have experienced communion with God
     a. Objections answered
  2. Oppression and idolatry have been removed
  3. Gospel light has come into the darkness
     a. Objection answered
  4. The evidence suggests that prophecy is being fulfilled

V. First main application: Examination of the response to this special coming of Christ
- A. The response of the nation in general
- B. The response of the saints in particular
  1. Division, rather than unity, and even the suggestion of persecution
  2. Many different forms of worldliness
  3. Failures with respect to the propagation of the gospel

                4. Scandalous sin
                5. Spiritual backsliding
- VI. Second main application: Exhortation and direction
    - A. Two initial premises about special motivations to comprehensive holiness
    - B. First direction: Serious consideration must be given to the promotion of generational holiness
        - 1. Words of caution
            - a. Beware the theological and practical dangers
                - i. Evidences of the prevalence of those dangers
            - b. Beware the danger of ceasing to serve God in this generation
            - c. Beware the danger of talking about holiness for unholy reasons
        - 2. Conclusion to the first direction
    - C. Second direction: Two essential ingredients for true holiness
        - 1. Stop loving earthly things
        - 2. Stop caring for perishing things
        - 3. Conclusion: Enlarge the heart with love for Christ
    - D. Third direction: Three motivations for this duty
        - 1. Holiness brings the inner peace that sustains the soul even in the loss of outer peace
        - 2. Holiness is the only way to save and reform the three nations
        - 3. Holiness will bring glory to Christ

THE GLORY AND INTEREST OF NATIONS PROFESSING THE GOSPEL

- I. Introduction and context
    - A. Promises made to a remnant in great distress
    - B. Promises of safety and preservation
- II. Opening the text to raise two doctrinal propositions
    - A. God is the source and pledge of these promises
        - 1. The creative power of God will preserve the remnant
        - 2. God will be present to guide and protect
    - B. Promises to a holy people
    - C. Exposition of the final clause of the text
    - D. Summary statement of the two doctrinal propositions

- III. Treatment of the main doctrine: The presence of Christ is the glory of any people
    - A. The glory of a people is not found in numbers, wisdom, strength, or wealth
    - B. The glory of a nation is Christ's presence with his people
        1. Empty profession is not the glory of a nation
        2. The fruitful profession of those united to Christ is the glory of a nation
    - C. Three reasons why the presence of Christ is the glory of a people
        1. The saints are precious in the eyes of God and have a great inheritance
        2. God's instruments may endure reproach, but by grace they are glorious
        3. The godly remnant preserves the nation and brings prosperity
    - D. The godly remnant preserved the nation during the English Revolution
    - E. Two applications of the doctrine
        1. Promote the interest of Christ in England, Scotland, and Ireland
            - a. Personal commitment to Christ is required, especially from those in power
            - b. Much is to be done because of declension and apostasy
            - c. A commitment to all the godly, regardless of their differences
            - d. First objection: Who is to be counted among the godly?
            - e. Response: Six considerations
            - f. Second objection: Are not the godly hopelessly divided?
            - g. Response: Three considerations
        2. Reassurance to the godly remnant

THE STEADFASTNESS OF THE PROMISES, AND THE SINFULNESS OF STAGGERING: OPENED IN A SERMON PREACHED AT MARGARET'S IN WESTMINSTER BEFORE PARLIAMENT FEBR. 28 1649

Being a Day Set Apart for Solemn Humiliation throughout the Nation

---

By John Owen minister of the gospel

London:
Printed by Peter Cole, and are to be
sold at his shop at the sign of
the printing press in Cornhill, near the Royal
Exchange, 1650

[Dedication][1]

TO THE COMMONS OF ENGLAND in Parliament assembled.

Sirs,

That God in whose hands your breath is, and whose are all your ways, having caused various seasons to pass over you, and in them all manifested that his "works are truth and his ways judgment,"[2] calls earnestly by them for that walking before him, which is required from them, who with other distinguishing mercies, are interested in the specialty of his protecting providence. As in a view of present enjoyments, to sacrifice to your net, and burn incense to your drag, as though by them your portion were fat and plenteous, is an exceeding provocation to the eyes of his glory.[3] So to press to the residue of your desires and expectations, by an arm of flesh, the designings and contrivances of carnal reason, with outwardly appearing mediums of their accomplishment, is no less an abomination to him. Though there may be a present sweetness to them that find "the life of the hand,"[4] yet their latter end will be, "to lie down in sorrow."[5] That you might be prevailed on to give glory to God by steadfastness in believing, committing all your ways to him,[6] with patience in well doing,[7] to the contempt of

1 In the original, the words "Promises" and "Staggering" on the title page are set in all caps for emphasis. Further, the year 1649 should be corrected to 1650.

2 Dan. 4:37.

3 Hab. 1:16.

4 Isa. 57:10.

5 Isa. 50:11.

6 Ps. 37:5.

7 Gal. 6:9.

the most varnished appearance of carnal policy, was my peculiar aim, in this ensuing sermon.

That which added ready willingness to my obedience unto your commands for the preaching and publishing hereof, being a serious proposal for the advancement and propagation of the gospel in another nation,[8] is here again recommended to your thoughts, by

Your most humble servant,
in our common Master,

J. O.

March 8, 1650.[9]

8 A reference to Ireland.

9 In the text: 1649.—Owen. This was the date on which the ordinance for the propagation of the gospel in Ireland was passed. See *Acts and Ordinances of the Interregnum*, eds. C. H. Firth and R. S. Rait, 3 vols. (London: HMSO, 1911), 2:355–57.

[Sermon]

The Steadfastness of the Promises, and the Sinfulness of Staggering[1]

Opened in a Sermon Preached at Margaret's in Westminster, before Parliament 28 February 1650[2]

He staggered not at the promise of God through unbelief.

ROMANS 4:20

INTRODUCTION AND CONTEXTUALIZATION

In the first chapters of this epistle, the apostle from Scripture and the constant practice of all sorts of men, of all ages, Jews and Gentiles, wise and barbarians,[3] proves all the world, and every individual therein, to "have sinned and come short of the glory of God":[4] and not only so, but that it was utterly impossible, that by their own strength, or by virtue of any assistance communicated, or privileges enjoyed, they should ever attain to a righteousness of their own,[5] that might be acceptable unto God.

Hereupon he concludes that discourse with these two positive assertions:

1. That for what is past, "every mouth must be stopped, and all the world become guilty before God." Chapter 3:19.

1 In the original, the words "Promises" and "Staggering" are, again, set in all caps for emphasis.

2 In the text: Febr. 28 1649.—Owen. At the time, the new year was taken to begin on Lady Day, March 25.

3 Rom. 1:14.

4 Rom. 3:23.

5 Rom. 1:17; cf. Rom. 10:3; Phil. 3:9.

2. For the future, though they should labor to amend their ways, and improve their assistances and privileges to a better advantage than formerly, "yet by the deeds of the law, shall no flesh be justified in the sight of God," verse 20.

Now it being the main drift of the apostle, in this epistle, and in his whole employment, to manifest that God has not shut up all the sons of men, hopeless and remediless under this condition; he immediately, discovers and opens the rich supply, which God in free grace, has made and provided, for the delivery of his own from this calamitous estate, even by the righteousness of faith in Christ;[6] which he unfolds, asserts, proves, and vindicates from objections, to the end of the third chapter.

This being a matter of so great weight, as, comprising in itself the sum of the gospel wherewith he was entrusted; the honor and exaltation of Christ, which above all he desired; the great design of God to be glorious in his saints;[7] and, in a word, the chief subject of the ambassage[8] from Christ, to him committed (to wit, that they who neither have, nor by any means can attain, a righteousness of their own, by the utmost of their workings, may yet have that which is complete and unrefusable in Christ, by believing), he therefore strongly confirms it in the fourth chapter, by testimony and example of the Scripture, with the saints that were of old: thereby also declaring, that though the manifestation of this mystery,[9] were now more fully opened by Christ from "the bosom of the Father,"[10] yet indeed this was the only way for any to appear in the presence of God, ever since sin entered the world.

To make his demonstrations the more evident, he singles out one for an example, who was eminently known, and confessed by all to have been "the friend of God,"[11] to have been righteous and justified before him, and thereon to have held sweet communion with him all his days; to wit, Abraham, the father according to the flesh,[12] of all those who put in the strongest of all men for a share in righteousness, by the privileges they did enjoy, and the works they did perform.

Now concerning him, the apostle proves abundantly in the beginning of the fourth chapter, that the justification which he found, and the righteousness he attained, was purely that, and no other, which he before described; to wit, a righteousness in the forgiveness of sins through faith in the blood of Christ.[13]

6 Rom. 3:22.
7 2 Thess. 1:10.
8 I.e., the message entrusted to an ambassador.
9 Col. 1:26.
10 John 1:18.
11 James 2:23.
12 Rom. 4:1.
13 Rom. 3:25.

Yea, and that all the privileges and exaltations of this Abraham, which made him so signal and eminent among the saints of God, as to be called the father of the faithful, were merely from hence, that this righteousness of grace, was freely discovered, and fully established unto him: an enjoyment being granted him in a peculiar manner, by faith, of that promise, wherein the Lord Christ with the whole spring of the righteousness mentioned, was enwrapped.

This the apostle pursues with sundry and various inferences, and conclusions, to the end of verse 17, chapter 4.

A THREEFOLD DESCRIPTION OF ABRAHAM'S FAITH

Having laid down this, in the next place he gives us a description of that faith of Abraham, whereby he became inheritor of those excellent things, from the adjuncts of it. That as his justification was proposed as an example of God's dealing with us by his grace, so his faith might be laid down as a pattern for us, in the receiving that grace.

Now, this he does, from—

1. The foundation of it, whereon it rested.
2. The matter of it, what he believed.
3. The manner of it, or how he believed.

Abraham's Faith Rested on the All-Sufficiency of God

1. From the bottom and foundation on which it rested, viz., the omnipotency or all-sufficiency of God, whereby he was able to fulfill whatever he had engaged himself unto by promise, and which he called him to believe, "He believed him who quickeneth the dead, and calleth those things which be not as though they were," verse 14.[14]

Two great testimonies are here of the power of God: (1) That he "quickeneth the dead," able he is to raise up those that are dead to life again. (2) He "calleth things that are not, as though they were": by his very call or word, gives being to those things which before were not: as when he said, "Let there be light, and there was light" (Gen. 1:3), by that very word "commanding light to shine out of darkness" (2 Cor. 4:6).

These demonstrations of God's all-sufficiency he considers in peculiar reference to what he was to believe; to wit, that "he might be the father of many nations," verse 11, of the Jews, "according to the flesh" of Jews and Gentiles, according to the faith whereof we speak.

14 Following Goold, this should be corrected to verse 17.

(1) For the first, "his body being now dead, and Sarah's womb dead," verse 19, he rests on God "as quickening the dead," in believing that he "shall be the father of many nations."

(2) For the other, that he should be a father of the Gentiles by faith, the Holy Ghost witnesses that they "were not a people" (Hos. 2:23), the implanting of them in his stock must be by a power "that calleth things that are not, as though they were":[15] giving a new nature, and being unto them, which before they had not.

To bottom ourselves upon the all-sufficiency of God, for the accomplishment of such things, as are altogether impossible to anything, but that all-sufficiency, is faith indeed, and worthy our imitation: it is also the wisdom of faith, to pitch peculiarly on that in God, which is accommodated to the difficulties wherewith it is to wrestle: is Abraham to believe that from his dead body, must spring a whole nation? He rests on God, as "him that quickeneth the dead."[16]

Abraham Believed the Promise of God

2. His faith is commended from the matter of it, or what he did believe: which is said in general to be "the promise of God": "He staggered not at the promise of God through unbelief," verse 20. And particularly the matter of that promise is pointed at, verses 11, 18, that he should be "the father of many nations": that was, his being a "father of many nations," of having "all nations blessed in his seed." A matter entangled with a world of difficulties, considering the natural inability of his body, and the body of Sarah, to be parents of children.

When God calls for believing, his truth and all-sufficiency being engaged, no difficulty nor seeming impossibilities, that the thing to be believed is or may be attended withal, ought to be of any weight with us. He who has promised, is able.[17]

A Fourfold Description of the Manner in Which Abraham Believed

3. From the manner of his believing, which is expressed four ways.

Abraham Had Hope

(1) "Against hope, he believed in hope": verse 18. Here is a twofold hope mentioned, one that was against him, the other, that was for him.

[1] He "believed against hope," that is, when all arguments that might beget hope in him, were against him. "Against hope," is against all motives unto hope

15 Rom. 4:17.

16 Rom. 4:17.

17 The italicization of the original is preserved because it marks out what Owen would, typically, refer to as an observation.

whatever. All reasons of natural hope were against him: what hope could arise, in, or by reason, that two dead bodies, should be the source and fountain of many nations? So that against all inducements of a natural hope he believed.

[2] He "believed in hope": that is such hope as arose as his faith did from the consideration of God's all-sufficiency; this is an adjunct of his faith, it was such a faith as had hope adjoined with it: and this believing in hope, when all reasons of hope were away, is the first thing that is set down, of the manner of his faith.

In a decay of all natural helps, the deadness of all means, an appearance of an utter impossibility, that ever the promise should be accomplished, then to believe with unfeigned hope, is a commendable faith.

Abraham's Faith Was Strong

(2) He was "not weak in faith": verse 19, μὴ ἀσθενήσας, "not weak," is the second thing. *Minime debilis*:[18] Beza. He was by "no means weak." A negation that, by a figure (μείωσις)[19] does strongly assert the contrary, to that which is denied. He was no way weak; that is, he was very strong in faith, as is afterward expressed, verse 20, he "was strong in faith, giving glory to God."

And the apostle tells you, wherein this his "not weakness" did appear: says he, "He considered not his own body being now dead, when he was about a hundred years old, neither yet the deadness of Sara's womb": verse 19. It was seen in this, that his faith carried him above the consideration of all impediments, that might lie in the way to the accomplishment of the promise.

It is mere weakness of faith, that makes a man lie poring on the difficulties and seeming impossibilities that lie upon the promise. We think it our wisdom, and our strength, to consider, weigh and look into the bottom of oppositions, and temptations, that arise against the promise. Perhaps it may be the strength of our fleshly, carnal reason; but certainly, it is the weakness of our faith: he that is "strong in faith," will not so much as debate or consider the things, that cast the greatest seeming improbability, yea impossibility, on the fulfilling of the promise. It will not afford a debate or dispute of the cause, nor any consideration. "Being not weak in faith, he considered not."

Abraham Was Fully Resolved

(3) He was "fully persuaded," verse 21, πληροφορηθεὶς, he was *persuasionis plenus*,[20] fully persuaded: this is the third thing that is observed in the manner

18 Theodore Beza, *Annotationes majores in Nouum Jesu Christi Testamentum*, "Ad Romanos" (Geneva, 1594), 53.

19 Gk. *meiosis*, a figure of speech involving understatement.

20 Beza, "Ad Romanos," 54.

of his believing. He fully, quietly, resolvedly cast himself on this, that "he who had promised was able to perform it." As a ship at sea (for so the word imports), looking about, and seeing storms and winds arising, sets up all her sails, and with all speed, makes to the harbor. Abraham seeing the storms of doubts and temptations, likely to rise against the promise made unto him, with full sail breaks through all, to lie down quietly in God's all-sufficiency. And this is the third.

Abraham Did Not Stagger

(4) The fourth is, that "he staggered not," verse 20. This is that which I have chosen to insist on unto you, as a choice part of the commendation of Abraham's faith, which is proposed for our imitation: "He staggered not at the promise of God through unbelief."

MAIN DOCTRINAL OBSERVATION

The words may be briefly resolved into this doctrinal proposition:

Obs[ervation]. *All staggering at the promises of God is from unbelief.*

What is of any difficulty in the text, will be cleared in opening the parts of the observation.

Men are apt to pretend sundry other reasons and causes of their staggering. The promises do not belong unto them, God intends not their souls in them, they are not such, and such, and this makes them stagger: when the truth is, it is their unbelief, and that alone, that puts them into this staggering condition. As in other things, so in this, we are apt to have many fair pretenses for foul faults. To lay the burden on the right shoulders, I shall demonstrate by God's assistance, that it is not this, or that, but unbelief alone, that makes us stagger at the promises.

To make this the more plain, I must open these two things:

1. What is the promise here intended?
2. What it is, to stagger at the promise?

The Promise That Abraham Would Have Seed of His Own

Abraham's Situation When This Promise Was Made

1. The promise here mentioned is principally that which Abraham believing, it was said eminently that "it was accounted to him for righteousness": so the apostle tells us, verse 5 of this chapter: When this was, you may see Genesis 15:6; there it is affirmed, that "he believed the Lord, and it was accounted

to him for righteousness." That which God had there spoken to him of, was about "the multiplying of his seed as the stars of heaven,"[21] whereas he was yet childless.

The last verse of chapter 14 leaves Abraham full of earthly glory. He had newly conquered five kings with all their host: honored by the king of Sodom, and blessed by the king of Salem; and yet in the first verse of chapter 15, God, "appearing to him in a vision," in the very entrance, bids him "fear not":[22] plainly intimating, that notwithstanding all his outward success and glory, he had still many perplexities upon his spirit, and had need of great consolation and establishment: Abraham was not clear in the accomplishment of former promises about the blessed seed, and so though he have all outward advancements, yet he cannot rest in them. Until a child of God be clear in the main, in the matter of the great promise, the business of Christ, the greatest outward successes and advantages, will be so far from quieting and settling his mind, that they rather increase his perplexities. They do but occasion him to cry, "Here is this and that; here is victory and success; here is wealth and peace; but here is not Christ."

That this was Abraham's condition, appears from verse 2 of that chapter, where God having told him that he was his "shield," and his "exceeding great reward," he replies, "Lord God, what wilt thou give me, seeing I go childless?" As if he should have said, "Lord God, you told me when I was in Haran, now 19 years ago, that in me and my seed all the families of the earth should be blessed," (Gen. 12:3). "That the blessed, blessing seed, should be of me: but now I wax old, all appearances grow up against the direct accomplishment of that word, and it was that which above all in following you, I aimed at; if I am disappointed therein, what shall I do? And what will all these things avail me? What will it benefit me to have a multitude of earthly enjoyments, and leave them in the close to my servant?"

I cannot but observe, that this sighing mournful complaint of Abraham, has much infirmity, and something of diffidence, mixed with it. He shakes in the very bottom of his soul, that improbabilities were growing up as he thought to impossibilities against him in the way of promise: yet hence also mark these two things:

(1) That he does not repine in himself, and keep up his burning thoughts in his breast, but sweetly breathes out the burden of his soul into the bosom

21 Gen. 22:17.

22 In the original, this is set in all caps for emphasis.

of his God: "Lord God," says he, "what wilt thou give me seeing I go childless?" *It is of sincere faith, to unlade our unbelief in the bosom of our God.*[23]

(2) That God takes not his servant at the advantage of his complaining and diffidence: but lets that pass, until having renewed the promise to him, and settled his faith, then he gives in his testimony, that he believed God. *The Lord overlooks the weakness and causeless wailings of his, takes them at the best, and then gives his witness to them.*

The Three Elements of This Promise of Seed

This I say was the promise whereof we spoke, that he should have a seed of his own, "like the stars that cannot be numbered" (Gen. 15:4–5). And herein are contained three things.

(1) The purely spiritual part of it, that concerned his own soul in Christ. God engaging about his seed, minds him of his own interest, in that seed which brings the blessing. Jesus Christ, with his whole mediation, and his whole work of redemption, is in this promise, with the enjoyment of God in covenant, "as a shield, and as an exceeding great reward."[24]

(2) The kingdom of Christ, in respect of the propagation and establishment of it, with the multitude of his subjects, that also is in this promise.

(3) The temporal part of it, multitudes of children to a childless man: and "an heir from his own bowels."[25]

General and Specific Application

Now this promise, in these three branches, takes up your whole interest, comprises all you are to believe for, be you considered either as believers, or as rulers.

(1) As believers: so your interest lies in these two things: 1. that your own souls have a share and portion in the Lord Christ: 2. that the kingdom of the Lord Jesus be exalted and established.

(2) As rulers: that peace and prosperity may be the inheritance of the nation, is in your desires: look upon this in subordination to the kingdom of Christ, and so all these are in this promise.

To make this more plain, these being the three main things that you aim at, I shall lay before you three promises, suited to these several things, which or the like, you are to view in all your actings, all staggering at them being from unbelief.

23 Samuel Parker challenged Owen on this point in *A Defence and Continuation of the Ecclesiastical Politie* (London, 1671), 208.

24 Gen. 15:1.

25 Gen. 15:4.

(1) The first thing you are to believe for, is the interest of your own souls in the covenant of grace, by Christ: as to this I shall only point unto that promise of the covenant, "I will be merciful to their unrighteousness, and their sins, and their iniquities, I will remember no more" (Heb. 8:12).

(2) The second is the establishment of the kingdom of Christ, in despite of all opposition: and for this among innumerable, take that of Isaiah 60:11. "Therefore thy gates shall be open continually, they shall not be shut day nor night, that men may bring unto thee the forces of the Gentiles, and that their kings may be brought; for the nation and kingdom that will not serve thee, shall perish."[26]

(3) The quiet and peace of the nation, which you regard as rulers, as it stands in subordination to the kingdom of Christ, comes also under the promise, for which take that of Jeremiah 30:20–21.

These being your three main aims, let your eye be fixed on these three, or the like promises; for in the demonstration and the use of the point, I shall carry along all three together: desiring that what is instanced in anyone, may be always extended to both the others.

Staggering Comes from Unbelief

2. What is it to stagger at the promise: "He staggered not," οὐ διεκρίθη, "he disputed not"; διακρίνομαι is properly to make use of our own judgment and reason, in discerning of things, of what sort they be. It is sometimes rendered, "to doubt" (Matt. 21:21); "If ye have faith" καὶ μὴ διακριθῆτε, "and doubt not"; that is, not use arguings and reasonings in yourselves concerning the promise and things promised. Sometimes it simply denotes to discern a thing as it is: so the word is used, διακρίνων τὸ σῶμα, "Discerning the body" (1 Cor. 11:29).

In the sense wherein it is here used, as also Matthew 21:21, it holds out, as I said, a self-consultation and dispute, concerning those contrary things that are proposed to us. So also Acts 10:20, Peter is commanded to obey the vision, μηδὲν διακρινόμενος, "nothing doubting": what is that? Why, a not continuing to do, what he is said to have done, verse 17, "He doubted in himself what the vision he had seen should mean": he rolled, and disputed it in his own thoughts, he staggered at it.

To stagger then at the promise, is to take into consideration the promise itself, and withal, all the difficulties that lie in the way for the accomplishment of it, as to a man's own particular, and then so to dispute it in his thoughts, as not fully to cast it off, nor fully to close with it. For instance, the

26 Isa. 60:11–12.

soul considers the promise of free grace in the blood of Jesus, looks upon it, weighs as well as it is able, the truth of God, who makes the promise, with those other considerations, which might lead the heart to rest firmly upon it; but withal, takes into his thoughts, his own unworthiness, sinfulness, unbelief, hypocrisy, and the like; which as he supposes, powerfully stave off the efficacy of the promise from him. Hence he knows not what to conclude: if he add a grain of faith, the scale turns on the side of the promise; the like quantity of unbelief, makes it turn upon him; and what to do he knows not: let go the promise he cannot, take fast hold he dares not; but here he staggers and wavers to and fro.

Proof of This Principle

Thus the soul comes to be like Paul, in another case (Phil. 1:23). He considered his own advantage on the one side by his dissolution, and the profit of the churches by his abiding in the flesh on the other; and taking in these various thoughts, he cries out, he is in a strait, he staggered, he was betwixt two, and knew not which to choose: or as David, when he had a tender of several corrections made to him, says, "I am in a great strait" (2 Sam. 24:14); he sees evil in every one, and knows not which to choose.

A poor creature looking upon the promise sees, as he supposes, in a steadfast closing with the promise, that there lies presumption; on the other hand, certain destruction, if he believes not: and now he staggers, he is in a great strait: arguments arise on both sides, he knows not how to determine them, and so hanging in suspense, he staggers.

Like a man traveling a journey, and meeting with two several paths, that promise both fairly, and he knows not which is his proper way; he guesses, and guesses, and at length cries, "Well, I know not which of these ways I should go, but this is certain, if I mistake, I am undone, I'll go in neither, but here I'll sit down, and not move one step in either of them, until someone come, that can give me direction." The soul very frequently sits down in this hesitation, and refuses to step one step forward, till God come mightily and lead out the spirit to the promise, or the devil turn it aside to unbelief.

It is, as a thing of small weight in the air: the weight that it has, carries it downward; and the air, with some breath of wind, bears it up again: so that it waves to and fro: sometimes it seems as though it would fall, by its own weight, and sometimes again, as though it would mount quite out of sight, but poised between both, it tosses up and down, without any great gaining either way.

The promise, draws the soul upward, and the weight of its unbelief, that sinks it downward: sometimes the promise attracts so powerfully, you would think the heart quite drawn up into it: and sometimes again unbelief presses down, that you would think it gone forever; but neither prevails utterly, the poor creature swags[27] between both, this is to stagger: like the two disciples going to Emmaus, "They talked together of the things that were happened" (Luke 24:14): debated the business: and verse 22 they gave up the result of their thoughts; they "trusted it had been he that should have redeemed Israel."[28] They trusted once, but now seeing him slain and crucified, they know not what to say to it: What then? Do they quite give over all trusting in him? No, they cannot do so, verses [22–24]. Certain women had astonished them, and affirmed that he was risen: yea, and others also, going to his grave, found it so: hereupon they have communication within themselves, and are sad, verse 17, that is, they staggered; they were in a staggering condition: much appears for them, something against them, they know not what to do.

A poor soul that has been long perplexed in trouble and anxiety of mind, finds a sweet promise, Christ in a promise suited to all his wants, coming with mercy to pardon him, with love to embrace him, with blood to purge him, and is raised up to roll himself in some measure upon this promise: on a sudden, terrors arise, temptations grow strong, new corruptions break out, Christ in the promise dies to him, Christ in the promise is slain, is in the grave as to him; so that he can only sigh, and say, "I trusted for deliverance by Christ, but now all is gone again, I have little or no hope, Christ in the promise is slain to me." What then? Shall he give over, never more inquire after this buried Christ, but sit down in darkness and sorrow? No, he cannot do so: this morning some new arguments of Christ's appearance again upon the soul, are made out; it may be, Christ is not forever lost to him. What does he then? Steadfastly believe he cannot, totally give over he will not: he staggers: he is full of self-consultations and is sad. This it is to stagger at the promise of God. I come now to prove, that notwithstanding any pretenses whatever, all this staggering is from unbelief.

The two disciples, whom we now mentioned that staggered and disputed between themselves in their journey to Emmaus, thought they had a good reason, and a sufficient appearing cause of all their doubtings: "We hoped," say they, "that it was he, that should have delivered Israel." What do they now stand at? Alas! The "chief priests and rulers have condemned him to death, and crucified him" (Luke 24:20). And is it possible that deliverance should arise from a crucified man? This makes them stagger. But when our Savior

27 I.e., moves unsteadily without control.

28 Following Goold, the citation should be corrected to Luke 24:21.

himself draws nigh to them, and gives them the ground of all this, he tells them it is all from hence; they are "foolish and slow of heart to believe," verse 25. Here is the rise of all their doubtings, even their unbelief. While you are slow of heart to believe, do not once think of establishment.

Peter venturing upon the waves at the command of Christ (Matt. 14), seeing "the wind to grow boisterous," verse 29,[29] he also has a storm within, and cries out, "Oh save me": what was now the cause of Peter's fear and crying out? Why the wind and sea grew boisterous, and he was ready to sink: no such thing; but merely unbelief, want of faith: verse 31. "O thou of little faith" (says our Savior) "wherefore didst thou doubt?" It was not the great winds, but your little faith that made you stagger. And in three or four other places, upon several occasions, does our Savior lay all the wavering and staggering of his followers, as to any promised mercy, upon this score, as Matthew 6:30 and 8:26.

Ahaz being afraid of the combination of Syria and Ephraim against him, received a promise of deliverance by Isaiah (Isa. 7:7) whereupon the prophet tells him, and all Judah, that "if they will not believe, surely they shall not be established," verse 9. He does not say, "If Damascus and Ephraim be not broken, you shall not be established"; no, the stick is not there: the fear that you will not be established, arises merely from your unbelief, that keeps you off from closing with the promise, which would certainly bring you establishment.

And this is the sole reason the apostle gives, why the word of promise being preached, becomes unprofitable; even because of unbelief: it was not "mixed with faith" (Heb. 4:2).

A Twofold Demonstration of the Principle

But these things will be more clear under the demonstration of the point; which are two:

Five Theological Reasons for Confidence in the Promises

(1) Dem[onstration]. When a man doubts, hesitates and disputes, anything in himself, his reasonings must have their rise, either from something within himself, or from something in the things concerning which he staggers: either *certitudo mentis*, "the assurance of his mind," or *certitudo entis*, the "certainty of the thing itself," is wanting.[30]

He that doubts whether his friend in a far country be alive or no, his staggering arises from the uncertainty of the thing itself: when that is made out,

29 Following Goold, this should be corrected to verse 30.

30 A distinction between the certainty of the object (*certitudo entis*) and the certainty of the mind about that object (*certitudo mentis*).

he is resolved, as it was with Jacob in the case of Joseph.[31] But he that doubts whether the needle in the compass, being touched with the lodestone,[32] will turn northward; all the uncertainty is in his own mind.

When men stagger at the promises, this must arise either from within themselves, or some occasion must be administered hereunto, from the promise. If from within themselves, that can be nothing but unbelief; an inbred obstacle to closing with, and resting on the promise, that is unbelief. If then we demonstrate that there is nothing in the promise, either as to matter or manner, or any attendancy of it, that should occasion any such staggering, we lay the burden and blame on the right shoulders, the sin of staggering on unbelief.

Now that any occasion is not administered, nor cause given, of this staggering, from the promise, will appear if we consider seriously whence any such occasion or cause should arise. All the stability of a promise, depends upon the qualifications of the promiser, to the ends and purposes of the promise. If a man make me a promise to do such and such things for me, and I question, whether ever it will be so, or no; it must be from a doubt of the want of one of these things in him that makes the promise: either [1] of truth, or [2] of ability to make good his word, because of the difficulty of the thing itself; or [3] of sincerity to intend me really, what he speaks of; or [4] of constant memory to take the opportunity of doing the thing intended; or [5] of stableness to be still of the same mind. Now if there be no want of any of these in him whose promises we speak of, there is then certainly no ground of our staggering, but only from our own unbelief.

God Has Done All That Is Necessary by Way of Confirmation

Let us now see whether any of these things, be wanting to the promises of God: and begin we with the first:

[1] Is there truth in these promises? If there be the least occasion in the world, to suspect the truth of the promises, or the veracity of the promiser, then may our staggering at them arise from thence, and not from our own unbelief. On this ground it is, that all human faith, that is bottomed merely on the testimony of man, is at best but a probable opinion: for every man is a liar, and possibly may lie, in that very thing, he is engaged to us in. Though a good man will not do so, to save his life, yet it is possible, he may be tempted, he may do so: but now the author of the promises whereof we speak is

31 Gen. 45:27.

32 I.e., iron oxide used as a magnet.

truth itself. The God of truth. Who has taken this as his special attribute, to distinguish him, from all other. He is the very God of truth; and holds out this very attribute in a special manner, in this very thing, in making of his promise. "He is faithful to forgive us our sins" (1 John 1:9) whence his word is said not only to be true, but "truth" (John 17:17), truth itself: "All flesh is as grass," but his "word abides for ever" (Isa. 40:6, 8).

But yet farther, that it may be evident, that from hence there can be no occasion of staggering. This God of truth, whose word is truth, has in his infinite wisdom, condescended to our weakness, and used all possible means, to cause us to apprehend the truth of his promises. The Lord might have left us in the dark, to have gathered out his mind and will toward us, from obscure expressions: and knowing of what value his kindness is, it might justly be expected that we should do so. Men in misery, are glad to lay hold of the least word, that drops from him that can relieve them, and to take courage and advantage upon it: as the servants of Ben-hadad, watched diligently, what would fall from the mouth of Ahab, concerning their master, then in fear of death: and when he had occasionally called him his brother, they presently laid hold of it, and cry, "Thy brother Benhadad" (1 Kings 20:33). God might have left us, and yet have manifested much free grace, to have gathered up falling crumbs or occasional droppings of mercy, and supply: that we should have rejoiced to have found out one word looking that way: but to shut up all objections, and to stop forever the mouth of unbelief, he has not only spoken plainly, but has condescended to use all the ways of confirming the truth of what he says and speaks, that ever were in use among the sons of men.

There be four ways, whereby men seek to obtain credit to what they speak, as an undoubted truth, that there may be no occasion of staggering.

{1} By often averring and affirming of the same thing. When a man says the same thing again and again, it is a sign that he speaks the truth, or, at least, that he would be thought so to do. Yea, if an honest man do clearly, fully, plainly, often engage himself to us in the same thing, we count it a vile jealousy not to believe the real truth of his intentions. Now the Lord in his promises often speaks the same things, he speaks once and twice. There is not anything that he has promised us, but he has done it, again, and again. For instance; as if he should say, "I will be merciful to your sins;" I pray believe me, for "I will pardon your iniquities," yea, it shall be so, "I will blot out your transgressions as a cloud."[33] There is not any want, whereunto we are liable, but thus he has dealt concerning it. As his command is line upon

33 Isa. 44:22.

line, so is his promise. And this is one way, whereby God causes the truth of his promises to appear. To take away all color of staggering, he speaks once, yea twice, if we will hear.

{2} The second way of confirming any truth, is by an oath. Though we fear the truth of some men in their assertions, yet when once they come to swear anything in justice and judgment, there are very few so knownly profligate, and past all sense of God, but that their asseverations[34] do gain credit, and pass for truth. Hence the apostle tells us, that "an oath for confirmation, is to men an end of all strife" (Heb. 6:16). Though the truth be before, ambiguous and doubtful, yet when any interposes with an oath, there is no more contest among men. That nothing may be wanting to win our belief to the promises of God, he has taken this course also, he has sworn to their truth, "When God made promise to Abraham, because he could swear by no greater, he sware by himself" (Heb. 6:13). He confirms his promise by an oath. "Oh blessed we, for whose sake God swears! Oh most miserable, if we believe not the Lord even when He swears!"[35] When Christ came, "in whom all the promises of God, are, yea and amen,"[36] to make sure work of the truth of them, he is confirmed in his administration by an oath (Heb. 7:21). He was made a priest by "an oath by him that said, 'The Lord sware, and will not repent, thou art a priest for ever' ": Now I pray, what is the cause of this great condescension in the God of heaven, to confirm that word, which in itself, is truth, by an oath? The apostle satisfies us as to the end aimed at (Heb. 6:17–18). This was (says he) the aim of God herein, that his people seeing him engaged by "two such immutable things" as his promise and his oath, may be assured that there is an utter impossibility, that any one word of his should come short of its truth; or that they firmly resting upon it, should be deceived thereby. And this is a second way.

{3} Another course whereby men confirm the truth of what they speak, is, by entering into covenant to accomplish what they have spoken. A covenant gives strength to the truth of any engagement. When a man has but told you he will do such and such things for you, you are full of doubts and fears, that he may break with you: but when he has indented in a covenant, and you can

34 I.e., solemn affirmation or declaration.

35 In the text: *O felices nos, quorum causâ Deus jurat; O infelices, si nec juranti Deo credimus*! This is a quotation from Tertullian *On Repentance* 4.8. For the Latin text, see Tertullian, *De paenitentia*, ed. Philippus Borleffs, Corpus Scriptorum Ecclesiasticorum Latinorum 76 (Vienna: Hoelder-Pichler-Tempsky, 1957), 149. For the English translation, see Tertullian, *On Repentance*, in *Ante-Nicene Fathers: The Writings of the Fathers Down to A.D. 325*, 10 vols., ed. Alexander Roberts and James Donaldson (1886; repr., Peabody, MA: Hendrickson, 1995), 3:660.

36 2 Cor. 1:20.

show it under his hand and seal, you look upon that, consider that, and are very secure. Even this way also has the Lord taken to confirm and establish his truths and promises, that all doubtings and staggerings may be excluded, he has wrapped them all up in a covenant, and brought himself into a federal engagement, that upon every occasion, and at every temptation, we may draw out his hand and seal, and say to Satan and our own false hearts: "See here, behold God engaged in covenant, to make good the word wherein he has caused me to put my trust: and this is his property, that he is a God keeping covenant": so that having his promise redoubled, and that confirmed by an oath, all sealed and made sure by an unchangeable covenant, what can we require more, to assure us of the truth of these things: But yet further.

{4} In things of very great weight, and concernment, such as whereon lives, and the peace of nations do depend, men use to give hostages, for the securing each other of the faith and truth of all their engagements; that they may be mutual pledges of their truth and fidelity. Neither has the Lord left this way unused to confirm his promise. He has given us a hostage to secure us of his truth: one exceedingly dear to him; one always in his bosom, of whose honor, he is as careful, as of his own. Jesus Christ is the great hostage of his Father's truth: the pledge of his fidelity in his promises. God has set him forth, and given him to us for this end. "Behold the Lord himself shall give you a sign" (a sign that he will fulfill his word), "a virgin shall conceive, and bear a son, and shall call his name Immanuel" (Isa. 7:14). That you may be assured of my truth, the virgin's son shall be a hostage of it. "In him are all the promises of God yea and amen." Thus also to his saints he gives the farther hostage of his Spirit, and the firstfruits of glory; that the full accomplishment of all his promises, may be contracted in a little, and presented to their view: as the Israelites had the pleasures of Canaan in the clusters of grapes brought from thence.[37]

Now from all this it is apparent, not only that there is truth in all the promises of God, but also that truth so confirmed, so made out, established, that not the least occasion imaginable, is thence administered to staggering or doubting. He that disputes the promise, and knows not how to close with them, must find out another cause of his so doing: as to the truth of the promise, there is no doubt at all, nor place for any.

God Has the Power and Means to Accomplish His Promises

[2] But secondly, though there be truth in the promise, yet there may want ability in the promiser to accomplish the thing promised, because of its

37 Num. 13:23–24.

manifold difficulties. This may be a second cause of staggering, if the thing itself engaged for, be not compassable, by the ability of the engager. As if a skillful physician, should promise a sick man recovery from his disease, though he could rely upon the truth and sincerity of his friend, yet he cannot but question his ability as to this, knowing that to cure the least distemper, is not absolutely in his power: but when he promises, who is able to perform, then all doubting in this kind, is removed. See then whether it be so, in respect of these promises whereof we speak. When God comes to Abraham, to engage himself in that covenant of grace, from whence flow all the promises whereof we treat: he lays this down as the bottom of all, "I am," (says he) "God Almighty" (Gen. 17:1) or "God all-sufficient," very well able to go through with whatever I promise. When difficulties, temptations, and troubles arise, remember who it is that has promised; not only he that is true and faithful, but he that is "God Almighty," before whom nothing can stand, when he will accomplish his word. And that this was a bottom of great confidence to Abraham, the apostle tells you, "Being fully persuaded that he who had promised, was able also to perform" (Rom. 4:21). When God is engaged by his word, his ability is especially to be eyed. The soul is apt to ask, "How can this be? It is impossible it should be so to me": but, "he is able that hath promised." And this, the same apostle holds out to us, to fix our faith upon, in reference to that great promise of recalling the Jews, and reimplanting them into the vine. "God," (says he) "is able to graft them in" (Rom. 11:23): though now they seem as dead bones, yet the Lord knows they may live; for he is able to breathe upon them,[38] and make them "terrible as an army with banners":[39] yea so excellent is this all-sufficiency, this ability of God to accomplish his whole word, that the apostle cautions us, that we do not bound it, as though it could go so far only, or so far: nay says he, "He is able to do exceeding abundantly, above all that we ask or think" (Eph. 3:20).

When men come to close with the promise indeed, to make a life upon it, they are very ready to question and inquire, whether it be possible that ever the word of it, should be made good to them. He that sees a little boat swimming at sea, observes no great difficulty in it, looks upon it without any solicitousness of mind at all, beholds how it tosses up and down, without any fears of its sinking: but now, let this man commit his own life to sea in that bottom, what inquiries will he make? What a search into the vessel? "Is it possible," (says he) "this little thing should safeguard my life in the ocean?" It is so with us, in our view of the promises: while we consider them at large,

38 Ezek. 37:1–10.

39 Song 6:4.

as they lie in the word, alas! They are all true, all "yea and amen," shall be all accomplished: but when we go to venture our souls upon a promise, in an ocean of wrath and temptations, then every blast we think will overturn it: it will not bear us above all these waves; is it possible we should swim safely upon the plank of a pinnace[40] in the midst of the ocean?

Now here we are apt to deceive ourselves, and mistake the whole thing in question, which is the bottom of many corrupted reasonings and perplexed thoughts. We inquire whether it can be so to us as the word holds out; when the truth is, the question is not about the nature of the thing; but about the power of God. Place the doubt aright, and it is this, is God able to accomplish what he has spoken? Can he heal my backslidings? Can he pardon my sins? Can he save my soul? Now that there may be no occasion, or color of staggering upon this point, you see God reveals himself as an all-sufficient God: as one that is able to go through with all his engagements. If you will stagger, you may so do; this is certain, you have no cause to do so from hence; there is not any promise that ever God entered into, but he is able to perform it.

Object[ion]. But you will say, "Though God be thus able, thus all-sufficient, yet may there not be defects in the means whereby he works? As a man may have a strong arm able to strike his enemies to the ground, but yet if he strike with a feather, or a straw, it will not be done; not for want of strength in his arm, but of fitness and suitableness in the instrument, whereby he acts." But,

Answ[er]. {1} God using instruments, they do not act according to their own virtue, but according to the influence of virtue by him to them communicated. Look to what end soever God is pleased to use any means, his choosing of them, fills them with efficacy to that purpose. Let the way and means of accomplishing what you expectest by the promise, be in themselves never so weak, yet know that, from God's choosing of them, to that end, they shall be filled with virtue and efficacy to the accomplishment of it.

{2} It is expressly affirmed of the great mediums of the promise, that they also are able, that there is no want of power in them, for the accomplishment of the thing promised.

1st. There is the means procuring it, and that is Jesus Christ: the promises, as to the good things contained in them, are all purchased by him: and of him the apostle affirms expressly, that "he is able to save them to the uttermost, them that come to God by him" (Heb. 7:25).[41] No want here: no defect: he is able to do it to the uttermost; able to save them that are tempted (Heb. 2:18).

40 I.e., a small light sailing vessel.

41 In the original, the word "able" is set in all caps for emphasis.

2nd. There is the great means of manifestation, and that is the word of God: and of this also it is affirmed, that it is able. It has an all-sufficiency in its kind. Paul tells the elders of Ephesus, that "the word of grace is able to build them up, and to give them an inheritance among them that are sanctified" (Acts 20:32).

3rd. There is the great means of operation, and that is the Spirit of grace: he works the mercy of the promise upon the soul: he also is able, exceeding powerful, to effect the end appointed. He has no bounds, nor measure of operation, but only his own will (1 Cor. 12:11).

Hence then it is apparent, in the second place, that there is no occasion for doubting; yea, that all staggering is excluded, from the consideration of the ability of the promiser, and the means whereby he works: if you continuest to stagger, you must get a better plea than this, "It cannot be, it is impossible": I tell you, nay, but God is able to accomplish the whole word of his promise. But,

God Is Sincere in What He Promises

[3] There may be want of sincerity in promises and engagements, which while we do but suspect, we cannot choose but stagger at them. If a man make a promise to me, and I can suppose that he intends not as he says, but has reserves to himself of another purpose, I must needs doubt as to the accomplishment of what he has spoken. If the soul may surmise, that the Lord intends not him sincerely in his promises, but reserves some other thing in his mind, or that it shall be so to others and not to him, he must needs dispute in himself, stagger, and keep off from believing. This, then must be demonstrated, in the third place, that the promises of God; and God in all his promises, are full of sincerity, so that none need fear to cast himself on them, they shall be real unto him. Now, concerning this, observe,

{1} That God's promises are not declarative of his secret purposes and intentions. When God holds out to any a promise of the pardon of sin, this does not signify to any singular man, that it is the purpose of God, that his sin shall be pardoned. For if so, then either all men must be pardoned to whom the word of promise comes, which is not: or else God fails of his purposes, and comes short of his intendments; which would render him, either impotent, that he could not; or mutable, that he would not, establish them: but, "who hath resisted his will?" (Rom. 9:19). He is the Lord, and he changes not (Mal. 1).[42] So that though everyone, to whom the promise is held out, has not the fruit of the promise; yet this derogates[43] not at all, from the sincerity of

42 Following Goold, the citation should be corrected to Mal. 3:6.

43 I.e., detracts.

God in his promises; for, he does not hold them forth to any such end and purpose, as to declare his intentions, concerning particular persons.

{2} There are some absolute promises, comprehensive of the covenant of grace, which, as to all those that belong to that covenant, do hold out thus much of the mind of God, that they shall certainly be accomplished in and toward them all. The soul may freely be invited to venture on these promises, with assurance of their efficacy toward him.

{3} This God principally declares in all his promises, of his mind and purpose, that every soul, to whom they shall come, may freely rest on; to wit, that faith in the promises, and the accomplishment of the promises, are inseparable. He that believes, shall enjoy; this is most certain, this God declares of his mind, his heart, toward us, that as for all the good things he has spoken of to us, it shall be to us, according to our faith. This I say the promises of God do signify of his purpose, that the believer of them shall be the enjoyer of them: in them "the righteousness of God is revealed from faith to faith" (Rom. 1:17). From the faith of God revealing, to the faith of man receiving: so that, upon the making out of any promise, you may safely conclude, that upon believing, the mercy, the Christ, the deliverance of this promise, is mine. It is true, if a man stand disputing and staggering, whether he have any share in a promise, and close not with it by faith, he may come short of it; and yet without the least impeachment of the truth of the promise, or sincerity of the promiser: for God has not signified by them, that men shall enjoy the good things of them, whether they believe, or not Thus far the promises of grace are general, and carry a truth to all, that there is an inviolable connection between believing, and the enjoyment of the things in them contained. And in this truth, is the sincerity of the promiser, which can never be questioned, without sin and folly. And this wholly shuts up the spirit from any occasion of staggering. "O ye of little faith! Wherefore do ye doubt?"[44] Ah! Lest our share be not in this promise; lest we are not intended in it: poor creatures! There is but this one way of keeping you off from it, that is, disputing it in yourselves by unbelief. Here lies the sincerity of God toward you, that believing, you shalt not come short of what you aim at. Here, then, is no room for staggering. If proclamation be made, granting pardon to all such rebels, as shall come in by such a season, do men use to stand questioning whether the state bear them any goodwill, or not? "No," says the poor creature, "I will cast myself upon their faith and truth engaged in their proclamation whatever I have deserved in particular, I know they will be faithful in their promises." The gospel proclamation is of pardon to

44 Matt. 14:31.

all comers in, to all believers: it is not for you, poor staggerer, to question, what is the intendment toward you in particular, but roll yourself on this, there is an absolute sincerity in the engagement[45] which you mayest freely rest upon. But,

God Never Forgets His Promises

[4] Though all be present, truth, power, sincerity; yet if he that makes the promise should forget, this were a ground of staggering. Pharaoh's butler, without doubt, made large promises to Joseph, and probably spoke the truth according to his present intention: afterward standing in the presence of Pharaoh, restored to favor, he had doubtless power enough to have procured the liberty of a poor innocent prisoner: but yet this would not do, it did not profit Joseph; because, as the text says, he "did not remember Joseph, but forgat him" (Gen. 40:23). This forgetting made all other things useless. But neither has this, the least color in divine promises. It was Zion's infirmity to say, "The Lord hath forsaken me, and my God hath forgotten me" (Isa. 49:14): for, says the Lord, "Can a woman forget her sucking child, that she should not have compassion on the son of her womb? Yea, they may forget, but I will not forget thee: behold, I have graven thee upon the palms of my hands, thy walls are continually before me": verses 15–16.

The causes of forgetfulness are,

{1} Want of love. The things that men love not, they care not for: the matters of their love are continually in their thoughts. Now says God to Zion, "Why sayest you, 'I have forgotten you'? Is it for want of love? Alas! The love of a most tender mother to her sucking child, comes infinitely short of my love to you: my love to you, is more fixed than so, and how should you be out of my mind? How should you be forgotten?" Infinite love will have infinite thoughtfulness and remembrance.

{2} Multiplicity of business: this with men is a cause of forgetting. I had done says one, as I promised, but multiplicity of occasions thrust it out of my mind, I pray excuse me: alas! "Though I rule all the world, yet you are graven upon the palms of my hands, and therefore your walls are continually before me." See also Psalm 77:9. Neither then is there as to this the least color given us, to stagger at the promise of God.

Divine Immutability Ensures That the Promises Will Not Change

[5] But lastly, where all other things concur, yet if the person promising be changeable, if he may alter his resolution, a man may justly doubt and debate

45 In the original, the word "engagement" is set in all caps for emphasis.

in himself, the accomplishment of any promise made to him: "It is true," may he say, "he now speaks his heart and mind, but who can say he will be of this mind tomorrow? May he not be turned, and then what becomes of the golden mountains, that I promised myself upon his engagement?" Wherefore in the last place, the Lord carefully rejects all sinful surmises concerning the least change or alteration in him or any of his engagements. He is "the Father of lights, with whom is no variableness, nor shadow of turning" (James 1:18); no shadow, no appearance of any such thing.[46] "I am the Lord," (says he) "I change not; therefore ye sons of Jacob are not consumed" (Mal. 3:6). The Lord knows, that if anything in us, might prevail with him to alter the word that is gone out of his mouth, we should surely perish. We are poor provoking creatures, therefore he lays out, not being consumed, only on this, even his own unchangeableness: this we may rest upon, "He is in one mind, and who can turn him?"[47]

And in these observations, have I given you the first demonstration of the point: *all staggering is from our own unbelief.*

Various Providential Reasons for Confidence in the Promises

(2) Dem[onstration]. The experience which we have of the mighty workings of God, for the accomplishment of all his promises, gives light unto this thing. We have found it true, that where he is once engaged, he will certainly go through unto the appointed issue, though it stand him in the laying out of his power and wisdom to the uttermost, "Thy bow was made quite naked according to the oaths of the tribes, thy word" (Hab. 3:9).[48] If God's oath be passed, and his word engaged; he will surely accomplish it, though it cost him the making of his bow quite naked, the manifestation of his power to the utmost.

It is true: never did any wait upon God for the accomplishment and fulfilling of a promise, but he found many difficulties fall out between the word and the thing. So was it with Abraham in the business of a son: and so with David in the matter of a kingdom. God will have his promised mercies to fall, as the dews upon the parched gasping earth, or "as the shadow of a great rock in a weary land" (Isa. 32:2), very welcome unto the traveler, who has had the sun beat upon his head in his travel all the day. Zion is "a crown of glory in the hand of the Lord," as "a royal diadem in the hand of her God" (Isa. 62:3). The precious stones of a diadem, must be cut and polished, before they be set in beauty and glory. God will have ofttimes the precious living stones of

46 Following Goold, the citation should be corrected to James 1:17.

47 Job 23:13.

48 Owen's text from his thanksgiving sermons after the siege of Colchester was published as *Ebenezer* (1648). See *Complete Works of John Owen*, 18:225.

Zion, to have many a sharp cutting, before they come to be fully fixed in his diadem: but yet in the close, whatever obstacles stand in the way, the promise has still wrought out its passage: as a river, all the while it is stopped with a dam, is still working higher and higher, still getting more and more strength, until it bear down all before it, and obtain a free course to its appointed place: every time opposition lies against the fulfilling of the promise, and so seems to impede it for a season, it gets more and more power, until the appointed hour be come, and then the promise bears down all before it.

Were there anything imaginable, whereof we had not experience, that it had been conquered to open a door for the fulfilling of every word of God, we might possibly, as to the apprehension of that thing, stagger from some other principle, than that of unbelief.

What is there in heaven or earth, but God and his ministering spirits, that has not one time or other, stood up to its utmost opposition, for the frustrating of the word, wherein some or other of the saints of God have put their trust? Devils in their temptations, baits, subtleties, accusations, and oppositions: men in their counsels, reasonings, contrivances, interests, dominions, combinations, armies, multitudes, and the utmost of their endeavors: the whole frame of nature, in its primitive instituted course, fire, water, day, night, age, sickness, death; all in their courses have fought against the accomplishment of the promises: and what have they obtained by all their contendings? All disappointed, frustrated, turned back, changed, and served only to make the mercy of the promise, more amiable and glorious.

I would willingly illustrate this demonstration with an instance, that the almighty, all-conquering power that is in the promise, settling all staggering upon its own basis of unbelief,[49] might be the more evident.

I might here mention Abraham, with all the difficulties and appearing impossibilities, which the promise unto him did pass through, and cast to the ground, the mercy of it at length, arising out of the grave; for he received his son from the dead "in a figure" (Heb. 11:19): or I might speak of Joseph, Moses, or David: but I shall rather choose a precedent from among the works of God, in the days wherein we live: and that in a business concerning which we may set up our Ebenezer,[50] and say, "Thus far has God been a helper."[51]

Look upon the affair of Ireland. The engagement of the great God of revenges against murder and treachery, the interest of the Lord Christ and his

49 In the original, the word "unbelief" is set in all caps for emphasis.

50 *Ebenezer* was the title of the published version of Owen's thanksgiving sermons after the siege of Colchester.

51 1 Sam. 7:12.

kingdom against the man of sin,[52] furnished the undertakers with manifold promises to carry them out to a desired, a blessed issue. Take now a brief view of some mountains of opposition, that lie in the way against any success in that place; and hear the Lord saying to every one of them, "Who art thou, O great mountain? Before my people thou shalt be made a plain" (Zech. 4:7).

Not to mention the strivings and stragglings of two manner of people in the womb of this nation, totally obstructing for a long time the bringing forth of any deliverance for Ireland:[53] nor yet, that mighty mountain (which some misnamed a Level) that thought at once to have locked an everlasting door upon that expedition:[54] I shall propose some few (of many) that have attended it.

[1] The silence that has been in heaven for half an hour as to this business:[55] the great cessation of prayers in the heavens, of many churches, has been no small mountain in the way of the promise. When God will do good for Zion, he requires that his remembrancers give him no rest, until he do it (Isa. 62:7). And yet sometimes in the close of their supplications, gives them an answer "by terrible things" (Ps. 65:5). He is sometimes "silent" to the prayers of his people (Ps. 28:1). Is not then a grant rare, when his people are silent as to prayers? Of how many congregations in this nation, may the prayers, tears, and supplications for carrying on of the work of God in Ireland,[56] be written with the lines of emptiness? What a silence has been in the heaven of many churches, for this last half hour? How many that began with the Lord in that work, did never sacrifice at the altar of Jehovah-nissi:[57] nor consider that the Lord has sworn to have war with such Amalekites as are there "from generation to generation" (Ex. 17:15–16)? They have forgotten, that Ireland was the first of the nations that laid wait for the blood of God's people desiring to enter into his rest; and therefore "their latter end shall be to perish for ever" (Num. 24:20). Many are as angry as Jonah,[58] not that Babylon is spared, but that it is not spared. Has not this been held out as a mountain? What will you now do, when such or such, these and those men, of this or that party, look upon you "as the grass upon the house-tops, which withereth afore it

52 2 Thess. 2:3.

53 Gen. 25:22. The Long Parliament had planned to take action against the rebels in Ireland in the spring of 1642, but this had been delayed because of the civil wars in England.

54 The Burford Mutiny of May 1649 involved the refusal of Leveller-inspired soldiers to participate in the Cromwellian conquest of Ireland.

55 Rev. 8:1.

56 In the original, the word "Ireland" is set in all caps for emphasis.

57 I.e., the Lord is my banner.

58 Jonah 4:9.

groweth up: wherewith the mower filleth not his hand, nor he that bindeth sheaves his bosom,"[59] that will not so much as say, "The blessing of the Lord be upon you, we bless you in the name of the Lord"?[60] But now! Shall the faithlessness of men, make the "faith of God of none effect"?[61] Shall the kingdom of Christ suffer because some of those that are his, what through carnal wisdom, what through spiritual folly, refuse to come forth "to his help against the mighty"?[62] No, doubtless! "The Lord sees it, and it displeases him; he sees that "there is no man, and wonders that there is no intercessor": (even marvels that there are no more supplications on this behalf) "Therefore his own arm brought salvation to him, and his own righteousness it sustained him: he put on righteousness as a breastplate, and an helmet of salvation upon his head: and he put on the garments of vengeance for clothing, and was clad with zeal as a cloak: according to their deeds, accordingly he will repay, fury to his adversaries, recompense to his enemies, to the islands he will repay recompense" (Isa. 59:15–18).[63] Some men's not praying, shall not hinder the promises accomplishing. They may sooner discover an idol in themselves, than disappoint the living God. This was a mountain.

[2] Our own advices and counsels have often stood in the way of the promises bringing forth: this is not a time nor place for narrations: so I shall only say to this in general; that if the choicest and most rational advices of the army, had not been overswayed by the providence of God, in all probabilities, your affairs had been more than ten degrees backward, to the condition wherein they are.[64]

[3] The visible opposition of the combined enemy in that nation seemed, as to our strength, unconquerable. The wise man tells us, "A threefold cord is not easily broken"[65] Ireland had a fivefold cord to make strong bands for Zion, twisted together: never (I think) did such different interests bear with one another, for the compassing of one common end.

He that met the lion, the fox, and the ass traveling together, wondered *quo unâ iter facerent*:[66] whither these ill-matched associates did bend their

59 Ps. 129:6–7.

60 Ps. 129:8.

61 Rom. 3:3.

62 Judg. 5:23.

63 Owen appealed to this text in *The Branch of the Lord* (1650), which is included in this volume, as he presented Christ as "the great avenger of his house."

64 See the comments in the editor's introduction to the sermon about these various factors.

65 Eccl. 4:12.

66 Lat. "where they were going together." Owen also uses this quotation and illustration in his sermon preaching at the thanksgiving for the suppression of the Levellers. This an allusion to

course! Neither did his marveling cease, when he heard they were going a pilgrimage, in a business of devotion.

He that should meet Protestants, covenanted Protestants, that had sworn in the presence of the great God to extirpate popery and prelacy, as the Scots in Ulster;[67] others, that counted themselves under no less sacred bond, for the maintenance of prelates, service book, and the like; as the whole party of Ormond's adherents:[68] joined with a mighty number, that had for eight years together, sealed their vows to the Romish religion, with our blood and their own;[69] adding to them those that were profound to revolt up and down, as suited their own interest, as some in Munster;[70] all closing with that party, which themselves had labored to render most odious and execrable, as most defiled with innocent blood: he, I say, that should see all these, after seven years' mutual conflicting, and imbruing their hands in each other's blood, to march all one way together, cannot but marvel, *quo unâ iter facerent*, whither they should journey so friendly together. Neither surely, would his admiration be lessened, when he should hear, that the first thing they intended and agreed upon, was, to cover the innocent blood of forty-one;[71] contrary to that promise: "Behold, the Lord cometh out of his place, to punish the inhabitants of the

---

the fable of the lion, the ass, and the fox who went hunting together, agreeing to divide the spoil equally among themselves. The ass divided the large fat stag into three equal measures, but then the lion killed the ass and asked the fox to divide the spoil. For this version of the fable, see Geffrey Whitney, *A Choice of Emblemes* [. . .] (London, 1586), 154.

67 The Ulster Scots, who had sworn the Solemn League and Covenant, were so horrified by the regicide that they joined a coalition against the English Parliament. For the formal condemnation of the actions of the English Parliament by the Belfast Presbytery, see *A Necessary Representation of the Present Evills, and Eminent Dangers to Religion, Lawes, and Liberties, Arising from the Late, and Present Practises of the Sectarian Party in England: Together with and Exhortation to Duties Relating to the Covenant, unto All within Our Charge; and to All the Well-Affected within This Kingdome, by the Presbytery at Belfast, February 15th 1649* (Belfast, 1649).

68 James Butler, Marquis of Ormond (1610–1688), had returned to Ireland in October 1648 and was at the head of the largely Protestant Old English "Ormondists."

69 This is a reference to the Catholic Confederacy, established at Kilkenny in 1642, which in 1648 had its own internal conflict between those who put loyalty to the king first and those who prioritized papal loyalty. In early January 1649, Ormond signed a peace treaty with the Irish Confederates that promised toleration for Roman Catholics in return for support in the royalist cause. For analysis of what is termed the second Ormond peace of 1649, see Mícheál Ó Siochrú, *Confederate Ireland, 1642–49: A Constitutional and Political Analysis* (Dublin: *Four Courts*, 1999), 198–200.

70 The southern Protestant port towns of Munster—such as Youghal, Cork, and Kinsale—had sided with the English Parliament for much of the 1640s, but in April 1648, under the command of Lord Inchiquin, they switched allegiance to the royalist cause. Patrick Little, *Lord Broghill and the Cromwellian Union with Ireland and Scotland* (Woodbridge, UK: Boydell, 2004), 51–52.

71 Those who had died in the 1641 Irish Rebellion.

earth, for their iniquity: the earth also shall disclose her blood, and shall no more cover her slain" (Isa. 26:21). And nextly, to establish Catholic religion, or the kingdom of Babel, in the whole nation, in opposition to the engaged truth, and, in our days, visibly manifested power of the Lord Jesus: with sundry such like things, contrary to their science[72] and conscience, their covenant and light,[73] yea the trust and honesty, of most of the chief leaders of them.

Now how can the promise stand in the way of this hydra? What says it to this combined opposition?

{1} Why first, says the Lord, "Though hand join in hand, the wicked shall not be unpunished" (Prov. 11:21). Their covering shall be too short, and narrow, to hide the blood which God will have disclosed.

{2} And nextly, though they will give their power to the beast, and fight against the Lamb,[74] consenting in this, who agree in nothing else in the world; yet they shall be broken in pieces; though they associate themselves, they shall be broken in pieces. If Rezin, and the son of Remaliah, Syria and Ephraim, old adversaries, combine together for a new enmity against Judah;[75] if covenant and prelacy, popery and treachery, blood and (as to that) innocency, join hand in hand,[76] to stand in the way of the promise; yet I will not in this join with them says the Lord. Though they were preserved all distinctly in their several interests for seven years, in their mutual conflicts, that they might be scourges to one another; yet if they close, to keep off the engagement of God in the word of his promise, not much more than the fourth part of one year, shall consume some of them to nothing, and fill the residue with indignation and anguish.

By what means God has mightily and effectually wrought, by mixing folly with their counsels, putting fear, terror, and amazedness upon all their undertakings, to carry on his own purpose, I could easily give considerable instances. That which has been spoken in general may suffice to bottom us on this, that while we are in the way of God, all staggering at the issue, is from unbelief; for he can, he will do more such things as these.

72 I.e., knowledge; understanding of truth.

73 The Solemn League and Covenant contained the pledge "to endeavour the extirpation of popery." S. R. Gardiner, *Constitutional Documents of the Puritan Revolution, 1625–60*, 3rd rev. ed. (Oxford: Clarendon, 1958), 188.

74 Rev. 17:13–14.

75 2 Kings 16:5.

76 Here "covenant" refers to the Ulster Scots Presbyterians; "prelacy" to Protestant royalists under Ormond; "popery" to the Irish Catholic Confederates, particularly under the influence of Rinuccini; "treachery" to the likes of Lord Inchiquin; and "blood" to those who had participated in the violence of 1641. See Martyn Calvin Cowan, *John Owen and the Civil War Apocalypse: Preaching, Prophecy and Politics* (London: Routledge, 2017), 39.

Five Applications of This Principle

Those in Power Must Learn to Live by Faith in All Matters of Policy and Politics

Use 1. My first use shall be as unto temporals; for they also (as I told you) come under the promise, not to be staggered at, with the limitations before mentioned. Learn hence then to live more by faith in all your actings: believe, and you shall be established.[77] I have in the days of my pilgrimage, seen this evil under the sun: many professors of the gospel, called out to public actings, have made it their great design to manage all their affairs with wisdom and policy, like the men of the residue of the nations. Living by faith, upon the promises has appeared to them, as too low a thing, for the condition and employment wherein they now are: now they must plot, and contrive, and design, lay down principles of carnal fleshly wisdom, to be pursued to the uttermost: and what I pray has been the issue of such undertakings?

(1) First, the power of religion has totally been devoured, by that lean, hungry, never-to-be-satisfied beast of carnal policy: no signs left that it was ever in their bosoms. Conformity unto Christ in gospel graces, is looked on as a mean contemptible thing: some of them have fallen to downright atheism, most of them to wretched formality in the things of God. And then,

(2) Secondly, their plots and undertakings, have generally proved tympanous[78] and birthless: vexation and disappointment has been the portion of the residue of their days. The ceasing to lean upon the Lord, and striving to be wise in our actings, like the men of the world, has made more Rehoboams,[79] than any one thing in this generation.

What now lies at the bottom of all this? Merely staggering at the promise through unbelief. What building is that like to be, which has a staggering foundation? When God answers not Saul, he goes to the devil.[80] When the promise will not support us, we go to carnal policy: neither can it otherwise be. Engaged men, finding one way to disappoint them, presently betake themselves to another. If men begin once to stagger at the promise, and to conclude in their fears, that it will not receive accomplishment, that the fountain will be dry, they cannot but think it high time to dig cisterns for themselves.[81] When David says, he shall one day perish by the hand of Saul

77 2 Chron. 20:20.

78 I.e., hollow and empty.

79 1 Kings 12 records how Rehoboam went out to war against Israel with one hundred eighty thousand troops but then turned back.

80 1 Sam. 28:6–7.

81 Jer. 2:13.

(whatever God had said to the contrary) his next advice is, "Let me go to the Philistines":[82] and what success he had in that undertaking, you know. Political diversions from pure dependence on the promise, do always draw after them a long time of entanglements.

Give me leave to give a word of caution, against one or two things, which men staggering at the promises through unbelief, do usually in their carnal wisdom run into, for the compassing of the thing aimed at, that they may not be found in your honorable assembly.

[1] Take heed of a various[83] management of religion, of the things of God, to the advantage of the present posture and condition of your affairs. The things of Christ should be as Joseph's sheaf, to which all others should bow.[84] When they are made to cringe, and bend, and put on a flattering countenance, to allure any sort of men into their interest, they are no more the things of Christ. I would it had not been too evident formerly, that men entangled in their affairs, enjoying authority, have with all industry and diligence, pursued such and such an appearance of religion; not that themselves were so passionately affected with it, but merely for the satisfaction of some in that, whose assistance and compliance they needed for other things.[85] Oh let not the things of God, be immixed any more with carnal reasonings. His truths are all eternal and unchangeable. Give them at once the sovereignty of your souls, and have not the least thought of making them bend, to serve your own ends, though good and righteous. Think not to get the promise like Jacob,[86] by representing yourselves in the things of God, for other than you are.

[2] Hide no truth of God as to that way of manifestation which to you is committed, for fear it should prove prejudicial to your affairs. That influence and signature of your power, which is due to any truth of God, let it not be withheld by carnal reasonings. I might farther draw out these, and such like things as these; the warning is, to live upon the faith of that promise, which shall surely be established, without turning aside to needless, crooked paths of your own.

God Is Faithful, So Those in Power Must Be Faithful in Propagation of the Gospel, Especially in Ireland

Use 2. Secondly. Be faithful in doing all the work of God whereunto you are engaged, as he is faithful in working all your works whereunto he is engaged.

82 1 Sam. 27:1.

83 I.e., characterized by change or vacillation.

84 Gen. 37:7.

85 Perhaps a reference to some in Parliament making concessions to the Presbyterian interest.

86 Gen. 27.

Your work whereunto (while you are in his ways) God is engaged, is your safety and protection. God's work whereunto you are engaged is the propagating of the kingdom of Christ, and the setting up of the standard of the gospel. So far as you find God going on with your work, go you on with his. How is it that Jesus Christ, is in Ireland only as a lion staining all his garments with the blood of his enemies? And none to hold him out as a lamb sprinkled with his own blood to his friends? Is it the sovereignty and interest of England that is alone to be there transacted? For my part, I see no farther into the mystery of these things,[87] but that I could heartily rejoice, that innocent blood being expiated, the Irish might enjoy Ireland so long as the moon endures,[88] so that Jesus Christ might possess the Irish. But God having suffered those sworn vassals of the man of sin, to break out into such ways of villainy, as render them obnoxious unto vengeance, upon such rules of government among men, as he has appointed; is there therefore nothing to be done but to give a cup of blood into their hands?[89] Doubtless the way whereby God will bring the followers after the beast to condign destruction, for all their enmity to the Lord Jesus, will be, by suffering them to run into such practices against men, as shall righteously expose them to vengeance, according to acknowledged principles among the sons of men. But is this all? Has he no farther aim? Is not all this to make way for the Lord Jesus to take possession of his long since promised inheritance? And shall we stop at the first part? Is this to deal fairly with the Lord Jesus? Call him out to the battle, and then keep away his crown? God has been faithful in doing great things for you, be faithful in this one, do your utmost for the preaching of the gospel in Ireland.

Give me leave to add a few motives to this duty.

(1) They want it: no want like theirs who want the gospel. I would there were for the present, one gospel preacher, for every walled town in the English possession in Ireland.[90] The land mourns, and the people perish for want of knowledge.[91] Many run to and fro, but it is upon other designs; knowledge is not increased.

(2) They are sensible of their wants, and cry out for supply. The tears and cries of the inhabitants of Dublin after the manifestations of Christ, are ever in

87 The word "mystery" is set in all caps for emphasis and presumably is designed to call to mind the mystery of iniquity (2 Thess. 2:7).

88 Ps. 72:5. In Powell's sermon he held out the hope for the people of Ireland "that those people that were so contemptible, are like to have the greatest presence of God amongst them." See Powell, *Christ Exalted Above All Creatures*, 96.

89 Ps. 75:8.

90 In the original, the word "Ireland" is set in all caps for emphasis.

91 Hos. 4:6.

my view. If they were in the dark, and loved to have it so, it might something close a door upon the bowels of our compassion; but they cry out of their darkness, and are ready to follow everyone whosoever, to have a candle. If their being gospelless, move not our hearts, it is hoped, their importunate[92] cries will disquiet our rest: and wrest help, as a beggar does an alms.

(3) Seducers and blasphemers will not be wanting to sow their tares,[93] which those fallowed fields will receive, if there be none to cast in the seed of the word. Some are come over thither already without call, without employments, to no other end, but only to vaunt themselves to be God; as they have done in the open streets, with detestable pride, atheism, and folly: so that as Ireland[94] was heretofore termed by some in civil things a frippery[95] of bankrupts, for the great number of persons of broken estates that went thither: so doubtless in religion, it will prove a frippery of monstrous, enormous, contradictious opinions,[96] if the work of preaching the word of truth, and soberness be not carried on. And if this be the issue of your present undertakings, will it be acceptable, think you, to the Lord Jesus, that you have used his power and might, to make way for such things, as his soul abhors?[97]

[1] Will it be for his honor, that the people whom he has sought to himself with so high a hand, should at the very entrance of his taking possession, be leavened with those high and heavenly notions, which have an open, and experimented tendency to earthly, fleshly, dunghill practices?[98] Or,

[2] Will it be for the credit and honor of your profession of the gospel,[99] that such a breach should be under your hand? That it should be (as it were) by your means? Will it not be a sword, and an arrow, and a maul[100] in the hands of your observers? Who can bear the just scandal that would accrue? Scandal to the magistrates, scandal to the ministers of this generation, in neglecting such an opportunity of advancing the gospel, sleeping all the day while others sow tares?[101]

92 I.e., persistent and pressing in making requests.

93 Matt. 13:24–30.

94 In the original, the word "Ireland" is, again, set in all caps for emphasis.

95 I.e., cheap ostentation

96 For a discussion of chronic issues of debt and bankruptcy in Ireland at this time, see P. Roebuck, "Landlord Indebtedness in Ulster in the Seventeenth and Eighteenth Centuries," in *Irish Population, Economy and Society: Essays in Honour of the Late K. H. Connell*, ed. J. M. Goldstrom and L. A. Clarkson (Oxford: Oxford University Press, 1981), 135–55.

97 In the original, "Lord Jesus," "power," "might," and "things" are set in all caps for emphasis.

98 Perhaps a reference to the so-called Ranter phenomenon.

99 In the original, the two references to "gospel" in this paragraph are set in all caps for emphasis.

100 I.e., a heavy hammer or a mace.

101 Matt. 13:25.

[3] Where will be the hoped, the expected consolation of this great affair, when the testimony and pledge of the peculiar presence of Christ among us upon such an issue shall be wanting?[102]

What then shall we do? This thing is often spoken of, seldom driven to any close!

{1} Pray; "Pray the Lord of the harvest, that he would send out," that he would thrust forth, "labourers into his harvest."[103] The laborers are ready to say, "There is a lion in the way":[104] difficulties to be contended withal: and to some men it is hard seeing a call of God through difficulties:[105] when if it would but clothe itself with a few carnal advantages, how apparent is it to them? They can see it through a little cranny. Be earnest then with the Master of these laborers, in whose hand is their life and breath, and all their ways; that he would powerfully constrain them, to be willing to enter into the fields that are white for the harvest.[106]

{2} Make such provision, that those who will go may be fenced from outward straits and fears, so far as the uncertainty of human affairs in general, and the present tumultuating[107] perturbations[108] will admit. And let not I beseech you, this be the business of an unpursued order. But,

{3} Let some be appointed (generals die and sink by themselves) to consider this thing, and to hear what sober proposals may be made by any, whose hearts God shall stir up to so good a work.[109]

This I say is a work wherein God expects faithfulness from you: stagger not at his promises, nor your own duty. However by all means possible, in this business, I have striven to deliver my own soul.

Once more, to this of faith, let me stir you up to another work of love: and that in the behalf of many poor perishing creatures, that want all things needful for the sustentation of life. Poor parentless children, that lie begging, starving, rotting in the streets, and find no relief; yea, persons of quality, that have lost their dearest relations in your service, seeking for bread, and finding none. Oh that some thoughts of this also, might be seriously committed to them that shall take care for the gospel.

102 In the original, "Christ" and "issue" are set in all caps for emphasis.

103 Matt. 9:38.

104 Prov. 26:13.

105 In the original, "God" is set in all caps for emphasis.

106 John 4:35.

107 I.e., stirred up and disturbed.

108 I.e., irregular unrest and disorder.

109 In the original, "proposals" is set in all caps for emphasis. This is a reference to the proposals for the propagation of the gospel in Ireland.

Those in Power Must Believe the Promises of the Gospel

Use 3. I desire now to make more particular application of the doctrine, as to things purely spiritual: until you know how to believe for your own souls, you will scarcely know how to believe for a nation. Let this then teach us, to lay the burden and trouble of our lives upon the right shoulder. In our staggerings,[110] our doubtings, our disputes, we are apt to assign this and that reason of them; when the sole reason indeed is our unbelief. Were it not for such a cause, or such a cause, I could believe; that is, were there no need of faith. That is faith must remove the mountains that lie in the way, and then all will be plain.[111] It is not the greatness of sin, nor continuance in sin, nor backsliding into sin, that is the true cause of your staggering, whatever you pretend: the removal of all these is from that promise, whose stability and certainty, I before laid forth: but solely from your unbelief, that "root of bitterness" which springs up and troubles you.[112] It is not the distance of the earth from the sun, nor the sun's withdrawing itself, that makes a dark and gloomy day, but the interposition of clouds and vaporous exhalations. Neither is your soul beyond the reach of the promise; nor does God withdraw himself, but the vapors of your carnal, unbelieving heart, do cloud you. It is said of one place, "Christ could do no great work there": Why so? For want of power in him? Not at all: but merely for want of faith in them; it was "because of their unbelief."[113] The promise can do no great work upon your heart, to humble you, to pardon, to quiet you; is it for want of fullness and truth therein? Not at all: but merely for want of faith in you, that keeps it off. Men complain, that were it not for such things, and such things, they could believe; when it is their unbelief that casts those rubs[114] in the way. As if a man should cast nails and sharp stones in his own way, and say, verily I could run, were it not for those nails and stones; when he continues himself to cast them there. You could believe, were it not for these doubts, and difficulties, these staggering perplexities, when alas! They are all from your unbelief.

Warnings about the Consequences of Staggering in Unbelief

Use 4. See the sinfulness of all those staggering doubts and perplexities, wherewith many poor souls have almost all their thoughts taken up: such as is the root, such is the fruit. If the tree be evil, so will the fruit be also. Men

110 In the original, "staggerings" is set in all caps for emphasis.

111 Isa. 40:4; Matt. 17:20–21.

112 Heb. 12:15.

113 Mark 6:5–6.

114 I.e., obstacles and impediments.

do not gather grapes from brambles.[115] What is the root that bears this fruit of staggering? Is it not the evil root of unbelief? And can any good come from thence? Are not all the streams of the same nature with the fountain? If that be bitter, can they be sweet? If the body be full of poison, will not the branches have their venom also? Surely if the mother (unbelief) be the mouth of hell, the daughters (staggerings) are not the gates of heaven.

Of the sin of unbelief, I shall not now speak at large: it is in sum, the universal opposition of the soul unto God: all other sins arise against something or other of his revealed will: only unbelief sets up itself in a direct contradiction, to all of him that is known. Hence the weight of condemnation in the gospel, is constantly laid on this sin: "He that believeth not, on him the wrath of God abideth; he shall be damned."[116] Now as every drop of seawater retains the brackishness[117] and saltness of the whole, so every staggering doubt that is an issue of this unbelief, has in it the unsavoriness and distastefulness unto God, that is in the whole.

Further, to give you a little light into what acceptance our staggering thoughts find with the Lord, according to which must be our esteem of all that is in us.

Observe, that—

(1) They grieve him.
(2) They provoke him.
(3) They dishonor him.

(1) Such a frame grieves the Lord. Nothing more presses true love, than to have an appearance of suspicion. Christ comes to Peter and asks him, "Simon, son of Jonas, lovest thou me?" (John 21:15). Peter seems glad of an opportunity to confess him, and his love to him, whom not long since he had denied; and answers readily, "Yea, Lord, thou knowest that I love thee."[118] But when Christ comes with the same question again and again, the Holy Ghost tells us, "Peter was grieved because he said unto him the 3rd time, 'Lovest thou me?' "[119] It exceedingly troubled Peter, that his love should come under so many questionings, which he knew to be sincere. The love of Christ to his, is infinitely beyond the love of his, to him. All our doubtings are nothing

115 Luke 6:44.
116 John 3:36.
117 I.e., salty or unpleasant taste.
118 John 21:16.
119 John 21:17.

but so many questionings of his love. We cry, "Lord Jesus, lovest you us?" And again, "Lord Jesus, lovest you us?" And that with distrustful hearts and thoughts, that it is not, it cannot be. Speaking of the unbelieving Jews, the Holy Ghost tells us, Jesus was "grieved for the hardness of their hearts" (Mark 3:5). And as it is bitter to him in the root, so also in the fruit. Our staggerings and debates when we have a word of promise; is a grief to his Holy Spirit, as the unkindest return we can make unto his love.

(2) It provokes him. "How can this be," (says Zacharias) "that I should have a son?" "This shall be," (says the Lord) "and you yourself for your questioning shalt be a sign of it, thou shalt be dumb and not speak" (Luke 1).[120] His doubting was a provocation: and our Savior expresses no less in that bitter reproof to his disciples upon their wavering, "O faithless and perverse generation, how long shall I be with you? how long shall I suffer you?" (Matt. 17:17). That is, in this unbelieving frame. Poor souls are apt to admire the patience of God in other matters; that he spared them in such and such sins, at such and such times of danger, but his exceeding patience toward them in their carnal reasonings, and fleshly objections against believing; this they admire not. Nay, generally they think it should be so: God would not have them one step further. Nay, they could be more steadfast in believing as they suppose, might it stand with the good will of God: when all this while, this frame of all others, is the greatest provocation to the Lord; he never exercises more forbearance, than about this kind of unbelief.

When the spies had gone into Canaan, had seen the land, and brought of the good fruit of it, then to repine, then to question whether God would bring them into it or no:[121] this caused the Lord "to swear in his wrath, that they should not enter into his rest."[122] When God has brought men to the borders of heaven, discovered to them the riches and excellency of his grace, admitted them to enter as spies into the kingdom of glory, then to fall a staggering, whether he intends them an entrance or no; is that which lies heavy on him. The like may be said of all promised mercies, and deliverances whatsoever.

That this is a provocation, the Lord has abundantly testified, inasmuch as for it he has oftentimes snatched sweet morsels from the mouths of men, and turned aside the stream of mercies, when it was ready to flow in upon them. "If," (says he) "ye will not believe, surely ye shall not he established" (Isa. 7:9). The very mercy but now promised, concerning your deliverance, shall be withheld. Oh stop not success from Ireland, by unbelief.

120 Luke 1:18–20.

121 Num. 13–14.

122 Ps. 95:11.

(3) It dishonors God. In the close of this verse, it is said, Abraham was "strong in faith" (or staggered not), "giving glory to God." To be established in believing, is to give God the greatest glory possible. Every staggering thought that arises from this root of unbelief, robs God of his glory.

[1] It robs him of the glory of his truth: "He that believeth not, hath made him a liar, because he believeth not his record" (1 John 5:10). Let men pretend what they please (as most an end,[123] we give in specious pretenses for our unbelief), the bottom of all is, the questioning of the truth of God in our false hearts.

[2] It robs him of the glory of his fidelity or faithfulness in the discharge of his promises: "If we confess our sins, he is faithful to forgive us our sins" (1 John 1:9). He has engaged his faithfulness in this business of the forgiveness of iniquities: he whose right it is, calling that in question, calls the faithfulness of God in question.

[3] It robs him of the glory of his grace: in a word, if a man should choose to set himself in a universal opposition unto God, he can think of no more compendious[124] way than this. This then is the fruit, this the advantage of all our staggering, we rob God of glory, and our own souls of mercy.

Those in Power Must Repent of All Staggering in Unbelief

Use 5. Be ashamed of, and humbled for, all your staggerings at the promises of God, with all your fleshly reasonings, and carnal contrivances issuing therefrom. For the most part, we live upon successes, not promises: unless we see and feel the print of victories, we will not believe. The engagement of God, is almost quite forgotten in our affairs. We travel on without Christ, like his mother, and suppose him only to be in the crowd: but we must return to seek him where we left him, or our journeying on, will be to no purpose.[125] When Job, after all his complaining, had seen "the end of the Lord,"[126] he cries out, "Now I abhor myself in dust and ashes."[127] You have seen "the end of the Lord" in many of his promises: oh that it might prevail to make you abhor yourselves in dust and ashes, for all your carnal fears and corrupt reasonings, upon your staggerings.

When David enjoyed his promised mercy, he especially shames himself, for every thought of unbelief, that he had while he waited for it: "I said," (says he) "in my haste, that all men were liars."[128] And now he is humbled for

123 I.e., as almost always.
124 I.e., direct and concise.
125 Luke 2:44–46.
126 James 5:11.
127 Job 42:6.
128 Ps. 116:11.

it. Is this to be thankful, to forget our provoking thoughts of unbelief, when the mercy is enjoyed? The Lord set it home upon your spirits, and give it to receive its due manifestation.

(1) If there be any counsels, designs, contrivances, on foot among us, that are bottomed on our staggering at the promise under which we are, oh let them be instantly cast down to the ground. Let not any be so foolish, as to suppose that unbelief will be a foundation for quiet habitations. You are careful to avoid all ways that might dishonor you, as the rulers of so great a nation: oh be much more careful about such things as will dishonor you as believers: that's your greatest title, that's your chiefest privilege. Search your own thoughts, and if any contrivance, any compliance be found springing up, whose seed was sown by staggering at the promise; root them up, and cast them out, before it be too late.

(2) Engage your hearts against all such ways for the future: say unto God, "How faithful are you in all your ways! How able to perform all your promises! How have you established your word in heaven and earth! Who would not put their trust in you? We desire to be ashamed, that ever we should admit in our hearts, the least staggering at the stability of your word."

(3) Act as men bottomed upon unshaken things: that are not at all moved by the greatest appearing oppositions: "He that believeth will not make haste":[129] be not hasty in your resolves, in any distress. Wait for the accomplishment of the vision, for it will come.[130] So long as you are in the way of God, and do the work of God, let not so much as your desires be too hasty, after appearing strengthenings, and assistance. Whence is it that there is among us, such bleating after the compliance of this or that party of the sons of men, perhaps priding themselves in our actings upon unbelief;[131] as though we proclaimed, that without such and such, we cannot be protected in the things of God? Let us (I beseech you) live above those things, that are unworthy of the great name, that is called upon us.

Oh that by these, and the like ways, we might manifest our self-condemnation, and abhorrency, for all that distrust and staggering at the word of God, which arising from unbelief, has had such deplorable issues upon all our counsels and undertakings.

FINIS.[132]

129 Isa. 28:16.
130 Hab. 2:3.
131 1 Sam. 15:14.
132 Lat. "The End."

THE BRANCH OF THE LORD, THE BEAUTY OF SION: OR, THE GLORY OF THE CHURCH, IN ITS RELATION UNTO CHRIST

Opened in Two Sermons; One Preached at Berwick, the Other at Edinburgh

---

By John Owen, minister of the gospel

Walk about Sion, and go round about her: tell the towers thereof.

Mark ye well her bulwarks, consider her palaces, that you may tell it to the generation following.

For this is our God for ever and ever: he will be our guide unto death.

PSALM 48:12–14

Edinburgh,
Printed by Evan Tyler, in the year 1650

[Dedication]

TO HIS EXCELLENCY the Lord General Cromwell etc.[1]

My lord,

It was with thoughts of peace, that I embraced my call, to this place, and time of war. As all peace that is from God is precious to my spirit, so incomparably, that between the Father and his elect, which is established, and carried on in the blood and grace of Jesus Christ. The ministerial dispensation of this peace, being through free grace committed even unto me also, I desire that in every place, my whole may be, to declare it to the men of God's good pleasure. That this was my chief design, in answer to the call of God upon me, even to pour out a savor of the gospel upon the sons of peace in this place, I hope is manifest to the consciences of all with whom (since my coming hither) in the work of the ministry I have had to do. The enmity between God and us, began on our part: the peace which he has made, begins and ends with himself. This is the way of God with sinners, when he might justly continue their enemy, and fight against them to their eternal ruin, he draws forth love, and beseeches them to be reconciled, who have done the wrong, and them to accept of peace, who cannot abide the battle. Certainly, the bearing forth of this message, which is so "worthy of all acceptation,"[2] and ought to be so welcome, cannot but have sweetness enough to season all the pressures and temptations wherewith it is sometimes attended. This it has been my desire

1 Oliver Cromwell became Lord General of all Parliament's forces on June 26, 1650. See *Journals of the House of Commons*, 13 vols. (London: HMSO, 1802–1803), 6:432; *Acts and Ordinances of the Interregnum*, eds. C. H. Firth and R. S. Rait, 3 vols. (London: HMSO, 1911), 2:393.

2 1 Tim. 1:15.

to pursue, and that, with the weapons which are not carnal.[3] And though some may be so seasoned with the leaven of contention about carnal things, or at best the tithing of mint and cumin, as to disrelish the weightier things of the gospel,[4] yet the great owner of the vineyard, has not left me without a comfortable assurance, that even this labor in the Lord has not been in vain.[5] The following sermons, which I desire to present unto your excellency, were preached one at Berwick upon your first advance into Scotland; the other at Edinburgh. My willingness to serve the inheritance of Christ here, even in my absence, caused me to close with the desires, that were held out to this purpose. And I do present them to your excellency, not only because the rise of my call to this service, under God was from you; but also, because in the carrying of it on, I have received from you in the weaknesses and temptations wherewith I am encompassed, that daily spiritual refreshment and support, by inquiry into, and discovery of the deep and hidden dispensations of God toward his secret ones, which my spirit is taught to value. The carrying on of the interest of the Lord Jesus among his saints, in all his ways, which are truth and righteousness, the matter pointed at in this discourse, being the aim of your spirit in your great undertakings, it bears another respect unto you. I am not unacquainted with its meanness yea its coming short in respect of use and fruit, of what the Lord has since, and by others drawn forth; but such as it is, having by providence stepped first into the world, I wholly commend it to him for an incense, who graciously "supplied the seed to the sower":[6] beseeching him that we may have joy unspeakable and glorious[7] in the acceptance of that peace, which he gives us in the Son of his love, while the peace whose desire in the midst of war, you continually bear forth to him, and to others, is by them rejected to their hurt.

Your excellency's most humble servant in our dearest Lord,

John Owen

Edinburgh, November 26, 1650.[8]

3 2 Cor. 10:4.
4 Matt. 23:23.
5 1 Cor. 15:58.
6 2 Cor. 9:10.
7 1 Pet. 1:8.
8 In the text: Edinb. Nov.—Owen.

[Sermon]

For mine house shall be called an house of prayer for all people.[1]

ISAIAH 56:7

INTRODUCTION AND CONTEXTUALIZATION

From the third verse of this chapter to the eighth,[2] you have promises and predictions of calling in Gentiles and strangers to the church of God, notwithstanding any objections, or hindrances laid in their way, by ceremonial and typical constitutions, they being all to be removed in the cross of Christ (Eph. 2:13–16; Col. 2:14), making way for the accomplishment of that signal promise which is given in the second chapter of this prophecy, [verses] 2–3. "And it shall come to pass in the last days, that the mountain of the house of the Lord shall be established in the top of the mountains, and shall be exalted above the hills, and all nations shall flow unto it: and many people shall go,[3] and say, Come ye, and let us go up," etc.[4]

The words of seventh verse, are a recapitulation of the whole, holding out summarily the calling of the Gentiles to the holy mount, or spiritual church of Christ: where also you have a description of the services performed by them upon their coming: "Their burnt offerings and sacrifices shall be accepted

1 Rutherford had contested the interpretation of this chapter by the Congregationalists in *Due Right of Presbyteries* (London, 1644), 113. Samuel Parker contended that Owen sought to guarantee "Success to *Cromwel's* Army against their *Soveraign*, by dark passages out of the old Prophets." See his *A Defence and Continuation of the Ecclesiastical Politie* (London, 1671), 114.

2 Isa. 56:3–8.

3 In the original, "all nations" and "many people" have been set in all caps for emphasis.

4 Isa. 2:2–3.

upon mine altar":[5] answerable to that eminent prediction of the solemn worship of the called Gentiles, Malachi 1:11:

> For, from the rising of the sun, even unto the going down of the same, my name shall be great among the Gentiles, and in every place incense shall be offered unto my name, and a pure offering: for my name shall be great among the heathen, saith the Lord of hosts.[6]

The spiritual services of the saints of the Gentiles, are in each place set forth by those ceremonial ordinances, of incense, altar and sacrifice, as were then most acceptable, from the Lord's own appointment.

Now this whole promise is once again strengthened, without loss of life or beauty, and comprised in the words of the text.

That which before he termed "sacrifice and burnt-offerings," here he calls "prayer": and those who before were, "the sons of the stranger,"[7] are here "all people": some, many of all sorts, the whole world, all men, without distinction, the partition wall being broken down.[8]

The thing here spoken of is God's house, described—

1. By its appropriation unto him, it is his peculiar, "My house."
2. By its extent of receipt in respect of others; it is "for all people."
3. By the employment of its inhabitants, that is, prayer, it "shall be called an house of prayer."

"House," here may be taken two ways.

1. Properly, as it was in the type for the material temple at Jerusalem: whereunto these words are applied by our Savior, Matthew 21,[9] but that is no farther concerned herein, but as the spiritual holiness of the antitype,[10] could not be represented without a ceremonial holiness of the type.

5 Isa. 56:7.

6 Mal. 1:11. Holmes describes how the "watchword" of the English forces at Dunbar had been "the Lord of Hosts." See Clive Holmes, *Why Was Charles I Executed?* (London: Hambledon Continuum, 2007), 130. The commemorative medals struck in celebration of the victory at Dunbar had the caption, "The Lord of Hosts." See *Mercurius Politicus* 14 (September 5–12, 1650), 223; Laura Lunger Knoppers, *Constructing Cromwell: Ceremony, Portrait, and Print, 1645–1661* (Cambridge: Cambridge University Press, 2000), 57. Another contemporary account in London spoke of the victory as the doing of "the Lord of Hosts," therefore regarding it as "marvellous in our eyes." See *A True Relation of the Routing the Scotish Army Near Dunbar* (London, 1650), 5.

7 Isa. 56:6.

8 Eph. 2:14.

9 Matt. 21:13.

10 I.e., that which is represented by the type.

2. Spiritually, for the church of Christ to be gathered to him out of all nations: the house wherein *juge sacrificium*,[11] a continual spiritual sacrifice, is to be offered to him: this is peculiarly intended: so then observe:

1. Christ's church of saints, of believers, is God's house.
2. The church of Christ under the gospel is to be gathered out of all nations.
3. There are established ordinances and appointed worship for the church of Christ under the gospel.

It is the first that I shall speak unto.

OBSERVATION: CHRIST'S CHURCH OF SAINTS IS GOD'S HOUSE

Christ's church of saints, of believers, is God's house.

That his church, is of saints, and believers, will appear in the issue.

By the church of Christ, I understand, primarily the whole multitude of them, who antecedently, are chosen of his Father, and given unto him: consequently, are redeemed, called, and justified in his blood: the church which he loved, "and gave himself for it," "that he might sanctify and cleanse it with the washing of water by the word. That he might present it unto himself a glorious church, not having spot or wrinkle, or any such thing, but that it should be holy, and without blemish" (Eph. 5:25–26).[12] And secondarily also, every holy assembly of Mount Zion, whereunto, the Lord Christ is made beauty and glory: every particular church of his saints, inasmuch as they partake of the nature of the whole, being purchased by his blood, Acts 20:28.[13]

A Threefold Demonstration That the Church Is God's House

That this church belongs unto God, I shall only leave evidenced under the claim whereby he here appropriates it to himself, he calls it his, "My house"; that it is his house, I shall further demonstrate:

Three things are required to the making of a house:

11 Lat. "a perpetual sacrifice," From the Latin text of Dan. 8:11.

12 Following Goold, the full reference is Eph. 5:25–27.

13 The English Army spoke of the true spiritual church of Christ "which he hath by his own most precious Blood." See *Declaration of the English Army Now in Scotland* (London, 1650), sig. B2r.

1. A foundation.
2. Materials for a superstruction.[14]
3. An orderly framing of both into a useful building.

And all these concur to the church of Christ:

1. It has a foundation: "I have laid the foundation," says Paul (1 Cor. 3:10) and, "Other foundation can no man lay, save that which is laid, which is Jesus Christ," verse 11. That which Paul laid ministerially, God himself laid primarily and efficiently: "Thus saith the Lord God, Behold I lay in Zion for a foundation a stone, a tried stone, a precious corner-stone, a sure foundation" (Isa. 28:16). Now, this foundation is no other but the rock upon which the church is built (Matt. 16:18), which makes it impregnable to "the gates of hell," communicating strength, and permanency, continually to every part of the building.

2. A foundation only will not make a house, there must also be materials for a superstruction: those you have, "Ye are," (says he) "lively stones" (1 Pet. 2:5): all God's elect, are stones, in due time to be hewed, and fitted for this building. For—

3. Materials themselves will not serve: they must be fitly framed, and wisely disposed, or they will be a heap, not a house. This then is not wanting.

You "are built upon the foundation of the prophets, and apostles, Jesus Christ himself being the chief corner-stone, in whom all the building fitly framed together, groweth unto an holy temple in the Lord: in whom also ye are builded together, for an habitation to God by the Spirit" (Eph. 2:20–22).

There is much spiritual and heavenly architecture in these three verses. I shall only touch on some particulars.

1. The foundation of this house, this temple, is laid, and that is Jesus Christ, "Other foundation can no man lay":[15] he is here called "the chief corner-stone": and, "The foundation of the prophets and apostles,"[16] it is not which they were, but which they laid: it is *genitivus efficientis*,[17] not *materiae*:[18] that expression holds out, the persons working, not the thing wrought.

2. The materials of this building, elect, believers: said in the former verse to be "fellow-citizens with the saints, and of the household of God":[19] they

14 I.e., a structure built on a foundation.

15 1 Cor. 3:11.

16 Eph. 2:20.

17 I.e., a genitive that denotes the efficient or instrumental cause.

18 I.e., a genitive of material that denotes composition or contents.

19 Eph. 2:19.

alone are built on Christ, and thereby have union with him: not one dead rotten stone in all this building, as shall be declared.

3. The architects or builders are of two sorts.

(1) Principal, "the Spirit," we are framed "for an habitation of God by the Spirit":[20] he is the principal workman in this fabric: without him, is not one stone laid therein.

(2) Secondary and instrumental, "the prophets and apostles,"[21] and this they were two ways:

[1] Personally, in their several generations: this was their work, their labor, to lay the foundation, and carry on the building of this house.

[2] Doctrinally: so they labor in it to this very day: their doctrine in the Scripture holds out the only foundation, and the only way of building thereon.

4. The manner of the building, it is "fitly framed together," συναρμολογουμένη: closely jointed and knit in together: sweetly closed together with Christ, "the head, from which, all the body by joints and bands having nourishment ministered, and knit together, increaseth with the increase of God" (Col. 2:19).[22]

5. What kind of a house it is: it receives here a twofold title, (1) "an holy temple":[23] (2) "an habitation," or tabernacle, because of its allusion to both those holy places of the worship of God, fulfilling the types of them both.

Hence it is most evident that this church of Christ is a house, and being appropriated unto God, God's house.

To make this the more evident, I shall do these two things:

(1) Show you what are the chief properties of this house.

(2) Declare what is the relation, wherein Jesus Christ stands to this house, having called it all along the church of Christ.

Three Characteristics of God's House

(1) For the properties, or chief qualities of this house, they are three:

[1] It is a living house:

[2] It is strong:

[3] It is glorious.

20 Eph. 2:22. Rutherford contested the Congregationalists' interpretation of this text. See *Due Right of Presbyteries*, 257–58.

21 Eph. 2:20.

22 In May 1679, Owen told his congregation, "I have often thought and sometimes said that he that rightly understands these two texts of Scripture [Col. 2:19 and Eph. 4:14–16], knows his duty in church relations." See Dr. Williams' Library, London, MS L6/2, 257.

23 Eph. 2:21.

The Church Is a Living House

[1] It is a living house: "Unto whom coming as unto a living stone, ye also as lively stones are built up a spiritual house" (1 Pet. 2:4–5). Christ the foundation is a living stone, and they that are built upon him, are living stones. Hence they are said to grow together into an house: growth is a sign of life: growing from an inward principle: such as the growth of anything is, such is its life: the growth of this house is spiritual, so therefore also is its life: it lives with a spiritual life: a life whose fullness, is in its foundation, he has "life in himself" (John 5:26): and from him, in them: "I am crucified with Christ: nevertheless I live" (Gal. 2:20); yea it is himself in them; "yet not I, but Christ liveth in me." It is true those stones are dead in the rock as well as others: "by nature children of wrath as well as they" (Eph. 2:3): being "dead in trespasses and sins": verse 1.[24] He who hews them out gives them life: he quickens them when dead in trespasses and sins:[25] there is not one rotten dead stone in all this building: however some such may, by the advantage of their outward appearance, crowd in, yet they are not of the house itself.

The Church Is a Strong House

[2] It is a strong house: "The gates of hell cannot prevail against it" (Matt. 16:18), though the rain descend, and the floods come, and the winds blow upon this house, yet it will not fall, because it is founded on a rock (Matt. 7:25). We were all once a house built upon Adam: and when the wind came, and beat upon us, we fell, and the fall of that house was very great:[26] he in his best estate was found to be but sand: now we are built upon a rock that will abide all trials: the waves may make a noise, and dash themselves against him, but it will be to their own ruin.

But you will say, "May not weak and inconsistent materials be built upon a rock, which yet may have never the more strength for their foundation?" Answer 1. It is not so here, for the whole building is framed together in the foundation (Eph. 2:22), not only *on* it, but also *in* it, and so not to be prevailed against, unless the rock itself be overthrown. 2. And it is a living rock, that this house is built on: a rock continually communicating strength unto every stone in the building, that it may be enabled to abide in him: I should proceed too far, should

24 Eph. 2:1.

25 When Cromwell wrote to the Commissioners of the Kirk at the beginning of August, he told them that "it is the Spirit that quickens and giveth life." Oliver Cromwell, *Letters, Writings, and Speeches of Oliver Cromwell*, ed. John Morrill et al., 3 vols. (Oxford: Oxford University Press, 2022), 2:302–3.

26 Matt. 7:27.

I go to declare the mighty defense and fortification of this house: what has been spoken from the foundation, is enough to demonstrate it to be a strong house.

The Church Is a Glorious House

[3] It is a glorious house, and that in a threefold respect:

{1} It is glorious in respect of inward glory brought unto it of God in the face of Jesus Christ: being beautiful, through the comeliness that he puts upon it. Hence Christ speaking of it says, "How fair art thou O love for delights," (Cant. 7:6),[27] and "Thou art all fair my love, there is no spot in thee," chapter 4:7, and how I pray comes that about, why Christ washes it in his own blood, that it might be wholly "a glorious church" (Eph. 5:26–27). And further he being "The branch of the Lord and fruit of the earth" is made beauty and glory, excellency and comeliness thereunto ([Isa.] 4:2).

It has the beauty and glory of justification, which does not only take away all filthy garments, causing iniquity to pass away, but also gives fair "change of raiment" (Zech. 3:4–5), even the "garments of salvation," and the "robe of righteousness" (Isa. 61:10).[28] And then it has, the glory, and beauty of sanctification, whence "the King's daughter is all glorious within" (Ps. 45:13). The comeliness and beauty that is in a sanctified soul, is above all the glory of the world. This house is all overlaid with gold within: Christ is unto it "a head of gold" (Cant. 5:11). His house is not like Nebuchadnezzar's image, that the head should be of gold, and the members some of them of clay:[29] they all partake of his nature, and are very glorious therein.

{2} In respect of its outward structure; which it eminently has in all the peculiar assemblies thereof: "O thou afflicted and tossed with tempest and not comforted, behold I will lay thy stones with fair colours, and thy foundations with sapphires: I will make thy windows of agates and carbuncles, and all thy borders of pleasant stones" (Isa. 54:11–12). So also where it is called the new Hierusalem,[30] (a city from its laws and policy) this city is said to be of "pure gold," (not dross and mire) "the building of the wall of jasper, and the foundations of the wall garnished with all manner of precious stones" (Rev. 21:18–19). This is that which the psalmist calls, "The beauty of holiness" (Ps. 110:3). The glory of the ordinances of the gospel is their vigor and

27 This is a reference to Song of Songs 7:6.

28 The English army alluded to this verse as it spoke of how the Lord was about to put "beautiful garments" on the saints, making them a praise in the earth and binding them up as "his Jewels." *Declaration of the English Army Now in Scotland*, sig. B4v.

29 Dan. 2:32–33.

30 I.e., Jerusalem.

purity:[31] there is nothing so glorious as our King on his throne: Christ in his court; this house, reigning in the administration of his ordinances: then "all his garments smell of myrrh, aloes, and cassia, out of the ivory palaces whereby they have made him glad. Kings' daughters are among his honorable women, upon his right hand doth stand the queen in gold of Ophir" (Ps. 45:8–9). His goings are seen, the goings of our God and King in the sanctuary (Ps. 68:24–25), etc. The apostle exalts the glory of gospel administrations exceedingly above the old tabernacle and temple worship, which yet was exceeding pompous and glorious. "If," (says he) "the ministration of death, written and engraven in stones was glorious, so that the children of Israel could not steadfastly behold the face of Moses, for the glory of his countenance, which glory was to be done away, how shall not the ministration of the Spirit be rather glorious: for if the ministration of condemnation be glory, much more doth the ministration of righteousness exceed in glory: for even that which was made glorious, had no glory in this respect, by reason of the glory that excelleth, for if that which was done away was glorious, much more that which remaineth is glorious" (2 Cor. 3:7–11). Let men think as meanly as they please of the spiritual service of God among his people: all glory that ever yet appeared in the world, was but a bubble to it: all that God ever instituted before, came exceeding short of it: he delights in it, who beholds the proud afar off.[32]

{3} It is glorious in respect of the exaltation it has above, and the triumph over all its opposers: to see a house, a palace hung round about with ensigns, spoils, and banners taken from the enemies that have come against it, is a glorious thing: thus is this house of God decked: "Kings of armies did flee apace, and she that tarried at home, divided the spoil" (Ps. 68:12).[33] "She that tarries at home," the mother of the family, the church of God, she "hath all the spoils."[34] The Lord has affirmed, that not only every one that opposes, but all that do not serve this house, shall be utterly destroyed (Isa. 60:12).[35] There you have the spoil of Pharaoh, and all his host, gathered on the shore of the Red Sea, and dedicated in this house (Ex. 15). There you have the robes of

31 The English Army stated that one of the purposes of the invasion of Scotland had been "the Establishment of his Ordinances amongst them, in purity according to his Word." See *Declaration of the Army Now in Scotland*, sig. B2r.

32 Ps. 138:6.

33 Cromwell began the battle of Dunbar with the words of the first verse of this psalm: "Let God arise and his enemies be scattered." See Ian Gentles, *The New Model Army: Agent of Revolution* (New Haven, CT: Yale University Press, 2022), 212.

34 Ps. 68:12.

35 Owen made a similar point from this text in *Ebenezer* (1648), *Of Toleration* (1649), and *The Shaking and Translating of Heaven and Earth* (1649). See *Complete Works of John Owen*, vol. 18.

Nebuchadnezzar here referred when himself was turned into a beast (Dan. [4]). There you have the imperial ornaments of Diocletian, and his companion casting aside their dominion for very madness that they could not prevail against this house:[36] there is the blood of Julian kept for a monument of vengeance against apostates:[37] there you have the rochets[38] of the prelates of this land, hung up of late, with other garments of their adherents rolled in blood: there is a place reserved for the remaining spoils of the great whore, when she shall be burned and made naked, and desolate (Rev. 11).[39] Never any rose, or shall arise against this house, and go forth unto final prosperity: let the men of the world take heed how they burden themselves with the foundation stone of this house, it will assuredly break them all in pieces.

Thus have I given you a glimpse of this house, with the chief properties of it, which as God assumes as his own, so also peculiarly it belongs unto the Lord Christ; yea what relation it stands in unto him, or rather he unto it, is the main thing I intend.

The Church's Relation to Jesus Christ

(2) Jesus Christ stands in a twofold relation unto this house,

[1] In respect of its fabric and building.
[2] In respect of its state and condition.

[1] In the first regard Christ relates to this house in a fourfold respect. As—

{1} Its foundation.
{2} Its ark.

36 The emperors Diocletian (ca. 244–311) and Maximian (ca. 250–310). Owen made the same point in *Ebenezer* (1648), and in *A Sermon Preached* [. . .] *January 31* (1649) he referred to Diocletian as one "smitten with madness." See *Complete Works of John Owen*, 18:270, 382.

37 Flavius Claudius Julianus (ca. 331–363), better known as Julian "the Apostate." His rejection of Christianity and attempts to restore traditional Roman values were taken as implied support for paganism. His dying words, according to Theodoret, were "*Vicisti Galilaee*" (Thou hast won, O Galilean). See Theodoret, *Ecclesiastical History* 3.20. For the English text, see *The Ecclesiastical History of Theodoret*, in *Nicene and Post-Nicene Fathers, Second Series*, ed. Philip Schaff and Henry Wace, 14 vols. (1890–1900; repr., Peabody: Hendrickson, 2004), 3:106. Sozomen recorded how, having been fatally wounded, Julian flung a handful of his own blood in the air toward heaven as if to accuse Christ of his death. See Sozomen, *Ecclesiastical History* 6.3 For the English text, see *The Ecclesiastical History of Sozomen*, in *Nicene and Post-Nicene Fathers, Second Series*, 2:347. Owen also referred to the death of the tyrant Julian in *A Sermon Preached* [. . .] *January 31* (1649).

38 I.e., white ecclesiastical vestments, similar to a surplice but with gathered sleeves, worn and favored by the Laudian bishops.

39 Rev. 17:16. The reference in the text to Rev. 11 may be a typographical error.

{3} Its altar.
{4} Its candlestick.

[2] In respect of its state and condition, Christ relates unto this house of God in a fivefold regard. [As—]

{1} The owner thereof
{2} The builder thereof
{3} The inhabiter thereof
{4} The watchman or keeper thereof[40]
{5} The avenger thereof

I shall pass through these (God assisting) in order: and begin with what was first laid down, his relation to this house in respect of its fabric and building as—

Christ Is the Foundation, Ark, Altar, and Candlestick of This House

Christ Is the Hidden Foundation, Supporting the Whole Weight of the Building

{1} The foundation of it: this was in part declared before: he is the stone which the builders rejected, but made of the Lord the head of the corner (Ps. 118:22). He is the lowest in the bottom to bear up the weight of the building, and the highest in the corner to couple the whole together: "Other foundation can no man lay but that which is laid, which is Jesus Christ" (1 Cor. 3:11). He is the rock, on which he builds his church (Matt. 16:18).

Now there are three things required to a foundation, all which are eminently seen in the Lord Christ, in reference to this house.

1st. That it be first laid in the building: it were a course exceeding preposterous, first to build a house, and then to lay the foundation. Jesus Christ is the first that is laid in this holy fabric, and that in a fourfold respect.

(1st)[41] He is the first, in respect of God's eternal purpose: the Lord purposed that "he should have the pre-eminence" in this as well as in all other things (Col. 1:15).[42] He is in that respect "the first-born among many brethren" (Rom. 8:29), the residue of this house, being predestinated to be made

40 In the treatment that follows, Owen reverses the order of his treatment of Christ as inhabiter and watchman.

41 As is explained in the *Works* preface, the numbering order is 1, (1), [1], {1}, and 1st. In this volume, the numbering goes deeper, with the next number being (1st).

42 Following Goold, the reference should be corrected to Col. 1:18.

conformable unto him. "He is before all things, by him all things," (that is all spiritual things, all the things of this house) "consist":[43] "He is the head of the body, the church":[44] this I mean, God purposed that Christ should be the bottom and foundation of this whole building, that it should be all laid on him: I do not mean that God first intended Christ for a foundation, and then his elect for building. The order of intention and execution is as to first, and last, inverted by all agents: but this I say, God purposing to build his elect into a holy temple, purposed that Jesus Christ should be the foundation.

(2nd) In respect of outward manifestation: God first manifests and declares him, before he laid one stone in this building. "The seed," (says he) "of the woman shall bruise the serpent's head" (Gen. 3:15): in that was laid the first stone of this building: then was the "Lamb slain," ἀπὸ καταβολῆς κόσμου, presently "after the foundation of the world" (Rev. 13:8), and thence, is grace in him said to be given to the elect, πρὸ χρόνων αἰωνίων, "many ages ago" (Titus 1:2).

(3rd) Because in order of nature, Christ must be first laid in the heart of every individual stone, before they are laid up in this building. If Christ be not in men, they are ἀδόκιμοι[45] (2 Cor. 15:1),[46] altogether useless for this building; try them never so often, they must at last be rejected, and laid aside.

(4th) In respect of every particular assembly, and little sanctuary of Mount Zion: if he be not first laid in the midst of such assemblies, they will prove to be pinnacles of Babel,[47] not towers of Zion:[48] this therefore was the way of the saints of old, first to give up themselves to the Lord Christ, and then to one another, by the will of God (2 Cor. 8:5).

In these respects Christ the foundation, is first laid in this spiritual building: which is the first property of a foundation.

2nd. A foundation must be hidden, and out of sight unto all those that outwardly look upon the house: they cannot perceive it, though every part of the house does rest upon it: and this has occasioned many mistakes in the world. An unwise man coming to a great house, seeing the antics[49] and pictures[50] stand crouching under the windows and sides of the house, may

43 Col. 1:17.

44 Col. 1:18.

45 Gk. "reprobates or worthless."

46 Following Goold, the reference should be corrected to 2 Cor. 13:7.

47 Gen. 11:4.

48 Ps. 48:12.

49 I.e., an ornamental architectural representation of creatures or vegetation; e.g., a gargoyle.

50 I.e., sculptured architectural representations.

happily[51] think that they bear up the weight of the house, when indeed they are for the most part pargeted[52] posts; they bear not the house, the house bears them. By their bowing and outward appearance, the man thinks the burden is on them, and supposes, that it would be an easy thing, at any time, by taking them away, to demolish the house itself; but, when he sets himself to work, he finds these things of no value, there is a foundation in the bottom, which bears up the whole, that he thought not of: against that he may waste himself, until he be broken in pieces.

Men looking upon the church, do find that it is a fair fabric indeed, but cannot imagine how it should stand. A few supporters it seems to have in the world, like crouching antics under the windows, that make some show of underpropping it: here you have a magistrate, there an army, or so: think the men of the world, "Can we but remove these props, the whole would quickly topple to the ground": yea, so foolish have I been myself; and so void of understanding before the Lord, as to take a view of some goodly appearing props of this building, and to think, how shall the house be preserved if these should be removed: they looked unto me like the mariners in Paul's ship without whose abode therein they could not be saved:[53] when lo, suddenly some have been manifested to be pargeted posts, and the very best, to be held up by the house, and not to hold it up.

On this account, the men of the world, think it no great matter to demolish the spiritual church of Christ to the ground: they encourage one another to the work, never thinking of the foundation that lies hidden, against which they dash themselves all to pieces. I say then, Christ as the foundation of this house, is hidden to the men of the world, they see it not, they believe it not: there is nothing more remote from their apprehension, than that Christ should be at the bottom of them and their ways, whom they so much despise.

3rd. The foundation is that which bears up the whole weight of the building. What part of the house soever, is not directly poised upon it, has no strength at all: take a goodly stone, hew it, square it, make it every way fit for your fabric,[54] so that it may seem to be the best of all your materials; yet if you do not lay it upon the foundation, answerable to that, which may give

51 I.e., possibly, or by chance.

52 Pargeted posts were frequently covered in lime plaster or mortar. One of the English counties with which decorative pargework was particularly associated was Essex, where Owen ministered. See George Bankart, *The Art of the Plasterer* (London: Routledge, 2002), 77. Owen used the same illustration in *A Sermon Preached* [. . .] *January 31* (1649). See *Complete Works of John Owen*, 18:338.

53 Acts 27:31.

54 I.e., building.

it a solid basis, and bear up the weight and poise thereof, it will be useless, cumbersome, and quickly fall to the ground.

Let a man be hewed and squared by the word and ordinances into outward conformity, never so exactly, that he seems one of the most beautiful saints in the world, yet if he be not laid rightly by faith upon the foundation, to derive from thence strength, supportment, and vigor, he will quickly fall to the ground: what then will become of their building, who heap up all sorts of rubbish to make a house for the Lord.

Christ Is the Ark and Mercy Seat of This House

{2} Christ is the ark of this house: the ark in the tabernacle, and afterward in the temple, was the most holy thing, in the Most Holy Place. There was nothing in it but the two tables of stone written with the finger of God: before it was Aaron's rod that budded, with a pot full of manna:[55] over it was the propitiatory or mercy seat, being a plate of gold as long and as broad as the ark, covering it, being shadowed with the cherubims of glory.[56] Now all this glorious fabric, did signify, that unless the law with its condemning power were hid in the ark, and covered with the mercy seat, no person could stand before the Lord: besides, the law was the old covenant of works, and being renewed unto them chiefly to be subservient to the gospel, and partly, with its appurtenances[57] and carnal administration, to be the tenure of the Israelites' holding the land of Canaan, and this being in the ark, it was said to contain the covenant, and is frequently called the ark of the covenant.

Jesus Christ is the ark of this spiritual house. When the temple was opened in heaven, there was seen in the temple the ark of God's testament (Rev. 11:19), Jesus Christ made conspicuous to all, who lay much hid under the Old Testament (Rom. 3:25). God is said to set forth Christ to be ἱλαστήριον, "a propitiation," or mercy seat; for by that very term is the mercy seat expressed (Heb. 9:5). He is then the ark, and the mercy seat covering it. He, then, does these two things:

1st. In behalf of this house, and every stone thereof, he hides the law with its condemning power, that nothing from thence shall be laid to their charge. If a man have a suit to be tried in any court, and a powerful friend engage himself, that the only evidence which is against him, shall not be produced, will it not give him encouragement to proceed? In that great and tremendous trial, which is to be above, there is but one principal evidence against us, which gives life to all others, which if it be removed all the rest must fail. This is the

55 Heb. 9:4.

56 Heb. 9:5.

57 I.e., appendages.

law: Christ as the ark and mercy seat, hides this law: it shall not (I speak in respect to this house) be produced at the day of trial: will not this be a great encouragement to them to appear at the throne of God? Christ hides the law as being "the end" of it (Rom. 10:4), "that the righteousness thereof might be fulfilled in us" (Rom. 8:4). He has so far answered all that the law required, that none from thence can "lay anything to the charge of God's elect" (Rom. 8:33–34). Let not poor sinners fear; it will not be with them as with Uzzah: he touched the ark, and died;[58] touch this ark, and live forever.

And 2nd. He is the ark of this house, as containing in himself the new covenant; it is made with him, originally: established in him, irreversibly; made out through him in all the grace of it, faithfully.

Christ Is the Altar of This House through His Atonement and Intercession

{3} He is the altar of this house: there were two altars in the old tabernacle, and temple: an altar for sacrifice, and an altar for incense, Exodus chapter 29 and 30. The first was the great brazen altar, that stood without the holy place, whereon the burnt offerings, and all sacrifices of blood, for remission were offered. The other less made of shittimwood, all overlaid with pure gold, and a crown of beaten gold upon it,[59] on which they were to burn pure incense unto the Lord always: and they were both most holy, sanctifying the gifts with legal sanctification, that were offered on them (Matt. 23:19). Now both these does our Savior supply in this house: (1) He is the great altar of sacrifice, the altar of offerings for expiation and atonement: "We have an altar, whereof they have no right to eat, who serve the tabernacle," (Heb. 13:10). That is even he who sanctified the people with his own blood, and suffered without the gate, verse 11. The goodwill and soul of Christ "offering up himself, through the eternal Spirit,"[60] a pure oblation and sacrifice, "by one offering to perfect for ever them that are sanctified,"[61] is all our altar. (2) He is also the golden altar of incense. Incense is prayer, "Let my prayer come before thee as incense" (Ps. 141:2). Jesus Christ is the golden altar, whereon that incense is offered (Rev. 8:3, 4), even that altar which is always before God (Rev. 9:13), as by being the former, he makes our persons accepted; so by the latter he makes our duties accepted: and all the living stones of this house, are priests to offer sacrifice on these altars:[62] by him as priests, they have approximation to the

58 2 Sam. 6:7.

59 Ex. 30:3–4.

60 Heb. 9:14.

61 Heb. 10:14.

62 1 Pet. 2:5.

holy place: there they have a share and participation in all the sacrifices that are offered upon, or by him.

Christ Is the Candlestick, Bringing Light That Shines Out to the World

{4} He is the candlestick of this house. The making, fashioning, and use of the candlestick, in the holy place of the tabernacle, you have, Exodus 25:31, etc. It was one of the most glorious utensils of that frame: made of pure and beaten gold, with much variety of works, knops,[63] flowers and lamps. The use of it was to bear out light, for all the worship of God in that Most Holy Place. The tabernacle was made close, without any window: it was not to receive light from without: it had all its own light from within. It is true, this candlestick, with its seven lamps, did secondarily represent the churches of Christ, which hold out his light among themselves, and unto others, "The seven candlesticks thou sawest are the seven churches" (Rev. 1 last):[64] therefore Solomon made "ten candlesticks of pure gold" (1 Kings 7:49), to set out yet further the increase and multiplying of the churches of God. Upon this account also, the two witnesses are said to be "two candlesticks" (Rev. 11:4), and "the two anointed ones that stand before the God of the whole earth" (Zech. 4:3).[65] Whence that in the Revelation is taken, there is mention indeed of two anointed ones, but of one candlestick: the Holy Ghost plainly intimating, that though the churches and witnesses of Christ are also candlesticks in a second sense, yet there is one eminent candlestick which has light originally in itself, which also it communicates unto all others. And this is that which is mentioned in Zechariah 4, which has the "two olive-trees,"[66] or the two anointed churches of Jews and Gentiles, standing by it, receiving light from it, to communicate to others: they empty the golden oil out of themselves, which they receive from the candlestick. For this candlestick has "seven lamps," verse 2,[67] which lamps that burn before the throne, are the "seven Spirits of God" (Rev. 4:5), seven Spirits that is, the perfection and completeness of the Spirit of God, in all his graces and operations. Now who has these seven Spirits? Even he who received not the Spirit "by measure" (John 3:34), being the "stone" upon which are the "seven eyes" (Zech. 3:9). He alone then is this candlestick, and all the light which this house has, it is from him.

63 I.e., small rounded protuberances on candlesticks.

64 Rev. 1:20

65 The correct reference is Zech. 4:14.

66 Zech. 4:3.

67 Zech. 4:2.

There are two ways whereby Jesus Christ makes out light to this house.

1st. By way of doctrinal revelation:
2nd. Of real communication.

1st. He alone discovers light to all the stones of this building: "No man hath seen God at any time: the only begotten Son which is in the bosom of the Father, he hath declared him" (John 1:18). No saving discovery of God, of his nature, his will, his love, but what is by Christ. The moon and stars give light, but it is only what they receive from the sun. The prophets and apostles held out light, but it was all received from him. They spoke by "the Spirit of Christ that was in them."[68] "I have received of the Lord that which I have delivered unto you" (1 Cor. 11:23). The same apostle curses everyone that shall bring in any other light into this house, be they angels or men (Gal. 1:8-9). Christ alone fully knows the mind of God, as being always "in the bosom of his Father" (John 1:18). Yea he knows it to the uttermost, being one with his Father (John 10:30). And he is willing to reveal it, for even "for this end came he into the world, that he might bear witness to the truth."[69] And he had ability enough to do it, for "in him were hid all the treasures of wisdom and knowledge" (Col. 2:3). He alone is the author of all light to this his holy habitation.

Many attempts have been to set up light in this house, and not from Christ. Some would kindle their traditions for the doctrine of this house:[70] some their prudentials for the government of it:[71] some their ceremonials for the

68 1 Pet. 1:11.

69 John 18:37.

70 The Roman Catholic view was that tradition, written and unwritten, was a source of authority on doctrine.

71 In the debates about the nature of church government, some believed that it was sufficient to invoke prudence as the basis for certain aspects of polity. For example, the Westminster Assembly described the office of the ruling elder as something "prudential" rather than something with clear and direct scriptural warrant (much to the horror of divine right Presbyterians). See Elliot Vernon, "Presbyterians in the English Revolution," in John Coffey ed., *The Oxford History of Protestant Dissenting Traditions*, vol. 1, *The Post-Reformation Era, c. 1559–c. 1689* (Oxford: Oxford University Press, 2020), 62. William Prynne was prepared to accept a Presbyterian settlement in which ministers had the power to keep the ignorant and scandalous from the Lord's Table but granted this power only "in a prudential way" and did not believe its authority was derived from the New Testament. See Prynne, *Suspension Suspended* [. . .] (London, 1646), sig. A2r. When Alexander Jaffray justified his embrace of Congregationalism, he described Presbyterian polity as "a human invention, composed with much prudence and policy of men's wit." See *Diary of Alexander Jaffray*, ed. J. M. G. Barclay (Aberdeen, 1856), 62–63.

worship of it:[72] all candles in the sun. Shall men think to compass themselves with sparks, and walk in the light of the fire which themselves have kindled,[73] in the face of the Sun of Righteousness?[74] Shall not such men lie down in sorrow?[75] Beloved, take heed of such *ignes fatui*,[76] foolish misguiding fires.

2nd. By way of real communication, he is "the true light, which lighteth every man" (John 1:9). Everyone that has any spiritual light really communicated to him, has it from Christ. It is part of his work to "recover sight to the blind" (Luke 4:18). And therefore he advises the church of Laodicea to come to him for eye salve, that she might see (Rev. 3:18). At his coming, Zion shines forth (Isa. 60:1), because his light arises upon her, verse 2. The former doctrinal teaching of itself will not suffice. That light may shine in darkness, and the darkness not comprehend it (John 1:5). All the light the sun can give, will not make a blind man see. There must be a visive[77] faculty within as well as light without: the stones of this building are by nature all blind, yea darkened, yea darkness itself. If the Lord Christ do not by the mighty efficacy of his Spirit create a visive power within them, as well as reveal the will of his Father to them, they will never spiritually discern the things of God. The natural man discerns not the things of God, nor indeed can do (1 Cor. 2:14).

It is true, men by the help of common gifts, with the use of the former doctrinal revelation, may attain to such a knowledge of the mind of God, as may in a sense be called illumination (Heb. 6:4). Far may they go, much may they do, by his light. They may teach others, and be cast away themselves: they may dispute for truth, yea die for truth, and all this while have but the first common anointing, see nothing clearly, but men walking like trees.[78] A spiritual insight into the mind of God, is not to be obtained, without an almighty act of the Spirit of Christ, creating a new power of life, and light upon the soul.

Some indeed think that they have this seeing power in themselves. Do but show them outwardly what is to be seen, and let them alone for the discerning

72 The Laudians had sought to justify and impose certain ceremonial and liturgical aspects of worship on the basis of "direct divine authority." See Anthony Milton, *Catholic and Reformed: The Roman and Protestant Churches in English Protestant Thought, 1600–1640* (Cambridge: Cambridge University Press, 2002), 497.

73 Isa. 50:11.

74 Mal. 4:2.

75 Isa. 50:11.

76 Lat. "foolish fires," like the phosphorescent light seen over marshy ground popularly called will-o'-the-wisp.

77 I.e., the faculty of sight.

78 Mark 8:24.

of it. Well then, let them alone, if ever they are stones of this living house, I am deceived. You that are so, know whence is all your light: and if you are anything in the dark, draw nigh to the candlestick, from whence all light is: thence must your light come, yea and thence it shall come: the secrets of the Lord shall make their abode with you.

And this is the fourfold relation wherein the Lord Christ stands unto this house, as it is a spiritual building.

Christ Is the Owner, Builder, Watchman, Inhabitant, and Avenger of His House

[2] In respect of state and condition, Jesus Christ stands in a fivefold relation to this house: which I shall unfold in order.

Christ Is the Owner with a Threefold Title to This House by Inheritance, Purchase, and Conquest

{1} He is the owner of it. He calls it "his":[79] "Upon this rock will I build my church" (Matt. 16:18). "Moses verily was faithful in all etc. but Christ as a Son over his own house, whose house are we" (Heb. 3:4–5).[80] And that you may see that he does not own it as his, without good right and title, know that in the great *oeconomie*[81] of grace, Jesus Christ has a threefold right and title to this house.

1st. Of inheritance, he is by his Father "appointed heir of all things" (Heb. 1:3).[82] By inheritance he obtains this excellent name, to be Lord of this house. God sends him to the vineyard as the heir, after his servants were refused.[83] And he has an engagement from his Father, that he shall enjoy his whole inheritance upon demand (Ps. 2:8). For the Father appointed, "in the fulness of times, to gather together all things in Christ, both which are in heaven, and which are on earth, even in him" (Eph. 1:10). So that as Christ is "the first-begotten" of the Father (Heb. 1:6), and "the first-born of every creature" (Col. 1:15), the right of heirship is his. But this will not do: for—

2nd. When he should come to take possession of this house, he finds that it is mortgaged, and that a great debt lies upon it, which he must pay to "the uttermost farthing,"[84] if he ever intend to have it. To the former title, there

79 In the original, "his" is set in all caps for emphasis.

80 In the original, "own" is set in all caps for emphasis. Following Goold, the reference should be corrected to Heb. 3:5–6.

81 I.e., economy.

82 The correct reference is Heb. 1:2.

83 Matt. 21:38.

84 Matt. 5:26. A farthing was an English coin worth a quarter of a penny.

must also be added a right of purchase. He must purchase this house, and pay a great price for it. And what is this price? What is required of him? No less than his dearest blood (Acts 20:28). Yea he must make "his soul an offering for sin";[85] and charge himself with the whole debt, all the curse and punishment, which this house had in part actually contracted upon itself, and wholly deserved. He must put his shoulders under the burden due to it, and "his back" to the "stripes" prepared for it.[86] A hard task. But Jesus Christ being the heir, the right of redemption belonged unto him. It was not for his honor that it should lie unredeemed. Full well he knew that if he did it not, the whole creation was too beggarly to make this purchase. 'Tis true, that nature of ours, which he assumed to pay that by, which he never took, was startled for a while, and would have deprecated this grievous price, crying out, "If it be possible, let this cup pass from me";[87] but he recollects himself, and says, "I am content to do thy will O God:" and so, through the eternal Spirit, he offered himself up unto God for a ransom.[88] He likes the house, and will have it to dwell in, whatever it cost him. "Here," (says he) "shall be my habitation and my dwelling for ever" (Ps. 132).[89] "Know ye not," (says the apostle) "that ye are the temple of the Spirit of Christ?" Well, and how come we so to be? "Ye are bought with a price" (2 Cor. 6:19).[90] They who affirm that he also purchased the unclean sties of the devil, wot not what they say.[91]

3rd. Unto purchase, he must also add conquest. An unjust usurper had taken possession of this house, and kept it in bondage: Satan had seized on it, and brought it, through the wrath of God, under his power. He then must be conquered, that the Lord Christ may have complete possession of his own house. "For this purpose," (then) "was the Son of God manifest, that he might destroy the works of the devil" (1 John 3:8). And how does he do it? (1) He overpowers him, and destroys him, in that "through death he destroyed him that had the power of death, that is, the devil" (Heb. 2:14). (2) He spoiled him having overcome him, he bound the strong man, and then spoiled his goods (Matt. 12:27).[92] All that darkness, unbelief, sin, and hardness, that he had stuffed this house withal, Christ spoils them, and scatters them all

85 Isa. 53:10.

86 Isa. 50:6; 53:5.

87 Matt. 26:39.

88 Heb. 9:14.

89 Here Owen paraphrases what is said in Ps. 132:5 and 132:11.

90 Following Goold, this should be corrected to 1 Cor. 6:19–20.

91 I.e., do not know what.

92 Following Goold, this should be corrected to Matt. 12:29.

away. (3) And to make his conquest complete, he triumphs over his enemy, and like a mighty conqueror makes an open show of him to his everlasting shame, "Having spoiled principalities and powers, he made a show of them openly, triumphing over them in his cross" (Col. 2:15): and by this means strengthens his title to his inheritance.

I might also farther insist on the donation of his Father, and the actual possession he takes of it by his Spirit, but these are sufficient, to prove this house to be Christ's. I shall take some observations hence.

Three Observations Arising

Christ Will Defend His House

[Observation] 1. Is this the house of Christ? Is he the owner of it? Let men take heed how they spoil it for themselves. The psalmist makes this a great argument in his pleading against opposers, that they came into the Lord's "inheritance" (Ps. 79:1). The title of Christ's purchase was not then so clearly known, as that of his inheritance, and therefore they of old pleaded chiefly by that title. Now he has proclaimed to all, his other titles also: the whole right he has to this house, to his saints. Who then shall meddle with it and go free? Among men, everyone with all his might will defend his own possession. And shall we think that the Lord Christ will suffer his to be spoiled at an easy rate? Shall not men pay dear for their encroachment? How has he in our days frustrated all attempts for the persecution of his? "Touch not," (says he) "mine anointed."[93] Men may upon various pretenses claim this privilege, to such a land, nation, or faction; it will in the end appear to be theirs and only theirs, who are living stones of this house: dogs may scramble for their bread, but shall not enjoy it:[94] it is Christ in this house that will make every stone of it a "burdensome stone":[95] he has done it that men may learn μὴ θεομαχεῖν.[96] Do not think it will excuse you to say, you were mistaken.[97]

93 Ps. 105:15. Owen made the same point in *Ebenezer* (1648) and *The Shaking and Translating of Heaven and Earth* (1649). See *Complete Works of John Owen*, 18:250, 459.

94 See Matt. 15:26–27.

95 Zech. 12:3.

96 Gk. "Not to fight against God." This is a quotation from Tertullian's *Ad Scapulam* 4.1. For the English translation, see Tertullian, *To Scapula*, in *Ante-Nicene Fathers: The Writings of the Fathers Down to A.D. 325*, 10 vols., ed. Alexander Roberts and James Donaldson (1886; repr., Peabody, MA: Hendrickson, 1995), 3:106. Owen made the same point in *Of Toleration*, the tract appended to his postregicide sermon, *A Sermon Preached* [. . .] *January 31* (1649). See *Complete Works of John Owen*, 18:383.

97 This is striking in the context of Cromwell's appeal to the Scots on August 3, 1650: "I beseech you in the bowels of Christ, think it possible you may be mistaken." See *The Letters, Writings, and Speeches of Oliver Cromwell*, 2:309.

Christ Has the Right to Order His House

[Observation] 2. Is Christ the owner of this house, let the order and disposal of it, be left to himself. Men are apt to be tampering with his house and household. They will be so kind and careful, as to lay out their wisdom and prudence about it: "Thus and thus shall it be," "These are parts and members of it." Christ is exceeding jealous of his honor in this particular: he cannot bear it, that men pretending to his glory, should think him so wanting in love, or wisdom, toward his own, as not exactly to dispose of all things that concern the reglement[98] thereof. Men would not be so dealt withal in their own houses, as they deal with Christ in his. We have all wisdom enough (as we suppose) to order our own houses: only the wisdom and love of the Father, leaves his to the discretion of others: these thoughts are not from above.

Christ Is Jealous for His House

[Observation] 3. Has Christ taken his own house to himself upon so many titles, let not men put those buildings on him for his, which are not so, which he holds not by these titles. Go to a man that dwells in a stately palace of his own, show him a hog sty, tell him, "This is your house, here you dwell, this is yours"; can you put a greater indignity on him? "No," says the man, "that is not mine, I dwell in yonder sumptuous palace." And shall we deal thus with the Lord Jesus? He has bought and adorned his own house: a glorious house it is. If now men shall hold out to him a sty of swine, a den of unclean beasts, a ruinous heap, whereof the far greatest part are dead stones, and tell him, this is his church, his house, will it not exceedingly provoke him? Will he bear such a reproach? Nay, he will reject such tenders, to their ruin.

Christ Builds His House with Living Stones

{2} Jesus Christ is the builder of this house. "This man was counted worthy of more glory than Moses, inasmuch as he who hath buildeth the house, hath more honour than the house" (Heb. 3:3). "I," (says he) "will build my church" (Matt. 16:18). This is not a fabric for any workman but Christ. It is true, there are others employed under him: and some so excellent that they may be said to be "wise master-builders" (2 Cor. 3:10),[99] but yet all the efficacy of their labor in this building is not from themselves, but merely from him by whom

98 I.e., regulation.

99 Following Goold, this should be corrected to 1 Cor. 3:10. The English invasion force spoke of the godly "Master Builders of the Churches of Jesus Christ." The *Declaration of the Army Now in Scotland*, sig. B2r.

they are employed. "Except the Lord build this house, they labor in vain that go about to build it."[100]

Now this house receives a twofold building. 1st. Spiritual, of all the stones thereof into one mystical house: of this I chiefly treat. 2nd. Ecclesiastical, of some particular stones into several tabernacles, which are useful partitions in the great mystical house, called assemblies and dwelling places of Mount Zion.[101] Both these it has from Christ alone.

1st. For the first. If all the most skillful workmen in the world should go to the pit of nature, by their own strength to hew out stones for this building, they will never with all their skill and diligence, lay one stone upon it. There is life required to those stones, which none can give but Christ. The Father has given into his hand alone "to give life eternal to whom he will" (John 17:2). He alone can turn stones into children of Abraham.[102] To him is committed all dispensation of quickening power. He brings us from the dust of death, and no man has quickened his own soul. With spiritual power, all spiritual life is vested in Christ. If dead stones live, it must be, by hearing the voice of the Son of God.[103] Christ's building of his mystical house, is his giving life unto dead stones, or rather, being life unto them. Of those who will attempt to build themselves, and draw a principle of spiritual life, from the broken cisterns of nature,[104] I shall speak afterward.

2nd. For the second, or the communion of living stones one with another, and all with Christ, in the order and worship appointed by the gospel, so becoming assemblies and dwelling places of Mount Zion,[105] this also is of him.[106] This is for his outward solemn worship: and he would never allow, that the will of any creature, should be the measure of his honor. He sets up the candlesticks, and holds the stars in his hand.[107] Look to the institution of this building, it is from Christ: look for directions about this building, it is

100 Ps. 127:1.

101 Isa. 4:5. Rutherford engaged with Congregationalists who claimed that a visible assembly of Mount Zion was a "covenanted, sanctified, and separated people." See Rutherford, *Due Right of Presbyteries*, 250.

102 Matt. 3:9.

103 John 5:25.

104 Jer. 2:13.

105 Isa. 4:5.

106 Rutherford adopted a different understanding of communion within the visible church: "The faithfull may become and stand members, and have a spirituall communion with a people . . . that are Idolaters, thieves, murtherers, worshippers of Baal, so being they worship the true God publickly as he commandeth, and be in externall covenant with him." See Samuel Rutherford, *A Peaceable and Temperate Plea for Pauls Presbyterie in Scotland* (London, 1642), 136.

107 Rev. 1:20.

wholly from him. From him, his word, his Spirit, is the institution, direction, and perfection of it: from hence now take some observations.

Two Observations Arising from This

The Master-Builder Puts Life into Dead Stones

[Observation] 1. Is Christ the builder of this house? Can he alone fit us for this building? Can he alone, and that by his almighty power, put life into dead stones, that they may grow up to be a holy and living habitation unto him? What then becomes of that famous workman "free-will," and a power of believing in ourselves? Do not they work effectually in this temple? As it was in Solomon's temple, "There was neither axe, nor hammer, nor any tool of iron heard in the house while it was in building" (1 Kings 6:7).[108] So in this spiritual house, that iron tool of free will, is not once heard: it comes not nigh the work, Christ does all alone. He gives life to whom he pleases.[109] Shall a dead will be thought to have a quickening, life-giving power in it? Shall a spirit of life be spun out of the bowels of nature? Is it the will of man, or the will of God that draws men unto Christ? And is it his Spirit or flesh that unites us to him? Where then is this workman employed that makes all this noise in the world? Even there where men cry, "Go to, let us build us a city and a tower whose top may reach unto heaven" (Gen. 11:4)? Among those who would build a Babel, a tower of their own to get to heaven by. The Lord comes down and scatters all their undertakings.[110] This workman never placed stone in the house of Christ. Nay, it is like the foolish woman, that pulls down her house with both her hands.[111] What free grace sets up, that free will strives to demolish.

Vows, Promises, Resolutions, and Engagements Are Insufficient

[Observation 2.] See hence a great mistake of many poor creatures, who would fain be stones in this house: what course take they? They hew and square themselves, strive to cut off this and that rubbish, which (as they suppose) alone hinders them from being fitted to this building.[112] They pare themselves with vows, promises, resolutions, and engagements,[113] beautify

108 This was an important text in debates over ecclesiology. See Rutherford, *Due Right of Presbyteries*, 265. Advocates of gathered churches argued that rough stones were not laid in the temple until they had been suitably prepared.

109 John 5:21.

110 Gen. 11:7–8.

111 Prov. 14:1.

112 This is suggestive of the attempts both before and after Dunbar to purge the Covenanter army.

113 "Vow" and "promises" is suggestive of the National Covenant (1638) and the Solemn League and Covenant (1643). The reference to "engagements" is striking language in the context of the

themselves with duties and services: and then with many perplexing fears present themselves to the building: never knowing whether they are admitted or no. All this while, the great Master-builder stands by, scarcely dealt withal. What now is the issue of such attempts? What they build one day, falls down in another. When they have oftentimes in their own thoughts, brought the building to such a pass,[114] as that they are ready to think, it will be well with them, now surely they shall have a share and interest in this living and glorious house, when all on a sudden they fall again to the ground: their hopes wither, and they suppose themselves in the world's rubbish again. There is no end of this alternation. Would now this poor soul see where its great defect lies? It has not applied itself aright to the only builder. Would you be a stone in this fabric, lay yourself before the Lord Jesus: say to him, that you are in yourself altogether unfit for the great building he has in hand, that you have often attempted to put yourself upon it, but all in vain: "Now Lord Jesus, do thou take me into thine own hand: if you cast me away, I cannot complain: I must justify you in all your ways: but you 'callest things that are not as though they were.'[115] You turn dead stones into children of Abraham:[116] oh turn my dead, into a living stone." Fear not; he will in no wise cast you out.[117]

The vanity of men attempting to mix their power and wisdom in the heaping up tabernacles for Christ, might be hence discovered, but I forbear.

Christ Watches Over His House in Order to Supply the Needs of His People and to Protect and Avenge Them

{3} Jesus Christ is the great watchman or keeper of this house. There are indeed other watchmen, and that of God's own appointment for the use of this house. "Son of man, I have made thee a watchman" (Ezek. 2:11).[118] "I have set watchmen upon thy walls" (Isa. 61:6–7),[119] which in a special manner are the pastors of the churches, "they watch" (Heb. 13:17). As the priests and Levites heretofore kept the watch of the Lord: it cannot be denied but that many who have taken upon them to be these watchmen, have watched only for their own advantage, have been very dogs, yea, dumb dogs, the very worst

---

defeat of the Scottish Engager army (1648). Similarly, the mention of "resolutions" is significant in the split in the Kirk between Protesters and Resolutioners, which occurred when the Commission of the General Assembly made two "public resolutions" on December 14, 1650.

114 I.e., a situation or point in the course of events.

115 Rom. 4:17.

116 Matt. 3:9.

117 John 6:37.

118 Following Goold, this should be corrected to Ezek. 3:17.

119 Following Goold, this should be corrected to Isa. 62:6–7.

of dogs (Isa. 66:10).[120] Yea they have been, and oftentimes are, under various pretenses, great "smiters and wounders of the spouse of Christ" (Cant. 5),[121] but yet were they never so good and true to their trusts, they were never able all to watch and keep this house, had it not another watchman: "Except the Lord keep the city, these watchmen watch in vain" (Ps. 127:1). He that "keeps Israel," who does "neither slumber nor sleep,"[122] must keep this house, or it will be destroyed. Christ, then, is that "holy one," and that "watcher," that "came down from heaven," and commanded to cut down the tree and the branches (Dan. 4:13–14), Nebuchadnezzar and his great power, for meddling with this house.[123]

Now, Christ watches his house for two ends.

1st. To see what it wants, "The eyes of the Lord run to and fro, throughout the whole earth, to show himself strong in its behalf" (2 Chron. 16:9). He looks down from heaven to behold them that fear him (Ps. 14).[124] He is that stone upon which are "seven eyes" (Zech. 3:9). A sufficiency, in perfection of wisdom, inspection, and government, for the good of his house. And those seven eyes of his "run to and fro through the whole earth" for this very purpose (Zech. 4:10). He takes notice of the state and condition of his people, to eye them in their distresses, and to give them timely and suitable deliverance. They may call every spring of their refreshment, Beer-lahai-roi.[125]

2nd. To see that the son of violence draw not nigh unto it, and if he do, to require it at his hands, to make him eat his own flesh, and drink his own blood, that he may learn to devour no more.[126] Observe then,

Three Observations Arising

Christ Tries His Church

[Observation] 1. Whence it is that this house, which seems so often to be nigh to destruction, is yet preserved from ruin. Ofttimes it is brought into a condition, that all that look on say, "Now it is gone for ever": but still it recovers and gets up again. The Lord Christ looks on all the while: he knows how far things may proceed for trial. When it comes to that pass, that if pressures

120 The correct reference is Isa. 56:10.

121 The reference is to Song 5:7.

122 Ps. 121:4.

123 In the original, "watcher" is set in all caps for emphasis.

124 Ps. 14:2.

125 I.e., the well of him that lives and sees me (Gen. 16:14; 24:62; 25:11).

126 Isa. 49:26. Owen appealed to this text in *The Shaking and Translating of Heaven and Earth* (1649) as he dealt with "the day of vengeance." See *Complete Works of John Owen*, 18:438.

and troubles should continue, the house will be overborne indeed, then he puts in, rebukes the winds and waves, and makes all things still again.[127] Like a father who looks upon his child in a difficult and dangerous business, knows that he can relieve him when he pleases, but would willingly see him try his strength and cunning, lets him alone, until perhaps the child thinks himself quite lost, and wonders his father does not help him: but when the condition comes to be such, that without help, he will be lost indeed, instantly the father puts in his hand and saves him. So deals the Lord Jesus with his house, lets it oftentimes strive and wrestle with great oppositions, to draw out and exercise all the graces thereof: but yet all this while he looks on, and when danger is nigh indeed, he is not far off.

Christ Protects His Church

[Observation] 2. Let all the enemies of the church know, that there is one, who has an eye over them in all their counsels and undertakings. While they are digging deep,[128] he looks on and laughs them to scorn.[129] How perplexed was the king of Syria when he found that the prophet was acquainted with all his designs, and made them known to the king of Israel![130] It cannot but be a matter of perplexity to the enemies of this house, when they shall find that the great friend and protector thereof, is continually present in all their advisoes.[131] Let them not wonder at their birthless undertakings, the eye of Christ is still upon them.

Christ Preserves His Church

[Observation] 3. Let the saints see their privilege, whoever they are, in what condition soever, the eye of Christ is upon them. He watches over them for good, and knows their souls in adversity. When no eye sees them, he looks on them, they cannot be cast out of his care, nor hid from his sight. There

127 Mark 4:39.

128 Leslie had put considerable effort into building trenches and fortifying a defensive line barring Cromwell access to Edinburgh and Leith. See Kenneth Charles Corsar, "David Leslie's Defence of Edinburgh," *Journal of the Society for Army Historical Research* 25, no. 103 (Autumn, 1947): 97. The Scots were entrenched behind "a nearly impregnable fortified line." See Ian Gentles, *The English Revolution and the Wars in the Three Kingdoms* (Harlow, UK: Pearson Longman, 2007), 418.

129 Ps. 2:4.

130 2 Kings 6:12. The Parliamentary army found itself trapped between the sea and the Covenanters, but intelligence reports enabled Cromwell to identify the weakness of Leslie's forces. See Martyn Calvin Cowan, *John Owen and the Civil War Apocalypse: Preaching, Prophecy and Politics* (London: Routledge, 2017), 41.

131 I.e., advices and counsels, particularly in dispatches or intelligence.

are many poor souls, who go heavily all the day long; that mourn in their spirits unknown, unregarded, unpitied: the eye of Christ is on them for good continually: they cannot be thrown out of his watchful care.

Christ Inhabits His House by the Holy Spirit

{4} Christ is the indweller of this house, he has not built it, and framed it for no use. It is for a habitation for himself. He has "chosen Zion, he has desired it for his habitation, this is my rest," (says he) "here will I dwell" (Ps. 132:13–14). This house is built up, to be a habitation unto him (Eph. 2:22). He is the "King of saints,"[132] and this house is his court. It is true for his human nature, "the heaven must receive him until the time of the restitution of all things" (Acts 4:27),[133] but yet, he dwells in this house three ways.

1st. By his Spirit, Christ dwells in this house, and every stone of it, by his Spirit, "Know ye not that Christ is in you, except ye be reprobates" (2 Cor. 13:5). "Christ in you" that is, the Spirit of Christ; Christ by his Spirit. So the Holy Ghost expounds it (Rom. 8:9), "If the Spirit of God dwell in you": which verse 10 is "If Christ be in you": Christ and his Spirit, as to indwelling, are all one: for he dwells in us by his Spirit. "The love of God is shed abroad in our hearts by the Holy Ghost that is given unto us" (Rom. 5:5). There is not only the "love of God," a grace of the Spirit, "shed abroad" in us, but there is also the "Holy Spirit given unto us." This is fully asserted, "The Spirit of him that raised up Jesus, dwells in you" (Rom. 8:11): as also, "Keep the good thing committed to thee by the Holy Ghost which dwelleth in us" (2 Tim. 1:14). Hence the saints are said to be "temples of the Holy Ghost."[134] Jesus Christ does not build temples, merely for graces, created graces, he dwells in them himself, he dwells in them by his Spirit. And this is a glorious privilege of this house, that Jesus Christ in a mystical and wonderful manner should dwell in it, and every stone of it. Hereby all believers become to be not one personal, but one mystical Christ (1 Cor. 12:6).[135] However we are distanced in respect of his human nature, yet mystically we are one, one body, one mystical Christ, because we have one Spirit, dwelling in us and him. If a man were never so tall, so that his head should reach the stars, and his feet stand upon the ground, yet, having but one soul, he is but one man still. Though Christ in his human nature be exceedingly distanced from us, yet there being one and the same Spirit in him and us, we are one mystical Christ. Yet observe,

132 Rev. 15:3.

133 Following Goold, this should be corrected to Acts 3:21.

134 1 Cor. 6:19.

135 Following Goold, this should be corrected to 1 Cor. 12:12.

Two Observations Arising

Clarifying the Nature of Union with Christ

[Observation] 1. Though Christ be united unto the persons of the saints, by the indwelling of the Spirit, yet the saints have not that which is called personal union with him, nor with the Spirit. Personal union is by a person of the Deity, assuming the nature of man into one personality with itself, that having of its own no personal subsistence.[136] Things are here clean otherwise: Christ does not assume the saints into a personal subsistence with himself, but dwells in their persons by his Spirit.[137]

The Spirit Is Free to Work as He Pleases

[Observation] 2. That the operations of the indwelling Spirit of Christ, and all his manifestations are voluntary. He works as he will, and reveals what he will, even where he dwells. He does not work in us naturally, but voluntarily, unto what proportion he pleases: therefore though he dwell equally in all saints, in respect of truth and reality, yet he does not in respect of working and efficacy.

Christ Graciously Makes the Believer's Heart His Dwelling Place

2nd. By his graces. Christ dwells in this house, and in all the stones thereof by his graces. He "dwells in our hearts by faith" (Eph. 3:17). He dwells in us by his word "in all wisdom" (Col. 3:16). All the graces we are made partakers of, we receive from his fullness, and by them he inhabits, in us. They are indeed the ornaments of the living stones of this house, to make them meet and fit for such an indweller as the Lord Christ. Christ will not dwell in a soul, whose mind is darkness, his will stubbornness, and his affections carnal and sensual. He puts light, and life, and love, upon the soul, that it may be meet for him to dwell in: Christ dwells in all the world by his power, and presence, but he dwells only in his saints, by his Spirit, and grace.

136 Congregationalists argued that the visible church consisted only of those who were "partakers of the divine nature." Owen's point is that it should not be inferred from the doctrine of union with Christ that believers ontologically participate in Christ's deity. For a similar point, see Samuel Rutherford, *A Survey of the Spirituall Antichrist. Opening the Secrets of Familisme and Antinomianisme* [. . .] (London, 1648), 167–68. Rutherford also engaged with the Congregationalists' use of this terminology in *Due Right of Presbyteries*, 250, 267.

137 Here Owen explicitly rejects the teaching of some of the sects such as the so-called Ranters and Familists. Here he concurs with Rutherford, *Survey of the Spirituall Antichrist*, 167–68. For examples of some of those who claimed something like theosis or divinization, see Nigel Smith, *Perfection Proclaimed: Language and Literature in English Radical Religion, 1640–1660* (Oxford: Oxford University Press, 1989), 144–84.

Christ Inhabits the Church as His Royal Court

3rd. By his ordinances. Where two or three of his are assembled together, there is he in the midst of them.[138] The ordinances of Christ, are the great ornaments of his kingly court: by them he is glorious in all the assemblies of Mount Zion.[139] Some would fain cast out this indwelling of Christ from among his saints: in due time he will thoroughly rebuke them: some again would thrust him out into the world: but he will make men know, that his ordinances are given unto his: it is true the benefit of some of them, extends to the world, but the right and enjoyment of them, that, is the privilege of his saints: thus Christ dwells in his house: hence observe,

Three Observations Arising

The Intimacy of Communion with Christ

[Observation] 1. The intimacy of the Lord Jesus with his saint[s], and the delight he takes in them: he dwells *with* them: he dwells *in* them. He takes them to the nearest union with himself possible. He in them, they in him, that they may be one. He has made many an admirable change with us. He took our sin, and gives us his righteousness; he took our nature, and gives us his Spirit. Neither is it a bare indwelling neither: he thereby holds with us all acts of the choicest communion. "If," (says he) "any man hear my voice, and open to me, I will come in to him": and what then? "I will sup with him, and he with me" (Rev. 3:20).[140]

(1) "I will sup with him." I will delight and satisfy myself with him. Jesus Christ takes abundance of delight and contentment in the hearts of his saints. When they are faithful, when they are fruitful, he is marvelously refreshed with it. Hence is that prayer of the spouse, "Awake O north wind and come thou south, blow upon my garden, that the spices thereof may flow out, let my beloved come and eat of his spices" (Cant. 4:16).[141] She would have the spices, the graces she has received, breathed on by a fresh gale of the Spirit, that they might yield a sweet savor. And why so? That her Beloved may have something for his entertainment, that he may come and sup, "and eat of his pleasant fruits."[142] A poor soul, that has received Christ, has not any desire

138 Matt. 18:20.

139 Isa. 4:5. Congregationalists understood each church to be a "dwelling place of Mount Zion." See John Dury, *A Model of Church-Government: or, The Grounds of the Spirituall Frame and Government of the House of God* [. . .] (London, 1647), 1.

140 William Strong utilized this text in *The Saints Communion with God and Gods Communion with Them in Ordinances* [. . .] (London, 1655), 69, 103–4, 110.

141 Song 4:16.

142 Song 4:16. Owen engaged with this text in *Communion with God*, describing it as the "prayer of the spouse that she may have something for his entertainment." William Strong appealed to

so fervent, as that it may have something for the entertainment of him: that he who filled it when it was hungry, may not (as it were) be sent away empty. And the Lord Jesus is exceedingly taken with those refreshments. "The King is held in the galleries" (Cant. 4:5).[143] He is detained, yea bound with delight, he knows not how to pass away. Therefore "he rests in his love" (Zeph. 3:17). He is exceedingly satiated in the delight he takes in his saints: neither is this all, that when Christ comes he will sup with us, (though this be a great deal; O what are we that we should entertain our Lord) but also,

(2) The saints sup with him. He provides choice refreshments for them also. When Christ comes in unto us, he will entertain a soul bounteously. He provides love for us. When the Spirit of Christ, is bestowed on us, he sheds abroad the love of God in our hearts (Rom. 5:5). He sheds it abroad, pours it out abundantly. Friends, love is a choice dainty.[144] He that knows it not is a stranger to all spiritual banquets: it is a choice dish in the feast of fat things, that Christ prepares: he provides "righteousness, and peace, and joy in the Holy Ghost," for us. That his "kingdom," (Rom. 14:17) and, this "kingdom of his is within us."[145] Of such precious things as these does Christ provide a supper for them, with whom he dwells. If Christ be in you, more or less, you shall not want this entertainment. We are indeed sometimes like mad[146] guests, that when meat is set on the table, cast it all down, without tasting a morsel. When Christ has prepared sweet and precious dainties for us, we cast them on the ground. We throw away our peace, our joy, by folly and unbelief; but this makes not the truth of God of none effect.

The Danger of Grieving His Spirit

[Observation] 2. Does Christ dwell in us by his Spirit, should we not be careful lest we grieve that Spirit of his? The Spirit of Christ is very tender. Did the saints continually consider this, that Christ dwells in them, that he is grieved, and troubled, at all their unbelief, unruly passions, worldly desires, foolish imaginations, surely they could not but be much more watchful over

---

this verse as he dealt with the communion the saints had with God as they approached him in ordinances. See Strong, *Saints Communion with God*, 30–31, 108, 110.

143 The correct reference is Song 7:5. William Strong interpreted this verse in a similar manner—namely, speaking of how Christ and his people enjoy "intimate converse, where friends walke together, and enjoy communion one with another." See Strong, *Saints Communion with God*, 22–23.

144 I.e., a fine delicacy.

145 Luke 17:21.

146 Following the editorial decision of Goold, "made" is altered to "mad." See *The Works of John Owen*, ed. William H. Goold, 24 vols. (Edinburgh: Johnstone and Hunter, 1850–1855), 8:306.

themselves, than generally they are. He is refreshed when we walk with him, and hold fellowship with him. To turn aside from him, to hold fellowship with the world or flesh, this grieves him, and burdens him.[147] Oh, "grieve not the Spirit of God, whereby you are sealed to the day of redemption."[148] And let me tell you, if you do, though he will not utterly depart from you, nor take his kindness away for evermore, yet he will do that which shall make your heart ache, your joints tremble, and break all your bones in pieces:[149] for,

(1) He will depart from you, as to all sense of his presence: that you shall have neither joy, nor comfort, nor peace. He will hide his face, and make you believe (as we say) that he is gone utterly from you. And this he will do, not for a day or a night, or so, but for a great while together. You shall go to seek him, and you shall not find him.[150] Yea beg, and cry, and have no answer: now all the world for one smile from Christ, for one impression of his presence upon my heart, and all in vain. When the Spirit of Christ was thus departed from David upon his miscarriage, as to the sense and joy of it, how does he cry out, "Make me to hear the voice of joy and gladness, that the bones which thou hast broken may rejoice," (Ps. 51:8). If you value the presence of Christ at no greater rate, but to jeopard[151] it upon every occasion, you may haply[152] go without the comfort of it all your days. Examine yourselves, is it not so with some of you? Have you not lost the sense of the presence of Christ by your folly and uneven walking? Perhaps you value it not much, but go on as Samson with his hair cut, and think to do as at other times: but if the Philistines set upon you, it will be sorrow and trouble.[153] In every assault you will find yourself a lost man. Sooner or later it will be bitterness to you.

(2) He will depart, as to the efficacy of his working in you, and leave you so weak that you shalt not be able to walk with God. His Spirit is "a Spirit of grace and supplications."[154] He will so withdraw it, that you shalt find your heart in a poor condition, as to those things. To be cold in prayer, dead in hearing, estranged from meditation, slight in all duties, this shall be your portion. A frame that a tender soul would tremble to think of. Ah! How many poor creatures are come to this state in these days, by their neglect and contempt

147 Owen may have been thinking of those considering entering into an agreement with former supporters of the Engagement or with so-called royalist malignants.

148 Eph. 4:30.

149 See Isa. 38:13.

150 Hos. 5:6.

151 I.e., to put in jeopardy, to risk.

152 I.e., by chance, accidently.

153 Judg. 16:20.

154 Zech. 12:10.

of Christ dwelling in them, they have lost their first love,[155] their first life, their graces are ready to die, and their whole soul is asleep, in a heartless, lifeless, zealless frame. They shall be saved, but "yet as through fire."[156]

(3) He will depart as to assurance of what is to come, as well as to a sense of what is present. It is the indwelling Spirit of Christ that gives assurance: hereby are we "sealed to the day of redemption."[157] He "beareth witness with our spirits, that we are the children of God."[158] Upon our grieving him, he will withdraw as to this also. We shall be bewildered, and in the dark, not knowing what will become of our souls to eternity. For if Christ by his Spirit do not speak peace, who shall?

The Value of the Graces of Christ

[Observation 3.][159] Does he dwell in us by his grace?

(1) Let us first know whence all graces are, that in a want, or weakness of them, we may know whither to go for a supply. "Of his fulness we receive, and grace for grace."[160] All supplies of graces are from Christ. "Lord, increase our faith,"[161] say the apostles: not only faith originally is from him, but all increases of it also. "I believe, help thou my unbelief," says the poor man.[162] We wrestle and struggle with a little grace, a little faith, a little love, a little joy, and are contented if we can keep our heads above water, that we be not quite sunk and lost. How sweet would it be with us, if upon a serious consideration from whence all these graces flow, we would apply ourselves to draw out farther degrees and heightenings of them, whereby he might dwell more plentifully in us, and we might always converse with him in his gracious train of attendants. How this may be done in particular, is not my business now to show.

(2) Learn to tender[163] the graces of Christ, as those which hold out his presence to us. Let us tender them in our own hearts, and prize them in whomsoever they are. They are pledges of the indwelling of Christ. Certainly if men valued Christ, they would more value his graces. Many pretend to love him, to honor him, yea with Peter to be ready to die with him, or for

155 Rev. 2:4.
156 1 Cor. 3:15.
157 Eph. 4:30.
158 Rom. 8:16.
159 In the text: 2.—Owen.
160 John 1:16.
161 Luke 17:5.
162 Mark 9:24.
163 I.e., to hold dear, to value.

him:[164] but what evil surmises have they of the graces of Christ appearing in others: how do they call them hypocrisy, humor,[165] folly, pride, singularity,[166] with other terms of a later invention. I cannot so easily believe, that anyone can love the Lord Jesus, and hate the appearances of him in others. Where is anything of Christ, there is also Christ.

Christ Brings Vengeance on All Who Persecute the Saints of His House

{5} Jesus Christ is the great avenger of this house, and of all the injuries or wrongs that are done unto it. "All," (says he) "that devour Israel shall offend" (Jer. 2:3). He will not hold him guiltless that rises up against it: see Isaiah 59:15–18.[167] He takes upon him the avenging of his house, as his own proper work. "Shall he not avenge his elect?" He will do it "speedily":[168] see also Isaiah 63:2–6.[169] How dreadful is he in the execution of his revenging judgments against the enemies thereof. So also is he described [in] Revelation 19:13–15. He has promised to make the stones of this house heavy stones, they shall "burden" all that touch them (Zech. 12:3). He comes forth of "the myrtle trees in the bottom" (his lowly people in a low condition) with the "red horse" following him (Zech. 1:8). Upon this account he fearfully broke the old Roman pagan empire (Rev. 6:13–17);[170] and will as fearfully destroy the anti-Christian Roman power, with all its adherents, Revelation 17, 18, 19.[171] Sooner or later he will call to an account every instrument of persecution in the world. Hence he is said to be "a lion" in the behalf of this house, that treads down all before him (Mic. 5:8). Jacob says of him in Judah, "He is a lion, as an old lion, who shall rouse him up?" (Gen. 49:9). Suppose any do rouse him up, how then? "He will not lie down, until he eat of the prey, and drink the blood of the slain" (Num. 23:24). Many poor creatures have by their opposition to his house, roused up this lion: and what has been the issue? What attempts have been to cause him to lie down again: all in vain:

164 Matt. 26:35 etc.

165 I.e., a whimsical fancy with no apparent ground in reason.

166 I.e., dissension from what is acceptable.

167 Owen appealed to this text in *The Steadfastness of the Promises* (1650) to make a similar point about God bringing "fury to his adversaries [and] recompense to his enemies."

168 Luke 18:7–8.

169 Owen appealed to this text in *The Shaking and Translating of Heaven and Earth* (1649) as he spoke of divine "recompense and vengeance," linking it, as he does here, to Zech. 12.

170 Owen made the same point about the judgment of pagan Rome in *Ebenezer* (1648) and *The Shaking and Translating of Heaven and Earth* (1649).

171 This appears to be a reference to Revelation 17–19. Owen gave considerable attention to these chapters in *The Shaking and Translating of Heaven and Earth* (1649).

if he be once roused up, he will not couch down, until he eat and drink the blood of the slain. But suppose great opposition he made unto him, will he not give over? Not at all: as a lion that comes upon his prey, "if a multitude of shepherds be called forth against him, he will not be afraid at their voice, nor abase himself at their noise" (Isa. 31:4). In brief, sooner or later, temporally or eternally, he will avenge all the injuries, and destroy all the enemies of his holy dwelling (1 Thess. 1:6–10).[172]

And these are some of the relations wherein the Lord Christ stands unto this house of God, being made thereby unto it, beauty and glory, comeliness and excellency. The carrying on of this building, by the union of all the stones thereof to the foundation, and their cementing one to another by faith, love, and order, I shall not now treat of: nor of the following points of the text. The general uses of what has been said are three, the heads whereof I shall name.

Three General Points of Application

The Privilege of Being a Living Stone in This House

[Use] 1. See the eminent privilege of them which are indeed stones of this house, which is living, strong, and glorious, which is so nearly related to the Lord Christ: there is more of duty, dignity, and safety in this thing, than can easily be expressed. To do service unto Christ, as his, to have the honor of being his, and to be safeguarded as his, are great privileges: let them who have any sense of these things, further draw out these particulars, from what has been spoken.

Not All Assemblies Have Such Status and Privilege

[Use] 2. Learn hence the vanity of resting upon outward church privileges, if we are not withal, interested in this spiritual estate: where men are living stones indeed, they lie in beauty and order in the assemblies: where they are otherwise, where assemblies are made up of dead rubbish, and yet cry, "The house of the Lord, the house of the Lord,"[173] the Lord Jesus abhors those assemblies, he stands not in those relations unto them.

History Teaches Persecutors of the True Church Will Be Destroyed

[Use] 3. See hence the ruin of persecution, that has appeared in the world in various forms. It has put on all manner of colors and pretenses, and prevailed with all sorts of persons at one time or other to close with it: what has been

172 The correct reference is 2 Thess. 1:6–10.

173 Jer. 7:4.

the issue? What is like to be? The house indeed has been battered sometimes, but they who have come against it, have been broken all to pieces. Shall the residue of men, who under new pretenses, or old ones new painted, drive on the same design, shall they prosper? You, O Lord Jesus, in thine anger, will cut them off. The Lord open the eyes of the sons of men, that they may not hope any more to separate between Christ, and his saints, between whom there are so many everlasting relations.

To the only wise God through Jesus Christ to whom be the glory forever. Amen.[174]

FINIS.[175]

174 In the text: Μόνῳ σοφῷ Θεῷ, διὰ Ἰησοῦ Χριστοῦ, ᾧ ἡ δόξα εἰς τοὺς αἰῶνας. Ἀμήν.—Owen. This is the Greek text of Rom. 16:27.

175 Lat. "The End."

THE ADVANTAGE OF THE KINGDOM OF CHRIST IN THE SHAKING OF THE KINGDOMS OF THE WORLD: OR, PROVIDENTIAL ALTERATIONS IN THEIR SUBSERVIENCY TO CHRIST'S EXALTATION. OPENED, IN A SERMON PREACHED TO THE PARLIAMENT OCTOB. 24. 1651.

A Solemn Day of Thanksgiving for the Destruction of the Scots Army at Worcester with Sundry Other Mercies, by John Owen Minister of the Gospel

---

Oxford, printed by Leon. Lichfield
printer to the university,
For Tho. Robinson.
Anno Dom. 1651.

[Parliamentary Order]

Tuesday the 28 of October 1651.

Ordered by the Parliament.

That the thanks of this House be given to Mr Owen, dean of Christ Church in Oxford, for his great pains taken in his sermon preached before the Parliament at Margaret's Westminster, on Friday the XXIVth of October (being a day set apart for public thanksgiving), and that he be desired to print his sermon, and that he have the like privilege in printing the same, as others in like case have usually had, and that the Lord General do give him the thanks of this House, and desire him to print his sermon accordingly.[1]

Hen. Scobell
Cler. Parliament.[2]

1 See also *Journals of the House of Commons*, 13 vols. (London: HMSO, 1802–1803), 7:30–31. Oliver Cromwell, the Lord General, was also charged with conveying thanks to Thomas Goodwin, who was likewise invited to print his sermon.

2 I.e., Henry Scobell, Clerk or Parliament. Henry Scobell (ca. 1610–1660) was an active supporter of the parliamentary cause and, in May 1649, had been appointed Clerk of the Parliament for life.

[Dedication]

TO THE SUPREME AUTHORITY of the nation, the Common assembled in Parliament.

Right Honorable,

Of all the times which the Holy One of Israel has caused to pass over the nations of the world, there has not any (from the days of old) been so filled with eminent discoveries of his presence, power, and providence, in disposing of all affairs here below according "to the counsel of his own will,"[1] as the season wherein he has made you a spectacle unto men and angels,[2] being the instrument in his hand to perform all his pleasure. Neither in this season has he upon any opportunity, so gloriously laid hold upon his own strength and goodness, to manifest the fixedness of his eye on those who are as the apple of it,[3] as in that mighty deliverance the high praises whereof, according to his good hand upon you, you lately rendered unto him.

The more beauty and desirableness any design against the Lord Christ is clothed withal, the more power and subtlety it is supported with, the greater is the brightness of his coming for its wasting and desolation. With what deceivableness of unrighteousness and lies in hypocrisy the late grand attempt of those in Scotland, with their adherents (which also was of the former, and is gone into destruction), was carried on, is in some measure now made naked to the loathing of its abominations. In digging deep, to

1 Eph. 1:11.

2 1 Cor. 4:9.

3 Zech. 2:8.

lay a foundation for blood and revenge, in covering private and sordid ends with a pretense of things public and glorious; in limning[4] a face of religion upon a worldly stock; in concealing distant aims, and bloody animosities, to compass one common end, that a theatre might be provided to act several parts upon, in pleading a necessity from an oath of God, unto most desperate undertakings against God,[5] and such like things as these, perhaps it gives not place to any which former ages have been acquainted withal.[6] Now to reject all the claims of the authors, and abettors thereof to any commission from above, to divest them of all pretenses to religion and zeal thereof, to disappoint them in their expected associations, and to make all their strength to become as tow[7] that has smelt the fire, has been his work alone who takes to himself his great power, to carry on the interest of his kingdom against all opposers. Under the shadow of this mercy, composed of as many branches of wisdom, power, goodness, and faithfulness, as any outward dispensation has brought forth since the name of Christian was known, do you now sit in council, and the residue of the nation in peace. What obligations from the Lord? What cords of love are upon us?[8] The returnal and improvement of all his dealings with us, which he requires and expects from us, I have pointed you unto in the following sermon. For the present, I shall only add, that as whatever there has been, of beauty, glory, or advantage unto the people of God, in the late transactions, has been eminently of undeserved grace; so the dreadful vengeance which the Lord has executed against the men of his enmity and warfare, has been most righteously procured, by their clothing cursed designs of revenge, persecution, bondage in soul and body, spoil and rapine,[9] with the most glorious pretenses of zeal, covenant,[10] reformation,[11] and such like things, which never came into their hearts. Therefore, that the

4 I.e., painting.

5 The Solemn League and Covenant (1643).

6 Samuel Parker understood Owen to be referring to "the Covenanting Brethren of the Kirk, when they joyn'd in with the Royal Interest in opposition to the designs of the Republican and Independent Party." See Parker, *A Defence and Continuation of the Ecclesiastical Politie* (London, 1671), 584.

7 I.e., short fibers of flax or hemp. See Judg. 16:9.

8 See Hos. 11:4.

9 I.e., plunder and pillage.

10 The National Covenant of Scotland (1638) and the Solemn League and Covenant (1643).

11 The Solemn League and Covenant spoke of working for "the preservation of the reformed religion in the Church of Scotland" and "the reformation of religion in the kingdoms of England and Ireland, in doctrine, worship, discipline, and government, according to the Word of God, and the example of the best reformed churches." See David Cressy and Lori Anne Ferrell, *Religion and Society in Early Modern England: A Sourcebook* (London: Routledge, 1996), 181.

God of all our mercies and deliverances, would forever keep alive in your hearts, a faithful acknowledgment of his grace, and a practical detestation of those ways which are such a provocation to the eyes of his glory, shall be the constant prayer of

From my study, Christ Church, Oxford.[12]
Nov. 7.

Your most humble servant in our dearest Lord,

John Owen.

12 In the text: Ch. Ch., OXON.—Owen. Owen was appointed dean of Christ Church in March 1651. See *Perfect Account* (March 12–19, 1651), 77. Blair Worden, "Cromwellian Oxford," in *The History of the University of Oxford*, vol. 4, *Seventeenth-Century Oxford*, ed. Nicholas Tyacke (Oxford: Clarendon, 1997), 737.

[Sermon]

Providential Alterations in Their Subserviency to Christ's Exaltation, Opened Etc.

And all the trees of the field shall know that I the Lord have brought down the high tree, have exalted the low tree, have dried up the green tree, and have made the dry tree to flourish: I the Lord have spoken it and have done it.

EZEKIEL 17:24

GOD'S WORKS OF PROVIDENCE

Although all the works of God's providence (which are great "and sought out of all that have pleasure in them")[1] have such a stamp and impress of his own image on them, his wisdom, goodness, power, love, that they declare their author, and reveal from heaven his kindness and wrath toward the children of men;[2] yet such are the prejudices, lusts, inordinacy of affections, and interest of many, that it has always been a long and difficult task to convince them of his presence in them, when it has been most uncontrollably evident.

The Egyptians will wrestle with many a plague, by thinking the "magicians can do so":[3] and the Philistines will try to the utmost whether it be

1 In the margin: Psal. 111:2.—Owen.

2 In the margin: Psal. 19:1–2; Rom. 1:18; Acts 27:26–27.—Owen. Although Goold plausibly corrected this to Acts 14:16–17, it is more likely a reference to Acts 17:26–27 or, perhaps, 17:24–27.

3 In the margin: Exod. 7:11–12.—Owen.

"his hand," or "a chance that happened" to them.[4] "Lord," says the prophet, "when thy hand is lifted up, they will not see" (Isa. 26:11).[5]

Yea, oftentimes (especially when judicial blindness is gone forth upon them),[6] though they cannot but see his arm awaked as of old, and made bare,[7] they will not rest in his sovereign disposal of things, but rise up against the works of his revenge and holiness: like wild beasts that are pursued, when all ways of escape and turning are shut up, they fly in the face of him that follows them. They "repent not of their evil deeds," but bite their tongues for anger, "and blaspheme the God of heaven" (Rev. 16:10–11).

Yea such is the power of deceivable lusts, that many will admire at the blindness of others in former generations, who considered not the works of God (as the Jews in the wilderness), when themselves are under actual contempt of no less glorious dispensations, like the Pharisees who bewailed the folly of their fathers in persecuting the prophets, when themselves were endeavoring to kill the Son of God (Matt. 23:29–30).

To bring then upon the spirits of men a conviction of the works of God, and his righteousness therein, so as to prevail with them to rest in his determination of things, is a task meet only for him, who knows all their hearts within them, and can carry on the issues of his providence, until to a man they shall say, "Verily there is a reward for the righteous, verily he is a God who judgeth in the earth" (Ps. 58:11).[8] And this is that which the Lord here undertakes to accomplish, "And," says he, "all the trees," etc.[9]

THE CONTEXT OF THE TEXT FROM EZEKIEL

In the preaching and prophesying of Ezekiel, this one thing among others is eminent, that he was *artifex parabolarum*,[10] a wonderful framer of similitudes and parables; a way of teaching attended with much evidence, clearness and power.[11]

In particular, he frequently compares the world to a field, or a forest, and the inhabitants of it to the trees therein. An allusion exceedingly proper,

4 In the margin: 1 Sam. 6:9.—Owen.

5 Owen quoted this text in *Ebenezer* (1648). See *Complete Works of John Owen*, vol. 18.

6 In the margin: Isa. 6:11–12.—Owen. This is most likely a reference to verses 9–10.

7 Isa. 51:9.

8 Owen had appealed to this text in *Ebenezer* (1648).

9 Ezek. 17:24.

10 Lat. "An artist of parables."—Owen. This is from Tremellius's Latin translation of the Old Testament, and according to Tremellius's chapter divisions this is Ezek. 21:5. See *Testamenta Veteris Biblia sacra* (Frankfurt, 1579).

11 In the margin: Ezek. 20:45.—Owen. This should be corrected to Ezek. 20:49.

considering the great variety and difference of condition both of the one and the other. The trees of the field are some high, some low, some green, some dry, some strong, some weak, some lofty, some contemptible, some fruitful, some barren, some useful, some altogether useless: so that you have all sorts of persons, high and low, of what condition, relation, or interest soever, clearly represented by the trees of the field, and these are the trees in my text.

This chapter, unto verse 22,[12] is taken up in a riddle, a parable, with the exposition of it. The time being come, that God would destroy the outward visible monarchy of the Jews, for their false worship, tyranny, persecution, and oppression, he employs the king of Babylon in that work,[13] who subdues the nation, takes away two kings, one after another,[14] and appoints Zedekiah a titulary governor under him:[15] but the wrath of God being to come upon them to the uttermost,[16] he also closes with Aegypt,[17] rebels against him by whose appointment alone he had any right to be a ruler, verse 16, so way is made by his ruin, to put an end to the kingly reign of the house of David in Jerusalem (Jer. 29:16–17).[18]

The Lord had of old erected a kingly government in the house of David: not for any eminency in the government itself,[19] or for the civil advantage of that people; for he had long before chosen and established another, consisting of "seventy elders of the people" (Num. 11:24), to whom he added prophets and judges extraordinarily raised up in several generations, according to his promise (Deut. 18:18), which when the people rejected, he said they rejected him, or his institution (1 Sam. 8:7); but that it might be a type of the spiritual dominion of their Messiah,[20] and so was a part of their pedagogy and bondage, as were the residue of their types, every one of

12 In the margin: Cap. 17.2.—Owen. I.e., Ezek. 17:2.

13 In the margin: 2 Chron. 36:17.—Owen.

14 Striking in the context of the death of Charles I and the defeat of Charles II at Worcester.

15 In the margin: 2 Chron. 36:17; 2 Kings 14:1–3.—Owen. The final reference should, following Goold, be corrected to 2 Kings 24:1–3.

16 In the margin: Jerem. 37:1; 2 Kings 24:17; 2 Chron. 36:10.—Owen.

17 I.e., Egypt.

18 In the margin: 2 Sam. 1. 81. 12. 10.—Owen. It is unclear which verses are intended. In the 1721 edition of Owen's sermons, these references were simply omitted. See *A Complete Collection of the Sermons of the Reverend and Learned John Owen* [. . .], ed. John Asty (London: John Clark, 1721), 400. Goold glossed it as 1 Sam. 16:1; 2 Sam. 12:7. See *The Works of John Owen*, ed. William H. Goold, 24 vols. (Edinburgh: Johnstone and Hunter, 1850–1855), 8:316. While the reference to "1. 81." is unclear, contextually the second part of the marginal note does appear to be to 2 Sam. 12:10.

19 An important statement in the political context of 1650.

20 In the margin: Psal. 45:6; Hos. 3:5; Isai. 9:7 & 16:5, Ch. 22:22; Jerem. 23:5; Amos 9:11; Ezek. 34:23–24, Ch. 37:24–25.—Owen.

them.[21] Yea the most glorious enjoyments whatsoever, which were granted them, which did yet represent something that was afterward to be brought in, was part of that servile estate wherein God kept that people, that without us they should not be made perfect.[22] But now this carnal people beholding the outward beauty luster and glory of the type, began to rest in it, to the neglect of the spiritual kingdom of Christ represented thereby.[23] And thus did they with the rest of their types, until the Lord destroyed all their outward pomp and glory (Isa. 1:11–12; Jer. 7:4, 14–15).

So in particular dealt he with their kingly government, when once they began to account their bondage, their glory, and to embrace the shadow instead of the substance. And this did he to recall them to a serious consideration of the tendency of all typical institutions, and the design he was carrying on, concerning the kingdom of Christ.

Hence verse 22 of this chapter, he calls them from their thoughtfulness about the destructions, desolations, and contentions, that were among them in reference to their civil rule, to the consideration of that design, which he was secretly, and silently carrying on, under all these dispensations. "I will also take of the highest branch of the high cedar and will set it, I will crop off from the top of his young twigs a tender one and will plant it upon an high mountain and eminent. In the mountain of the height of Israel will I plant it, and it shall bring forth boughs, and bear fruit, and be a goodly cedar, and under it shall dwell all fowl of every wing: in the shadow of the branches thereof shall they dwell."

As if the Lord should say, "There is a great noise in the world, about setting up, and plucking down of kings, in this their carnal rule, and many of you see nothing else, you will look no farther; but I also have my work in hand, my design is not bounded within these limits, and outward appearances, I am setting up a King that shall have another manner of dominion and rule than these worms of the earth. He shall stand," as Micah 5:4.[24]

Two Observations Arising from a Brief Exposition of Ezekiel 17:22–23

The setting up, then, of this kingdom of Christ, who is "the highest branch of the high cedar," and planting it in the church, the "mountain of Israel,"

21 Samuel Parker understood Owen to be claiming that "Monarchic Governments being a Jewish Ceremony, a part of their Pedagogy and Bondage, and [was] abolish't by the coming of the *Messiah.*" See Parker, *A Defence and Continuation of the Ecclesiastical Politie* (London, 1671), 115.

22 Heb. 11:40.

23 In the margin: 1 Cor. 10:11; Acts 15:10; Gal. 3:4.—Owen.

24 Owen would return to this text in his sermon one year later in *The Kingdom of Christ, and the Power of the Civil Magistrate* (1652), which is included in this volume.

with the prosperity hereof, and safety of him that shall dwell therein, is the subject of verses 22–23.

This being that, to the consideration whereof, God here calls his people at such a season, I shall name one or two observations from this connection of the words.

God's Special Work of Advancing the Kingdom of Christ

Obs[ervation] 1. *In the midst of all the tumults and embroilments of the nations, that which the Lord takes peculiarly as his own design, into his own management, is the carrying on of the kingdom of the Lord Jesus.* "You are about your work," (says the Lord) "I also am about mine; you have your branches and cedars, I also have one to plant, that shall flourish."

"In the days of these kings shall the God of heaven set up a kingdom that shall never be destroyed" (Dan. 2:44) etc. Were not those kings and kingdoms also of his setting up, that it is said, "in their days" he shall set up one of his own? Yea doubtless, "He changeth the times and the seasons, he setteth up kings, and removeth kings" (Dan. 2:21). He "ruleth in the kingdom of men, and giveth it to whomsoever he will," chap[ter] 4:25. There is not a persecuting Pharaoh, but he raises him up for his own purpose (Ex. 9:16). But yet, in respect of the kingdom of his Son, he speaks of them, as if he had nothing to do with them. "In their days I will do my own work, advance the kingdom of the Lord Christ."

There are great and mighty works in hand in this nation, tyrants are punished, the jaws of oppressors are broken,[25] bloody, revengeful persecutors disappointed, and we hope, governors set up that may be "just, ruling in the fear of the Lord, that they may be as the light of the morning," etc. (2 Sam. 23:3–4).[26] The hand of the Lord has been wonderfully exalted in all these things: but yet should we rest in them, should they not be brought into an immediate subserviency, to the kingdom of the Lord Jesus, the Lord will quickly distinguish between them, and his own peculiar design, and say, "In the days of these changes, I will do so, and so, speak of them, as if he had nothing to do with them." The carrying on of the interest of Christ, is his peculiar aim; he of his goodness make it ours also.

All the Nations Will Be Brought into Christ's Possession

Obs[ervation] 2. *Among all the designs that are on foot in the world, there is none that has either stability, fixedness, or final success, but only the design*

25 Job 29:17.

26 Owen referred to this text in *Of Toleration* (1649) and described how magistrates would only be taught such fear by the word of God. See *Complete Works of John Owen*, 18:384.

of God concerning the kingdom of Christ.[27] Other branches may be set, but the branch of the Lord only prospers: the likeliest appearances of other undertakings, are but as the glorious rising of the sun in the morning, quickly clouded. The interest of Christ is like Joseph (Gen. 49:23–24). Ofttimes the archers shoot at it, and grieve it;[28] but in the close, the bow thereof abides in strength;[29] and therefore this is the issue of all these dispensations, that the kingdoms and nations are at length to be possessed by the Lord Christ;[30] his sheaf standing up, and all others bowing thereunto.[31]

And unto the consideration of these things, in the midst of all the tumults in the world, does God effectually recall his people, and withal tells them how he will carry it on, in the words of my text, "And all the trees," etc.

EXPOSITION OF THE TEXT

In the words three things are to be observed.

1. The work that God ascribes to himself, and that he sets down under a twofold similitude.

(1) Of pulling down the "high tree," and setting up the "low tree";

(2) Of drying up the "green tree," and making the "dry tree" to flourish.

And both these similitudes are coincident, serving only in this redoubling, for the clearer illustration of that, which they shadow out.

2. There is the issue that God will carry this out unto in respect of others: "All the trees of the field shall know."

3. A particular assurance that the Lord gives for the accomplishment of all this, from the engagement of his name: "I the Lord," etc.

The Work That God Is Doing

1. For the first, the expression of the work of the Lord, may be taken two ways: (1) Strictly and properly. (2) Largely, and by the way of analogy and proportion.

In the first way you may consider,

(1) The tree that is to be cast down and withered, and that is the "high tree," and the "green tree": a tree that in their eyes had both beauty and vigor, high

27 In the margin: Hagg. 2:6–7; Heb. 12:26–27; Isa. 8:9–10, Ch. 9:7, Chap. 46:10, Chap. 53:10; Psal. 33:11; Prov. 19:21, Chap. 21:30; Job 23:13.—Owen.

28 Gen. 49:23.

29 Gen. 49:24.

30 In the margin: Isa. 60:12–13; Revel. 11:15.—Owen.

31 See Gen. 37:7.

and green: this was the Judaical kingdom, admired and delighted in by the Jews: "This," says God, "I will reject"; as also he will many a tall Eliab, that even some Samuels may think to be his anointed.[32]

(2) The tree that is to be exalted and made to flourish, and that is the "low tree," the "dry tree," contemptible for growth, it is low, useless for fruit, it is dry. And this is the spiritual kingdom of the Messiah, contemned, despised. "This," says God, "I will exalt, carry on, and make glorious"; for though the interest of Christ and the gospel may seem low, and dry for a season, in comparison of the glory of other flourishing interests, yet in the issue, it shall be exalted above them all.

2. As taken more largely, and by the way of analogy; (1) and so the high and the green tree are the things of the most glorious appearance in the world, persons and states, that seem to be exceedingly suited for the work that God has to do; that are in the greatest probability to be eminently instrumental in his hand: but, "Alas," says God, "These will I pull down and cause to wither. Perhaps you will think it strange, that a mighty monarchy,[33] a triumphing prelacy,[34] a thriving conformity,[35] should all be brought down; but so it shall be, 'Every mountain shall be made a plain.' "[36]

(2) The "low tree," and the "dry tree," are things, persons, assemblies, outwardly, weak and contemptible, such as wise men do verily believe that God will never use; they will not understand that such Moseses shall be deliverers, but cry, "Who made them judges and rulers?"[37] But even these will God exalt and cause to flourish: "Every valley shall be exalted."[38]

Introduction to the Two Main Observations

Two observations flow from hence, which I shall insist upon.

[Observation] 1. *In the carrying on of the interest of Christ and the gospel, God will work wonderful providential alterations.*

32 1 Sam. 16:6. Although Charles II was not anointed at his coronation at Scone (this was considered superstitious), the moderator of the Scottish Kirk made it clear in his sermon that this did not undermine Charles's role as "the anoynted of the Lord." See Robert Douglas, *The Form and Order of the Coronation of Charles the Second, King of Scotland, England, France, and Ireland: As It Was Acted and Done at Schoone, the First Day of January, 1651* (Aberdeen, 1651), 12–13.

33 I.e., the House of Stuart.

34 I.e., the Laudian episcopacy.

35 I.e., the imposition of ecclesiastical conformity.

36 Isa. 40:4.

37 In the margin: Exod. 2:14; Acts 7:25.—Owen. Following Goold, the final Acts reference should be corrected to 7:27.

38 Isa. 40:4.

[Observation] 2. *The actings of God's providence in carrying on the interest of Christ, shall be exceedingly unsuited to the reasonings and expectations of the most of the sons of men.*

Some trees must be plucked down, and some raised up; yea, high trees thrown down, and the low caused to flourish.

The Reason for God's Great Works of Providence

2. There is the issue of God's thus dealing in respect of others, "All the trees of the field," etc. By the "trees of the field" are meant men of all sorts, that are concerned in these transactions; and herein you may observe two things.

(1) Something intimated, and that is, an unwillingness in men to own these dispensations of God; hence the Lord undertakes himself to set on a conviction upon them, as a thing of great difficulty.

(2) Something expressed, which is the conviction itself, that shall in the issue fall upon them, notwithstanding all their reluctancy. Hence also are these two observations.

[Observation] 1. *Men are exceeding unwilling to see and own the hand of God, in those works of his providence, which answer not their reasonings, interests and expectations.*

[Observation] 2. *The Lord will not cease walking contrary to the carnal reasonings of men, in his mighty works for the carrying on the interest of the Lord Jesus, until his hand be seen, owned, and confessed.*

The Assurance That God's Great Work Will Be Accomplished

For what remains concerning the assurance of the accomplishment of all this from the engagement of his name, I shall only add,

[Observation] *That the power and faithfulness of God are engaged in the carrying on the things of the kingdom of Christ, to the conviction of the most stubborn opposers.*

FIRST OBSERVATION: IN CARRYING ON THE INTEREST OF CHRIST AND THE GOSPEL, GOD WILL WORK WONDERFUL PROVIDENTIAL ALTERATIONS

I begin with the first.

1. *In the carrying on the interest of Christ and the gospel, God will work wonderful providential alterations.* Alterations among the trees of the field, nations, states, and men on earth.

When the beginning of the saints' departure from under the dominion of Antichrist, was followed with wars, tumults, and destructions, it was objected to Luther, that that doctrine could not be of God, which was attended with such desolations; he replied, according to the vigor of his spirit, "Did he not see those tumults, he would not believe that Christ was come forth into the world."[39]

The Lord tells you how he will bring on his kingdom (Hag. 2:6–7), "I will shake the heavens, and the earth, and the sea, and the dry land. And I will shake all nations, and the desire of all nations shall come," etc. The "desire of the nations," is to be brought in, by the "shaking of the nations." They are to be civilly moved, that they may be spiritually established. Neither are they only to be shaken, but also to undergo great alterations in their shakings, "This word yet once more signifies the removing of those things that are shaken, as of things that are made, that those things that cannot be shaken may remain" (Heb. 12:27). They must have a removal as well as a shaking; μετάθεσιν, "a change," "a translation." Most nations in their civil constitution lie out of order, for the bringing in of the interest of Christ: they must be shaken up and new disposed of, that all obstacles may be taken away. The day of the gospel is not only terrible in its discovering light, and as it is a trying furnace (Mal. 3:2), but also in its devouring fury, as it is a consuming oven (Mal. 4:1).[40]

The Three Seasons in Which These Providential Alterations Take Place

There are three principal seasons of the Lord's eminent appearance to carry on the kingdom of Christ, and the gospel, and all attended with dreadful providential alterations; and unto one of these heads, may all particular actings be reduced.

The Time of Christ and the Apostles

(1) The first is, the promulgation of the gospel among the Jews, by the Lord Christ himself and his apostles: what this was attended withal, is graphically described, "And ye shall hear of wars, and rumours of wars; for nation shall

39 In the text: *Ego nisi istos tumultus viderem, verbum Dei in mundo non esse dicerem.*—Owen. This is a quotation from Martin Luther, *De servo arbitrio* (*The Bondage of the Will*, 1525). For the Latin text, see *D. Martin Luthers Werke, Kritische Gesamtausgabe*, 127 vols. (Weimar: Hermann Böhlau und Nachfolger, 1883–2009), 18:625–27. The translation is Owen's. For an English translation, see Luther, *The Bondage of the Will: A New Translation of "De servo arbitrio" (1525); Martin Luther's Reply to Erasmus of Rotterdam*, trans. J. I. Packer and O. R. Johnston (Cambridge: James Clarke, 1957), 90–92.

40 This paragraph summarizes the overall thesis of Owen's sermon *The Shaking and Translating of Heaven and Earth* (1649). See *Complete Works of John Owen*, 18:411–62.

rise against nation, and kingdom against kingdom, and there shall be famines, and pestilences, and earthquakes in divers places" (Matt. 24:6–7). And the close of it you have, verse 29, "Immediately after the tribulation of those days, shall the sun be darkened, and the moon shall not give her light, and the stars shall fall from heaven, and the powers of heaven shall be shaken." The Judaical state in all the height and glory of it, was utterly consumed; so that all flesh, all the Jews, were in danger of utter destruction, verse 22. Their own historian himself a Jew, affirming, that from the foundation of the world never was there such destruction and desolation brought upon any nation.[41] Which words of his are a comment on that prediction of our Savior, (Matt. 24:21) and the reason of this eminent desolation you have (Isa. 9:5–6).[42]

The Growth of the Church and the Fall of the Roman Empire

(2) The second is, in the farther carrying on of the gospel, after the destruction of Jerusalem, throughout the world of the Gentiles, subject then in a great proportion to the Roman Empire. And what is the issue hereof? The opening of the six seals, immediately follows thereon, Revelation 6.[43] Which (after manifold and various alterations) end in that dreadful dissolution of the pagan empire, which you have described from verse 14 to the end.[44]

The Reformation and Post-Reformation Era

(3) The most signal is the coming of the Lord Christ, to recover his people from anti-Christian idolatry and oppression; which of all others, is and shall be, attended with the most astonishing alterations and desolations, pulling down of high trees, and exalting them that are low: thence is that war described [in] Revelation 17:14).[45] And that mighty vengeance poured out

41 Josephus wrote in his preface to *The Jewish War* that "The war of the Jews against the Romans—the greatest not only of the wars of our own time, but, so far as accounts have reached us, well nigh of all that ever broke out between cities or nations." Josephus, *The Jewish War*, vol. 1, *Books 1–2*, trans. H. St. J. Thackeray, Loeb Classical Library 203 (Cambridge, MA: Harvard University Press, 1927), 3.

42 In *The Shaking and Translating of Heaven and Earth* (1649), Owen utilized these verses from Isaiah and Matthew in his description of "a civil shaking of civil constitutions."

43 Owen had engaged with Revelation 6 in *A Vision of Unchangeable Free Mercy* (1646), *Ebenezer* (1648), *Sermon Preached* [. . .] *January 31* (1649), *The Shaking and Translating of Heaven and Earth* (1649), and the *Branch of the Lord* (1650). For the first four sermons, see *Complete Works of John Owen*, 18:209, 270, 307, 438–39, 457, 460.

44 Rev. 6:14–17.

45 Owen had engaged with Rev. 17:14 in *Sermon Preached* [. . .] *January 31* (1649), *The Shaking and Translating of Heaven and Earth* (1649), and his June 1649 sermon *Human Power Defeated*. See *Complete Works of John Owen*, 18:330, 436, 440, 460, 474–75.

by the Lord Christ on the nations, their kings and captains, chapter 19:11 to the end; which the Holy Ghost describes by a collection of all the most dreadful expressions which are anywhere used to set out great devastations in the Old Testament.[46]

And this is the head whereunto the present actings of providence in this nation are to be referred, they all tend to the accomplishment of his main design therein. He that thinks Babylon is confined to Rome, and its open idolatry, knows nothing of Babylon, nor of the new Jerusalem: the depth of subtle mystery does not lie in gross visible folly: it has been insinuating itself into all the nations for 1,600 years, and to most of them is now become as the marrow in their bones: before it be wholly shaken out, these "heavens" must be dissolved, and "the earth shaken"; their "tall trees" hewed down, and set a howling (Rev. 18), and the residue of them transplanted from one end of the earth to another.[47]

This I say then is the work that the Lord has now in hand; and this is a day of thankfulness in reference to what he has done for us in this nation. I know no better way of praising God for any work, than the finding out of his design therein, and closing with him in it. God has gone with you (I hope) now to the end of your work, leave him not until he comes to the end of his. He has compelled you "to go with him one mile" for your own good, go with him two for his glory.[48] The two tribes and a half sat not down in their own possessions until the whole work of the Lord was done.[49] I speak not with respect to any engagements of war with foreign nations; what have I to do with things that are above me? You will find work enough for your zeal to the kingdom of Christ at home; and this is the work of thankfulness which you are called unto.

Two Reasons for This Observation

Now, the reasons of this are,

Christ Must Take His Inheritance Out of the Hands of His Enemies

Reas[on] (1) Because among all men, where the kingdom of Christ is to be set up, there is something or other possessed, that he alone must and will

46 Owen had appealed to Rev. 19:11–21 in *Ebenezer* (1648) and *The Shaking and Translating of Heaven and Earth* (1649). See *Complete Works of John Owen*, 18:271, 438–39.

47 See Owen's treatment of this in *The Shaking and Translating of Heaven and Earth* (1649), in *Complete Works of John Owen*, 18:437–38, 445. Samuel Parker understood that by speaking of "tall trees," Owen was referring to "kings and princes." See *Defence and Continuation*, 60.

48 Matt. 5:41.

49 This is a reference to the Reubenites, Gadites, and the half tribe of Manasseh.

have: and therefore the Lord, giving Jesus Christ but his own inheritance, it must needs be attended with great alterations. I dare say, until of late (whatever now is) there was not any state or nation in the world, where the name of Christ is known, but that there was an entrenchment upon that which is the pure portion and inheritance of the Lord Christ, and that detained with falsehood and force. Yea such is the folly and blindness of the most of men, that they think their greatest interest lies, in holding that fast, which Christ will take from them: Pharaoh-like, that thought it the great advantage of his kingdom, not to let the people go, when it proved the ruin of him and his land.[50] This I dare say will in the issue be the ruin of all, or most of the tall trees of Europe; they have grasped much of the power of Christ, and endeavor to impose on the consciences of his in the worship of God, or otherwise oppress them in what he has purchased for them; and, by a dreadful mistake, they suppose their own interest lies therein, which makes them hold fast, until Christ has shaken them all to pieces, and taken away even that also which was their own. The late king[51] had learned a saying from his predecessor, "No bishop, no king":[52] hence he supposes his main interest to lie in holding fast prelacy;[53] whatever he seems to part withal, that he will not let go, that's his main interest: and what is this prelacy, a mere anti-Christian encroachment upon the inheritance of Christ.[54] Christ coming to take his own, shakes the other to pieces; those who would have been our oppressors in Scotland, but that God has crushed the cockatrice[55] in the shell, and filled the pit with their dead bodies which they had digged for us, they also had prepared a Procrustes' bed,[56] a heavy yoke, a beast that had it grown to perfection, would have had horns and hoofs,[57] and in maintaining this, they think their great interest to lie.

50 Ex. 11:10.

51 In the original, "king" is set in all caps for emphasis.

52 An aphorism said to have been used by King James at the Hampton Court Conference (1604) by which the king emphasized his commitment to episcopacy. See Charles Howard McIlwain, *The Political Works of James I* (Union, NJ: Lawbook Exchange, 2002), xc. Charles II had seemingly abandoned his father's commitment to the episcopal church by swearing to uphold the Covenant.

53 I.e., the system of episcopal church government, often used pejoratively to refer to the eminence and authority conferred on bishops.

54 This sentence was provocative enough for Roger L'Estrange to include it in his *The Dissenters Saying* [. . .] (London, 1681), 25.

55 I.e., a mythical dragon hatched by a serpent. See Isa. 14:29. Others had employed this description. For example, a pamphlet argued that Presbyterians and the other sons of the antichrist were hatched from "eggs of the same Cockatrice." See *Shrill Cry in the Eares of Cavaliers, Apostates, and Presbyters* [. . .] (London, [February] 1649), 12.

56 I.e., figurative of enforcing conformity without regard to legitimate variation.

57 Dan. 7:19.

And in holding this fast, are they after all their associations broken in pieces, and this is one cause:

The Nature of This Work Involves Vengeance, Deliverance, and Trial

Reas[on] (2) The works that God has to do in such a season, require it: God has three great works to do, in the day of his carrying on the interest of Christ and the gospel:

[1] He has great revenges to take.
[2] He has great deliverances to work.
[3] He has great discoveries to make. I shall but touch on each.

[1] He has great revenges to take: and that on three sorts of persons:

{1} On oppressing Babylonians; false worshipers and persecutors: while the bride is preparing for the Lord Christ, he goes forth with the armies of heaven following him to take vengeance on these his enemies (Rev. 19:11).[58] These are the Absaloms, the usurpers of his throne, the Hamans,[59] the forcers of his spouse, the chiefest adversaries of his kingdom: "He shall fill the places with dead bodies" of these, and upon this account "wound the heads over many countries" (Ps. 110:6).[60] The axe is laid to the root of many a tall tree on this score,[61] even in this nation where he is reckoning for blood, and imposition of yokes; and he has found out men, inheriting this spirit from one generation to another.

{2} Scoffing Edomites: there is a twofold quarrel that God has with that generation of men.

1st. Their rejoicing at Zion's distress, and desiring its increase (Ps. 137:7).

2nd. Their endeavor to destroy the residue, when at any time straitened (Obad. 14). How many in the late trial, rejoiced in the straits of Zion? That sat expecting our destruction, that they might have risen to "stand in the cross ways to have cut off them that escaped,"[62] wherewith should they have reconciled themselves to their master, but with the heads of the servants of Christ? God has vengeance in such a day as this for Edom also.

58 In the margin: Isai 43:14; Jerem. 25:12; Chap. 51:35; Rev. 16:19.—Owen. Owen had linked the final two references in *Ebenezer* (1648). See *Complete Works of John Owen*, 18:267.

59 In *Ebenezer* (1648), Owen had spoken of how with "open opposers" and "secret apostates" the story of Haman "must be acted over again." See *Complete Works of John Owen*, 18:266.

60 Owen would return to Ps. 110:6 and Rev. 19:11 in *The Kingdom of Christ, and the Power of the Civil Magistrate* (1652), which is included in this volume.

61 Matt. 3:10.

62 Obad. 14.

{3} Lukewarm Laodiceans,[63] neutralists, that "drink wine in bowls," and are no way moved at the "suffering of Joseph"?[64] Gallios that "care for none of these things."[65] There is not a generation in the world with whom the Lord is more provoked than with this Meroz generation:[66] when God is jealous for Zion, he is "displeased with them that are at ease" (Zech. 1:14–15). Now consider how many persons of all these sorts are fixed in the nation, and you will see that vengeance cannot be taken on them, without great alterations.

[2] He has deliverances to work: it is the time of "visiting the prisoners of hope":[67] the prey must be taken out of the jaws of the terrible:[68] every "staff of the oppressor broken in pieces":[69] yea he delivers his saints, not only from all that they have suffered, but from all that was in the contrivance of their enemies to bring upon them, which is greater than they can execute: and this will cost something before the Pharaohs of the nation, will let his people go.

[3] He has great trials to make.

{1} Of his own that they may be purged.

{2} Of hypocrites, that they may be discovered.

{1} The day of carrying on the interest of Christ, is a day of purifying and purging, "Many shall be purified and made white and tried" (Dan. 12:10), that is a day like "a furnace" (Mal. 3:3),[70] that will consume dross and tin.[71] The remainder of the people must be brought through the fire (Zech. 13:9). Joshua's garments are defiled by dwelling in Babylon:[72] many of Christ's own, have contracted rust and soil, have got carnal interests and engagements that must be scoured from them.

{2} Of the discovery of hypocrites: it is emphatically said of the saints, that they "follow the Lamb whether ever he goes."[73] All sorts of professors will follow him in some paths, in such as are consistent with their power, dominion, and advantages, they are even ready to run before him: but he has some paths

63 Rev. 3:16.
64 Amos 6:6.
65 Acts 18:17.
66 Judg. 5:23.
67 Zech. 9:12.
68 Isa. 49:24.
69 Isa. 9:4.
70 The reference should probably be expanded to Mal. 3:2–3.
71 Ezek. 22:18–20.
72 In the margin: Zach. 3:3.—Owen. I.e., Zech 3:3.
73 In the margin: Revel. 14:4.—Owen.

that are unpleasing to flesh and blood, paths that he gives no loaves in;[74] here men that say they are "Jews and are not, but lie,"[75] give quite out from him. Now upon all these several accounts, must that day of the gospel of necessity be attended with great providential alteration.

Two Applications Arising

In the British Civil Wars, God Has Been Bringing Down Oppressors and Raising Up the Saints

Us[e] 1. To discover where dwells that spirit that actuates all the great alterations that have been in these nations. Such things have been brought to pass as have filled the world with amazement. A monarchy of some hundred years' continuance,[76] always affecting and at length wholly degenerated into tyranny, destroyed, pulled down, swallowed up, a great and mighty potentate, that had caused "terror in the land of the living," and "laid his sword under his head,"[77] brought to punishment for blood,[78] hypocrites and selfish men abundantly discovered, wise men made fools, and the strong as water;[79] a nation (that of Scotland) engaging for and against the same cause, backward and forward twice or thrice,[80] always seeking where to find their own gain and interest in it, at length totally broken in opposition to that cause wherewith at first they closed: multitudes of professors, one year praying, fasting, mightily rejoicing upon the least success, bearing it out as a sign of the presence of God; another year while the same work is carried on, cursing, repining, slighting the marvelous appearance of God in answer unto prayers and most solemn appeals, being very angry at the deliverances of Zion: on the other side, all the mighty successes that God has followed poor despised ones withal, being with them as with those in days of old. "Who through faith subdued kingdoms, wrought righteousness, obtained promises, stopped the mouths of lions, quenched the violence of fire, escaped the edge of the sword, out of weakness were made strong, waxed valiant in fight, turned to flight the

74 In the margin: John 6:26.—Owen.

75 Rev. 2:9; 3:9.

76 The House of Stuart. James Stuart was king of Scotland from 1567 and also King of England and Ireland from 1603.

77 Ezek. 32:26–27. Roger L'Estrange included this sentence in his section of what dissenters had said to encourage and justify the regicide. See his *Dissenters Saying*, 44.

78 The trial and execution of Charles I.

79 Ezek. 7:17.

80 The Scots fought against Charles I in the Bishops' Wars (1639–1640), formed an alliance with the English Parliament in the first Civil War (1644–1646), and then allied with the English royalists (1647–1651).

armies of the aliens" (Heb. 11:33). He I say that shall consider all this, may well inquire after that principle which, being regularly carried on, yet meeting with the corruption and lusts of men, should so wheel them about, and work so many mighty alterations: now what is this, but the most effectual design of the Lord, to carry on the interest of Christ and the gospel, whatever stands in the way? This bears down all before it, wraps up some in blood, some in hardness, and is most eminently straight and holy in all these transactions. "What shall one then answer the messengers of the nation? That the Lord hath founded Zion, and the poor of his people shall trust in it" (Isa. 14:32).[81]

Reasons to Rejoice in These Providential Alterations

Us[e] 2. To magnify the goodness of God, who unto us has sweetened and seasoned all his dreadful dispensations, and all the alterations in those nations, with this his gracious design running through them all: this is that which puts all their beauty and luster on them, being outwardly dreadful and horrible. The carrying on of this (which is hidden from the men of the world, who have therefore no joy) is the only thing we have to rejoice at in this day, our victories have no glory, but what they receive from hence (Isa. 4:2).[82] That blood which is an acceptable sacrifice to the Lord, is the blood of the enemies of this design of his: the vengeance that is to be delighted in, is "the vengeance of the temple":[83] heaven and all that is in it, is called to rejoice, when Babylon "is destroyed with violence and fury" (Rev. 18:20–21), when those who would not have the King of saints reign, are brought forth and slain before his face: and in this God makes distinguishing work, and calls to rejoicing:

> Therefore thus saith the Lord God, my servants shall eat, but ye shall be hungry, my servants shall drink, but ye shall be thirsty: behold my servants shall rejoice but ye shall be ashamed: behold my servants shall sing for joy of heart, but ye shall cry for sorrow of heart and shall howl for vexation of spirit. (Isa. 65:13–14)[84]

Thus the saints are called to sing "the song of Moses the servant of God, and the song of the Lamb" (Rev. 15:3). The deliverance by Moses was a temporal deliverance from outward yokes and bondage: the deliverance of

81 This would be Owen's text for his sermon at the opening of the second Protectorate Parliament published as *God's Work in Founding Zion* (1656), which is included in this volume.

82 This verse provided the title for the published sermon, *The Branch of the Lord* (1650).

83 Jer. 50:28.

84 Owen had quoted this text in *Ebenezer* (1648). See *Complete Works of John Owen*, 18:264.

the Lamb, was a spiritual deliverance, from spiritual bondage: the deliverance that God will give his saints from this oppression shall be mixed; as their bondage partakes of both, so shall their deliverance be: and therefore they shall "sing the song of Moses and the Lamb": if ever any persons in the world had cause to sing "the song of Moses and the Lamb," we have this day, the bondage prepared for us was both in spirituals and temporals: about a tyrant full of revenge,[85] and a discipline full of persecution,[86] has been our contest: whether the yoke of the one and the other, should by the sword and violence be put upon our necks, and consciences, is our controversy: there was both Aegypt and Babel in the bondage prepared: and both these enraged: Pharaoh doubled the task of the Israelites when they did speak of liberty.[87] What would he have done had he recovered them under his hand after they were escaped? What would the thoughts of that man of blood have been, and his ways, had he prevailed, after so many provocations? *Caede ac sanguine,*[88] *quisquis ab exilio.*[89] And what would their ways have been, who thought to sit on his right hand and his left in his kingdom:[90] but of this afterward; now God having broken both the one snare and the other, surely we have cause to sing "the song of Moses and of the Lamb" this day: when others are in the condition mentioned [in] Isaiah 8:21–22.

It is true, all things are not clear to all perhaps, that serve the Lord: some cannot rejoice in the works of our God, but they are not the first on whom that sin has been charged: nothing more frequent in the Scripture,[91] than the laying this sin at the door of professors, that "they set not their hearts to the work of the Lord":[92] if they are of the armies in heaven, they will at length

85 A reference to King Charles II.

86 A reference to Presbyterian polity.

87 Ex. 5:7.

88 Lat. "slaughter and carnage." This is a reference to Juvenal, *Satires* 10.112, which states that few kings go down to the underworld without slaughter and blood. For the text and English translation, see Juvenal, *Satires*, in Juvenal, Persius, *Juvenal and Persius*, ed. and trans. Susanna Morton Braund, Loeb Classical Library 91 (Cambridge, MA: Harvard University Press, 2004), 374–75.

89 Lat. "he has come out of exile." This is a reference to Suetonius' *Life of Tiberius* 59.2. It describes one who "always reigned with great bloodshed," who came "to kingship out of exile," and who retired from government to indulge in sexual vice and excess. For the Latin text and English translation, see Suetonius, *Lives of the Caesars*, vol. 1, *Julius. Augustus. Tiberius. Gaius Caligula*, trans. J. C. Rolfe, Loeb Classical Library 31 (Cambridge, MA: Harvard University Press, 1914), 392–93. Marchamont Nedham had utilized this "old Saying" about revengeful kings in his *The Case of the Common-Wealth of England Stated* (London, 1650), 44.

90 Matt. 20:21.

91 In the margin: Isai 43:18; Psal. 48:42–44.—Owen. Following Goold, the final reference should be corrected to Ps. 78:42–44.

92 Ps. 78:8.

learn to follow the Lamb:[93] and for the present, music with some discords, may make melody for the Lord: the song of Deborah is full of complaint: divisions of Reuben: Gilead, Dan, and Asher, slow in their helps: Meroz wholly neutral:[94] though we have of all these sorts, yet may we make a song to the Lord, that in Jesus Christ may be acceptable this day.

And the Lord I hope will open the eyes of them, among us, and give them to cry for mercy when his righteous judgments have driven them from all their holds. When the mighty army was destroyed in the north about three years ago,[95] many would see nothing in it, but that they had not the blessing of the church.[96] Hence they began to think of it as Balak did of Balaam, "whom he blessed they were blessed, and whom he cursed they were cursed."[97] God could not bear the robbing him of his glory, and giving it unto selfish men: they shall bless and bless again, and be no more heard than the Baalists' cry: even to the Lord shall they cry but he will not regard them:[98] the Lord I say will drive them from such holds as these, that they may acknowledge his hand: let then the great work of the Lord be owned, be rejoiced in, for it will certainly bear down all that stand in the way of it. Neither is there the least true consolation in any of these alterations, but what arises from a closing with it.

SECOND OBSERVATION: THESE PROVIDENTIAL ALTERATIONS DO NOT CONFORM TO THE THOUGHTS AND EXPECTATIONS OF MANY

Come we to the second observation.

Ob[servation] 2. *The actings of God's providence in carrying on the interest of Christ, are and shall be exceedingly unsuited to the reasonings and expectations of the most of men.*

He has a glorious work here to be accomplished: of whom should he now make use? Surely the "high tree," the "green tree" will be employed? If one

93 Rev. 14:4.

94 In the margin: Judges 5:15, 17, 23.—Owen.

95 The Battle of Preston in Lancashire (August 1648) saw the Scottish Engager army defeated.

96 After Preston, the Kirk Party regime came to power in Scotland and, confident in God's blessing, its ministers urged David Leslie to engage Cromwell at Dunbar against his better judgment. Spurlock describes how the Covenanter Army "marched out with the ministers in the fore like a righteous shield or a righteous guarantee of victory." See R. Scott Spurlock, *Cromwell and Scotland: Conquest and Religion, 1650–1660* (Edinburgh: John Donald, 2007), 34.

97 In the margin: Numb. 22:6.—Owen.

98 In the margin: 1 King. 18:26.—Owen.

be to be anointed in the family of Jesse, will it not be goodly Eliab?[99] If the king will honor any, who should it be but I, says Haman?[100] But all on the contrary, the low, dry tree is taken, David from the flock,[101] and Mordecai from the gate.[102] The thoughts of God are "not as our thoughts,"[103] neither does he look on "outward appearances."[104]

Examples of This Principle

To give some instances in his most signal actings in this kind.

Examples from Biblical History

The Jews knew that God had a great work to do in giving of a Messiah the Savior of the world: they are raised up to expectation of it: upon every considerable appearance, they cry, "Is this he?"[105] And what withal did they expect? Outward glory, beauty, deliverance, carnal power and dominion. God at length comes to do his work, and brings forth a poor man, that had not where to lay his head,[106] followed by a few fishermen and simple women, that had "neither form nor comeliness that he should be desired," persecuted, despised, crucified, from the beginning to the end, quite another thing than what they looked for.[107] Thus lays he the foundation of the gospel, in the person of his Son, by frustrating the expectations of the most of men: "The stone which the builders refused," etc.[108]

Again seeing salvation is of the Jews, "the rod of Christ's strength being to be sent out of Zion," and that "living waters" were to flow forth from Jerusalem;[109] the gospel being from thence to be published through the world, whom should the Lord choose to do it? Surely the great, the wise, the learned of that nation; the high priests, learned scribes, devout Pharisees, that might have won their message some repute and credit in the world. But contrary to all the wisdom of the flesh, he takes a few ignorant, weak, unlearned fishermen, despised upon all accounts, and commits this great work unto them:

99 1 Sam. 16:6.

100 Esth. 6:6.

101 1 Sam. 16:11.

102 Esth. 6:10.

103 Isa. 55:8.

104 1 Sam. 16:7.

105 In the margin: Luk 3:15; Joh. 1:19–20.—Owen.

106 Matt. 8:20.

107 In the margin: Acts 1:6; Mat. 20:21–22, Mat. 13:55, Ch 8:20; Joh. 4:28, 29; Isai 53:2–3; Phil. 2:7–8, etc.—Owen.

108 Ps. 118:22. A text Owen had referred to in *The Branch of the Lord* (1650), which is included in this volume.

109 In the margin: Joh. 4:22; Psal. 110:2; Ezek. 47:1; Zech. 14:8: Acts 4:13; 1 Cor. 1:20, 26–28.—Owen.

and accordingly out they go friendless, helpless, harborless, unto their great employment: the like instruments for the most part, did he employ to make an entrance upon the great work of casting down false worship and idolatry.

Moreover in that great work for the Lord Christ, which is to be accomplished in the ruin and destruction of Babel, when it must be done with might, power and strength, with armies and blood, will not now the Lord use the "high and green tree?" Many kings and potentates having in profession embraced the doctrine of the gospel; nobles and great ones having given up their names in appearance unto Christ, who but they, shall now be used in this work of the Lord? But yet plainly the Lord tells them the contrary (Rev. 18:9)—all these persons bewail the judgments of God that are executed on Babel, which shall be done by low, dry trees.

An Example from Recent History

To give one instance in the mighty works which God has lately wrought in these nations, a work of reformation and carrying on the interest of Christ is here undertaken: what upon this are the thoughts of the most of men? Whither were their eyes turned? Tall trees, green trees are pitched on. This and that great lord, popular with the multitude, Eliabs in their eyes,[110] they must do it; the Scots shall certainly effect it:[111] the king shall be taken from his evil counsel,[112] he shall be active in it. A church government shall be set up, and no man suffered to live in the nation that will not submit unto it.[113] Some, like the sons of Zebedee, shall sit on the right and left hand of Christ, in the kingdom they were setting up for him;[114] these, and those, sound good men, shall be next the king,[115] then all will be great and glorious indeed. What now,

110 1 Sam. 16:6.

111 Charles was proclaimed king on February 5, 1649, at the Mercat Cross of Edinburgh, and in the Treaty of Breda of May 1650 he agreed to the rigid terms set down by the Covenanters.

112 The Kirk Party in Scotland intended that the king's "malignant" advisors be removed from the royal court—e.g., John Maitland, Duke of Lauderdale, was separated from the king until after the defeat at Dunbar. See David Stevenson, *Revolution and Counter-Revolution, 1644–1651* (Edinburgh: John Donald, 2003), 171.

113 The imposition of Presbyterian church government in England.

114 Matt. 20:21. Owen may be thinking of someone like Archibald Campbell, the Marquess of Argyll. In the wake of the defeat at Dunbar, Charles had maintained the support of Argyll by the promise of a dukedom if he was restored to his throne, and it was Argyll who had placed the crown on Charles at his coronation at Scone in January 1651. See John Willcock, *The Great Marquess: Life and Times of Archibald, 8th Earl, and 1st (and only) Marquess of Argyll (1607–1661)* (Edinburgh: Oliphant, 1903), 253; Ronald Hutton, *Charles the Second: King of England, Scotland and Ireland* (Oxford: Clarendon, 1989), 59.

115 According to the Treaty of Breda (1650), all members of the royal court were to be Presbyterian.

I pray? Do all things indeed suit and answer these expectations and reasonings of men? Does God accomplish the thoughts of their hearts? Alas the high trees rested on, proved for the most part, "broken reeds, that ran into our hands,"[116] and let out our blood in abundance to no purpose; the top bough, hoped for, fallen as an abominable branch; the Scots shaken and broken with unparalleled destruction, in the maintenance of the interest and cause, which at first they prosperously opposed;[117] the iron yoke,[118] pretended to be that of Christ (though it be fleshly carnal and cruel, suited to the wisdom of a man, and his rule be spiritual meek and gentle), cast off and thrown away: low trees, dry trees, despised ones, contemned ones, without form or comeliness, exalted, used, employed, and the hand of the Lord evidently lifted up, in all these transactions.

Three Reasons for This Observation

Some reasons of this may be given, and the first is taken,

The Corrupt Heart Given Over to Judgment

1. From the corruptions of the hearts of men, squaring the works of God to their fleshly reasonings, corrupt interests and principles: they are bold with the wisdom of God, and conclude thus, and thus things ought to be, ordering their thoughts for the most part, according to their corrupt and carnal advantages: I shall instance both as to carnal advantages and principles.

(1) Carnal power and glory seem excellent to the Jews: hence think they, "When God gives us our Messiah, all this must be accomplished": their affections are disordered by corrupt lusts and desires, and that enslaves their minds to strange apprehensions: God comes in his own way, and how cross do things run to their expectations? What was the corrupt design of many in Scotland? That they might set up a son of Tabeal in England,[119] and themselves be great under him; that they and their partakers, might impose on the residue of the nation, especially in the things of God: their great desire that things should be thus, corrupts their minds to think, that it ought to be so, and shall be so: hence, ambition to rule and to have all under their power, even in conscience,

116 2 Kings 18:21.

117 The Scottish Covenanters had initially opposed the royalist cause.

118 This is another reference to the establishment of Presbyterian church government. John Goodwin also regarded the Scottish clergy as seeking to impose an iron yoke. See Goodwin's *Two Hymnas, or Spiritual Songs* (London, 1651), 10–11. Milton had also spoken of the "iron yoke of outward conformity" in *Areopagitica* (London, 1644), in *Complete Prose Works of John Milton*, vol. 2, ed. Ernest Sirluck (New Haven, CT: Yale University Press, 1959), 563–64.

119 Isa. 7:6. Samuel Parker discussed Owen's use of this title to describe "one who would have usurpt the Crown without Right or Title." See Parker, *Defence and Continuation*, 114–15.

is quickly mistaken for zeal to the kingdom of Christ, reenthroning of tyranny, is loyalty, and all according to covenant.[120] As if men had sworn to be good to themselves, and to be true to their own interests all their days, which surely few need to be sworn to. Thus men's minds and judgments are distempered[121] by their lusts and interests, which makes them frame a way for God to proceed in, which when he does not, how are they surprised.

(2) For principles; men take up principles that they will adhere unto: wise principles forsooth, yea and very righteous too: all things whatever that fall out, must be squared unto their principles; they expect that nothing must be done, but what suits unto them; and if anything contrary be wrought, even of God himself, how deceived, how disappointed are they?[122]

The most tremendous judgment of God in this world, is the hardening of the hearts of men; this seals them up for the most part to destruction: a thing it is often mentioned in the Scripture, and many subtle disputes there are, how it should come forth from him, who is most holy, seeing it is the greatest sin of the creature? I shall give you my thoughts in a most eminent instance or two, as to one particular of it.

(1) Look on Pharaoh, of whom it is most signally spoken, that God "hardened his heart": how did the Lord accomplish this? Pharaoh settles himself upon as righteous principles as ever any of the sons of men could do: one is, "That it belongs to the chief ruler of a nation to see to the profit and glory of the nation." What more righteous principle is there in the world? You that talk of your principles, give me one more righteous than this: hence he concludes, that if it be incumbent on him to see that the realm receive no detriment, he must not let the people go by whom they received so many great advantages: God confirms his heart in these principles, which are good in themselves, but abominable when taken up against the mind and providence of God:[123] Hence he and his, perished in their principles, acting against the appearance of God.

(2) It is also said of Sihon the king of the Amorites, that "his heart was hardened that he would not let the people go through his land."[124] How I pray? Even by adhering to that wise principle, "That it is not meet to let a potent enemy into the bowels of a people." And this made way for his ruin.

120 The Solemn League and Covenant (1643).

121 I.e., disordered.

122 Owen here concludes his examination of (1) carnal advantages and (2) principles. The following paragraph begins a new thought.

123 Parker judged this to be another particularly provocative point in the sermon. See *Defence and Continuation*, 115.

124 Deut. 2:30.

Thus is it with many; they fix on principles, good in general, and in their season. Old bounds must not be broken up; order must not be disturbed: let God appear never so eminently, so mightily, they will keep to their principle, what is this, but judicial hardness? And this, (I say) is one reason why the actings of God in such a day as this, are so unsuited to the expectations of men; they square his works, to the interests and principles, which it will not answer.

The Glory of God

2. God chooses thus to do things above and besides the expectations of men, that his presence, and the presence of the Lord Christ, may be the more conspicuous in the world. Did the Lord always walk in paths that men had rationally, that is, foolishly (for such is our wisdom in the ways of God) allotted to him, the appearances of his glory would be exceedingly eclipsed. It is hard for men to have a clear and naked view of the power of God in effecting anything, when there is great help of means to do it:[125] but it is much harder, to discern the wisdom of God in an affair, when men's own wisdom and designing is all accomplished. But now, when the way of God is "like the way of an eagle in the air";[126] when "his paths are in the deep, and his footsteps are not known":[127] then is he glorious in his goings. Men think all things would be very glorious, if they might be done according to their mind; perhaps indeed they would, but with their glory, not the glory of God.

Judicial Hardening

3. God will do it for the hardening of many false, empty professors, and others in the world, that the judgments appointed may come upon them to the uttermost.[128] The hardening of men to their destruction, being a close and inward work, is one of the most eminent acts of the providence of God, in governing the world: by this, he accomplishes most of the judgments that he has threatened. Now there is not any dispensation of God toward man, but he can, and does sometimes cause it to be so managed, and ordered, that it shall be a way and means of hardening such as he has appointed thereunto: some are hardened by the word, some by mercies, some by judgments. Among other ways that he uses for this purpose, this is

125 In the margin: Jud. 7:4.—Owen.

126 Prov. 30:19.

127 Ps. 77:19.

128 In the marginal note: Rom. 9:18; Deut. 2:30; Ps. 81:12 & 69:22; Josh. 11:20; Isa. 6:9–12; Joh. 12:4–43; Deut. 32:15.—Owen.

one, the disposal of the works of his providence contrary to the reasonings of men, doing things unlikely and unfitly in the eyes of flesh and blood, that so they may despise those ways of his, and be broken in opposition unto them. Take an instance in Pharaoh's last hardening for destruction: When he brought the people out of Aegypt, he did not lead them the direct way to Canaan, but carries them into the wilderness, and shuts them up between the mountains and the sea: Pharaoh justly concludes, that they are entangled beyond escape, and that he shall surely overtake them and destroy them; this draws him out to his ruin: had God led them in the straight path, probably he had not pursued after them, but the Lord lays this as a plot for his destruction.[129] God will harden Jeroboam, and therefore a lion shall slay the prophet, that preached against his idolatry.[130] So was it with the Jews, they expect all glory to attend the coming of the Messiah; and after the coming of him indeed, God follows them with judgments to a total desolation; which being so unsuited unto the dispensation they expected, hardness thereby is come upon them to the uttermost. Tertullian says, he dares say, that the Scriptures were on purpose framed in many things, to give occasion to proud and curious unhumbled wits to stumble and fall.[131] And I dare say, that the Lord does order many of his works in the world, in "ways past finding out,"[132] on purpose to give occasion to many to stumble and fall. God fulfills many mighty works, that could not otherwise be brought about, by hardening the hearts of men. The hardening of the late king's heart was an engine whereby he wrought mighty things and alterations:[133] had not God laid obdurateness[134] and stubbornness upon his spirit, we had long since in all probability been ruined.[135] To accomplish this end then, God will so order the works of his providence, that men shall reason themselves into

129 Ex. 14:4.

130 1 Kings 13:26.

131 E.g., in *De praescriptione haereticorum* (The prescription against heretics) 14, Tertullian writes about how restless curiosity is one way of falling into heresy. For the English text, see Tertullian, *Against all Heresies*, in *Ante-Nicene Fathers: The Writings of the Fathers Down to A.D. 325*, 10 vols., ed. Alexander Roberts and James Donaldson (1886; repr., Peabody, MA: Hendrickson, 1995), 3:249–50.

132 Rom. 11:33.

133 In the original, "king's" is set in all caps for emphasis. This is a reference to king Charles I and the events of the British Civil Wars.

134 I.e., stubborn persistence in wrongdoing.

135 Samuel Parker understood Owen to be arguing that the king's heart had been hardened in order "to carry on the Mighty Work of a Thorough Reformation; and of laying stubbornness and obdurateness upon his Spirit, to preserve us from ruine and final destruction." See Parker, *Defence and Continuation*, 115.

unreasonable and brutish hardness and stupidity. Thus God has done, in the days wherein we live; his mighty acts that he has wrought, both for the *matter* of the things done, and the *manner* of their doing, have been so contrary to men's principles, interest, expectations and reasons, that they have slighted them to such a degree of hardening, that they seem to have no reason left at all; and when it comes to that, God will fall judicially upon the very faculties of their souls; he will blind their eyes, deprive them of their judgment and insight into things, that they shall be as incapable of God's mind as fools; and "give them up to vile affections,"[136] to do the things that are not seemly,[137] as it has fallen out with too many among us. Let us now make some use of this point. It serves then,

One Application Arising: It Is a Foolish Provocation to Reject the Work of God

[Use] 1. To discover the vanity of those men, who because the works of God have not been carried on in ways suitable to their reasonings and expectations, do utterly reject them, disown them, and oppose him in them. Can these men give any one instance, of any one eminent work of God, that he has brought about by such ways, and means, as men would rationally allot thereunto? Especially in things that are in immediate subserviency to the kingdom of the Lord Christ? Can they instance, that they have been so managed? Nay has not this been a means to harden multitudes to their destruction, that have limited the Holy One, and chalked out paths for him to walk in? I cannot but fear, that it was a great provocation of the eyes of God's glory, that at the beginning, and in the carrying on of the great alterations that have been wrought by his providence among us, we did speak of confirming and continuing under any condition whatsoever, any things or persons, which it was in his design to evert: we must be promising to keep up the high tree, and to keep down the low tree, which was not at all in his thoughts, neither ever came it into his heart. I hope he has taught us (though with thorns)[138] to follow him sometimes, like Abraham, "not knowing whither we go."[139] Now the Lord convince them who are yet under this darkness; that think the ways of God not equal,[140] because not measured by their line; that bring their crooked rules unto that which is really straight,

136 Rom. 1:26.
137 Rom. 1:28.
138 See Judg. 8:16.
139 Heb. 11:8.
140 Ezek. 18:25, 29; 33:20.

and cast it away, as abominable. The children of Israel had got a proverb against the ways of God; it was so taken for granted that the ways of his providence were not right and straight, that it was grown into a common byword:[141] a little discovery of the pride and hypocrisy of their own hearts undeceived them at last.

I shall not say to our brethren, that they have showed this day, that if Absalom had lived, and all we had been slain, it would have been well-pleasing to them:[142] but this I shall say, that it is a sad sign, that our ways please not God, when his ways please not us at all.

There being not space for handling the two remaining propositions,[143] I shall go forth to one general use, and so conclude.

GENERAL CONCLUSION: PREPARE TO MEET GOD

[Use 2.] Now this I shall take from that of the prophet Amos (4:12). The generality of the people being exercised with various judgments, the residue of them are said to be saved "as a firebrand out of the burning";[144] that is, powerfully, effectually, from a very terrible, and a very near destruction. After all the Lord's great dispensation of providence, in carrying on his own design, this being the condition of the people of this nation, many being destroyed by foregoing judgments, and the residue now saved like a firebrand out of the burning, God having given us this issue of his mighty works, in pulling down the high tree, and exalting the low tree, it cannot but be our wisdom to close with the counsel which God gives in such a condition; and that you have, I say, "Because I will do this unto thee, prepare to meet thy God, O Israel" (Amos 4:12). Seeing that all this is done, prepare to meet your God, O England; prepare to meet your God, O Parliament: prepare to meet your God, O army: to lead you a little toward the performance of this duty, it being that, and that alone, which is incumbent on you, I shall show you these two things.

1. What it is wherein we are to meet our God.
2. How we must meet him therein.

141 In the margin: Ezek. 18:2.—Owen.

142 2 Sam. 19:6.

143 The other two observations were to be: "First, Men are exceeding unwilling to see and own the hand of God, in those works of his providence, which answer not their reasonings, interests and expectations. Second. The Lord will not cease walking contrary to the carnal reasonings of men, in his mighty works for the carrying on the interest of the Lord Jesus, until his hand be seen, owned, and confessed."

144 Amos 4:11.

A Summary of What It Means to Prepare to Meet the Lord

1. For the first, there are three ways wherein we must meet the Lord, if we desire to answer his mind in any of these dispensations.

(1) In the way of his providence.
(2) In the way of his worship.
(3) In the way of his holiness.

(1) First, the eminent ways of the providence of God in these days, may be referred unto three heads:

[1] His general design, to pull down all those high oppositions to the kingdom of his Son, which I have mentioned.

[2] His peculiar aim, to stain the glory of all flesh,[145] to pull down high trees, that no flesh may glory.[146]

[3] His shaking of all endearments and enjoyments here below, that the hearts of his may be fixed only on the things that cannot be shaken.[147]

And these upon all accounts and considerations whatever, appear to be the main tendencies of the actings of providence in these our days.

(2) Secondly, there is the way of his worship, wherein also he will be met: it is most remote from my thoughts to enter into contests concerning that peculiar way of gospel worship which Christ has appointed. It suffices me, that seeing God has promised that in these days he will have his "tabernacle with men,"[148] and that barrenness and drought shall be on every soul "that comes not up to his feast of tabernacles,"[149] it is bottom sufficient to press men to meet him in that way, according as he shall graciously make out light unto them.

(3) There is the way of his holiness; as he is holy, so are all his ways holy, so he will be met and walked with, in all ways of holiness and obedience to Jesus Christ; and these are the ways wherein God will be met by his remnant, his delivered remnant.

2. What then is it to meet the Lord in any of these ways? What is it to meet him in the way of his providence, his worship, his holiness? To meet one in

145 Isa. 23:9.

146 1 Cor. 1:29.

147 Heb. 12:27.

148 Rev. 21:3. Owen had cited this text in *The Shaking and Translating of Heaven and Earth* (1649). See *Complete Works of John Owen*, 18:432.

149 Zech. 14:16–19. Owen also had cited this text in *The Shaking and Translating of Heaven and Earth* (1649) as a promise of God dwelling with his church by his ordinances. See *Complete Works of John Owen*, 18:440.

anything, is to close with him in that thing: we say, "Herein I meet you, when we are of one mind." To meet the Lord in these things, is to close with the will and mind of God in them; this is that which I would exhort you unto, yea lay the charge of God upon you this day, even on you and your companions, who are as a brand snatched out of the burning.[150]

Meet God in His Works of Providence

Cast Down All Opposition to Christ's Kingdom in Anticipation of the Latter-Day Glory

[1] Meet him in his general design of casting down all combined opposition to the kingdom of his Son; that God in his appointed time will bring forth the kingdom of the Lord Christ, unto more glory and power, than in former days, I presume you are persuaded: whatever will be more, these six things are clearly promised.

{1} Fullness of peace unto the gospel and the professors thereof (Isa. 11:6–7; 54:23;[151] 33:20–21; Rev. 21:25).

{2} Purity and beauty of ordinances and gospel worship (Rev. 11:1; 21:5).[152] The tabernacle was wholly made by appointment (Mal. 3:3–4; Zech. 14:16;[153] Rev. 21:27; Zech. 14:23;[154] Isa. 35:8).

{3} Multitudes of converts, many persons, yea, nations (Isa. 60:7–8; 66:8; 49:18–22;[155] Rev. 7:9).

{4} The full casting out and rejecting of all will-worship, and their attendant abominations (Rev. 11:2).[156]

{5} Professed subjection of the nations throughout the whole world unto the Lord Christ (Dan. 2:4; Ch. 7 last;[157] Isa. 60:6–8):[158] the kingdoms become

150 Amos 4:11.

151 Following Goold, this reference should probably be corrected to Isa. 54:13.

152 Following Goold, this reference should probably be taken as Rev. 21:3.

153 Owen referenced these first two texts in *The Shaking and Translating of Heaven and Earth* (1649) as a promise of God dwelling with his church by his ordinances. See *Complete Works of John Owen*, 18:440, 432.

154 Following Goold, this reference should be corrected to Zech. 14:20

155 Owen referenced this text in *The Shaking and Translating of Heaven and Earth* (1649). See *Complete Works of John Owen*, 18:432.

156 Owen appealed to this text about the remeasuring of the temple twice in this section and also in *Ebenezer* (1648) and *The Shaking and Translating of Heaven and Earth* (1649). For a discussion of its significance, see Cowan, *John Owen and the Civil War Apocalypse*, 49–51.

157 I.e., Dan. 7:27. Owen referenced this text in *Sermon Preached* [. . .] *January 31* (1649) and *The Shaking and Translating of Heaven and Earth* (1649). See *The Complete Works of John Owen*, 18:298, 435.

158 Following Goold, this reference should probably be Isa. 60:6–9.

etc.,[159] among whom his appearance shall be so glorious, that David himself shall be said to reign.

{6} A most glorious and dreadful breaking of all that rise in opposition unto him (Isa. 60:12):[160] never such desolations (Rev. 16:17–19).

Now in order to the bringing in of this his rule and kingdom, with its attendances, the Lord Christ goes forth, in the first place, to cast down the things that stand in his way, dashing his enemies "in pieces like a potter's vessel":[161] this is a part of the design of providence, wherein we are to meet him in these days: I shall speak a word, 1st. unto them who are enabled to look through the clouds and darkness, whereby his paths are encompassed, 2nd. unto them who cannot.

Believe and Pray, and Those in Power Must Be Active in Reformation

1st. Be you persuaded to meet the Lord in this his design, yet to continue steadfast in helping him against the mighty:[162] I speak not only to you who are in authority, nor unto you to whom the sword is girded:[163] but unto all that wish well to Zion: we have every one our mite that we may cast into this treasury:[164] we may be all princes in this case, all Israels, prevailers with God and men.[165] There be three things whereby even you, who are but as the number, the common soldiers of Christ, may meet the Lord in this design.

(1st)[166] By faith; believe the promises, close with them, act faith upon them,[167] and you will believe the beast unto destruction,[168] Antichrist into the pit, and Magog to ruin;[169] believe that the enemies of Christ shall be made his footstool,[170] that the nations shall be his inheritance,[171] that he shall reign

159 Rev. 11:15.

160 This is an important text for Owen, which he referenced in *Ebenezer* (1648), *Of Toleration* (1649), *The Shaking and Translating of Heaven and Earth* (1649), and *The Branch of the Lord* (1650). For the first three sermons, see *Complete Works of John Owen*, 18:271, 390, 429. He would employ it again in *The Kingdom of Christ, and the Power of the Civil Magistrate* (1652).

161 Ps. 2:9. Owen used this text in *The Shaking and Translating of Heaven and Earth* (1649). See *Complete Works of John Owen*, 18:440.

162 Judg. 5:23.

163 See Rom. 13:4. This is a reference to both Parliament and the army.

164 Mark 12:41–42.

165 Gen. 32:28.

166 As is explained in the *Works* preface, the numbering order is 1, (1), [1], {1}, and 1st. In this volume, the numbering goes deeper, with the next number being (1st).

167 In the margin: Ps. 110:1, 4; Ps. 2:7–8; Mic. 5:3–4; Isa. 60:12—Owen.

168 Rev. 17:8, 11.

169 Rev. 20:8.

170 Ps. 110:1.

171 Ps. 2:8.

gloriously in beauty, that he shall smite in pieces the heads over divers nations; live in the faith of these things, and as it will give you the sweetness of them before they come, so it will hasten their coming beyond the endeavors of thousands, yea millions of armed men.

(2nd) Meet him with your supplications. Cry unto him, as Psalm 45:3–5,

> Gird thy sword upon thy thigh, O most Mighty, with thy glory and thy majesty. And in thy majesty ride prosperously, because of truth and meekness, and righteousness, and thy right hand shall teach thee terrible things. Thine arrows are sharp in the heart of the King's enemies, whereby the people fall under thee.

This will make you be the armies of heaven, that follow him in his great undertakings (Rev. 19:14). It is his praying people, that are his conquering armies that follow him: now you find it coming, leave not pulling with all your strength, lest it roll back again, "Shoot not two or three arrows," and so give over; but never leave shooting until the enemies of the Lord be all destroyed.[172]

(3rd) Seeing it is his gospel whose advancement the Lord Jesus aims at in all these dispensations, and whose quarrel alone he revenges (whatever men may do), help on to the advancement of that gospel of his, which as formerly it was oppressed by the height and tyranny of the tower of Babel, so for the present is exceedingly denied and cumbered by the rubbish of it, being in some measure cast down.

(4th) Whereas in these dispensations, it is most eminently and frequently, in the praise of Christ, said that he is just and righteous in all his ways, as you may see in all the acclamations of the saints upon the execution of his judgments on his enemies ("Just and righteous art thou");[173] which is signally done on this account, because the ways whereby he does it, are counted most unrighteous in the world, in this then also, is he to be met, even in the administration of justice and judgment: you will otherwise certainly be found in a cross path unto him, and be borne down before him. This is that wisdom which he calls for among the judges of the earth, when he is set to reign on his holy hill (Ps. 2:10–11).

Consider the Lessons of Providence

2nd. I shall add one word or two unto them who, either from the darkness of the things themselves, or from the prejudices and temptations of their

172 See 2 Kings 13:17–19.

173 The prayer for a time of affliction in John Knox's liturgy began with this phrase. See *The Works of John Knox*, ed. David Laing, 6 vols. (Edinburgh: Bannatyne, 1816–1864), 6:375.

own spirits, are not able to discern the righteousness of the ways of God, but rather lift up themselves against him.

First, then, consider the constant appearing of God against every party that, under any color or pretense whatever have lifted up themselves for the reinforcement of things, as in former days what color or pretense soever they have put on, or which way soever they have turned themselves, God has still appeared against them.[174] Can you not discern his leavening their counsels with folly and madness, weakening their hearts and hands, making the strong become as tow, and the successful a reproach: though they have gone from mountain to mountain to seek for divination, and changed their pretenses as often as Laban did Jacob's wages,[175] yet they find neither fraud nor enchantment that will prevail: and does not this proclaim, that the design which God had in hand is as yet marvelously above you?

Secondly, consider the constant answer of prayers which those which have waited on God in these dispensations (to their unspeakable consolation) have received; finding God to be "nigh unto them in all that they call upon him" for:[176] if in this thing, they "regarded iniquity in their hearts, surely God would not have heard them":[177] others also cry, even to the Lord do they cry; but he will not bear witness to the abomination of their hearts: O that upon these and such like considerations, you would at last take the counsel of the psalmist, "Be still and know that he is God" (Ps. 46:10): be silent before him for he is risen out of his holy habitation. Say, God "has done great things for these";[178] "who has hardened himself against him and prospered?"[179] And this is the first particular.

Reject All Worldly Glory

[2] The 2nd design of Providence in these dispensations, is evidently "to stain the glory of all flesh," so Isaiah 23:9.[180] Never did the Lord any work more

174 The Parliamentary Act, which established the thanksgiving, spoke of "the glorious Appearances of God" in the recent victories. See *An Act for Setting Apart Friday the Four and Twentieth Day of October, One Thousand Six Hundred Fifty One* [. . .] (London, 1651), 1440.

175 Gen. 31:7.

176 Ps. 145:18.

177 Ps. 66:18.

178 Ps. 126:3.

179 Job 9:4.

180 In *A Sermon Preached* [. . .] *January 31* (1649), Owen utilized this text to explain how all opposition to the work of God was folly. In *The Shaking and Translating of Heaven and Earth* (1649), he used the verse to caution members of Parliament against anxiously seeking honor since God was working "to lay all the honor of the earth in the dust." See *Complete Works of John Owen*, 18:299, 327, 450, 462.

eminently? What sort of men is there among us, whose glory God has not stained? I had rather leave this unto a silent thought, than give you particular instances of it: otherwise it were very easy to make it as clear as the sun, that God has left neither self-honor nor glory to any of the sons of men: meet him then in this also.

{1} Cease putting confidence in man, say, "He is a worm, and the son of man is but a worm;"[181] "his breath is in his nostrils, and wherein is he to be accounted of?"[182] This use does the church make of mercies, "Some trust in horses, and some in chariots, but we will remember the name of the Lord" (Ps. 20:6–7): we will not trust in parliaments or armies. "All flesh is grass" (Isa. 40), let it have its withering time and away:[183] see no wisdom, but the wisdom of God, no strength but the strength of God, no glory but his.

{2} Have any of us, any glory, any crowns, any gifts, any graces, any wisdom or valor, any useful endowments, let us cast them all down at the feet of Jesus Christ; if we look on them, if we keep them as our own, God withers all their beauty and their glory: thus do the elders who worship the Lamb forever (Rom. 4:10–11),[184] say to him, "Lord Jesus, thine is the glory, thine are all the mighty works which have been wrought in our days, thine are all the means whereby they have been accomplished; we are nothing, we can do nothing, you are all, and in all:" and this is the second.

Treasure the Things of the Kingdom

[3] He aims at the shaking of all these things here below: he is taking down the rate and price of all things here below, on that which was worth a 1,000l[185] he takes his bill and writes down scarce the 1,000th part: he has laid his hand upon the nests of the nation, and has fitted wings unto all their treasures; and so eminently written vanity and uncertainty on them all, as must needs lessen their esteem, were not men blinded by the god of this world.[186] In this also are we to meet the Lord.

{1} By getting a low esteem of the things that God is thus shaking, and that upon this account, that he shakes them for this very end and purpose, that we should find neither rest nor peace in them: perhaps you have had a desire to be somebody in the world, you see yourself come short of what you

181 Job 25:6.

182 Isa. 2:22.

183 Isa. 40:6–8.

184 Following Goold, this should be corrected to Rev. 4:10–11.

185 I.e., £1,000.

186 2 Cor. 4:4.

aim at: say now with Mephibosheth upon the return of David, "'Not only half, but let all go, seeing that' the Lord Jesus shall reign with glory."[187] A man may sometimes beat a servant for the instruction of his son: God has shaken the enjoyments of his enemies, to lead his friends to disesteem them: God forbid, the quite contrary should be found upon any of us.

{2} By laboring to find all riches and treasures in the Lord Christ: the earth staggers like a drunken man: the princes of it are reduced to a morsel of bread: all that is seen, is of no value: does not God direct us to the hidden paths, to the treasures that cannot be destroyed? "Many say, 'Who will show us any good?' Lord, lift thou up the light of thy countenance upon us."[188]

Meet God in Worship

(2) We are to meet the Lord in the way of his ordinances, in the way of gospel worship, the exalting of the Lord Christ herein is the issue of all the mighty works of God: this is given in as the end of all: "The tabernacle of God" (Rev. 21:3) etc.[189] After great shakings, the promise still is of "a new heaven and earth" (Isa. 65:17; Rev. 21:1), and this is that the people of God put themselves upon in the days wherein Babylon is to be destroyed (Jer. 50:4–8). That is the work they then take in hand: the end of all is the building of the temple, Ezekiel 47, and this is the conclusion that the people of God do make, Isaiah 2:3–4,[190] and if this be neglected, the Lord will say of us as David of Nabal, "Surely in vain have I kept these men, and all that they have":[191] to meet the Lord in this also.

[1] Inquire diligently into his mind and will, that you may know his paths, and be acquainted with his statutes; I dare say, no temptation in the world, presses with more color and violence upon men under mercies, than that to a neglect of walking and holding communion with God in his ordinances: the devil thinks thus to revenge himself of the Lord Jesus: his own yoke being broken, he thinks to prevail to the casting away of his: Christ has a yoke, though it be gentle and easy.[192]

[2] You that do enjoy holy ordinances, labor to have holy hearts answerable thereunto: you have heavenly institutions, labor to have heavenly conversations: if we be like the world in our walking, it is no great matter, if we be like the world in our worship: it is sad walking contrary to God in his own paths,

187 2 Sam. 19:30.

188 Ps. 4:6.

189 Owen has referred to this verse earlier in the sermon.

190 Owen opened his sermon *The Branch of the Lord* (1650) with reference to these verses.

191 1 Sam. 25:21.

192 Matt. 11:29–30.

show out the power and efficacy of all gospel institutions, in a frame of spirit, course of life, and equability[193] of spiritual temper, all your days.

[3] Keep up the power of private worship, both personal and family. I have seen many good laws for the Sabbath,[194] and hope I shall see some good examples: look what the roots are, in the family, such will the fruit be, in the church and commonwealth: if your spirits are not well manured there, you will be utterly barren elsewhere: that is done most clearly to God, which is done within doors.

Meet God through Holy Living

(3) Meet him in the way of his holiness; in the cry of the saints unto the Lord for the execution of his judgments and vengeance, they in an especial manner invocate his holiness, "How long, O Lord, holy and true, dost thou not judge and avenge our blood on them that dwell on the earth?" (Rev. 6:10). And in their rendering praises to him, they still make mention of his holiness and righteousness in all his ways. Though the ways of God are commonly traduced as unequal and unholy ways, yet in the close there is no property of his, that he will more vindicate in all his works, than that of his holiness; in this then we are also to meet the Lord in this day of our deliverance, the day wherein he has wrought such great and wonderful alterations.

This use the Holy Ghost makes upon such like dispensations, "Seeing that all these things" etc. (2 Pet. 3:11), and so also, "And this word, 'yet once more,' signifieth the removing of those things that are shaken, as of things that are made, that those things which cannot be shaken, may remain. Wherefore we receiving a kingdom which cannot be moved, let us have grace, whereby we may serve God acceptably, with reverence and godly fear" (Heb. 12:27–28). All things opposing removed, a freedom established, therefore "let us have grace":[195] God is the thrice holy one, holy in his nature, holy in his word, and

193 I.e., well-balanced condition.

194 In April 1650, the Rump Parliament passed new laws about Sabbath keeping. Travel was forbidden, and there were fines for those found working, drinking, or dancing. Local magistrates were responsible for the enforcement of the ordinance. See "An Act for the Better Observation of the Lords-Day, Days of Thanksgiving and Humiliation," in *Acts and Ordinances of the Interregnum*, eds. C. H. Firth and R. S. Rait, 3 vols. (London: HMSO, 1911), 2:383–87. Printed as *An Additional Act for the Better Observation of the Lords-Day, Days of Humiliation and Thanksgiving Together with a Collection of Former Laws, Statutes and Ordinances Now in Force for Observation of the Said Days* (London, [April] 1650). Nonetheless, by 1651 anti-Sabbatarianism was becoming increasingly popular among certain religious radicals, and Owen was adding his voice to others calling for better observance of the Sabbath.

195 Heb. 12:28.

holy in all his works, and he requires that his people be a holy people. To this he still urged his ancient people, from the argument of his presence among them. Oh that the Spirit of the Lord would bring forth this one fruit of all his dealing with us, that we might be a holy people: if we put God's pure and clean mercies into impure and unclean vessels, they will to us be defiled. Let us take heed of prostituting the mighty works of God to the service of our lusts: should we now make such conclusions to ourselves, as the rich fool in the gospel, and say, "Well, we have now peace and prosperity laid up for some years, 'Soul take your ease, eat, drink, and be merry,[196] grow rich and great, follow after vanity, pride, folly, uncleanness, enjoy with delight the things which we have, and heap up thereto.' " Why, as this is to labor to draw the Lord God into a partnership with our abominations, and to enforce his mighty works to bear witness to our lusts, so certainly it is such a frame, as he will surely and speedily revenge: the end why God delivers us from all our enemies, is, not that we may serve our lusts and ourselves without fear, but that we "may serve him without fear, in righteousness and holiness, all the days of our lives":[197] let then this be the issue upon our hearts, of all the victories, and successes, and returns of prayers, that we have received; that we give up ourselves to the Lord in all manner of holiness; this is that which the Lord's voice calls us unto: let not now him that is filthy be filthy still;[198] let not him that is worldly be worldly still; let not him that is loose, and has cast off the yoke of Christ be so still: let not him that has sought himself, do so still, let not him who has contemned the institutions of Christ, do so still, let not him that has been lifted up above his brethren, be so still, but let everyone forsake his evil way, and the iniquity that is in his hand, that we who were not a people at all may be a people to the praise of the God of all;[199] that you who rule over men may be just, "ruling in the fear of the Lord,"[200] that you may be "as the light of the morning when the sun is risen, even as a morning without clouds, as the tender grass springing out of the earth by clear shining after rain":[201] that we who are under rule, may "sit under our vines and fig-trees,"[202] speaking well of the name of God, and laboring to carry on the kingdom of the Prince of Peace, even "every one as we are called, and abiding therein

196 Luke 12:19.

197 Luke 1:74–75.

198 Rev. 22:11.

199 See 1 Pet. 2:9–10.

200 2 Sam. 23:3. Owen has referred to this text earlier in the sermon.

201 2 Sam. 23:4.

202 Mic. 4:4.

with God";[203] that as when you sought this mercy of God which we rejoice in, in solemn humbling of yourselves before the Lord, I made it appear unto you, that it was "the remnant of Jacob,"[204] God's secret and holy ones, lying in the bowels of the nation, that must be the rise of all our deliverances, so we would now, everyone strive to be of that number, for they alone enjoy the sweetness of this and every mercy.

FINIS.[205]

203 1 Cor. 7:24.

204 Mic. 5:7. Owen would return to this verse and its implications in *God's Work in Founding Zion* (1656).

205 Lat. "The End."

THE LABORING SAINT'S DISMISSION TO REST. A SERMON PREACHED AT THE FUNERAL OF THE RIGHT HONORABLE HENRY IRETON, LORD DEPUTY OF IRELAND:

In the Abbey Church at Westminster,
the 6th Day of February 1651

By
John Owen, minister of the gospel.
Licensed and entered according to order.

London,
Printed by R. and W. Leybourn,
for Philemon Stephens, at
the gilded lion in Paul's Churchyard, 1652

[Dedication]

To the Honorable, and My Worthy Friend Colonel Henry Cromwell[1]

SIR,[2]

The ensuing sermon was preached upon as sad an occasion, as on any particular account has been given to this nation in this our generation. It is now published, as at the desire of very many who love the savor of that perfume which is diffused with the memory of the noble person peculiarly mentioned therein: so also upon the requests of such others, as enables me justly to entitle the doing of it, obedience. Being come abroad, it was in my thoughts to have directed it immediately in the first place to her, who of any individual person was most nearly concerned in him.[3] But having observed how near she has been to be swallowed up of sorrow, and what slow progress, he who took care to seal up instruction to her soul by all dispensations, has given her hitherto toward a conquest thereof: I was not willing to offer directly a new occasion unto the multitude of her perplexed thoughts about this thing. No doubt, her loss being as great as it could be upon the account of one subject to the law of mortality, as many grains of grief and sorrow are to be allowed her in the balance of the sanctuary, as God does permit to be laid out and dispended about any of the sons of men. He who is able to make sweet the bitterest, waters, and to give a gracious issue to the most grievous trial, will certainly, in due

1 The year on the title page should be corrected from 1651 to 1652. This is because, at the time, the New Year was taken to begin on Lady Day, March 25.

2 Colonel Henry Cromwell (1628–1674) was a son of Oliver Cromwell who had fought alongside his brother-in-law, Ireton.

3 Bridget Ireton (ca. 1624–1662), daughter of Oliver Cromwell, had married Ireton in 1646.

time, eminently bring forth that good upon her spirit, which he is causing all these things to work together for.[4] In the meantime, sir, these lines are to you: your near relation to that rare example of righteousness, faith, holiness, zeal, courage, self-denial, love to his country, wisdom and industry, mentioned in the ensuing sermon, the mutual tender affection between you while he was living; your presence with him in his last trial and conflict,[5] the deserved regard you bear to his worth and memory; your design of looking into, and following after his steps and purpose in the work of God in his generation, as such an accomplished pattern, as few ages have produced the like; with many other reasons of the like nature, did easily induce me hereunto. That which is here printed is but the notes which I first took, not having had leisure since to give them a serious perusal, and upon that account, must beg a candid interpretation unto anything that may appear not so well digested therein as might be expected. I have not anything to express concerning yourself, but only my desire that your heart may be fixed to the Lord God of your fathers, and that in the midst of all your temptations and oppositions wherewith your pilgrimage will be attended,[6] you may be carried on and established in your inward subjection unto, and outward contending for, the kingdom of the dearly beloved of our souls; not fainting, or waxing weary until you received your dismission to rest, for your lot in the end of the days.[7]

Sir,

Your most humble and affectionate servant,

John Owen.
Oxford, Christ Church.[8]
April 2nd.

4 Rom. 8:28.

5 Henry Cromwell had been at the siege of Limerick and was with Ireton when he died.

6 In 1651, Thomas Patient, a preacher with the Cromwellian army in Ireland, reported to Oliver Cromwell about God's work of grace in Henry's life and how "he hath had inward temtations in his soule, and many words of grace made very precious and comfortable to his soule." See *The Original Letters and Papers of State, Addressed to Oliver Cromwell: Concerning the Affairs of Great Britain*, ed. J. Nickolls (London, 1743), 6–7.

7 Dan. 12:13.

8 In the text: OX. CH. CH.—Owen.

[Sermon]

The Laboring Saint's Dismission to Rest

But go thou thy way till the end be, for thou shalt rest,
and stand in thy lot at the end of the days.

DANIEL 12:13

INTRODUCTION AND OPENING OF THE TEXT

The words of my text having no dependence (as to their sense and meaning, but only as to the occasion of them) on the verses foregoing, I shall not at all look backward into the chapter, but fall immediately upon them, that I be not hindered from my principal intendment; being unwilling to detain you long, though willing to speak a word from the Lord, to such a congregation, gathered together by such an eminent act of the providence of God.

The words are the Lord's dismission[1] given to a most eminent servant, from a most eminent employment, wherein these four things are observable.

1. The dismission itself in the first words, "Go thou thy ways."
2. The term allotted for his continuance, under that dismission, "Until the end be."
3. His state and condition under that dismission, "For thou shalt rest."
4. The utmost issue of all this dispensation, both as to his foregoing labor, his dismission and rest following, "Stand in thy lot at the end of the days."

1 I.e., discharge, formally taking leave.

The Servant Is Dismissed from His Service

1. In the first, I shall consider two things.

(1) The person dismissed, (Thou) "Go thou thy ways."
(2) The dismission itself, "Go thou thy ways."

The Godly Character and Work of This Servant

(1) The person dismissed is Daniel, the writer of this prophecy, who received all the great visions of God mentioned therein, and I desire to observe concerning him, as to our purpose in hand, two things.

[1] His qualifications.
[2] His employment.

A Loving, Wise, and Upright Servant

[1] For the first, I shall only name some of them that were most eminent in him, and they are three.

{1} Wisdom.
{2} Love to his people.
{3} "Uprightness and righteousness in the discharge of that high place whereunto he was advanced."

{1} For the first, the Holy Ghost bears ample testimony thereunto, "As for these four children, God gave them knowledge and skill in all learning and wisdom, and Daniel had understanding in all visions and dreams. And in all matters of wisdom, and understanding that the king inquired of them, he found them ten times better than all the magicians and astrologers that were in all his realm" (Dan. 1:17, 20).

In "all matters of wisdom and understanding," none in the whole Babylonian empire full of wise men and artists, were to be compared unto Daniel and his companions, and Ezekiel, (28:3), rebuking the pride and arrogancy of Tyrus with a bitter scorn, he says; " 'Behold, thou art wiser than Daniel,' or you thinkest yourself so," intimating that none in wisdom was to be compared unto him.

{2} Love to his people. On this account was his most diligent inquiry into the time of their deliverance, and his earnest contending with God upon the discovery of the season when it was to be accomplished, chapter 9:1–4.[2]

2 Dan. 9:1–4.

Hence he is reckoned among them, who in their generation stood in the gap in the behalf of others,[3] Noah, Daniel, and Job.[4] Hence God calls the people of the Jews, his people, "Seventy weeks are determined on thy people" (Dan. 9:24): the people of your affections and desires, the people of whom you are, and who are so dear unto you.

{3} For his righteousness in discharging of his trust and office, you have the joint testimony of God and man: his high place and preferment you have, chapter 6:2. He was the first of the three presidents who were set over the hundred and twenty other princes of the provinces;[5] and the Holy Ghost tells you that in the discharge of this high trust and great employment, he was faithful to the utmost, "Then the presidents and princes sought to find occasion against Daniel concerning the kingdom, but they could find none occasion nor fault: forasmuch as he was faithful, neither was there any error or fault found in him" (Dan. 6:4). Which also his enemies confessed, verse 3.[6] "Then said these men, We shall not find any occasion against this Daniel, except we find it against him concerning the law of his God."

These qualifications I say among others were most eminent in this person who here received his dismission from his employment.

A Servant Who Rightly Understood God's Providential Alterations

[2] There is his employment itself, from which he is dismissed, and herein I shall observe these two things.

{1} The nature of the employment itself.
{2} Some considerable circumstances of it.

{1} For the first, it consisted in receiving from God, and holding out to others, clear and express visions concerning God's wonderful providential alterations in kingdoms, and nations, which were to be accomplished, from the days wherein he lived, to the end of the world. All the prophets together had not so many clear discoveries, as this one Daniel concerning these things.

{2} For the latter, this is observable, that all his visions still close with some eminent exaltation of the kingdom of Christ; that is the center where all the lines of his visions do meet, as is to be seen in the close almost of every chapter; and this was the great intendment of the Spirit in all those glorious

3 Ezek. 22:30.

4 Ezek. 14:14.

5 Dan. 6:1.

6 Following Goold, this should be corrected to Dan. 6:5.

revelations unto Daniel, to manifest the subserviency of all civil revolutions unto the interest of the kingdom of the Lord Christ.[7]

This then is the person concerning whom these words were used, and this was his employment.

A Servant Who Died in Service

(2) There is his dismission itself, "Go thou thy ways." Now this may be considered two ways,

[1] Singly, relating to his employment only.
[2] In reference to his life also.

[1] In the first sense, the Lord discharges Daniel from his farther attendance on him, in this way of receiving visions and revelations concerning things that were shortly to come to pass, although happily his portion might yet be continued in the land of the living: as if the Lord should say, "You are an inquiring man, you are still seeking for farther acquaintance with my mind in these things, but content yourself, you shalt receive no more visions; I will now employ Haggai, Zechariah, and others, you shalt receive no more." But I cannot close with this sense, for;

{1} This is not the manner of God to lay aside those whom he has found faithful in his service, men indeed do so, but God changes not: whom he has begun to honor with any employment, he continues them in it, while they are faithful to him.

{2} Daniel was now above a hundred years old, as may be easily demonstrated by comparing the time of his captivity, which was in the third year of the reign of Jehoiakim (Dan. 1:1), with the time of his writing this prophecy, which is expressly said to be in the reign of Cyrus the king of Persia (Dan. 10:1), and therefore probably his end was very nigh; and after this you hear of him no more; who had he lived many days, it had been his sin, not to have gone up to Jerusalem, the decree of Cyrus giving liberty for a return being passed.

[2] It is not then God's laying him aside from his office simply, but also his intimation that he must shortly lay down his mortality, and so come into the condition wherein he was to "rest" until the end; this then is his dismission, he died in his work, life and employment go together, "Go thou thy ways."

7 Owen took the opportunity to repeat a point from his sermon delivered just over three months previously, captured in the title of the published sermon, *The Advantage of the Kingdom of Christ* (1651).

Observation: There Is an Appointed Time for All Servants to Be Dismissed

Obs[ervation] 1. *There is an appointed season wherein the saints of the most eminent abilities, in the most useful employments, must receive their dismission,* be their work of never so great importance, be their abilities never so choice and eminent, they must in their season receive their dismission.

Before I handle this proposition, or proceed to open the following words, I shall crave leave to bring the work of God, and the word of God, a little close together, and lay the parallel between the persons dismissed, the one in our text, the other in a present providence, which is very near, only that the one lived not out half the days of the other.[8]

Daniel and Ireton Were Servants of Similar Character

Three personal qualifications we observed in Daniel, all which were very eminent in the person of our desires.

Men of Wisdom

1. Wisdom.[9] There is a manifold wisdom which God imparts to the sons of men; there is spiritual wisdom, that by the way of eminency is said to be "from above" (James 3:17), which is nothing but the gracious acquaintance of the soul with the hidden wisdom of God in Christ (1 Cor. 2:7), and there is a civil wisdom, or a sound ability of mind for the management of the affairs of men in subordination to the providence, and righteousness of God. Though both these were in Daniel, yet it is in respect of the latter that his wisdom is so peculiarly extolled. And though I am very far from assuming to myself the skill of judging of the abilities of men, and would be far from holding forth things of mere common report, yet, upon assured grounds I suppose this gift of God, ability of mind, and dexterous industry for the management of human affairs may be ascribed to our departed friend.

There are sundry things that distinguish this wisdom from that policy which God abhors, which is "carnal, sensual, and devilish" (James 3:15), though it be the great darling of the men of the world; I shall name one or two of them.

(1) A gracious discerning of the mind of God, according to his appearance in the affairs wherein men are employed, "The Lord's voice crieth unto the city, and the man of wisdom shall see thy name, hear ye the rod, and who

8 Ireton was forty years old when he died.

9 Gentles describes Ireton as "the army's chief theoretician, writer and political draftsman." See Ian Gentles, *The English Revolution and the Wars in the Three Kingdoms, 1638–1652* (Harlow, UK: Pearson Longman, 2007), 312.

hath appointed it" (Mic. 6:9). It is the wisdom of a man, to see the name of God, to be acquainted with his will, his mind, his aim in things, when his providential voice cries to the city. All the works of God have their voice, have their instruction: those of signal providences speak aloud, they cry to the city; "Here is the wisdom of a man," he is a man of substance, a substantial man, that can see his name in such dispensations. This carnal policy inquires not into, but is wholly swallowed up in the concatenation of things among themselves, applying secondary causes unto events, without once looking to the "name" of God, like swine following acorns under the tree, not at all looking up to the tree from whence they fall.[10]

(2) Such acquaintance with the seasons of providence, as to know the duty of the people of God in them, "The children of Issachar, men that had understanding of the times, to know what Israel ought to do" (1 Chron. 12:32): this it is indeed to be a man of understanding, to know in any season the duty of Israel, that they may walk up to acceptation with God in the performance thereof. A thing which is neither prescribed in the rules, nor followed in the practice of men, wise only with that cursed policy which God abhors: to have a mind suited unto all seasons and tempers, so as to compass their own selfish ends, is the utmost of their aim.

Now in both these did this gift of God shine in this deceased saint.

(1) He ever counted it his wisdom to look after the name of God, and the testification of his will, in every dispensation of providence, wherein he was called to serve: for this were his wakings, watchings, inquiries; when that was made out, he counted not his business half done, but even accomplished, and that the issue was ready at the door; not "What says this man?" or, "What says that man?" but "What says the Lord?" That being evident. He consulted not with flesh and blood,[11] and the wisdom of it (whereof perhaps, would he have leaned to it, he was as little destitute as any in his generation, I mean the whole wisdom of a man). The name of God was as land in every storm, in the discovery whereof he had as happy an eye at the greatest seeming distance when the clouds were blackest, and the waves highest, as any.

10 An adaption from the proverb: The hog never looks up to him that threshes down the acorns. John Cardell used this illustration when preaching alongside Owen in January 1649. See Cardell, *Gods Wisdom Justified, and Mans Folly Condemned, Touching All Maner of Outward Providential Administrations* [. . .] (London, 1649), 19. Swine browsing the mast of an oak tree is memorably illustrated in the satirical engraving "The Royall Oake of Brittayne," which appeared as the frontispiece to Clement Walker's *Anarchia Anglicana, or, The History of Independency, the Second Part* [. . .] (London, 1649).

11 Gal. 1:16; cf. Matt. 16:17.

(2) Neither did he rest here: "What Israel ought to do"[12] in every season, was also his inquiry; some men have a wisdom to know things, but not seasons, in any measure; surely a thing in season, is no less beautiful than a word in season: "as apples of gold in pictures of silver":[13] there are few things that belong to civil affairs, but are alterable upon the incomprehensible variety of circumstances. These alter and change the very nature of them, and make them good or bad, that is useful or destructive. He that will have the garment that was made for him one year, serve and fit him the next, must be sure that he neither increase nor wane. Importune[14] insisting on the most useful things, without respect to alterations of seasons, is a sad sign of a narrow heart. He of whom we speak was wise to "discern the seasons," and performed things, when both themselves, and the ways of carrying them on were excellently suited unto all coincidences of their season. And indeed, what is most wisely proposed in one season, may be most foolishly pursued in another.[15] It had been wisdom in Joshua not to have made any compact, but to have slain all the Gibeonites;[16] but it was a folly sorely revenged in Saul, who attempted to do the same.[17] He who thinks the most righteous and suitable proposals or principles, that ever were in the world (setting aside general rules of unchangeable righteousness, and equity compassing all times, places, ways and forms of government), must be performed as desirable, because once they were so, is certainly a stranger to the affairs of human kind.

Some things are universally unchangeable and indispensable among men, supposing them to live answerable to the general principles of their kind: as that a government must be, without which, everyone is the enemy of everyone; and all tend to mutual destruction, which are appointed of God for mutual preservation, that in government some do rule, and some be in subjection, that all rule be for the good of them that are ruled, and the like principles, that flow necessarily from the very nature of political society.

Some things again are alterable and dispensable merely upon the account of preserving the former principles, or the like: if any of them are out of course, it is a vacuum in nature politic, for which all particular elements instantly dislodge and transpose themselves to supply, and such are all forms of governments among men, which if either they so degenerate of themselves that

12 1 Chron. 12:32.

13 Prov. 25:11.

14 I.e., persistently.

15 Owen appears to be seeking to justify some of Ireton's changes in policy.

16 Josh. 10:1.

17 1 Sam. 15:9.

they become directly opposite, or are so shattered by providential revolutions as to become useless to their proper end, may and ought to be changed, and not upon other accounts: but now for other things in government, as the particular way, whereby persons shall be designed unto it, the continuance of the same persons in it, for a less or greater proportion of time, the exercise of more or less power by some sorts, or the whole body of them that are ruled, the uniting of men for some particular end by bonds and engagements, and the like occasional emergencies, the universal disposal of them is rolled on prudence to act according to present circumstances.

Lovers of God's People

2. Love to his people: this was the second qualification, wherein Daniel was so eminent. And our deceased friend, not to enter into comparison with them that went before, had clearly such a proportion, as we may heartily desire that those who follow after, may drink but equal draughts of the same cup; that his pains, labor, travail, jeopards[18] of his life, and all that was dear to him, relinquishment of relations and contentments, had sweetness and life from this motive, even intenseness of affection to his people, the people of whom he was, and whose prosperity he did desire, needs no farther demonstration, than the great neglect of self and all self-concernments which dwelt upon him, in all his tremendous undertakings: *vicit amor patriae*,[19] or certainly he who had upon his breast and all his undertakings self-contempt so eminently engraven, could not have persisted wrestling with so many difficulties, to the end of his days: it was Jerusalem and the prosperity thereof, which was preferred to his chief joy. Neither—

Righteous in Public Service

3. Did he come short in righteousness in the administration of that high place whereto he was called? Nay, than this, there was not a more eminent stone

18 I.e., risks.

19 Lat. "love of country drove him." This is adapted from a Virgil's *Aeneid* 6.823, which reads "*Vincet amor patriae*" (love of his fatherland will conquer). This describes Aeneas's vision of the Elysian fields of Rome. For the Latin text and English translation, see Virgil, *Eclogues. Georgics. Aeneid: Books 1–6*, trans. H. Rushton Fairclough, rev. G. P. Goold, Loeb Classical Library 63 (Cambridge, MA: Harvard University Press, 1999), 590–91. Augustine had echoed this phrase in *De civitate Dei* 5.18 but changed the tense of the verb from *vincet to vincit*. The latter is the form that is found here. For the Latin text, see Augustine, *The City of God*, vol. 2, *Books 4–7*, trans William M. Green, Loeb Classical Library 412 (Cambridge, MA: Harvard University Press, 1963), 226. For an English translation, see *Augustine: The City of God against the Pagans*, ed. R. W. Dyson, Cambridge Texts in the History of Political Thought (Cambridge: Cambridge University Press, 1998), 219.

in that diadem which he had in the earth. If he lay not at the bottom, yet at least he had a signal concurrence in such acts of justice, as antiquity has not known, and posterity will admire. Neither was it this or that particular act that did in this bespeak his praise, but a constant will and purpose of rendering to everyone his due.

I shall not insist upon particulars, in these and sundry other personal qualifications, between the persons mentioned a parallel may lie.

Daniel and Ireton Both Understood Providential Alterations

2. As to employment, that of Daniel was mentioned before: it was the receiving and holding out from God visions of providential alterations, disposing and transposing of states, nations, kingdoms, and dominions; what he had in speculation, was this man's part to follow in action, he was an eminent instrument in the hand of God in as tremendous providential alterations, as such a spot of the world has at any time received since Daniel, foresaw in general them all: and this, not as many have been carried along with the stream, or led by outward motives, and considerations far above their own principles and desires, but seeingly and knowingly, he closed with the mind of God, with full purpose of heart to serve the will of the Lord in his generation.[20] And on this account did he see every mountain made a plain beforehand by the Spirit of the Lord,[21] and "staggered not" at the greatest difficulties "through unbelief, but being steadfast in faith, he gave glory to God."[22] And to complete the parallel, as Daniel's visions were still terminated in the kingdom of Christ, so all his actions had the same aim and intendment. This was that which gave life, and sweetness to all the most dismal and black engagements that at any time he was called out unto.[23] All made way to the coming in of the promised glory. It was all the "vengeance of the Lord and his temple."[24] A Davidical preparation of his paths in blood,[25] that he might forever reign in righteousness and peace; but be he so or so, the truth of our proposition is confirmed toward him.

That there is an appointed season, when the saints of the most eminent abilities, in the most useful employments, shall receive their dismission, etc.

20 Acts 13:36.

21 Zech. 4:7. Owen referenced this text in *A Vision of Unchangeable Free Mercy* (1646), *Ebenezer* (1648), and his June 1649 sermon *Human Power Defeated.* See *Complete Works of John Owen,* 18:110, 127, 271, 473–74.

22 Rom. 4:20. This was the theme of Owen's February 1650 sermon, *The Steadfastness of the Promises.*

23 Ireton participated in the brutal sieges of Colchester, Drogheda, Wexford, and Limerick.

24 Jer. 50:28; 51:11.

25 1 Chron. 28:3.

I shall briefly open the rest of the words, and so take up the proposition again which was first laid down.

The Servant Is Dismissed Before the Completion of His Work

2. Then, there is the term allotted to him in this state of his dismission: "Until the end be."

The Meaning of "The End"

Three things may be here intended in this word, "end."

(1) The end of his life, "Go thou thy ways to the end of thy life and days;" but this we before disallowed, not consenting that Daniel received a dismission from his employment, before the end of his life and pilgrimage.

(2) The end of the world, "Go thy ways to the end of the world: till then thou shalt rest in thy grave"; but neither yet does this seem to be particularly intended in these words. The words in the close of the text do expressly mention that, calling it "the end of days;" and in so few words, the same thing is not needlessly repeated: besides, had this expression held out the whole time of his abode in the state of rest here signified, it must have been, "Go thou thy ways, for thou shalt rest until the end be;" so that,

(3) Thirdly, the "end" here is to be accommodated unto the things, whereof the Holy Ghost is peculiarly dealing with Daniel; and that is the accomplishment of the great visions which he had received, in breaking the kingdoms of the world, and setting up the kingdom of "the Holy One of God."[26] Daniel is dismissed from farther attendance in this service, he shall not see the actual accomplishment of the things mentioned, but is dismissed and laid aside unto the end of them. The word "until," in the Scripture, is not such a limitation of time, as to assert the contrary to what is excepted, upon its accomplishment: "Until the end," does not signify, that he should not rest after the end of the things intimated, no more than it is affirmed that Michal had children after her death, because it is said that until her death she had none (2 Sam. 6:23). This then is that end that he is dismissed unto; the appointed season for the accomplishment of those glorious things which he had foreshown.

Observation: Servants Often Do Not See Their Work Completed

Obs[ervation 2]. *God oftentimes suffers not his choicest servants to see the issue and accomplishment of those glorious things wherein themselves have been most eminently engaged.*

26 Mark 1:24; Luke 4:34.

The Servant Is Released to Rest

3. The third thing (that we may make haste) is his state and condition, during the time which he lies under this dismission, in these words, "For thou shalt rest."

There is nothing of difficulty in these words, but what will naturally fall under consideration in the opening of the proposition which they hold out; which is—

Observation: Dismissed Servants Are at Rest

Obs[ervation] 3. *The condition of a dismissed saint is a condition of rest: "Thou shalt rest until the end be."* What this rest is, and from what, with wherein it consists, shall be afterward explained.

The Servant Is Dismissed to Rest Until the End of Days

4. The last thing in the text is; the utmost issue of all these dispensations, both as to his foregoing labor, and his present dismission, and following rest. "Thou shalt stand in thy lot," etc.

Here are two things considerable in these words,¶[27]

Observation: The Intermediate State Precedes the Eternal State

1. The season of the accomplishment of what is here foretold, and promised unto Daniel, and that is "in the end of the days," that is, when time shall be no more, when a period shall be put to the days of the world: called "the last day," "the great day," "the day of judgment;" that is the season of the accomplishment of this promise, "The day wherein God will judge the world by the man whom he hath ordained."[28]

Obs[ervation 4]. *There is an appointed, determinate season, wherein all things and persons according to the will of God will run into their utmost issue and everlasting condition.*

Observations concerning the Appointed Lot

2. The thing foretold, and promised, that is, that he should "stand in his lot."

Obs[ervation 5]. *There is an appointed lot for everyone to stand in, and measured portion, which in the end they shall receive.*

[Observation 6].[29] *There is an eminent lot hereafter, for men of eminent employment for God here.*

27 The ¶ symbol indicates that a paragraph break has been added to Owen's original text.

28 Acts 17:31.

29 In the text this is numbered as "2," but, following Goold, it is presented here as "Observation 6."

TREATMENT OF THE FIRST OBSERVATION: THERE IS AN APPOINTED TIME FOR ALL SERVANTS TO BE DISMISSED

I shall not be able to handle all these several truths which lie in the words;[30] those only which are of most importance, and most suitable, may briefly be handled unto you, and the first is,

There is an appointed season wherein the saints of the most eminent abilities, in the most useful employments, must receive their dismission. "Your fathers where are they? And the prophets do they live for ever?" (Zech. 1:5). Fathers, and prophets have but their season, and they are not: they have their dismission; so old Simeon professes, "*Nunc Dimittis*"[31] (Luke 2:29). Now you give me a dismission. They are placed of God in their station, as a sentinel in his watchtower; and they have their appointed season, and are then dismissed from their watch. The great "Captain of their salvation" comes,[32] and says, "Go you your ways: you have faithfully discharged your duty; go now unto your rest." Some have harder service: some have harder duty than others: some keep guard in the winter, a time of storms and temptations, trials and great pressures: others in the sunshine, the summer of a more flourishing estate and condition; yet duty they all do; all attend in the service; all endure some hardship, and have their appointed season for their dismission: and be they never so excellent at the discharging of their duty, they shall not abide one moment beyond the bounds which he has set them, who says to all his creatures, "Thus far shall you go, and no further."[33] Oftentimes this dismission is in the midst of their work, for which they seem to be most eminently qualified.

The three most eminent works of God, in and about his children, in the days of old, were—(1) His giving his people the law, and settling them in the land of Canaan. (2) His recovering them from the Babylonish captivity, and (3) his promulgation of the gospel unto them. In these three works, he employed three most eminent persons; Moses in the first; Daniel in the second; and John Baptist in the third, and [none] of them saw the work accomplished, wherein they were so eminently employed: Moses died the year before the people entered Canaan: Daniel, some few years before the foundation of the temple: and John Baptist in the first year of the baptism of our Savior, when the gospel which he began to preach, was to be published in its beauty and glory. They had all but their appointed seasons, though their abilities were

30 In other words, the observations that are here presented as numbers 5 and 6.

31 The opening words of the canticle from Luke 2:29–32 of the Latin Vulgate: *Nunc dimittis servum tuum Domine* ("Lord, now you let your servant depart in peace").

32 Heb. 2:10.

33 Job 38:11.

eminent: who like unto them, and their employment excellent, what like it in the earth? Yet at their seasons, they must go their ways to rest, and lie down, "till they stand in their lot at the end of the days."

Three Reasons for This Doctrine

Reas[on] 1. The general condition of their mortality does require that it should be so: "It is appointed to all men once to die" (Heb. 9:27). There is a stable law fixed concerning the sons of men, that is not upon the account of any usefulness here to be dispensed withal, "The number of our months" is with God; he has fixed our "bounds," which we shall not "pass."[34] Our days are as "the days of an hireling,"[35] that have a certain prefixed, and determinate end: their strength is not the strength of stones, neither is their flesh of brass, that they should endure forever. See Job 14:10–12. This (I say) requires that there should be an appointed season for their employment, for it is so for their lives: and yet there is more in it than this: for in the course of five thousand years, God has exempted two persons by his sovereignty from the condition of mortality, who walked with him in their generations.[36] So that the bounds fixed to them were not upon the account of their lives, but merely of the work they had in hand.

[Reason] 2. God does it, that he may be the more eminently seen in the carrying on his own works, which in their season he commits to them. Should he leave his work always on one hand it would seem at length to be the work of the instrument only. Though the people opposed Moses at the first, yet it is thought they would have worshiped him at the last: and therefore God buried him where his body could not be found.[37] Yet indeed he had but the lot of most, who faithfully serve God in their generations:[38] despised while they are present, idolized when they are gone. I do not know of any great work, that the Lord carried out the same persons to be the beginners and enders of. He gave them all their seasons, that his power and wisdom might the more evidently appear in carrying it from one hand to another.

[Reason] 3. God makes room as it were in his vineyard, for the budding, flourishing and fruit bearing of other plants which he has planted. Great employments call for great exercise of graces. Even in employments in and about providential things, there is the exercise of spiritual grace: as much

34 Job 14:5.

35 Job 7:1.

36 Enoch (Gen. 5:24) and Elijah (2 Kings 2:11).

37 Deut. 34:6.

38 Acts 13:36.

faith and prayer, as much communion with God, walking before him[39] and wrestling with him,[40] may be used in casting down of armies, as in setting up of churches: God exercises all the graces of his, in the work he calls them out unto. He principles[41] them, by faith and fellowship with himself, for their employment; and therefore he gives each individual, but his appointed season, that others in whose hearts he has lodged the same spirit wherewith they are endued, may come forth, and show the fruits thereof. Daniel lies down in the dust, in rest and peace, and why so? The spirit of prophecy is poured out on Haggai and Zechariah, etc., they must also carry on this work, and bear my name before my people.[42] Consider the use of this.

Two Applications

Servants Should Improve the Time That Has Been Allotted to Them

Use 1. Of exhortation unto all that are employed in the work of God, especially such as with eminent abilities are engaged in eminent employments, you have but your allotted season for your work: your day has its close, its evening: your night comes, wherein none can work:[43] "The grave cannot praise the Lord; death cannot celebrate him": it is the living, the living that are fitted for that work (Isa. 38:18–19). It is true, men may allot you your season, and all in vain; but your "times are in the hand of God";[44] that which he has appointed out unto you shall stand; be you never so excellent, never so useful, yet the days of your service "are as the days of an hireling," that will expire at the "appointed" season:[45] be wise then to improve the time that is in your hands; this is the praise of a man, the only praise whereof in this world he is partaker, that he does the will of God before he fall asleep: that he faithfully serves his generation,[46] until he be no more.

For a dying man to wrestle with the rebukes of God, and the complaints of his own conscience, for meeting with the end of his days, before he has attained the midst of his duty, is a sad condition.

You have your season, and you have but your season, neither can you lie down in peace, until you have some persuasion that your work as well as your

39 Gen. 17:1.
40 Gen. 32:24
41 I.e., trains and instructs for a course of action.
42 Cf. Acts 9:15.
43 John 9:4.
44 Ps. 31:15.
45 Job 7:1.
46 Acts 13:36.

life is at an end; whatever then you find to do, do it with all your strength; for there is neither wisdom nor power in the grave, whither you are going (Eccl. 9:10).

Some particular rules may direct you herein.

Take Ireton as an Example

(1) Compare yourselves with the saints of God, who were faithful in their generations, and are now fallen asleep; what a deal of work did Josiah do in a short season?[47] What a light did John set up in a few years?[48] With what unwearied pains and industry did our deceased friend serve his generation?[49] It is said of Caesar, that he was ashamed of his own sloth, when he found that Alexander had conquered the eastern world at the age wherein he had done nothing.[50] Behold here, one receiving his dismission about the age of forty years, and what a world of work for God, and the interest of the Lord Christ did he in that season? And how well, in the close, has he parted with a temporal life for him, who by his death procured for him an eternal life. And now rest is sweet unto this laboring man. Provoke one another by examples.

A Call to Diligence

(2) Be diligent to pass through your work, and let it not too long hang upon your hands: your appointed season may come before you bring it to the close; yea search out work for God.[51] You that are entrusted in power, trifle not away your season. Is there no oppressed person that with diligence you might relieve? Is there no poor distressed widow or orphan, whose righteous requests you might expedite and dispatch? Are there no stout offenders against God and man that might be chastised? Are there no slack and slow counties and cities in the execution of justice, that might be quickened by

47 2 Kings 22–23.

48 John 5:35.

49 John Cook described Ireton by saying "there was never a more able painefull, provident and industrious servant." See Cook, *Monarchy No Creature of Gods Making* (London, 1652), sig. G1r.

50 According to Suetonius, *The Deified Julius* 7, it was said that the young Caesar wept when saw a statue of Alexander the Great because he had accomplished so little in comparison to Alexander, who had, by the age of thirty, "brought the world to his feet" in conquering the Persian empire. See Suetonius, *Lives of the Caesars*, vol. 1, *Julius. Augustus. Tiberius. Gaius Caligula*, trans. J. C. Rolfe, Loeb Classical Library 31 (Cambridge, MA: Harvard University Press, 1914), 43.

51 Days after this sermon was preached, Owen and a group of other ministers appeared before Parliament, and, as a result, the Rump created a Committee for the Propagation of the Gospel. See Martin Calvin Cowan, *John Owen and the Civil War Apocalypse: Preaching, Prophecy and Politics* (London: Routledge, 2017), 135.

your example? No places destitute of the gospel that might be furnished and supplied by your industry and wisdom? Can you not find out something of this or the like nature to be despatched with vigor and diligence? Nay do not innumerable particulars in each kind lie upon your hands? And is not your nonperformance of them such a sacrifice as wherewith God is not well pleased? Your time is limited and appointed, you know not how soon you may be overtaken with it; and would it not be desirable unto you, that you had done these things? Will it be bitterness in the end, that you so laid out your endeavors?

Servants Come and Go, but the Work Is God's

Use 2.[52] All men have but their seasons in any work, only God abides in it forever: in every undertaking let your eye still be on him, with whom is the fullness and the residue of the Spirit.[53] Jeremiah's great bewailing of Josiah's death was doubtless made upon the account of his discerning that none would come after him to carry on the work which he had begun,[54] but the wickedness of that people was to come to its height: else God can raise up yet more Josiahs: let him be eyed as the principal and only abiding agent in any great undertaking.

In the residue of the observations I shall be very brief. The next is.

TREATMENT OF THE SECOND OBSERVATION: SERVANTS OFTEN DO NOT SEE THEIR WORK COMPLETED

Obs[ervation] 2. *God oftentimes suffers not the choicest of his servants to see the accomplishment of those glorious things wherein themselves have been most eminently engaged.*

The case of Moses is most eminently known, he had a large share in suffering the persecutions which were allotted to the people: forty years' banishment he endured in the wilderness, under the reproach of Christ—[55] forty years more spent in wrestling with innumerable difficulties, dangerous perils, mutinies, wars, and contentions. At the close when he comes to look upon the land, when the end of all that dispensation was to be wound up, and the rest and reward of all his toil and labor to be had, which formerly he had undergone for twice forty years; "Go thou thy ways," says the Lord, "thou

52 Corrected from "Use 3."

53 Mal. 2:15.

54 2 Chron. 35:25.

55 Heb. 11:26.

shalt rest," take your dismission, you shalt not enter into the good land, lie down here in the wilderness in peace.

John Baptist goes and preaches the drawing nigh of the kingdom of God,[56] but lived only to point out Christ with his finger; cries, "Behold the Lamb of God,"[57] "I must decrease,"[58] and is cut off. David makes the great preparation for the temple, but he shall not see so much as the foundation laid.[59] Men must take their appointed lot. God will send "by the hand of him whom he will send."[60] Daniel must rest until the end be. It is said of some, they began to deliver Israel. The case of Zerubbabel was very rare, who saw the foundation and also the topstone of the temple laid,[61] and yet the work of Jerusalem was not half finished in his days, as you may see, Zechariah chap[ter] 1.

Two Reasons for This Doctrine

Reason 1. God oftentimes receives secret provocations from the choicest of his servants, which move him to take them short of their desires. Those of his own whom he employs in great works, have great and close communion with him. God usually exercises their spirits in near acts of fellowship with himself: they receive much from him, and are constrained to unburden themselves frequently upon him; now when men are brought into an intimacy with God, and have received great engagements from him, the Lord takes notice of every working and acting of their souls in an especial manner, and is oftentimes grieved and provoked with that in them which others can take no notice of: let a man read the story of that action of Moses upon which the Lord told him directly he should not see the finishing of the work he had in hand, nor enter into Canaan (Num. 20:7–8, 11).[62] It will be a hard matter, to find out wherein the failing was: he smote the rock with the rod, with some words of impatience, when he should only have spoken to it, and this with some secret unbelief, as to the thing he had in hand: God deals with others visibly, according to their outward actions, but in his own he takes notice of all their unbelief, fears, withdrawings, as proceeding from a frame in no measure answering those gracious discoveries of himself, which he has made unto them, and on this account it is that some are taken off in the midst of their work.

56 Matt. 3:2.

57 John 1:36.

58 John 3:30.

59 2 Sam. 7:5–13.

60 Ex. 4:13.

61 Ezra 5:2; Zech. 4:7.

62 The reference should probably also include verse 12. See *A Sermon Preached* [. . .] *January 31* (1649), in *Complete Works of John Owen*, 18:325.

[Reason] 2. To manifest that he has better things in store for his saints than the best and utmost of what they can desire or aim at here below. He had a heaven for Moses, and therefore might in love and mercy deny him Canaan. He employs some eminently, their work is great, their end glorious, at the very last step almost of their journey, he takes off one and another, lets them not see the things aimed at: this may be thought hard measure, strict severity, exact justice, yea as Job complains, "taking advantages against them";[63] but see what he calls them to, in calling them off from their greatest glories and excellencies on the earth, and all this will appear to be love, tenderness and favor in the highest. While you are laboring for a handful of firstfruits, he gives you the full harvest; while you are laboring for the figure here below, he gives you the substance above. Should you see the greatest work, wherein any of you were ever engaged brought to perfection, yet all were but a few drops compared with that fullness which he has prepared for you. The Lord then does it to witness to the children of men, that the things which are seen—the best of them, are not to be compared with the things that are not seen, yea the least of them,[64] inasmuch as he takes them whom he will honor, from the very door of the one, to bear them into the other. The meanest enjoyment in heaven is to be preferred before the richest on earth, even then when the kingdom of Christ shall come in most beauty and glory.

Two Applications

Servants Should Seek Their Reward in the Service Itself

Use 1.[65] You that are engaged in the work of God, seek for a reward of your service in the service itself. Few of you may live to see that beauty and glory which perhaps you aim at as the end of all your great undertakings for God, whereunto you have been engaged. God will proceed at his own pace, and calls on us to go along with him, and in the meantime, until the determinate end come, to wait in faith, and not make haste.[66] Those whose minds are so fixed on, and swallowed up with some end (though good) which they have proposed to themselves, do seldom see good days, and serene in their own souls, they have bitterness, wrath and trouble all their days: are still pressing to the end proposed, and commonly are dismissed from their station before it be attained. There is a sweetness, there is wages to be found in the work of God itself: men who have learned to hold communion with God in every work

63 Job 35:3.

64 2 Cor. 4:18.

65 Corrected from "Use 2."

66 Hab. 2:3; Isa. 28:16.

he calls them out unto, though they never see the main harvest they aim at in general, yet such will rest satisfied and submit to the Lord's limitation of their time: they bear their own sheaves in their bosoms.[67] Seeing God oftentimes dismisses his choicest servants, before they see, or taste of the main fruits of their endeavors; I see not upon what account consolation can be had in following the Lord in difficult dispensations, but only in that reward which every duty brings along with it, by communion with God in its performance. Make then this your aim, that in sincerity of heart, you do the work of God in your generation:[68] find his presence with you, his Spirit guiding you, his love accepting you, in the Lord Christ, and whenever you receive your dismission, it will be rest and peace, in the meantime, you will not make haste.

Servants Should Be Confident in Their Eternal Hope

[Use] 2. See a bottom and ground of consolation, when such eminent instruments as this departed worthy, are called off from their station, when ready to enter upon the harvest of all their labors, watchings, toilings, and expense of blood, God has better things for them in store, abiding things, that they shall not enjoy for a day or two, which is the best of what they could hope for here, had they lived to see all their desires accomplished; but such as in the fullness whereof, they may lie down in peace to eternity. Why do we complain? For our own loss? Is not the residue, and fullness of the Spirit with him, who gave him his dismission? For his loss, he lived not to see Ireland in peace,[69] but enjoys the glory of that eternal kingdom that was prepared for him before the foundation of the world, which is the condition held out in the third observation.

TREATMENT OF THE THIRD OBSERVATION: SAINTS ARE DISMISSED TO THEIR REST

Obs[ervation 3]. *The condition of a dismissed saint is a condition of rest: "Go thy way until the end be; for thou shalt rest."* The apostle gives it in as the issue of a discourse from a passage in the Psalms, "There remaineth therefore a rest for the people of God" (Heb. 4:9), it remains and is reserved for them, this the Lord has solemnly proclaimed from heaven, "Blessed are the dead

67 Ps. 126:6.

68 Acts 13:36.

69 At this point, the Cromwellian conquest of Ireland was almost complete except for Galway (which had yet to surrender) and the ongoing harassing of the English army by bands of Irish raiders known as Tories.

which die in the Lord from henceforth, yea, saith the Spirit, that they may rest from their labours, and their works do follow them" (Rev. 14:13): they go into a blessed condition of rest; there is not any notion under which the state of a dismissed saint, is so frequently described as this, of "rest," which indeed is the proper end and tendency of all things; their happiness is their rest; their rest is all the happiness they can be partakers of: "You have made us for yourself, O Lord, and our heart is restless until it rests in you."[70]

Now "rest" holds out two things unto us: (1) A freedom from what is opposite thereunto, wherein those that are at rest, have been exercised, in reference whereunto they are said to be at rest. (2) Something which suits them, and satisfies their nature in the condition wherein they are; and therefore they are at rest, which they could not be, were it not so with them, for nothing can rest, but in the full fruition, and enjoyment of that which satiates the whole nature of it in all its extent and capacity. We must briefly inquire, 1. What it is that the saints are at rest from, and secondly, what it is that they are at rest in, which I shall do very speedily.

This Rest Is Freedom from Sin, Oppression, and Grief

1. The many particulars which they are at rest from, may be referred unto two general heads, (1) Sin. (2) Labor, and travail.

(1) Sin; this on all considerations, whatever, is the main disquietness of the soul; temptations to it, actings in it, troubles for it, they are the very Egypt of the soul, its house and place of bondage, and vexation; either the power of it indwelling, or the guilt of it pressing, are here still disquieting the soul. For the first, [1][71] how does Paul complain, lament, yea cry out concerning it, "O wretched man that I am!" (Rom. 7:24), and what a sad, restless, and tumultuating condition upon this account does he describe in the verses foregoing? The best, the wisest, the holiest of the saints, on this account are in a restless condition.

Suppose a man a conqueror in every battle, in every combat that he is engaged in, yet while he has any fighting, though he be never foiled, he has not peace. Though the saints should have success in every engagement against sin, yet because it will still be rebelling, still be fighting, it will disturb their peace.

70 In the text: *Fecisti nos ad te, Domine, et inquietum est cor nostrum, donec veniat ad te.*—Owen. This is a quotation from Augustine's *Confessiones* 1.1. For the Latin text, see Augustine, *Confessions*, vol. 1, *Introduction and Text*, trans. James J. O'Donnell (Oxford: Clarendon, 1992), 3. For the English translation, see Saint Augustine, *Confessions*, trans. Henry Chadwick (Oxford: Oxford University Press, 1992), 3.

71 The number is inserted for clarity.

[2] So also does the guilt of it; our Savior testifies, that a sense of it will make a man to be "weary and heavy laden" (Matt. 11:28). This oftentimes makes the inhabitants of Zion say they are sick, for though an end be made of sin as to the guilt of it in the blood of Christ, yet by reason of our darkness, folly, and unbelief, and the hiding of the countenance of God, the conscience is oftentimes pressed with it, no less than if it lay indeed under the whole weight and burden of it.

I shall not instance in more particulars, concerning this cause of want of rest, and disquietness, the perplexity of temptations, buffetings and winnowings of Satan, allurements and affrightments of the world, darkness and sorrows of unbelief, and the like, do all set in against us upon this account.

This in general is the first thing that the dismissed saints are at rest from: they, sin no more, they wound the Lord Jesus no more, they trouble their own souls no more, they grieve the Spirit no more, they dishonor the gospel no more, they are troubled no more with Satan's temptations without, no more with their own corruption within, but lie down in a constant enjoyment of one everlasting victory over sin, with all its attendants: says the Spirit, "They rest from their labours," Revelation 14,[72] those labors which make them faint and weary, their contending with sin to the uttermost; they are no more cold in communion; they have not one thought that wanders off from God to eternity; they lose him no more, but always lie down in his bosom, without the least possibility of disturbance. Even the very remembrance of sin is sweet unto them, when they see God infinitely exalted, and admired in the pardon thereof.

They are free from trouble, and that both as to doing, and suffering: few of the saints but are called out in one kind or another to both these. Everyone is either doing for God, or suffering for God, some both do and suffer great things for him: in either of them there is pain, weariness, travail, labor, trouble, sorrow and anxiety of spirit; neither is there any eminent doing or working for God, but is carried on with much suffering to the outward man.

What a life of labor and trouble did our deceased friend lead for many years in the flesh? How were his days consumed in travail? God calling him to his foot,[73] and exercising him to understand the sweetness of that promise, that they that die in him, shall have rest.[74] Many spend their days deliciously,[75] with so much contentment to the flesh, that it is impossible they should have any foretaste and sweet relish of their rest that is to come.

72 Rev. 14:13.

73 Isa. 41:2.

74 Rev. 14:13.

75 I.e., in a manner characterized by pleasure, comfort, and indulgence.

The apostle tells us that "there remaineth a rest for the people of God";[76] and yet withal, that they who believe are entered into that rest,[77] those who in their labors, in their travails do take in the sweetness of that promise of rest, do even in their labor make an entrance thereinto.

(2)[78] This then secondly, they rest from all trouble and anxiety that attend them in their pilgrimage, either in doing or suffering for God. They enter into rest, and cease from their works (Heb. 4:10). God wipes all tears from their eyes,[79] there is no more watching, no more fasting, no more wrestling, no more fighting, no more blood, no more sorrow, "the ransomed of the Lord do return with everlasting joy on their heads, and sorrow and sighing flee away."[80] There tyrants pretend no more title to their kingdom; rebels lie not in wait for their blood; they are no more awakened by the sound of the trumpet, nor the noise of the instruments of death: they fear not for their relations, they weep not for their friends, the Lamb is their temple,[81] and God is all in all unto them.[82] Yet—

This Glorious and Satisfying Rest Is in God

2. This will not complete their rest, something farther is required thereto: even something to satisfy, everlastingly content and fill them in the state and condition wherein they are. Free them in your thoughts from what you please, without this they are not at rest. This then you have in the second place, God is the rest of their souls, "Return to thy rest, O my soul" (Ps. 116).[83] Dismissed saints rest in the bosom of God,[84] because in the fruition and enjoyment of him they are everlastingly satisfied, as having attained the utmost end whereto they were created, all the blessedness whereof they are capable. I could almost beg for liberty a little to expatiate in this meditation of the sweet, gracious, glorious, satisfied condition of a dismissed saint.

76 Heb. 4:9.

77 Heb. 4:3.

78 This numeral is added for the purposes of clarity and consistency.

79 Rev. 21:4.

80 Isa. 35:10; 51:11.

81 Rev. 21:22.

82 1 Cor. 15:28.

83 Ps. 116:7.

84 For a treatment of debates about the nature of Abraham's Bosom, see Peter Marshall, "'The Map of God's Word': Geographies of the Afterlife in Tudor and Early Stuart England," in *The Place of The Dead: Death and Remembrance in Late Medieval and Early Modern Europe*, ed. Bruce Gordon and Peter Marshall (Cambridge: Cambridge University Press, 2000), 121–22.

But the time is spent, and therefore without holding out one drop of water to quench the feigned fire of purgatory,[85] or drawing forth anything to discover the vanity of their assertion who affirm the soul to sleep,[86] or to be nothing until the resurrection;[87] or theirs who assigning to them a state of subsistence and perception,[88] do yet exclude them from the fruition of God,[89] without which there is no rest, until the end of all, with such other by-persuasions, as would disquiet the condition or abridge the glory of those blessed souls, which yet were a facile undertaking, I shall draw toward a close.

There are three points yet remaining.[90] I shall speak only to the first of them, and that as a use of the doctrine last proposed, and I have done.

TREATMENT OF THE FOURTH OBSERVATION: THE INTERMEDIATE STATE PRECEDES THE ETERNAL STATE

[Observation 4.][91] Then you see *there is an appointed determinate season, wherein all things and persons, according to the will of God, will run into their utmost issue and everlasting condition*. You are going, whoever you are, into an abiding condition, and there is a lot appointed for you, wherein lies an estate everlastingly unchangeable. It is the utmost end whereunto you are designed, and when once you are entered into that lot, you are everlastingly engaged: no more change, no more alteration, if it be well with you, it will

85 According to the doctrine of purgatory as defined by the Second Council of Lyons (1274) and the Council of Florence (1439), this was "a place and condition of temporal, purgative punishment reserved for those Christians who die with the stain of venial sin still on them or who die without having completed temporal satisfaction or penance for their sins." See Richard A. Muller, *Dictionary of Latin and Greek Theological Terms: Drawn Principally from Protestant Scholastic Theology*, second edition (Grand Rapids, MI: Baker, 2017), s.v. "*Purgatorium*."

86 Soul sleep (*psychopannychism*) was a form of Christian mortalism in which the soul was said to lapse into a state of unconsciousness from the hour of death until the day of judgment. See Norman T. Burns, *Christian Mortalism from Tyndale to Milton* (Cambridge MA: Harvard University Press, 1972), 18.

87 Another form of Christian mortalism was *thnetopsychism*, the belief that the soul dies with the body before being raised at the last judgment. This view was associated with Richard Overton, Thomas Hobbes, and John Biddle. See Richard Sugg, *The Smoke of the Soul: Medicine, Physiology and Religion in Early Modern England* (Basingstoke, UK: Palgrave Macmillan, 2013), 207–23.

88 The state of limbo, both *limbus patrum* (the limbo of the fathers) and *limbus infantum* (the limbo of infants), was said to be without suffering but also without the beatific vision. Muller, *Dictionary of Latin and Greek Theological Terms*, s.v. "*limbus*."

89 The fruition of God through the enjoyment of the *visio Dei*, the beatific vision.

90 These points are observations 4–6.

91 Following Goold, this first of "the three points yet remaining" is presented as "Observation 4," which is how Owen had described it earlier in the sermon.

abide: if otherwise expect not any relief. In our few days we live for eternity, in our mutable estate we deal for an unchangeable condition. It is not thus only in respect of particulars, but God has "appointed a day, wherein he will judge all the world by the man whom he hath ordained."[92] An end is coming unto all that whole dispensation under which we are. To you who by the riches of free grace have obtained union and communion with the Lord Jesus, rest and peace, when God shall everlastingly "rain snares, fire and brimstone,"[93] upon the workers of iniquity. Some mock indeed, and say, "Where is the promise of his coming?"[94] But we know, "the Lord is not slack, as some men count slackness,"[95] but exercises patience until the appointed season, for the bringing about of his own glorious ends, which he has determined concerning his creatures. Why should we then complain, when anyone, perhaps before our expectation, but yet according to God's determination, makes an entrance into the end of all? All things work to that season. This state of things is not for continuance. That which is incumbent, is in this uncertain space of time allotted to us, to "give all diligence to make our calling and election sure,"[96] as also to serve the Lord faithfully in our generations,[97] wherein we cannot be surprised: we have an example in him who is gone before; it is true, the Lord Jesus is our primitive pattern and example: but those also who have followed him, wherein they have followed him, are to be eyed and marked as provocations to the same labor of faith and love, wherein they were exercised. And that this use may be made by this assembly, I shall add one word concerning him from whom is the occasion thereof.

CONCLUDING APPLICATION FROM IRETON'S EXAMPLE

Every man stands in a threefold capacity. 1. natural, 2. civil, 3. religious. And there are distinct qualifications that are suited unto these several capacities.¶[98]

1.[99] To the first as the ornaments and perfections of nature, are suited some seeds of those heroical virtues, as courage, permanency in business, etc., which being in themselves morally indifferent, have their foundations

92 Acts 17:31.

93 Ps. 11:6.

94 2 Pet. 3:4.

95 2 Pet. 3:9.

96 2 Pet. 1:10.

97 Acts 13:36.

98 The ¶ symbol indicates that a paragraph break has been added to Owen's original text.

99 This numeral is added for the purposes of clarity and consistency.

eminently laid in the natures of some persons, which yet hinders not, but that their good improvement is of grace.

2. To the second, or man's civil capacity, there are many eminencies relating as peculiar endowments, which may be referred unto the three heads of ability, faithfulness, and industry, that through them neither by weakness, treachery nor sloth the works and employments incumbent on men in their civil state and condition may suffer.

3. Men's peculiar ornament and improvement, in their religious capacity, lies in those fruits of the Spirit which we call Christian graces: of these in respect of usefulness there are three most eminent, viz., faith, love, and self-denial. I speak of them upon another account than the apostle does, where he places hope among the first three of Christian graces.[100] Now all these in their several kinds were as eminent in the person deceased in his several capacities, as perhaps is usually found in anyone in a generation. My business is not to make a funeral oration, only I suppose that without offense I may desire, that in courage and permanency in business (which I name in opposition to that unsettled, pragmatical shuffling disposition which is in some men) in ability for wisdom and counsel, in faithfulness to his trust and in his trust, in indefatigable industry in the pursuit of the work committed to him, in faith on the promises of God, and acquaintance with his mind in his mighty works of providence, in love to the Lord Jesus and all his saints, in a tender regard to their interest, delight in their society, contempt of himself and all his for the gospel's sake, with eminent self-denial in all his concernments, in impartiality and sincerity in the execution of justice, that in these and the like things we may have many raised up in the power and spirit wherein he walked before the Lord, and the inhabitants of this nation. This (I say) I hope I may speak without offense here upon such an occasion as this; my business being occasionally to preach the word, not to carry on a part of a funeral ceremony, I shall add no more, but commit you to him, who is able to prepare you for your eternal condition.

FINIS.[101]

100 1 Cor. 13:13.
101 Lat. "The End."

A SERMON PREACHED TO THE PARLIAMENT, OCTOB. 13. 1652. A DAY OF SOLEMN HUMILIATION. CONCERNING THE KINGDOM OF CHRIST, AND THE POWER OF THE CIVIL MAGISTRATE ABOUT THE THINGS OF THE WORSHIP OF GOD.

By John Owen

Oxford,
Printed by Leonard Lichfield printer to the University, for Thomas Robinson.
Anno Dom. 1652.

[Sermon]

I Daniel was grieved in my spirit, in the midst of my body, and the visions of my head troubled me. I came near unto one of them that stood by, and asked him the truth of all this: so he told me, and made me know the interpretation of the things.

DANIEL 7:15–16

INTRODUCTION AND OPENING OF THE TEXT

What there is of concernment for the right understanding of these words, in that part of the chapter which goes before, may be considered in the opening of the words themselves, and therefore I shall immediately attend thereunto.

There are in them four things considerable.

1. The state and condition which Daniel the penman of this prophecy, expresses himself to be in, wherein he has companions in the days wherein we live: "He was grieved in his spirit in the midst of his body."

2. The cause and means whereby he was brought into this perplexed frame of spirit: "The visions of his head troubled him."

3. The remedy he used for his delivery from that entangled condition of spirit wherein he was: "He went nigh to one of them that stood by, and asked him the truth of all this."

4. The issue of that application, he made to that one that stood by for redress: "He told him, and made him know the interpretation of the things."

All these I shall briefly open unto you, that I may lay a foundation for the truth which the Lord has furnished me with, to hold out unto you this day.

The Perplexing Nature of the Shaking of the Nations

1. In the first, the person spoken of is Daniel himself. "I Daniel;" he bears this testimony concerning himself, and his condition was, that "he was grieved in his spirit."

The person himself was a man highly favored of God, above all in his generation: so richly furnished with gifts and graces, that he is once and again brought forth as an example, and instanced in by God himself, upon the account of eminence in wisdom and piety. Yet all this preserves him not, from falling into this perplexed condition (Dan. 1:17–20; Ezek. 9:24;[1] 28:3).

Now as the principal work of all the holy prophets, which have been since the world began (Luke 1:70; 1 Pet. 1:10–12), was to preach, set forth, and declare the Lord Jesus Christ, the Messiah, who was for to come, so some especial concernments of his person, righteousness, and kingdom, were in especial manner committed unto them respectively. His passion and righteousness to Isaiah, the covenant of grace in him to Jeremiah, and to this Daniel most eminently the great works of the providence of God, in the shaking and overturning of kingdoms and nations, in a subserviency to his kingdom; with the revelation hereof for the consolation of the church in all ages, did the Lord honor him of whom we speak.

For the present he describes himself in a somewhat perplexed condition. His spirit (mind and soul) was grieved, sick, troubled, or disquieted in the midst of his body; that is, deeply, nearly, closely: it sets out the greatness of his trouble, the anxiety of his thoughts within him: like David when he expostulated[2] with his soul about it. "Why art thou so sad my soul, and why art thou so disquieted within me" (Ps. 43:5): he knew not what to say, what to do, nor wherewith to relieve himself. He was filled with sad thoughts, sad apprehensions of what was to come to pass, and what might be the issue of the things that had been discovered unto him. This I say is the frame and temper he describes himself to be in: a man under sad apprehensions of the issues and events of things, and the dispensations of God, as many are at this day: and upon that account closely, and nearly perplexed.

A Survey of the Establishment of the Kingdom of Christ

2. The cause of this perturbation of mind, and spirit was from the visions of his head: "The visions of his head troubled him." He calls them "visions of the head," because that is the seat of the internal senses, and fantasy, whereby

1 Following Goold, this should be corrected to Ezek. 14:14.

2 I.e., debated as an aggrieved person.

visions are received. So he calls them, "a dream," verse 1, and "visions of his head upon his bed": yet such visions, such a dream it was, as being immediately from God, and containing a no less certain discovery of his will, and mind, than if the things mentioned in them, had been spoken face to face, he writes them by the inspiration of the Holy Ghost, verse 2, for the use of the church.

I shall not take the advantage of going forth unto any discourse, of dreams, visions, oracles, and those other "divers ways and manners" (Heb. 1:1) of revealing his mind and will, which God was pleased to use with his prophets of old (Num. 12:6–8): my aim lies another way: it suffices only to take notice, that God gave him in his sleep a representation of the things here expressed, which he was to give over, for the use of the church in following ages. The matter of these visions which did so much trouble him, falls more directly under our consideration.

A Survey of the Progress within Daniel's Vision

(1) Now the subject of these perplexing visions, is a representation of the four great empires of the world, which had, and were to have dominion, in and over the places of the church's greatest concernments, and were all to receive their period, and destruction by the Lord Christ and his revenging hand: and these three things he mentions of them therein.

[1] Rise.
[2] Nature.
[3] Destruction.

[1] [In] verse 2 he describes their rise and original: it was "from the strivings of the four winds of the heavens, upon the great sea";[3] he compares them to the most violent, uncontrollable, and tumultuating things in the whole creation: winds and seas![4] What waves, what horrible storms, what mixing of heaven and earth, what confusion, and destruction must needs ensue the fierce contest of all contrary winds upon the great sea? Such are the springs of empires, and governments for the most part among men, such their entrances and advancements. In particular, such were the beginnings of the four empires here spoken of. Wars, tumults, confusions, blood, destruction, desolation, were the seeds of their greatness ("He made a wilderness and

3 Dan. 7:2.

4 This is striking language in the context of the Anglo-Dutch sea war.

called it peace").[5] Seas and great waters do, in the Scripture represent people, and nations, "The waters which thou sawest, where the whore sitteth, are peoples, and multitudes, and nations, and tongues" (Rev. 17:15); as "waters," they are unstable, fierce, restless, tumultuating, and when God mingles his judgments among them, they are as "a sea of glass mingled with fire";[6] brittle, uncertain, devouring, and implacable.

It is a demonstration of the sovereignty of God, that he is above them, "The floods have lifted up, O Lord, the floods have lifted up their voice, the floods lift up their waves. The Lord on high is mightier than the noise of many waters, yea than the mighty waves of the sea" (Ps. 93:3–4). Now from these, tossed with the winds of commotions, seditions, oppressions, passions, do flow the governments of the world, the Spirit of God moving upon the face of those waters,[7] to bring forth those forms and frames of rule, which he will make use of.

[2] Unto verse 9 he describes them in order, as to their nature and kind: one of them being then ready to be destroyed, and the other to succeed, until the utter desolation of them all, and all power rising in their spirit and principle.

I shall not pass through their particular description, nor stay to prove that the fourth beast, without name or special form, is the Roman Empire, which I have elsewhere demonstrated,[8] and it is something else which at this time I aim at. This is that which troubles and grieves the spirit of Daniel in the midst of his body. He saw what worldly powers should arise, by what horrible tumults, shakings, confusions, and violence they should spring up, with what fierceness, cruelty, and persecution, they should rule in the world, and stamp all under their feet.[9]

[3] Their end and destruction is revealed unto him, from verse 10 unto verses 12–13. And this by the appearance of "the Ancient of days" (the eternal God) in judgment against them: which he sets out with that solemnity and

5 In the text: *vastitiem ubi-fecerunt, pacem vocant*, Galgac. apud Tacit.—Owen. This is a version of the words of the first-century Caledonian war leader Calgacus (Galgacus) from Tacitus' *Life of Julius Agricola* 30.5. For the Latin text and English translation, from which this translation is adapted, see Tacitus, *Agricola. Germania. Dialogue on Oratory*, trans. M. Hutton and W. Peterson, rev. R. M. Ogilvie, E. H. Warmington, Michael Winterbottom, Loeb Classical Library 35 (Cambridge, MA: Harvard University Press, 1914), 80–81.

6 Rev. 15:2.

7 Gen. 1:2.

8 In the margin: Sermon on Heb. 12:27–28.—Owen. This is a reference to Owen's sermon from April 1649, *The Shaking and Translating of Heaven and Earth* (1649). See *Complete Works of John Owen*, 18:411–62.

9 Dan. 7:7.

glory, as if it were the great judgment of the last day: God indeed thereby giving a pledge unto the world, of that universal judgment he will one day exercise toward all, "by the man whom he hath ordained" (Acts 17:31). And this increases the terror of the vision, to have such a representation of the glory of God, as no creature is able to bear: God also manifests hereby his immediate actings, in the setting up, and pulling down the powers of this world, which he does as fully and effectually, as if he sat upon a throne of judgment, calling them all by name to appear in his presence, and, upon the evidence of their ways, cruelties and oppression, pronouncing sentence against them: "Be wise therefore O ye kings, be instructed, ye judges of the earth: serve the Lord with fear and rejoice with trembling";[10] "He changeth the times and seasons" (Dan. 2:21): "He ruleth in the kingdom of men, and setteth over it whom he pleaseth," chapter 5:21. And this is the first thing in this vision, at which the prophet was perplexed.

The Climax of the Vision and a Threefold Analysis of Christ's Kingdom

(2) There is the approach of the Lord Christ unto the Father, with his entrance into his kingdom and dominion, which is everlasting, and passes not away, verse 14. This being the end of the vision, I must a little insist upon it; not that I intend purposely to handle the kingdom of Christ as mediator, but only a little to consider it, as it lies here in the vision, and is needful for the right bottoming of the truth in our intendment.

Various have been the thoughts of men about the kingdom of Christ in all ages. That the Messiah was to be a King, a Prince, a Ruler, that he was to have a kingdom, and that the government was to be on his shoulders,[11] is evident from the Old Testament. That all this was, and is accomplished in Jesus of Nazareth, whom God exalted, made a Prince and a Savior,[12] is no less evident in the New.

But about the nature of this kingdom, its rise, and manner of government, have been and are the contests of men.

The Jews to this very day expect it, as a thing carnal, and temporal, visible, outwardly glorious, wherein, in all manner of pleasure, they shall bear rule over the nations, at their will; such another thing, of all the world, as the popedom, which the Gentile or idolatrous worshipers of Christ set up for his kingdom: and of some such thing it may be supposed, the apostles themselves were not without thoughts, until they had conversed with the

10 In the margin: Ps. 2:11–12.—Owen.

11 Isa. 9:6.

12 Acts 5:31.

Lord after the resurrection (Luke 9:46; Acts 1:6). Neither are all among us free from them at this day.[13]

Those who with any simplicity profess the name of Christ, do generally agree, that there are three parts of it.

[1] First and principally; in that which is internal and spiritual, in and over the souls of men, over spirits both good and bad, in reference unto the ends which he has to accomplish upon them: of that which is direct and immediate upon the hearts and souls of men, there are two parts.

{1} That which he exercises toward his elect, who are given unto him of his Father, converting, ruling, preserving them, under and through great variety of dispensations, internal and external, until he brings them unto himself: "He stands and feeds them in the strength of the Lord, in the majesty of the name of the Lord his God" (Mic. 5:4), even he who is the "Ruler in Israel" (Mic. 5:2). He is exalted and made "a Prince and a Saviour, to give repentance to Israel, and the forgiveness of sins" (Acts 5:31). He makes his people "a willing people in the day of his power" (Ps. 110:3). Sending out his Holy Spirit to lead them into all truth,[14] and making his word and ordinances "mighty through God, to the pulling down of strongholds" in their hearts, "casting down imaginations, and every high thing that exalts itself against the knowledge of God; and bringing into captivity every thought to the obedience of himself" (2 Cor. 10:4–5). He takes possession of their hearts by his power, dwelling in them by his Spirit, making them kings in his kingdom, and bringing them infallibly into glory: oh that this rule, this kingdom of his, might be carried on in our hearts! We busy ourselves about many things, we shall find at length this one thing necessary: this is that part of the kingdom of Christ, which we are principally to aim at in the preaching of the gospel: "We preach Christ Jesus the Lord" (1 Cor. 4:5),[15] him to be Lord and King, though others have had dominion over us: they are the grains of Israel which the Lord seeks for in his sifting the nations by his word, as well as by his providence:[16] and we are, in the work of the gospel, to "endure all things for the elect's sakes" (2 Cor. 2:10).[17]

{2} In the power which he exercises toward others, to whom the word of the gospel does come, calling, convincing, enlightening, hardening many,

13 This is a reference to the Fifth Monarchists, not least among them Owen's fellow preacher at the parliamentary fast, Christopher Feake.

14 John 16:13.

15 Following Goold, this should be corrected to 2 Cor. 4:5.

16 Amos 9:9.

17 Following Goold, this should be corrected to 2 Tim. 2:10.

whom yet being not his sheep, nor of his fold, he will never take to himself: but leaves to themselves, under aggravations of condemnation, which they pull upon themselves by the contempt of the gospel (2 Cor. 2:16; Heb. 10:29). He sends his Spirit to convince even the perishing "world of sin, righteousness, and judgment" (John 16:8). He sends "sharp" arrows into the very hearts of his enemies (Ps. 45:5)—making them stoop, bow, and fall under him: so bounding their rage, overbearing their lusts, leaving them without excuse in themselves, and his people, oftentimes not without profit from them: with some dealing even in this life more severely, causing the "witnesses" of the gospel to torment them by the preaching of the word (Rev. 11:10), yet giving them up to "strong delusions," that they may believe lies, and be damned (2 Thess. 2:11–12) etc.

{3} In carrying on of this work toward the one and the other, he puts forth the power, rule, and dominion, which he has of his Father over spirits, both good and bad. 1st. Being made head of "principalities and powers," and exalted far above "every name in heaven or earth,"[18] being made the "first-born of every creature,"[19] and all the angels of God being commanded to worship him (Heb. 1:6) and put in subjection under his feet; he sends them forth, and uses them "as ministering spirits for them who shall be heirs of salvation," verse 14, "appointing them to behold the face of his Father," ready for his commands on their behalf (Matt. 18:10), attending in their assemblies (1 Cor. 11:10), and to give them their assistance in the time of danger and trouble (Acts 12:9), destroying their adversaries (Acts 12:23), with innumerable other advantageous administrations, which he has not thought good to acquaint us withal in particular, that our dependence might be on our King himself, and not on any of our "fellow-servants," though never so glorious and excellent (Rev. 22:9).

2nd. For Satan as he came "to bind the strong man" armed, and to "spoil his goods" (Matt. 12:29), "to destroy him that had the power of death" (Heb. 2:14), and being made manifest to this end, "that he might destroy his works" (1 John 3:8) in the souls of men in this world (2 Cor. 10:4–5), so having in his own person conquered these "principalities and powers" of darkness, making "an open show of them" in his cross, and "triumphing over them" (Col. 2:15) he continues overruling and judging him and them, in their opposition to his church, and will do so until he bring them to a full conquest and subjection, that they shall be judged and sentenced by the

18 Col. 1:16–18; Phil. 2:9–10.

19 Col. 1:15.

poor creatures, whom in this world they continually pursue with all manner of enmity (1 Cor. 6:3).

And this looks to the inward substance of the kingdom of Christ, which is given him of his Father, and "is not of this world,"[20] though he exercise it in the world to the last day: a kingdom, which can never be shaken nor removed.[21] "The government of it is upon his shoulder," and "of the increase of it there shall be no end."[22]

[2] That rule or government, which in his word he has appointed and ordained, for all his saints and chosen ones to walk in, to testify their inward subjection to him, and to be fitted for usefulness one to another. Now of this part the administration is wrapped up in the laws, ordinances, institutions, and appointments of the gospel, and it is frequently called "The kingdom of God." That Jesus Christ does not rule in these things, and is not to be obeyed as a king in them, is but a late darkness, which though it should spread as a cloud over the face of the heavens, and pour forth some showers and tempests, yet it would be as a cloud still, which will speedily scatter and vanish into nothing.

And this is that, whose propagation, as the means of carrying on the former spiritual ends of Christ, which you desire strength and direction for this day, etc.[23]

Men may gather together unto Christ and say, with heads full of hopes, poor souls, and eyes fixed on the right hand and left, "Lord wilt thou at this time restore the kingdom to Israel?" Take you his answer, and be contented with it, "It is not for you to know the times or the seasons, which the Father has put in his own power," but do your work faithfully.[24]

I know in this thing, it is far easier to complain of you for not doing, than to direct you what to do; the Lord be your guide, and give you straw wherever bricks are required of you.[25]

[3] In the universal judgment, which the Father has committed to him over all: which he will most eminently exercise at the last day; rewarding, crowning, receiving some to himself, judging, condemning, casting others into utter darkness (John 5:22–27; Acts 2:36; Rom. 14:9; Acts 17:31).

20 John 18:36.

21 Heb. 12:28.

22 Isa. 9:6–7.

23 One of the reasons for the fast was to discover "how the saving truth of the Gospel may be best advanced and propagated, and whatsoever is contrast to sound Doctrine & the power of Godliness suppressed." See *An Act For setting apart Wednesday the Thirteenth day of October, 1652, For a Day of Publique Fasting and Humiliation* [. . .] (London, 1652).

24 In the margin: Acts 1:6–7.—Owen.

25 Ex. 5:7.

And of this universal righteous judgment, he gives many warnings unto the world, by pouring forth sundry vials of his wrath upon great Nimrods and oppressors (Ps. 110:6; Mic. 4:3; Rev. 19:11–13).[26] And in the holding forth these three parts of the kingdom of the Lord Jesus, does the Scripture abound.

Five Observations about the Nature of Christ's Kingdom

But now whether over and beyond all these the Lord Christ shall not bear an outward, visible, glorious rule? Setting up a kingdom like those of the world, to be ruled by strength and power? And if so; when, or how it shall be brought in, into whose hands the administration of it shall be committed, and upon what account, whether he will personally walk therein or no, whether it shall be clearly distinct from the rule he now bears in the world, or only differenced by more glorious degrees and manifestations of his power? Endless and irreconcilable, are the contests of those that profess his name: this we find, by woeful experience, that all who from the spirituality of the rule of Christ, and delight therein, have degenerated into carnal apprehensions of the beauty and glory of it, have for the most part, been given up to carnal actings, suited to such apprehensions, and have been so dazzled, with gazing after temporal glory, that the kingdom which comes not by observation, has been vile in their eyes.[27]

Now because it is here fallen in my way, and is part of the vision, at which the prophet was so much troubled, I shall give you some brief observations, of what is clear and certain from Scripture relating hereunto, and so pass on: it is then certain;

(1) That the interest of particular men as to this kingdom of Christ, is to look wherein the universal concernment of all saints, in all ages does lie: this undoubtedly they may attain, and it does belong to them: now certainly this is in that part of it, which comes not by "observation" (Luke 17:20), but is "within" us,[28] which "is righteousness, and peace, and joy in the Holy Ghost" (Rom. 14:17). This may be possessed in a dungeon, as well as on a throne. What outward glory soever may be brought in, it is but a shadow of this: this is the kingdom that cannot be moved, which requires grace in us to "serve God acceptably with reverence and godly fear" (Heb. 12:28). Many have failed in grasping after outward appearances: never any failed of blessedness, who made this their portion: oh that this were more pursued and followed after!

26 The Micah reference should probably be corrected to 5:6, a text Owen would appeal to in *God's Presence with a People*, which is contained in this volume.

27 This is an oblique reference to the Fifth Monarchists.

28 Luke 17:21.

Let not any think to set up the kingdom of Christ in the world, while they pull it down in their own hearts, by sin and folly: in this let "the lines fall to me,"[29] and let my inheritance be among those that are sanctified:[30] yet,

(2) This is certain, that all nations whatever, which in their present state and government, have given their power to the dragon and the beast to oppose the Lord Christ withal,[31] shall be shaken, broken, translated, and turned off their old foundations, and constitutions, into which the anti-Christian interest has been woven for a long season.[32] God will shake the heavens and the earth of the nations round about, until all the Babylonish rubbish, all their original engagements to the man of sin be taken away.[33]

This I have fully demonstrated elsewhere.[34] All those great wars which you have foretold, wherein the saints of God shall be eminently engaged, are upon this account.

(3) That the civil powers of the world after fearful shakings and desolations shall be disposed of into a useful subserviency to the interest, power, and kingdom of Jesus Christ: hence they are said to be his kingdoms (Rev. 11:15). That is, to be disposed of, for the behoof[35] of his interest, rule, and dominion: of this you have plentiful promises [in] Isaiah 60 and elsewhere; when the nations are broken in opposition to Zion, "their gain must be consecrated to the Lord, and their substance to the Lord of the whole earth" (Mic. 4:15).[36] Even judges and rulers, (as such) must "kiss the Son,"[37] and own his scepter, and advance his ways: some think, if you were well settled,[38] you ought not in anything, as rulers of the nations, to put forth your power for the interest of Christ: the good Lord keep your hearts from that apprehension. Have you ever in your affairs, received any encouragement from the promises of God, have you in times of greatest distress been refreshed with the testimony of a good conscience, that in godly simplicity, you have

29 Ps. 16:6.

30 Acts 20:32.

31 Rev. 17:13.

32 Owen employed the trope of such weaving of the Antichristian interest in *A Sermon Preached* [...] *January 31* (1649), where he spoke of it as a web that needed to be untangled. See *Complete Works of John Owen*, 18:299, 308, 335.

33 Heb. 12:27.

34 In the margin: Serm. on Heb. 12:28.—Owen. This is a further reference to Owen's sermon from April 1649, *The Shaking and Translating of Heaven and Earth* (1649). See *Complete Works of John Owen*, 18:411–62.

35 I.e., use or benefit.

36 Following Goold, this should be corrected to Mic. 4:13.

37 Ps. 2:12.

38 I.e., the desire to see the Parliament was well settled.

sought the advancement of the Lord Christ; do you believe that he ever owned the cause as the head of his church? Do not now profess you have nothing to do with him: had he so professed of you and your affairs, what had been your portion long since!

(4) Look what kingdom soever, the Lord Christ will advance in the world, and exercise among his holy ones, the beginning of it must be with the Jews; they are to be *caput imperii*,[39] the head and seat of this empire must be among them; these are the "saints of the Most High," mentioned by Daniel:[40] and therefore in that part of his prophecy, which he wrote in the Chaldean tongue,[41] then commonly known and spoken in the East, being the language of the Babylonish empire, he speaks of them obscurely, and under borrowed expressions; but coming to those visions which he wrote in Hebrew, for the sole use of the church, he is much more express concerning the people of whom he spoke. The "rod" of Christ's "strength" goes out of Zion, and thence he proceeds "to rule those that were his enemies" (Ps. 110:2). All the promises of the glorious kingdom of Christ, are to be accomplished in the gathering of the Gentiles, with the glory of the Jews. The Redeemer comes to Zion, and to them "that turn from transgression" (that great transgression of unbelief) "in Jacob" (Isa. 59:20). Then shall "the Lord rise" upon them, and "his glory shall be seen" upon them, "the Gentiles shall come to their light, and kings to the brightness of their rising" (Isa. 60:2–3). I dare say there is not any promise anywhere of raising up a kingdom unto the Lord Christ in this world, but it is either expressed or clearly intimated, that the beginning of it must be with the Jews, and that in contradistinction[42] to the nations: so eminently in that glorious description of it, "I will make her that halted a remnant, and her that was cast a far off a strong nation, and the Lord shall reign over them in mount Zion, from henceforth even for ever: and thou O tower of the flock, the strong hold of the daughter of Zion, unto thee shall it come, even the first dominion, the kingdom shall come to the daughter of Jerusalem" (Mic. 4:7–8). When the great hunter Nimrod set up a kingdom, the beginning of it was Babel (Gen. 10:10) and when the great shepherd sets up his kingdom, the beginning of it shall be Zion: so farther it is at large expressed, Micah 5:7–8. Nothing is more clear to any, who, being not carried away with weak, carnal apprehensions of things present, have once seriously weighed the promises of God to this purpose: what the Lord Christ will do with them,

39 Lat. "The head of the empire."

40 Dan. 7:18.

41 Daniel 2:4b–7:28 was written in Aramaic.

42 I.e., distinction by means of contrast.

and by them, is not so clear, this is certain, that their return shall be marvelous, glorious, as life from the dead.[43] When then Euphrates shall be dried up, Turkish power, and popish idolatry be taken out of the world, and these "kings of the east" are come,[44] when the seed of Abraham, being multiplied "like the stars of heaven and the sands of the sea-shore," shall "possess the gates of their enemies,"[45] and shall have peace in their borders,[46] we may lift up our heads toward the fullness of our redemption: but while these things are or may be (for anything we know), afar off, to dream of setting up an outward, glorious, visible kingdom of Christ, which he must bear rule in, and over the world, be it in Germany or in England,[47] is but an ungrounded presumption. The Jews not called, Antichrist not destroyed, the nations of the world generally wrapped up in idolatry and false worship, little dreaming of their deliverance: will the Lord Christ leave the world in this state, and set up his kingdom here on a molehill?[48]

(5) This is a perpetual antithesis, and opposition that is put between the kingdoms of the world, and the kingdom of Christ; that they rise out of the strivings of the winds upon the sea;[49] he comes "with the clouds of heaven":[50] they are brought in by commotions, tumults, wars, desolations, and so shall all the shakings of the nations be, to punish them for their old opposition, and to translate them into a subserviency to his interest: the coming in of the kingdom of Christ, shall not be by the arm of flesh, nor shall it be the product of the strifes and contests of men which are in the world: it is not to be done by "might" or "power," but by the Spirit of the Lord of hosts (Zech. 4:6). Great wars, desolations, alterations, shall precede it: but it is not the sons of men that by outward force, shall build the new Jerusalem: that comes down from heaven "adorned as a bride" for Christ, fitted and "prepared" by himself:[51] certainly the strivings of men about this business shall have no

43 Rom. 11:15.

44 Rev. 16:12. Compare with Owen's very similar section in *The Shaking and Translating of Heaven and Earth* (1649), in which he argued that the drying up of the Euphrates primarily involved the withering of the Roman Catholic Church, which would advance the conversion of the Jews. See *Complete Works of John Owen*, 18:443–44.

45 Gen. 22:17.

46 Ps. 147:14.

47 This is an allusion to the events surrounding the Anabaptist Kingdom in Münster (1534–1535). See James M. Stayer, *The German Peasants' War and Anabaptist Community of Goods* (Montreal: McGill-Queen's University Press, 1991), 123–38.

48 Owen used the trope of the molehill in a number of other sermons.

49 Dan. 7:2.

50 Dan. 7:13.

51 Rev. 21:2.

influence into it. It shall be by the glorious manifestation of his own power, and that by his Spirit subduing the souls of men unto it; not by the sword of man setting up a few to rule over others. Hence it is everywhere called a creating of "new heavens, and a new earth" (Isa. 65:17): a work doubtless too difficult for the worms of the earth to undertake. There is nothing more opposite to the spirit of the gospel, than to suppose that Jesus Christ will take to himself a kingdom by the carnal sword and bow of the sons of men. The raising of "the tabernacle of David, which is fallen down," and the setting up the decayed places of it (Acts 15:16), is done by his visiting the people with his Spirit and word, verse 14. It is by the pouring out of his Spirit in a covenant of mercy (Isa. 59:21).

Thus the Lord sets up one shepherd of his people, "and he shall feed them, even," (says he) "my servant David, he shall feed them, and he shall be their shepherd, and the Lord will be their God, and my servant David a prince among them" (Ezek. 34:23–24): he brings in the kingdom of his Son by making the children of Israel "seek the Lord their God, and David their king, and to fear the Lord and his goodness" (Hos. 3:5).[52] Who now can fathom the counsels of the Almighty, who has searched his bosom, and can by computation tell us, when he shall pour out his Spirit for the accomplishment of these things?

This then is the last thing in this vision, whose consideration brought the prophet, into so great perplexity and distress of spirit.

Seeking the Mind of God

3. There is the means that Daniel used for redress, in that sad condition whereunto he was brought by the consideration of this vision: he drew "near to one of them that stood by, and asked him the truth of all this."[53]

This also was done in vision: there is no mention of his waking before his making this address: but the vision continuing, he draws nigh in the same manner "to one of them that stood by"; one of those angels or holy ones, that stood ministering before the throne of God, who was commissionated to acquaint him with the mind and will of God in the things represented to him. This then is the remedy he applies himself unto: he labors to know the mind and will of God, in the things that were to be done: this it seems he pitched on, as the only way for quieting his grieved and troubled spirit; and hereupon,

52 Owen appealed to these texts from Ezekiel and Hosea in both *The Shaking and Translating of Heaven and Earth* (1649) and *The Advantage of the Kingdom of Christ* (1651). For the first sermon, see *Complete Works of John Owen*, 18:443. The second sermon is included in this volume.

53 Dan. 7:16.

The Peace That Comes from a Revelation of the Mind of God

4. He is "told and made to know the interpretation of the things," so far, at least, as might quiet his spirit in the will of God:[54] not that he is clearly instructed in every particular, for he tells them in the close of the chapter, that he had troublesome thoughts about the whole—his "cogitations troubled" him, and "his countenance changed," verse 28, but having received what light God was willing to communicate to him, he inquires no farther, but addresses himself to his own duty.

Take then from the words thus opened in these propositions, some whereof I shall do little more than name unto you.

Summary of the Three Doctrines Raised from the Text

Observation 1. *In the consideration of God's marvelous actings in the world, in order to the carrying on of the gospel and the interest of the Lord Jesus Christ, the hearts of his saints are oftentimes filled with perplexity and trouble.* They know not what will be the issue, nor sometimes what well to do. Daniel receives a vision of the things which in part we live under: and if they fill his heart with astonishment, is it any wonder if they come close to us, and fill us with anxious perplexing thoughts, upon whom the things themselves are fallen?

Observation 2. *The only way to deliver and extricate our spirits from under such perplexities, and entanglements, is to draw nigh to God in Christ, for discovery of his will*; so did Daniel here: he went to one of them that ministered before the Lord, to be acquainted with his will, otherwise thoughts and contrivances will but farther perplex you; like men in the mire, while they pluck one leg out, the other sticks faster in: while you relieve yourselves in one thing, you will be more hampered in another.

Yea "he that increases wisdom, increases sorrow,"[55] the larger the visions are, the greater will be their troubles; until being consumed in your own fears, cares and contrivances, you grow useless in your generation: those who see only the outside of your affairs, sleep securely: those who come nigher, to look into the spirits of men, rest is taken from them: and many are not quiet, because they will not: the great healing of all is in God.

Observation 3. *When God makes known the interpretations of things, it will quiet your spirits, in your walking before him, and actings with him.* This was that which brought the spirit of Daniel into a settlement. How God reveals his mind in these things, by what means, how it may be known by

54 Dan. 7:16.
55 Eccl. 1:18.

individual persons, for their quiet and settlement, how all God's revelations are quieting, and tend to the calming of men's spirits, not making them foam like the waves of the sea, should be handled on this observation, but I begin with the first.[56]

TREATMENT OF THE MAIN DOCTRINE: THE ADVANCEMENT OF THE KINGDOM OF CHRIST OFTEN LEAVES THE SAINTS TROUBLED AND PERPLEXED

When John received his book of visions in reference to the great things that were to be done, and the alterations that were to be brought about, though it were "sweet in his mouth," and he rejoiced in his employment, yet it made his "belly bitter" (Rev. 10:9–10): it filled him with perplexity, as our prophet speaks, in the midst of his body; he saw blood and confusion, strife and violence; it made his very belly bitter.

Poor Jeremiah, upon the same account, is so oppressed, that it makes him break out of all bounds of faith and patience, to curse the day of his birth, to wax quite weary of his employment; chapter 15.[57]

Our Savior describing such a season, tells us, that "men's hearts shall fail them for fear, and for looking after those things that are coming upon the earth" (Luke 21:26): they will be thinking what will become of them, and what will be the issue of God's dispensations; fearing that the whole frame of things will be wrapped up in darkness, and confusion. Hence our Savior bids his disciples not be "troubled" when they hear of "these things" (Matt. 24:6), intimating that they will be very apt, so to be.

Four Reasons Why the Saints Find Themselves in Such a Condition

The Astonishing Nature of What God Is Doing

Now the causes and occasions (which are the reasons of the point) arise, 1. First from the greatness and astonishableness of the things themselves which God will do: even great and "terrible things, which men looked not for" (Isa. 64:2–3). When he comes "to make his name known" to "the nations," that his "adversaries" may "tremble at his presence," and does "terrible things," quite above and beyond the expectation of men, which they never once looked for; no wonder if their hearts be surprised with amazement. It has of late

56 The first doctrine is "In the consideration of God's marvelous actings in the world, in order to the carrying on of the gospel, the hearts of his saints are oftentimes filled with perplexity and trouble."

57 Jer. 15:10.

been so with this nation: all professors at the beginning of these days, joined earnestly in that prayer [of] Isaiah 63:17–19; 64:1. God, in answer hereunto, "comes down" and "rends the heavens," and "the mountains flow down at his presence," according to the desire of their souls: yet withal he does "terrible things, things that we looked not for"; how many poor creatures are turned back with astonishment, and know not how to abide with him? When our Savior Christ came in the flesh, who had been the desire of all nations,[58] for four thousand years, and most importunately sought after by the men of that generation wherein he came, yet doing great and unexpected things at his coming, who was able to abide it? This, says Simeon, will be the issue of it, "He shall be for the fall and rise of many; and the thoughts of many hearts shall be revealed" (Luke 2:34–35). Hence is that exclamation, "Who may abide the day of his coming, and who shall stand when he appeareth?" (Mal. 3:2): his coming is desired indeed, but few can bear it: his day will "burn as an oven," as a furnace (Mal. 4:1): some are overheated by it, some consume in it, blessed are they that abide: this is one cause of the perplexing of the spirits of men: the consideration of the things themselves that are done, being above and beyond their expectations; and this even many of the saints of God are borne down under at this day: they little looked for the blood and banishment of kings,[59] change of government,[60] alteration of nations, such shakings of heaven and earth as have ensued;[61] not considering that he who does these things weighs all the nations in a "balance," and the rulers of them are as the "dust" thereof before him.[62]

The Mysterious Manner in Which God Works

2. From the manner whereby God will do these things: many perplexing, killing circumstances attend his dispensations: I shall instance only in one: and that is darkness and obscurity, whereby he holds the minds of men in uncertainty, and suspense, for his own glorious ends: such he tells us shall his day, and the works thereof, be. "And it shall come to pass in that day, that the light shall not be clear, nor dark. But it shall be one day which shall be known to the Lord, not day, nor night: but it shall come to

58 Hag. 2:7.

59 The execution of Charles I (1649) and the flight of Charles II to the continent (1651).

60 E.g., the establishment of the Commonwealth and the Acts abolishing the office of the King and the House of Lords (1649).

61 E.g., the Cromwellian conquests of Ireland and Scotland, and the beginning of the First Anglo-Dutch War.

62 Isa. 40:15.

pass that at evening-time it shall be light" (Zech. 14:6–7).[63] Men shall not know what to make of it, nor what to judge: he brings not forth his work all at once, but by degrees, and sometimes sets it backward, and leads it up and down, as he did his people of old in the wilderness, that none might know where they should fall or settle: and "he that believeth will not make haste."[64] When God is doing great things, he delights to wrap them up in the clouds, to keep the minds of men in uncertainties, that he may set on work all that is in them; and try them to the utmost, whether they can live upon his care and wisdom, when they see their own care and wisdom will do no good. Men would fain come to some certainty, and commonly by the thoughts and ways whereby they press unto it, they put all things into more uncertainty than ever, and so promote the design of God, which they so studiously endeavor to decline: hence is that description of the presence of the Lord in his mighty works, "Darkness was under his feet"; men could not see his paths, etc. (Ps. 18:9, 11). He has ends of surprisal, hardening, and destruction toward some, for which they must be left unto their own spirits, and led into many snares and bypaths, for their trial, and the exercise of others, which could not be accomplished, did he not come in the clouds, and were not "darkness his pavilion" and "his secret place":[65] on this account, is that cry of men of profane and hardened spirits, "Let him make speed, and hasten his work that we may see it, and let the counsel of the Holy One of Israel draw nigh and come, that we may know it" (Isa. 5:19). They know not what to make, of what they see; of all that is yet done or accomplished, they would have the whole work out, that they might once see the end of it, and so know what to judge: they would be at a point with him, and not always kept at those perplexing uncertainties: and this is another cause of the trouble of men's spirits, in consideration of the dispensations of God: God still keeps a cloud hanging over, and they know not when it will fall, nor what will be done in the issue of things; this makes some weary of waiting on him, and with the profane king of Israel, to cry, "This evil is of the Lord," there is no end, confusion will be the issue of all, "Why should I abide any longer?"[66]

63 Owen made similar comments in *A Vision of Unchangeable Free Mercy* (1646) and *Ebenezer* (1648). See *Complete Works of John Owen*, 18:129, 232.

64 Isa. 28:16. Owen appealed to this verse in *Ebenezer* (1648), *The Steadfastness of the Promises* (1650), and *The Laboring Saint's Dismission to Rest* (1652). For the first sermon, see *Complete Works of John Owen*, 18:237. The other two are included in this volume.

65 Ps. 18:11.

66 2 Kings 6:33.

The Unsettling Influence of the Ungodly

3. The lusts of men, do commonly under such dispensations, fearfully and desperately tumultuate,[67] to the disturbance of the most settled and weighed spirits: Satan takes advantage to draw them out in such a season to the utmost, both in spirituals and civils. What will be the constant deportment of men of corrupt minds in such a time, our Savior sets forth (Matt. 24:8).[68] "They shall come in the name of Christ" to deceive; and "shall deceive many," and cause "iniquity to abound."[69] In such a day Edom will appear an enemy, and Ephraim with the son of Remaliah will join with Syria for the vexing of Judah:[70] hence are perplexities, and swords piercing through the very souls of men. Take an instance in the days wherein we live. From the beginning of the contests in this nation, when God had caused your spirits to resolve, that the liberties, privileges, and rights of this nation, wherewith you were entrusted, should not (by his assistance) be wrested out of your hands by violence, oppression, and injustice; this he also put upon your hearts, to vindicate and assert the gospel of Jesus Christ, his ways and his ordinances, against all opposition, though you were but inquiring the way to Zion, "with your faces thitherward":[71] God secretly entwining the interest of Christ with yours, wrapped up with you the whole generation of them that seek his face, and prospered your affairs on that account:[72] so that whereas causes of as clear a righteousness among the sons of men as yours, have come to nothing, yet your undertaking has been like the sheaf of Joseph, in the midst of the nations, which has stood up when all the others have bowed to the ground:[73] being then convinced, that your affairs have fallen under his promises, and have come up to an acceptance before him, solely upon the account of their subserviency to the interest of Christ; God has put it into your hearts, to seek the propagation of his gospel. What now by the lusts of men is the state of things? Say some, "There is no gospel at all": say others, "If there be, you have nothing to do with it": some

67 I.e., be put into a state of tumult.

68 Following Goold, this should be corrected to Matt. 24:5.

69 Matt. 24:12.

70 In the margin: Obad. 12–13; Isa. 6.—Owen. Following Goold, the final reference should be corrected to Isa. 7—in particular, 7:6. Owen made a similar point in *The Steadfastness of the Promises* (1650), which is included in this volume.

71 Jer. 50:5.

72 Crawford Gribben describes this as "homiletical flattery [that] offered a rather more positive view of the Rump Parliament than that maintained among the army elite." See Gribben, "Owen and Politics," in *The T&T Clark Handbook of John Owen*, ed. Crawford Gribben and John Tweeddale (London: T&T Clark, 2022), 93.

73 Gen. 37:7. Owen employed the same illustration in *The Steadfastness of the Promises* (1650).

say, "Lo, here is Christ"; others "Lo, there":[74] some make religion a color for one thing; some for another: say some, "The magistrate must not support the gospel"; say others, "The gospel must subvert the magistrate": say some, "Your rule is only for men, as men, you have nothing to do with the interest of Christ and the church": say others, "You have nothing to do to rule men but upon the account of being saints." "If you will have the gospel," say some, "down with the ministers of it, chemarims,[75] locusts, etc."[76] and "if you will have light, take care that you may have ignorance and darkness: things being carried on as if it were the care of men, that there might be no trouble in the world, but what the name of religion might lie in the bottom of." Now those that ponder these things, their spirits are grieved in the midst of their bodies; the visions of their heads trouble them,[77] they looked for other things from them that professed Christ; but "the summer is ended," and "the harvest is past," and we are not refreshed.[78] Again; God had so stated your affairs, that you were the mark of the anti-Christian world to shoot at, in the beginning; and their terror in the close: and when you thought only to have pursued Sheba the son of Bichri, the man of your first warfare, behold one Abel after another, undertakes the quarrel against you:[79] yea such Abels as Scotland and Holland,[80] of whom we said in old times, "We will inquire of them, and so ended the matter: and there is not a wise man or woman among them that can dissuade them." Strange! That Ephraim should join with Syria to "vex" Judah their brother:[81] that the Netherlands, whose being is founded merely upon the interest you have undertaken, should join with the great anti-Christian interest, which cannot possibly be set up again, without their inevitable ruin. Hence also are deep thoughts of heart, men are perplexed, disquieted, and know not what to do.

74 Matt. 24:23.

75 *Chemarim* is a term from Zeph. 1:4 (also used in 2 Kings 23:5), sometimes rendered as those who go about in black. Here it is a reference to the traditional clothing of the clergy.

76 The other preacher at this fast was the Fifth Monarchist Christopher Feake. His associate, John Simpson (1614/15–1662), had called clergy by such names. See Martyn Calvin Cowan, *John Owen and the Civil War Apocalypse: Preaching, Prophecy and Politics* (London: Routledge, 2017), 142.

77 See Dan. 7:15.

78 Jer. 8:20.

79 2 Sam. 20:1–2, 14–18.

80 In 1650, with the Treaty of Breda, the Scottish Covenanters had agreed to support Charles II's claim to his throne, and months before this sermon was preached, the Commonwealth had declared war against the United Provinces (July 1652). The Battle of the Kentish Knock had been fought only weeks beforehand on September 28, 1652.

81 Isa. 7:6.

I could mention other lusts, and tumultuatings of the spirits of men, that have an influence into the disturbance of the hearts of the most precious in this nation, but I forbear.

The Unsettling Effects of Sin

4. Men's own lusts disquiet their spirits in such a season as this: I could instance in many, I shall name only four.

(1) Unstableness of mind.
(2) Carnal fears.
(3) Love of the world.
(4) Desire of preeminence.[82]

(1) Unstableness of mind, which makes men like the waves of the sea, that cannot rest.[83] The Scripture calls it ἀκαταστασίαν,[84] "tumultuatingness" of spirit: there is something of that which Jude speaks of, in better persons than those he describes, "raging like waves of the sea, and foaming out their own shame," verse 13. If God give men up to a restless spirit, no condition imaginable can quiet them, still they think they see something beyond it, that is desirable. Annibal said of Marcellus, that he could never be quiet conqueror nor conquered;[85] some men's desires are so enlarged, that nothing can satiate them. Wise men, that look upon sundry godly persons in this nation, and beholding how every yoke of the oppressor is broken from off their necks,[86] that no man makes them afraid,[87] that they are looked on as the head, not as the tail,[88] enjoying the ordinances of God according to the light of their minds, and desires of their hearts, no man forbidding them, are ready to wonder, (I speak of private persons) what they can find to do in their several places and callings, but to serve the Lord "in righteousness and holiness," being "without fear,"

82 Owen discusses only the first two particulars in this list and states on the following page that he will not discuss the latter two.

83 The language is suggestive given that the First Anglo-Dutch War was fought entirely at sea.

84 Gk. "Instability, disturbance, confusion"—e.g., Luke 21:9; James 3:16.

85 According to Livy's *History of Rome* 27.14, Hannibal, the Carthaginian general, said of Marcus Claudius Marcellus, the consul of the Roman Republic, "Winning, he puts fierce pressure on his defeated foe; losing, he renews the fight with his victors." For the text, see Livy, *History of Rome*, vol. 8, *Books 26–27*, trans. J. C. Yardley, Loeb Classical Library 367 (Cambridge, MA: Harvard University Press, 2020), 257.

86 Isa. 9:4.

87 Ezek. 34:28.

88 Deut. 28:13.

all the days of their lives.[89] But alas when poor creatures are given up, to the power of an unquiet, and unstable mind, they think scarce anything vile, but being wise unto sobriety: nothing desirable, but what is without their proper bounds, and what leads to that confusion, which themselves in the issue are least able of many to undergo.[90] It is impossible but that men's hearts should be pierced with disquietness and trouble, that are given up to this frame.

(2) Carnal fears: these even devour and eat up the hearts of men: "What shall we do? What shall become of us?" Ephraim is confederate with Syria, and the hearts of men are shaken "as the trees of the wood that are moved with the wind":[91] "What new troubles still, new unsettlements?" "This storm will not be avoided, this will be worse than all, that has befallen us from the youth of our undertaking." God has not yet won upon men's spirits to trust him in shakings, perplexities, alterations: they remember not the manifestations of his wisdom, power, and goodness in former days; and how tender hitherto he has been of the interest of Christ, that their hearts might be established. Could we but do our duty, and trust the Lord, with the performance of his promises, what quietness, what sweetness might we have? I shall not instance in the other two particulars: it is too manifest that many of our piercing and perplexing thoughts, are from the tumultuating and disorder of our own lusts. So that what remains of the time allotted to me, I shall spend only in the use of this point, and proceed no farther.

Application: Instruction in How to Find Peace

Use 1. Of instruction; to direct you into ways and means of quietness, in reference unto all these causes and occasions of piercing, dividing thoughts, in such a season as this. The good Lord seal up instruction to your souls, that you may know "the things that belong to your peace,"[92] and "what Israel ought to do"[93] at this, even at this time: "For my brethren's and companions' sake,"[94] I wish you prosperity: though my own portion should be in the dust, for the true spiritual, not imaginary, carnal interest of the church of God in this nation, and the nations about, I wish you prosperity.

89 Luke 1:74–75.

90 This description of transgressive belief and behavior is typical of what was reported about the "Ranters" in 1652. See J. C. Davis, *Fear, Myth and History: The Ranters and the Historians* (Cambridge: Cambridge University Press, 1986), 76–83.

91 Isa. 7:2.

92 Luke 19:42.

93 1 Chron. 12:32. In the *Laboring Saint* (1652), which is included in this volume, Owen held up Ireton as an example of one who asked this very question.

94 Ps. 122:8.

Be Guided by the Second Observation: Draw Near to God in Prayer

(1) First then, in reference to the things that God is doing, both as to their greatness, and their manner of doing; whose consideration fills men with thoughts, that grieve their spirits in the midst of their bodies![95] Would you have your hearts quieted in this respect? Take my second observation for your direction; the only way to extricate and deliver our spirits from under such perplexities, and entanglements, is to draw nigh to God in Christ for the discovery of his will. So did Daniel here in my text, I fear this is too much neglected. You take counsel with your own hearts, you advise with one another, hearken unto men under a repute of wisdom; and all this does but increase your trouble, you do but more and more entangle and disquiet your own spirits. God stands by and says, "I am wise also"; and little notice is taken of him: we think we are grown wise ourselves, and do not remember, we never prospered, but only when we went unto God, and told him plainly we knew not what to do. Public fastings are neglected, despised, spoken against; and when appointed, practiced according as men's hearts are principled to such a duty, coldly, deadly, unacceptably: life, heat, warmth is gone; and shall not blood and all go after? The Lord prevent it: private meetings are used to show ourselves wise in the debate of things, with a form of godly words; sometimes for strife, tumult, division, disorder; and shall we think there is much closet inquiring after God,[96] when all other actings of that principle, which should carry out thereunto, are opposed and slighted? When we do sometimes wait upon God, do not many seem to ask amiss, to spend it on their lusts;[97] not waiting on him poor, hungry, empty, to know his will, to receive direction from him; but rather going full, fixed, resolved, settled on thoughts, perhaps prejudices, of our own, almost taking upon us to prescribe unto the Almighty, and to impose our poor, low, carnal thoughts upon his wisdom and care of his church? Oh where is that holy, and that humble frame, wherewith at first we followed our God into the wilderness, where we have been fed, and clothed, preserved and protected for so many years?[98] Hence is it that the works of God are become strange, and terrible, and dark unto us: and of necessity, some of us, many of us, must shut up all with disappointment and sorrow: we fill our souls boldly, confidently, with cross and contrary apprehensions,

95 Daniel's experience as described in the text of this sermon.

96 Matt. 6:6.

97 James 4:3.

98 Worden describes this as "Owen's *crie de Coeur* [which] echoed his bewildered sense of loss." See Blair Worden, *The Rump Parliament, 1648–1653* (Cambridge: Cambridge University Press, 1977), 294.

of the intendments of God, and of the mediums whereby he will accomplish his ends; and do not consider, that this is not a frame of men, who had given up themselves to the all-sufficiency of God. Some perhaps will say, "This belongs not unto them, they have waited upon God, and they do know his mind, and what are the things he will do, and are not blind also, nor in the dark, as other men." But if it be so, "What means this bleating of sheep and oxen in mine ears?"[99] Yea; what means that roaring and foaming of unquiet waves which we hear and see:[100] hard speeches, passionate reproaches, sharp revilings of their brethren, in boundless confidence, endless enmity, causing evil surmises, biting, tearing, devouring terms and expressions, casting out the names of men upright in their generations, saying, "The Lord be praised"? When the Lord discovers his mind, and will, it settles the heart, composes the mind, fills the soul with reverence and godly fear, conforms the heart unto itself, fills it with peace, love, meekness, gentleness etc. And shall we be thought to have received the mind, the will of God, when our hearts, words, ways, are full of contrary qualities? Let it be called what it will, I shall not desire to share in that, which would bring my heart into such a frame. Well, then, beloved, take this for your first direction: be more abundant with God in faith and prayer: deal with him in public and private, take counsel of him, bend your hearts through his grace, to your old frame, when it was your joy to meet in this place, which now I fear to many is their burden: seek the Lord and his face, "seek him while he may be found":[101] and hereby;

Three Reasons to Seek God in Public and Private Prayer

[1] You will empty your hearts, of many perplexing contrivances of your own, and you will find faith in this communion with God, by little and little working out, killing, slaying these prejudices and presumptions which you may be strong in, that are not according to the will of God; so you be sure to come not to have your own lusts, and carnal conceptions answered, but to have the will of God fulfilled. When men come unto the Lord to have their own visions fulfilled, it is righteous with God to answer them according to those visions, and confirm them in them, to their own disturbance, and the disturbance of others.

[2] You shall certainly have peace in your own hearts in the all-sufficiency of God: this he will give in upon your spirits, that whatever he does, all his ways shall be to you, mercy, truth, faithfulness, and peace, yea the discoveries which you shall have of his own fullness, sweetness, suitableness, and the

99 1 Sam. 15:14.

100 Once again, this is striking language in the context of the Anglo-Dutch sea war.

101 Isa. 55:6.

excellency of "things which are not seen,"[102] will work your hearts to such a frame, that you shall attend to the things here below, merely upon the account of duty, with the greatest calmness, and quietness of mind imaginable.

[3] You shall surely know your own particular paths, wherein you ought to walk in serving God in your generation,[103] those that wait upon him, "he will guide in judgment":[104] he will not leave them in the dark, nor to distracted, divided, piercing thoughts: but what ere others do, you shall be guided into ways of peace:[105] this you shall have when the lusts of men will neither let themselves, nor others be at quiet. Oh, then return to your rest, look to Him from whom you have gone astray: take no more disturbing counsel with yourselves, or others; renew your old frame of humble dependence on God, and earnest seeking his face; you have certainly backslidden in this thing.

Is the Lord not the God of counsel and wisdom, as well as the God of force and power, that you run to him when in a strait in your actions, but when your counsels seem sometimes to be mixed with a spirit of difficulty and trouble, he is neglected: only come with humble depending hearts, not everyone to bring the devices, imaginations, opinions, prejudices, and lusts of their own hearts, before him:

The Magistrate Should Advance the Cause of the Gospel

(2) For the troubles that arise from the lusts of other men: and that about the gospel and the propagation thereof: the tumultuating of the lusts of men in reference hereunto, I gave you an account of formerly: there are many piercing thoughts of heart. What extremes, I had almost said extravagances, men have in this matter run out into, I shall now not insist upon: only I shall give you a few directions for your own practice.

Protect, Promote, and Propagate the Gospel

[1] If once it comes to that, that you shall say, you have nothing to do with religion as rulers of the nation,[106] God will quickly manifest that he has nothing to do with you as rulers of the nation: the great promise of Christ is, that in these latter days of the world, he will lay the nations in a subserviency to him, the kingdoms of the world shall become his;[107] that is, act as kingdoms

102 2 Cor. 4:18.
103 Acts 13:36.
104 Ps. 25:5, 9.
105 Luke 1:79.
106 There had been a barrage of criticism directed against Owen's proposals.
107 Rev. 11:15.

and governments no longer against him, but for him: surely those promises will scarcely be accomplished in bringing commonwealths, of men professing his name, to be of Gallio's frame, "to care for none of those things":[108] or as the Turk, in an absolute indifferency what any profess: I mean that are not his own, for in respect of them he changes not his God: not that I would you should go and set up forms of government, to compel men to come under the line of them, or to thrust in your sword to cut the lesser differences of brethren; not that I think truth ever the more the truth, or to have anything the more of authority upon the conscience, for having the stamp of your authority annexed to it, for its allowance to pass in these nations. Nor do I speak a word of what is, may, or may not be incumbent on you, in respect of the most profligate opposers of the truths of the gospel:[109] but only this, that, not being such as are "always learning, never coming to the knowledge of the truth,"[110] but being "fully persuaded in your own minds,"[111] certainly it is incumbent on you, to take care that the faith which you have received, which was "once delivered to the saints,"[112] in all the necessary concernments of it, may be protected, preserved, propagated to and among the people which God has set you over.[113] If a father as a father is bound to do what answers this in his family, unto his children; a master as a master to his servants; if you will justify yourselves as fathers, or rulers of your country, you will find in your account this to be incumbent on you.

Allow the Church to Be the Church

[2] Take heed of them that would temper clay and iron, things that will not mingle,[114] that would compound carnal and fleshly things, with heavenly things and spiritual, that they may not entangle your spirits: the great design of grasping temporal power, upon a spiritual account, will prove at last to be the greatest badge of Antichrist: hitherto God has appeared against it, and

108 Acts 18:17.

109 John Coffey deals with Owen's evolving views on the magistrate's response to heresy and blasphemy in "The Toleration Controversy during the English Revolution," in *Religion in Revolutionary England*, ed. Christopher Durston and Judith Maltby (Manchester: Manchester University Press, 2006), 50.

110 2 Tim. 3:7.

111 Rom. 14:5.

112 Jude 3.

113 Similar language would be employed in chapter 24 of the Savoy Declaration of 1658. It stated that the magistrate was bound "to incourage, promote and protect the professors and profession of the Gospel." See *The Savoy Declaration of Faith and Order 1658*, ed. A. G. Matthews (Letchworth, UK: Independent Press, 1959), 37.

114 Dan. 2:43.

will, no doubt to the end; if either you, by the authority God has given you in the world, shall take upon you to rule the house of God, as formally such, as his house, though you rule the persons, whereof it is made up, or those who are, or pretend to be, of that house, to rule the world on that account, your day and theirs will be nigh at hand.

Specific Guidance to Parliament in the Propagation of the Gospel and in Dealing with Religious Heterodoxy

(3)[115] Now because you wait on God for direction in reference to the propagation of the gospel, and the preventing that which is contrary to sound doctrine and godliness,[116] I shall very briefly give you to this end, some principles whereon you may rest in your actings; and some rules, for your direction, and so draw to a close.[117]

Understand the Promises about God Raising Up Godly Rulers

[1] Take in the first place what God has promised concerning magistrates, kings, rulers, judges, and nations, and their subserviency to the church; what God has promised they shall do, that is their duty to do; he has not measured out an inheritance for his people, out of the sins of other men: let us a little view some of these promises, and then consider their application to the truth we have in hand, and what is cleared out unto us by them: they are many; I shall instance in the most obvious and eminent. "I will restore their judges and priests and counsellors as at the beginning" (Isa. 1:26): it is to Zion redeemed, purged, washed in the blood of Christ, that this promise is made.

"Kings shall see and arise, and princes shall bow down themselves" (Isa. 49:7). The Jews being for the greatest part of them rejected upon the coming of Christ, this promise is made unto him upon his pouring out of the Spirit, for the bringing in of the Gentiles: as it is farther enlarged, verses 22–23: "Kings shall be thy nursing-fathers, and their queens thy nursing-mothers."[118]

Isaiah 60 looks wholly this way:[119] taste of the nature and intendment of the whole; "And the Gentiles shall come to thy light, and kings to the brightness

115 In the first edition this was numbered as point 4, and the discrepancy may have occurred because Owen handled both the "greatness" and the "manner" together under point 1 when, earlier in the sermon, he had treated these as points 1 and 2.

116 1 Tim. 1:10.

117 This was one of the express purposes for the day of fasting.

118 Owen appealed to these texts from Isaiah in *Of Toleration* 1649) and *The Shaking and Translating of Heaven and Earth* (1649). See *Complete Works of John Owen*, 18:388–89, 432, 440.

119 Owen had appealed to this chapter from Isaiah in all his published sermons from 1648 to this point.

of thy rising. Therefore thy gates shall be open continually, they shall not be shut day nor night, that men may bring unto thee the forces of the Gentiles, and that their kings may be brought. Thou shalt also suck the milk of the Gentiles, and shalt suck the breast of kings, and thou shalt know that I the Lord am thy Saviour and thy Redeemer, the mighty one of Jacob. For brass I will bring gold, and for iron I will bring silver, and for wood brass, and for stones iron: I will also make thy officers peace, and thine exactors righteousness," verse 3 and the 11 and the 16–17. To which add the accomplishment of all those promises mentioned [in] Revelation 11:15 and 21:24.

You see here are glorious promises, in the literal expression looking directly to what we assert concerning the subserviency of rulers to the gospel, and the duty of magistrates in supporting the interest of the church: let us concerning them, observe these three things as—{1} to whom they are made: {2} on what occasion they are given: {3} what is the subject or matter of them in general.

These Promises Are for Today

{1} Then they are all given and made to the church of Christ after his coming in the flesh, and his putting an end to all ceremonial typical carnal institutions; for,

1st. They are every way attended with the circumstances of calling the Gentiles, and their flowing into the church; which were not accomplished till after the destruction of the Jewish church etc.

So is the case in that which you have, "The children which thou shalt have, after thou hast lost the other, shall say again in thine ears, The place is too strait for me: give place to me that I may dwell" (Isa. 49:20). It shall be when the church shall have received the new children of the Gentiles, having lost the other of the Jews: which he expresses more at large, verse 22, "Thus saith the Lord God, Behold, I will lift up mine hand to the Gentiles, and set up my standard to the people: and they shall bring thy sons in their arms, and thy daughters shall be carried upon their shoulders." So also are the rest. When God gives the nations to be the inheritance of Christ, the Holy Ghost cautions rulers and judges to "kiss the Son," and pay the homage due to him in his kingdom (Ps. 2:10–11).[120]

2nd. Because these promises are pointed unto, as accomplished to the Christian church in that place of the Revelation, before mentioned, "And the seventh angel sounded, and there were great voices in heaven, saying, The kingdoms of this world are become the kingdoms of our Lord, and of his Christ, and he shall

120 The reference should be expanded to include Ps. 2:12.

reign for ever and ever," chapter 11:15.[121] "And the nations of them which are saved, shall walk in the light of it: and the kings of the earth do bring their glory and honour into it": chapter 21:24. So that there are plainly promises of kings and princes, judges and rulers to be given to the church, and to be made useful thereunto, and kingdoms and nations, people in their rules and governments to be instrumental in the good thereof: so that these promises belong directly to us, and our rulers, if under any notion, we belong to the church of Christ.

Magistrates Are Entrusted with Particular Responsibilities in Matters of Religion

{2} For the occasion of these promises; it is well known what a trust by God's own appointment there was invested in the rulers, judges, kings, and magistrates, of the judicial state and church under the Old Testament, in reference unto the ways and worship of God: the prosecution and the execution of the laws of God, concerning his house and service being committed to them; further when they faithfully discharged their trust, promoting the worship of God according to his institutions, encouraging, supporting, directing, reproving others, to whom the immediate and peculiar administration of things sacred was committed, destroying, removing whatever was an abomination unto the Lord, it was well with the whole people and church, they flourished in peace, and the Lord delighted in them, and rejoiced over them to do them good:[122] and on the other side, their neglect in the discharge of their duty, was then commonly attended with the apostasy of the church, and great breakings forth of the indignation of the Lord: this the church found in those days and bewailed. To hold out therefore the happy state of his people, that he would bring in, he promises them such rulers, and judges as he gave at first,[123] who faithfully discharged the trust committed to them: not that I suppose them bound to the Mosaical rules of penalties in reference to transgressions and offenses against gospel institutions, but only that a duty in general is incumbent on them, in reference to the church and truth of God, which they should faithfully discharge; of which afterward.

This then being the occasion of those promises, and their accomplishment being as before, in a peculiar manner pointed at, upon the shaking, calling, and new molding of the kingdoms and nations of the world,[124] which had

121 Owen cited these verses in *The Shaking and Translating of Heaven and Earth* (1649) and *The Advantage of the Kingdom of Christ* (1651). For the first sermon, see *Complete Works of John Owen*, 18:440, 459. The second sermon is included in this volume.

122 Deut. 28:63.

123 Isa. 1:26.

124 Heb. 12:27.

given their power to the beast,[125] and thereupon framed anew into a due subserviency to the interest of Christ, here is not the least shadow or color left, for the turning off, and rejecting the sweetness of all these promises, upon account of their being merely metaphorical, and shadowing out spiritual glories: neither their beginning nor ending, neither their rise, nor fall, will bear any such gloss or corrupting interpretation.

Magistrates Have a Duty to Use Their Power for the Good of the Church

{3} As to the matter of these promises, I shall only assert this in general: that the Lord engages, that judges, rulers, magistrates; and such like, shall put forth their power, and act clearly for the good, welfare, and prosperity of the church; this is plainly held out in every one of them: hence kingdoms are said to serve the church; that is all kingdoms, they must do so, or be broken in pieces, and cease to be kingdoms: and how can a kingdom as a kingdom (for it is taken formally, and not materially, merely for the individuals of it, as appears by the threatening of its being broken in pieces) serve the church, but by putting forth its power and strength in her behalf (Isa. 60:12), and therefore upon the accomplishment of that promise, they are said to become the kingdoms of the Lord Christ (Rev. 11:15), because, as kingdoms, they serve him with their power and authority; having before, as such, and by their power, opposed him to the utmost. They must nurse the church not with dry breasts, nor feed it with stones and scorpions, but with the good things committed to them. Their power and substance, in protection and supportment, are to be engaged in the behalf thereof: hence God is said to give these judges, rulers, princes, kings, queens to the church, not setting them in the church, as officers thereof, but ordering their state in the world (Rev. 11:15), to its behoof. In sum, there is not any one of the promises recited, but holds forth the utmost of what I intend to assert from them all; viz. that the Lord has promised, *that the magistrates whom he will give, own, and bless, shall put forth their power, and act in that capacity, wherein he has placed them in the world, for the good, furtherance, and prosperity of the truth and church of Christ*: they shall protect them with their power, feed them with their substance, adorn them with their favor, and the privileges wherewith they are entrusted: they shall break their forcibly oppressing adversaries, and take care that those who walk in the truth of the Lord, may lead a "peaceable life, in all godliness and honesty."[126] If then you are such magistrates as God has

125 Rev. 17:13.

126 1 Tim. 2:2.

promised, (as, woe be unto you if you are not) know that he has undertaken for you, that you shall perform this part of your duty, and I pray that you may rule with him therein, and be found faithful.

Understand Five Relevant Principles

[2] The second ground that I would point unto, as a bottom of your actings in this thing arises from sundry undoubted principles, which I shall briefly mention: and the first is:

The Gospel Should Be Preached to Every Nation

{1} *That the gospel of Jesus Christ has a right to be preached and propagated in every nation, and to every creature under heaven.* Jesus Christ is the "Lord of lords, and King of kings" (Rev. 17:14): the nations are given to be his inheritance, and the utmost parts of the earth to be his possession (Ps. 2:8–9). He is appointed the "heir of all things" (Heb. 1:2). God has set him over the works of his hands, and put all things in subjection under his feet (Ps. 8:7).[127] And upon this account he gives commission to his messengers, to preach the gospel "to all nations" (Matt. 28:19), or, "to every creature under heaven" (Mark 16:17).[128] The nations of the world being of the Father given to him, he may deal with them as he pleases, and either, bruise them with a rod of iron, and "break them in pieces as a potter's vessel" (Ps. 2:9), he may "fill the places" of the earth with their "dead bodies," and strike in pieces "the heads of the countries" (Ps. 110:6). Or he may make them his own, and bring them into subjection unto himself; which toward some of them he will effect (Rev. 11:19).[129] Now the gospel being "the rod of his power,"[130] and "the scepter of his kingdom,"[131] the grand instrument whereby he accomplishes all his designs in the world, whether they be for life or for death (2 Cor. 2:16), he has given that a right to take possession in his name, and authority, of all that he will own in any nation under heaven. (And indeed, he has in all of them, some that are his peculiar purchase (Rev. 5:9). Whom in despite of all the world, he will bring in unto himself.) To have free passage into all nations, is the undoubted right of the gospel; and the persons of Christ's goodwill, have such a right to it, and interest in it, that look from whomsoever they may claim protection in reference unto any other of their most undoubted concernments among

127 Following Goold, this should be corrected to Ps. 8:6.

128 Following Goold, this should be corrected to Mark 16:15.

129 Following Goold, this should probably be corrected to Rev. 11:15.

130 Ps. 110:2. Here Owen appears to be citing from the Geneva Bible (GNV).

131 Ps. 45:6; Heb. 1:8.

men, of them may they claim protection in respect of their quiet enjoyment, and possession of the gospel.

Blessing and Prosperity Come to a Nation That Embraces the Gospel

{2} *That wherever the gospel is by any nation owned, received, embraced, it is the blessing, benefit, prosperity and advantage of that nation*: they that love Zion shall prosper (Ps. 122:6): godliness has the promise of this life, and is profitable unto all things (1 Tim. 4:8): the reception of the word of truth, and subjection to Christ therein, causing a people to become "willing in the day of his power,"[132] entitle that people to all the promises, that ever God made to his church: they shall be "established in righteousness"; they shall be "far from oppression," and for fear and terror, they shall not draw nigh unto them; whosoever contends against such a people, shall fall thereby: "no weapon that is formed against them shall prosper," "every tongue that shall rise against them in judgment, they shall condemn," for this is the inheritance of the servants of the Lord (Isa. 54:14–15, 17). To the prosperity of a nation two things are required.

1st. That they be freed from oppression, injustice, cruelty, disorder, confusion in themselves, from their rulers, or others.

2nd. That they be protected from the sword and violence, of them that seek their ruin from without. And both these do a people receive by receiving the gospel.

(1st)[133] For the first, they have the promise of God that they shall have "judges as at the first" (Isa. 1:26): such injustice and judgment shall bear rule over them and among them, as the first judges whom he stirred up, and gave to his ancient people: their "officers" shall be "peace," and their "exactors righteousness" (Isa. 60:17):[134] even the very gospel which they do receive, is only able to instruct them to be just, ruling in the fear of the Lord,[135] for that only effectually teaches the sons of men "to live righteously, soberly, and godly in this present world" (Titus 2:12).

(2nd) And for the second, innumerable are the promises, that are given to such a people; whence the psalmist concludes upon the consideration of the mercies; they do and shall enjoy, "Happy is the people whose God is the Lord" (Ps. 144:15). "The glorious Lord will be to them a place of broad rivers and

132 Ps. 110:3.

133 As is explained in the *Works* preface, the numbering order is 1, (1), [1], {1}, and 1st. In this volume, the numbering goes deeper, with the next number being (1st).

134 Owen had appealed to this text in *Of Toleration* (1649) and *The Shaking and Translating of Heaven and Earth* (1649). See Complete Works of John Owen, 18:389, 435, 440, 459.

135 2 Sam. 23:3.

waters, in which no galley with oars, nor gallant ship shall pass by," the Lord will be their redeemer, lawgiver, king, and Savior (Isa. 33:21). It will interest any people in all the promises, that are made for the using of the church to thrash, break, destroy, burden, fire, consume, and slay the enemies thereof: so far shall a people be from suffering under the hands of oppressors, that the Lord will use them for the breaking and destruction of the Nimrods of the earth,[136] and this blessing of the nations do they receive by the faith of Abraham.

A Nation That Rejects the Gospel Will Be Rejected by God

{3} *The rejection of the gospel by any people or nation to whom it is tendered, is always attended with the certain and inevitable destruction of that people or nation, which sooner or later, shall without any help or deliverance be brought upon them by the revenging hand of Christ.*

When the word of grace was rejected and despised by the Jews, the messengers of it professedly turning to the Gentiles: Acts 13:46; and chapter 28:28. God removing it from them, unto "a nation that would bring forth fruit" (Matt. 21:43): "as it did in all the world," or among all nations, for a season (Col. 1:6), with what a fearful and tremendous desolation he quickly wasted that people, is known to all: he quickly slew and destroyed "those husbandmen" that spoiled his vineyard, and "let it forth unto others, that might bring him his fruit in due season."[137]

Hence, when Christ is tendered in the gospel, the judges and rulers of the nations, are exhorted to obedience to him, upon pain of being destroyed upon the refusal thereof (Ps. 2:12). And we have the experience of all ages, ever since the day, that the gospel began to be propagated in the world: the quarrel of it was revenged on the Jews by the Romans,[138] upon the Romans by the Goths, Vandals, and innumerable barbarous nations;[139] and the vengeance due to the anti-Christian world is at hand, even at the door. The Lord will certainly make good his promise to the utmost, that the kingdom and nations, which will not serve the church, even that kingdom and those nations shall utterly perish (Isa. 60:12).

Magistrates Have Specific Responsibilities in These Matters

{4} *That it is the duty of magistrates to seek the good, peace, and prosperity of the people committed to their charge, and to prevent, obviate, remove, take*

136 See Mic. 5:6.

137 Matt. 21:40–41.

138 In the destruction of Jerusalem in AD 70.

139 Rome was sacked by the Visigoths in 410 and by the Vandals in 455.

away everything, that will bring confusion, destruction, desolation upon them; as Mordecai procured good things for his people, and prosperity to his kindred (Est. 10:4):[140] and David describes himself with all earnestness, pursuing the same design (Ps. 101).[141] Magistrates are the "ministers of God" for the "good," universal good, of them to whom they are given (Rom. 13:1–4); and they are to watch and apply themselves to this very thing, verse 6. And the reason the apostle gives to stir up the saints of God to pray, among all sorts of men, in special "for kings, and those that are in authority," to wit, that they may, in general, "come to the knowledge" of the faith, and "be saved," and, in particular discharge the duty and trust committed to them (for on that account are they to pray for them as kings and men in authority) is, "that we may lead a quiet and peaceable life, in all godliness and honesty" (1 Tim. 2:1–4). It being incumbent on them, to act even as kings and men in authority, that we may so do: they are to feed the people committed to their charge with all their might, unto universal peace, and welfare: now the things that are opposite to the good of any nation or people, are of two sorts.

1st. First; such as are really, directly, and immediately opposed to that state and condition, wherein they close together, and find prosperity. In general, seditions, tumults, disorders; in particular, violent, or fraudulent breakings in upon the respective designed bounds, privileges, and enjoyments of singular persons, without any consideration of him who rules all things, are of this kind: if nations and rulers might be supposed to be atheists, yet such evils as these, tending to their dissolution, and not-being, they would with all their strength labor to prevent, either by watching against their commission, or inflicting vengeance on them that commit them, that others may hear, and fear, and do so no more.

2nd. Such as are morally and meritoriously opposed to their good and welfare; in that they will certainly pluck down the judgments and wrath of God upon that nation or people, where they are practiced, and allowed: there are sins for which "the wrath of God" will be assuredly "revealed from heaven" against the children of disobedience:[142] Sodom and Gomorrah are set forth as examples of his righteous judgment in this kind.[143] And shall he be thought a magistrate, to bear out the name, authority, and presence of God to men, that so he, and his people have present peace, like a herd of swine, cares not though such things as will certainly first eat and devour their strength, and then utterly

140 Following Goold, this should be corrected to Est. 10:3.

141 Here Owen probably has Ps. 101:8 in view.

142 Rom. 1:18.

143 Gen. 19:24; 2 Pet. 2:6.

consume them, do pass for current?[144] Seeing that they that "rule over men must be just, ruling in the fear of the Lord,"[145] the sole reason why they sheathe the sword of justice in the bowels of thieves, murderers, adulterers, is not because their outward peace is actually disturbed by them, and therefore they must give example of terror to others, who being likeminded, are not yet actually given up to the practice of the like abomination, but also, yea principally, because he in whose stead they stand and minister to the world, is provoked by such wickedness to destroy both the one and the other: and if there be the same reason to be evidenced concerning other things, they also call for the same procedure.

To gather up now what has been spoken: considering the gospel's right and title, *to be propagated, with all its concernments, in every nation under heaven, the blessing, peace, prosperity, and protection wherewith it is attended, when, and where received, and the certain destruction, and desolation, which accompanies the rejection and contempt thereof, considering the duty that by God's appointment, is incumbent on them that rule over men, that in the fear of the Lord they ought to seek the good, peace, and welfare, and prosperity of them committed to their charge; to prevent, obviate, remove, revenge that which tends to their hurt, perturbation, dissolution, destruction, immediate from heaven, or from the hand of men, and in the whole administration to take care, that the worshipers of God in Christ, may lead a quiet and peaceable life in all godliness and honesty,*[146] let anyone, who has the least sense upon his spirit, of the account which he must one day make to the great King and Judge of all the world, of the authority and power wherewith he was entrusted, determine, whether it be not incumbent on him by all the protection, he can afford, by all the privileges he can indulge, the supportment that he can grant, by all that encouragement, which upon the highest account imaginable, he is required or allowed to give to any person whatsoever, to further the propagation of the gospel, which upon the matter is the only thing of concernment, as well unto this life, as that which is to come. And if anything be allowed in a nation, which in God's esteem may amount to a contempt and despising thereof, men may be taught by sad experience, what will be the issue of such allowance.

Rightly Understood, the Old Testament Teaches These Principles

{5} I shall only propose one thing more to your consideration. *Although the institutions and examples of the Old Testament, of the duty of magistrates, in the things and about the worship of God,* are not in their whole latitude and

144 I.e., to be accepted as genuine.

145 2 Sam. 23:3.

146 1 Tim. 2:2.

extent, to be drawn into rules, that should be obligatory to all magistrates now under the administration of the gospel; and that because the magistrate then was keeper, avenger and administrator of the judicial laws and polity of Moses,[147] from which, as most think, we are freed; yet doubtless there is something moral in those institutions, which being unclothed of their Judaical form, is still binding to all in the like kind, as to some analogy and proportion: subduct[148] from those administrations, what was proper to, and lies upon the account of the church and nation of the Jews, and what remains, upon the general notion of a church and nation, must be everlastingly binding: and this amounts thus far at least, that judges, rulers, and magistrates, which are promised under the New Testament, to be given in mercy, and to be of singular usefulness, as the judges were under the Old, are to take care that the gospel church may, in its concernment as such, be supported and promoted, and the truth propagated, wherewith they are entrusted; as the others took care, that it might be well with the Judaical church, as such. And on these, and such like principles as these are, may you safely bottom yourselves in that undertaking, wherein you seek for direction from God this day.

Three Rules for Parliament in the Propagation of the Gospel and in Dealing with Religious Heterodoxy

For the rules which I intimated I shall but name them, having some years since delivered my thoughts to the world at large on this subject;[149] and I see no cause as yet to recede from anything then so delivered. Take only then for the present, these brief directions following.

Be Committed to the Truth of the Gospel

[1] Labor to be fully persuaded in your own minds, that you be not carried up and down with every wind of doctrine,[150] and be tempted to hearken after every spirit, as though you had received no truth, as it is in Jesus.[151] It is a sad condition, when men have no zeal for truth, nor against that which is opposite to it, whatever they seem to profess; because indeed having not taken in any truth in the power and principle of it, they are upon sad thoughts, wholly at

147 In the text: *custos, vindex, et administrator legis judicialis, et politiae Mosaicae.*—Owen.

148 I.e., take away.

149 In the margin: *Discourse on Toleration.*—Owen. This was the discourse appended to the published version of Owen's *A Sermon Preached* [. . .] *January 31* (1649). See *Complete Works of John Owen*, 18:339–410.

150 Eph. 4:14.

151 Eph. 4:21.

a loss, whether there be any truth or no: this is an unhappy frame indeed, the proper condition of them whom God will spew out of his mouth.[152]

There Are No Grounds for Formally Supporting Error

[2] Know that error and falsehood have no right or title, either from God, or man, unto any privilege, protection, advantage, liberty, or any good thing you are entrusted withal: to dispose that unto a lie, which is the right of and due to truth, is to deal treacherously with him by whom you are employed: all the tenderness, and forbearance unto such persons as are infected with such abominations, is solely upon a civil account, and that plea which they have for tranquility, while neither directly nor morally they are a disturbance unto others.

The Plea of Conscience Is Insufficient Grounds for Rejecting This

[3] Know that in things of practice, so of persuasion, that are impious and wicked, either in themselves or in their natural and unconstrained consequences, the plea of conscience is an aggravation of the crime: if men's "consciences are seared,"[153] and themselves "given up to a reprobate mind,"[154] to do those things that are "not convenient,"[155] there is no doubt but they ought to suffer such things, as to such practices are assigned and appointed.

Conclusion

Should I now descend unto particulars, in all the things mentioned, and insist on them, time would wholly fail me, neither is it a work for a single sermon: and therefore in one word I shall wind up the whole matter and end.

Know them then, that are faithful and "quiet in the land";[156] regard the truth of the gospel: remember the days of old, what has done you good, quieted your heart in distress, crowned your undertakings with sweetness: lose not your first love;[157] draw not out your own thoughts for the counsel of God: seek not great things for yourselves: be not moved at the lusts of men, keep peace what in you lies, with all that fear the Lord: let the glory of Christ be the end of all your undertakings, etc.

FINIS.[158]

152 Rev. 3:16.
153 1 Tim. 4:2.
154 Rom. 1:28.
155 Eph. 5:4.
156 Ps. 35:20.
157 Rev. 2:4.
158 Lat. "The End."

GOD'S WORK IN FOUNDING ZION, AND HIS PEOPLE'S DUTY THEREUPON

A Sermon Preached in the Abbey Church at Westminster, at the Opening of the Parliament Septemb. 17th 1656

By John Owen: a servant of Jesus Christ in the work of the gospel

---

Walk about Zion, and go round about her, tell the towers thereof. Mark ye well her bulwarks, consider her places, that ye may tell it to the generation following.

For this God is our God for ever and ever; he will be our guide even unto death.

PSAL. 48. 12–14

Oxford,
Printed by Leon: Lichfield printer to the University, for Tho: Robinson 1656

[Parliamentary Order]

Wednesday the 17th of September 1656.[1]

Ordered by the Parliament, that Mr. Maidstone,[2] and the lieutenant of the Tower,[3] do give the hearty thanks of the House to Doctor Owen, Dean of Christ Church, and vice-chancellor of the University of Oxford, for his great pains taken in his sermon preached this day in the Abbey Church at Westminster, before his Highness the Lord Protector,[4] and the members elected to sit this present Parliament. And that he be desired to print his sermon. And that no man presume to print it without his leave.

Hen. Scobell,[5] Clerk of the Parliament.

1 This order is also recorded in *Journals of the House of Commons*, 13 vols. (London: HMSO, 1802–1803), 7:423.

2 John Maidstone (1606–1667), the member of Parliament for Colchester and steward of the Lord Protector's household.

3 Major General Sir John Barkstead (d. 1662), who sat in this Parliament as the member of Parliament for Middlesex.

4 Oliver Cromwell was Lord Protector from 1653 until his death in 1658.

5 I.e., Henry Scobell (ca. 1610–1660), the clerk of the Protectorate Parliaments.

[Dedicatory Epistle]

To His Highness, the Lord Protector, and to The Parliament of the Commonwealth of England, Scotland, and Ireland, Etc.

ALTHOUGH I NEED PLEAD NO OTHER REASON for the publishing of the ensuing discourse, but your order and command for my so doing, yet because I know that your peculiar interest, as governors of this commonwealth, in the several stations wherein you are placed of God, is truly stated therein, in the pursuit whereof, your peace, and the peace of these nations will be found to lie; I crave leave to add that consideration also. Being fully acquainted, in, and with what weakness it was composed and delivered, I cannot but conclude, that it was merely for the truth's sake therein contained, which is of God, and its suitableness through his wise providence, to the present state of things, in these nations, that it found acceptance and entertainment with you, which also makes me willing to be therein your remembrancer a second time. From the day wherein I received a command and call unto the service of preaching unto you, unto this issue of it, wherein it is clothed anew with obedience to your order, I found mercy with God to have that caution, of the great apostle abiding in my heart and thoughts, "If I yet please men, I am not a servant of God";[1] hence I can with boldness profess, that influenced in some measure with the power of that direction, I studiously avoided whatever might be suggested, with the least unsuitableness thereunto, with respect either to myself or others.

1 Gal. 1:10.

It was for Zion's sake, that I was willing to undertake this duty, and service: rejoicing that I had once more an opportunity to give public testimony to the great concernment of the great God, and our dear Lord Jesus Christ, in all the concussions of the nations in the world, and peculiarly in his wonderful providential dispensations, in these wherein we live. And here as the sum of all, to use plainness and liberty of speech, I say, if there be anything, in any person whatever, in these nations, that cannot stand with, that can stand without, the general interest of the people of God pleaded for, let it fall and rise no more: and the Lord I know will send his blessing out of Zion on whatever in singleness of heart, is done in a tendency to the establishment thereof.

Farther I shall not need to suggest anything of the ensuing discourse: they who take themselves to be concerned therein, will acquaint themselves with it, by its perusal. I shall only add, if the general principles asserted therein be in your hearts, if in pursuit thereof you endeavor, that in no corner of the nation it may be said, "This is Zion, that no man cares for,"[2] but that those who love the Lord Jesus Christ in sincerity,[3] and are, by faith and obedience, separated from the perishing world, following the Lamb,[4] according to the light which he is graciously pleased to impart unto them and engaged by the providence of God, in that work which he has undertaken to accomplish among us; be not overborne by a spirit of profaneness, and contempt of the power of godliness,[5] raging in the earth; that they may be preserved and secured, from the return of a hand of violence, and encouraged in the testimony they have to bear to the kingdom of Christ, in opposition to the world and all the ways which the men thereof have received by tradition from their fathers, that are not according to his mind, you will undoubtedly in your several conditions, receive blessing from God; which also that you may, in all your concernments, is the daily prayer of—

Your humble servant in the work of our dear Lord Jesus,[6]

John Owen.

2 Jer. 30:17.
3 Eph. 6:24.
4 Rev. 14:4.
5 2 Tim. 3:5. Cromwell alluded to this text in his address to members of Parliament at the opening of the Parliament. See *Letters, Writings, and Speeches of Oliver Cromwell*, vol. 3, *16 December 1653 to 2 September 1658*, ed. Joel Halcomb, Patrick Little, and David L. Smith (Oxford: Oxford University Press, 2022), 314.
6 Falconer Madan observed "the humility of the D.D., Dean of Christ Church, and Vice-Chancellor of the University, when addressing his great patron." See Falconer Madan, *Oxford Books: A Bibliography of Printed Works Relating to the University and City of Oxford or Printed or Published There*, vol. 3, *Oxford Literature, 1651–1680* (Oxford: Clarendon, 1931), 55.

[Sermon]

What shall one then answer the messengers of the nation? That the Lord hath founded Zion and the poor of his people shall trust in it.

ISAIAH 14:32

INTRODUCTION AND CONTEXT

The head of the prophecy, whereof these words are the close, lies in verse 28, ("In the year that king Ahaz died was this burden") which gives us the season, and just time of its revelation and delivery.

The kingdom of Judah was at that season low, and broken. Foreign invasions, and intestine[1] divisions had made it so; an account hereof is given us [in] 2 Chronicles chapter 28, throughout; as it is especially summed up, verse 19 of that chapter, "For the Lord brought Judah low because of Ahaz king of Israel, for he made Judah naked, and transgressed sore against the Lord."

Among their oppressing neighbors that took advantage of their low and divided condition, their old enemies the Philistines, the posterity of Cham in Canaan,[2] had no small share, as verse 18 of that chapter.

"The Philistines also had invaded the cities of the low country, and of the south of Judah, and had taken Bethshemesh, and Ajalon, and Gederoth, and Shocho with the villages thereof, and Timnah with the villages thereof, Gimzo also and the villages thereof, and they dwelt there."[3]

In this state of things, God takes notice of the joy, and triumphing of the whole land of Palestina, that is, the country of the Philistines. In that "the rod of

1 I.e., internal (in this context of domestic affairs).

2 The sons of Ham (Gen. 9:18).

3 2 Chron. 28:18.

him that smote them was broken":[4] that is the power of the kings and kingdom of Judah, which for many generations had prevailed against them, especially in the days of David (2 Sam. 5) and of Uzziah (2 Chron. 26:6) and kept them under, was made weak and insufficient for that purpose, "Rejoice not thou whole land of Palestina, because the rod of him that smote thee is broken" (Isa. 14:29).

It is no wonder, if Palestina, that was to be smitten, and broken by the rod of God among his people, rejoice at their perplexities and distresses, when we have seen men so to do, who pretend to dwell in Judah.

To take them off from their pride and boasting, their triumph and rejoicing, the Lord lets them know, that from the people whom they despised, and that broken rod they trampled upon, their desolation was at hand, though they seem to be perplexed, and forsaken for a season, verses 29–31.

> Rejoice not thou whole Palestina, because the rod of him that smote thee is broken, for out of the serpent's root shall come forth a cockatrice,[5] and his fruit shall be a fiery flying serpent, and the first-born of the poor shall feed, and the needy shall lie down in safety, and I will kill thy root with famine, and he shall slay thy remnant. Howl O gate, cry O city, thou whole Palestina art dissolved, for there shall come from the north a smoke, and none shall be alone in his appointed times.[6]

That it is Hezekiah who is principally intended in these lofty allegorical expressions, that was then rising up from the broken rod of Judah, is evident. He is termed a "cockatrice," and a "fiery flying serpent," not from his own nature, which was tender, meek, and gentle, wherein the comparison does not at all lie, nor hold; but in respect of the mischief[7] that he should do unto, the irrecoverable destruction that he should bring on, the land of Palestina: which accordingly, he performed "He smote the Philistines, even unto Gaza, and the borders thereof, from the tower of the watchmen to the fenced cities" (2 Kings 18:8): that is he wasted and destroyed the whole land, from one end even to the other.

It is it seems, no new thing, that the season of the enemies' rejoicing,[8] built upon the outward appearance, and state of things among the people of God,

4 Isa. 14:29.

5 I.e., a mythical dragon hatched by a serpent (see Isa. 11:8; 14:29; 59:5; Jer. 8:17).

6 Isa. 14:29–31.

7 I.e., attack and infliction of injury.

8 Perhaps the Spanish rejoicing over the recent humiliation of the Protectorate's previously victorious forces in the Caribbean. See Blair Worden, "Oliver Cromwell and the Sin of Achan," in *God's Instruments: Political Conduct in the England of Oliver Cromwell* (Oxford: Oxford University Press, 2012), 22.

is the beginning of their disappointment and desolation; the Lord make it so in this day of England's expectation, that the rod of it may be strengthened again, yet to smite the whole land of Palestina.[9]

The words of my text, are the result of things, upon God's dealings and dispensations before mentioned. Uncertain it is, whether they ought to be restrained, to the immediate prophecy before-going concerning Palestina, or whether they relate not also, to that in the beginning of the chapter, concerning the destruction of the Assyrian, which is summed up, verses 24–26. "The Lord of hosts hath sworn, saying, as I have thought so shall it come to pass, and as I have purposed, so shall it stand: that I will break the Assyrian in my land, and upon my mountains tread him under foot: then shall his yoke depart from off them, and his burden depart from off their shoulders." It is the ruining of Sennacherib and his army in the days of Hezekiah, that is foretold. Yea and this seems to claim a peculiar share and influence into this ἐπινίκιον,[10] or triumphant close; because eminently and signally, not long after, messengers were thus sent from Babylon, to inquire of the health and congratulate the good success of Hezekiah.[11] And well had it been for him, and his posterity, had he given those messengers the return to their inquiry, which was here prepared for him, some years before. His mistake herein, was the fatal ruin of Judah's prosperity.

Let not then that consideration be excluded, though the other insisted on, be principally intended.

OPENING OF THE TEXT AND RAISING OF FOUR DOCTRINES

The words you see have in them, an inquiry and a resolution thereof. I shall open them briefly as they lie, in the text.

Exposition of the Inquiry: What Shall One Answer the Messengers of the Nations?

First, there is an inquiry.[12]

1. "What *shall* one": what shall, or what ought? What is it their duty to do or to say? Or what shall they, upon the evidence of the things done, so do or

9 This could well be a reference to the plans to attack the Spanish ruled Flemish North Sea Coast. See Adam Quibell, "The Grounds, Method, Scope, and Impact of Independentism's Efforts for Union, 1654–1659," (PhD diss., Queen's University Belfast, 2024), 58.

10 Gk. "victory ode or song of triumph."

11 2 Kings 20:12; Isa. 39:1.

12 In the five exegetical points that follow, in the original the italicized terms were set in all caps for emphasis.

say: either their duty, or the event is denoted, or both, as in such predictions it often falls out.

2. "What shall *one*"? That is anyone, or everyone; the answer spoken of is either the duty of everyone to give, or it will be so evident, that anyone shall be able to give it. The word "one," I confess, is not expressly in the original, but is evidently included in the verb וּמַה־יַּעֲנֶה: "what shall be answered," that is, by any one whatever. There is no more in the translation, than is eminently enfolded in the original expression of this thing.

3. "What shall one *then*"? That is, in the season when God has disappointed the hopes and expectations of the enemies of his people, and has "strengthened their rod" to bruise them again more than ever. That is a season wherein great inquiry will be made about those things; "What shall one then answer?" This word also, is included in the interrogation; and much of the emphasis of it consists therein.

4. "Answer the messengers:" that is men coming on set purpose to make inquiry after the state of affairs among God's people; ambassadors, agents, spies, messengers, inquirers of any sort; or the word may be taken more largely, for any stranger that came to Jerusalem. The Septuagint render these words, βασιλεῖς ἐθνῶν; "the kings of the nations," what shall they say in this case, τί ἀποκριθήσονται; "what shall they answer," or "say?"[13] So that word is sometimes used: some think that for מַלְאֲכֵי, which they should have rendered ἄγγελοι, or "messengers," they read מַלְכֵי, or "kings," by an evident mistake: but all things are clear in the original.

5. "Of the *nations*": that is of this, or that nation, of any nation that shall send to make inquiry: גּוֹי, "of the heathen," say some; those commonly so called, or "the nations estranged from God," are usually denoted by this word in the plural number: yet not always under that consideration: so that there may be an enallagy of number,[14] the nation for the nations, which is usual.

"What shall one answer them?" They come to make inquiry after the work of God among his people, and it is fit that an answer be given to them: two things are observable in this interrogation.

Two Doctrines Raised from the Exposition of the Inquiry

Ob[servation] 1. *The nations about will be diligently inquiring after God's dispensations among his people*; besides what reports they receive at home, they will have messengers, agents, or spies,[15] to make inquiry.

13 In other words, the Septuagint translates Isa. 14:32 as "And what will the kings of the nations answer?"

14 I.e., a change of the number—the singular for the plural.

15 The secretary of state, John Thurloe (d. 1668), ran an international espionage network. The lieutenant of the Tower, John Barkstead, who was charged with thanking Owen for his sermon,

Ob[servation] 2. *The issues of God's dispensations among his people shall be so evident and glorious, that everyone, anyone though never so weak, if not blinded by prejudice, shall be able to give a convincing answer concerning them, to the inquiries of men.*

Something shall be spoken to these propositions in the process of our discourse.

First Part of the Exposition of the Answer to the Question: The Lord Has Founded Zion

Secondly, there is the resolution given of the inquiry made in this interrogation, hereof are two parts.

1. What God has done.
2. What his people shall, or ought to do.

Wrap up at any time, the work of God, and the duty of his people together, and they will be a sufficient answer to any man's inquiry after the state of things among them. As to our wisdom in reference unto providential dispensations, this is the whole of man.

1. The first thing in the answer to be given is the work of God. "The Lord hath founded Zion." Zion; that is his church, his people his chosen ones, called Zion from the place of their solemn worship in the days of David, the figure and type of the gospel church. "Ye are come unto Mount Zion, and unto the city of the living God, the heavenly Jerusalem" (Heb. 12:22).

It is generally used, not for the whole body of that people, unless as they were typically considered, in which respect they were all holy: but for the secret covenanted ones of that people, as is evident from all the promises made thereunto, yet with special regard to the ordinances of worship.

This God "hath founded": founded, or established, strengthened, that it shall not be removed. Psalm 87 is a comment on these words: he "hath founded" it; that is in faithful promises, and powerful performances, sufficient for its preservation and establishment.

Now this expression, (The Lord hath founded Zion) as it is an answer to the inquiries of "the messengers of the nations," may be taken two ways.

(1) As giving an account of the work itself done; or what it is that God has done, in and among his people. What is the work that is so famed

---

was also known for his intelligence work. For example, in the speech that he made after Owen's sermon, the Lord Protector praised Barkstead, noting "There was never any designe, but we could heare of it out of the Tower." See *The Letters, Writings, and Speeches of Oliver Cromwell*, 3:298.

abroad, and spoken of throughout the world? That being attempted in many places, and proving abortive, is here accomplished? This is it, shall one say: "God has established his people and their interest"; it is no such thing as you suppose, that some are set up, and some pulled down; that new fabrics of government or ruling are erected for their own sakes, or their sakes, who are interested in them. But this is the thing that God has done; he "hath founded Zion," established his people and their interest, in despite of all opposition.

(2) As giving a reason of the work done; whence is it that the Lord has wrought so mightily for you, among you, in your behalf, preserved you, recovered you, supported you, given you success and victory; when all nations conspired your ruin? Why this is the reason of it. "God hath founded Zion." He bore it goodwill, has taken care of the interest of his church and people.

The words may be taken in either sense; the issue of their intendment, as to our instruction, will be the same. This is the answer to be given to "the messengers of the nation," who perhaps expected to have heard of their strength and policy, of their counselors and armies, of their wealth and their riches, of their triumphs and enjoyments; no! "God hath founded Zion." And well had it been for Hezekiah, had he given this answer, prepared for him so long before, to the messengers of Babylon.[16]

Doctrine Raised from This First Part of the Answer

[Observation] 3. *The great design of God in his mighty works, and dispensations in the world; is the establishment of his people, and their proper interest, in their several generations.*

Give me leave to say; it is not for this or that form of government, or civil administration of human affairs; it is not for these, or those governors, much less for the advantage of one or other sort of men: for the enthroning of anyone, or other persuasion, gainful, or helpful to some few, or more, that God has wrought his mighty works among us. But it is that Zion may be founded, and the general interest of all the sons and daughters of Zion be preserved; and so far as anything lies in a subserviency thereunto, so far, and no farther is it with him accepted. And whatever, on what account soever sets up against it, shall be broken in pieces.

What answer then should we give to inquirers? "That the Lord hath founded Zion." This is that, and that alone, which we should insist upon, and take notice of, as the peculiar work of God among us. Let the reports

16 Isa. 39:2.

from other nations be what they will, let them acquaint the messengers of one another, with their glory, triumphs, enlarging of their empires and dominions.

When it is inquired what he has done in England, let us say, "He hath founded Zion." And he will not leave until every man concerned in the work shall be able to say, "We have busied ourselves about things of no moment; and consumed our days, and strength in setting up sheaves that must bow hereunto."[17] This is the main of God's intendment, and while it is safe, he has the glory and end of his dispensations.

Second Part of the Exposition of the Answer to the Question: The Poor of His People Shall Trust in It

2. The other part of the answer relates to the people; "The poor of his people shall trust in it."

The words contain either their duty, they ought to do so, or the event, they shall do so; or both jointly.

(1) "The poor of his people," [in] verse 30, they are called, "The firstborn of the poor" and "needy": that is, those who are very poor. Now this expression may denote either the people in general, who had been poor and afflicted; and so "the poor of his people," is as much, as "his poor people": or some in particular, that partly upon the account of their low outward condition, partly on the account of their lowliness of mind, are called "the poor of his people": and so the words are excellently paraphrased, "I will also leave in the midst of thee an afflicted, and poor people; and they shall trust in the name of the Lord: the remnant of Israel shall not do iniquity, nor speak lies: neither shall a deceitful tongue be found in their mouth, and none shall make them afraid" (Zeph. 3:12–13). We may take the words in a sense comprising both these: namely for the poor preserved remnant, carried through the fiery trial, and preserved to see some comfortable issue of God's dealing with them, though yet wrestling with difficulties and perplexities.

(2) What shall they do? They "shall trust in it"; וּבָהּ יֶחֱסוּ, "and in it they shall trust"; that is, being "in it," they shall trust, confide, acquiesce, namely in the Lord, who has wrought this work: or "in it," that is, either in the work of God, or in Zion so established by God.

The word here used for "trusting," is sometimes taken for to "repair," or to retreat to anything, and not properly to put trust, affiance,[18] or confidence, and

17 Gen. 37:7.

18 I.e., trust or faith in a person or thing.

so it is rendered in the margin of your books,[19] they shall "betake themselves to it." So is the word used [in] Judges 9:15; Psalm 36:7.

So the intendment is, that the poor preserved people of God, seeing his design to found Zion, and to establish the interest of his chosen, shall leave off all other designs, aims, and contrivances, and wind up all on the same bottom; they shall not, at least they ought not (for I told you the words might denote either their duty, what they ought to do, or the event what they shall do) set up designs, and aims of their own, and contend about other things! But betake their hopes to that which is the main intendment of God, the establishment of the interest of his people, and cast all other things in a subserviency thereunto. The sum is,

Doctrine Raised from This Second Part of the Answer

Ob[servation] 4. *It is the duty of God's poor preserved remnant, laying aside all other aims and contrivances, to betake themselves to the work of God, founding Zion and preserving the common interest of his people.*

TREATMENT OF THE FIRST DOCTRINE

Of the propositions thus drawn from the words, I shall treat severally, so far, as they may be foundations of the inferences intended.

Statement of the Doctrine

The first is this: *the nations about, will be diligently inquiring concerning God's dispensations among his people*; their eyes are upon them, and they will be inquiring after them.

In the handling of this, and all that follows, I humbly desire, that you would consider in what capacity, as to the discharge of this work, I look upon myself, and you. As you are hearers of the word of God, (in which state alone at present, though with reference to your designed employment, I look upon you) as you are not at all distinguished from others, or among yourselves: but as you are believers, or not; regenerate persons, or coming short thereof. And on this account, as I shall not speak of my rulers without reverence, so I shall endeavor to speak to my hearers with authority. I say then,

There are certain affections, and principles, that are active in the nations, that will make them restless, and always put them upon this inquiry. The people of God, on one account or other, shall be in all seasons, a separated

19 The marginal reading of Isa. 14:32 in the Authorized Version (KJV).

people. "Lo the people shall dwell alone, and shall not be reckoned among the nations" (Num. 23:9); yea they are separated from them, while they are in their bowels, and dwell "in the midst" of them (Mic. 5:7–8). Whether they are among them, as the spring of their mercies, or the rise of their destruction, (one of which they will always be) yet they are not of them. No sooner then is any people, or portion of them, thus dedicated to God; but all the nations about, and those among them not engaged in the same way with them, instantly look on them, as utterly severed from them: having other ways, ends, and interests than they, being built up wholly on another account and foundation: they reckon not of them as a people and a nation. The conclusion they make concerning them is that of Haman, "There is a certain people scattered abroad, and dispersed among the people in all the provinces of thy kingdom, and their laws are diverse from all people" (Est. 3:8). Not their moral and judicial laws, which were the sum of that perfection, which all nations aimed at; on which account they said of them, "Surely this great nation is a wise and understanding people" (Deut. 4:6) and the keeping of those laws was their wisdom and understanding among all nations: nor yet merely the laws of their religious worship: but the whole way, interest, design, profession of that people, is comprised in this expression, they "are diverse from all people." Looking on them in this state, they have principles (as I said) that will carry them out to an inquiry into their state and condition.

Two Reasons Why the Nations Make Such Inquiries

The Nations Are Prompted by Envy

1. They are full of envy against them; "They shall be ashamed for their envy at the people" (Isa. 26:11).[20] Looking on them, as wholly separated from them, and standing on another account than they do, they are full of "envy" at them. Envy is a restless passion, full of inquiries and jealousies; the more it finds of poison, the more it swells and feeds. It will search into the bottom of that which its eye is fixed on. The transaction of the whole business between Nehemiah and Sanballat, gives light to this consideration. See Nehemiah 4:1–6.

And ever the nearer any nation is to this people, the greater is their envy. It was Edom, and Moab, and Ammon, the nations round about, that were most filled with wrath and envy against Israel. Yea when that people was divided

20 Owen appealed to this text in *Ebenezer* (1648) and *The Advantage of the Kingdom of Christ* (1651). For the first sermon, see *Complete Works of John Owen*, 18:264. The second sermon is included in this volume.

among themselves, and the true worship of God remained with Judah, and they became the separated people, Ephraim was instantly filled with envy against them, "The envy also of Ephraim shall depart, and the adversaries of Judah shall be cut off. Ephraim shall not envy Judah" (Isa. 11:13): for there must be a desire of the same thing, or something answering it (which befalls in proximity of habitation) that a man is envied for, in him that envies him. This is one fountain of the nations' inquiry after your affairs.

Through the providence of God you "dwell alone";[21] that is, as to your main design and interest. You are not reckoned among the nations, as to the state of being the people of God; so far, and under that consideration, they count you not worthy to be reckoned or esteemed a nation. They envy to see the men of their contempt exalted, blessed. The same is the condition of Ephraim among us;[22] men not engaged in the same cause and way with you, they are full of envy. Wherefore do they inquire of your welfare, of your state and condition, of your affairs? Is it that they love you, that they desire your prosperity, that they would have you an established nation? No, only their envy makes them restless. And as it is in general: so no sooner does any man upon a private account separate himself from the public interest of the people of God, but he is instantly filled with envy against the managers of it. And notwithstanding all our animosities, if this has not befallen us, in our differences and divisions; I no way doubt a peaceable composure, and blessed issue of the whole. If envy be not at work, we shall have establishment.

The Nations Are Driven by Fear

2. A second principle, whereby they are put upon their inquiries, is fear. They fear them, and therefore will know how things stand with them, and what are the works of God among them. "I saw the tents of Cushan in affliction, and the curtains of the land of Midian did tremble" (Hab. 3:7); "I saw" it; when God was doing the great work described in that chapter with many lofty allegorical expressions, of bringing his people out of bondage, to settle them in a new state and condition; the nations round about, that looked on them, were filled with affliction, fear, and trembling.[23] They were afraid whither these things would grow.

21 Num. 23:9.

22 Isa. 7:4–6. For a discussion of the motif of the false brother, see Martyn Calvin Cowan, *John Owen and the Civil War Apocalypse: Preaching, Prophecy and Politics* (London: Routledge, 2017), 166–67.

23 This was Owen's text from his post-Colchester sermons of 1648, published as *Ebenezer* (1648). See *Complete Works of John Owen*, 18:225.

> Great is the Lord, and greatly to be praised in the city of our God, in the mountain of his holiness; beautiful for situation, the joy of the whole earth is Mount Zion, on the sides of the north, the city of the great King; God is known in her palaces for a refuge. For lo, the kings were assembled, they passed by together; they saw it and so they marvelled, they were troubled and hasted away; for fear took hold upon them there, and pain as of a woman in travail. (Ps. 48:1–6)

The close of all the considerations of these kings, and their attendants, is, that "fear took hold upon them." Fear is solicitous and inquiring; it will leave nothing unsearched, unlooked into, it would find the inside and bottom of everything wherein it is concerned. Though the more it finds, the more it is increased, yet the greater still are its inquiries; fearing more what it knows not, than what it knows, what is behind, than what appears. This puts the nations upon their inquiry, they are afraid what these things will grow to. "Then was our mouth filled with laughter, and our tongue with singing, then said they among the heathen, the Lord hath done great things for them" (Ps. 126:2): they are the words of men pondering their affairs, and filled with fear at the issue: if God does such things as these for them, what think you will be the issue? I dare say of the proudest adversaries of the people of God at this day; notwithstanding all their anger they are more afraid than angry. The like also may be said concerning their wrath, revenge, and curiosity, all pressing them to such inquiries.

Application of the First Doctrine

This is the issue of this proposal. If we are not a separated people unto God, if our portion be as the portion of the men of the world, and we are also as they, reckoned among the nations, if we have had only national works, in the execution of wrath on men fitted thereunto among us; woe unto us that we were ever engaged in the whole affair that for some years we have been interested in. It will be bitterness and disappointment in the latter end. If we be the Lord's peculiar lot, separate unto him, the nations about, and many among ourselves, on the manifold accounts before mentioned, will be inquiring into our state and condition, and the work of God among us. Let us consider what we shall answer them, what we shall say unto them, what is the account we give of God's dealings with us, and of his mighty works among us? What is the profession we make? If we seek ourselves, if we are full of complaints and repinings one against another: if everyone has his own aims, his own designs, (for what we do, not what we say, is the answer we make) if we measure the work of God by its suitableness to our private interests; if this be the issue of all the dealings of God among us, we shall not have wherein to rejoice: but of these things afterward. The second proposition is—

TREATMENT OF THE SECOND DOCTRINE

Statement of the Doctrine

Ob[servation] 2. *The issue of God's dealing with, and dispensations among his people, shall be so perspicuous and glorious, that one, anyone, everyone, shall be able to give an answer to them that make inquiries about them.* "What shall one then say;" whether it be for judgment, or mercy, all is one: he will make the event to be evident and glorious. He "is our rock, and his work is perfect";[24] and he will have his works so known, as that they may all praise him. Be it in judgment; see what issue he will bring his work unto. "Even all nations shall say, 'Wherefore hath the Lord done thus unto this land? What meaneth the heat of this great anger;' Then men shall say, 'Because they have forsaken the covenant of the Lord God of their fathers, which he made with them, when he brought them forth out of the land of Egypt'" (Deut. 29:24–25). "*Men* shall say,"[25] ordinary men shall be able to give this sad account of the reason of the works of God, and his dealings with his people. So also as to his dispensations in mercy, "Lord, when thy hand is lifted up, they will not see: but they shall see, and be ashamed for their envy at the people, yea, the fire of thine enemies shall devour them" (Isa. 26:11). He will not leave the work of his favor toward his people, until those who are willing to shut their eyes against it, do see and acknowledge his hand and counsel therein.

I do not say this will hold in every dispensation of God, in all seasons, from the beginning to the ending of them. In many works of his power and righteousness, he will have us bow our souls to the law of his providence, and his sovereignty, wisdom, and goodness therein, when his footsteps are in the deep, and his paths are not known;[26] which is the reasonablest thing in the world.

But this generally is the way of his proceedings; especially in the common concernments of his people, and in the disposal of their public interests; his works his will and counsels therein, shall be eminent and glorious.

24 Deut. 32:4.

25 In the original, the word "men" is set in all caps for emphasis.

26 Ps. 77:19.

It is chiefly from ourselves, and our own follies that we come short of such an acquaintance with the works of God, as to be able to give an answer to everyone that shall demand an account of them. When David was staggered at the works of God, he gives this reason of it, "I was foolish and as a beast before him" (Ps. 73:22). That thoughtfulness and wisdom which keeps us in darkness, is our folly.

Two Reasons Why God's Glorious Works of Providence May Not Be Seen

There are sundry things that are apt to cloud our apprehensions, as to the mind of God in his dealing with his people. As,

People May Be Blinded by Selfishness

1. Self-fulness of our own private apprehensions and designs; a private design and aim in the works of providence, is like a private, by-opinion[27] in matters of religion.

You seldom see a man take up a by-opinion (if I may so speak), but he instantly lays more weight upon it than upon all religion besides. If that be not enthroned, be it a matter of never so small importance, he scarce cares what becomes of all other truths which he does embrace. When men have fixed to themselves, that this, or that particular, must be the product of God's providential dispensations, that alone fills their aims and desires, and leaves no room for any other apprehension. Have we not seen persons in the days wherein we live, so fixed on a reign, a kingdom,[28] I know not what, that they would scarce allow God himself to be wise, if their minds were not satisfied? "Give me this child, or I die."[29] Now is it probable, that when men's whole souls, are possessed with a design[30] and desire of their own, so fully that they are cast into the mold of it, are transformed into the image and likeness of it, they can see, hear, think, talk, dream nothing else; they shall be able to discern aright, and acquiesce in the general issue of God's dispensations, or be able to "answer the messengers of the nations," making inquiry concerning them. Fear, hope, wrath, anger, discontentment, with a rabble of the like mind-darkening affections, are the attendants of such a frame. He who

27 I.e., a distorted or erroneous opinion.

28 This is quite possibly a reference to Presbyterians seeking reformation under a covenanted king.

29 Gen. 30:1. Owen would make the same point the following month in *God's Presence with a People* (1656), which is included in this volume.

30 The language of design is striking in the context of the failure of the exorbitantly costly so-called Western Design against the Spanish Caribbean (1654–1655).

knows anything of the power of prejudices in diverting the minds of men, from passing a right judgment on things proposed to them, and the efficacy of disordered affections for the creating and confirming of such prejudices; will discern the power of this darkening disturbance.

People May Be Distracted by Strife

2. Private enmities, private disappointments, private prejudices, are things of the same consideration; let a man of a free and large heart and spirit, abstract his thoughts from the differences that are among the people of God in this nation, and keep himself from an engagement into any particular design and desire: it is almost impossible that he should wink so hard,[31] but that the issue and reason of God's dealing with us, will shine in upon his understanding; so that he shall be able to give an account of them, to them that shall make inquiry. Will he not be able to say to "the messengers of the nations"; and all other observers of the providential alterations of the late times that have passed over us: The people of God in this nation were despised, but are now in esteem: they were under subjection to cruel task-masters, some in prisons, some banished to the ends of the earth, merely on the account of the worship of their God; the consciences of all inthralled, and of many defiled and broken on the scandals laid before them, while iniquity and superstition were established by law.[32] But this is that which God has now done and accomplished: the imprisoned are set at liberty,[33] the banished are recalled,[34] they that "have lain among the pots" have got "doves wings,"[35] conscience is no more enthralled, their sacrifices are not "mixed with their blood,"[36] nor do they meet with trembling in the worship of God. O you "messengers of the nations," this is that which the Lord has done! Who (I say) not entangled with one prejudicate[37] engagement or other, may not see this with half an eye? But such is our state and condition, such our frame and temper, so full are

31 I.e., to shut one's eyes.

32 For an account of the experience of the suffering, and consequent diaspora, of the godly during the Laudian regime of the 1630s, see Tom Webster, *Godly Clergy in Early Stuart England: The Caroline Puritan Movement, c. 1620–1643* (Cambridge: Cambridge University Press, 1997).

33 Alexander Leighton, William Prynne, John Bastwick, and Henry Burton had all been imprisoned for their attacks on the Laudian regime.

34 Some of the exiled victims of Laudian uniformity returned: Samuel Eaton, Sir Henry Vane, and Hugh Peter from New England; and Jeremiah Burroughes, Thomas Goodwin, Philip Nye, Sidrach Simpson, William Bridge, and Joseph Symonds from the Netherlands.

35 Ps. 68:13.

36 Luke 13:1.

37 I.e., obsolete form of prejudice.

we of our own desires, and so perplexed with our own disappointments, that we can see nothing, know nothing nor are able to give any word of account, that may tend to the glory of our God, to them that inquire of us; but every one vents his own discontentments, his own fears, his own perplexities. The Lord look down in mercy, and let us not be found despisers of the work of his power and goodness. Ah! How many glorious appearances have I seen, of which I said, "Under the shadow hereof shall we live among the heathen"?[38] But in a short space they have passed away." Shall we, therefore, choose us a captain, and go down again into Egypt?[39] The third proposition ensues.

TREATMENT OF THE THIRD DOCTRINE

Statement of the Doctrine

Ob[servation] 3. *The great design of God in his mighty works and dispensations, is the establishment of his people and their proper interest, in their several generations.*

Three Premises for This Doctrine

To make this clear, some few things are previously to be considered, as:

The People of God Are to Glorify Him in Their Generation

1. The proper interest of the people of God, is to glorify him in their several places, stations, and generations; none of us are to live unto ourselves. It is for this end that God has taken a peculiar people to himself in this world, that his name may be borne forth by them, that he might be glorified by them and upon them.[40] This is the great end whereunto they are designed, and that which they ought to aim at only, even to glorify God.

If this be not done, they fall off from, and are beside their proper interest. Besides innumerable testimonies to this purpose I might give evidence to this assertion, from God's eternal electing love toward them, with his intendment therein; from their redemption out of every kindred, tribe, and family under heaven, by the blood of Christ,[41] from their separation from the world, by

38 Lam. 4:20.

39 Num. 14:4. Later that day Cromwell made mention of Owen's use of this passage and told those gathered in the Painted Chamber that Owen had given them "some hints" about "return-ing to all those things that we thinke we have ben fighting against, & destroying of all that good . . . we have attayned unto." See *The Letters, Writings, and Speeches of Oliver Cromwell*, 3:294.

40 1 Pet. 2:9.

41 Rev. 5:9.

their effectual calling, and the like considerations; but I have the consenting voice of them all in general, and of every individual in particular, crying out, "This is our, this is my proper interest, that we may glorify God; fail we and come short in this, we come short, and fail in the whole: so that I shall not need further to confirm it."

This Generation Should Glorify God in the Midst of Divisions

2. God is the only proper and infallible judge in what state and condition his people will best, and most glorify his name, in their several generations. I think I need not insist on the proof of this assertion; "Should it be according to thy mind," says he in Job 34:33 or according to the mind of God? Should the disposal of things be according to his will, or ours? Whose end is to be obtained in the issue of all? Is it not his glory? Who has the most wisdom to order things aright, he or we? Who has the chief interest in, and right unto the things contended about? Who sees what will be the event of all things, he or we? Might men be judges would they not universally practically conclude, that the condition wherein they might best glorify God would be, that they might have peace and rest from their enemies, union and a good understanding among themselves: that they might dwell peaceably in the world, without control, and have the necks of their adversaries under their feet. This in general. In particular: that this, or that persuasion that they are peculiarly engaged in, might be always enthroned, that their proper sheaf might stand upright, and all others bow thereunto,[42] and that nothing is contrary to the glory of God, but what disturbs this condition of affairs. I know not what may be accomplished before the end of the world, from the beginning of it hitherto for the most part the thoughts of God, have not been as these thoughts of ours: he has judged otherwise as to the condition wherein his people should glorify him. God is judge himself, let us I pray you leave the determination of this difference to him; and if it be so as to our general condition, much more is it so as to our peculiar designs and aims, wherein we are divided.

The People of God Must Submit to Providence

3. Providential dispensations are discoveries of the wisdom of God in disposing of the condition of his people so as, they may best glorify him. To dispute against the condition wherein at any time we are cast by his providence, is to rise up against his wisdom in disposing of things to his own glory.

42 Gen. 37:7.

Reasons for This Doctrine

These things being premised, it is easy to give light and evidence to the assertion laid down.

I might go through the stories of God's dealings with the nations of the world, and his own people among them, and manifest in each particular, that still his design was, the establishment of his people's proper interest. But instead of instances take two or three testimonies that occur. "When the most high divided to the nations their inheritance, when he separated the sons of Adam, he set the bounds of the people according to the number of the children of Israel" (Deut. 32:8). From the beginning, God has so ordered all the nations of the world that they may bear a proportion to what he has to do with his people; that he may so order and dispose of them, as that his design toward his own may be accomplished. "For lo I will command and I will sift the house of Israel among all nations like as corn is sifted in a sieve, yet shall not the least grain fall upon the earth" (Amos 9:9);[43] all the stirs and commotions that are in the world, are but God's siftings of all the nations, that his chosen ones may be fitted for himself, and not lost in the chaff and rubbish.

"Whose voice then shook the earth, but now he hath promised saying, 'Yet once more I shake not the earth only, but also heaven'; and this word, 'Yet once more,' signifieth the removing of those things that are shaken, as of things that are made, that those things which cannot be shaken may remain" (Heb. 12:26–27): all the shakings of the nations are, that the unshaken interest of the saints may be established.[44] "But I am the Lord thy God that divided the sea whose waves roared, the Lord of hosts is his name. And I have put my words in thy mouth, and I have covered thee in the shadow of mine hand, that I may plant the heavens, and lay the foundations of the earth, and say unto Zion, 'Thou art my people'" (Isa. 51:15–16). Heaven, and earth, and all things therein, are disposed of, that Zion may be built and established. All God's works in this world, lie in a subserviency to this end and purpose.

Does God at any time prosper an evil or a wicked nation? An anti-Christian nation?[45] Is it for their own sakes? "Does God take care for

43 Owen had alluded to this text in *A Sermon Preached* [. . .] *January 31* (1649), *The Shaking and Translating of Heaven and Earth* (1649), and his June 1649 sermon *Human Power Defeated*. See *Complete Works of John Owen*, 18:308, 458, 465.

44 The text of Owen's sermon, *The Shaking and Translating of Heaven and Earth* (1649). In that sermon, Owen also appealed to the verses that he goes on to mention in Isaiah 51.

45 At this point, the war with Spain was not advancing as hoped, and later that day Cromwell would seek to encourage the new Parliament to support it financially. He told members of Parliament that Spain was "head of the Papall Interest, the head of the Antichristian Interest". See *The Letters, Writings, and Speeches of Oliver Cromwell*, 3:295.

oxen?"[46] Has he delight in the prosperity of his enemies? No: it is only that they may be a rod in his hand for a little moment, and a staff for his indignation against the miscarriages of his people, "O Assyrian, the rod of mine anger, and the staff in their hand is mine indignation" (Isa. 10:5, 12). This in such a season is their proper interest, to glorify God in distress. Does he break, ruin, and destroy them, as sooner or later he will "leave them neither root nor branch"?[47] All that he does to them is a recompense for the controversy of Zion. "For it is the day of the Lord's vengeance, and the year of recompenses for the controversy of Zion" (Isa. 34:8).

We see not perhaps at this day, wherein the concernments of the remnant of God's people do lie, in the great concussions of the nations in the world; we know not what design in reference to them may lie therein: alas! We are poor shortsighted creatures, we know nothing that is before us, much less can we make a judgment of the work of God, in the midst of the darkness and confusion, that is in the world, until he has brought it to perfection. All lies open and naked to his eye;[48] and the beauty of all his works will one day appear. The true and proper interest of his people, so as they may best glorify him in the world, is that, which he is pursuing in all these dispensations.

Application of the Third Doctrine, Particularly to Those in Power

The grounds, reasons, and foundations of this truth, in the counsel, from the love and attributes of God, the redemption in the blood of Jesus, I must not now pursue, this one thing I shall only offer.

The state of Zion, of the people of God, being much to depend upon the disposals of them, whom God by his providence raises up to rule and government among the nations; though sometimes he sets up men, whose hearts and minds are upright with himself, yet he will not trust his own to their mercy, and the variableness of their wills in general: but will so dispose, alter, weaken and strengthen them, to set them up, and pull down, that it shall be their interest, to which they will always abide faithful, so to deal with his people, as he will have them dealt with, that they may best glorify him in their generations.

If it be in the infinite wise counsel of God, to give his saints in this nation peace and tranquility, they shall not have it precariously upon the wills of men; for he will not leave molding and disposing of the affairs of the nation, until it find, that it is its proper interest to give, and measure out unto them,

46 1 Cor. 9:9.
47 Mal. 4:1.
48 Heb. 4:13.

what is to the mind of God. All that has been done among us, all that we are in expectation of, turns on this hinge alone. But lastly,

TREATMENT OF THE FOURTH DOCTRINE

Statement of the Doctrine

Ob[servation] 4. *It is the duty of God's preserved remnant, laying aside all other aims and contrivances, to betake themselves to the work of God, founding Zion, and preserving the common interest of his people.*

"God hath founded Zion, and the poor of the people shall trust therein," or betake themselves unto it.

We are apt to wander on hills and mountains, everyone walking in the imagination of his own heart,[49] forgetting our resting place.

When God was bringing the power of the Babylonian upon his people, the prophet Jeremiah could neither persuade the whole nation to submit to his government, nor many individuals among them, to fall to him in particular. And when the time of their deliverance from that captivity was accomplished, how hardly were they persuaded to embrace the liberty tendered; notwithstanding all encouragements and advantages, the greatest part of them abide in that place of their bondage to this day. So hardly are we brought to close with God's peculiar work, and our own proper interest, although his glory, and our own safety lie therein. The reasons of this frame, I have in part touched before, I shall add but two more.

Two Reasons Why Those in Power Have Been Slow to Be Persuaded

Unwillingness to Pursue the Common Interest of God's People

1. Discontentment with our peculiar lot and portion, in the work of the Lord and common interest of his people. It is with us, in our civil affairs, as the apostle says it is not in the natural body, nor ought to be in the spiritual, or church body: the foot does not say, "Because I am not the head, I am not of the body";[50] no, it does not, but is content with its own place and usefulness. It is so with the rest of the members, that are more noble, and yet are not the head neither. It is otherwise with us: I interpose not my thoughts, as to your present constitution, and the order of things among us. I speak no more than I have sundry years since, sundry times complained of to a parliament of this commonwealth. Everyone, if not personally, yet in association with them, of

49 Jer. 3:17.

50 1 Cor. 12:15.

some peculiar persuasion with himself, would be the head; and because they are not, they conclude they are not of the body, nor will care for the body, but rather endeavor its ruin. Because their peculiar interest does not reign, the common interest shall be despised; and this has been the temper or rather distemper, of the people of God in this nation now for sundry years; and what it may yet produce I know not. Only for the present the work of God in founding Zion, in pursuing his people's common interest, is despised, thought light of, and all the pleasant things thereof trodden under foot. Unless God end this frame, my expectations, I confess, of a happy issue of the great work of God among us will wither day by day.

The Presumption That Seeks to Determine How God Should Work

2. The suffering of our wills and judgments, as to the products of providence, to run before the will of God. This, the experience of these days has taught us. Those who have a forwardness in prescribing to God what he should do, as to the *modus*, or manner of the work, which at any time he has to accomplish, are stubbornly backward, in closing with what he does actually produce. These and the like things, which might be in large catalogues reckoned up, one after another, detain the minds of men, from acquiescing in the common interest of Zion, whose preservation is the whole peculiar design of the great work of God, in any place or season. These foundations being laid in the words of the text, let us now see what inferences from them may be made, for our advantage and instruction.

First Application: Those in Power Should Be Able to Give an Account of God's Work in the English Revolution

Use 1. Let us then consider diligently what we shall "answer the messengers of the nations"; some think that by the "nation," is peculiarly intended the nation of the Jews themselves, whose messengers from all parts came to Jerusalem to inquire of the work of God, and to advise about the affairs of the whole. In this sense you are the messengers of this nation, to whom an answer is to be returned: and because the text says, "*one*" shall do it,[51] that is, anyone, I shall make bold before we close, to give an answer to your inquiries; and endeavor to satisfy your expectations: in the meantime as the words seem more directly to respect the inquiries of other nations: so it is in a special manner incumbent on you, who will be especially inquired of, to return an answer to them. Be provided then I pray in your own hearts, to give an answer in this business; and

51 In the original, "one" is set in all caps for emphasis.

oh that you could do it with one heart and lip, with one consent and judgment. On whom are the eyes of this nation and of those round about? From whom are the expectations of men? To whom should we go to inquire what God has done in this nation, what he is doing, what are the effects of his power, if not of you? Some of you have been engaged in this work with the Lord from the beginning: and I hope none of you have been engaged in heart or hand against it; and you speak still with living affections, to the old and common cause.[52] If you will be able to steer your course aright, if you would take one straight step, have in a readiness an acquaintance with the work of God, what it is that he aims at, by which you may be guided in all your undertakings. Suppose now a man, or men, should come and ask of you, what God has done in these nations? What he has wrought, and effected? What is brought forth? Have you an answer in readiness? Certainly God has done so much as that he expects you should be able to give an account of it. Take heed that every one of you be not ready to speak the disquietness of your own spirits, and so cast contempt on the work of God. Something else is required of you. I have sometimes in darkness and under temptations myself, begun to think, that what has been, is the thing that is, and there is no new thing under the sun.[53] As it has been among the heathen of old, so it has been among us; or as it was with Israel, "Then were the people of Israel divided into two parts: half of the people followed Tibni the son of Ginath to make him king, and half followed Omri: but the people that followed Omri prevailed against the people that followed Tibni the son of Ginath: so Tibni died and Omri reigned" (1 Kings 16:21–22):[54] that a common thing and frequent in the world had befallen us, wherein God had no hand, but that of common providence, in dashing one sort of men against another. So foolish have I been, and as a beast, so ready to condemn "the generation of the righteous,"[55] so unbelieving and ready to cast away the faith and prayer of ten thousand saints; one of whose sighs shall not be lost. But such fearful effects, sometimes trouble disquietment, disappointment, and carnal fear will produce. But certain it is, none of the many

52 This is a reference to the "good old cause," which became a shorthand for the civil war struggle, particularly to rally opposition to the Cromwellian Protectorate. Months beforehand, Sir Henry Vane used it in the pamphlet *A Healing Question* (London, [May] 1656). The terminology was ambiguous because, as Tim Cooper points out, "the language of the 'good old cause' was wide open to interpretation." See Cooper, *John Owen, Richard Baxter and the Formation of Nonconformity* (Farnham, UK: Ashgate, 2011), 291.

53 Eccl. 1:9.

54 Owen had engaged with this text in *A Sermon Preached* [. . .] *January 31* (1649). See *Complete Works of John Owen*, 18:308, 458, 465.

55 Ps. 14:5.

cries of the people of God shall be lost, nor their faith be disappointed. God has a peculiar design in hand, and we are to find it out, that we may be able to answer them that make inquiries. If you lay not this foundation of your procedures, I shall not wonder if you err in your ways; it is your polestar[56] and will be so, by which your whole course is to be steered; your shield, which while it is safe, though you die, your glory abides.

Objections Answered

But you will say! "What then is this great design of God among his people: 'let the Holy One of Israel bring nigh his work, that we may know it';[57] what is that true and general interest of Zion that he has founded; let us know it, that we may be able to give an answer to them that inquire after it."

Ask themselves, those who have prayed for it, waited for it, expected it, are made partakers of it, do enjoy it, live upon it, probably they will be able to give you an account what is their peculiar and only interest, as to these providential dispensations; surely they cannot but know that which they enjoy, and live upon.

But you will say, "Of all others this is the most unlikely, and irrational course, a way to perplex and entangle, not to inform us at all. Is it not clear, that they are divided among themselves? Is not their language, is not their voice, like that of the Jews at the building of the second temple; some shouted for joy, and some wept at the remembrance of the former temple.[58] Are not their desires rather like that, and those of theirs, who built Babel, than of those who cry 'Grace, grace,'[59] while God is founding Zion? Do not many of them utterly deny any work or design of God (I mean that is peculiar) in the affairs of this nation; and utterly fall away from the society of them, who are otherwise persuaded? And is it likely that we can gather any resolution from them? Does not the greatest danger of our own miscarriage lie in this? That we may be apt to attend to their peculiar desires, and so to divide among ourselves, as they are divided?"

And is this the return that indeed is to be made! Oh that mine eyes might run down with water day and night on this account,[60] that my heart might be moved within me, for the folly of my people. Ah "foolish people and unwise, do we thus requite the Lord?"[61]

56 I.e., a prominent star serving as a guiding light.

57 Isa. 5:19.

58 Ezra 3:12.

59 Zech. 4:7.

60 Ps. 119:136.

61 Deut. 32:6.

It is true, many at all times have desired the day of the Lord, who, when it has come, have not been able to abide it, it has consumed them,[62] and all the principles, whereon they have acted, and upon which they did desire it;[63] but that those who have their share in it indeed, should be thus broken among themselves, should "bite" one another, "devour" one another,[64] and scarce allow one another to be sharers in the common interest of the saints in that day; "This is a lamentation, and shall be for a lamentation."[65]

Summary of What God Has Done for All the Saints

But yet something may be farther pressed on them in this business. When one went to demand of the philosophers of the several sects, which was the best of them, everyone named his own sect and party in the first place; but all of them, in the second place, granted that of Plato to be the most eminent. The inquirer knew quickly what to conclude; setting aside prejudicate affections, self-love, and by-interests, he saw that the judgment of all, ran on that of Plato, as the best and most eminent sect, and which thereupon he preferred before the rest.[66]

May not some inquiry of the like nature be made of the people of God among us? Ask them, what is the common interest of Zion, that God takes care of, that he has founded in the days wherein we live, in the great transactions of providence that have passed over us. Say some: "That such a form of church worship and discipline be established, such a rule of doctrine confirmed, and all men whatever compelled to submit unto them: herein lies that kingdom of Christ which he takes care of, this is that which God will have founded and established: and what this form, what this rule is, we are to declare."[67]

"That that discipline be eradicated, the ministers' provision destroyed,"[68] and the men of such a persuasion enthroned, to rule all the rest at their

62 Mal. 3:2.

63 This is most probably a reference to the Fifth Monarchists.

64 Gal. 5:15.

65 Ezek. 19:14.

66 This argument, attributed to Cicero, is preserved in Augustine's *Contra academicos* (*Against the Academicians*) 3.7.15–16 and is included as fragment 20 in Cicero, *On the Nature of the God. Academics*, ed. H. Rackham, Loeb Classical Library 268 (Cambridge, MA: Harvard University Press, 1933), 460–61. It is also expounded by Francis Bacon in his 1597 work *The Colours of Good and Evil*. See *Bacon's Essays and Colours of Good and Evil*, ed. W. Aldis Wright (Cambridge: Macmillan, 1862), 247–48.

67 This is a description of the views of some Presbyterians.

68 This is a reference to the call for the abolition of tithes. Both Fifth Monarchists and Quakers were particularly prominent in calling for a ministry that was not state (or compulsorily) financed.

pleasure, seeing, that notwithstanding all their pretended reformation, they are yet anti-Christian, say others.[69]

Say some: "That a kingdom and rule be set up in our hands, to be exercised in the name and authority of Jesus Christ, taking away all law and magistracy already established, to bring forth the law of righteousness conceived in our minds, and therein to be preserved"; all uniting only in this, that a sovereignty as unto administration of the things of God is to be theirs.[70]

Say others, lastly, "That the people of God be 'delivered from the hands of their cruel enemies,' that they 'may serve the Lord without fear all the days of their lives, in righteousness and holiness,'[71] that, notwithstanding their present differences, they may live peaceably one with, or at least one by another, enjoying rule and promotion, as they are fitted for employments, and as he gives promotion, in whose hand it is, that godliness and the love of the Lord Jesus Christ be preserved, protected, and secured, from a return of the hand of violence upon it"; herein say some lies the common interest of the people of God; this he has wrought out for them, herein he has founded Zion. Ask now the people of God in this nation, I say or any of them, one, or more, at any time? What he, or they, look upon as the chief thing aimed at in the mighty dispensations of God among us; will they not everyone answer in the first place, that is aimed at, that is to be enthroned, that so doing is the will of God, the end of his works among them, wherein their, or his particular engagement and interest lies. But ask them now again, in the second place, which of the remaining persuasions concerning the work of God, and the common interest of his people, they would prefer next to their own: will they not all unanimously fix on that mentioned in the last place, rather than any of the others. Is it not then evident that setting aside prejudicate affections, and such determinations, as may reasonably be supposed to arise from them, laying away all private animosities, and desire of rule and preeminence, with other worldly and selfish designs; the universality of the people of God, do answer to them that inquire, that in the last persuasion lies the aim, and work of God in our generation. For my own part, on this and other considerations hereafter to be mentioned, I shall dare freely to give this answer to the

69 This is a description of the views of early Quakers. As Hughes explains, in the 1650s "Fox and other early Quakers like Richard Farnworth rejected and harassed the 'hireling' anti-Christian ministry." See Ann Hughes, *Politics, Society and Civil War in Warwickshire, 1620–1660* (Cambridge: Cambridge University Press, 1987), 319.

70 This is a description of the views of Fifth Monarchists. In his speech later that day, Cromwell was critical of the Fifth Monarchists. *The Letters, Writings, and Speeches of Oliver Cromwell*, 3:301–2.

71 Luke 1:74–75.

messengers of this, or any nation in the world, who shall make inquisition after the work of God among us, and his design in reference to his people; and it is no other than my heart has been fixed upon for many years, and which I have several times, on one account or other intimated, or pressed unto the parliament, which first undertook to manage, and successfully carried on that cause, in whose protection you are now engaged.

Specific Application to Those in Power, Supported by Five Reasons

This I say then; "God hath founded Zion," he has taken care of "the generation of the righteous,"[72] "the children of Zion,"[73] however differenced among themselves; has "broken the yoke" of their oppressors,[74] given them peace, ordered the affairs of this nation so, that they do, or may, all of them enjoy quietness, one not envying the other, nor they vexing them, but serving God according to the light, which he is graciously pleased to afford them, they wait for farther manifestations of the glorious gospel; and that God has broken, and will break, every design that, either openly, and professedly, or under specious pretenses of crying, "Lo, here is Christ, or, Lo, there,"[75] has sought, or shall seek and endeavor, to subvert this his work, to the preservation whereof, he will certainly mold the government, and interest of this nation, ordering its affairs in a peculiar manner on that account only: and not that he delights in one way or form, whereinto it has been cast, more than another. And whatever high-minded men, full of their own apprehensions and wisdom, may do, to this work of God "the poor of his people" shall repair.[76] And for my insisting on this answer, and this only, I have these further reasons to add for my justification.

(1) This is an interest comprehensive of all the sons of Zion, whose founding God intends; it excludes none that can claim a share in "the city of the living God."[77] God takes equal care of all the "dwelling-places of Zion;" every dwelling place of Zion has its beauty, has its glory (Isa. 4:5). The glory of one, may be as the glory of the sun, of another as the moon, of others as the stars, and those differing from one another in glory; yet each has its glory; and upon it there "shall be a defence," a covering, a protection. This is the promise; this has been the work of God.

72 Ps. 14:5.
73 Ps. 149:2.
74 Isa. 9:4.
75 Matt. 24:23.
76 I.e., return to habitually.
77 Heb. 12:22.

(2) This comprises all them, who have lived by faith, and abode in supplications in reference to God's late dispensations among us. Who dare "despise" any one of "those little ones,"[78] and say, "God has heard me, not you, regarded me, not you, you have no share or portion in the returns of supplications which we enjoy."

(3) This alone preserves the dwellers of Zion from offering violence one to another; from taking the work of Babylon out of its hands, and devouring one another. Let any other apprehension whatever, of the work of God be embraced, and the first work that thereby men will be engaged in, is the oppressing, persecuting, ruining of their brethren, which whether it be the founding of Zion, or no, the day of judgment shall determine.

(4) This is that which the common enemy seeks to destroy.[79] It is not this, or that party that he would devour; it is not this or that persuasion he would cast down; his hatred is πρὸς τὸ γένος, "against the whole race" and kind; this is that which he would accomplish, that all the children of God, however differenced among themselves, might be ruined, destroyed, cast down, and rooted out for ever: "that the name of Israel might no more be had in remembrance":[80] this then is that which God, in their disappointment, aims to establish.

(5) Because the founding of Zion, does not consist in this or that form of the civil administration of human affairs, there being nothing promised, nor designed concerning them, but that they be laid in an orderly subserviency, to the common interest of the saints; which let men do what they will, yea what they can, all governments shall at last be brought unto.[81] And who is there among us, that in singleness of heart, dares make such an answer to "the messengers of the nations" inquiring after the peculiar work of God among us; namely, that it consists in the establishment of this or that form of civil administration, though much of the work of God lies therein in relation to this general end.¶[82]

Summary of the Answer That Should Be Given

This then is the answer which I "shall give to the messengers of the nations," and of it there are these three parts.

78 Matt. 18:10.

79 In his speech later that day, Cromwell also spoke about "the Common Enmity." *The Letters, Writings, and Speeches of Oliver Cromwell*, 3:290.

80 Ps. 83:4.

81 This is a tacit rebuke to one hundred elected members who were excluded from the Parliament because of their refusal to accept the Protectorate. For Owen's ambivalence to particular political forms, see Cowan, *John Owen and the Civil War Apocalypse*, 104–5.

82 The ¶ symbol indicates that a paragraph break has been added to Owen's original text.

(1) God has broken, destroyed, ruined them and their contrivances, who made it their business to overthrow Zion, and to root out "the generation of the righteous,"[83] not under this, or that way or form, whereby they are differenced among themselves, but as such, as the saints of the Holy One, and will continue so to do.

(2) He has given to them, to "the poor of his people," peace, liberty, freedom from impositions on their consciences, with much glorious light in several degrees, in his worship and service.

(3) He has cast (as he has promised) the power of the nation, into a subserviency to this common interest of Christ and his people in this world, and has made, or will make them to understand, that as the peace of Zion lies in their peace, so their peace lies in the peace of Zion, and what to say more "to the messengers of the nations," I know not.

Second Application: Directions to Those in Power about How to Respond to What God Is Doing

Use 2. If this then be the work of God, let us repair[84] to it; "The poor of the people shall trust therein," or join themselves thereunto. That you may do this in judgment, be pleased to take these directions, which with all humility I offer to you, and I hope from the Lord.

First Direction: Reject Any Proposals for a Church Settlement That Is Incompatible with the Common Interest of the Saints

(1) Engage in no way, no counsels, be the reasonings and pretenses for them never so specious,[85] which have an inconsistency with this common interest of Zion, in this generation. If instead of repairing to the work of God, you should be found contending against it, and setting up your own wisdom, in the place of the wisdom of God, it would not be to your advantage. I know many things will be suggested unto you: settling of religion, establishing a discipline in the church, not to tolerate errors, and the like: from which discourses, I know what conclusions some men are apt to draw, if no otherwise, yet from what they have been doing for many years; do we then plead for errors and unsettlement?[86] God forbid! God has undertaken to found

83 Ps. 14:5.

84 I.e., proceed or go to.

85 I.e., attractive in appearance.

86 Worden comments that as the new Parliament met there was a renewed drive for "an authoritative ecclesiastical settlement" and that the Presbyterians were "well prepared with their own solution." See Worden, "Toleration and the Protectorate," in *God's Instruments*, 82.

and establish Zion, to settle it, and he will do it, and I pray God you may be instrumental therein according to his mind. He will also give his people "one heart and one way";[87] and I pray that you by your example of union in love, and by all other good means may be instrumental toward the accomplishment of that promise among us.

It is only the liberty and protection of the people of God as such, that is pleaded for, and he that shall set up anything inconsistent therewith as so set up, will lay the foundation of his building in the firstborn of his peace, and set up the gate of it in the utmost and last of his welfare.[88] In a word; the people of God may possibly in this nation devour one another, and wash their hands in the blood of one another, by widening the breaches that are among them; and woe be to them that shall be instrumental therein: but if ever they come to a coalescency in love and truth, it must be by their mutual forbearance of one another, "until the Spirit be poured down from on high," and the fruits of "peace" be brought forth thereby;[89] and herein the Lord make you as "the mountains" that bring forth "righteousness," and "the little hills" that bring forth "peace unto his people."[90]

Three Words of Caution

There are some things that I am afraid of, that lie contrary to what I am exhorting you unto! I wish the event manifest that I am afraid without cause; however give me leave to caution you of them, because I cannot be faithful to my call, if I do not.

[1] Take heed, lest that evil be still abiding upon any of our spirits, that we should be crying out and calling for reformation, without a due consideration of what it is, and how it is to be brought about.[91] I wish one of many of them, who have prayed for it, and complained for want of it, had endeavored to carry it on as they might; would you have a reformation; be you more humble, more holy, more zealous, delight more in the ways, worship, ordinances of God: reform your persons in your lives, relations, families, parishes, as to gospel obedience, and you will see a glorious reformation indeed: what mean you by a reformation, is it the hurting of others, or doing good to

87 Jer. 32:39.

88 Josh. 6:26.

89 Isa. 32:15–18.

90 Ps. 72:3.

91 In his speech later that day the Lord Protector expressed his desire that members of Parliament would have a God-given "spirit of Reformacion." See *The Letters, Writings, and Speeches of Oliver Cromwell*, 3:316.

ourselves? Is it a power over other men's persons, or our own lusts? God has now for sundry years tried us, whether indeed we love reformation or no; have any provoked us, or compelled us to defile the worship of God, with ceremonies or superstitions, and our own consciences therewithal? Have we been imposed on in the ways of God, by men ignorant of them? Has not God said to us! "You that have prayed under persecution for reformation, you that have fought in the high places of the field for reformation, you that have covenanted and sworn for reformation, go now, reform yourselves; you ministers, preach as often as you will, as freely as you please, no man shall control you, live as holily as you can, pray as often, fast as often as you will; be full of bounty and good works, giving examples to your flock, none shall trouble you; 'be instant in season, out of season,'[92] preach the whole counsel of God without control;[93] you people, be holy, serve God in holiness, keep close to his worship and ordinances, love them, delight in them, bring forth such fruits as men may glorify God on your account, condemn the world,[94] justify the cause of God by a gospel conversation; take seven years' peace and plenty, and see what you can do."[95] If after all this, we still cry out, Give us a reformation, and complain not of our own negligence, folly and hatred of personal reformation, to be the only cause of that want, it is easy to judge what we would have, had we our desires.

[2] Take heed lest any who have formerly desired the day of the Lord,[96] considering the purity and holiness wherewith it will be attended, grow weary of it and its work, as not being able to abide it; and so lay aside all thoughts of growing up with it in the will of God: lest any say, "Is this the day of the Lord, that holiness, godliness, exact obedience, should be prized, exalted, esteemed; that profaneness, pride, selfishness, formality should be despised, consumed, devoured, we will have none of this day."

[3] Take heed that there rise not up a generation "that knew not Joseph";[97] that knew us not in the days of our distress, and contending with those who would have destroyed us; who were not engaged with us in praying, fasting, fighting, in England, Scotland, and Ireland, but were unconcerned in

92 2 Tim. 4:2.

93 Acts 20:27.

94 Heb. 11:7.

95 Gen. 41:29.

96 Amos 5:18. Owen referenced this text in *A Sermon Preached* [...] *January 31* (1649), *The Shaking and Translating of Heaven and Earth* (1649), and the 1657 sermon *Providential Changes*. For the first two sermons, see *Complete Works of John Owen*, 18:313, 459. The last sermon mentioned is included in this volume.

97 Ex. 1:8.

all our affairs; who know nothing of the cries, tears, trembling, and fears, wherewith this cause has been managed; can we expect that they should be acted by the spirit of it, or have a due sense of what they must be engaged in: what know they of the communion we have had with God in this business all along, what answers he has given us, what obligations he has put upon us thereby; the whole business is to them as a story only of that which is past, wherein they are not concerned: there are such abiding impressions left on the souls of as many as have been engaged in the work of God in this nation from the beginning to the end, as will never be blotted out. If a spirit not sensible of former ways should arise among us, and prevail, it would be sad with the interest of Christ, and his people in this nation: to return to my directions.

Second Direction: Be Guided by the Work of God in Both Domestic and Foreign Policy

(2) Make this work of God your polestar, that you may steer and guide your course by it? In all your consultations and actions, whatever is proposed, whatever is to be done, let this consideration attend it; "But how will it suit the design of God in establishing Zion; men speaking of a thing of manifest evidence, say that it is written with the beams of the sun." Give me leave to tell you of a thing, that is written in the prayers of the saints, the fears of your enemies, the condition of this nation, the counsels of princes of the earth, the affairs of the nations abroad in the world, all the issues of the providence of God in these days, all which concurring, I suppose will give as good an evidence as anything in the like kind is capable of. What is this you will say? It is in brief, let the work of God as stated, be your guide in all your consultations, and it will direct you to aim at these two ends.

[1] To preserve peace, to compose differences, to make up breaches, to avoid all occasions of divisions at home.

[2] To make up, unite, gather into one common interest, the Protestant nations abroad in the world, that we may stand or fall together, and not be devoured one after another. That these are the things which God calls you to mind, and do, if you will bear any regard to his present work is, I say, written with all the beams of providence before mentioned. If the Lord should suffer you to be regardless either to the one or the other, know you not that it would be bitterness in the latter end. Ask your friends what they desire, your enemies what they fear, the nations abroad what they are doing: consider Babylon, consider Zion, and if one and the same voice come from them all; not to attend unto it, would be not to attend to the voice of God. It is indeed,

an easy thing for you, to gratify Satan, satiate the desire of your enemies, lay a foundation of troubles; it is but attending to the clamors of men without, and the tumultuating of lusts, and carnal wisdom within and the whole work is done. But to carry on the work of God in the particulars mentioned, this is not so easy a task: self must be denied, many glorious pretenses laid aside, contrary reasonings answered, men's weaknesses, miscarriages, failings borne withal, because they are men; and which is more than all, our own particular darling desires it may be let go unsatisfied, though molded into contrivances for many years. The truth is, the combinations of the anti-Christian party in the world, are so evident, their successes so notorious, their designs so fixed, their advantages to carry them on, so many; that to persuade with them, who have power for that end and purpose, to make it their business to keep union among ourselves, on all good and honest terms, and to endeavor the union of all that call on the name of the Lord Jesus Christ, their Lord and ours, in the world; were to cast a reproach upon their wisdom, foresight, and zeal; so that it suffices me to have mentioned these things.

Third Application: Those in Power Must Encourage, Preserve, Promote, and Defend the Work of the Gospel

Use 3.[98] Encourage all things that lie in a tendency and subserviency to the work of God, unfolded and insisted on.[99] For instance.

(1) Wherever you see any work of real reformation, tending to the advancement of the gospel, discarding of old useless forms, received by tradition from our fathers, separating the precious from the vile, according to the several measures of light, which God in his infinite wisdom, has graciously imparted; let not needless objections and hindrances lie in the way, but give in all due encouragements, to the men of such engagements. Perhaps the business of carrying on reformation is grievous to some, who in their anger and wrath, revenge and disappointment, may make complaints of it to you, in private or in public; the Lord give you wisdom, that you may never weaken the hands or sadden the hearts, of men who are willing to join hearts and hands with you, to save a poor nation, and to keep life in the work of God in the midst thereof.

(2) What you find established already in this kind, encourage, preserve, improve, that the work fail not.

(3) Find out what is wanting, and pursue it, as God gives you advantage and opportunity.

98 In the original, "Use 4." Following Goold, the numbering has been corrected.

99 Later, in his speech to the members of Parliament, Cromwell appealed to them to "encourage whatsoever is of Godlynesse." *The Letters, Writings, and Speeches of Oliver Cromwell*, 3:314.

(4) Where men under pretense of religion, make it their business to defile themselves, or disturb the civil peace, and quiet of others, let them know that the sword is not borne in vain.[100] I can but name these things.

CONCLUDING GENERAL DIRECTIONS

Honorable: my heart's desire and prayer to God for you is, that you may be the repairers of breaches, and the restorers of paths for men to walk in; that you may be the preservers of the Good Old Cause of England,[101] according to the growth it received in and under several providential dispensations. Many particulars lie in my heart, to propose unto you, but on very many considerations, I shall name none at present of them; but close all with some few general directions.

(1) Secure your spirits, that in sincerity you seek the public good of the nations, and the prosperity of the good people therein, who have adhered to the good cause of liberty and religion; if this be in your eye, as that which is principally intended, as you may pray in faith, for the presence of God with you, and have a comfortable expectation of his protection and favor; so if in the pursuit of it, through human frailty you should err, or mistake in the choice of means, paths, ways, tending to that end, God will guide you, and lead you, and not leave you until he has made straight paths for your feet: but if at the bottom, there lie secret animosities, self-will, desire of obtaining greatness or power, on the one hand, or other; if every such thing be not on all hands subdued unto public good, prayers will be weakened, carnal wisdom increased, the counsel of God rejected, and you will wander in all your ways without success.

(2) Keep alive this principle (which whether any will hear, or whether any will forbear, I know not; but this I am sure of, in the latter end it will be found to be true) according as you regard, cleave to, promote, protect, on the one side, or despise, contemn, and oppose on the other, the common interest of Zion, the people of God, before laid down, so will your affairs either flourish, prosper, and succeed on the one hand, or wither, decay, and be fruitless, on the other. In all other things that shall fall under your consideration, that relate to the civil government of the nations, prudence, conjecture, probability, consideration of circumstances, and the present posture of things

100 Rom. 13:4.

101 In the original, "good old Cause of England" is italicized, and this is a significant early use of this precise terminology making a further reference to what Owen had already described as "the old and common cause."

may take place. This is capable of no framing to the one hand or other, upon any pretense whatever.

(3) If it be possible, keep up a spirit of love and forbearance among yourselves, love "thinketh no evil";[102] do not impose designs on one another, and then interpret everything that is spoken, though in never so much sincerity, and simplicity of spirit, in a proportion to that design; this will "turn judgment into wormwood,"[103] and truth "into hemlock."[104]

FINIS.[105]

102 1 Cor. 13:5.
103 Amos 5:7.
104 Amos 6:12.
105 Lat. "The End."

GOD'S PRESENCE WITH A PEOPLE, THE SPRING OF THEIR PROSPERITY; WITH THEIR SPECIAL INTEREST IN ABIDING WITH HIM

A Sermon, Preached to the Parliament of the Commonwealth of England, Scotland and Ireland, at Westminster, Octob. 30 1656. A Day of Solemn Humiliation.

By John Owen, DD a servant of
Jesus Christ, in the work
of the gospel

Printed by order of Parliament.
London
Printed by R. N. for Philemon
Stephens, at the gilded
lion in Paul's Churchyard. 1656.

[Parliamentary Order]

Friday, the 31st October 1656.

Ordered by the Parliament, that the thanks of this House be given unto Dr. Owen, dean of Christ Church, and vice-chancellor of the University of Oxon,[1] for his great pains taken in his sermon preached before this House yesterday in Margaret's Church, Westminster, being a day set apart for solemn fasting and humiliation, and that he be desired to print his sermon; and that he have the like privilege in printing thereof, as has been formerly allowed to others in like cases.

And Major General Kelsey[2] is desired to give him the thanks of this House accordingly.

Hen. Scobell.[3] Clerk of the Parliament.

1 I.e., Oxford.

2 Major General Thomas Kelsey was the member of Parliament for Dover in this Parliament and served on a number of important committees. He recommended that ministers like Owen, Philip Nye, and George Griffith preach to the house. See *History of Parliament: The House of Commons 1640–1660*, ed. Stephen K. Roberts, 9 vols. (Woodbridge, UK: Boydell and Brewer, 2023), *1660*, s.v. "Kelsey, Thomas (c. 1616–?1687)."

3 I.e., Henry Scobell (ca. 1610–1660), who was clerk of the Protectorate Parliaments and was active in publishing a series of works on parliamentary procedure.

[Dedicatory Epistle]

To the Parliament of the Commonwealth of England, Scotland, and Ireland, with the Dominions Thereunto Belonging

SIRS,

My hope that some impression may possibly remain upon your hearts and spirits, of, and from the things delivered unto you in the ensuing sermon, makes me willing unto the obedience of presenting it unto you, upon your command in this manner. Were I not persuaded, that your peace, interest and concernment is expressed therein, and knew not with what simplicity of heart you were minded thereof, I should have chosen on many accounts to have waived this duty. But having now performed what is incumbent on me, to render this service useful, recommending it yet farther to the grace of God, I humbly beg that it may not in this return unto you, be looked on as a thing of course and so laid aside, but be reviewed with that intension of spirit which is necessary in duties of this importance; whereby you may manifest that your command unto this service, was grounded on a sense of some advantage to be made by that performance of it. Sundry things I confess that were spoken unto you, are gone beyond my recovery, having had their rise from the present assistance which God was pleased to afford in the management of the work itself.[1] The sum of what was provided beforehand

1 Samuel Parker was dismissive of Owen at this point, claiming that he was seeking to "fasten his own raw Effusions upon the wisdom of the Spirit of God, and to stamp a divine Authority

and no otherwise, without the least addition, is here presented unto you, with hearty desires, that the vision of the truth herein considered may be to them that love you, and the accomplishment thereof be found in the midst of you. So prays

Novemb 17.[2]

Your humblest servant

In our dear Lord Jesus:

John Owen.

upon the Extravagances of his own roving fancy." See Parker, *A Defence and Continuation of the Ecclesiastical Politie* (London, 1671), 330–31.

2 I.e., November 17, 1656.

[Sermon]

A Sermon Preached to the Parliament of England, at their Public Fast, held the 30 October 1656

And he went out to meet Asa, and said unto him; "Hear ye me, Asa, and all Judah and Benjamin, the Lord is with you, while ye be with him: and if ye seek him, he will be found of you; but if ye forsake him, he will forsake you.[1]

2 CHRONICLES 15:2

INTRODUCTION AND CONTEXT

It will not, I am sure, seem strange to any, that I have taken a text to preach on in a day of humiliation, out of a thanksgiving sermon, such as this discourse of Azariah[2] seems to be; if they shall but consider the suitableness of the instruction given therein, to any great and solemn occasion, whether of humiliation or rejoicing. The words indeed are the sum of all directions that in such cases can be given; the standard of all rules, and exhortations, wherein any nation, or people in any condition are, or may be concerned, so plainly measuring out our fate and lot, the event, and issue of our affairs, with all the great undertakings of the people of God in this nation, that of themselves I hope they will make some passage to the hearts of them, to whom the inferences from them, shall this day be applied.

1 Owen had quoted this text in *A Sermon Preached* [. . .] *January 31* (1649). See *Complete Works of John Owen*, 18:323.

2 Azariah the prophet (2 Chron. 15:1).

In the foregoing chapter, we have an account of a great victory that Asa and the people of Judah fighting in faith and with prayer obtained against the huge host of the Ethiopians, with the abundant spoils which they took, and carried away thereupon.[3]

In their triumphant return to Jerusalem, the Spirit of God stirs up a prophet to go out, and meet them, to give them an account of the rise, and cause of their success, and direction for their future deportment under the enjoyment of such mercies and deliverances.

The Lord knows how apt even the best of men, are to forget the spring of their mercies; how negligent in making suitable returns by a due improvement of the advantages put into their hands, unto the Lord of all mercies. Therefore are they in all seasons to be minded of their proper interest, and duty; this is done in my text to Asa and Judah by Oded,[4] and I desire in my sermon, that it may with the same spirit, and the same success, be done by me unto you.

The words I intend principally to insist on, having the same thing for substance three times repeated in them, the opening of the first clause with the general tendency of the whole, will suffice as to their exposition, and the grounding of that general proposition which I shall improve. Two things are, then, principally to be inquired into.

First, what it is for God to be with any people. Secondly, what it is for a people to be or abide with God; and according to the analogy of these two the following assertions of seeking the Lord, and forsaking him will be easily understood. For though the words differ in expression, yet they are all of the same way of assertion: they are three, hypothetical propositions, or promissory assertions on supposition. "If you abide with the Lord, he will be with you," "If you seek the Lord, he will be found of you," "If you forsake the Lord, he will forsake you":[5] the same matter is trebled for the fuller and surer confirmation of the thing asserted. Only whereas the last proposition supposes a thing possible, namely that they might forsake the Lord; the first supposes a thing present, and therefore it is so expressed, "whilst you are with him"; because they had abode with God in their late war and trial.

Doctrinal Proposition Raised from the Preface

Before I enter upon the opening of the words themselves, I cannot pass by the earnest preface of the prophet; "Hear ye me O Asa": he saw the people upon their success, taken up with many thoughts, thinking of many businesses,

3 2 Chron. 14:8–15.

4 2 Chron. 15:8.

5 2 Chron. 15:2.

full of many contrivances, one imagining one thing, another another; all of them (it may be) how they should use and improve their peace, and success to their advantage, interest, profit, or security. Or the princes, and rulers, as it is probable, and usual in such cases, might be considering how to carry on their victory, how to make the best advantage of it, in their dealing with neighboring princes, and nations, in making peace or war.[6] In the midst of these thoughts the prophet meets them and diverts them with all earnestness, to things quite of another nature, and of unspeakably greater importance and concernment to them. "Hear ye me," says he; it is not your own counsel nor your own valor, that has brought about this great work, this mighty victory; the Lord himself has done it, by his presence with you. It is not of any concernment unto you, what other nations do, or may do, but the presence of God concerns you alone to look after.

Obs[ervation]. *The great concernment of any people or nation, is to know, that all their prosperity is from the presence of God among them, and to attend to that which will give continuance thereunto.* You may tire yourselves in the imaginations and contrivances of your own hearts, and lay out your thoughts and time about things that will not profit, nor advantage you, this is your interest, this is your concernment, "Hear ye me Asa, and all Judah and Benjamin." Of this proposition afterward.

OPENING OF THE TEXT IN ORDER TO RAISE THE MAIN DOCTRINAL OBSERVATION

Distinguishing the Four Ways in Which God May Be Said to Be with a People

For the words themselves, the first thing proposed to be inquired into for their explanation is this; what is it for God to be with a people? God may be said to be with men, or present with them, in sundry respects.

By Divine Omnipresence

1. First, he may be said to be with them in respect of the omnipresence of his essence; so he is naturally, and necessarily present with all creatures; indistant from them, present with them. The ubiquity and immensity of his essence, will not allow that he should be distant from anything to which he has given a being. "The heaven, even the heaven of heavens, cannot contain

6 The First Anglo-Dutch War had ended in 1654, and a defensive treaty had been signed between England and France in 1655. The war with Spain was ongoing.

him" (1 Kings 8:27). Does he not fill heaven and earth? Is he a God at hand only, and not afar off, as to the ends of the earth? This presence of God with all things David emphatically declares (Ps. 139:7–12). But it is not that, that is here intended: that is universal, to all creatures, natural, and necessary, this especial to some, voluntary, and of mercy; that of nature and essence, this of will and operation.

By the Incarnation

2. Secondly, God may be said to be with one in respect of personal union, so he was with, and only with, the man Jesus Christ. Θεὸς ἦν μετ' αὐτοῦ, "God was with him," (Acts 10:38), that is, in personal union; the human nature being taken into subsistence with the Son of God.[7]

By Means of the Covenant of Grace

3. Thirdly, God is present, or with any in respect of the covenant of grace. He is with them to be their God in covenant, the tenor whereof is, that he will not leave them, nor shall they forsake him, he will be for them, and they shall be for him, and not for another. He is with them for all the ends of mercy, love, kindness, pardon, salvation, that are proposed and exhibited in it: but neither is this the presence of God here intended, though this be something that flows from it, and does attend it: for,

(1) First, that presence of God with his people has not such a conditional establishment, as this here mentioned: it stands on other terms, and better security than that here proposed; it has received an eternal ratification in the blood of Christ; is founded in the immutable purpose of grace, and is not left to the conditionality here expressed, as we shall see afterward.

(2) Secondly, the presence here mentioned, respects the whole body of the people; all Judah and Benjamin in their national state, and consideration, unto whom, as such, the effectual covenant of grace was never extended; for they were not all Israel who were of Israel.[8]

(3) Thirdly, the presence here promised respects immediately the peculiar end of blessing the whole people with success in their wars and undertakings; so the occasion of the words, and the context, with regard to the following discourse do undeniably evince; it is not then this presence of God only that is intended, though, as it will afterward appear, it is not to be separated from it.

7 This text was significant in the context of the arguments about John Biddle and the Racovian Catechism. See Owen's *Vindiciae Evangelicae* (1655), chap. 7. See *Complete Works of John Owen*, vol. 2.

8 Rom. 9:6.

By Means of Providence

4. Fourthly, there is a presence of God in respect of providential dispensations, and this is twofold.

(1) First, general; ordering, disposing, guiding, ruling all things, according to his own wisdom, by his own power, unto his own glory; thus he is also present with all the world; he disposes of all the affairs of all the sons of men as he pleases; sets up one and pulls down another;[9] changes times, seasons, kingdoms,[10] bounds of nations,[11] as seems good to him. The help that is given to any he does it himself. "The shields of the earth belong unto God";[12] he works "deliverance in the earth,"[13] even among them that know him not.

And the evils, desolations and destruction, that the earth is full of, are but the effects of his wrath and indignation, revealing itself against the ungodliness of men.[14] He is thus present with every person in the world, holds his breath, and all his ways in his hand;[15] disposes of his life, death, and all his concernments, as he pleases. He is present in all nations, to set them up, pluck them down, alter, turn, change, weaken, establish, strengthen, enlarge their bounds as he sees good; and the day is coming, when all his works will praise him:[16] neither is this here intended: it is necessary, and belongs to God, as God; and cannot be promised to any; it is a branch of God's natural dominion, that every creature be ruled and disposed of, agreeably to its nature, unto the end whereunto it is appointed.

(2) Secondly, special; attended with peculiar love, favor, good-will; special care toward them with whom he is so present: so Abimelech observed that he was with Abraham, "God is with thee in all that thou doest" (Gen. 21:22): with you, to guide you, bless you, preserve you, as we shall see afterward: so he promised to be with Joshua, chapter 1:5 and so he was with Gideon, Judges 6:12 to bless him in his great undertaking; and so with Jeremy, chapter 15:2.[17] This is fully expressed [in] Isaiah 43:1-3. "I have redeemed thee, I have called thee by thy name, thou art mine: when thou passest through the waters, I will be with thee, and through the rivers, they shall

9 Ps. 75:7.
10 Dan. 2:21.
11 Acts 17:26.
12 Ps. 47:9.
13 Isa. 26:18.
14 Rom. 1:18.
15 Dan. 5:23.
16 Ps. 145:10.
17 Jer. 15:2.

not overflow thee;" and this is the presence of God here intimated; his presence with the people, as to special providential dispensations, as is manifest from the whole discourse of the prophet; and wherein this consists, shall be afterward at large declared.

Distinguishing the Two Ways in Which a People May Abide with God

Secondly, what is a people's abiding with God? There is a twofold abiding with God.

Personally

1. First, in personal obedience, according to the tenor of the covenant, this is not here intended, but supposed: there is no abiding in anything with God, where there is not an abiding in this thing: yet this, as I said, is not here principally intended, but supposed, something further is intended: for as has been declared, it is national work, and national abiding, that is intended; so that—

Nationally

2. Secondly, there is an abiding with God in national administrations: this is a fruit of the other, in those who are called to them; and that this is principally here intended, is evident, from that use that Asa made of this information, and exhortation of the prophet: he did not only look to his personal walking thereupon; but also immediately set upon the work of ordering the whole affairs of the kingdom; so as God might be glorified thereby; how this may be effected shall at large afterward be declared; what has already been spoken may suffice for a foundation of that proposition, which I shall this day insist upon: and it is this.

Main Doctrine Raised from the Text

Observation. *The presence of God with a people in special providential dispensations for their good, depends on their obediential presence with him, in national administrations to his glory*: "The Lord is with you, while ye be with him."

TREATMENT OF THE MAIN DOCTRINE

Three Initial Premises

For the explication of this proposition some few things are to be premised.

The Conditional Nature of God's Presence in Respect of Providential Dispensations

1. First, the presence of God with his people, as to special grace in the covenant; and his presence with them, as to special assistance in providence, proceed on very different accounts.

(1) First, they have a very different rise: the foundation, and principal law of special grace dispensed in the covenant is this; that some sinned, and another was punished. So it is laid down expressly, "All we like sheep have gone astray, we have turned every one to his own way, and the Lord hath laid on him the iniquity of us all" (Isa. 53:6). "He was made sin for us, that we might be made the righteousness of God in him" (2 Cor. 5:21). "A curse for us," that the blessing of faithful Abraham might come on them that believe (Gal. 3:13–14). This is the great and sovereign principle of the covenant of grace, that a commutation should be made of persons, as to punishments, and rewards; that sinners should be provided of a substitute; one that should undergo the punishment due to them, that they might go free and procure a reward for them who could procure none for themselves (1 Pet. 2:24).

Now the supreme, and sovereign law of providential dispensations is utterly diverse and alien from this of the covenant of grace. This you have asserted, Ezekiel 18:20. "The soul that sinneth it shall die": one shall not bear the iniquity of another: "the righteousness of the righteous shall be upon him, and the wickedness of the wicked shall be upon him": take this for a law of universal right and indispensable, extend it to the covenant of grace, and it is absolutely exclusive of the substitution and satisfaction of Christ. But it is the ground, rule, and law of providential dispensations, that God is there treating about; and vindicating his dealing with any people as to his presence with them, and acting toward them therein; which is diverse, as you see, from the foundation of the covenant before mentioned.

(2) Secondly, as the foundations are diverse, so is the rule of their continuance. What is the rule and measure of God's continuance with his people in the covenant of grace? Plainly this; that he will never forsake them; and on that account will take care that they shall never forsake him, but abide with him forever. It is not while they do so, and so, he will abide with them, and when they cease so to do, he will forsake them, as to his federal and covenant presence: there is not such a sandy foundation left us, of our abiding with God in Christ. See the tenor of the covenant [in] Jeremiah 31:33; 32:38–40. The sum is, that God will be with them, and take care that they always abide

with him; and therefore he has provided for all interveniences[18] imaginable, that nothing shall violate this union: God lays his unchangeableness as the foundation of the covenant (Mal. 3:6), and he therein makes us unchangeable; not absolutely so, for we change every moment; but with respect to the terms and bounds of the covenant; he has undertaken that we shall never leave him. The law of God's presence in respect of providential dispensations, and all special privileges attending it, is quite of another importance: it is purely conditional, as you may see in my text. The tenor of it is expressed to the height, "I said indeed that thy house and the house of thy father should walk before me for ever: but now the Lord saith, that be it far from me, for them that honour me, I will honour, and they that despise me shall be lightly esteemed" (1 Sam. 2:30).[19] Here is no alteration of counsel, or purpose in God: but merely an explanation of the rule, law, and tenor of providential dispensations; no interpretation of the covenant of grace; Eli held not the priesthood by that covenant; but an explication of the tenor of a privilege given in special providence (Ps. 89:32–33). Hence is that variety of God's dealings with men mentioned in the Scripture which yet are always righteous, according to one or other of these rules, and laws. [In] Isaiah 43:23–24 says God of his people;

> Thou hast not called upon me, O Jacob, but thou hast been weary of me, O Israel. Thou hast not brought me the small cattle of thy burnt-offerings, neither hast thou honoured me with thy sacrifices: thou hast bought me no sweet cane with money, neither hast thou filled me with the fat of thy sacrifices: but thou hast made me to serve with thy sins, thou hast wearied me with thine iniquities.

What then shall be done with this people? Depart from them, destroy them, let them die; no, verse 25, "I, even I, am he that blotteth out thy transgressions for mine own sake, and will not remember thy sins." So also, chapter 57 verse 17. "For the iniquity of his covetousness was I wroth, and smote him: I hid me, and was wroth, and he went on frowardly in the way of his heart." Surely now God will utterly consume them, root, and branch, as persons incorrigible and irrecoverable: no, the case is quite otherwise, verses 18–19. "I have seen his ways, and will heal him, I will lead him also,

18 I.e., interventions.

19 In *A Sermon Preached* [. . .] *January 31* (1649), Owen appealed to this verse in association with 2 Chron. 15:2, the text on which this sermon is based. See *Complete Works of John Owen*, 18:325.

and restore comforts unto him": I will pity him, pardon him, save, sanctify him, and fill him with consolation. Go now to Ezekiel chapter 33:18, "When the righteous turns from his righteousness"; what then? God will heal him and restore comforts unto him, as it was in the places before mentioned. No, no! "He shall die"; he shall be cut off: What is the reason of this diversity? Why! In the first place, God speaks of his dealings unto their souls as to his covenant of grace, and all the mercies of it; in this last, as to his dealings with their persons, and their outward concernments, in the dispensations of his providence. And the not heeding hereof has made some pronounce inconsiderately, the covenant of grace to be merely conditional; because they find many mercies, and privileges spoken of under such a notion; not considering that all those proposals belong to the law of outward providence, and not to the nature of the covenant of promise established in the blood of Christ. And unless this be allowed, nothing can be more contrary to my text, than that promise, and such as that which we have [in] Isaiah 54:9 where provision is made for God's abiding with his people notwithstanding all their backslidings, and provocations, which he will so far heal, as that he may not forsake them; and this is first to be observed, that we do not in the consideration of God's presence and withdrawings, as to providential dispensations, cast any reflection on the stability, and unchangeableness of the covenant of grace. David has fully stated this business [in] 2 Samuel 23:5 he says, "Although my house be not so with God, yet he hath made with me an everlasting covenant, ordered in all things and sure, for this is all my salvation, and all my desire, although he make it not to grow":[20] David had a promise for the prosperity of his house: he had also an engagement of the sure mercies of the covenant. The different tenor of these engagements, as to their success and establishment, he gives us this account of. The covenant is absolute and unchangeable, that is, ordered in all things and sure: the prosperity of his house depends on another law and rule, that is, subject to alteration.

God's Presence in Providential Dispensations Is on the Basis of Mercy Rather Than Merit

2. Secondly, observe the nature of this dependence of God's presence on our abiding with him: it does not depend upon it, as the effect upon its proper cause, as though it were procured by it, merited by it; we enjoy not the least morsel of bread on any such account, much less such eminent privileges as attend God's special providential presence; we deserve nothing

20 Owen would expound this text in June 1669. See *Complete Works of John Owen*, vol. 20.

at the hand of God, and therefore if he should take us in the midst of the choicest obedience, and fill us with the fiercest of miseries, he does us no wrong; and therefore the Lord does so deal sometimes with his; and that not only with particular persons, as in the case of Job, but also with his people in general, as Psalm 44:17–19, "All this is come upon us, yet have we not forgotten thee, neither have we dealt falsely in thy covenant. Our heart is not turned back, neither have our steps declined from thy way. Though thou hast sore broken us in the place of dragons, and covered us with the shadow of death." Though he requires our duty at our hands, yet he is not tied to any such present reward. This is all: it ordinarily depends upon it as a consequent upon an antecedent, which allows an interposition of grace and mercy, as Nehemiah 9:19. Nevertheless, you being merciful, "forsookest them not"; so elsewhere, that good man prays, "Remember me for good, and spare me according to the multitude of thy mercies":[21] for the glory of his righteousness, and of his ways in the world, God has ordered, that his people shall walk with him, when he abides eminently and conspicuously in a special manner with them.

God Gives the Ability to Perform the Conditions

3. Thirdly, observe, that our abiding with God, even in national administrations, is the proper effect of his presence with us in covenant dispensations; so that all in the issue is of mere mercy and grace; though the condition seems to be imposed on us, yet it is from him alone that we have strength for its performance. It is in this, and such like cases, as David said it was with them, at their dedicating their silver, and gold for the building of the temple; Τὰ σὰ, ἐκ τῶν σῶν,[22] "Of thine own, Lord, have we given unto thee"; we do but return him his own, we give him but the fruits of his own grace, and without it, we can make no return whatever.

These things being premised, I shall give the proposition some confirmation, and so descend to the due improvement of it.

Proofs Confirming This Doctrine

I suppose I need not go for proof, beyond the observation of the constant tenor of God's proceedings with his people of old. When did he not deal thus with them? What instance can be given of transgressing this rule? Is the whole story of the nation of the Jews, anything but the illustration of this proposition;

21 Neh. 13:22.

22 Gk. "Yours and of your things," the Septuagint text of 1 Chron. 29:14.

some ruled well, and sought the Lord, and the Lord was with them; and prospered them in all their ways; some fell from him, and walked according to their own imaginations, and the Lord cut them short on that account. Yea, sometimes the same man, as Solomon, Asa, Uzziah, experienced both these states, and conditions. Has not the state of all nations, since they came into the power of men professing the knowledge of him, been the same? Look on the Roman Empire, did it not flourish under the hand of men who ruled with God, and were faithful with the saints? Is not the present distraction of it under the fury and cruelty of Turk and pope,[23] the issue of the violence, unrighteousness, idolatry, luxury, and persecution of ill governors? Does not the demonstration of all God's people in the world, the consideration whereof in particular, might be insisted on as the ground and reason of the truth insisted on, require that it should be thus? Leviticus 26, and almost the whole book of Deuteronomy, are sermons on this text, and every verse almost in them, would afford a new confirmation of the truth in hand, I shall need rather then to caution from mistakes, than further to confirm the proposition. For this end, take these ensuing observations.

Two Qualifications

Outward Prosperity Is Not Necessarily Evidence of God's Special Presence

1. First, all outward flourishing, or prosperity of a people, does not always argue the special presence of God with them. There are sundry things required to make success and prosperity an evidence of the presence of God.

(1) First, that the people themselves prospered, be his people, his peculiar. How many wicked nations are there in the world, that for a long season have received blessings (as it were) and success in their undertakings? Is the Lord among them by his special presence? Not at all: he is using them indeed for his own end, and purposes, to break others, or fill up the measure of their own iniquities;[24] that their destruction may be an evident demonstration of his vengeance, and righteous judgment to all the world, but present with them in the sense contended about; he is not. The case is stated [in] Habakkuk 1–2, as you may see in those chapters at large. It is the same case with the anti-Christian,[25] and Mohammedan[26] nations in the world at this day:

23 The Holy Roman Empire had been devastated by the Thirty Years' War (1618–1648), and the Ottoman empire was once again beginning to pursue its expansionist ambitions.

24 Gen. 15:16; Matt. 23:32.

25 I.e., Roman Catholic (in this context).

26 I.e., Islamic. This was the very beginning of the period of the Köprülü revival of the Ottoman Empire (1656–1702).

their prosperity is no evidence of God's presence, because themselves are his enemies. Other bottoms, reasons, and grounds there are of their successes; God's owning of them, is none of them.

(2) Secondly, that the whole work be good, and have a tendency to God's glory; wherein they are engaged. David's counsel for the killing of Uriah prospered, and took effect, yet was not God with him therein;[27] the work engaged in, must be according to his mind: and—

(3) Thirdly, made useful and subservient to his glory: when the hearts of a people can secure themselves in these things, then may they rejoice in their prosperity, as a pledge of God's presence with them.

Trials Do Not Necessarily Mean That God Has Withdrawn His Special Presence

2. Secondly, even great afflictions, eminent distresses, long perplexities, may have a consistency with God's special presence; though the wheel goes on, yet it may have a cross wheel in it, that may cause rubs and disturbances. The rule of God's acting in his presence, is his own wisdom, and our good in the issue, not our partial self-destroying desires. Had the best people in the world, all their own desires, they would be every way ruined. When God is nigh to us he knows what is best for us. Security from destroying evils, not trying evils, he gives to them with whom he is.

And this is all that I shall offer for the explication, confirmation, and cautioning of the proposition insisted on, what remains further to be opened, will fall in under the uses of it: which now ensue.

Application of the Doctrine: Instruction

Use 1. This special presence of God, being (as you have heard) the great and only concernment of any people, the tenure, or condition thereof being our abiding with him, let our first use be to instruct us particularly.

(1) First, what this special presence of God is, and wherein it does consist.
(2) Secondly, what it is for us to abide with God, so as we may enjoy it.

Understand the Nature of God's Special Presence with a Nation

(1) For the full discovery of the first, I shall consider it in that eminent instance, wherein of old he did grant his presence to his people. The bottom of that stupendous undertaking of the Israelites in leaving Egypt, and

27 2 Sam. 11.

journeying through the wilderness into Canaan, lay in the promise of the presence of God with them (Ex. 3:10–12): on this one consideration, their whole undertaking and affair turned; to this issue it is put by Moses, "If thy presence go not with us, carry us not up hence" (Ex. 33:15). They will not move one step without him; and with him they care not whither they go. Now this presence of God with them, symbolically did consist in, or rather was represented by, two things:

[1] First, the pillar of the cloud, and fire which was with them ordinarily.
[2] Secondly, the appearance of his glory which they enjoyed on extraordinary occasions.

God Will Be Present to Guide and Protect, Even through Political Uncertainty

[1] The first, with the first use of it is mentioned [in] Exodus 13:21–22. "And the Lord went before them by day in a pillar of a cloud, to lead them the way, and by night in a pillar of fire to give them light, to go by day and night: he took not away the pillar of the cloud by day; nor the pillar of fire by night, from before the people."

There is mention here, as if it were of two pillars, one by day, and another by night, but it seems to have been the same pillar with several properties: for chapter 14:19–20 the same pillar at the same time, performs both these offices, in respect of several persons; to some it was on the one side a cloud and darkness, to others bright, and shining as fire. "The pillar of the cloud went from before their face, and stood behind them; and it came between the camp of the Egyptians and the camp of Israel, and it was a cloud and darkness to them, but it gave light by night to these."

After this when the ark was made, and the tabernacle erected, this cloud, which until then went before the camp, came, and covered the tabernacle night and day, as it stood in the midst of the camp, or the congregation; as a cloud it was by day and as a pillar of fire by night (Ex. 40:34–38) and there it continued with the people all the while they were in the wilderness (Neh. 9:19). This being the first eminent pledge of the presence of God, with that people, let us consider what was indulged or granted to them thereby.

{1} First, they had hereby constant direction in all their journeyings, and undertakings, they were by this pillar directed in their way; so at large it is expressed [in] Numbers 10:33, as also Exodus 40. God by this pledge of his presence, was the beginning of all their rest, and motion: the guide, and director of all their undertakings: so that they moved, acted, rested, proceeded, according to his will and counsel; he "guided them by his eye," and led them by his counsel (Ps. 32:[8]). Sometimes perhaps they would be forward, they would be up, acting, doing, their hearts are full of desires; and they are impatient of delay. If it be not according to his mind, he will cause a cloud to abide on their tabernacle, or their assemblies and meetings; a cloud that shall darken them, and distract them in their consultations, that they shall not be able to take one step forward. Though their desires be great, their intentions good, yet the cloud shall be upon them, and they shall not know their way.

Sometimes perhaps they are heavy, fearful, slothful, "there is a lion in the way,"[28] giants are in the land;[29] difficulties, and perplexities lie in the way before them in such and such undertakings, they have no heart to them, the way is long, and perilous, better return than go forward. Would God now have them pass on, and engage? The cloud shall break up, and go before them, they shall see so far on their way, as to go forth with cheerfulness. Only observe this! That when the cloud was taken up, they knew they were to go on in the way wherein they were, and journeyed accordingly; yet they knew not whither they should go, nor what would be the end of their journey:[30] and therefore it is said, that when they journeyed the ark went before them, to seek out a resting place for them (Num. 10:33). It was carried on, to see where the pillar or cloud of direction would stay, and there they rested wherever it was. When God gives a people so much direction, as that they see it is their duty to go on, and to trust him in so doing, though they see not the end, nor know what their resting place will be, yet it is a pledge of God's presence with them. I suppose in your assembly you have had the cloud taken off, as to your engagements in some undertakings, concerning which you are to trust that the ark of God's presence, the Lord Jesus Christ, will find you out a resting place, which as yet appears not unto you.[31]

What a full experience have we had of this kind of proceeding among us? In the last assembly of Parliament, how many had no less real intentions to be at work for God, than now? God saw that it would not be for the advantage of the people that they should proceed: hence the cloud rested on that as-

28 Prov. 26:13.

29 Num. 13:33.

30 Heb. 11:8.

31 Owen employs the motif of the cloud guiding the journey through the wilderness to provide an account of why the first Protectorate Parliament (1654–1655) had made little progress, and he expressed his desire that this new Parliament would be led toward its promised rest. The trope of the cloud being lifted is similar to that offered by Cromwell, who spoke of "all Mists being dispelled and cleered." See *Declaration of His Highnes, By the Advice of His Council; Setting Forth* [. . .] *the Justice of Their Cause against Spain* [. . .] (London, [Oct. 26] 1655), 142.

sembly, that they could not see how to take one step forward.[32] He was still present with us, but it was by a darkening cloud, that we could not journey toward our rest. Nor is it the will, or counsel of man, but of God, that is to be looked to in these things. We now hope the cloud is up, and we are journeying toward our rest. The great angel of his presence will find a rest for us in the good providence of God.

This then lies in God's special presence, he is with us to give us direction in all our undertakings; to take away darkness, perplexities, difficulties from our counsels, or to cause us to rest and cease from whatever may come into our hearts, that is not according to his mind; the Lord give us ever more of this his presence!

I cannot stay to show you the several ways whereby God now communicates direction to a people, how he inclines their hearts insensibly, yet powerfully; fixes the bent of their spirits effectually, (their hearts being in his hand "as the rivers of water, which he turns as he pleases")[33] supplies them with reasonings and consultations beyond the verge of their own wisdom, proposes, occasions, invitations, provocations; gives them spirit and courage, beyond their natural frames and tempers; enlarges them in prayer, or shuts them up; makes walls on the one hand, and open paths on the other; with innumerable such ways, and means as in his infinite wisdom, he is pleased to make effectual for their guidance. It suffices, that in the use of means, through patience and waiting upon him, they shall be directed to that which is pleasing to him: so is he with them.

{2} The second use of this pillar was, to give them protection and defense in their way. So Exodus 14:19–20, 24. This protected them from the Egyptians, and from thence God troubled their enemies; out of the pillar, that is from his especial presence. This use of it is insisted on [in] Isaiah 4:5–6. The cloud that was as "smoke by day," and as "fire by night;" was also "a shadow," "a place of refuge," and "a covert"; in one word: a protection or a defense.

And this is a second thing, which is in God's special presence; he will protect, or defend them with whom he is so present. He is their "dwelling-place" (Ps. 90),[34] then when in this world they have none; their "refuge in the time of trouble."[35] So Isaiah 25:4; 26:1; 31:4. Promises and instances to make this good abound; they are known to all: the time would fail me to insist upon them.

32 The first Protectorate Parliament met from September 1654 to January 1655 and enacted no legislation during its entire sitting.

33 Prov. 21:1.

34 Ps. 90:1.

35 Ps. 9:9.

I might go over all the causes, means, and ways of the fears, dangers, ruin of such a people, and show you how a defense is provided against them all.

Are their fears from themselves, because of their folly, weakness, and division, or from pretended friends, because of their envy and desertion, or from open enemies; because of their power, cruelty, malice, and revenge, a defense is provided on every account, heat, rain, tempests, storms, adversity, prosperity, all are provided against where God is present (Isa. 32:1–2). And if any people in the world have experience of this truth, we have it this day. Had not the Lord been with us, who had not destroyed us? Enemies, friends, abroad, at home, our own follies, all, any of them, had done the work, had not the Lord himself been with us.

Only observe, that the presence of God, as to these effects, may sometimes in some particulars, be eclipsed and the effects themselves, for some season be entangled, though there be not an utter breach between him and his people.[36] How often did the Israelites attempt things without his direction? How often did he break in upon them to their woe and sorrow? Yet for the main, he forsook them not, until the great work intended by them was accomplished (Neh. 9:19). It is not every entanglement, every disappointment, every defeat, that argues God's departure, as to his special presence. It may be good for us sometimes to be in such a condition, and then that desertion that carries into it, is from the presence of God; we are now grown to that, that if everything immediately surmount not our imagination, say some, "God is gone from them," not because it is so, but because they would have it so, but he is merciful with whom we have to do, and will not cast off his people forever.

Special Manifestations of God's Presence with a Nation, as Seen in His Works of Providence, Strengthen the Saints

[2] Secondly, the people with whom God was, had the glory of Jehovah, as a pledge of his presence with them; this appeared only at extraordinary seasons, so it did at the giving of the law (Ex. 24:16). So also at the setting up of the tabernacle. It differed from the cloud, for when the cloud was upon the tabernacle, the glory of the Lord filled it. It appeared again to all the people (Lev. 9:23). I shall not now inquire what was this visible representation of the majesty of God, it suffices as to the purpose in hand, that when God gives his presence to a people, at extraordinary seasons, he affords them extraordinary manifestations of his glory. So in Ezekiel's vision of those dreadful wheels

36 This may be Owen's assessment of the failure of the campaign against the Spanish Empire known as the "Western Design."

of providence, the glory of the Lord is said to appear in the temple; and as his especial presence departed from the temple, and the city, so the glory, by several degrees, departed also, chapter 2; 10:10, 18–19; chapter 11:23.

Eminent, and glorious appearances with, and for a people in extraordinary seasons, is then another thing that accompanies God's special providential presence with them; when they are at an utter loss in their counsels, at a stand in their motions, disappointed in their undertakings, deserted in their enterprises, pressed on every side above measure; or called to some extraordinary work, so that their ordinary direction and protection will not carry them on, nor bear them up; then will God relieve them by some especial appearance of his glory. "In the mount will the Lord be seen."[37] This will give a relief, when all is at a loss. And in this lies the most discriminating evidence of special providence. Glorious appearances in great straits are eminent testimonies of God's regard. Could I now insist on some of the instances, that might be given, of this kind of dealing with us in England, in the pursuit of the cause we have in hand, it would make us ashamed of all our unworthiness, carnal fears, and unbelief.

This is the second evidence of God's presence. He is with a people to direct them, to protect, to manifest his glory among them; his glory in balancing the issues of providence one in respect of another; so that all shall acknowledge that of a truth the Lord is among them. "Blessed is the people, that is in such a case; yea, blessed is the people whose God is the Lord."[38] What would you have more? Here is ease of all cares, a remedy for all sores, security in the midst of troubles, rest, and peace, and assured dwelling places, though the Assyrian should be in the land.[39]

Thus you see what is this great concernment of any people:

Understand How a Nation Can Obtain and Enjoy God's Special Presence

(2) Let us now consider the tenure of this blessedness: on what account it is to be obtained, or enjoyed: now this is, our abiding with God; this then is next to be considered, What it is for a people, what it is for you, and us, so to abide with God, as that we may in all our affairs, enjoy his presence in the ways before described.

Now something is hereunto previously required: something it consists in.

An Essential Prerequisite Is a Nation Having Godly Rulers

[1] First, that we may abide with God, this is indispensably required? That we may have peace with him in Jesus Christ. If we are never with him, we cannot

37 Gen. 22:14.

38 Ps. 33:12.

39 Mic. 5:6.

abide with him; no man can abide, where he never comes. The acceptance of our persons, lies at the bottom of the acceptance of our duties. As the special presence of God with any, is in, and by Christ, and no otherwise: so is our abiding with God, in, and through him. "God with us" is the name of Christ:[40] our being with God, is in him who is our peace. Two cannot walk together, unless they be agreed (Amos 3:3). Now because this is not to be expected from all the individuals of a nation: yet this thing is to be endeavored.

That the rulers of it be such as have this interest. I do not divest of a share in government, those who have no share in Christ, if lawfully called thereunto.[41] But I say, when God gives governors, whom he intends to make a blessing unto a people, they shall be such as are blessed of him in Christ. And if ever the government of this nation, in this present constitution,[42] suppose it the most exactly framed, and balanced, in the several parts of it, for the furtherance of public good, be devolved into the hands of men, not interested in God by Christ, though the constitution may be absolutely good, yet the government will not be blessed, and the nation will be ruined: for God and his glory will depart. It is Christ that is our peace, even in outward troubles? They are "seven shepherds under him," and "eight principal men," accepted with him, that are to be our relief (Mic. 5:5–6).

It is true, for some particular actions, or works, a wicked man may be anointed particularly; as Jehu,[43] and Jeroboam the son of Joash:[44] but you have no instance that ever God was with a people to bless them indeed, in a course of special providence, when wicked men by their own consent were their rulers; where the union and relation, between them and the people is considerable. I confess unto you, I never think of the state of England, but my heart trembles at this thing; namely, that those who have, and it is fit should have, so great a share in the government of this commonwealth, should have their rise from the body of the people, that is dark and profane, and full of enmity against the remnant; did not God overrule men contrary to their own inward principles, and lusts, how soon would ruin, and desolation break in upon that hand. And give me leave to say, that God, in his sovereign providence, having called so many at this time to the place of rule, and authority, who indeed (as

40 Matt. 1:23.

41 Fifth Monarchists advocated the rule of the saints over the masses. See Bernard Capp, *The Fifth Monarchy Men: A Study in Seventeenth-Century English Millenarianism* (London: Faber 2008), 15–16, 20, 82, 175.

42 The constitution under which the Parliament met was the Instrument of Government (1653–1657).

43 1 Kings 19:16.

44 2 Kings 14:23–25.

we believe) love the Lord Jesus in sincerity, it seems to me, to look as your duty, to consider all ways and means whereby the power of these nations may be in succeeding seasons, devolved on men of the like spirit and condition.

I shall not interpose in that, which by some is so much spoken of; the reign of the saints; I am sure the means used, and attempted by some, to set upon, and to set up such a rule and dominion, have not become sober men, much less saints of Christ;[45] yet this I must say, and in the saying of it, I dare say, "Hear ye me, Asa, and all Judah and Benjamin"; if ever God cease to call saints, that is, men interested personally in Christ, to places of chief authority in this nation, or commit the power of it into other hands; and when those called to power, cease to exert it in a subserviency to the kingdom of Christ, for the true spiritual advantage of his people, there will be an end of England's glory and happiness. I say, "Hear you this, all you people."

This I have delivered long ago, and many times in this place, this I say still, and in this persuasion hope to live and die.[46]

The Lord guide you in this thing: however we shall live on the good providence of our God, who has hitherto taken care for us.

This then I say, is prerequired, as a qualification of any person to the performance of this duty of abiding with God. It is the psalmist's advice (Ps. 2:11–12).[47] Let this principle be always owned among you: by it, honor Christ in the world; give him the preeminence, it is the Father's will he should have it in all things. Expect not the presence of God, but upon this account. Bear testimony herein against the world of profane men, who despise these things. Seeing then it cannot be expected, to have this qualification diffused universally as yet through the body of the people, let the rulers take care, that they be not the cause of God's departure from us.

Those in Power Must Seek God's Direction, Trust Him for Protection, and Submit to Providence

[2] Secondly, what is it now for such persons to abide with God; so as they may expect comfortably the continuance of his presence with them, which is their all, that they need or desire: I shall name some few things that are signally required thereunto.

45 Fifth Monarchism was viewed as a significant security threat at the time.

46 While these themes have characterized much of Owen's parliamentary preaching, the language of the previous paragraph recalls the full title of his sermon preached at the celebration of the battle of Worcester in October 1651: *The Advantage of the Kingdom of Christ in the Shaking of the Kingdoms of the World: or, Providential Alterations in Their Subserviency to Christ's Exaltation* (1651).

47 Owen referenced these verses in *The Kingdom of Christ, and the Power of the Civil Magistrate* (1652).

{1} First, that they inquire of God, ask counsel at his hand, look to him for direction in all their affairs. He is present with them to give them direction; not to seek for it at his hand, is exceedingly to despise him. It must arise from one of these two apprehensions, either he cares not for us, or he knows not how to direct us. When he gave direction by the cloud on the tabernacle, the people being reproved for their carnal fears, and unbelief, upon the return of the spies; some of them would needs instantly into the mountain, and fight with the Canaanites: but says the Holy Ghost, the "ark abode in the camp";[48] they went without God's direction, and prospered accordingly. With what contempt does God speak of the wisdom, and counsels of the sons of men, when they will adhere unto them? How does he make it his glory to turn all their consultations into folly? And to make them err in their ways, like a drunken man?[49] How does he bid them take counsel together, when he intends to destroy them? What instances may be given of all good and prosperous rulers of old, of their seeking direction from God? What promises of a success, and a blessed issue in so doing are there? The words of my text will suffice as an instance in every kind.

Objections Answered

But you will say; "How shall we inquire of God? The nations had their oracles, whereby they deluded themselves. The people of God had their Urim and Thummim,[50] their prophets and oracle. 'Bring hither the ephod, and inquire of God,' was the word with them.[51] But alas! What is all this to the advantage we have of seeking counsel of God; and taking direction from him?" We have a high priest always present with us, by whom we may inquire. Our high priest is "the angel of God's presence,"[52] the mighty counselor,[53] the power, and eternal wisdom of God himself? And where is he? He appears in the presence of God for us, in the holy place, not made with hands,[54] having made a new and living way for us to come within the veil,[55] to inquire of the oracle. What would we have more? He is our captain, our leader, our high priest, Urim, and Thummim, our oracle, our ark, on whom the cloud of direction rests, and abides forever.

Would you, then, be with God? Take direction from him by Christ in all your undertakings; so do in deed, and not in word, or profession only.

48 Num. 14:40, 44.
49 Isa. 19:14.
50 Ex. 28:20; Lev. 8:8.
51 1 Sam. 23:9; 30:7.
52 Isa. 63:9.
53 Isa. 9:6.
54 Heb. 9:24.
55 Heb. 10:20.

I hope, I need not stay to give you directions, how this duty is to be performed, the "unction" will teach it you,[56] and your "fellowship," I hope, "is with the Father, and with his Son Jesus Christ";[57] only now take these few words with you.

1st. First, captivate all your desires to his glory: set your hearts on nothing, but with this express reserve, if it is consistent with, and expedient unto the glory of Christ, and his kingdom. Be not sick of your own violent desires, but lay all your aims and designs at his feet always; becoming as "weaned children before him."[58]

2nd. Secondly, bear before him a real sense of your own weakness, and folly both severally and jointly, if not directed by him; that in his pity and compassion, he may relieve you.

3rd. Thirdly, keep your hearts in that integrity, that you may always press and urge him with his own concernment in all your affairs, this is a thing that none but upright hearts can do uprightly.

4th. Fourthly, actually inquire by faith and prayer, what is his will and mind; do it severally, and jointly; do it privately, publicly; do it every day, and in days set apart for that purpose;[59] he will assuredly "be found of you."[60] You know how easy it were to exemplify all these things, by testimonies, and instances, but time will not permit.

If instead of these things, you bear yourselves up on the wings of your own wisdom, and contrivances; though you may seem for a season to have attained a fair pitch and flight; you will be entangled, and brought down in the midst of your course with shame and sorrow; for the Lord will not be with you.

{2} Secondly, another thing wherein we are to be with God is by trusting in him for protection. "O trust in the Lord for ever, for in the Lord Jehovah there is everlasting strength.[61] This man made the Lord his refuge.[62] He that trusts in the Lord "shall be as mount Zion, that shall never be removed."[63] Commit your ways to the Lord,[64] roll your burden on him,[65] "stand still and

56 1 John 2:20.
57 1 John 1:3.
58 Ps. 131:2.
59 This sermon was delivered on one such day of public humiliation.
60 Jer. 29:14.
61 Isa. 26:4.
62 Ps. 91:9.
63 Ps. 125:1.
64 Ps. 37:5.
65 Ps. 22:8; 37:5. In both texts, the marginal reading in the Authorized Version uses the language of rolling.

see his salvation."[66] What glorious things are spoken of this trusting to the Lord for protection, you all know. It were endless to insist on commands and promises to this purpose; and to single out one, or two, were but to weaken the cause in hand, seeing hereunto the whole Scriptures bear witness. I shall only show you what it is so to do, in some few particulars.

1st. First, it is to strengthen and encourage your hearts in difficult affairs, a comfortable issue whereof, you cannot on visible causes conjecture, on the account of God's engagement for your good. To omit the instances of Asa,[67] Jehoshaphat,[68] and many others; take that signal one of David in his great distress at Ziklag (1 Sam. 30). You know the story: his habitation was burnt and spoiled, his wives and children captived,[69] his people consulting to stone him, so that he was greatly distressed, the enemy numerous and without his reach; all means of relieving his condition and bringing it to a comfortable issue, far removed; but what course did he now take? Did he despond? Did he give over? Did he rest on his own counsel and strength? No, says the Holy Ghost; "But David encouraged himself in the Lord his God."[70] Have you any affair that lies before you that is good, and honest, but yet dreadful, difficult, entangled? Your hearts are ready to faint, whenever you think of it; it is almost beyond your imaginations, to contrive a comfortable issue: in such a season, if you will be with God, he will be with you; if you so trust him as to encourage your hearts on the account of his wisdom, goodness, power; that he can find out, and bring about a comfortable glorious end; this is to trust him for protection. Psalm 46 is this doctrine delivered to the full.[71]

2nd. Secondly, to trust God for protection, is to wait under discouragements, and disappointments for a desired issue, of the affairs we commit to him. "He that believeth will not make haste" (Isa. 28:16).[72] This the Lord pleads for (Hab. 2:3–4).[73] Men will have their desires precisely accomplished this year, this month, this week, or they will wait no longer; "These," says God, "are proud men, their hearts are lifted up in them, they trust not to me for protection."

66 Ex. 14:13.

67 2 Chron. 14:10–11.

68 2 Chron. 20:3–5.

69 1 Sam. 30:3.

70 1 Sam. 30:6.

71 Owen briefly expounded Psalm 46:6–8 in *Ebenezer* (1648). See *Complete Works of John Owen*, 18:261.

72 Owen cited this call to patience on many occasions: *Ebenezer* (1648), *The Steadfastness of the Promises* (1650), *The Labouring Saint's Dismission* (1652), and *The Kingdom of Christ, and the Power of the Civil Magistrate* (1652).

73 Owen also made the point in *Ebenezer* (1648). See *Complete Works of John Owen*, 18:236.

Men love to trust God (as they profess) for what they have in their hands, in possession, or what lies in an easy view; place their desires afar off, carry their accomplishment behind the clouds, out of their sight, interpose difficulties, and perplexities, their hearts are instantly sick, they cannot wait for God; they do not trust him, nor ever did. Would you have the presence of God with you; learn to "wait quietly for the salvation" you expect from him.[74] Then indeed is he glorified, when he is trusted in a storm; when he is waited for under long perplexities, and distresses. Want of this ruined the Israelites in the wilderness; their work was long, their difficulties, and entanglements many, they would have had an immediate end of their troubles. "What! More difficulties, more hardships! Nay then 'let us choose a captain, and go down again into Egypt;' we know the worst of that, where this will end we know not."[75] This laid "their carcases in the wilderness,"[76] and deprived them of enjoying the good land.

3rd. Thirdly, it is to commit your affairs to the Lord with submission to his will, as to their issue and accomplishment. Trust respects protection, but it prescribes not, as to particular events. It is to commit our affairs to God, with thoughts of his infinite wisdom, sovereignty and goodness; with resolutions thereupon, that the product of his will, is that which will be good, be best for us, though it should not at all fall in with our present desires. It is true the Psalmist says, "Commit your ways unto the Lord, trust also in him, he shall bring it to pass" (Ps. 37:5). And so he shall and will, in all such cases, as that there particularly insisted on by the Psalmist, wherein his own glory is particularly engaged. But this prescribes not, as to all cases that we should cry, "Give me this child, or I die."[77] The rule is known; abide in this frame, and we shall have that we desire, or that which is better for us; but I must not abide in these things. See Psalm 37:3–5; 73:23–26.

And these are some of those ways wherewith we abide with God, as to our trusting of him in reference to special protection.

Those in Power Must Prioritize the Interest of Christ and His Church

{3} A third thing I should fix upon is, a people's universal owning of God's concernments in the world. His presence with them is, his owning their concernments, and certainly he expects that they abide with him in the owning

74 Lam. 3:26.

75 Num. 14:4, 29.

76 Heb. 3:17.

77 Gen. 30:1. Owen also quoted this as an example of impatient prescriptiveness in *A Vision of Unchangeable Free Mercy* (1646) and, the previous month, in *God's Work in Founding Zion* (1656). For the first sermon, see *Complete Works of John Owen*, 18:153.

of his. God's concernment in the world, is his people as invested with the privileges purchased for them by Christ. "The Lord's portion is his people" (Deut. 32:9). This is that which the Lord has particularly kept to himself. The vineyard that he has chosen out of all the forests of the world;[78] the handful that he has taken to himself, his sons, and daughters, his family; these he expects that you should abide by, if you would have him abide by you; yea it is most certain, as your respect, and regard shall be to them and their interest, as his people; so will his respect, and regard be to you, and your interest, as the people of this nation. But I have formerly spoken hereof unto you, and therefore, though it be a matter of the greatest importance, I shall not further insist upon it.[79]

And these are some of the conditions of God's special presence with you, pleasant conditions, their performance is your glory, your rest, your blessedness, not your bondage, not your burden. Not one duty does God on this account require of you, but it is also your reward. O blessed terms of peace and agreement. Blessed be the great Peacemaker, cursed be the breakers of this blessed agreement. Is this all indeed that is required, that we may have the special presence of God with us forever? O how inexcusable shall we be, if we neglect these terms? How just will be our ruin? Behold, I have "set before you life and death this day." The life, or death of these nations. O "choose life," seeing it may be had on such easy, such blessed terms:[80] terms wherein in doing good to others, you will also do good to your own souls; you will give peace to the nation, and have peace and rest in your own souls.

THREE CONCLUDING APPLICATIONS

Prioritize Abiding with God at a National Level in Order to Maintain God's Special Presence

Use 1. Look on this presence of God as your main concernment? This is that which the prophet calls for in the words of the text; so the psalmist, "There are many that say, 'Who will show us any good?' Lord lift thou up the light of thy countenance upon us" (Ps. 4).[81] Let other men make what inquiries they please, look for good, for rest, for peace in what they best fancy; acquiesce you in this, that the light of God's countenance, a pledge of his presence with you,

78 See 2 Esdras 5:23.

79 This was a prominent theme in Owen's sermon delivered the previous month at the opening of this Parliament, *God's Work in Founding Zion* (1656).

80 Deut. 30:19.

81 Ps. 4:6.

is that alone which you are to inquire after. I remember since the beginning of these last wonderful days, how often we have thought ourselves utterly ruined; if such alterations come, we are undone; if such men die, fall off, oppose, there is little hope of carrying on the work wherein we are engaged. If such shakings, such divisions befall us, our ruin is at hand; if we break with such, and such foreign nations, what hope remains: but alas we have found by experience, that our affairs have turned on none of these things; our prosperity has been built on none of those principles: such desertions, as we feared, have happened; such alterations, such divisions have befallen us; we have been sometimes almost reduced to Gideon's number;[82] such breaches with foreign nations have ensued;[83] one party that was with us has gone off, and asked, "What will you now do?"[84] And then another party has gone off, and asked us, "What will you do now?"[85] And no sooner do any fall off, but instantly they expect, and foretell destruction to them that do abide; as though they were God and not man, or as though God were bound to follow them with his presence in all their passions, in all their wanderings. It would I confess be more desirable unto me than life itself, to see all those at least, who stuck to the cause of God in its greatest difficulties, and trials, and then when it ceased to be carried on in the ordinary paths of nations, united again in the same common interest; to see their passions and prejudices cured, and their persons returned to their former usefulness: but this is that which is the result of all this discourse. It is not this, or that thing, or anything whatever; but the presence of God alone with a people, that is their life, their preservation, their protection and prosperity. If our strength had lain in anything else in this world, our light had gone out long ago, and it had departed from us: but hence it is that "we are not consumed."[86] Now if you are so careful not to lose these, and those friends, this, and that party of the nation, not to provoke this, or that people causelessly; oh what weight ought it to have upon your hearts and souls, that you provoke not the Lord to depart from you, that you take care for the continuance of his presence with you. This is your life, your safety, your success, your peace. Learn to prize it, value it etc.

82 Judg. 7:7.

83 For example, the Scots had, through the Solemn League and Covenant, been former allies of the English Parliament in the First Civil War but then turned to support the king in the hope of a covenanted settlement. Similarly, the Commonwealth had proposed an Anglo-Dutch union in 1651, but within a year, the two nations entered into war (1652–1654). In response Scotland had been conquered, and there was naval success in the first Anglo-Dutch war.

84 Perhaps a reference to those who had refused to accept the Commonwealth in 1649.

85 Perhaps a reference to those who refused to accept the Protectorate in 1653.

86 Lam. 3:22.

Be Reassured by Providential Signs of God's Special Presence with the Nation

[Use] 2. Secondly. While you have any pledge of the presence of God with you, be not greatly moved, nor troubled by any difficulties that you may meet withal: be not moved with any terror, but "sanctify the Lord of hosts" in your hearts, and make him "your dread and your fear," and he shall be a refuge and a hiding place unto you.[87]

Some pretend to visions of God, and they prophesy your ruin, and destruction; yea, they have limited times thereof, to the shame of their prognostications:[88] some are full of revenge, and they threaten your ruin, and talk what a catholic interest is complicating, and rising up against you:[89] some are troubled at your proceedings, that they are not in such equal paths as might be desired; as though that were a work and way of yesterday; as though we had not been turned and driven out of old tracks and paths above ten years ago; and as though the old paths were not so worn to the interest of a profane multitude, that it is yet impossible to keep the burden upright in them, whose guidance you are entrusted with.

Some say you will never be able to go through with the charge[90] of your undertakings?[91] As though God had never said, "The gold and silver are mine."[92] Should these things busy or distract you: does the issue of the business in hand, depend on the thoughts of these men? Will the end be according to their contrivances? Have these things indeed any influence at all into the determination of this controversy? Will not this one consideration guide your hearts, and spirits, when all these waves roll all together upon you? Yea but the

87 Isa. 8:13–14.

88 A reference to millenarian critics of the Protectorate. The year 1656 had a particular significance in English eschatological thought. For example, the Fifth Monarchist John Rogers had prophesied that fire would come into the world in 1656, and the Fifth Monarchist prophetess Mary Cary stated that the Jews would be converted that year. See David S. Katz, "English Redemption and Jewish Readmission in 1656," *Journal of Jewish Studies* 34, no.1 (1983), 73–76; David Loewenstein, "Scriptural Exegesis, Female Prophecy, and Radical Politics in Mary Cary," *Studies in English Literature, 1500–1900* 46, no. 1 (2006), 141.

89 In the summer of 1656, intelligence reports suggested that the recently elected pope, Alexander VII, was seeking to unite Roman Catholic powers against England. See John Thurloe, *Collection of the State Papers of John Thurloe* [. . .], ed. Thomas Birch, 7 vols. (London, 1742), 5:93–94, 292. In Owen's Parliamentary sermon from the previous month, he had called for efforts to be made to build a pan-Protestant alliance.

90 I.e., expense.

91 There had been considerable debates about how the war with Spain would be financed, but now some new funds were available through the captured Spanish treasure.

92 Hag. 2:8.

whole of this affair must be ordered, and will fall out according as the presence of God is with us, or otherwise. "If God be with us, who can be against us?"[93] How may you on this account, triumph against all oppositions whatsoever.

Maintain God's Special Presence through the Cromwellian Church Settlement and Legal Reform

[Use] 3. Thirdly, fix then your thoughts on the things which lie in a tendency toward the confirming of God's special providential presence with you; you have heard of the tenure of it, the means whereby it is procured, and retained. These things I have spoken to in general before; besides your own dependence on God, and comportment with his providence, the things incumbent on you, are such as respect either persons or things.

(1) First, for persons! It is that which I have minded you of before, and which I shall do, while I have life, and opportunity to speak to you or any concerned in the government of this nation, in public or private, because I know it is your life, your peace, your duty; and that is, that the end, and aim of all your consultations be the protection, encouragement, liberty of the seed of Jacob, the remnant, the hidden people! Those whom God has owned, accepted, blessed, given his presence unto, and among them. I plead not for their exaltation, promotion, preferment, I know not what! But charge it as your duty to take care, that they be not trodden underfoot, nor swallowed up, nor exposed to the rage and contempt of the men of the earth;[94] it is not this or that party of them that I speak of, but the generation of them that seek the face of God,[95] whose cause alone it is, and not of any other men, or frame of things, that is through the mighty power of God triumphant in these nations. They are to God as the apple of his eye;[96] and let their safety be so also to you; and you will not fail of the presence of God.[97]

(2) Secondly, for things, they are either the things of God, or men; of each a word.

[1] First, for the things of God, or the public profession of religion in the land, my time is too far spent for me to enter into a serious discourse on the

93 Rom. 8:31.

94 Ps. 10:18.

95 In the sermon from the previous month, Owen made three references to "the generation of the righteous." See *God's Work in Founding Zion* (1656).

96 Zech. 2:8.

97 Three months later, in January 1657, Cromwell reflected on how there was "in the midst of this People, a people . . . that are to God as the aple of his Eye, & hee sayes soe of them, bee they many or be they few: but they are many a people of the blessing of God, a People under his safety & protection." See *The Letters, Writings, and Speeches of Oliver Cromwell*, 3:332.

subject: some things have of late been done, which when envy, and anger, and disappointment shall cease to operate, the whole people of God in this nation will have cause to rejoice in.[98]

Let it not be thought amiss, if I mind you of one part of the nation in especial, the example of the saints allows us a special regard to those of our own nation, our kinsfolks in the flesh. It is for Wales I speak,[99] where the unhappiness of almost all men running into extremes has disadvantaged the advancement of the gospel, and the progress of it, when we had great ground, for the expectation of better things. Some are still zealous of the traditions of their fathers, and nothing almost will satisfy them, but their old road of beggarly readers in every parish:[100] others again, perhaps out of a good zeal, have hurried the people with violence beyond their principles, and sometimes it may be beyond the truth; and as Jacob said; overdriving the cattle, and young ones, has almost destroyed the whole flock;[101] between complaints on one side, and the other, I fear between misguided zeal, and formality, the whole work is almost cast to the ground, the business of Zion, as such, is scarce by any cared for. The good Lord guide you to somewhat for its relief, that those who are godly may be encouraged: and those that need instruction may not be neglected.

[2] Secondly the things of man, or righteous administrations of justice in things relating to this present pilgrimage. These wheels also, are you to

98 Owen's language recalls that of the Instrument of Government and its provisions for "the public profession of these nations."

99 There was considerable resistance to attempts to bring godly religion to Wales at this time.

100 Samuel Parker understood this to be a reference to "the episcopal clergy." See Parker, *A Defence and Continuation of the Ecclesiastical Politie* (London, 1671), 331. More specifically, in this context, those Owen describes as marked by "formality," a zeal for "the traditions of their fathers," and a desire for "beggarly readers in every parish," may have a particular Welsh focus. The gentry of the northeast of Wales "sheltered clergymen, enabled their private chapels to be used for banned ceremonies or prayer book worship, and used their remaining religious authority to resist ecclesiastical appointments of which they did not approve." Owen spoke of a desire for "their old road," and this sentiment was expressed by the clergyman Archibald Sparke, who wrote of his commitment "to tread in beaten paths." Those prosecuted for using the prayer book include George Griffith, future bishop of St Asaph. See Sarah Ward Clavier, "'Horrid Rebellion' and 'Holie Cheate': Royalist Gentry Responses to Interregnum Government in North-East Wales, 1646–1660," *The Welsh History Review* 29, no. 1 (June 2018), 52, 54, 69. One example of those whom Owen describes as being marked by a "good" but "misguided zeal" might be Vavasor Powell (1617–1670), "a firebrand by any measure." See Densil Morgan, "Nonconformity in Wales," *T&T Clark Companion to Nonconformity*, ed. Robert Pope (London: T&T Clark, 2013), 29. Owen appears to share something of the attitude of Berry, who described Vavasor Powell's Welsh Fifth Monarchists to Thurloe as "affectionate, tender-spirited people that want judgement." See Thurloe, *Collection of the State Papers of John Thurloe*, 4:215, 394.

101 Gen. 33:13.

set going. Many particulars lie before you; more will present themselves, troublesome times have always produced good laws;[102] your wisdom will be to provide for good execution, that not only the generations to come, but the present, may eat of the fruit of your labors and travail.

The End.

102 The "particulars" before Parliament were those suggested by William Sheppard for a fundamental reform of English law that would establish a new and decentralized legal system.

[Sermon]

Providential Changes, an Argument for Universal Holiness

Seeing then that all these things shall be dissolved, what manner of persons ought ye to be in all holy conversation and godliness?

2 PETER 3:11

INTRODUCTION AND CONTEXT

Peter's Audience

That this second epistle was written unto the same persons to whom the former was directed, the apostle himself informs us (2 Pet. 3:1).[1] Who they were to whom the first was directed, he declares fully, "Peter, an apostle of Jesus Christ, to the strangers scattered throughout Pontus, Galatia &c" (1 Pet. 1:1–2).

Scattered Strangers

"Strangers" are taken two ways: first, in a large, general, and spiritual sense. So all believers are said to be strangers and pilgrims in this world, because they are not of the world, but they look for another country,[2] another city,[3] another house, whose framer and builder is God.[4] Secondly, in a proper, natural sense; for those who abide or dwell in a land that is not their own,

1 In *A Complete Collection of the Sermons of the Reverend and Learned John Owen* [. . .], ed. John Asty (London: John Clark, 1721), this material was presented as sermons 8–11, running pp. 49–78, and was given the title *Providential Changes, an Argument for Universal Holiness.*

2 Heb. 11:14.

3 Heb. 13:14.

4 See Heb. 11:10.

wherein they have not right of inheritance with the natives and citizens of it. In this sense the patriarchs were strangers in the land of Canaan, before it came to be the possession of their posterity: and the children of Israel were strangers four hundred years in the land of Egypt.[5]

Now though the persons to whom the apostle wrote, were strangers in the first sense; pilgrims whose conversation and country was in heaven, yet they were no more so than all other believers in the world; so that there was no just cause of saluting them peculiarly under that style and title, were there not some other special reason of that appellation. They were therefore also strangers in the latter sense, persons who had no inheritance in the place of their abode, that were not the free and privileged natives of the country where they dwelt and inhabited, that is, they were Jews scattered abroad in those parts of the world.

The people of Israel in those days were under various distributions and appellations. First, they were the natives of Jerusalem, and the parts adjacent; and these were in the gospel, peculiarly called Jews. You have it often mentioned, that in our Savior's discourse with them, the Jews answered so and so,[6] that is, the natives of Jerusalem, and places adjoining. Secondly, those who inhabited the seacoasts of the country, whom the others much despised, and called them, from the place of their habitation, as if they had been men of another nation, "Galileans."[7] Thirdly, those who lived in several dispersions up and down the world among other nations. Of these there were two chief sorts, 1. Those who lived in some parts of Europe, in Asia the less, also at Alexandria, and other Greek colonies. These are in the Scripture sometimes called Greeks, Acts 17 and elsewhere,[8] commonly termed Hellenists, because they used the Greek language, and the Greek Bible then in use.[9] 2. Those who lived in the greater Asia, in and about Babylon; as also in the countries here enumerated by the apostle: the Jews converted to the faith, that lived scatteredly up and down in those parts of Asia.

Peter being in a special manner designed by the Holy Ghost the apostle of the circumcision,[10] and being now "at Babylon" in the discharge of his apostolical office and duty (1 Pet. 5:13), and being now nigh unto death, which he also knew (2 Pet. 1:14), and not perhaps having time to pass through, and personally visit these scattered believers; he wrote unto them these two

5 Gen. 15:13.
6 John 2:18; 8:48; 10:33; 19:7.
7 Luke 13:1–2; Acts 2:7.
8 Acts 17:4, 12.
9 A reference to the Septuagint.
10 Gal. 2:8.

epistles, partly about the main and important truths of the gospel, and partly about their own particular and immediate concernment, as to the temptations and afflictions wherewith they were exercised.

Scoffed At by Their Countrymen

It is evident from sundry places in the New Testament, what extreme oppositions the believing Jews met withal all the world over from their own countrymen, with and among whom they lived. They in the meantime, no doubt, warned them of the wrath of Christ against them for their cursed unbelief and persecutions; particularly letting them know, that Christ would come in vengeance ere long according as he had threatened, to the ruin of his enemies. And because the persecuting Jews all the world over upbraided the believers with the temple and the holy city, Jerusalem, their worship and service instituted of God, which they had defiled; they were given to know, that even all these things also should be destroyed, for their rejection of the Son of God. After some continuance of time, the threatening denounced being not yet accomplished, as is the manner of profane persons and hardened sinners (Eccl. 8:11), they began to mock and scoff, as if they were all but the vain pretenses, or loose, causeless fears of the Christians. That this was the state with them, or shortly would be, the apostle declares in this chapter, verses 3–4. Because things continued in the old state without alteration, and judgment was not speedily executed, they scoffed at all the threats about the coming of the Lord, that had been denounced against them.

Peter's Threefold Purpose

Hereupon the apostle undertakes these three things:

First, he convinces the scoffers of folly by an instance of the like presumption in persons not unlike them, and the dealings of God in a case of the same nature.

Secondly, he instructs believers in the truth of what they had before been told concerning the coming of Christ, and the destruction of ungodly men.

Thirdly, he informs them in the due use and improvement, that ought practically to be made of the certainty of this threatening of the coming of Christ.

Excursus: Consideration of the Prophetic Idiom of "Heaven and Earth"

For the first he minds them, as I said, of the old world, verses 5–6. Before the destruction of that world, God sent "Noah a preacher of righteousness,"[11]

11 2 Pet. 2:5.

who both in word and deed, effectually admonished men of the judgment of God, that was ready to come upon them; but they scoffed at his preaching and practice, in building the ark, and persisted in their security. "Now," says he, "this they willingly are ignorant of,"[12] it is through the obstinacy and stubbornness of their will, they do not consider it; for otherwise they had the Scripture, and knew the story. There is no ignorance like that, where men's obstinacy and hardness in sin keeps them from a due improvement of what they ought to have improved to its proper purpose. They are to this day willingly ignorant of the flood, who live securely in sin, under the denunciation of the judgments of God against sin.

I shall only observe by the way, not to look into the difficulties of these verses, that I be not too long detained from my principal intendment, that the apostle makes a distribution of the world into heaven and earth, and says, they were destroyed with water, and "perished." We know that neither the fabric or substance of the one or other was destroyed, but only men that lived on the earth; and the apostle tells us, verse 7 of "the heavens and earth" that were then, and were destroyed by water, distinct from "the heavens and the earth" that were "now," and were to be consumed by "fire":[13] and yet as to the visible fabric of heaven and earth, they were the same both before the flood and in the apostle's time, and continue so to this day; when yet it is certain that the heavens and earth whereof he speaks, were to be destroyed and consumed by fire in that generation. We must then for the clearing our foundation, a little consider what the apostle intends by "the heavens and the earth" in these two places.

1. It is certain, that what the apostle intends by the world, with its heavens and earth, verses 5–6, which was destroyed; the same or somewhat of that kind he intends by the heavens and the earth that were to be consumed and destroyed by fire, verse 7, otherwise there would be no coherence in the apostle's discourse, nor any kind of argument, but a mere fallacy of words.

2. It is certain, that by the flood, the world, or the fabric of heaven and earth, was not destroyed, but only the inhabitants of the world; and therefore the destruction intimated to succeed by fire, is not of the substance of the heavens and the earth, which shall not be consumed until the last day, but of persons or men living in the world.

3. Then we must consider, in what sense men living in the world are said to be "the world," and "the heavens and earth" of it. I shall only insist

12 2 Pet. 3:5.

13 2 Pet. 3:7.

on one instance to this purpose, among many that may be produced (Isa. 51:15–16).[14] The time when the work here mentioned of planting the heavens, and laying the foundation of the earth, was performed by God, was when he "divided the sea," verse 15, and gave the law, verse 16, and said to Zion, "Thou art my people;" that is, when he took the children of Israel out of Egypt, and formed them in the wilderness into a church and state; then he planted the heavens, and laid the foundation of the earth; made the new world; that is, brought forth order, and government, and beauty, from the confusion wherein before they were. This is the planting of the heavens, and laying the foundation of the earth in the world. And hence it is, that when mention is made of the destruction of a state and government, it is in that language that seems to set forth the end of the world. So Isaiah 34:4, which is yet but the destruction of the state of Edom.[15] The like also is affirmed of the Roman Empire (Rev. 6:14),[16] which the Jews constantly affirm to be intended by Edom in the prophets. And in our Savior Christ's prediction of the destruction of Jerusalem (Matt. 24), he sets it out by expressions of the same importance. It is evident then, that in the prophetical idiom and manner of speech, by "heavens and earth," the civil and religious state and combination of men in the world, and the men of them, are often understood. So were the heavens and earth that world which then was destroyed by the flood.

4. On this foundation, I affirm, that the heavens and earth here intended in this prophecy of Peter, the coming of the Lord, "the day of judgment, and perdition of ungodly men," mentioned in the destruction of that heaven and earth, do all of them relate, not to the last and final judgment of the world, but to that utter desolation and destruction that was to be made of the Judaical church and state; for which I shall offer these two reasons, of many that might be insisted on from the text.

(1) Because whatever is here mentioned, was to have its peculiar influence on the men of that generation. He speaks of that wherein both the profane scoffers, and those scoffed at, were concerned, and that as Jews; some of them

14 Owen also appealed to these verses in *The Shaking and Translating of Heaven and Earth* (1649) and *God's Work in Founding Zion* (1656).

15 In *The Shaking and Translating of Heaven and Earth* (1649), Owen made the same point, explaining that this refers to the destruction of Edom's "power and heights"—i.e., its "government and tyranny." See *Complete Works of John Owen*, 18:426.

16 In *The Shaking and Translating of Heaven and Earth* (1649), Owen stated that it was "eminently apparent" that these verses referred to "the destruction and wasting of the Pagan-Romish state, the plagues and commotions of her people, the dethroning her idol worship, and destruction of persecuting emperors and captains, with the transition of power and sovereignty from one sort to another." See *Complete Works of John Owen*, 18:427.

believing, others opposing the faith. Now there was no particular concernment of that generation in that sin, nor in that scoffing, as to the day of judgment in general; but there was a peculiar relief for the one, and a peculiar dread for the other at hand in the destruction of the Jewish nation; and besides an ample testimony both to the one and the other of the power and dominion of the Lord Jesus Christ, which was the thing in question between them.

(2) Peter tells them, that, after the destruction and judgment that he speaks of, verse 13, "We, according to his promise, look for new heavens and a new earth," etc., they had this expectation. But what is that promise? Where may we find it? Why we have it in the very words and letter [in] Isaiah 65:17. Now when shall this be that God will create these "new heavens and new earth, wherein dwelleth righteousness?" Says Peter, "It shall be after the coming of the Lord, after that judgment and destruction of ungodly men, who obey not the gospel, that I foretell." But now it is evident from this place of Isaiah, with chapter 66:21–22, that this is a prophecy of gospel times only; and that the planting of these new heavens, is nothing but the creation of gospel ordinances, to endure forever. The same thing is so expressed [in] Hebrews 12:26–28.

This being, then, the design of the place, I shall not insist longer on the context, but briefly open the words proposed, and fix upon the truth contained in them.

OPENING THE TEXT IN ORDER TO RAISE A DOCTRINE

The Foundation: Providential Alterations Will Come, Despite What Scoffers Say

First, there is the foundation of the apostle's inference and exhortation, "Seeing then that all these things shall be dissolved":[17] "Seeing that I have evinced that all these things, however precious they seem, or what value soever any put upon them, shall be dissolved, that is, destroyed; and that in that dreadful and fearful manner before mentioned, in a way of judgment, wrath, and vengeance, by fire and sword; let others mock at the threats of Christ's coming, he will come, he will not tarry:[18] and then the heavens and earth that God himself planted, the sun, moon, and stars of the Judaical polity and church, the whole old world of worship and worshipers that stand out in their obstinacy against the Lord Christ, shall be sensibly dissolved and destroyed; this we know shall be the end of these things, and that shortly."

17 In the text: Τούτων οὖν πάντων λυομένων.—Owen.

18 Hab. 2:3.

There is no outward constitution nor frame of things in governments or nations, but it is subject to a dissolution, and may receive it, and that in a way of judgment. If any might plead exemption, that on many accounts of which the apostle was discoursing, in prophetical terms (for it was not yet time to speak it openly to all), might interpose for its share. But that also, though of God's creation, yet standing in the way of, and in opposition to the interest of Christ, that also shall be dissolved: and certainly there is no greater folly in the world, than for a mere human creation, a mere product of the sayings and the wisdom of men, to pretend for eternity, or any duration beyond the coincidence of its usefulness to the great ends that Christ has to accomplish in the world. But this is not my business.

The Inference: This Necessitates a Heightened Response of Holiness

Secondly, there is the apostle's inference from, or exhortation on this supposition, expressed emphatically by way of interrogation: "What manner?"

Now, herein two things are included.

1. The evidence of the inference. It follows necessarily, unavoidably; everyone must needs make this conclusion: so that he leaves it to themselves to determine whose concernment it is. So the apostle Paul in another case, Hebrews 10:29, leaves it to themselves to determine, as a case clear, plain, unquestionable. So here: and this is a most effectual way of insinuating an inference and conclusion, when the parties themselves who are pressed with it, are made judges of its necessary consequence. Judge ye whether holiness becomes not all them who are like to be concerned in such providential alterations.

2. The extent and perfection of the duty in its universality and compass, is in this manner of expression strongly insinuated: "What manner of persons?" That is, such as indeed it is not easy to express, what attainments in this kind we ought on this account to press after. This apostle uses the same kind of expression to set forth the greatness and height of what he would deliver to the thoughts of men (1 Pet. 4:17–18). There is in this kind of expression somewhat more insinuated to the mind, than we know how to clothe with any words whatever.

Two things seem principally to be intended.

(1) That even the saints themselves in such cases ought to be other manner of men than usually they are, under ordinary dispensations of providence. Mistake not; our old measures will not serve; another manner of progress than as yet we have made, is expected from us; it is not ordinary holiness and godliness that is expected from us, under extraordinary calls from God and Christ.

(2) That our endeavors to be godly and holy, ought to be boundless and endless. No less is included in this apostrophe, "What manner of persons ought we to be?" Not resting in what we have attained, nor what may seem sufficient to keep our heads above water, but an endless and boundless pressing on. Alas! It will hardly enter into our hearts to think what manner of men we ought to be.

The Exhortation: This Is a Call to Comprehensive Holiness

Thirdly, for the matter of this exhortation and inference from the former principle, couched in this interrogation, it is, "All holy conversation and godliness." The word "all" is not in the original; but both the other words are in the plural number, "In holy conversations and godlinesses." Now these expressions being not proper in our language, the translators have supplied the emphasis and force of them by the addition of the word, "all": and there is no just cause of quarrel with them for so doing: only in the original the words are more weighty and emphatical than that supply does readily reach unto. That which is principally intended, is, that all the concernments whatever of holiness and godliness, are couched in the words. So that two things are in them.

1. The two general parts of that universal duty that we owe to God; and they are these. First, holiness of conversation; which is comprehensive of all holiness and righteousness, both in principle and practice; for no conversation is holy, but what comes from a holy heart, and is carried on to that great and holy end, the glory of God. Secondly, godliness, or the worship of God according to the appointment and institution of Christ. This is the proper importance of εὐσέβείαις,[19] as distinct from holiness of conversation; a due adherence to, and observance of the instituted worship of God.

2. The extent and compass of them both and their degrees. It is not in this or that part of conversation; to be holy in one thing, and loose in another; to be holy in one capacity, and vain in another; to be godly as a private person, and ungodly or selfish as a magistrate; nor is it to observe one part of worship, and despise another: but in all concernments of conversation, in all parts of worship, does this duty lie: "In all holy conversation and godliness."

The Call to Universal Holiness

Fourthly, there is the relation that we ought to bear to the universality of holiness and godliness. We ought to be in them: δεῖ ὑπάρχειν ὑμᾶς, You "ought to be," "to exist," in them. In these things is your life; they are not to

19 Gk. "godliness or piety."

be followed now and then, as your leisure will serve; but in all that you do, you ought to be still in these, as in the clothes that you wear, the garment that is on you; be what you will, or where you will, or employed as you are called, yet still you ought to be in holiness and godliness; and what persons you ought to be in them, or how, has been declared.

TREATMENT OF THE DOCTRINE RAISED FROM THE TEXT

Statement of the Doctrine

Observation. *Great providential alterations or destructions made upon the account of Christ and his church, call for eminency of universal holiness and godliness in all believers.*

I esteem it my duty to speak somewhat to this proposition, as containing the direction of our great duty in this day. That we have had many providential alterations among us, is known to all. What light I have about their relation to Christ and his church, I shall make bold to communicate when I come to the application of the truth in hand, and thereby make way for the pressing of the duty of the text on ourselves in particular: for the present, I confess, I am ashamed and astonished at the deportment of many who are professors in these days; they see and talk of the alterations and dissolutions that God is pleased to make; but what is the improvement that is made hereof? Many take advantage to vent their lusts and passions, some one way, some another; one rejoicing at the ruin of another, as if that were his duty; others repining at the exaltation of another, as if that were their duty; some contriving one form of outward constitutions, others for another. (I speak of private persons) but who almost looks to that which is the special call of God under such dispensations? Let us then, I pray you, take a little view of our duty, and the grounds of it; and who knows but that the Lord may by it enlarge and fix our hearts to the love and prosecution of it?

Defining the Two Great Periods of Providential Alterations

The two great providential alterations and dissolutions that have been, and shall be made on the account of Christ and his church, to which all lesser are either consequent, or do lie in a tendency, are that first of the Judaical church and state, whereof I have spoken; and secondly, that of the anti-Christian state and worship, whereunto all the shakings of these nations seem to tend in the wisdom of God, although we are not able to discern their influence thereunto.

The Destruction of the Jewish Church and State in AD 70

1. Now for the first of these, we may consider it in its coming as foretold, and as accomplished.

(1) As it was foretold and threatened by Christ. How were believers cautioned to be ready for it with eminent holiness and watchfulness therein? So Luke 21:34, 36, "Take heed to yourselves; watch therefore." Why so? "Christ is coming," verse 27. When? "Why, 'in this generation,'" verse 32. What to do? "Why to dissolve heaven and earth," verse 25, "to dissolve the Jewish church and state. Watch therefore; give all diligence." So also Matthew 24:42. "Watch, therefore." Oh! on this account what manner of persons ought we to be?

(2) As accomplished. See what use the apostle upon it directs believers unto (Heb. 12:26–28). This is the use, this the call of providence, in all these mighty alterations: "Let us have grace," strive for it; the nature of the works of God call aloud for an eminent frame of holiness, and close adherence unto God in his worship. I could show how both the duties of my text are here expressed; but I need not.

The Destruction of the Antichrist's Church and State

2. So is it also in reference to that other great work of God in the world relating to Christ and his church, which is the ocean of providence whereinto all the rivulets of lesser alterations do run; I mean the destruction of Antichrist and his Babylonish kingdom.

What a frame shall be in the saints on the close of that work, the Holy Ghost declares at large [in] Revelation 19. All rejoicing and spiritual communion with God; and while the work is on the wheel, those whom God will own in it, he sets his mark on as holy, called, and chosen.[20]

The grounds hereof are—

First Ground of This Doctrine: In Providential Alterations There Is a Special Coming of Christ

1. Because in every such providential alteration or dissolution of things on the account of Christ and his church, there is a peculiar coming of Christ himself. He comes into the world for the work he has to do: he comes among his own to fulfill his pleasure among them. Hence such works are called "his coming"; and "the coming of his day." Thus James exhorts these very Jews to whom Peter here writes, with reference to the same things, "Be patient unto the coming of the Lord" (James 5:7–9). But how could that generation

20 Cf. Rev. 17:14.

extend their patience to the day of judgment? "Nay," says he, "that is not the work I design, but his coming to take vengeance on his stubborn adversaries," which he says, verse 8, " 'draweth nigh,' is even, at hand: yea, Christ, 'the judge, standeth before the door,' verse 9, ready to enter"; which also he did within a few years. So upon, or in the destruction of Jerusalem, the same work, the Son of man is said to "come in the clouds, and great glory" (Luke 21:27); and they that escape in that "desolation"[21] are said to "stand before the Son of man," verse 36. So, in the ruin and destruction of the Roman Empire on the account of their persecution, it is said that "the day of the wrath of the Lamb was come" (Rev. 6:16–17).[22]

In all such dispensations then, there is a peculiar coming of Christ, a peculiar drawing nigh of him to deal with all sorts of persons in a special manner; though he be oftentimes encompassed with many clouds, and with much darkness, yet he is present exerting his authority, power, wisdom, righteousness, and grace in an eminent manner. It is with him as it is with God in other works, though all "see him not, perceive him not," yet "he goeth by," and "passeth on" (Job 9:11). The lusts, prejudices, corruptions, selfishness, injustice, oppressions of men; the darkness, unbelief, fears, carnal wisdom, of the saints themselves; the depth, compass, height, unsearchableness, of the path of the wisdom of Christ himself, keep us in the dark as to his presence in this and that particular; but yet in such dispensations he is come, and passes on toward the accomplishment of his work, though we perceive it not. Now, "what manner of persons ought we to be in all holy conversation and godliness," to meet this great King of saints at his coming? What preparation ought there to be? What solemnity of universal holiness for his entertainment? He is in such dispensations continually nigh us, whether we take notice of it or not.

I say then, if there be a special coming, and a special meeting of Christ in such dispensations, I suppose, I may leave the inference unto all holy conversation and godliness with the apostle to the breasts and judgment of them that are concerned. Are we in this work to meet the Lord Jesus? What manner of persons ought we to be?

It may be observed, that Christ puts very great weight on the present frame and course, which he finds men in at his coming. "Blessed is that servant whom his Lord, when he cometh, shall find so doing" (Matt. 24:46). He

21 Luke 21:20.

22 Owen frequently appealed to Rev. 6:12–17 as a prophetic account of the fall of the pagan Roman Empire. See *Ebenezer* (1648), *The Shaking and Translating of Heaven and Earth* (1649), *The Branch of the Lord* (1650), and *The Advantage of the Kingdom of Christ* (1651). For the first two sermons, see *Complete Works of John Owen*, 18:270, 438, 457.

annexes blessedness to the frame and course he finds men in at his coming; and waits for that hour, verse 42. Be not asleep when the thief comes to break up the house;[23] take heed that that day take you not unprovided, that you be not overtaken in the midst of the cares of this world. And he complains, that when he comes, he shall not "find faith on the earth."[24]

Objection Answered

But you will say, "Is this enough then, that we look to be found in all godliness and holiness at his coming? May we indulge ourselves and our lusts at other seasons, so we be sure to be then provided? Is not the command of duty equal and universal as to all times and seasons? Or is it pointed only unto such dispensations?"

Answ[er] 1. The inference for preparedness for the coming of Christ, is to universal holiness at all seasons, and that upon the account of the uncertainty of it. This our Savior presses again and again. "You know not at all when it will be, nor how; no not in the least; you believe it not when it is come: 'I shall not find faith of it on the earth,'" says Christ. "Men will not take notice of it, nor acknowledge it, nor own it, as my coming; wherefore you have no way to be prepared for it, but by universal, perpetual watchfulness."

Answ[er] 2. The exhortation lies not unto holiness and godliness in general; but as to the degrees of it, what manner of men we ought to be in them. It is not a godly conversation at an ordinary rate that may find acceptance at another time, which will suffice to meet Christ at his coming, and that on sundry accounts afterward to be mentioned.

I shall at present only treat of some grounds of it from his own person who comes, and whom we are to meet; and speak of the work he has to do in his coming afterward.

The One Who Comes Is Holy

(1) On the account of his personal excellencies and holiness. Consider how he is described when he comes to walk among his churches (Rev. 1:13–17). He is full of beauty and glory. When Isaiah saw him, he cries out, "I am undone, I am a man of unclean lips" (Isa. 6);[25] because of the dread and terror of his holiness. And Peter also, "Depart from me, Lord, for I am a sinful man."[26] They were not able to bear the thoughts of his glorious holiness so nigh to

23 Matt. 24:43.

24 Luke 18:8.

25 Isa. 6:5.

26 Luke 5:8.

them. When the holy God of old was to come down among the people at the giving of the law, all the people were to sanctify themselves, and to wash their clothes (Ex. 19:10–11). And order was still taken that no unclean thing might be in the camp, because of the presence of the holy God, though but in a type and resemblance. Whether we observe it or no, if there be any dissolving dispensations among us, that relate to Christ or his church, there is a holy one in the midst of us; or there will be when any such dispensations shall pass over us. And to think to have to do in the works and ways wherein he has to do, with hearts unlike and unsuitable unto him, to act our lusts and follies immediately under the eye of his holiness, to set our defiled hands to his pure and holy hands, his soul will abhor it. This is a boldness which he will revenge, that we should bring our neglect and lusts into his holy presence. Christ is in every corner, in every turn of our affairs; and it is incumbent on us to consider how it is fit for us to behave ourselves in his special presence.

The One Who Comes Has Kingly Power and Authority

(2) Upon the account of his authority. He who thus comes is the King of saints,[27] and he comes as the King of saints: he comes to exert his regal power and authority, to give a testimony to it in the world. So Isaiah 63:1–4.[28] He shows his glory, his might, his kingdom and authority in this work. So Revelation 19:12. When he comes to destroy his anti-Christian enemies, he has "many crowns" on his head; he exercises his regal power and authority. What is the duty of saints when their King is so nigh them, when he is come into the midst of them, while he puts forth the greatness of his power round about them? Will it become them to be neglective of him; to be each man in the pursuit of his own lusts, and ways, and works, in the presence of their King? Holiness and godliness has a due regard to the authority of Christ. Wherever there is a due subjection of soul unto Christ, all holy conversation and godliness will ensue. To be neglective in, or of any part of holy conversation, to be careless of any part of worship under the special eye of the Lord of our lives and our worship, is not to be borne with.

The One Who Comes Has a Loving Heart of Compassion

(3) On the account of the present care, kindness and love, that he is exerting in all such dispensations toward his. It is a time of care and love; the way of

27 Rev. 15:3.

28 Owen had also referred to this passage in his sermons *The Shaking and Translating of Heaven and Earth* (1649) and *The Branch of the Lord* (1650). For the first sermon, see *Complete Works of John Owen*, 18:438. The second sermon is included in this volume.

his working out the designs of his heart, are indeed ofttimes dark and hid; and his own do not see so clearly how things lie in a tendency to the event and fruits of love. But so it is; Christ comes not but with a design of love and pity toward his, with his heart full of compassion for them. Now, what this calls for at their hands, seeing their holiness and worship is all that his soul is delighted in, is evident unto all.

Summary of the First Ground of This Doctrinal Observation

Put now these things together: every such dispensation is a coming of Christ: the coming of Christ, as it is trying in itself, so it is the coming of the holy King of saints in his love and pity toward them; yea, be the dispensation what it will, never so sharp and severe unto them, yet it is in love and compassion to their souls: their work is to meet this their holy King in the works of his love and power: and "what manner of persons ought we to be?"

Second Ground of This Doctrine: In Providential Alterations Christ Comes as Judge

2.[29] The second ground is, because every such day, is a lesser day of judgment, a forerunner, pledge, and evidence of that great day of the Lord which is to come. God's great and signal judgments in the world, are to be looked on as pledges of the final judgment at the last day. So Jude tells us, that in the destruction of Sodom and Gomorrah, God "set forth an example" of them that shall suffer "the vengeance of eternal fire" (Jude 7). And Peter calls the time of the destruction of the Judaical church and state expressly "the day of judgment and perdition of ungodly men" (2 Pet. 3:7). So to the full is the destruction of the Roman persecuting state expressed (Dan. 7:9–10, 14). The solemnity of the work and whole procedure bespeaks a great day, a day of judgment; it is so, and a representation of that which is to come. And the like also is set forth [in Daniel] 12:1–3. And the same description have we of the like day of Christ (Mal. 4:1).

Every such day, I say then, is a lesser day of judgment, wherein much judging work is accomplished. This Daniel tells us (Dan. 12:10), it is a trying, a purifying, a teaching, a hardening, a bleeding time:[30] there are great works that are done upon the souls and consciences of men, by Christ, in such a day, as well as outwardly; and all in a way of judgment. To let pass then the

29 This is described as the second part of the sermon in the 1721 edition.

30 Owen made the same point from this verse in *Ebenezer* (1648), *The Shaking and Translating of Heaven and Earth* (1649), and *The Advantage of the Kingdom of Christ* (1651). For the first two sermons, see *Complete Works of John Owen*, 18:223, 437. The third sermon is in this volume.

outward, visible effects of his wrath and power, of his wisdom and righteousness; I shall consider some few of the more secret judiciary acts that the Lord Christ usually exerts in such a day.

Christ Pleads with Nations about Their Sin

(1) He pleads with all flesh that are concerned in the alterations and desolations he makes. God puts this as one act of his in judgment, that he pleads with men (Ezek. 38:22). In his judgments he pleads with and against men about their sins. And in that great representation of the day of judgment, God is said to "plead with all nations" (Joel 3:2). Now, I say, in general, Christ in such a day pleads with all men concerned. His providences have a voice, and that a contending, pleading voice: unless men are utterly blinded and hardened, as indeed the most are, they cannot but hear him in his great and mighty works contending with them about their sin and unbelief; representing to them his righteous judgment to come. Though men now cast off things, on this account and that, and being filled with their lusts, passions, fury, revenge, or ease, sensuality, and worldliness, think these things concern them not; yet the day will come, wherein they shall know, that the Lord Christ in his mighty works was pleading even with them also, and that in a way of judgment about their sin and folly.

Christ Exposes False Professions of Faith

(2) In such a day Christ judges and determines the profession of many a false hypocrite, who has deceived the church and people of God. One great work of the last day shall be the discovery of hypocrites: it is thence principally called, the day wherein the secrets of all hearts shall be revealed.[31] Many a fair pretender in the world, shall be found to have been an enemy of Christ and the gospel. So is the day of Christ's coming in the flesh represented (Mal. 3:1–2). All were high in their professions of desiring his coming, and of delighting in him; but when he came, what was the issue? How few endured the trial? The false, hypocritical, selfish hearts, who had treasured up the hopes of great things to themselves, being discovered by the trials and temptations wherewith his coming was attended, themselves were utterly cast off from their profession, into open enmity to God and his Son. So deals the Lord Christ in and under the dispensations whereof we speak, to this day. What by the fury of their own lusts, what by the temptations which lie in their way, what by the advantages they meet withal for the exercise of their

31 See Rom. 2:16.

vile affections, their hypocrisy is discovered, and themselves cast out of their profession. Notable effects of this acting of Christ as a judge have we seen in the dispensation that is passing over us: some he has judged by the sentence and judgment of his churches. How many false wretches have been cast out of churches, that have withered under their judgment, and returned no more? Some who have not walked in the order of his churches by him appointed, he has judged by the world itself, suffered their sin and folly so to break forth, that the world itself has cast them out from the number of professors, and owned them as its own.[32] Some have been judged as to their profession of him by strong temptations; that is, their lusts, ambition, selfishness, which have carried them into ways and compliances, wherein they have been compelled to desert, and almost renounce all their former profession. Some have been tried and judged by the errors and abominations of the times, and turned aside from the simplicity of the gospel. Now though there have been, and are these and many other ways and means of casting men out of, and from the profession that they have made, some good, some bad, some in themselves of a mere passive nature and indifferent; yet they all proceed from Christ, in a judiciary way, they are acts of his, in his day of judgment: and oh, that England might not yet be farther filled with instances and examples of this kind!

Christ Engages in Judicial Hardening of the Wicked

(3) He does exercise his judgment in blinding and hardening of wicked men; yet they shall not see nor perceive what he is doing, but shall have advantages to do wickedly, and prejudices to blind them therein. So expressly, "They shall do wickedly, and they shall not understand" (Dan. 12:10). There are two parts of his judgment in such a day, about and against them: first, his giving of them up to their own lusts, to do wickedly, "They shall do wickedly." Wicked they are, and they shall act accordingly; they shall do it in such a day to the purpose (Rev. 16:10–11).[33] Christ will providentially suffer occasions, advantages, provocations, to lie before them, so that they shall do wickedly to the purpose, they shall have daily fresh occasions to curse, repine, blaspheme, oppose Christ and his interest, or to seek themselves, and the satisfaction of their lusts, which at other times they shall not be able to do. Be they in what condition they will, high or low, exalted or depressed, in power or out of it, they shall in such a season do wickedly, according as their advantages and

32 This is a comment about the proliferation of the more radical sects.

33 Owen summarized his understanding of these verses in *The Advantage of the Kingdom of Christ* (1651). He argued that as a result of "judicial blindness" people "repent not of their evil deeds, but bite their tongues for anger, and blaspheme the God of heaven."

provocations are. And for men to be given up to their own hearts' lusts, is the next door to the judgment of the great day, when men shall be given up to sin, self, and Satan, unto eternity. Secondly, he blinds them: "None of the wicked shall understand."[34] Strange! Who seems so wise and so crafty as they? Who do understand the times, and their advantages in them, more than they? Who more prudent for the management of affairs than they? But the truth is, none of them, no not one of them, shall, or do, or can understand; that is, they understand not the work of Christ, the business and design that he has in hand; nor what is the true and proper interest of them who are concerned in these dispensations. There are many ways whereby Christ exerts this blinding and infatuating efficacy of his providence toward wicked men in such a day of judgment, that they shall not understand, or know, that he is at all concerned in the works that are in the world.

Sometimes the very things that he does, are such, and so contrary to the prejudicate[35] opinions of men, that they can never understand that they are things which he will own. How many have been kept from understanding anything of Christ in the world, in the days wherein we live, from their inveterate prejudices on the account of old superstitions, and forms of government which have been removed: they will rather die, than believe that Christ has any hand in these things: "They shall not understand."

Sometimes the persons by whom he does them, keep them from understanding. "Shall these men save us?" These whom they look upon as the offscouring[36] of the earth. "Sure if Christ had any work to do in the world, he would make use of other manner of instruments for the accomplishing of them." They are no less offended with the persons that do them, than the things that are done. Christ works all this, that they should not understand.

Sometimes the manner of doing what he has to do, the darkness wherewith it is attended, the strange process that he makes, sometimes weak, sometimes foolish, sometimes disorderly to the reasoning of flesh and blood, though all beautiful in itself, and in relation to him.

And sometimes Christ sends a spirit of giddiness into the midst of them,[37] that they shall err and wander in all their ways, and not see nor discern the things that are before them. "None of the wicked shall understand."

By these, and many such ways as these, does Christ in these days of his coming exercise judgment on ungodly men: not to mention the outward

34 Dan. 12:10.

35 I.e., prejudice.

36 I.e., those rejected and cast aside. See 1 Cor. 4:13.

37 Isa. 19:14.

destruction, desolation, and perdition, which usually in such seasons he brings upon them.

Christ Pleads with His People about Their Sins and Temptations through a Range of Different Ways and Means

(4) He exercises judgment at such a time, even among the saints themselves, he is judging in the great congregation (Ps. 82:1). So Psalm 50:4–8. All this solemnity of proceeding is for the judgment of his own people. And his judging of them is in a plea about their obedience and failing therein. The sum of this his dealing with them is expressed, [in] Revelation 3:9.[38]

We may, then, consider, [1] What it is that Christ pleads with his own people about his coming. [2] What are the ways and means whereby he does so.

[1] There are sundry things on the account whereof Christ at his coming pleads with his saints, one or more of them.

{1} On the account of some secret lusts that have defiled them, and which they have either indulged themselves in, or not so vigorously opposed as their loyalty unto Christ required. Times of peace and outward prosperity are usually times, wherein, through manifold temptations, even the saints themselves are apt to sully[39] their consciences, and to have breaches made upon their integrity; sometimes in things they do know, and sometimes in things they do not know, nor take notice of. Instances may be given in abundance of such things. In this condition Christ deals with them, as Isaiah 4:4. There is "blood" and "filth" upon them; "the spirit of judgment" and "burning" must be set at work, which as it principally aims at the internal efficacy of the Spirit in the cleansing of sin, so it respects a time of providential alterations and trials, wherein that work is effectually exerted. Christ in these dispensations speaks secretly to the consciences of his saints, and minds them of this and that folly and miscarriage, and deals with them about it. He asks them if things are not so and so with them? If they have not thus and thus defiled themselves? Whether these hearts are fit to converse with him? And leaves not until their dross and tin be consumed.[40]

{2} On the account of some way or ways wherein they may have been unadvisedly, or through temptation, or want of seeking counsel aright from him, engaged. They may be got, in their employments, in their callings, in the work that lies before them in this world, into ways and paths wherein Christ is not pleased they should make any progress: what through leaning to their

38 Those of "the synagogue of Satan" will come to know that the godly are loved by God.

39 I.e., defile.

40 Isa. 1:25.

own understandings,[41] what through an inclination of saying "A confederacy" to them to whom the people say "A confederacy,"[42] what through the common mistakes in the days wherein they live, even the saints may be engaged in ways that are not according to the mind and will of Christ. Now in such a day of Christ's coming, though he spares the souls of his saints, and forgives them, yet he "takes vengeance of their inventions" (Ps. 99:8). He will cast down all their idols, and destroy and consume every false way wherein they were: one is, it may be, in a way of superstition and false worship; another in a way of pride and ambition; another in a way of giving countenance to the men of the world, and things wherein God delights not. Christ will take vengeance of all these their inventions in the day of his coming.[43] He acts as "a refiner's fire," and as "fullers' soap."[44]

{3} On the account of inordinate cleaving unto the shaken, passing things of the world.[45] This is a peculiar controversy that Christ has with his, upon the account of adherence to the passing world; and it is a thing wherein, when he comes, too many will be found faulty. I might also insist on their unbelief, and other particulars; but—

[2] The ways and means whereby Christ judges and pleads with his own, on these accounts, are also various.

{1} He does it by the afflictions, trials, and troubles, that he exercises them with at his coming. The use of the furnace is to take away dross; and the issue of afflictions and trials, to take away sin: this is their fruit. So Daniel 12:1, the time of Christ's coming shall be a day of "trouble, such as never was." And what shall be the issue? "Many shall be purified, and made white, and tried" (Dan. 12:10). Their trials and troubles, their great tribulations, shall be purifying and cleansing. Though the design of Christ in the issue at the appointed season, be the peace and deliverance of his saints, yet in the carrying on of his work, great trials and tribulations may befall them all; and many may fall in the way, and perish as to the outward man. Hence there is an appointed time of "rest," and it will be a blessed thing for them that shall be preserved unto it; but while those days and seasons are coming to their period, there is often a time of great "trouble" (Dan. 12:1, 13). And "the power of the holy people" may be scattered, verse 7, and many afflictions and trials may befall them. Now by these does Christ plead with his for the consumption of their

41 Prov. 3:5.
42 Isa. 8:12.
43 Ps. 99:8.
44 Mal. 3:2.
45 Heb. 12:27–28.

lusts, and the destruction of their inventions,[46] for the purging and purifying of them. All our trials, pressures, troubles, disappointments, in such a day, are the actings of Christ to this end and purpose. The influences that affliction has unto these ends, are commonly spoken unto.

{2} He does it by pouring out of his Spirit in a singular manner, for this end and purpose, so to plead with, judge, and cleanse his saints. It is in the administration of his Spirit that at his coming "he sits as a refiner and purifier of silver" (Mal. 3:1–3); and we see what work he accomplishes thereby. The Holy Ghost, who is the great pleader for the saints, and in them, does at such a time effectually plead with them, by convictions, persuasions, arguings, application of the word, motions, strivings, and the like. Hence those who are unrefined at such a season are said in a peculiar manner "to vex," to grieve "the Holy Spirit" of God (Isa. 63:10). His design upon them, is a design of love; and to be rejected, resisted, opposed, in his actings and motions, this grieves and vexes him. Men know not what they do in neglecting the actings of the Holy Ghost, which are peculiarly suited to providential dispensations. When God is great in the world in the works of his providence, in alterations, dissolutions, shakings, changings, removals, and sends his Spirit to move and work in the hearts of men, answerably to his mind and will in these dispensations; so that there is a harmony in the voice of God without and within, both speaking aloud and clearly; then to neglect the workings of the Spirit, brings men into that condition complained of, "Because I have purged thee, and thou wast not purged, thou shalt not be purged any more" (Ezek. 24:13).

It may be observed, that at such seasons when Christ has any great and signal work to bring forth in the world, he does by his Spirit deal with the hearts and consciences of the most wicked and vile men; which, when the secrets of all hearts shall be discovered at the last day, will exceedingly exalt the glory of his wisdom, patience, goodness, holiness, and righteousness. So did he with them before the flood, as is evident from Genesis 6:3. When an utter destruction was to come, he says, his Spirit shall "strive" with them no more; that is, about their sin and rebellion. That this Spirit was the Spirit of Christ, and that the work of dealing with these ungodly men was the work of Christ, and that it was a fruit of long-suffering, Peter declares (1 Pet. 3:18–20). And if he deals thus with a perishing world, by a work that perishes also; how much more does he it in an effectual work upon the hearts of his own? It is the Spirit that speaks to the churches in all their trials (Rev. 2).

46 Ps. 99:8.

By this means, I say then, Christ pleads with his saints, secretly and powerfully judging their lusts, corruptions, failings, consuming and burning them up: he first by frequent motions and instructions gives them no rest in any unequal path; then discovers to them the beauty of holiness, the excellency of the love of Christ, the vanity and folly of everything that has interrupted their communion with him, and so fills them with godly sorrow, renunciation of sin, and cleaving unto God; which is the very promise that we have (Ezek. 6:10).

{3} As he does it by the inward, private, effectual operation of his Spirit; so he does it by the effusion of his light and gifts in the dispensation of the word. Christ seldom brings any great alteration upon the world, but together with it, or to prepare for it, he causes much effectual light to break forth in the dispensation of his word. Before the first destruction of Jerusalem by the Babylonians, how he dealt with them he declares, "And the Lord God of their fathers sent to them by his messengers, rising up betimes and sending, because he had compassion on his people and on his dwelling place" (2 Chron. 36:15). And before the final dissolution of the heavens and earth of that church and state, he preached to them himself in the flesh. A glorious light! Before the ruin of the anti-Christian world, he sends the angel with the everlasting gospel,[47] and his two witnesses to hold forth the light of the gospel:[48] and we must witness to this his way and wisdom in our generation. Now though there are many rebels against light, and many whose lusts are enraged by the breaking forth of truth in its beauty and luster; and many that being dazzled with it, do run out of its paths into ways of error and folly, and none of the wicked do understand; yet among the saints, the more light, the more holiness; for their light is transforming. This then is another means whereby, in such a day, Christ consumes the lusts, and judges the inordinate walking of his own, even by the light which in an eminent manner he sends forth in the dispensation of the word.

Conclusion of the Treatment of the First Doctrinal Observation

Now if the time and season whereof we speak, be such a day of judgment, wherein Christ thus pleads with all men, and with his own in an especial manner; I think the inference unto eminency in universal holiness, may be left upon the thoughts and minds of all that are concerned: especially from these considerations does the inference lie strong unto the ensuing

47 Rev. 14:6.

48 Rev. 11:3.

particulars, in the ways of holiness and godliness. First, of self-searching, and self-judging in reference to our state and condition. Dreadful are the actings of Christ in such a day on the souls and consciences, ofttimes on the names and lives of corrupt, unsound professors: in part I declared them before. If any now should be found in such a condition, his day of judgment is come, his sealing to destruction. This the apostle calls to in such a dispensation (1 Cor. 11:31–32). Self-judging, as to our state and condition, ways and practices, is a great principle of holy conversation and godliness. When Christ comes to judge, we ought surely to judge ourselves; and abounding in that work is a great means of preservation from the temptations of the days whereunto we are exposed. Secondly, of weanedness[49] from the world and the things thereof. Christ's coming puts vanity on all these passing things. This is surely contained in the text: "Seeing that these things shall be dissolved, what manner of persons, etc." At best they are vain and passing uncertain things; in such a dispensation as is spoken of, they are all obnoxious to dissolution, and many of them certainly to be removed and taken away. And why should the heart of anyone be set upon them? Why should we not fix our souls on things more profitable, more durable. It is no small matter to meet the Lord Christ at his coming (Mal. 3:1–3). They were all full of desires of the coming of Christ; they sought after him: "The Lord whom ye seek." They delighted in the thoughts of him: "Whom ye delight in." Well, he came according to their desires; he whom they sought was found. And what was the issue? Why very few of them could abide the day of his coming, or stand when he appeared. He had a work to do they could not away with. They desired his coming; they desired the day of the Lord; but as the prophet says, "Woe unto them, to what end have they desired it? It was darkness to them, not light" (Amos 5:18).[50] That was the coming of Christ in person to his temple; it is not otherwise in any of his other comings in providential dispensations. Many men long for it, delight in it; it is our duty so to do: but what is the issue? One is hardened in sin and lust; another is lifted up as though himself were something, when he is nothing; a third stumbles at the coming itself, and falls: "Woe unto them, the day of the Lord is darkness unto them, and not light."

49 I.e., spiritual detachment.

50 Owen appealed to this text in *A Sermon Preached* [. . .] *January 31* (1649), explaining that "in every generation many desirous of the accomplishment of God's work are shaken off from any share therein." He also referenced it in *The Shaking and Translating of Heaven and Earth* (1649) and the 1657 sermon *Providential Changes.* For the first two sermons, see *Complete Works of John Owen*, 18:313, 459. The third sermon is included in this volume.

THE PROVIDENTIAL ALTERATIONS OF THE MID-CENTURY CRISIS IS SUCH A COMING OF CHRIST

I proceed now to the use. But to make way for the due improvement of the apostle's exhortation unto us, some previous considerations must be laid down.

Two Initial Premises about What Has Occurred

England Has Been Shaken

First, it is known to all the world, that we have had great providential alterations and dissolutions in these nations. He must be a stranger, not in England only, but in Europe, almost in the whole world, that knows it not.[51] Our heavens and our earth, our sea and our dry land, have been not only shaken, but removed also.[52] The heavens of ancient and glorious fabric, both civil and ecclesiastical, have been taken down by fire and sword, and the fervent heat of God's displeasure. It is needless for me to declare, what destructions, what dissolutions, what unparalleled alterations we have had in these nations: persons, things, forms of government of old established, and newly framed constitutions,[53] we have seen all obnoxious to change or ruin.

This Is a Mighty Work of God

Secondly, it is no less certain, that we may say concerning all these things, "Come and see what God hath wrought." And as to these desolations of nations, ruin of families, alterations of governments, we may say of them all, as the psalmist, "Come, behold the works of the Lord, what desolations he hath made in the earth" (Ps. 46:8). It is his work, he has done it himself: there is no "evil in the city, and the Lord has not done it" (Amos 3:6). Have there been any exaltations of men, recoveries from depression, relief of the oppressed, establishments of new frames and order of things? It has been all from him (Dan. 2:21; 4:32). Indeed the days wherein we live are full of practical atheism; some out of mere stoutness of heart and innate unbelief will take no notice of God in all these things.[54] "The wicked through the pride of his countenance, will not seek after God: God is not in all his thoughts" (Ps. 10:4). As things have been, so they suppose they are, and will be; but as to the consideration of him who disposes of all as seems good unto him, they are strangers unto it. Some have had their lusts enraged, and themselves so provoked and disappointed,

51 See Luke 24:18.

52 Heb. 12:27.

53 The "newly framed constitutions" is probably a reference to the Instrument of Government (1653–1657).

54 Isa. 9:9.

that flying upon the instruments which God has used, they have been filled with prejudice, and utterly blinded as to any discovery of the ways or work of God in these revolutions. Some have been utterly cast down in their thoughts, because they have not been able to discover the righteousness, beauty, and order, of the ways of God; his footsteps having been in the deep, while his paths have not been known.[55] And some having found an open door for the satisfaction of their lusts, pride, covetousness, ambition, love of the world, reputation, vainglory, and uncleanness; have been so greedily engaged in the pursuit of them, that they have taken little or no notice of the hand of God in these things. And others are at a stand like the Philistine priests and diviners (1 Sam. 6:9).[56] They know not whether all this has been from the hand of God, or whether some chance has befallen us. I shall not need to mention those in Isaiah 47:13: "astrologers, star-gazers, and monthly prognosticators," who have endeavored also to divert the thoughts of unbelieving, foolish men, from a due consideration of the author of all our revolutions.[57] To all which I shall answer in general in the words of Hannah, "God hath done all these things" (1 Sam. 2:3–9); and men that will not take notice of him, and his proceedings, shall at length be forced so to do (Isa. 26:11).[58]

Statement of the Main Question to Determine

These things being premised; one principal inquiry, which must be the bottom and foundation of the ensuing directions, is, whether it may appear that

55 Ps. 77:19.

56 Owen appealed to this example of uncertainty in *Ebenezer* (1648) and *The Advantage of the Kingdom* (1651). For the first sermon, see *Complete Works of John Owen*, 18:288. The second sermon is included in this volume.

57 Earlier in the decade, Owen and his colleagues had spoken of "that abominable Cheat of Judiciall Astrology." See *The Humble Proposals of Mr Owen, Mr Tho Goodwin, Mr Nye, Mr Sympson and Other Ministers* (London, 1652), 6. Here, by the reference to Isaiah, Owen is locating astrology in the ongoing conflict between the true church of Christ and the false church of Babylon and presenting it as a kind of false prophecy that diverted the foolish away from a consideration of the work of divine providence in what is here referred to as "all our revolutions." At this time, there was significant interest in the judicial astrology practiced by people like William Lilly (1602–1681). See, e.g., Lilly's *Merlini Anglici Ephemeris: Astrological Predictions for the Year 1657* (London, 1657). At the time of this sermon, Lilly was selling thirty thousand almanacs each year, and his work was appearing in a number of newspapers and pamphlets. For further discussion, see Bernard S. Capp, *Astrology and the Popular Press: English Almanacs 1500–1800* (London: Faber and Faber, 1979), 44, 48, 72–88.

58 Owen appealed to this text on a number of occasions as he explained how "judicial blindness" resulted in "devouring envy." See *Ebenezer* (1648), *The Advantage of the Kingdom* (1651), and *God's Work in Founding Zion* (1656). For the first sermon, see *Complete Works of John Owen*, 18:264. The other two sermons are included in this volume.

these providential alterations and dissolutions have related to Christ and his interest in the world in an especial manner?

That we may yet a little farther clear our way, you may farther observe, what I intend, by relating unto Christ and his church in an especial manner.

1. Whereas the Lord Christ is, by the appointment of the Father, made "heir of all things" (Heb. 1:2), and "hath all judgment committed unto him,"[59] over all flesh, in all the world; which include his right to send his gospel into what nation and place he pleases: so all the alterations that are in the world, all things relate to him, and do lie in a remote tendency to the advancement of his glory. He will work out his own glorious ends from all the breakings of all the nations in the world; even where the interest of his gospel seems outwardly to be very little or nothing at all. But it is not in this sense that we make our inquiry; for so there would be nothing peculiar in the works that have been among us.

2. Things may relate unto Christ and his church, upon the account of special promise. Christ has a special and peculiar concernment in providential dissolutions, when they so relate to him; and that appears in these things:

(1) When the judgments that are exercised in such a dispensation, flow from provocations given unto the Lord Christ, upon the account of his church. So Isaiah 34:8.[60] All the dissolutions mentioned of the heavens and the earth (ver. 4),[61] were on Zion's account; and the controversy that Christ had with Idumea[62] about her. So the day of vengeance is the year of the redeemed (Isa. 63:4). Whence in such a day, the saints themselves are stirred up to take notice that the desolations wrought in the earth, are on their account (Jer. 51:35) and so it is fully expressed in the ruin of anti-Christian Babylon, in the Revelations:[63] where then there is a peculiar relation of any dissolving providence unto Christ and his church, the judgments exerted in and under it, regard the vengeance of the church, and proceed from the provocations of Christ on that account.

(2) Some promises made unto Christ concerning his inheritance; some promises of Christ unto his church are in such a day, brought forth unto

59 John 5:22.

60 Owen made the same point about the "recompense for the controversy of Zion" in *Ebenezer* (1648), *The Shaking and Translating of Heaven and Earth* (1649), and *God's Work in Founding Zion* (1656). For the first sermon, see *Complete Works of John Owen*, 18:267, and for the second, see 18:459. The third sermon is included in this volume.

61 I.e., Isa. 34:4. As he explained in *The Shaking and Translating of Heaven and Earth* (1649), these dissolutions were of the "government and tyranny . . . of Idumea." See *Complete Works of John Owen*, 18:426.

62 I.e., Edom.

63 In *Ebenezer* (1648) Owen linked Jer. 51:35 to Rev. 16:19–20. See *Complete Works of John Owen*, 18:267.

accomplishment. The promises of Christ to the church are of two sorts: first, general, essential to the new covenant: and these belong equally to all saints, of all ages, in all places, not to one more than another. Every saint has an equal right and interest in the essential promises of the covenant with any other saint whatever; there is no difference, but one God, Lord, and Father of all, is good unto them all alike. And, secondly, there are promises which are peculiarly suited to the several states and conditions into which the visible kingdom of Christ is in his wisdom to be brought in several ages. Such are the promises of the calling of the Jews, of the destruction of Antichrist, of the increase of light in the latter days, of the peace, rest, and prosperity of the church in some times or ages, after trials and tribulation. Now they are the promises of this latter sort, that relate unto providential dispensations.

Four Reasons for Confidence

Having premised these things, I shall now briefly offer some grounds of hope, that such have been the alterations and dissolutions wherein we have been exercised in this generation.

The Saints Have Experienced Communion with God

First, because very many of the saints of God have obtained real, evident, soul-refreshing communion with Christ in and about these things, on this foundation, that the things on the wheel among us have had a peculiar relation unto him. There is nothing of more certainty to the souls of any, than what they have real, spiritual experience of. When the things about which they are conversant lie only in notion, and are rationally discoursed or debated, much deceit may lie under all. But when things between God and the soul come to be realized by practical experience, they give a never-failing certainty of themselves. Now by holding communion about these things with Christ, I understand the exercise of faith, love, hope, expectation, delight on and in Christ on the one hand, and the receiving relief, supportment, consolation, joy, patience, perseverance on the other: from both which, holiness, faithfulness, and thankfulness have proceeded and been increased. Now this communion with Christ, in and about the works of his providence among us, very many of the saints have obtained; and, which is the height and complement of it, died in the clear visions of Christ in such communion. Now there are two things that offer sufficient security against any deceit or mistake in this thing.

1. The goodness, care and faithfulness of God toward his own, which will not suffer us to fear that he would lead all his people into such a temptation, wherein, in their chiefest communion, as they apprehended, with himself,

they should feed on the wind and delusion. If the foundation of all this intercourse with God, was false, and not according to his mind, then so was the whole superstructure. Now that God for many years should lead his people into a way of prayer, faith, hope, thankfulness, and yet all false and an abominable thing, because all leaning on a false ground and supposition, none that consider his goodness and tender pity toward his own, with the delight of his soul in their worship and ways, can once imagine. It is true, men may be zealously engaged in ways and acts of worship, and that all their lives, wherein they think they do God good service; and yet both they and their service be abominated by him forever. But men cannot do so in faith, love, obedience, thankfulness, which alone we speak of. At least, he will not suffer his saints to do so, of whom alone we speak. We have then the tender mercies and faithfulness of God to assure us in this case.

2. The self-evidencing efficacy of faith in spiritual experiences strengthens their persuasion. Many doubtless may persuade themselves that they have communion with God, and yet feed upon ashes, and a deceived heart turns them aside.[64] The principle of such a delusion, I shall not now lay open. But when it is indeed obtained by faith, it is always accompanied with a soul-quieting, refreshing evidence; for faith in its operation, will evince itself to the soul where it is. I do not say, it always does so. It may be so clouded with darkness of mind; so overpowered by temptations, that in its most spiritual and genuine acting, it may be hid from the soul wherein it is, which we find to be the condition of many a gracious soul; but in itself, it clears up its own actings. Things that have a self-evidencing power, may be hindered from exerting it; but when they do exert it, it is evident. Put a candle under a bushel, it cannot be seen; but take away the hindrance, and it manifests itself.[65] It is so in faith, and its actings. They may be so clouded to the soul itself in which they act; that it may not be able to attain any comforting evidence of it. But take away the bushel, fear, prejudices, temptations, corrupt reasonings, and it will assure the soul of itself and its working. Neither is its working more evident than its fruit, or the product of its operations in the soul; it brings forth love, rest, peace, all with a spiritual sense upon the heart and spirit. Now these have been in this thing so evident in the souls of the saints, that they have bespoken that faith which cannot deceive nor be deceived.

The bottom then of the communion which the saints had with Christ in this work, and have, must either be faith or fancy: if faith, then the communion

64 Isa. 44:20.

65 See Matt. 5:15.

was and is real, and the work true that it is built upon. That it was not, that it is not the fancy or imagination of a deluded heart, may appear from these considerations:

(1) From its extent. We know it possessed the minds of the universality of believers in this nation, who were not, nor are at this day combined in our political interest, but are woefully divided among themselves;[66] yet have all had, more or less, this persuasion of the work relating unto Christ. Now that this should be any corrupt imagination, seems to me impossible. I speak not of outward actions and proceedings; for so, I know whole nations may politically combine in evil; though I will not believe that ever the generality of the saints of Christ shall do so. But I speak of the frame of their hearts and spirits as to communion with Christ in faith and love, whereunto no outward reasonings or interests could influence them in the least: *Digitus Dei est hoc*.[67]

(2) It appears from the permanency, and flourishing of this principle in straits and difficulties. A corrupt imagination, be it never so strong and vigorous in its season, and while its food is administered to it, in the temptation it lives upon; yet in trials, great and pressing, it sinks and withers; or if the difficulty continue, for the most part, unless, where it falls on some natures of an unconquerable pertinacy,[68] utterly vanishes. But now, this principle of the saints' communion with Christ about the work of our generation, was never more active, vigorous, and flourishing, did never more evidence itself to be of a divine extract, than in the greatest straits and difficulties, in the mouth and entrance of the greatest deaths. Then did it commonly rise up to its greatest heights and assurance. Our temptations, whether Christ be in this work or no, have, for the most part, befallen us since we had deliverance from pressing, bloody troubles. And I think I may say, that there are very many saints in these nations, who can truly say, that the best and the most comfortable days that ever they saw in their lives, were those wherein they were exercised with the greatest fears, dangers and troubles, and that upon the account of the strengthening of this principle of communion with Christ. And in very many has it been tried out to the death, when corrupt fancies were of little worth.

(3) It appears from the fruits of this persuasion. Every corrupt imagination and fancy is of the flesh; and the works of the flesh are manifest.[69] Whatever

66 A reference to the divided political interests among the godly.

67 Lat. "This is the finger of God." See Ex. 8:19. Owen identified the *digitus Dei* in various works of providence in his sermons *Ebenezer* (1648) and his June 1649 sermon *Human Power Defeated*. For the first sermon, see *Complete Works of John Owen*, 18:262, and for the second, see 18:470.

68 I.e., adhering resolutely to an opinion.

69 Gal. 5:19.

it may do in conjunction with convictions and for a season, yet in itself, and in a course it will bring forth no fruit, but what tends to the satisfaction of the flesh. But now, the principle under consideration, did bring forth fruits unto God; in godliness and righteousness.

Objections Answered

But you will say, "Do we not see what fruit it has brought forth? Is not the land full of the steam of the lusts of men engaged in the work of this age? Can hell itself afford a worse savour than is sent forth by many of them?"

Answ[er] 1. Very many who have been engaged, never pretended to ought[70] of this principle, but followed professedly on carnal, at best rational and humane[71] accounts solely. Now these being men of the world, and being fallen into days of notable temptations, no wonder if their lusts work and tumultuate, and that to purpose. The principle is not to suffer for their miscarriages who renounce it.

Answ[er] 2. There was a mixed multitude which in this business went up with the people of God,[72] who pretended to this principle indeed, and talked, and spoke of the interest of Christ; but knowing nothing of the power of it, when these men were brought into the wilderness, and there met with provocations on the one hand, and temptations on the other, they fell a lusting:[73] and indeed they have pursued and acted their lusts to purpose also, which have been indeed the more abominable; in that some of them have still the impudence to pretend this principle of faith as to the interest of Christ, which teaches no such things, nor produces any such fruits as they abound withal.

Answ[er] 3. Many who have really the power of this principle in them, have yet been overpowered by temptations, and have brought forth fruits directly opposite unto that obedience, and holiness, and self-denial, which the principle spoken of tends unto. This, for the most part, has fallen out since deliverance came in, and so the vigor of faith, raised by daily exercise, was much decayed. None therefore of these things can be charged on the principle itself, whose natural, genuine effects we have experienced to be such as no corrupt fancy or imagination could produce.

Many other reasons of this nature might be insisted on; but this is my first ground.

70 I.e., anything.

71 I.e., civil and courteous.

72 Ex. 12:38.

73 Num. 11:4.

Oppression and Idolatry Have Been Removed

Secondly, because in this, much work has been really done for Christ. Whatever have been the designs of any, or all of the sons of men, Christ has done so much for himself, as I can from thence with confidence conclude, that the whole has related unto him. Indeed in the work he does, his interest ofttimes lies very much in the dark, yea, is utterly hid from the instruments he employs. Little did the Medes and Persians think, in the destruction of Babylon,[74] that they were executing the vengeance of Zion, and the blood of Jerusalem, a poor city ruined sixty or seventy years before.[75] And when the Romans destroyed Jerusalem, little did they think whose work they had in hand.[76] And whatever instruments thought or intended, Christ has done notable work for himself. The destruction, of false worship as established by a law, the casting down of combinations for persecution, are no small works.[77] I say, much work has been done for Christ. There was a generation of men that were risen to a strange height in the contempt of the Spirit, and ways of Christ, combined in a resolution to oppose and persecute all the appearance of him, either by light or holiness, in his saints, setting up an outside, formal worship, in opposition unto the spiritual worship of the gospel. And upon the account of the light and truth which he began to command forth in those days, an unspeakable aggravation attended their guilt; in the pursuit of whose design some were imprisoned, some banished into the ends of the earth, some beggared, many ruined and given up to death itself. Now what work has Christ made in these days on the men of that generation? What vengeance has he taken on them? This is certain, not to insist on particulars, that whatever new sort or combination of men may rise up in their spirit and design, and whatever success they may obtain, yet the generality of the men of that provocation, at least, the heads and rulers of it, are already sealed up under the indignation of the Lord Jesus, and the vengeance he takes for Zion. I shall not insist on more particulars; the wasting and destruction of the most eminent persecutors of the saints, the ruin and destruction of civil and ecclesiastical fabrics and combinations of men, designing the opposing and persecuting of the Spirit of Christ, the removal of all that false worship under the pretense whereof they persecuted all the spiritual appearances of Christ, has been all work done for him.

74 The fall of Babylon to the Medes and Persians under Cyrus, ca. 537 BC.

75 The destruction of Jerusalem by Nebuchadnezzar, ca. 588 BC, having initially carried away the treasures of the city, ca. 599 BC.

76 The fall of Jerusalem to Romans under Titus in AD 70.

77 This is a reference to the Laudian era of the 1630s.

Gospel Light Has Come into the Darkness

Thirdly, the breaking forth of much glorious gospel light under this dispensation, evinces its relation unto Christ. Look upon the like outward work at any other time in the world. What is the issue of war, blood, confusion? Is it not darkness, ignorance, blindness, barrenness? Has it not been so in other places of the world? But now, in the coming forth of Christ, though he has a sword in one hand, yet he has the sun in the other;[78] though he cause darkness in the destruction and desolation that attend his vengeance, yet he gives light and faith to his saints (Mal. 4:1–2). Christ never comes for vengeance only; his chief design is love. Love brings forth light; and that which reveals him more to his saints, and which endears his saints more to him. But I have manifested before, that he brings light with him; and he has done so in this dispensation. Light as to the mysteries of the gospel; light as to the riches of his grace; light as to the way of his worship, of his ordinances and institutions, has broken out among us. As Daniel 12:4. It is such a day he speaks of.

Objection Answered

I know how obnoxious this observation is to a sad objection. "Call you these days of light, and knowledge? Say you that truth has shined forth, or been diffused? Is it increased, or more scattered abroad? Is not the contrary true?"

Answ[er]. It cannot be denied, but that many grievous and enormous abominations have been broached in these times under the name and pretense of light and truth. But is that singular to these days? Has it not been so upon every appearance of Christ? As the light has been, so has been the pretense of it in error and darkness. No sooner was Christ come in the flesh, but instantly there were many false Christs: "Lo, here is Christ," and, "There is Christ,"[79] was common language in those days; as, "This is the only way," and "That is the only way," is now; and yet the true Christ was in the world. And whatever light at any time comes forth, some mock; false light about the same thing immediately breaks forth. So was it in the first spreading of the gospel; so in the late Reformation, and so in our days; and this is no evidence against the coming of Christ, but rather for it. For,

1. Satan pours out this flood of abominations on purpose to bring an ill report upon the truth and light that is sent out by Christ.[80] The great prejudice against truth in the world is, that it is new. "He seems to be a setter forth of

78 Rev. 1:16.

79 Matt. 24:23.

80 Rev. 12:15.

strange" or new "gods," say they of Paul, because he preached "Jesus and the resurrection."[81] To increase this prejudice, the devil with it or after it sends forth his darkness; which, first, enables the world to load the truth itself with reproaches, while it comes accompanied with such follies, as though it also were of the number. Secondly, it disables weak friends to find out and close with the truth amid so many false pretenders. Where much false money is abroad in the world, every man cannot discern, and receive only that which is good. Much less will men always keep safe, when they are so unstable, and uncertain, as they are for the most part, about choosing of truth.

2. God permits it so to be,

(1) For the trial of careless professors. There "must" be "heresies," that the "approved" may be tried.[82] Most men are apt to content themselves with a lazy profession. They will hold to the truth while nothing appears but truth. Let error come with the same pretenses and advantage, they are for that also. Now, God delights to judge such persons even in this world; to manifest that they are not of the truth, that they never received it in the love thereof. And he sifts and tries the elect by it, and that for many advantages, not now to be insisted on. As, first, that they may experiment the efficacy of truth: secondly, his power in their preservation: thirdly, that they may hold truth upon firm and abiding grounds.

(2) God permits it to set a greater luster and esteem upon truth. Truth, when it is sought after, when it is contended for, when it is experimented in its power and efficacy, is rendered glorious and beautiful; and all these with innumerable other advantages it has by the competition that is set up against it by error. When men keep to the truth by the power of God, and the sense of its sweetness and usefulness to their own souls, and shall see some by their errors turned aside to one abomination, some to another, some made to wither by them and under them, they discern the excellency of the truth they embrace. So that notwithstanding this exception, the observation stands good.

The Evidence Suggests That Prophecy Is Being Fulfilled

Fourthly, it appears from the general nature of the dispensation itself, which clearly answers the predictions that are of the great works to be accomplished in the latter days, upon the account of Christ and his church. This is a general head, whose particulars I shall not enter into. They cannot be managed without a consideration of all, at least, of the most principal prophecies of the last

81 Acts 17:18.

82 1 Cor. 11:19.

times, and of the kingdom of Christ as to its enlargement, beauty, and glory in them; too large a task for me to enter upon at present.

And these are some of the grounds on which I am persuaded, that the alterations and providential dissolutions of these days, have related unto and do lie in a subserviency to the interest of Christ and his church; whatever be the issue of the individual persons who have been engaged therein.

Come we now to the uses.[83]

FIRST MAIN APPLICATION: EXAMINATION OF THE RESPONSE TO THIS SPECIAL COMING OF CHRIST

Use 1. Of trial or examination.

Has Christ for many years now been in an especial manner come among us? Do these alterations relate to him and his interest; and so require universal holiness and godliness? Let us then in the first place see, whether in their several stations, the men of this generation have walked answerable to such a dispensation. Christ indeed has done his work; but have we done ours? He has destroyed many of his enemies, judged false professors, hardened and blinded the wicked world, sent out his Spirit to plead with his people, and taken vengeance on their inventions,[84] he has given out plentiful measures of truth and light: but now the whole inquiry is, whether all or any of us have answered the mind of Christ in these dispensations, and prepared ourselves to meet him as becomes his greatness and holiness?

The Response of the Nation in General

For the generality of the people of the nation, Christ has been pleading with them about their unbelief, worldliness, atheism, and contempt of the gospel. And what has been the issue? Alas! He that was filthy is filthy still;[85] he that was profane is so still; swearers, drunkards, and other vicious persons are so still. Where is that man in a thousand in the nation, that takes notice of any peculiar plea of Christ with him about his sin, in any of these dispensations? One cries out of one party of men, another curses another party,[86] a third is

83 In the 1721 edition, the following uses are described as the third part of the sermon.

84 Ps. 99:8.

85 Rev. 22:11.

86 For the types of parties that may be in view, consider the following examples: In Secretary Thurloe's account of the Sindercombe plot, he spoke of the two main parties involved in it as the "Levelling party" and "the late king's party." At this time the Cromwellian "court" party was dividing into rival civilian and army interests that would culminate in the offer of the crown to Cromwell. See Patrick Little, "John Thurloe and the Offer of the Crown to Oliver Cromwell,"

angry with God himself; but as to the call of Christ in his mighty appearances, who almost takes any notice of it? The abominable pride, folly, vanity, luxury that are found in this city, testify to their faces that the voice of wisdom is not heard in the cry of fools. And whereas Christ's peculiar controversy with this nation has been about the contempt of the gospel; is there any ground got upon the generality of men? Is any reformation wrought on this account among them? Nay, may we not say freely, that there is a greater spirit of hatred, enmity, and opposition to Christ, and the gospel risen up in the nation than ever before? Light has provoked and enraged them, so that they hate the gospel more than ever. How mad are the generality of the people on and after their idols, their old superstitious ways of worship, which Christ has witnessed against? What an enmity against the very doctrine of the gospel? What a combination in all places is there against the reforming dispensation of it? And is this any good omen of a comfortable issue of this dispensation? Is not Christ ready to say of such a people, "Why should you be smitten any more, you will revolt more and more?"[87] and to swear in his wrath that they shall not enter into his rest?[88] Nay, may he not justly take his gospel from us, and give it to a people that will bring forth fruit?[89] O England, that in this your day you had known the things of your peace! I fear they will be hidden from you.[90] The temptations of the day, the divisions of your teachers, with other their miscarriages, and your own lusts, have deceived thee, and without mercy, insuperable mercy, will ruin you. Shall this shame be your glory that Christ has not conquered you, that you have hardened yourself against him?

The Response of the Saints in Particular

But passing them let us inquire, whether the mind of Christ has in these dispensations, been answered in a due manner by the saints themselves? Have they made it their business to meet him "in all holy conversation and godliness?" Indeed to me, the contrary appears upon these considerations.

(1) Their great differences among themselves about lesser things.
(2) Their little difference from the world in great things.

---

in *Oliver Cromwell: New Perspectives*, ed. Patrick Little (Basingstoke, UK: Palgrave Macmillan, 2009), 220. There were also different parties and alliances within the Scottish Church that were a cause of debate in London. See Patrick Little, *Lord Broghill and the Cromwellian Union with Ireland and Scotland* (Woodbridge, UK: Boydell, 2004), 103–9.

87 Isa. 1:5.

88 Ps. 95:11; Heb. 3:11.

89 See Matt. 3:8; Luke 3:8.

90 See Luke 19:42.

(3) The general miscarriage of them all, in things prejudicial to the progress of the gospel.
(4) The particular deviation of some into ways of scandal and offense.
(5) The backsliding of most if not of all of them.

Division, Rather Than Unity, and Even the Suggestion of Persecution

(1) Consider their great differences among themselves about lesser things. I cannot insist on the weight that is laid by our Savior on the union of his disciples; with the condescension and love which he requires of them to that purpose; the motives and exhortations given by the Holy Ghost unto them on that account; the provision of principles and means made in the gospel for it; the necessity of it to the promotion of the interest of Christ in the world; the benefit and advantage of it to the saints themselves; the testimony given by it to the power of Christ, and truth of his word; the blasphemies and woeful soul-ruining offenses that ensue on the contrary frame; the weakening of faith, hindrance of prayer, quenching of zeal, strengthening of the men of the world, that attend the neglect of it. I must not, I say, insist on these things; but see John 17:21–23, and Philippians 2:1–3, of a hundred places that might be mentioned; how little the mind of Christ, and his expectation at his coming has been answered by his saints in this particular, is evident unto all.

[1] Who is there almost who having got any private opinion, true or false, wherein he differs from all or any of his brethren, who is not ready to proclaim it, without due regard to scandal and division, and even to quarrel with and divide from all that will not think as he thinks, and speak as he speaks? Now, the pride, self-fullness, vanity of mind, unlikeness to Christ, folly, want of faith and love that is in such a frame can never be expressed, nor sufficiently lamented. Christ abhors such a frame of spirit, as he does the pollution of the world.

[2] Neither is this all; but men will lay more weight on their mint and cummin,[91] on the lesser things wherein they differ from their brethren, spend more time about them, write more books of them, labor more in their prosecution, than they will do in and about the weighty things of law and gospel; all which will appear at length to have been but the laying of hay and stubble on the foundation, that must be consumed.[92]

[3] And farther; men fall to judging and censuring each other, as to their interest in Christ, or their eternal condition. By what rule? The everlasting gospel? The covenant of grace? No; but of the disciples: "Master, they follow

91 Matt. 23:23.

92 1 Cor. 3:12.

not with us."[93] They that believe not our opinion, we are apt to think believe not in Jesus Christ; and because we delight not in them, that Christ does not delight in them. This digs up the roots of love, weakens prayer, increases evil surmises, which are of the works of the flesh, genders strife, and contempt; things that the soul of Christ abhors.

[4] The abomination of this wickedness ends not here; persecution, banishment, the blood of one another, has on this account lain in the hearts and minds of some of the saints themselves:[94] not only have expressions to that purpose broken out from particular men; but it is to be feared, that designs for it have been managed by parties and combinations. And are they not ready to dress up one another with such names and titles as may fit them for ruin? Sectaries,[95] heretics, schismatics on the one side; priests, anti-Christian dogs on the other: and all this while Christ is in the midst of us! And does this answer the expectation of Christ? Is this a preparation to meet him "in all holy conversation and godliness?" Can we render ourselves more unlike him, more unmeet for communion with him? Are not saints ready to join with the world against saints? To take the vilest men into their bosom that will close with them in defaming, deriding, or it may be, destroying their brethren? Does Christ look for this usage in the house of his friends?

Many Different Forms of Worldliness

(2) Consider their little difference from the world in great things. The great separation that Christ requires and commands of his saints, is, from the world: he died to redeem them from it, and out of it; to deliver them from the present evil world, the ways, works, fellowship, and ends of it; so providing, that in all holy conversation his people should "dwell alone," and "not be reckoned among the nations."[96]

Now, there are five things wherein Christ calls for his own to be differenced from the world, and the men thereof.

[1] In spirit.
[2] In principle.

93 Luke 9:49.

94 The anti-Trinitarian John Biddle had been banished to the Isles of Scilly in October 1655 and there had been discussion about the banishment of James Nayler. See Gwenda Morgan and Peter Rushton, *Banishment in the Early Atlantic World: Convicts, Rebels and Slaves* (London: Bloomsbury, 2013), 25. The fact that so many members of Parliament were willing to support the death penalty for Nayler illustrates the grave concerns surrounding the spread of sectarianism.

95 I.e., adherents of schismatic or heretical groups.

96 Num. 23:9.

[3] In conversation.

[4] In ends.

[5] In worship.

[1] In spirit. He tells us everywhere, that it is one Spirit that is in his, another that is in the world. "Greater is he that is in you, than he that is in the world" (1 John 4:4). There is a "he" in you, and a "he" in the world, and they are different and opposite. There is dwelling in you "the Spirit of truth," which the world "cannot receive," nor doth it know him (John 14:17). And when his disciples began to act in the power of a carnal spirit, he tells them they knew not what spirit they were of.[97]

[2] In principle. The principle that Christ requires in his saints is faith, working by love,[98] and guided by that wisdom which is from above.[99] Here are the saints' principles, I mean, should be so of all their operations (1 Tim. 1:5). A pure heart, and love, which is the end of all faith, is their great principle; this cleanses the conscience, and so sets them on work; by this they take in strength for operation from Christ, without whom they can do nothing (John 15:5). By this they receive light and guidance from Christ, and that wisdom which is from above, enabling them to order their affairs with discretion (James 3:17–18). Now the principle that is in the world, is self, self-acted and guided by carnal wisdom, which is "sensual" and "devilish";[100] on the account whereof, they despise the principle and actings of the saints (Ps. 14:6).

[3] In conversation. He has redeemed us from a "vain conversation" (1 Pet. 1:18). There is a peculiar emphasis put upon a conversation that becomes the gospel. There is a twofold conversation; one that becomes the world and the men of the world; another that becomes the gospel, and the profession thereof: that these be kept unmixed is the great exhortation of the apostle (Rom. 12:2). And if you would know wherein a worldly conversation consists, the apostle tells us, 1 John 2:16. A conversation wherein any of these things bear sway, is a conversation of this world. That all holiness, all manner of holiness, universal holiness and godliness, is in the gospel conversation to which the saints are called, shall be afterward spoken unto.

[4] In ends. There is a double end of men's working and acting in this world: {1} General, which regulates the course of their lives and conversations: {2}

97 Luke 9:55.

98 Gal. 5:6.

99 James 3:17.

100 James 3:15.

Particular, which regulates their particular actings and works: and in both these are the saints and the world differenced.

{1} The general end of the saints is the glory of God; this lies in their eye, in their design: how God may be glorified by them, his name exalted, his interest promoted; this way the bent of their minds and spirits tends. The general end of the men of the world is self; all is resolved into self; whatever they do or act in public or private, whatever their pretense be, yet self is their end: self-admiration, self-ostentation, self-satisfaction, all centers in self: sometimes indeed they may perform things that seem to be of a public tendency, for the good of mankind, the good of nations, yea, it may be the good of the church; so that it is hard for themselves to discover, or for others to charge them, it may be, that they act for self. But there are these two things that will evince men to make self their general end and aim, even then when they act for public ends.

1st. This is a rule that will not fail men: whatever in public actings is not done with a single eye for the glory of God, is done for self. These two divide all the general ends of men; and where one is not enthroned, the other is. Now though some men may so far proceed in public actings, that it may not be evident wherein their self-interest lies, though that also be but seldom, yet if they do not eye the glory of God with a single eye in these their actings, it is all for self, and so it will be found at the last day. Now how few will be left not turning into self on this rule, now pretenses run so high of public aims, might be easily evinced. It were no hard matter to discover, how in things of a public tendency, men make some fleshly imagination or other the god they worship; so that be enthroned, they are little solicitous about the glory of God himself.[101]

2nd. The difference of these ends even in public actings may be seen from the ways, means, and frame of spirit in which they are carried on. Let men pretend what they will to public ends, yet if they press after them with a proud, carnal, wrathful, envious spirit, by the ways, wisdom, and in the spirit of the world, without faith and submission to God, it is self and not God that is their aim. And this also might be improved to strip men of

101 The double mention of enthronement in the context of "public actings" is suggestive in the context of the offer of the crown to Cromwell. In late March 1657, Parliament debated the clause of the new constitution that stated that Cromwell should "assume the Name, Style, Title, and Office of King of England, Scotland and Ireland." See Little, "John Thurloe and the Offer of the Crown to Oliver Cromwell," 216–43; Jonathan Fitzgibbons, "Hereditary Succession and the Cromwellian Protectorate: The Offer of the Crown Reconsidered," *English History Review* 128, no. 534 (2013): 1095–128.

glorying in their public designs, were that my present business. Jehu's spirit spoiled his work.[102]

{2} There is a particular end that regulates the public actings of men. This in the saints is their doing the work of their generation; that, as Noah, they may walk with God in their generation.[103] This is their integrity as to the special course of their lives, and their particular employment, how they may fulfill the work of their generation. The special end of the men of the world, is the satisfaction of one particular lust or other. "Will this increase my wealth, my power, my carnal interest in this world, my reputation for wisdom and ability, or give me advantage to grow in this or that corrupt end in particular?" This is the secret inquiry of their deceived hearts; this influences and regulates all their particular actings.

[5] As to their separation in worship, I shall only point to that one place, and leave it, 2 Corinthians 6:14–18 and 7:1, which belongs to that discourse.

Now I wish I had a more difficult task in hand: I wish it were harder for me to manage any principle of conviction, that we have not been prepared to meet Christ in his coming, from this consideration of our little difference from the world in these great things of principle, spirit, walking, ends, and worship. For—

What a fleshly, wrathful, carnal, worldly spirit has discovered itself in many professors; nay, in the most! How little of the humble, lowly, meek, loving spirit of Christ? Many think it their glory to be unlike Christ in the spirit of their minds, high, heady, self-full, proud, revengeful. What little difference between them and the men of the world? How like to one another? What oneness is found in them? Is this to learn Christ?[104] To put on Christ?[105] Is this the image of Christ that manifests itself in most professors? Nor—

Are they at a distance from the world, as to the principle of their walking and working. Do they walk by faith, and work by faith? Are they guided by the wisdom that is from above? Make they God their refuge? Or are any men more dipped into a principle of carnal wisdom, than most professors are? To seek counsel of God, to take the law of their proceedings at his mouth, to look up to him for guidance and direction, to derive strength from the Lord Christ by believing for the work of their employments; in how few are these things found? Their own wisdom, their own counsel, their own contrivance,

102 2 Kings 10:16.

103 Gen. 6:9.

104 Eph. 4:20.

105 Gal. 3:27.

their own abilities, shall do their work. Carnal policy and fleshly wisdom are "their net" and "drag."[106]

Moreover, what is our conversation? How like the world in our persons, in our families, in our spirits, callings, in whatever the world may properly call its own? Professors have justled[107] the men of the world out of the possession of the ways of the world. How few are found walking in a world-condemning conversation? A gospel-glorifying conversation? A fruitful, holy conversation? We are known from the world by word more than by deed; which is not the way that James directs us unto.[108]

I might go through with the rest of the considerations mentioned, and manifest that there is another evil found among us: for as we have great differences among ourselves about little things, so we have little difference from the world in those which are great and weighty.

Failures with Respect to the Propagation of the Gospel

(3) Consider the general miscarriage almost of all professors in things prejudicial to the advancement of the gospel; the pretense, whereof we have served ourselves all along, has been, of the furtherance, propagation, and advancement of the gospel. Our Lord Christ has sent out light, and given opportunities suitable unto such a design. Never greater advantages, nor greater opportunities from the foundation of the world. If ever they are required at the hands of this generation, they will be found to have been so: whence then has it been, that the work has not gone on and prospered? Why does it yet stick? Has it not been from the woeful miscarriage of those, who were looked on as the means and instruments of carrying it on? Have there been a few saints in a place? It is odds,[109] that they have been at variance among themselves, and made sport for the vain multitude by their divisions: or they have walked frowardly,[110] provokingly, uselessly, worldly, that their pretense for the gospel has been despised, because of their persons. Have they, as men concerned in the honor of Christ and the gospel, as men enjoying the blessed principle of his Spirit, labored to be useful, fruitful, to do good to all, to be meek, lowly, self-denying, charitable, abounding in good works, patient toward opposers, not reviling again, not returning evil for evil, bearing, suffering, committing all to Christ? Alas! How few are there who

106 Hab. 1:15–16.

107 I.e., contended for the best place by pushing another away from it, vied for advantage.

108 James 1:22.

109 I.e., it is likely.

110 I.e., perversely and unwillingly.

have so walked? Could some see believers making it their business to be like Christ in the world, to deny themselves as he did, to do good to all as he did, to be patient under persecution and reproaches as he was to be tender, pitiful, merciful, like him, to abide in faith and prayer as he did; what might we not expect, as to the advancement of the gospel among us? We complain of cold preaching among ministers, of dead and dull attendance in hearers, of contempt of the word in the most, whereby the power of the gospel is kept within narrow bounds; but the truth is, the prejudices that have been raised by the miscarriages of professors, have had a greater influence unto that evil event, than any of the rest. And has this been to meet Christ in his coming?

Scandalous Sin

(4) Of the like nature are the scandalous offenses of many. I shall not insist on the scandalous apostasies of many professors, who, some by one great sin, some by another, are fallen off from the profession of the gospel. I wish that too many other instances might not be found among them that remain. Are there not some proud unto scandal, or sensual unto scandal, or covetous unto scandal, or negligent of their families and relations unto scandal, or conformable to the ways, customs, and fashions of the world unto scandal? I wish no such things might be found among us.

Spiritual Backsliding

(5) Add hereunto, the general backsliding, or going back from God, that is among professors; we scarce seem to be the same generation of men that we were fifteen or sixteen years ago: some have utterly lost their principle.[111] Zeal for God, reformation, purity of ordinances, interest of Christ in his saints, are things to be despised, things that have no concernment in our condition and

111 This is most likely a reference to the events of 1641–1642. The year 1641 became identified as the "golden year" and *annus mirabilis* because it was the time of the following events: the move to suppress Arminian innovations (February); Parliament being made secure by the Triennial Act and the Act for Parliamentary continuance (May); and the abolition of the prerogative courts of Star Chamber and the ecclesiastical courts of High Commission (July). In November, the Commons passed its controversial Remonstrance of the State of the Kingdom, a scathing account of the people's grievances (among other things, it proposed that bishops be deprived of their votes in the House of Lords and that innovative religious ceremonies be removed). This sense was no doubt heightened by Owen's own profound religious experience when he heard an otherwise unknown preacher at St Mary's Aldermanbury during the winter of 1641–1642, at which time he appears to have gained assurance of salvation and therefore the conviction that he was among the saints. See John Asty, "Memoirs of the Life of John Owen," in *A Complete Collection of the Sermons of the Reverend and Learned John Owen* [. . .], ed. John Asty (London, 1721), v.

affairs; as though we had no more need of Christ, or his interest among us: and in the best, is not a fresh spirit of our present engagement almost lost?

But why should I insist farther on these things? Are not the things that have been spoken, sufficient for a rebuke, or a conviction at least, that the professing people of Christ have not walked as though they had a just respect to his coming, or his peculiar presence among them? May we not justly fear, that our multiplied provocations may at length prevail with him to withdraw, to put a stop to his work that is upon the wheel; not only to leave us to manifold entanglements in the carrying of it on, but also utterly to forsake it, to cast down the tower, and pluck up the hedge that he has made about his vineyard, and leave it to be laid waste?[112] He must have a heart like the flint in the rock of stone, that does not tremble at it. But complaints will not be our relief. That which is incumbent on us, if yet there may be hope, is our answering the exhortation in my text. If then any sense do fall upon our spirits, that Christ is come among us in a peculiar manner, in the providential alterations and dissolutions that have been among us; and that we have not hitherto demeaned ourselves as becomes them who are called to meet him, and to walk with him in such ways and paths as his among us have been; then, I say, let us apply ourselves in our next use to the exhortation that lies before us, to "all" manner of "holy conversation."

SECOND MAIN APPLICATION: EXHORTATION AND DIRECTION

Use 2. Of exhortation. That I say then which we are now to attend unto, is the exhortation that is included in this expression: "What manner of persons ought we to be?" To further the efficacy of this exhortation, give me leave to premise some few things.

Two Initial Premises about Special Motivations to Comprehensive Holiness

First, there are general reasons of holiness and godliness, and there are special motives unto them. I am not now dealing upon the general reasons of holiness on the account of the covenant of grace, and so shall not press it on those considerations, upon believers as such. But I speak of it in reference unto the peculiar motive mentioned in the text; namely, the providential dissolution of temporal concernments, and so speak to believers as men interested therein,

112 See Isa. 5:5; Matt. 21:33.

as persons whom Christ has a special regard unto in these his dispensations. It is one thing to say, "What manner of persons ought ye to be, whom God hath loved with an everlasting love,[113] whom Christ hath washed in his own blood,[114] who have received the Spirit of Christ?" and another to say, "Ye that are loved with an everlasting love, are washed in the blood of Christ, and made partakers of the Holy Ghost. Seeing that Christ is come among us, to the dissolution of the great things of the nations, what manner of persons ought you to be?" That is it in a peculiar pressing unto holiness on the account of the motive that is intended.

Secondly, there is a holiness and godliness that is required universally at all times, in all places and seasons, and in all persons whatever, by the gospel; and there is a peculiar improvement of that holiness and godliness at some seasons, and in some persons, that is not required at some times, and of some persons. Christ has work for all the grace of his people in this world; and according as opportunities for that work are presented unto them, they ought to stir up their grace for it. In the times of Christ's coming, he has great work to do for and by the holiness and godliness of his people: a great testimony is to be given to himself thereby; his work is much to be promoted by it; the world to be convinced, condemned; his judgments against them justified in the sight of all; and much more has Christ to do with the holiness of his people at such a season. Now it is this peculiar improvement of covenant gospel holiness that is required; not only that holiness that is indispensably incumbent on us by the virtue of the covenant, but that heightening and improvement of it which the season wherein we live, and the work that Christ has to do, do require of us.

These things being premised, let us now proceed to the management of our exhortation; and observe—

First Direction: Serious Consideration Must Be Given to The Promotion of Generational Holiness

(1) That the apostle calls us to a consideration how this work may be effected: "What manner of persons ought ye to be?" Consider with yourselves the equity of the matter, the greatness of the motive, and the ways whereby it may be answered. The business is not now to be left at an ordinary rate, nor unto private meditations; it is to be made a matter of solemn consideration and design; it is to be managed with advice and counsel: consider, I say, "what

113 Jer. 31:3.

114 See Rev. 1:5.

manner of persons." It is not about holiness in general that I speak, but about that holiness which becomes us in such a season. This then is the first part of this exhortation, that as to the improvement of holiness answerable to the season of this coming of Christ, we would carry it on by design, by counsel, by deliberate consideration; not only laboring to be holy ourselves, but to promote the work of holiness, the eminency, the activity, the usefulness of it, in one another, in all believers, so far as our prayers, exhortations, and examples, can reach. This the apostle pleads for on the same account [in] Hebrews 3:13 and Hebrews 10:23–24 to the same purpose. And we have the practice of it [in] Malachi 3:16. It was such a time and season as that we treat of, Christ was coming to his temple (Mal. 3:1–3). The earth was full of wickedness and contempt of him. What do the saints do? Do they content themselves with their ordinary measures? Do they keep all close to themselves? No, they confer, advise, consult, and that frequently, how, wherein, whereby, the expectation of their coming Lord may be answered.[115] The reasons, arguments, way of carrying on such a counsel and design, the apostle declares, "The time requires it, the duty is urgent, temptations are many, failings have been great, the Lord is nigh at hand" (Rom. 13:11–14). Let then believers enter together into this plot,[116] this design, draw as many as they can into it, promote it by all ways and means possible. Let them get together; make this their aim, their design, engage in it as the duty of their day, of their time and season. This would be a plot that the men of the world would have more just cause to fear, than ever they had of any, and yet dare not question, disturb, or interrupt. A design that would blow up their contrivance, disappoint their counsel, ruin their interest, shake heaven and earth.[117] Let everyone contribute the best of his counsel, the best of his grace, the best of his interest in heaven, the utmost of his self-denial, to the carrying of it on. Methinks we have dwelt long enough upon others' failings, fruitless, selfish designs; the world is full of the noise, the steam, the filth of them. Oh, that the stream of our endeavors might now be another way! Oh, that God would stir up some that might stand up and cry: "Who is for God? Who is on our

115 See Mal. 3:16.

116 It is plausible to see this language about a "plot" as alluding to the events surrounding Sindercombe's Plot to plant an incendiary bomb at the house of the Lord Protector in Whitehall. The plot had shown how central Cromwell was to the Protectorate and the future of the three nations. As Little puts it, "The protectorate was built around the protector, and his death would cause its collapse." This opened up the opportunity to revisit the question of the political (and religious) settlement. See Little, "John Thurloe and the Offer of the Crown to Oliver Cromwell," 220.

117 Heb. 12:26.

side, for holiness now?" If ministers at their meetings; if Christians at theirs would make this their business; if all would agree to sacrifice their lusts, their self-love, their by-opinions to this work, what glory would redound to Christ? What salvation would be wrought in the earth? Why do any of us lie complaining? Let us up and be doing, there is no doubt, no question to be made; this is that which Christ lengthens his controversy with us about, that he will bring us to, or ruin us, and destroy us as to this world. Ministers meet: What do they? Pray a while, and spend their time in and about differences, controversies, how they may do this or that which I shall not name. Christians meet, and pray, and go away as they came. Lusts are not sacrificed; faults are not confessed to one another; exhortations mutual are not used; no ground is got for holiness or godliness, but things remain as they did, or rather grow worse and worse every day; at best profession rises, and the power of religion falls and decreases.

I heartily wish professors would be persuaded to come together, to advise, to consult for God, for the glory of Christ and the gospel, and for their own interest in this thing: to consider what are the pressing temptations of the days wherein we live; what are the corruptions and lusts that are apt to be provoked and excited by these temptations, or by the state of things among us; what duties seem to be neglected; and what are the common, visible failings and scandal of professors, wherein themselves, through party, or neglect, or selfishness have been wanting: and to advise and pray for the remedying of all these evils. I wish they would seriously stir up and exhort one another, to contend mightily for the crucifying of all their secret lusts and bosom sins; for heart purity, and likeness to Christ in all things: that they would incite others, and draw all they can into their society and combination in all parts of the nation. In particular, let not us of this place[118] stand still, expecting when others will begin the work; the meaner, poorer, worse we are, the more incumbent is it on us to rise and be doing; the water is moved, teaching is in it, and we strive not who shall enter first,[119] but rather stand striving, contesting with others, to put them before us.

This is the first direction: let us make the matter of holiness and godliness, suited to the coming of Christ, a business of design, counsel, and common engagement. Whereunto everyone may contribute of the store which from God he has received. Blessed will be those servants, whom their Master, when he comes, shall find so doing.

118 An important interpretative question lies in what is the referent of "this place."

119 See John 5:3–7.

Words of Caution

I shall now add some cautions as to the pursuit of the first direction.[120]

Beware the Theological and Practical Dangers

[1] Take heed of a degeneration into self-righteousness. Intendments of holiness have more than once been ruined by Satan through this deceit; they have set out upon conviction, and ended in Pharisaism. Now this has been done many ways.

{1} Some really convinced of the vanity of an empty profession, and of boasting of saintship upon the account of faith and light without holiness and godliness, which was the way of many when James and John wrote their epistles, fall to dispute and contend, as well they may, for the absolute necessity of holiness and strict obedience, of fruitfulness and good works. But Satan here gets advantage upon men's natural spirits, their heats and contentions, and insinuates an inherent righteousness, upon the account whereof we should, under one pretense or other, expect acceptation with God, as to the justification of our persons. So he prevailed upon the Galatians. The way is narrow and strait that lies between the indispensable necessity of holiness, and its influence into our righteousness. Because no faith will justify us before God, but that also which will justify itself by fruitfulness before men, a great mistake arises, as though what it does for its own justification were to be reckoned unto ours. Many in our days have gone off from the mystery of the gospel on this account.[121]

{2} It prevails from a secret self-pleasing, that is apt to grow on the minds of men, from a singularity in the performance of duties. This is that which the heart-searcher aims to prevent in his command, that "when we have done all, we should say we are unprofitable servants";[122] that is, in the secrets of our hearts to sit down in a sense of our own worthlessness. And here lies another great practical difficulty, namely, to have the rejoicing of a good conscience in our integrity and constancy in duties, without a reflection upon something of self, that the soul may please itself, and rest in. Nehemiah fixes on the medium (Neh. 13:22). He had in the sight of God the testimony

120 In the 1721 edition, this is described as the fourth part of the sermon.

121 For a consideration of how an aversion to antinomianism led some to a neonomian denial of the doctrine of justification by faith alone in the 1650s, see Tim Cooper, *Fear and Polemic in Seventeenth-Century England: Richard Baxter and Antinomianism* (Aldershot, UK: Ashgate, 2001), 15–45; and Hans Boersma, *A Hot Pepper Corn: Richard Baxter's Doctrine of Justification in its Seventeenth-Century Context of Controversy* (Zoetermeer: Boekencentrum, 1993), 166–94.

122 Luke 17:10.

of his conscience, concerning the service he had done for the house of God; but as to the rest, he winds up all in mercy, pardon, and grace. "God, I thank thee I am not as other men,"[123] is apt to creep into the heart in a strict course of duties. And this self-pleasing is the very root of self-righteousness, which as it may defile the saints themselves, so it will destroy those who only in the strength of their convictions go forth after a holiness and righteousness; for it quickly produces the deadly poisonous effect of spiritual pride, which is the greatest assimilation to the nature of the devil that the nature of man is capable of.

{3} Our own holiness has an advantage upon spiritual sense against the righteousness of Christ. The righteousness of Christ, is utterly a strange thing to the best of unbelievers; and this puts them by all means upon the setting up of their own (Rom. 10:3). And believers themselves know it only by faith (Rom. 1:17), which is "of things not seen."[124] But what we are ourselves, what we do, what we aim at, and in what manner, this we have a near sense of. And holiness is apt to insinuate itself into the conscience with a beauty that is none of its own, to proffer itself to the soul's embraces instead of Jesus Christ. Its native beauty consists in its answering the will of God, conforming the soul to the likeness of Christ, and being useful in the world, in a covenant of mere mercy. From its presence, and the sense we have of it, the heart is apt to put a varnish and false beauty upon it, as to the relief of conscience upon the account of justification. As it was of old with the children of Israel, when Moses was in the mount, and not seen, nor had they any visible pledge of the presence of God, instantly they turned their gold into a calf that would be always present with them.[125] Being in the dark as to the righteousness of Christ, which is as it were, absent from them, men set up their own holiness in the stead of it; which, though of itself it be of God, yet turned into self-righteousness, is but a calf, an idol, that cannot save them.

This is my first caution. But that we may make the better improvement of it; as unto present practice, I shall add some evidences of the prevalency, or at least contending of self-righteousness for an interest in the soul, under a pretense of duty and holiness. As—

Evidences of the Prevalence of Those Dangers

1st. When, under a design of holiness, there is an increase of a bondage frame of spirit. When the mind begins to be enslaved to the duties which

123 Luke 18:11.

124 Heb. 11:1.

125 Ex. 32:1–4.

it does itself perform. When that amplitude,[126] freedom, and largeness of mind, which is in a gracious frame of heart, decays; and a servile[127] bondage frame grows in the room of it, so that the soul does what it does under this notion, that it dare not do otherwise. "Where the Spirit of the Lord is, there is liberty" (2 Cor. 3:17). Those that come to Christ, he makes "free" (John 8:36). There is freedom and spiritual largeness of heart unto obedience and duty. A will unto duty enlarged, dilated, and sweetened by love, delight, joy, complacency in the matter of obedience, is the freedom we speak of. This frame, I confess, is not always alike prevalent in gracious souls: they may have things ready to die; sin within, temptations without, desertion from God, all of them together, each of them may disturb this harmony, and bring them for a time, it may be a long time, under an indisposition unto such a frame: but this is for the most part predominant. When such a frame decays, or is not, all endeavors, pains, attempts, severities in duties, do all relate to the law; to bondage; and consequently lead to self-righteousness, fear, subjection of conscience to duties, not God in Christ in the duty, fluctuating of peace according to performances; the soul, in its strictest course, had need fear a snare.

2nd. Increasing in form, and withering in power. Forms are of three sorts. (1st)[128] Those of institution. (2nd) Moral. (3rd) Arbitrary, in conversation.

(1st) There are forms and ways of worship, whereof some are, and all pretend to be, of Christ's institution. Let us at present take it for granted, that they are all what they are apprehended to be, namely, from Christ. For a man to grow high, earnest, zealous, in and about them, to be strict and severe in contending for them, and yet find no spiritual refreshment in them, or communion with God, nor to grow in faith and love by them, is to dwell on the confines of self-righteousness, if not hypocrisy. This was the very sin of the Jews, about their institutions, so much condemned in the Scripture. None use instituted ways or forms of worship profitably, but such as find communion with God in them, or are seriously humbled because they do not.

(2nd) The outward form of moral duties, that depend not merely on institution, is the same. Such are praying, preaching, hearing, bounding in them without a suitable increase in grace, power, liberty, love, meekness, lowliness of mind, argues, though under the highest light to the contrary, a real mixture of self.

126 I.e., breadth and fullness.

127 I.e., of or belonging to a slave.

128 As is explained in the *Works* preface, the numbering order is 1, (1), [1], {1}, and 1st. In this volume, the numbering goes deeper, with the next number being (1st).

(3rd) There are also outward forms in conversation, that are used to the same purpose. We have had some who have changed their outward form in a few years, as often as Laban changed Jacob's wages.[129] What shape they will next turn themselves into, I know not. This is not going from strength to strength, and increasing in life and power, but from one shape to another; and their word and prophecy is directly proportioned, and answerable in its outward appearance to the administration of the Old Testament,[130] and not at all to the spiritual dispensation of the New. So it may be feared that in the principle of their obedience, they lie under a legal bondage and self-righteousness, which has utterly spoiled that which perhaps in its first design set out for mortification and holiness.

3rd. Where self-righteousness is getting ground, these two, bondage and form, at length bring forth burdensomeness and wearisomeness. This God charges on such justiciaries,[131] "Thou hast been weary of me" (Isa. 43:22). The ways and worship of God grow very grievous and burdensome to such a soul. He is a stranger to that of the apostle: "His commandments are not grievous":[132] and that of our Savior himself: "My yoke is easy, and my burden light."[133] The easiness of the yoke of Christ arises from the assistance that is given to him that bears it by the Holy Ghost; as also the connaturalness[134] that is wrought in the heart to all the duties of it. Both these accompany a gospel frame. But when a soul is deserted of these, the yoke grows heavy, and galls[135] him, but yet he must go on. This is from self-righteousness. Let this, then, be our first caution.

129 Gen. 31:7.

130 This could well be a reference to the Quakers. Ecstatic prophecy was a distinctive practice of the Quakers at this time. See Hilary Hinds, *George Fox and Early Quaker Culture* (Manchester: Manchester University Press, 2011), 93–94. Owen had to contend with early Quakers who walked seminaked through Oxford. See Peter Toon, *God's Statesman: The Life and Work of John Owen* (Exeter, UK: Paternoster, 1971), 76. See also Kenneth L.Carroll, "Early Quakers and Going Naked as a Sign," *Quaker History* 77 (1978): 69–79. James Nayler's prophetic acts had achieved infamy when, released from Exeter jail, he mounted a horse and was led by two female disciples in an attempt to recreate the events of Palm Sunday. Nayler was attempting to make the point that there was something of Christ in all people. See John Coffey, *Persecution and Toleration in Protestant England, 1558–1689* (Harlow, UK: Pearson, 2000), 153–54. It could also be a reference to the intense debates about the seventh day (Saturday) Sabbath that were taking place within the Fifth Monarchist movement in 1656–1657. See Bernard Capp, *Fifth Monarchy Men: A Study in Seventeenth-Century English Millenarianism* (London: Faber 2008), 162–71.

131 I.e., those who seek to establish their righteousness by the adherence to law.

132 1 John 5:3.

133 Matt. 11:30.

134 I.e., the state of being suited to the nature of a thing.

135 I.e., make sore or annoying by chafing or rubbing.

Beware the Danger of Ceasing to Serve God in This Generation

[2] Take heed of monastic uselessness. I am persuaded monkery[136] came into the world not only with a glorious pretense, but also with a sincere intention. Men weary of the ways, weary of the lusts, and sin of the world, designing personal holiness left their stations, and withdrew themselves into retirement. David was almost gone with this design, "O that I had wings" (Ps. 55:6). And Jeremiah, "O that I had a lodging in the wilderness" (Jer. 9:2). Whose heart has not been exercised with reasonings of this kind? Oh, that we could be freed from the encumbrances and provocations of this world; what manner of persons might we be in all holy conversation and godliness? But consider—

{1} What success this design prosecuted has had in others. How quickly did it degenerate into wretched superstition, and was thereon blasted and rejected of God?

{2} God can suffer temptation to pursue us into a wilderness, that shall more obstruct us in the progress of holiness, than all the difficulties we meet withal in this world. It is not of what kind our temptations are, but what assistance we are to expect under them, that we are to look after.

{3} Not our communion, but God's work is to be considered. God has work to do in this world, and to desert it because of its difficulties and entanglements, is to cast off his authority. Universal holiness is required of us, that we may do the will of God in our generation (Gen. 6:9). It is not enough that we be just, that we be righteous, and walk with God in holiness; but we must also serve our generation, as David did before he fell asleep.[137] God has a work to do, and not to help him, is to oppose him.

Beware the Danger of Talking about Holiness for Unholy Reasons

[3] Take heed of laying a design for holiness in a subserviency unto any carnal interest; of crying with Jehu, "Come see my zeal for the Lord of hosts,"[138] thereby to do our own work, and compass our own ends. The great scandal that has befallen the days wherein we live, and which has hardened the spirits of many against all the ways of God, is, that religion, godliness, zeal, holiness, have been made a cloak for carnal and secular ends. What of this has been really given, and what has been taken on false imaginations, the last day will discover. In the meantime this is certain,

136 I.e., monasticism, particularly with its faults or abuses.

137 Acts 13:36.

138 2 Kings 10:16.

that there is a corruption in the heart of man, rising up to such a visible prostitution of the whole profession of religion, which of all things must be carefully avoided.

Conclusion to the First Direction

And this is the grand exhortation that I shall insist on: let it be our design to promote generation holiness in ourselves and others, with the cautions insisted on.

Second Direction: Two Essential Ingredients for True Holiness

(2) That which in the next place is considerable, is the proposing of the ingredients that lie in the motive to holiness, here expressed by the apostle, "Seeing that these things shall be dissolved." As,

Stop Loving Earthly Things

[1] It will be a furtherance of holiness to take off our hearts from an esteem and valuation of all things, that are so obnoxious to dissolution. An estimation or valuation of earthly things is on all accounts the greatest hinderance to the promotion of holiness. Earthly-mindedness, pride of spirit, elation above our brethren, self-estimation, carnal confidence, contempt of the wisdom and grace of others, aptness to wrath and anger; some, or all of these, always accompany such a frame.

The apostle also makes this an effectual means of the improvement of holiness, that the mind be taken off from the delightful contemplation of visible things (2 Cor. 4:18). Things will work toward "a weight of glory":[139] in which words the apostle alludes to the Hebrew word כָּבוֹד, "glory," which comes from a root signifying to "weigh," or "to be heavy"; that being the only weighty thing, and all others light and of no moment. This way, I say, things will work, while our minds are taken off from things that are seen. The mind's valuation of them is as great an obstruction to the growth of holiness, as anything whatever that can beset us in our pilgrimage. Now what can give a greater allay[140] to the warmth of our thoughts and minds, than their continual obnoxiousness to dissolution and change? This the apostle makes his argument everywhere. "They are temporal things," says he, "things that abide not, things obnoxious to change and ruin: The world passeth away, and the figure of it. Wilt thou set thine heart upon that which

139 2 Cor. 4:17.

140 I.e., something that acts as a check or restraint.

is not?" And there lies the force of the inference under consideration: "Seeing that these things shall be dissolved," and it may be in a way of judgment, in a dreadful, fearful manner; how is it incumbent on us to fix our hearts on more durable things, to choose the better part,[141] the better portion? What advantage can it be to enlarge our hearts to the love of the things that are upon the wing? To cleave to parting things with our affections? To grow in our desires after that which withdraws itself from us continually? Let us then consider, how many duties have been omitted, how many temptations have been offered, and objected to us; how many spiritual frames of heart prevented or expelled; how much looseness and vanity of mind introduced; how much self-confidence promoted, by an overvaluation of these things: and we shall then see what influence a watching against it may have to the furtherance of a design of holiness.

Stop Caring for Perishing Things

[2] It will be so, to take off our care about them. This also is a worm that lies at the root of obedience, and is of itself able to wither it, if not removed. Our Lord Jesus Christ, giving us instruction how we should be prepared for the coming of such a day, as that whereof we are speaking, charges us, among other things, to take heed that we "be not overcharged with the cares of this life" (Luke 21:34). Indeed there is nothing so opposite to that peculiar holiness and godliness that is required of us in and under great providential dissolutions, as this of care about perishing things. The special holiness that we press after, is a due mixture of faith, love, self-denial, fruitfulness, all working in a peculiar and eminent manner. Now to every one of these is this care a canker and a gangrene, fitted to eat out and devour the life and spirit of them. The very nature of faith consists in a universal casting of our care on God, "Cast all your care on him" (1 Pet. 5:7). All our care about temporal, spiritual, eternal things, let us cast all this on God, our whole burden; this is believing, this is faith: and what is more opposite unto it, than this care and solicitousness of the soul about the obtaining or retaining of these things? Resignation, acquiescency, rest, all which are acts or effects of faith, are devoured by it. Trust in God, affiance,[142] delight in his will, [it] ruins them all. How can a soul glorify God in believing in a difficult season, that is overlaid with this distemper.[143] Nothing is more diametrically opposite thereunto.

141 Luke 10:42.

142 I.e., trust or faith.

143 I.e., disturbance or disorder.

Conclusion: Enlarge the Heart with Love for Christ

Love enlarges the heart to Christ, and everything of Christ; valuation, delight, satisfaction, accompany it: it makes the heart free, noble, ready for service, compassionate, zealous; nothing is more called for in such a day: and the decay of faith, in the trials and temptations of such a season, is called the "waxing cold of love";[144] as the fruit decays, when the root is consumed. To think of glorifying God in the days wherein we live, without hearts warmed, enlarged, made tender, compassionate, by gospel love, is to think to fly without wings, or to walk without feet. What day almost, what business, wherein our love is not put to the trial in all the properties of it; whether it can bear and forbear; whether it can pity and relieve; whether it can hope all things, and believe all things;[145] whether it can exercise itself toward friends and toward enemies; whether it can give allowance for men's weakness and temptations; whether it can value Christ above all, and rejoice in him in the loss of all; and many the like things is it continually tried withal. Now nothing so contracts and withers the heart, as to all these things, as the cares of this world do. Whatever is selfish, fearful, unbelieving, is enwrapped in them. They sometimes pine, wither, and render useless, the whole man, always drink up the spirit, and deprive it of any communion with God in anything it has to do.

The same may be said concerning self-denial and fruitfulness; which in an eminent manner Christ now calls upon us for. Love, care, and fear about the things that shall be dissolved,[146] unframes the soul for them.

On these considerations, and the like which might be added, may this direction be improved, and no small obstacle unto a course of universal holiness and godliness, be taken away. Is the power, are the riches, the pleasures of the world valuable? Alas! They are all passing away. It is "but yet a little while,"[147] "and their place shall know them no more."[148] Yet could we take off our hearts from an undue valuation of these things, and care about them, half our work were done.

Third Direction: Three Motivations for This Duty

(3) That which remains for the closing of our discourse on this subject, is to give some few motives unto the duty proposed: and I shall only mention three generals, [1] Relating unto ourselves. [2] Unto others. [3] Unto Christ himself.

144 Matt. 24:12.
145 1 Cor. 13:7.
146 2 Pet. 3:11.
147 Isa. 10:25.
148 Ps. 103:16.

Holiness Brings the Inner Peace That Sustains the Soul Even in the Loss of Outer Peace

[1] As to ourselves; this alone will maintain peace and quiet in our souls in and under those dissolutions of things that we are to be exercised with. We know what desolations, what ruin of families, what destruction of all outward enjoyments in many, they have already in these nations been attended with; and we know not how soon, nor by what ways or means, the bitterest part of the cup, as to outward pressures and calamities, may become our portion. We have seen somewhat of the beginning of the work of Christ; where he will cease, what he has yet farther to do, we know not. Our concernment then certainly was never greater than it is at this day, to keep up peace and rest within. If there should be a confederacy of outward and inward trouble, who can stand before it? A wounded body, a wounded, it may be ruined estate, and a wounded spirit altogether, who can bear? This is that alone which the world cannot take from us; which is not obnoxious to sword, fire, plots, conspiracies, nothing without us; even the peace that is left us, left to our own keeping, through the Holy Ghost, by Jesus Christ. It is not committed to parliaments, to armies, to rulers to keep for us;[149] it is committed to our own souls to keep, through the Holy Ghost, and no man can take it from us. Again, as it is valuable on this account, that it cannot be taken from us; so on this also, that it will countervail[150] and support us under the loss of all that can. Peace in God, rest in sole retirement, quietness, and security of mind on spiritual, gospel accounts, sense of God's love in Christ, will support and keep life and vigor in the soul in the loss of outward peace, with whatever is desirable and valuable unto us on any account that relates to this world.

Now there is no maintaining of this peace and rest in such a season, without the performance of this duty. So dealt Habakkuk, "I trembled in myself, that I might rest in the day of trouble" (Hab. 3:16). That which God required of him in that season, that he brought up his soul unto, that he might have rest; and his endeavor had the glorious issue mentioned, verses 17–18. Though spiritual peace may radically and virtually live under many sins and provocations; yet it will not flourish under them, or bring forth any refreshing fruit. To have the fruit and effect of peace under a continuance in any known sin, is impossible. Now the omission of any known duty, is a known sin; and that a peculiar pressing after eminency in universal holiness and godliness in such

149 A recognition of the limitations of Parliament, the rule of the Major Generals, and the Protector and his Council.

150 I.e., to counterbalance or ballast.

a season is a known duty, I have before evinced: no maintaining of inward peace, rest in God, without it: and we shall be sure to be tried, whether it be in us of a truth, or not. I discourse not what the carnal security of seared, blinded, hardened sinners will do; but I am sure the weak, tottering, uncertain peace of many believers, will not support them in such trials, as it is not only possible that we may, but probable that we shall meet withal. Would you now desire that your Master should find you unprepared; that he should make his entrance while all things were in disorder? If the heavens should thunder over you, and the earth tremble under you, and the sword stand ready to devour. Oh! What sad thoughts must you have, if at the same time you should be forced to say, "O my soul, is not God mine enemy also? May not wrath, and hell, and judgment be at the end of this dispensation?" What is the reason, that a very rumor, a noise oftentimes, is ready to fill many of our souls with such disturbances? Is it not because this peace does not flourish in the inward man? And what shall we do in the day of trial itself? Let us then endeavor as Peter exhorts, to "be found of Christ in peace" (2 Pet. 3:14). And what may we do that we may be found of him in peace? "Why," says he, "be 'without spot, and blameless.' "[151] Let him come when he will, in what way he pleases, we shall be found in a way of peace, if we be found spotless and blameless in a way of holiness. And "blessed is that servant, whom his Master, when he cometh shall find so doing."[152] This will give light in a dungeon, as it did to Paul and Silas;[153] ease in the fire, in the furnace, as to Shadrach, Meshach, and Abednego;[154] contentment in the loss of all, as it did to Job; satisfaction on the foresight of future trouble, as it did to David: "Although my house be not so with God, yet he hath made with me an everlasting covenant."[155] Whatever sword be in the hand of Christ; whatever fire or tempest be before him, and round about him; what vengeance soever he is to take on any, or all of the sons of men, this peace, kept up by the holiness he requires in such a season, will make a way to his bosom love, and there repose the soul in rest and quietness.

Holiness Is the Only Way to Save and Reform the Three Nations

[2] As to others, what Paul says to Timothy in another case about preaching of the gospel, may in some sense be spoken in this: "Take heed," says he, "to

151 2 Pet. 3:14.
152 Matt. 24:46.
153 Acts 16:25.
154 Dan. 3:25.
155 2 Sam. 23:5.

thy doctrine; for thereby thou shalt save thyself, and them that hear thee."[156] Who knows but that hereby we may save ourselves, and the nation wherein we live. The Lord Christ has certainly a controversy with these nations, he has begun to deal with them in his indignation; and we know that there are provocations enough among us, to stir him up unto our ruin. Who knows, I say, but that by meeting him in a way of generation holiness, we may divert deserved ruin, at least hinder that it be not brought upon us for the provocations of his sons and daughters?

Now there are several ways, whereby this may have an influence into the safety and deliverance of the nations themselves.

{1} By setting all things right between Christ and the saints, that he may have no need farther to shake the earth and dissolve the heavens of the nations,[157] to awaken his own from their security, to loosen them from perishing things, or to accomplish any other glorious end toward them. Christ sometimes sifts nations, that his wheat may be separated from the chaff: he sets nations on fire, that they may be a furnace for the trial of his own; and when their dross is cleansed, he will quench his fire. When there was but one saint in a ship, yet it was for his sake that a storm came on all the rest.[158] It is not always for the sins of the wicked, that they may be destroyed, that he comes in a way of judgment; but for the sins of his people, that they may be cleansed. So "judgment," as Peter speaks, "begins at the house of God" (1 Pet. 4:17). It is not unlikely, that our troubles were brought on these nations for the sins of the nations in their persecution of Christ, his truths, and saints against great light. Nor is it less unlikely, that troubles are continued on these nations for the sins of the saints themselves, such as those before insisted on. Now what is it that in such trials Christ calls for, and which he will not cease calling for, until he prevails? Is it not the work which we are in the pursuit of, weanedness from the world, self-denial, zeal for truth, humbleness, fruitfulness, faithfulness, universal holiness? If here then lies the root of Christ's controversy with these nations, as most probably it does; if this be the cause of our troubles, as to me questionless it is, an engagement into the pursuit of this work, is the only remedy and cure of the evils that we either feel or fear in these nations. Other remedies have been tried, and all in vain. O that we had hearts through the Holy Ghost to make trial of this, which the great physician Jesus Christ has prescribed unto us! Heaven and earth call for it at

156 1 Tim. 4:16.
157 Heb. 12:26.
158 Jonah 1:7.

our hands; the nations groan under our sin; if we regard not ourselves, yet let us make it our business to deliver England out of the hand of the Lord (Josh. 22:31).

{2} In that it may be an effectual means for the reformation of the nation. Reformation is the great thing that we have been talking of many years; and this has been our condition in our attempts after it; the more that light for it has broken forth among us, the more unreformed has the body of the people been, yea the more opposite for the most part unto reformation: and may not this, among other things, be one occasion, yea the principal cause of it; the light of truth has been accompanied with so many scandals in some, with so little power and evidence in the most, that prejudices have been strengthened in the minds of men against all that has been pretended or professed. I am persuaded, that a design for generation holiness, carried on according to the light that we have received, would have a greater influence on the minds of the men of the world to look after reformation, than any of our entreaties or exhortations have yet obtained. We are contemptible to the nation, in our pressing after reformation, while we are divided among ourselves, conformable to the world;[159] while we proclaim our unmortified lusts, pride, covetousness, ambition, revenge, self-seeking. Would all the people of God stir up themselves to show forth the power of that faith and life they have received, and so take away advantage from obdurate opposers of the gospel, and give an eminent example to others, who now abhor them on the account of many prejudices that they have taken; the nations would be more awakened unto their duty than now they are. Were we agreed and united on this principle, that we would jointly and severally make this our design; what work might be wrought in families, councils, counties, cities? Now reformation is acknowledged to be the means, the only means of the preservation of a nation, and this the only means of that.

{3} This is the most effectual way of standing in the gap,[160] to turn away the indignation of the Lord against the nation. Whatever is required thereunto, is contained in this design of holiness; there is reformation, there is wrestling by prayer, sundry promises improving our interest in Christ, all included in this duty. Now this is the most common way of saving nations. When wrath is ready to break forth, some Moses or Samuel stands up, and pleads for a deliverance, and prevails.[161] Says God, "Destroy not the cluster, there is a

159 Rom. 12:2.

160 Ezek. 22:30.

161 See Jer. 15:1.

blessing in it."[162] When the greatest and most dreadful judgment, that God ever executed on sinners in this world, was coming forth, had there been ten persons following after holiness, its accomplishment had been prevented.[163] Here then we have a project to save three nations by;[164] and without this, in vain shall they use any other remedies, they shall not be healed.

Holiness Will Bring Glory to Christ

[3] Consider this thing, how it relates unto Christ and his glory. All the revenue of glory or honor that we bring unto Christ in this world, is by our obedience or holiness. He did not die for us, that we might be great, or wise, or learned, or powerful in the world; but that he might purify us to be a peculiar people unto himself, zealous of good works.[165] This was his design and aim, that he might have a holy people, a faithful people in the world. He tells us that herein his Father is glorified, that we bear much fruit:[166] not that we be successful, that we rule and prevail, that we are in credit and reputation; but that we bring forth much fruit: and in the glory of the Father is the Son glorified also. It is this alone that adorns the doctrine of his gospel,[167] and lifts up his name in the world; but especially is Christ glorified by the holiness of his saints in such a season; because—

{1} Thereby we bear witness to the world that indeed we believe him to be come forth among us, and that the works that are on the wheel relate to his kingdom and interest. Let us talk of it while we please, unless we live and walk as those who have communion with Christ in the works he does, the world will yet think that whatever we profess, yet indeed we believe as they do, that it is a common thing that has befallen us. But when indeed they shall see, that there is a real reverence of his person upon our spirits, and that we bestir ourselves in his ways, like servants in the presence of their master; this

162 Isa. 65:8. Thomas Brooks helpfully describes the similitude of the new wine in the cluster: "When a Vine being blasted or otherwise decayed is grown so bad, and so barren, that scarce any good clusters of Grapes can be discerned on it, whereby it may be deemed to have any life, or of ever becoming fruitful again, and the Husband-man is about to grub it up, or cut it down to the ground; One standing by, sees here a cluster, and there a little cluster, and cryes out, O don't grub up the Vine, don't cut down the Vine, it hath a little life, and by good husbandry it may be made fruitful." See Brooks, *The Unsearchable Riches of Christ, or, Meat for Strong Men and Milke for Babes Held Forth in Twenty-Two Sermons from Ephesians III, VIII* (London, 1655), 80.

163 Gen. 18:32.

164 The Protectorate was officially the Commonwealth of England, Scotland, and Ireland.

165 Titus 2:14.

166 John 15:8.

167 Titus 2:10.

carries a conviction along with it. To hear men talk of the coming of Christ, and the day of Christ, and the great and terrible things that Christ has done in these days; and yet in the meantime to walk as the men of the world, in a spirit of pride, selfishness, and wrath, in sensuality or pleasure, in neglect of prayer and humiliation; yea of all gospel duties, swearers and drunkards do not so dishonor Christ, as such men do. But let men but see professors making it their business to be holy, humble, self-denying, useful in the world, condescending in love, resigning all to God, they cannot but say, "Well, this is a great day to the saints; they verily believe that Christ is among them." This is a professing that brings conviction; words are but as speaking with tongues, that work not out the glory of Christ.

{2} Thereby we bear witness unto what sort of kingdom it is, that Christ has in the world, and what a kind of king he is. I cannot but fear that our talking of the kingdom of Christ, and managing our notions of it, at least in the world's apprehensions, to carnal advantages, has been a notable hindrance of the coming of it forth in beauty and glory among us. Every party talks of the kingdom of Christ, some more, some less, all pretend unto it;[168] but it is evident that many would set him on his throne with the petition of Zebedee's children in their mouths, that they may sit on his right hand, and his left.[169] Hence the world does really persuade itself, and is hardened every day in that persuasion, that whatever is pretended of Christ, it is self-interest that carries all before it; and that men do entertain that notion for the promotion of self-ends. But now this design of abounding in real holiness sets up the pure, unmixed, interest of Christ, and casts a conviction upon the world to that purpose. When the world may read in our lives, that the kingdom we look for, though it be in this world, yet it is not indeed of this world,[170] but is righteousness, and peace, and joy in the Holy Ghost:[171] this brings that honor to Christ, wherein he is delighted; and the ignorance of foolish men is put to silence.

168 In 1657, there was renewed agitation by the Fifth Monarchists, a group that, as the name suggests, talked much about the kingdom of Christ. Some of this activity was centered around the parliamentary officer, regicide, and excluded member of parliament Thomas Harrison (1616–1660). Other Fifth Monarchists, led by Thomas Venner (1608/9–1661), had been planning an uprising during the winter of 1656–1657, but as the rebels assembled in April 1657, government forces arrested the leaders and seized their weapons. See David Farr, *Major-General Thomas Harrison: Millenarianism, Fifth Monarchism and the English Revolution 1616–1660* (Farnham, UK: Ashgate, 2014), 215–17.

169 Mark 10:35–37.

170 John 18:36.

171 Rom. 14:17.

{3} This brings honor unto Christ, and glorifies him in all the vengeance that he executes on his enemies, and all the care that he takes of his own. The world itself is hereby made to see, that there is a real difference indeed in them, between whom Christ puts a difference, and is convinced of the righteousness of his judgments. Everyone may answer them, when they inquire the reason of the dispensations among us. Yea, they may answer themselves: "'The Lord hath done great things for these,'[172] even these that serve him."

172 Ps. 126:2.

THE GLORY AND INTEREST OF NATIONS PROFESSING THE GOSPEL

Opened in a Sermon Preached at a Private Fast to the Commons Assembled in Parliament. Published by Their Command.

By John Owen, D.D.

London
Printed for Philemon Stephens,
at the gilded lion in
St Paul's Churchyard, 1659

[Epistle Dedicatory]

To the Right Honorable the Commons of England Assembled in Parliament

I NEED NOT GIVE ANY OTHER ACCOUNT of my publishing this ensuing short discourse, than that which was also the ground and reason of its preaching, namely your command. Those who are not satisfied therewith, I shall not endeavor to tender farther grounds of satisfaction unto, as not having any persuasion of prevailing if I should attempt it. Prejudice so far oftentimes prevails even on good soils, that satisfaction will not speedily thrive and grow in them. That which exempts me from solicitousness about the frame and temper of men's minds and spirits in the entertainment of discourses of this nature, is the annexing of that injunction unto our commission in delivering the word of God: it must be done, "whether men will hear or whether they will forbear."[1] Without therefore any plea or apology, for whatever may seem most to need it in this sermon, I devolve the whole account of the rise and issue it had, or may have on the providence of God in my call, and your command. Only I shall crave leave to add that in my waiting for a little leisure to recollect what I delivered, out of my own short notes and others' (that I might not preach one sermon and print another) there were some considerations that fell in exciting me to the obedience I had purposed. The desire I had to make more public at this time and season the testimony given in simplicity of spirit to the interest of Christ in these nations, and therein to the true real interest of these nations themselves, which was my naked design openly managed and

1 Ezek. 2:5.

pursued with all plainness of speech (as the small portion of time allotted to this exercise would allow) was the chief of them. Solicitations of some particular friends, gave also warmth unto that consideration. I must farther confess that I was a little moved by some mistakes that were delivered into the hands of report, to be managed to the discountenance of the honest and plain truth contended for, especially when I found them without due consideration exposed in print unto public view.[2] That is the manner of these days wherein we live. I know full well, that there is not anything from the beginning to the ending of this short discourse that does really interfere with any form of civil government in the world, administered according to righteousness and equity: as there is not in the gospel of Christ or in any of the concernments of it. And I am assured also that the truth proposed in it enwraps the whole ground of any just expectation of the continuance of the presence of God among us, and his acceptation of our endeavors about the allotment and just disposal of our civil affairs, let others lay what weight they will or please, upon the lesser differences that are among us on any account whatever; if this shield be safe,[3] this principle maintained and established, that is here laid down, and the just rights of the nation laid in a way of administration, suited unto its preservation and furtherance I, shall not easily be cast down from my hopes, that among us poor unprofitable, unthankful creatures as we are, we may yet see "the fruit of righteousness to be peace, and the effect of righteousness quietness and assurance for evermore."[4] For those then who shall cast their eye on this paper, I would beg of them to lay aside all those prejudices against persons or things, which their various contexture in our public affairs may possibly have raised in them. I know how vain, for the most part expectations of prevailing in such a desire, by naked requests, are. But sick men must be groaning though they look for no relief thereby. Wherefore committing it into that hand, wherein lie also your hearts and mine, I shall commend it

2 Owen may have in mind the comments which James Harrington made about the alleged contents of his sermon in *The Art of Lawgiving* (London, 1659), a work which was prepared for publication on February 20.

3 The motif of the Theban shield which Owen had employed his June 1649 sermon *Human Power Defeated.* See *Complete Works of John Owen*, 18:467. Epaminondas, a Greek general of Thebes, was fatally wounded by a Spartan javelin, and when he regained consciousness his first question was whether his shield was safe. Only then did he ask whether his army had won the battle. This incident is recorded in Diodorus of Sicily, *Library of History* 15.87.6. For text, Diodorus Siculus, *Library of History,* vol. 7, trans. Charles L. Sherman, Loeb Classical Library 389 (Cambridge, MA: Harvard University Press, 1952), 197.

4 Isa. 32:17.

for your use unto the sovereign grace of him, who is able to work all your present works for you, and which is more, "to give you an inheritance among them that are sanctified."[5] So prays

Your servant in the work of our Lord Jesus Christ and his gospel,

J. O.

5 Acts 20:32.

[Sermon]

A Sermon Preached within the Commons House of Parliament, at a Fast Them Solemnly Held upon the 4 of February, 1658[1]

Upon all the glory shall be a defence.

ISAIAH 4:5[2]

INTRODUCTION AND CONTEXT

The design of this chapter is to give in relief against outward perplexing extremities from gospel promises, and the presence of Christ with his people in those extremities.

The next intendment of the words in the type, seems to relate to the deliverance of the people of the Jews from the Babylonish captivity, and the presence of God among them upon their return; God frequently taking occasion from thence, to mind them of the covenant of grace, with the full ratification and publication of it by Christ, as is evident from Jeremiah 31 and 32, and sundry other places.

As to our purpose, we have considerable in the chapter, the persons to whom these promises are given; the condition wherein they were; and

1 By today's standards, the year would be 1659. At that time, the new year was taken to begin on Lady Day, March 25.

2 Owen had appealed to this text about the glory of the assemblies of Mount Zion in his June 1649 sermon *Human Power Defeated* and *God's Presence with a People* (1656). For the first sermon, see *Complete Works of John Owen*, 18:466. The second sermon is included in this volume.

the promises themselves, that are made to them for their supportment and consolation.

Promises Made to a Remnant in Great Distress

The persons intended are the remnant, "the escaping," the "evasion of Israel";[3] as the word signifies, verse 2. They that are "left," "that remain," verse 3, who escape the great desolation that was to come on the body of the people, the furnace they were to pass through. Only in the close of that verse, they have a farther description added of them, from the purpose of God concerning their grace and glory; they are "written among the living," or rather, written unto life; "every one that is written," that is, designed unto life in Jerusalem.

As to the persons in themselves considered, the application is easy unto this assembly: are you not the remnant, the escaping of England? Is not this "a brand plucked out of the fire?"[4] Are you not they that are "left," they "that remain," from great trials and desolations; the Lord grant that the application may hold out, and abide to the end of the prophecy.[5]

2. The condition that this remnant or "escaping" had been in is laid down in some figurative expressions concerning the smallness of this remnant, or the paucity of them that should escape, and the greatness of the extremities they should be exercised withal. I cannot insist on particulars; it may suffice that great distresses and calamities are intimated therein; and such have the days of our former trials and troubles been to some of us.

3. The promises here made to this people, thus escaped from great distresses, are of two sorts. (1) Original or fundamental; and then (2)[6] consequential thereon.

(1) There is the great spring or fountain promise, from which all others as lesser streams do flow; and that is the promise of Christ himself unto them, and among them, verse 2. He is that "branch of Jehovah," and that "fruit of the earth" which is there promised. He is the bottom and foundation, the spring and fountain of all the good that is or shall be communicated unto us, all other promises are but rivulets from that unsearchable ocean of grace and love, that is in the promise of Christ; of which afterward.

3 The "evasion of Israel" is the reading provided in the marginal note of the Authorized Version (KJV).

4 Zech. 3:2.

5 Probably what is held out in Isa. 4:4–6.

6 This numeral is added for the purposes of clarity and consistency.

(2) The promises that are derived and flow from hence may be referred unto three heads. [1] Of beauty and glory, verse 2. [2] Of holiness and purity, verses 3–4. [3] Of preservation and safety, verses 5–6.

Promises of Safety and Preservation

My text lies among the last sort; and not intending long to detain you, I shall pass over the others, and immediately close with that of our present concernment.

Now this promise of verse 5 is of a comprehensive nature, and relates to spiritual and temporal safety or preservation; "godliness" though it be not much believed, yet indeed has "the promise of this life, and that which is to come."[7]

OPENING THE TEXT TO RAISE TWO DOCTRINAL PROPOSITIONS

I shall a little open the words of the verse, and thereby give light to those which I have chosen peculiarly to insist upon. It is, as I have said safety and preservation both spiritual and temporal that is here engaged for; and concerning it we have considerable;

God Is the Source and Pledge of These Promises

The Creative Power of God Will Preserve the Remnant

1. The manner of its production; "I 'will create' it," says God. There is a creating power, needful to be exerted, for the preservation of Zion's remnant. Their preservation must be of God's creation. It is, not only, not to be educed out of any other principle or to be wrought by any other means; but it must, as it were by the almighty power of God, be brought out of nothing; God must create it. At least, as there were two sorts of God's creatures at the beginning, that dark body of matter,[8] whose rise was merely from nothing; and those things which from that dark confused heap, he made to be other things, than what they were therein;[9] it is of the last sort of creatures if not of the first. If the preservation of this remnant be not out of nothing, without any

7 1 Tim. 4:8.

8 Gen. 1:2.

9 Owen here distinguishes the divine act of creating all things out of nothing (*creatio ex nihilo*), also called "first creation" (*creatio prima*), which produced "indisposed plain matter," from the "second creation," the divine "work of distinction" (*distinctionis operatio*). See Andreas J. Beck, "God, Creation, and Providence in Post-Reformation Reformed Theology," in *The Oxford*

means at all; yet it is for the most part from that darkness and confusion of things, which contribute very little or nothing toward it; "I will create it" says God; and while he continues possessed of his creating power, it shall be well with his Israel.

God Will Be Present to Guide and Protect

2. For the nature of it, it is here set out, under the terms of that eminent pledge of the presence of God with his people in the wilderness, for their guidance and protection, in the midst of all their difficulties and hazards, by a pillar of cloud, and a flaming fire; this guided them through the sea, and continued with them after the setting up of the tabernacle in the wilderness forty years. The use, and efficacy of that pillar, the intendment of God in it, the advantage of the people by it, I cannot stay to unfold. It may suffice in general that it was a great and signal pledge of God's presence with them for their guidance and preservation; that they might act according to his will, and enjoy safety in so doing. Only whereas this promise here respects gospel times, the nature of the mercy promised is enlarged, and thereby somewhat changed. In the wilderness there was but one tabernacle; and so consequently one cloud by day, and one pillar of fire by night, was a sufficient pledge of the presence of God with the whole people: there are now many dwelling places, many assemblies of mount Zion; and in the enlargement of mercy and grace under the gospel, the same pledge of God's presence and favor is promised to every one of them as was before to the whole.[10] The word we have translated "a dwelling-place," denotes not a common habitation, but a place prepared for God; and is the same with the "assemblies" and congregations in the expression following. The sum of all is; God by his creating power, in despite of all opposition will bring forth preservation for his people, guiding them in paths wherein they shall find peace and safety.

Promises to a Holy People

Only you may observe the order and dependence of these promises; the promise of holiness, verse 4, lies in order, before that of safety, verse 5. Unless our "filth" and our "blood" be "purged" away by "a spirit of judgment and a spirit of burning," it is in vain for us, to look for the pillar and the cloud. If

---

Handbook of Early Modern Theology, 1600–1800, ed. Ulrich L. Lehner, Richard A. Muller, and A. G. Roeber (Oxford: Oxford University Press, 2016), 205–6.

10 This was a significant theme in *God's Presence with a People* (1656), which is included in this volume.

we are not interested in holiness, we shall not be interested in safety; I mean as it lies in the promise, and is a mercy washed in the blood of Jesus; for as for the peace of the world, I regard it not. Let not men of polluted hearts, and defiled hands, once imagine, that God cares for them in an especial manner. If our "filth" and our "blood," our sin and our corruption abide upon us, and we are delivered, it will be for a greater ruin; the way unto the cloud and pillar, is by "the spirit of judgment and burning."

Exposition of the Final Clause of the Text

The words of my text are a recapitulation of the whole verse; and are a gospel promise given out in law terms, or a New Testament mercy, under Old Testament expressions.

I shall then briefly show you these two things; 1. What is here expressed as to the type and figure. 2. What is here intended as to the substance of the mercy promised.

1. For the figure; by the "glory" and "defence," a double consort, or two pairs of things seem to be intended; (1) The ark and the mercy seat. (2) The tabernacle and the pillar of fire.

For the first; the ark is oftentimes called the "glory" of God; "He delivered his strength into captivity, and his glory into the enemy's hand" (Ps. 78:61). Where he speaks of the surprisal of the ark by the Philistines; which when it was accomplished, Phinehas's wife called her son "Ichabod, and said, "The glory is departed" (1 Sam. 4:21).

The word which we have rendered "a defence," properly signifies "a covering"; as was the mercy seat, the covering of the ark. So that, "Upon the glory shall be a defence," is as much as, "Unto you the mercy-seat shall be on the ark"; or, "You shall have the mercy represented and intimated thereby."

(2) The tabernacle and cloud, or pillar of fire, are also called to mind; so the words are expressive, of that figure of God's gracious presence with his people, which we have recounted, "Then a cloud covered the tent of the congregation, and the glory of the Lord filled the tabernacle" (Ex. 40:34). So it continued, the glory of God was in the tabernacle, and the cloud upon it, or over it; as the word here is; and so "upon all the glory there was a defence."

2. I need not stay to prove that all those things were typical of Christ. He was the "end of the law," represented by the ark, which did contain it (Rom. 10:3–4). He was "the mercy-seat"; as he is called, and said to be (Rom. 3:25; 1 John 2:2). Covering the law from the eye of justice, as to those that are interested in him; he was the tabernacle and temple wherein dwelt the glory of God, and which was replenished with all pledges of his gracious presence.

Summary Statement of the Two Doctrinal Propositions

Apply then this promise to gospel times, and the substance of it is comprehended in these two propositions.

1. *The presence of Christ with any people, is the glory of any people.* This is the glory here spoken of, as is evident to anyone that will but read over the second verse, and consider its influence unto these words: "The branch of the Lord shall be to them beautiful and glorious," and, "Upon all the glory shall be a defence."

2. *The presence of God in special providence over a people, attends the presence of Christ in grace with a people*; if Christ the glory be with them, a defense shall be upon them; what lies else in allusion to the mercy seat, not drawn forth in these propositions, may be afterward insisted on.

TREATMENT OF THE MAIN DOCTRINE: THE PRESENCE OF CHRIST IS THE GLORY OF ANY PEOPLE

The Glory of a People Is Not Found in Numbers, Wisdom, Strength, or Wealth

1. For the first; what I pray else should be so. This is their glory, or they have none; is it in their number, that they are great, many, and populous? God thinks not so, nor did he when he gave an account of his thoughts of his people of old: "The Lord did not set his love upon you, nor choose you, because you were more in number than any people, for you were the fewest of all people" (Deut. 7:7). God made no reckoning of numbers; he chose that people that was fewest of all. He esteemed well of them, when they were but "a few men in number; yea very few and strangers" (Ps. 105:12). You know what it cost David in being seduced by Satan into the contrary opinion. He thought the glory of his people had been in their number, and caused them to be reckoned; but God taught him his error, by taking off with a dreadful judgment no small portion of the number he sought after.[11] There is nothing more common in the Scripture than for the Lord to speak contempt of the multitude of any people, as a thing of nought; and he takes pleasure to confound them by weak and despised means. Is it in their wisdom and counsel, their understanding for the ordering of their affairs? Is that their glory? Why, see how God derides the prince of Tyrus, who was lifted up with an apprehension hereof; and counted himself as God, upon that account; Ezekiel 27:3–6 etc. The issue

11 2 Sam. 24:10.

of all is; "Thou shalt be a man and no God in the hand of him that slays thee";[12] God will let him see in his ruin and destruction, what a vain thing that was, which he thought his glory. Might I dwell upon it I could evince unto you these two things.

(1) That whereas the end of all human wisdom, in nations or the rulers of them, is to preserve human society in peace and quietness, within the several bounds and allotments that are given unto them by the providence of God, it so comes to pass for the most part through the righteous judgment and wise disposal of God, that it has a contrary end, and brings forth contrary effects throughout the world. Do not the inhabitants of the earth, generally owe all their disturbance, sorrow, and blood to the wise contrivance of a few men, not knowing how to take the law of their proceedings from the mouth of God, but laying their deep counsels and politic contrivances in a subserviency to their lusts and ambition. And what glory is there in that which almost constantly brings forth contrary effects to its own proper end and intendment?

(2) That God delights to mix a spirit of giddiness, error, and folly in the counsels of the wise men of the world; making them reel and stagger in their way like a drunken man, that they shall not know what to do,[13] but commonly in their greatest concernments, fix upon things as devoid of true reason and sound wisdom, as any children or fools could close withal. "He taketh the wise in their own craftiness, and the counsel of the froward is carried headlong" (Job 5:13–14); so at large Isaiah 19:11–14.[14] And now where is their glory? I could give instances of both these, and that plentifully, in the days and seasons that have passed over our own heads.

The like also may be said of the strength, the power, the armies of any people; if their number and wisdom be vain, be no glory, their strength which is but the result or exurgency[15] of their number and wisdom, must needs be so also. But you have all this summed up together. "Thus saith the Lord, let not the wise man glory in his wisdom, neither let the mighty man glory in his might, let not the rich man glory in his riches; but let him that glorieth, glory in this, that he understandeth and knoweth me, that I am the Lord" (Jer. 9:23–24): it is neither wisdom nor might nor riches, that is our glory; but our interest in Jehovah only.

12 Ezek. 28:9.

13 Ps. 107:27.

14 Owen appealed to this text in *Ebenezer* (1648) to describe the enemies of Parliament in the second Civil War. See *Complete Works of John Owen*, 18:483.

15 I.e., urgent force.

The Glory of a Nation Is Christ's Presence with His People

This I say is in the presence of Christ only: now Christ may be said to be present with a people two ways.

Empty Profession Is Not the Glory of a Nation

(1) In respect of the dispensation of his gospel among them, the profession of it, and subjection to the ordinances thereof. The gospel of Christ is a "blessed" gospel, a "glorious gospel" in itself,[16] and unto them that embrace it. But yet this profession separated from the root from which it ought to spring, is not the glory of any people; Christ is not their glory who are his shame. Empty profession is the shame of Christ in the world; and shall not be others' glory. The apostle tells us that this may consist with a litter of unclean lusts, making them in whom it is abominable to God and man (2 Tim. 3:4–5 etc.). If the bare profession of the truth, would render a nation glorious, oh how glorious were this nation. So would have been the people of old, who cried "The temple of the Lord, the temple of the Lord."[17] But when men profess the truth of Christ, but in their hearts and ways maintain and manifest an enmity to the power of that truth, and to all of Christ that is in reality in the world, this is no glory.

The Fruitful Profession of Those United to Christ Is the Glory of a Nation

(2) Christ is present with a people in and by his Spirit, dwelling in their hearts by his Spirit and faith, uniting them to himself: I do not distinguish this from the former as inconsistent with it; for though the former may be without this, yet where this is, there will be the former also. Profession may be without union, but union will bring forth profession. There may be a form of godliness without power:[18] but where the power is, there will be the appearance also. Now when Christ is thus present with a people, that is, they are united to him by his Spirit, they are members of his mystical body, that is their glory. Be they few or many in a nation that are so, they are the glory of that nation, and nothing else: and where there is the most of them, there is the most glory: and where they are diminished, there the glory is eclipsed. Christ mystical, the head, and his body is all the glory that is in the world. If any nation be glorious and honorable above others, it is because of this presence of Christ in that nation. Christ is the glory of his saints (Isa.

16 1 Tim. 1:11.
17 Jer. 7:4.
18 2 Tim. 3:5.

4:2). In him they glory (Isa. 45:25): and the saints are Christ's glory (2 Cor. 8:23). They are the glory of Christ: and he glories in them, as God of Job, to Satan. "Seest thou my servant Job" (Job 1:8). He does as it were glory in him against the wickedness of the world; and Christ in them, and they in him, are all the glory of this world.

So Zechariah 2:8, Christ was in the pursuit of the collection of his people from their dispersion: what seeks he after; what looks he for? He goes "after the glory." Even to find out them who are God's glory in the world.

Three Reasons Why the Presence of Christ Is the Glory of a People

Now this is the glory of any people upon a threefold account.

The Saints Are Precious in the Eyes of God and Have a Great Inheritance

(1) This alone makes them honorable and precious before God. So says God of them, "I have redeemed thee, I have called thee by thy name, thou art mine" (Isa. 43:1); those are they of whom I spoke: What then, verse 4. "Thou art precious in my sight, thou art honourable, and I have loved thee"; how does God manifest his valuation of them, verse 3. Why he will give all the world, the greatest, mightiest, wealthiest nations, "for them," verse 5, all is as nothing in comparison of them who are his portion, and the lot of his inheritance. The Lord keep this alive upon your hearts, that that may be in your eyes the glory of this nation, on the account whereof it is "precious" to God, and "honorable" in his sight.

God's Instruments May Endure Reproach, but by Grace They Are Glorious

(2) Because this presence of Christ makes men "comely" and "excellent" in themselves,[19] with what eye soever the world may look upon them. The whole world out of Christ, lies in evil, under the curse of God, and defilement of sin: in all the glittering shows of their wealth and riches, in the state and magnificence of their governments, the beauty of their laws and order (as they relate to their persons), they are in the eye of God a filthy and an abominable thing, a thing that his soul loathes.[20] Curse and sin will make anything to be so: but now Christ is to them and in them beautiful and glorious (Isa. 4:2). Christ is so in himself, and he is so unto them: and makes them to be so. There is through him beauty and excellency and comeliness, everything that may make them

19 Isa. 4:2.

20 Crawford Gribben suggests that Owen may be "remembering the pomp and circumstance of the recent funeral of the Protector." See Gribben, *John Owen and English Puritanism: Experiences of Defeat* (New York: Oxford University Press, 2016), 200.

lovely and acceptable. That the world looks not on them as such, is not their fault, but the world's misery: it looked on their master Christ himself, "the brightness of his Father's glory,"[21] who is "altogether lovely,"[22] "the chiefest of ten thousand,"[23] with no other eye (Isa. 53:2). They are so in themselves, and are so to Christ; being exposed indeed to many temptations, oftentimes they are made black and sully[24] by them: but yet they are "comely" still (Cant. 1:5).[25] The ways whereby they are made black for the most part, we have expressed, verse 6, when "the sun shines on them," and they are "made keepers of the vineyard," it comes upon them. Prosperity, and public employment oftentimes so sully them, that they are made black to the reproach of the world: but yet to Christ who forgives, and washes them, they are "comely." Yea this is all the excellency that is in the world. Sin with honor, with wealth, with power, with wisdom, is a deformed and contemptible thing: it is grace only that is beautiful and glorious: it is the gracious only that are "excellent" in the earth (Ps. 16:3).

The Godly Remnant Preserves the Nation and Brings Prosperity

(3) This alone makes any truly useful unto others; and that either for preservation, or prosperity.

[1] Here lies the preservation of any nation from ruin. "Thus saith the Lord, as the new wine is found in the cluster, and one saith, 'Destroy it not, for a blessing is in it:' so will I do for my servants' sakes, that I may not destroy them all" (Isa. 65:8). This is the blessing in the cluster, the hidden and secret blessing, for the sake whereof the whole is not destroyed.[26] The "remnant" left by the Lord of hosts (Isa. 1:9) that keeps the whole from being as Sodom or Gomorrah.

If Elisha a servant of the Lord told the king of Israel in his distress, that if he had not regarded the presence of Jehoshaphat the king of Judah he would not so much as have spoken to him;[27] how much more will the Lord himself let a people know in their distress, that were it not for the regard he has to his secret ones, he would not take the least notice (as to relief) of them or their concernments. Sodom could not be destroyed until Lot was delivered.[28] The

21 Heb. 1:3.

22 Song 5:16.

23 Song 5:10.

24 I.e., stained, polluted.

25 This is a reference to Song of Songs 1:5.

26 Owen appealed to this text to make the same point in *An Humble Testimony unto the Goodness and Severity of God in His Dealing with Sinful Churches and Nations* (1681). See *Complete Works of John Owen*, vol. 21.

27 2 Kings 3:14.

28 Gen. 18:32.

whole world owes its preservation and being, to them, whom they make it their business to root out of it: they are as the foolish woman, that pulls down her own house with both her hands.[29] It is not your councils, you know how they have been divided, entangled, ensnared, it is not your armies, as such; what have they been, to oppose against the mighty floods that have risen up in this nation; and they also have been as a reed driven to and fro, with the wind (mankind is no better; John the Baptist says it of himself),[30] but it is this presence of Christ in and with his, that has been the preservation of England, in the midst of all the changes and revolutions that we have been exercised withal (Mic. 5:5).

[2] Not only preservation but prosperity is from hence also. "And the remnant of Jacob shall be in the midst of many people, as a dew from the Lord, as the showers upon the grass, that tarrieth not for man, nor waiteth for the sons of men" (Mic. 5:7). It is "the remnant of Jacob," of whom he speaks, that is, this people of Christ, with whom he is so present as has been manifested; and where are they; they are "in the midst of many people," in their inside, in their bowels; they are woven by their relations and employments into the bowels of the nations; and on that account there is neither this nor any nation about us, but shall spin out their mercies or their misery from their own bowels; their providential fates lie in them; as is their deportment toward this remnant, such will their issue be. But what shall this remnant do? Why it shall be "as dew from the Lord," and "as showers, on the grass." It shall be that alone which makes them fruitful, flourishing and prosperous; it may be it will be so, provided there be good assistance, counsel and strength, to carry on their affairs: yea blessed be God for councils, and for armies, he has made them useful to us: but the truth is, the blessing of this dew depends not on them, it "tarries not for man; it waits not for the sons of men": it will be a blessing, let men do what they will; it depends not on their uncertain and unstable counsel, on their weak and feeble strength. This remnant is as the ark in the house of Obededom,[31] as Joseph in the house of Potiphar,[32] all is blessed and prospered for their sakes. It is not the glorious battlements, the painted windows, the crouching antics, that support a building, but the stones that lie unseen in, or upon the earth.[33] It is often those who are despised and

29 Prov. 14:1.

30 Matt. 11:7. Owen here references Jesus's words about John the Baptist, which he attributes to John.

31 2 Sam. 6:11.

32 Gen. 39:3.

33 This architectural trope was employed at greater length in *The Branch of the Lord* (1650), which is included in this volume.

trampled on, that bear up the weight of a whole nation. All the fresh springs of our blessings are in Zion.

The Godly Remnant Preserved the Nation during the English Revolution

It were easy to manifest, that in all our late revolutions we have turned on this hinge. According as the presence of Christ with his people, in the power of his Spirit, has received entertainment in these nations, so has our state and condition been. For many years before the beginning of these troubles, the land had been full of oppression, I mean, in respect to the people of God. Poverty, imprisonment, dangers, banishment, reproaches were their portion.[34] God was long patient; at length the height of their adversaries came to this, that they set not themselves so much against their persons or ways, as against the Spirit of Christ in and with them: that was made their reproach, that the byword wherewith they were despised in the mouths of their adversaries, and the profane multitude: when things were come to this, that the very presence of Christ with his people, was made the direct object of the hatred of men, the Lord could bear it no longer; but swore by himself, that time should be given them no more: in this very house[35] he raised up saviors and deliverers on mount Zion to judge the mount of Edom;[36] and how did he carry on this work, "Not by might, nor by power, but by the Spirit of the Lord of hosts": as Zechariah 4:6. Even by that very Spirit which had been reviled and despised. Give me leave to say, the work of judging this nation was carried on by the presence of the Spirit of Christ with his in faith and prayer: it was not by prudence of councils, or strength of armies above that of our enemies, that we prevailed, but by faith and prayer; and if anyone be otherwise minded, I leave him for his resolution to the judgment of the great day, when all transactions shall be called over again: the adversaries themselves I am sure acknowledged it, when they openly professed, that there was nothing left for them to overcome, or to overcome them, but the prayers of the fanatic crew.[37]

After some years' contending, when the Lord had begun to give us deliverance by breaking the power of the enemy, at least in this nation, besides those bitter divisions that fell out among the people of God themselves, and the

34 This is particularly a reference to the Laudian policies of the 1630s and their consequences for the godly.

35 The House of Commons of the English Parliament.

36 Obad. 21.

37 I.e., persons subject to enthusiasm.

backsliding of some, to the cause and principles they had opposed, this evil was also found rising again among us; slighting, blaspheming, contemning, under several pretenses, of the Spirit and presence of Christ in and with his saints: you know what ensued; what shakings, what revolutions, with new wars, bloodshed, and desolation, over the three nations.[38] And give me leave to remember you as one that had opportunity to make observations of the passages of providence in those days, in all the three nations, in the times of our greatest hazards, give me leave I say, to remember you, that the public declarations, of those employed in the affairs of this nation, in the face of the enemies, their addresses unto God among themselves, their prayers night and day, their private discourses one with another, were, that the preservation of the interest of Christ in and with his people was the great thing that lay in their eyes; and that if it were not so, they desired that God would stop them in their way, yea rather cause their carcasses to fall in the high places of the field, than to prosper them in that which should be contrary thereunto: and we know what ensued. How we have used our mercies is another matter: this was the principle that prevailed with God and man.

Two Applications of the Doctrine

Promote the Interest of Christ in England, Scotland, and Ireland

Use 1. If you desire the glory of these nations, labor to promote the interest of Christ in these nations; I am not speaking unto you about disputable things, differences among the people of God themselves, nor am I interposing my advice in your civil affairs, but I speak in general about those with whom Christ is present, by his Spirit, his chosen ones, against whom there is an old enmity in Satan and the world. The glory of these nations is, that there is a people "in" them, that have Christ in the midst of them; let it be your business to take care for that glory. But how shall we do it?

Personal Commitment to Christ Is Required, Especially from Those in Power

(1) Labor personally, every one of you to get Christ in your own hearts. I am very far from thinking that a man may not be lawfully called to magistracy, if he be not a believer; or that being called, he should be impeded in the execution of his trust, and place, because he is not so;[39] I shall not suspend my obedience while I inquire after my lawful governor's conversion; but yet

38 This is a reference to the second English Civil War (1648), the Cromwellian conquest of Ireland (1649–1653), and the Third Civil War (1650–1651).

39 This principle would not have been accepted by those like the Fifth Monarchists.

this I say considering that I cannot much value any good, but what comes in by the way of promise, I confess I can have no great expectation from them whom God loves not, delights not in; if any be otherwise minded, I shall not contend with him; but for this I will contend with all the world, that it is your duty to labor to assure Christ in your own hearts, even that you may be the better fitted for the work of God in the world. It is the promise of God to Zion; that "her officers shall be peace, and her exactors righteousness" (Isa. 60:17), and then shall she call her "walls Salvation, and her gates praise" (Isa. 60:18). It will be little advantage to any, to have the work of God raised in the world, and not to have the foundation stone laid in their hearts: if there should be in any of you an enmity unto Christ, and the power of godliness, a hatred and contempt of the people of God, "an evil heart of unbelief,"[40] an evil course of life, worldliness, oppression, "vanity of mind,"[41] etc. would it advantage you to be entrusted with power in these nations? Would it not hasten your destruction, and increase your account? It is a noble promise that we have, "And the work of righteousness shall be peace, and the effect of righteousness, quietness and assurance for ever" (Isa. 32:17). It is a gospel righteousness that is spoken of; and that not of the cause as such only, but of the persons; the persons being righteous, and that with the righteousness of Christ, the effects mentioned, shall follow their righteous undertakings; we have peace now, outward peace; but alas, we have not quietness; and if anything may be done that may give us quietness, yet perhaps we may not have assurance; we may be quickly shaken again; but when the righteousness of the persons, and cause meet, all the rest will follow.[42]

Much Is to Be Done Because of Declension and Apostasy

(2) Set yourselves to oppose that overflowing flood of profaneness, and opposition to the power of godliness, that is spreading itself over this nation. Know you not that the nation begins to be overwhelmed by the pourings out of a profane, wicked, carnal spirit, full of rage and contempt of all the work of reformation that has been attempted among us?[43] Do you not know that if

40 Heb. 3:12.

41 Eph. 4:17.

42 According to Goold, this "emphatic sentence lays bare the very heart of the nation, heaving and throbbing with painful uncertainty in regard to the issue of public events." See John Owen, *The Works of John Owen*, ed. William H. Goold, 24 vols. (Edinburgh: Johnstone and Hunter, 1850–1855), 8:454.

43 Here Owen's call to oppose ungodliness should be contrasted with the focus on many in the Commons on opposing heresy. Parliament had been debating holding a fast day, and the declaration before the House on April 2 described a nation "overspread with many blasphemies,

the former profane principle should prove predominant in this nation, that it will quickly return to its former station and condition, and that with the price of your dearest blood; and yet is there not already such a visible prevalency of it, that in many places the very profession of religion is become a scorn; and in others, those old forms and ways taken up with greediness, which are a badge of apostasy from all former engagements and actings; and are not these sad evidences of the Lord's departing from us; if I should lay before you a comparison between the degrees of the appearances of the glory of God in this nation, the steps whereby it came forth, and those whereby it seems almost to be departing, it would be a matter of admiration and lamentation; I pray God we lose not our ground faster than we won it. Were our hearts kept up to our good old principles on which we first engaged, it would not be so with us; but innumerable evils have laid hold upon us; and the temptations of these days have made us a woeful prey, "Gray hairs are here and there,"[44] and it will be no wonder if our ruin should come with more speed, than did our deliverance. O then set yourselves in the gap;[45] by all ways and means oppose the growth of an evil, profane, common, malignant spirit among us. But I haste.

A Commitment to All the Godly, Regardless of Their Differences

(3) Value, encourage, and close with them, in and with whom is this presence of Christ. They are the glory of the nation; its peace, safety and prosperity will be found wrapped up in them. I know there lie divers considerable objections against the practice of this duty;[46] I shall name some few of them, and leave the exhortation unto your considerations.

First Objection: Who Is to Be Counted among the Godly?

Who are those persons in whom is this presence of Christ? Are they such as profess indeed religion, but neglect all rules of righteousness; that would be accounted godly, but care not to be honest? The marks of whose miscarriages

---

and damnable heresies against God . . . by denying the authority thereof, and crying up the light in the hearts of sinfull men as the rule and guide of all their actions, besides many other abominable errours." This was exacerbated by "suffering persons under the abuse of Liberty of Conscience to distureb the publike Ordinances." See *A Declaration of the Lord Protector and Both Houses of Parliament for a Day of Solemn Fasting* [. . .] *upon the Eighteenth Day of May, 1659* (London, 1659), 4–5. This Declaration was published after the dissolution of the Parliament.

44 Hos. 7:9.

45 Ezek. 22:30.

46 As the *Declaration* for the fast suggested, the Presbyterians in the Commons were concerned about toleration and sought to enforce a degree of uniformity. See *A Declaration of the Lord Protector and Both Houses of Parliament for a Day of Solemn Fasting*, 4–5.

are written on their foreheads; are not these so far from being the glory, that they are the shame of any nation? I pray give me leave to endeavor the rolling away of this great stone of offense, in these few ensuing considerations.

Response: Six Considerations

[1] Then, I shall willingly lay this down for a principle, that he is not religious who is not also righteous; as also I shall not much value his righteousness, who is not religious. He that is righteous does righteousness; he does so, in the bent of his spirit, and course of his ways and walkings. If a man be froward,[47] heady, high-minded, sensual, unjust, oppressive, worldly, self-seeking, a hater of good men, false, treacherous, let him pretend to what he will; that man's religion is in vain; he may have a form of godliness, but he has not the power of it.[48] This principle we shall agree upon;

[2] There have been in the days wherein we live, many false professors, hypocrites, that have thought "gain to be godliness";[49] by reason of whose wicked lives, ways, and walking, the name of God has been evil spoken of; and "Woe to them by whom these offenses are come"; but yet also, "Woe to the world because of offenses";[50] if these offenses turn off men, from an esteem of the remnant of Christ, in whom is his presence, woe to them also. I acknowledge these days have abounded with offenses; but woe to them who are turned aside by them, from owning the portion and inheritance of Christ.

[3] It cannot be denied, but that many of them who do belong unto Christ, have woefully miscarried in these days. "O tell it not in Gath, publish it not in Askelon";[51] O that our souls could mourn in secret on that account, that we could go backward, and cover the nakedness and folly of one another;[52] but alas, this has been far from being our frame of spirit; we have everyone spread the failings of his brother, before the face of men and devils; but yet notwithstanding these miscarriages, those that are the people of Christ, are his people still; and he loves them still. Whether we will or no; and commonly those who are least able to bear with the miscarriages of others, have most of their own.

[4] That differences of judgments, in civil affairs, or church matters ought not presently to be made arguments of men; not being righteous. Some men think

47 I.e., perverse or peevish.

48 2 Tim. 3:5.

49 1 Tim. 6:5.

50 Matt. 18:7.

51 2 Sam. 1:20.

52 Gen. 9:23.

that none are righteous that are not of their principles; than which principle there is nothing more unrighteous. Let men that differ from them walk never so holily, profess never so strictly; yet if they are not of their mind, they are not righteous. If men are offended on such accounts, it is because they will be so.

[5] This has ever been the way of the men of the world; that when any have been unblamable and zealous upon the account of religion, they will attempt their reputation, though without any ground or color, upon the account of righteousness. So suffered the Christians of old; and so the Puritans of former days, unjustly and falsely, as God will judge and declare. The world then in this matter is not to be believed; the common reports of it are from the devil, "the accuser of the brethren"; who accuses them in the same manner "before God night and day."[53] These are but pretenses, whereby men ignorant of the mystery of the gospel and the power of grace, harden themselves to their ruin.

[6] This remnant of Christ with whom his presence is, who are the glory of a nation, is to be found only among the professors of a nation. For although of those who are professors, there may be many bad, yet of those that are not professors, there is not one good. Where there is faith there will be a profession. If I should not know well where to find them; I am sure I know where I cannot find them; I cannot find them in the ways of the world, and conformity to it; in darkness, ignorance, neglect of duty, and utter unacquaintedness with gospel truths, the gifts and graces of the Spirit; there I cannot find them; I shall not say of them, "Behold the Lord's anointed," let their outward, worldly appearance be what it will. Now by the help of these considerations, those who have in themselves principles of life and light in Christ, will or may be, setting aside their temptations, enabled to discover this generation of the Lord's delight; and for others, I cannot take down the enmity that God has set up. So then notwithstanding this objection, I shall certainly esteem this remnant of Christ to lie among those, who having received gospel light, and gospel gifts evidently, do make also profession of gospel grace, union and communion with Christ, separation from the world, and the ways of it, in a conversation acceptable unto God in Christ; and to this portion shall I say as Ruth to Naomi, "Let what will be glorious or uppermost in the world, 'Whether thou goest, I will go, where thou lodgest I will lodge; thy people shall be my people, and thy God my God; the Lord do so to me and more also, if ought part thee and me';[54] with them let my portion be, and the portion of my family, whatever their lot and condition in this world should be"; and the Lord say, "Amen."

53 Rev. 12:10.

54 Ruth 1:16–17.

Second Objection: Are Not the Godly Hopelessly Divided?

Objection. But it will be said secondly, "We are still at a loss; for what woeful divisions are there among this generation of professors? Some are for one way, and some for another; some say one sort are the people of God, some another; some say the Prelatists are so, some the Presbyterians, some the Independents, some the Anabaptists, some the Fifth Monarchy men, some others, and on whom should the valuation pleaded for be cast?"

Response: Three Considerations

Answer 1. Some do say so, and plead thus, it cannot be denied; but the truth is, the greater is their weakness and folly. It is impossible men acquainted with the Spirit of Christ and the gospel, should say so, unless they were under the power of one temptation or other. But it is no party, but the party of Christ in the world, and against the world, the seed of the woman against the seed of the serpent that I am pleading for;[55] that men as to their interest in Christ should be judged from such denominations, as though they make a great noise in the world, yet indeed signify very little things in themselves, is most unrighteous, and unequal; nor will men find peace, in such rash and precipitate judgments.

[Answer] 2. There may be many divisions among the people of God, and yet none of them be divided from Christ the head. The branches of a tree may be entangled by strong winds, and stricken against one another, and yet none of them be broken off from the tree itself; and when the storm is over everyone possesses its own place in quietness beauty and fruitfulness. While the strong winds of temptations are upon the followers of Christ, they may be tossed and entangled; but not being broken off from the root, when he shall say to the winds, "Peace, be still,"[56] they will flourish again in peace and beauty.

[Answer] 3. Let not Satan cheat you of your duty, by this trivial objection. If he can keep you from duty, while he can make divisions; he has you sure enough. They of whom I speak, be they under what reproach or obloquies[57] soever, they are all true men, all the children of one Father, though they are unhappily fallen out by the way.

Reassurance to the Godly Remnant

Use 2. Of encouragement to those that have the presence of Christ with them in the manner declared; they shall be safe; in vain it is for all the world

55 Gen. 3:15.

56 Mark 4:39.

57 I.e., verbal abuse.

to attempt their security; either they shall not prevail, or they shall mischief themselves by their own prevalency (Mic. 5:8). As they shall be "a dew" where they are appointed for a blessing; so, "as a lion" where they are oppressed.[58] Destruction will come forth on their account, and that terribly like the destruction of a lion, speedily, in passing through it shall be done. And whence is it that this feeble generation shall be "as a lion"? It is from the presence of Christ among them, who is "the lion of the tribe of Judah,"[59] and to honor them, he assigns that to them, which is his own proper work; let men take heed how they provoke this lion: for the present he is "gone up from the prey: he stoopeth down, he coucheth as a lion and as an old lion, who shall rouse him up?" (Gen. 49:9).[60] He has taken his prey in these nations, in the destruction of many of his enemies: he seems now to take his rest, to couch down, his indignation being overpast, but who shall rouse him up? Why what if he be provoked? What if he be stirred up? Why "he will not lie down, until he eat of the prey, and drink the blood of the slain" (Num. 23:24). There is no delivery from him: no, but what if there be a strong combination of many against him will he not cease and give over? (Isa. 31:4). Be they who they will, the "shepherds" of the people, be they never so many "a multitude" of them, let them lift up their "voice" and rage never so much, all is one, he will perform his work and accomplish it:[61] until you have him in the condition mentioned [in] Isaiah 63:1–6. Blessed are the people that are under his care and conduct, yea "Blessed are the people whose God is the Lord."[62]

FINIS.[63]

58 Mic. 5:7–8.

59 Rev. 5:5.

60 Owen employed this trope in *The Branch of the Lord* (1650), which is included in this volume.

61 Isa. 31:4.

62 Ps. 33:12.

63 Lat. "The End." This sermon was followed by a catalog of twelve works by Owen that Philemon Stephens was selling at his bookshop at St Paul's Churchyard. This was a shorter list than the one included at the end of *God's Presence with a People* (1656), which had included nineteen titles. Stephens was no longer listing for sale the following titles by Owen: *The Advantage of the Kingdom of Christ* (1651); *Diatriba de Justitia Divina* (1653); *The Doctrine of the Saints Perseverance* (1654); *Of Schisme* (1657); *Of Mortification* (1656); *Vindiciae Evangelicae* (1655); and *A Review of the Annotations of Hugo Grotius* (1656). Stephens was now also marketing *God's Presence with a People* (1656).

General Index

Scripture Index